Visions of the Heart

Fourth Edition

Visions of the Heart

Issues Involving Aboriginal Peoples in Canada

Edited by

David Long *and*
Olive Patricia Dickason

OXFORD
UNIVERSITY PRESS

OXFORD
UNIVERSITY PRESS

Oxford University Press is a department of the University of Oxford.
It furthers the University's objective of excellence in research, scholarship,
and education by publishing worldwide. Oxford is a registered trade mark of
Oxford University Press in the UK and in certain other countries.

Published in Canada by
Oxford University Press
8 Sampson Mews, Suite 204,
Don Mills, Ontario M3C 0H5 Canada

www.oupcanada.com

Copyright © Oxford University Press Canada 2016

The moral rights of the authors have been asserted

Database right Oxford University Press (maker)

First Edition published in 1996 © Harcourt Brace Canada
Second Edition published in 2000 © Harcourt Brace Canada
Third Edition published in 2011

Library and Archives Canada Cataloguing in Publication
Visions of the heart : issues involving Aboriginal peoples in Canada
/ edited by David Long and Olive Patricia Dickason. — Fourth edition.

Includes bibliographical references and index.
ISBN 978–0–19–901477–4 (paperback)

1. Native peoples—Canada—Textbooks. I. Long, David Alan, 1958–,
editor II. Dickason, Olive Patricia, 1920-, editor

E78.C2V58 2015   971.004'97   C2015-906445-7

Cover image: Darren Julian, 2010

Oxford University Press is committed to our environment.
This book is printed on Forest Stewardship Council® certified paper
and comes from responsible sources.

Printed and bound in the United States of America

1 2 3 4 — 19 18 17 16

Contents

4 | Elders' Teachings in the Twenty-First Century: A Personal Reflection   80

Marlene Brant Castellano

5 | Foundations: First Nation and Métis Families   99

Kim Anderson and Jessica Ball

6 | First Nations Women in Canada   127

Cora J. Voyageur

7 | Indigenous Men: Masculinity and Leadership   152

John Swift and Lee Maracle

8 | Aboriginal Demography   179

Don Kerr and Roderic Beaujot

9 | Aboriginal Languages in Canada: Generational and Community Perspectives on Language Maintenance, Loss, and Revitalization 209

Mary Jane Norris

10 | Learning from Indigenous Knowledge in Education 241

Jan Hare and Sara Florence Davidson

11 | Art and Reconciliation   263
Jonathan Dewar

12 | A Way Forward in Efforts to Support the Health and Well-Being of Canada's Aboriginal Peoples   291
Martin Cooke and David Long

13 | Aboriginal Communities in the City: Reflections along the Path to Self-Government 319

Kevin FitzMaurice and Don McCaskill

14 | The Failed Foreign System of Criminal Justice and the Problem with Canada 351

Lisa Monchalin

Preface

I vividly remember the first time I met my *Visions of the Heart* collaborator and mentor Olive Dickason. It was a typically wind-chilled Alberta day in March 1994. I had phoned Olive to ask if she would be interested in meeting with me to talk about an idea I had for a book of readings addressing issues involving Aboriginal peoples in Canada. Olive immediately said that she would be delighted to chat and invited me to come to her home. Even though this was the first time we had met, she welcomed me at the door with her genuinely warm and inviting smile as though we were long-time friends. Within a few minutes of sitting down we were engaged in a rather intense discussion of why we felt that it was important for the people of Canada to understand what Olive referred to as "a rather interesting though somewhat disconcerting blend of anger and optimism in the air." We both sensed, or at least hoped, that the discontent, frustration, and anger of many First Nations people that had boiled over during the Oka crisis had been at least partially quelled by the establishment of the Royal Commission on Aboriginal Peoples in 1993. We felt strongly that Canada was at a turning point in its history, and that there was need for people to engage in mutually respectful dialogue that sought clarity, honesty, and a deeper understanding of current relations between Aboriginal peoples and the rest of Canada. More importantly, we immediately liked each other and knew that we wanted to work together to promote a good way forward in those relations. And so it was that our book, *Visions of the Heart*, was born.

Needless to say, I have learned a great deal since my first conversation with Olive. I have always seen relations between Aboriginal people and the rest of Canada in a discerningly hopeful way, and so one of the most disheartening attitudes I have heard expressed many times over the years is that "the more things change, the more they stay the same." I am thankful that Olive and many other *Visions of the Heart* colleagues have helped me to learn that there is much more to human relations than meets the cynical eye. In particular, they have helped me to know that we are destined to see only what we are looking for if we do not attempt to see things from the perspective of others, and that if we are unwilling to listen and learn from others, it is impossible for us to walk respectfully together. While I recognize there are those who still believe that "the more things change, the more they stay the same," my *Visions of the Heart* collaborators have helped me to understand in a genuinely hopeful way that "the more things change in positive ways, the more chance this will continue to happen provided we stay committed to a process of reconciliation that is based on treating each another with dignity and respect."

That reconciliation is a complex and challenging process is clearly evident in the opening chapter by Peter Cole. Readers will note that while a superficial reading of Peter's story suggests that the rather mischievous and insightful Indigenous protagonist simply dismisses his miserably conceited and thoroughly naive Euro-Canadian antagonist, a more careful (re)reading enables us to see that the protagonist is animated by much the same critically hopeful vision expressed in 2013 by then national chief of the Assembly of First Nations, Shawn A-in-chut Atleo, in his open letter to Bernard Valcourt, minister of Aboriginal affairs and northern development:

> In the spirit of the statement of Apology [from Prime Minister Harper in 2008], I, together with First Nations leaders invite you to stand with us—in affirming for all Canadians a solemn commitment to reconciliation and to a path forward that never again will our children be victimized in the name of education, never again will our dignity, languages and cultures be denied and desecrated. Instead, we will rise anew in this new day that was the promise of the Apology, in partnership and pledge our dedication, together, to ensure these conditions are addressed, that we chart a path forward of partnership and respect and that we immediately seize this moment and this opportunity to achieve the change needed for our children—change that is essential for reconciliation and change that is essential for Canada.[1]

Contributors to this edition of *Visions of the Heart* acknowledge that current relations between Aboriginal peoples and the rest of Canada are in many ways quite challenging and fragile. Nonetheless, we are confident that the more people in Canada learn to view reconciliation as an ongoing process, the less concern there will be that current relations between Aboriginal peoples and the rest of Canada are far from "reconciled." It is therefore our hope that this edition of *Visions of the Heart* will enable readers to know that even though it may appear that "some things never change," those who are willing to walk with others in pursuit of justice, healing, and reconciliation will realize the hopeful, albeit for a time unsettling, visions of their hearts.

Note

1. Accessed 1 Apr. 2015, http://www.afn.ca/uploads/files/13-11-25_open_letter_to_minister_valcourt_final.pdf.

Acknowledgements

The good people at Oxford University Press have once again made it a pleasure to put together another edition of *Visions of the Heart*. I am thankful that they share my sense that *Visions of the Heart* is a project of the heart. I particularly appreciate the contributions and support I received from a couple of people at OUP, including Richard Tallman, who provided the most thoughtful, challenging, and detailed copy editing I have ever experienced. Thank you Richard, for helping each chapter in this collection to become better, as well as the collection as a whole. I am especially thankful to the *Visions* project manager, Tamara Capar. Her patience, encouragement, editorial insight, and good humour throughout the entire process helped all of us bring this project to fruition in a good way. We have never met face to face, Tamara, but thank you for being so good at your job and so wonderfully patient and supportive of me as well as our collaborators.

I am of the mind that good projects such as this are not simply created by those who put them together. Rather, they are gifts that have been passed on to those who are mindful of their importance and are willing to receive and then share them with gratitude. It was just over 20 years ago when I first approached Olive Dickason to ask if she had the time and inclination to work with me on putting together a book of readings that would engage current issues involving Aboriginal peoples in Canada. I told Olive that I was aware that a few books on the market at the time addressed "contemporary Native issues in Canada," though I felt strongly that our understanding of relations between Aboriginal peoples and the rest of Canada would benefit not only from more voices, but more importantly from the voices of those who were committed to working with others in cultivating a wise and hopeful vision of the future of our relations. I was elated as well as humbled when Olive phoned me the day after receiving my outline to say that she would be delighted to work with me on this "rather interesting looking collection."

It was a great privilege to edit the first three editions of *Visions of the Heart* with Olive, and I learned much that was good from her over the many years we worked together. She was the kind of mentor a young academic can only hope for, and I will always be grateful for the scholarly wisdom she shared with me. Olive was also a genuinely kind and humble person who treated everyone she met with respect and good, often quick-witted humour. She and I befriended each other in our own unique ways over the years, and for that I am deeply thankful. Unfortunately, this fourth edition of *Visions of the Heart* did not benefit from Olive's editorial acumen and unrelenting insistence that we "get the story straight," for she passed away peacefully on 12 March 2011 after 91 very full and incredibly interesting years. I do hope, however, that this edition carries Olive's ever hopeful spirit within it, and I trust that readers will learn to be thankful for all of her gifts and for her generosity of spirit in sharing them with us in a good way.

This edition is therefore not dedicated to Olive's memory, for she has become one of our ancestors that many will continue to draw wisdom and inspiration from. It is instead dedicated to all who seek to follow her good and wise path, and who will hopefully grow to understand the importance of passing along Olive's lesson to us all: that careful, respectful listening to other people's voices and stories invites us to enjoy the gift of all our relations.

Go raibh maith agat and chi meegwetch, Olive.

Contributors

Kim Anderson
Wilfrid Laurier University, Indigenous Studies

Jessica Ball
University of Victoria, School of Child and Youth Care

Roderic Beaujot
University of Western Ontario, Department of Sociology

Yale D. Belanger
University of Lethbridge, Political Science Department

Marlene Brant Castellano
Trent University, Professor Emerita

Peter Cole
University of British Columbia, Department of Curriculum and Pedagogy

Martin Cooke
University of Waterloo, Department of Sociology and Legal Studies

Sara Florence Davidson
University of British Columbia, Ph.D. Candidate

Jonathan Dewar
Algoma University, Shingwauk Residential Schools Centre

Kevin FitzMaurice
University of Sudbury, Department of Indigenous Studies

Jan Hare
University of British Columbia, Department of Language and Literacy Education

Don Kerr
King's University College, University of Western Ontario, Department of Sociology

David Long
The King's University, Edmonton, Department of Sociology

Lee Maracle
University of Toronto, First Nations House

Don McCaskill
Trent University, Department of Indigenous Studies

Deborah McGregor
University of Toronto, Department of Geography/Department of Aboriginal Studies

Lisa Monchalin
Kwantlen Polytechnic University, Department of Criminology

David Newhouse
Trent University, Department of Indigenous Studies

Mary Jane Norris
Independent research consultant

John Swift
Vancouver Island University, First Nations Studies

Cora J. Voyageur
University of Calgary, Department of Sociology

Introduction

David Long

All acts of justice are acts of reconciliation.

Contributors to this fourth edition of *Visions of the Heart* share a fundamental commitment to bringing justice, reconciliation, and hope to relations between Aboriginal peoples and the rest of Canada. While we agree that post-colonial analysis and action are essential to finding a good way forward in these relations, we also recognize that cultivating hope requires that people be mindful and respectful of one another. Learning to walk together in this way will inevitably confront us with "unsettling" differences in our perspectives and circumstances, and so it should come as little surprise to readers that the chapters in this collection do not flow in a smooth and uniform manner from beginning to end.

This is not to say that what follows is a haphazard and disconnected array of essays, for a number of key themes thread their way throughout. These themes emerged out of three rather basic questions that contributors were asked to engage in their particular issue area: What gives Aboriginal[1] individuals, families, communities, and/or nations hope? What factors hinder Aboriginal individuals, families, communities, and/or nations from experiencing hope? And what is a good way forward in relations between Aboriginal peoples and the rest of Canada? The particular themes these questions give rise to include:

- honouring the integrity of Aboriginal peoples' identity;
- interrogating how the ways and means of colonialism hinder the hope of Aboriginal peoples;
- understanding the spirit of current relations between Aboriginal peoples and the rest of Canada; and
- making sense of how current expressions of positive, transformational change are cultivating hope in the lives of Aboriginal peoples, including in their relations with the rest of Canada.

The remainder of this introduction describes of how our contributors engage these themes. Our hope throughout is that we do so in ways that invite as well as challenge readers to think and act in respectful, reconciling ways.

The Hill Times, Daniel León Rodríguez

Honouring the Integrity of Aboriginal Peoples' Identity

In our cultures, to vision quest is strong and good medicine. To have a vision for the people is powerful and to fulfil a vision for the people is sacred. Our ancestors were given visions by the Creator, which lead the people to govern themselves.[2]

Morningstar Mercredi

Where there is no guiding vision, a people will run unrestrained and perish.

Proverbs 29:18

One of the most challenging aspects of writing about the lives of others is honouring the integrity of a people's identity. This is a particularly difficult task for modern storytellers whose manner of inquiry is informed by Western scientific notions of objectivity and empirical verifiability, and whose relations with the people they seek to understand are largely regulated by ethical guidelines that emphasize the minimizing of risk rather than being animated by the wonderfully human ability to cultivate relations based on appreciation and respect. As Martin Cooke and I note in Chapter 12, the Western scientific approach to medicine has a particular way of understanding and addressing issues involving illness, health, and healing that is in many ways at odds with the traditional knowledge approach of Aboriginal people. Nonetheless, we discuss a number of examples in which a harmonizing of different experiences and perspectives is evident in the collaborative efforts of medical and social scientists, doctors, and traditional healers who are dedicated to bring healing and health to those who are struggling with illness.

Remaining mindful that different populations are comprised of a wide variety of whole human beings is another challenge to those committed to honouring people's identities. Post-colonial storytellers are committed to honouring the voices of those who have been marginalized and oppressed, and many of their stories often include critical descriptions and analyses of the ways and means of colonial oppressors. Contributors to this collection have thus sought to pay careful attention to the way they engage issues surrounding identity, for example, the tendency in much post-colonial writing to idealize the past and present lives of those who have experienced colonial oppression. It is clear that all contributors were mindful of this, and that they remained committed to giving honest account of not only how the lives of Aboriginal people have been affected by colonialism, but also how agency and choice are expressed in the midst of challenging and often oppressive circumstances.

Visions authors were also asked to be mindful of the tendency in a good deal of post-colonial writing to essentialize/demonize Europeans. Given our shared commitment to finding a good way forward in relations between Aboriginal peoples and the rest of Canada, all contributors acknowledge the difference between the harmful actions of "agents of colonization" and the masses of people whose lives benefit from colonial circumstances even though their attitudes and behaviours could hardly be described as intentionally malevolent and oppressive. Still, the analyses, insights, and questions presented throughout this edition pose a challenge to those who say they appreciate Canada and are committed to living justly but who then decide, for whatever reason, to remain "idle" in the face of the obvious injustices experienced by Aboriginal people in this country. The concluding dialogue between David Newhouse and myself (Chapter 15) as well as Lisa Monchalin's discussion in Chapter 14 of the criminal justice system engage the question of why it is difficult to meaningfully address inequality and injustice in our relations. At the same time, they along with our other contributors agree that there are many signs in current relations between Aboriginal peoples and the rest of Canada suggesting that justice, reconciliation, and peace are being realized.

Contributors also agree—given that the 500-year history of colonialism in the land that officially became Canada in 1867 is in many respects a history of European attempts to purge this land of Indigenous peoples and their history—that it is quite remarkable that Aboriginal peoples in all their diversity have lived and moved and often flourished throughout Turtle Island (i.e., present-day North America) for thousands of years. Eleven Indigenous language families developed 53 different languages, and as Mary Jane Norris notes in Chapter 9, each and every language and dialect has been given unique expression by people living in different times and places. Kim Anderson and Jessica Ball's discussion of First Nation and Métis families (Chapter 5) and Jan Hare and Sara Davidson's insights into Indigenous education initiatives (Chapter 10) underscore how the diversity and complexity of Aboriginal communities, settlements, and nations have always been expressed through their unique knowledge systems, cultural traditions and values, economic and political arrangements, familial and kin relationships, and languages. In other words, they note how all Aboriginal families, communities, settlements, bands, and nations have their own histories that have shaped their present-day culture and relations with the rest of Canada. John Swift and Lee Maracle (Chapter 7), Marlene Brant Castellano (Chapter 4), Deborah McGregor (Chapter 2), and Lisa Monchalin (Chapter 14) stress that to ignore the rich histories and vibrant cultures of Aboriginal peoples before and after European settlement is to ignore an essential element of the identity of this land. Moreover, David Newhouse and Yale Belanger (Chapter 3) affirm support in their analysis of Aboriginal politics for John Ralston Saul's rather intriguing and contentious view that a new kind of hope in Aboriginal/state relations will emerge when Canada acknowledges that it has become a Métis nation.

With our rich Aboriginal history in mind, it should not be surprising that most every contributor engages the resurgence of efforts to honour Indigenous wisdom. Many of these efforts are being expressed in wonderfully resourceful and thoroughly post-colonial ways. While each chapter draws our attention to the diverse ways and contexts in which the revitalization of traditional knowledge systems, cultural practices and values, and ancestral languages are occurring, Cole and numerous other contributors make it abundantly clear that the raison d'être of all revitalization efforts is to honour and cultivate the sacredness of Indigenous people's identity.

Indeed, each chapter engages current identity-related issues and activities involving Aboriginal people in its own way. For example, while Voyageur, Swift and Maracle, Anderson and Ball, as well as Norris invite readers to reflect on the everyday, grassroots experiences and perspectives of Aboriginal people, their chapters focus, respectively, on some of the peculiarly gendered dilemmas facing First Nations women, First Nations boys and men, traditionally based head start educational initiatives, and ancestral language revitalization efforts in particular First Nations communities. Castellano offers a personal reflection on how Elder wisdom provides guidance to those who are patiently and respectfully committed to one another over time. FitzMaurice and McCaskill explore the complex developments and questions surrounding Aboriginal identity in urban areas. In a different realm, Monchalin perceptively analyzes Aboriginal people's experience of (in)justice, suggesting how identity and the environment shaping it can operate negatively for many people. In related areas of cultural trauma, Dewar inquires into the relationship between art and reconciliation in the context of the Truth and Reconciliation Commission (TRC), and McGregor offers insights into the importance of Indigenous visions of environmental care in a time and place where resource development, regardless of the harm to Mother Earth, has become politically and economically expedient. All of these authors demonstrate that, despite large problems, misunderstandings, and troubles, critically hopeful analyses of diverse areas of Aboriginal life can deepen our appreciation of the creative determination that has been at the heart of Aboriginal people's identity since time immemorial.

Interrogating the Ways and Means of Colonization

As Olive Dickason (1997) notes, Europeans from France and England ventured across the ocean roughly 500 years ago to discover lands they could exploit. While history attests to countless genocidal visions based on a belief in the superiority of some and the inferiority of others, the ethnocentric vision that Europeans sought to impose on the Aboriginal peoples living on the land they "discovered" was also fundamentally colonizing in nature. This vision, by and large, was informed by a perspective that regarded the Aboriginal inhabitants of the lands as *l'homme sauvage*. Consequently, whether colonizers viewed the "savages" they sought to assimilate or exterminate as noble or hopelessly inferior, their "New World" vision had little if any room for Indigenous ways of thinking and acting. Unfortunately for the many descendants of the original peoples of this land, the spirit and imprint of a colonizing vision remain evident in virtually every spiritual, physical, cultural, relational, and structural area of Aboriginal life. The result, as discussed throughout *Visions of the Heart*, is a history of painful and even deadly experiences, broken and unhealthy relations, and deeply embedded and thoroughly oppressive cultural attitudes and institutional structures.

Contributors to *Visions of the Heart* thus agree that engaging in honest, post-colonial dialogue that seeks a hopeful way forward is vital. Such dialogue challenges and enables those who are involved to understand and seek to change the circumstances, social attitudes, processes, and structures that privilege some at the expense of "others." Post-colonial dialogue that envisions positive transformational change seeks not only to deconstruct and dismantle social relations and conditions that breed social injustice and inequality, but also to effect liberating social change by giving voice to the experiences, perspectives, and visions of those whose lives have been disadvantaged and in many respects devastated by colonialism. This vision—of deconstructing, dismantling, liberating, and positively reconstructing—informs our analyses of issues surrounding Aboriginal Elders, language, women, masculinities, education, family, urban identity, health, justice, and environmental identity. And while contributors to *Visions of the Heart* agree that there are clear indications over the past 50 or so years of a "post-colonial turn" in Canada, we think it important to reflect carefully on whether or not, and possibly in what respects, the age in which we live can properly be called "post-colonial." Two of the most obvious reasons for questioning if we have come this far are that: (1) clear evidence suggests that colonizing experiences, relations, processes, and structures continue to abound in Canada, and that Aboriginal individuals, communities, and nations have to fight each day for the right to have control over practically every area of their lives; and (2) government action after such official statements as the prime minister's 2008 apology for the Canadian government's role in Indian residential schools[3] and those in 2014 by the minister of Aboriginal affairs and northern development in relation to government support for Aboriginal education in Canada[4] show little evidence that official representatives of the Canadian state are sincere in their commitment to treat Aboriginal people with equality, dignity, and respect.

Referring to this or any other age as post-colonial assumes not only that large-scale movements of diverse people have managed to successfully challenge the basic ethnocentric tenet of colonialism, but also that their movements have resulted in a fundamental restructuring of colonial relations in ways that have enabled those who have been oppressed to gain meaningful control over the social and material conditions of their lives. Certainly there is much evidence presented throughout this collection of significant and very positive changes in the physical, social, political, legal, and economic conditions of Aboriginal peoples' lives in this country. However, the existence of post-colonial dialogue and developments does not necessarily indicate that we live in a post-colonial age. We thus invite readers to reflect carefully on what a post-colonial Canada would look like, and whether the evidence presented in this collection supports the view that the Canada in which we live can properly be termed "post-colonial."

The Spirit of Current Relations: Seeking Reconciliation, Speaking Truth, and Being Idle No More

The third theme that weaves its way through this collection is the spirit of reconciliation, which recently has been embodied in the work of the TRC as well as the actions of Idle No More participants. The critically hopeful vision of reconciliation between Aboriginal people and the rest of Canada was most clearly expressed in the introduction to the 1996 report of the Royal Commission on Aboriginal Peoples (RCAP):

> [A] vision of a balanced relationship has been a constant theme in our work as a Commission. . . . [W]e rejected the idea that the past can simply be put aside and forgotten as we seek to build a new relationship. What we should strive for instead is a renewed relationship. The concept of renewal expresses better the blend of historical sensitivity and creative initiative that should characterize future relations among Aboriginal and non-Aboriginal people in this country. It would be false and unjust to suggest that we start entirely anew, false and unjust to attempt to wipe the slate clean, ignoring both the wrongs of the past and the rights flowing from our previous relationships and interactions.

While we argued in the previous three editions of *Visions of the Heart* that the RCAP represented the first real watershed of hope for relations between Aboriginal people and the rest of Canada, there is agreement among contributors to this edition that there are similar signs of hope in the TRC and the Idle No More movement, though some are more skeptical and even critical of these signs than others. There is, however, full agreement that the TRC and Idle No More involve many thousands of Aboriginal people and their supporters from all across Canada walking together in their pursuit of justice and reconciliation. There is also agreement that the willingness of so many Aboriginal people to open their hearts and speak their truth signifies that they are willing to walk in a spirit of trust and hope. Much like the RCAP, the TRC foreshadows a Canada quite different from the one it testified to, since it envisions a Canada in which Aboriginal people have confidence and pride in themselves, their communities, their cultures, and their place in Canadian society. It also envisions a Canada in which Aboriginal peoples have autonomy and control over their individual and collective lives, and where everyone in Canada can learn to walk together in respect, appreciation, and hope.

While all contributors to this collection share this vision of Canada, they do not shy away from examining deeply personal and often painful stories of abuse and addiction and poverty and violence and loss—impassioned outbursts by sometimes enraged and often profoundly sad individuals who have lost their ancestral language, their traditions and cultural identity, their legal status, their means of subsistence and livelihood, and/or their immediate as well as extended familial relations. A number of contributors, including

Hare and Davidson as well as Dewar, recount some of the profoundly person-al and tragic stories told by residential school survivors to the TRC. Others, including Voyageur and Monchalin, engage in detailed historical analyses of socially devastating developments in pre- as well as post-Confederation rela-tions between Aboriginal and non-Aboriginal people in this country, while still others, such as Swift and Maracle, and Newhouse and Belanger, provide wide-ranging critique of the many ways that fundamentally racist legislation, policies, and programs have long affected the lives of Aboriginal individuals, families, communities, and nations.

Given the experiences and marginalized historical status of Aboriginal people in Canada, it is hardly surprising that relatively few comprehensive examinations of Aboriginal issues in this country had been undertaken pri-or to the RCAP. While a large number of national and provincial task forces, non-government organizations, and individual researchers had examined many different areas of Aboriginal life in Canada, none of them had sought to provide a "big picture" perspective that also honoured the everyday lives and experiences of Aboriginal people across the country. As highlighted through-out the fourth edition of *Visions of the Heart*, those who contributed to the RCAP joined together in a national-level attempt to pursue reconciliation in relations between Aboriginal peoples and the rest of Canada. Some con-tributors to the current collection view the TRC in a somewhat similar way, although Dewar, Newhouse, and Hare and Davidson remind us of the import-ance of reflecting critically on the meanings and processes of reconciliation.

In the concluding dialogue to this volume, David Newhouse and I suggest that the way forward in relations between Aboriginal people and the rest of Canada requires a shared commitment to base our relations on mutual re-spect, dignity, and an appreciation of difference. This was the clear message of the RCAP, and while some would say it is time to leave the RCAP behind and look to more recent developments, we believe that all who are truly interested in moving forward would do well to (re)acquaint themselves with the princi-ples, personal accounts, in-depth analyses, and forward-looking policy state-ments that comprise the five-volume RCAP final report. To ignore this report by claiming it is simply time to move on amounts to ignoring one of the most significant historical moments and documents in Canadian history. Simply "moving on" would also mean that we will gradually lose sight of the fact that Idle No More, the TRC, fracking protests, ongoing consultations and com-munity conversations, and countless community initiatives throughout the country represent the continuation of a centuries-long struggle by Aboriginal people to be treated with respect and to develop right relations with the rest of Canada.

Making Sense of Current Expressions of Positive, Transformational Change

Contributors to this edition of *Visions of the Heart* are well aware that there are many competing versions of "the truth" about relations between Aboriginal peoples and the rest of Canada, which is why they acknowledge the importance of paying attention both to the stories we tell and to how and why we tell the stories that we do. The following collection thus demonstrates that there are many different ways to tell the stories of Aboriginal peoples in Canada. The diverse sources and types of data that contributors draw upon provide a picture of the past and present life of Aboriginal people that is both broad and intimate. Quantitative data used by Norris, Monchalin, Kerr and Beaujot, FitzMaurice and McCaskill, and Cooke and Long come from a large number and variety of sources, including our own research, government-sponsored national, provincial, and territorial task forces and surveys, a variety of federal and provincial ministries; other academic and non-government studies, and numerous reports and discussion papers. Although our analyses provide important insight into trends and issues, we recognize the dangers of generalizing from data derived from regions, cities, reserves, settlements, and towns with vastly different geographical, historical, and social characteristics. Even though Norris, Kerr and Beaujot, and Cooke and Long employ sophisticated national-level demographic data, we all caution readers against generalizing our findings to all First Nation, non-status, Métis, or Inuit people.

As an important complement to statistical analysis, qualitative research serves to flesh out our understanding of human experiences and relationships. The contributions of Castellano, McGregor, Hare and Davidson, Anderson and Ball, Voyageur, Swift and Maracle, and Monchalin illustrate that giving voice to the unique of experiences and perspectives of Aboriginal individuals deepens our understanding of the individual as well as the spiritual and collective aspects of their lives. Moreover, Cole's wonderfully playful introduction to our collection reminds us that stories that honour the diverse and subtle character of human experience and relations can invite as well as challenge readers to reflect critically on the power as well as the validity of different kinds of stories and storytellers. This is fundamental to all postcolonial discourse, since it highlights not only that social analysis is a highly interpretive act, but also that the stories told by academics can all too easily cloud rather than clarify our understanding.

Our hope, therefore, is that readers will join this and other similar conversations that invite them to put their own understandings and perspectives of Aboriginal life in Canada to the test. To encourage dialogue beyond this book, questions specific to each contribution are included at the end of each chapter (except Cole's introductory chapter, for which readers are encouraged to engage directly with the author by posing their own questions). Beyond these specific questions, we encourage readers to reflect on the more general questions of who should be responsible to initiate change and how they should go about their tasks. The glossary at the end of the book is intended to clarify how contributors understand key terms, while the further readings section at the end of each chapter offers suggestions for those who want to pursue an issue area in more depth. *Visions of the Heart* thus continues to be more than a collection of papers by individuals writing on a common theme in their areas of expertise. Together, the chapters in this collection embody the kind of dialogue that values contributions from people with different experiences and sometimes quite divergent perspectives. The intent is to highlight that openness to different experiences, insights, and voices is essential to cultivating respect and appreciation for one another. As the success of the many initiatives involving the collaboration of Aboriginal and non-Aboriginal people indicates, openness to learning from our differences is also essential to positive and lasting transformational change in our relations.

Fortunately, there have been significant positive developments over the past 50 years in the experiences of Aboriginal people in Canada and in writing by and about them. Prior to the early 1960s, those who supported the dominant social scientific perspectives of the time assumed that social disorganization, cultural conflict, and feelings of inferiority experienced by minority group members reflected their inability and/or unwillingness to adjust to rapid social and cultural change. The assumption underlying the perspectives of main (white)stream social scientists, who were apparently blind to their own ethnocentrism, was in some respects the same as that held by those whose vision it had been to colonize the "New World." Theirs was a taken-for-granted superiority since they viewed it as their right and even destiny to dominate whatever individuals, groups, and societies they deemed inferior. Consequently, in much early writing about Aboriginal people in Canada, First Peoples were blamed for having inadequate skills, for lacking understanding of European ways, and for an apparent unwillingness to do anything to alleviate their personal and social problems. Scholars, government officials, and others perpetuated this "blaming the victim" perspective through their interpretations of the data they had gathered on everything from Aboriginal peoples' rates of physical and mental illness, family violence, suicide, homicide, and incarceration to unemployment and standards of living. Moreover, many academic and government representatives assumed that little would change, since along with blaming Aboriginal people for their own problems, they also saw them as lacking adequate technical and interpersonal skills—as well as the commitment needed—to address their own problems in constructive ways.

A different set of theoretical assumptions began to take hold during the 1960s in relation to the personal and social problems experienced by Aboriginal people in Canada. According to those writing out of this emerging post-colonial perspective (which was inspired in part by such diverse writers and movements as Frantz Fanon, Malcolm X, Paulo Freire, Vine Deloria Jr, Harold Cardinal, the US civil rights movement, the American Indian Movement, and even Quebec separatism), colonizing social structures and processes needed to be examined in light of the experiences and perspectives of those who had been disadvantaged by colonization. In their analysis of issues affecting Aboriginal people in Canada, Aboriginal and non-Aboriginal scholars noted the many ways that the colonizing project of Europeans had formally (re)organized all aspects of Aboriginal life through policies and legislation that primarily served the economic, political, legal, and cultural interests of the colonizers. Moreover, they clearly identified how the cultural ways and means of colonialism gradually, though sometimes quite forcefully, displaced the diverse cultural ways and means of Aboriginal people in this country. In doing so, they drew attention to the fact that colonialism represents a "totalizing" phenomenon since it leaves no area of social life unscathed, including the way that academics and others give account of the experiences and circumstances of Aboriginal people as well as their relations with the rest of Canada.

As Martin Cooke and I discuss in our chapter on illness, health, and healing, it would be naive and socially unjust to ignore the personal and social significance of research studies and reports that indicate disproportionately high rates of suicide, certain types of addiction and illness, unemployment, incarceration, and interpersonal violence among certain segments of the Aboriginal population in Canada. We also appreciate that it would be equally naive and unjust to assume that these reports and statistics provide a clear and fully informed sense of what life is like and what life ought to be like for Aboriginal people in this country. We all clearly need to be careful not to assume that life is as bleak as many statistics and news stories would seem to indicate. However, it is equally important to recognize the numerous problems and even dangers in assuming that "all is well" for Aboriginal people in this country and in thinking that only traditional knowledge and ceremony can bring healing and hope to those who are ill and suffering. In this light, the contributors to this collection remain committed to engaging in a "critically and cautiously hopeful" spirit of post-colonial dialogue and analysis.

It is in this spirit that our authors invite readers to become aware of issues surrounding the history of research and writing about Aboriginal people. One of the most basic of these issues is that historical and social scientific analysis does not merely provide an impersonal, detached approach to understanding social life in Canada. Contributors to this collection agree that in this somewhat tumultuous age of de/reconstruction, both academic writers and readers must take seriously our role in storytelling. We share the view that open, constructive dialogue depends on everyone involved having a sense of how and why they view the relationship between academic research and storytelling in the way they do. While this does not necessarily require everyone to tell their own personal story every time they speak or write, it does require those involved to reflect honestly on certain fundamental philosophical, methodological, and theoretical issues in research involving human subjects. The issues that contributors to *Visions of the Heart* engage in various ways include: (1) the challenges, benefits, and drawbacks of using certain types of data, such as oral and ethnographic accounts, interviews, surveys, and archival information, to name a few; (2) the challenges of conveying the inner workings of personal relationships, families, communities, and societies to "outsiders"; (3) general difficulties in doing inter- and cross-cultural research; (4) honouring the different experiences, concerns, and perspectives that Aboriginal and non-Aboriginal people have in relation to the lives of Aboriginal people; and (5) politically charged questions surrounding voice appropriation, all of which are fundamentally a question of the appropriateness and validity of telling another's story. Not all contributors articulate their position on all of these issues, nor do they answer them in the same way. However, all agree that their different experiences, perspectives, styles of writing, and approaches to exploring Canadian Aboriginal issues are important to the inclusive spirit and vision that animate this collection.

Concluding Remarks

Contributors to *Visions of the Heart* agree that it is the commitment of Aboriginal people to the visions of their hearts that has long animated their willingness and ability to seek personal and social justice, healing, and a hopeful way forward. Our shared hope is that *Visions of the Heart* will contribute to visionary post-colonial dialogue and to positive, transformational change in at least two ways: by offering a critically hopeful examination of past and present sources of oppression and injustice in the lives of Aboriginal people in Canada, and by challenging/enabling readers to see the many ways that Aboriginal people in this country, in the face of these experiences, have sought to realize the visions of their hearts.

Contributors to *Visions of the Heart* thus invite readers to reflect critically on how and why they and others make sense of relations between Aboriginal peoples and the rest of Canada the way they do. We regard this as one of the benefits of engaging the post-colonial perspective, for it helps us to recognize that even the most sensitive and respectful dialogue can cultivate diverse and sometimes competing versions of individual and collective experiences, circumstances, and events. We are aware that post-colonial dialogue privileges both the stories of those whose voices have been silenced and the wonderfully diverse ways and contexts in which these stories are often told. We are also aware that each story contributing to such dialogue is embedded within a wealth of larger narratives that may or may not promote a good way forward in relations between diverse peoples. As Dewar reminds us, one of the more significant implications of this is that what readers and listeners, and even casual bystanders, come to agree "actually" happened—and what we should do about it—is collectively shaped through the telling and hearing/reading of every story. Given the legally and politically charged character of past and present relations between Aboriginal peoples and the rest of Canada, it is important that we be mindful of the fact that we may not be as honest and discerning in our storytelling and reading as we could be.[5]

The hope of every contributor to *Visions of the Heart* is that this collection will contribute in positive ways to building a Canada in which there is a deep and shared commitment to reconciliation. Our hope is that there will be continued growth in the numbers of those who share the conviction that relations between Aboriginal people and the rest of Canada must be based on mutual respect and appreciation. Our hope is that there will be continued growth in the numbers of those who share the conviction that finding a good way forward in relations between Aboriginal people and the rest of Canada requires that we affirm the inherent right of all peoples to govern themselves. Our hope is that there will be continued growth in the numbers of those who understand that a good way forward requires "the rest of Canada" to accept the invitation to walk together with the many thousands of Aboriginal people across this country who have opened their hearts and shared the burdens that our colonial past has placed on them and all their relations. We are confident that doing so will enable us all to see and hear the many cries for justice across this land, and to know what we must all do to achieve peace. We are also confident that doing so will help us all to learn the wisdom of knowing that every act of justice is an act of reconciliation. And we are confident that this will grow hope among us, for we will gradually learn to know in our hearts that every act of reconciliation is an act of love.

Notes

1. "Aboriginal" is used throughout this edition when referring to First Nations, Inuit, and Métis individuals and/or peoples. On occasion, contributors use "First Nation," "Inuit," or "Métis" over "Aboriginal" to underscore separate identities and the diversities within these population groups. "Native" is sometimes used interchangeably with "Aboriginal," although it is a somewhat ambiguous term since it is used on occasion by a number of contributors when referring to First Nations or Indians. The same is true for the term "Indian." Writers also sometimes use the term "Indigenous," although it tends to be used in reference to indigeneity in an international context.
2. Accessed 12 Dec. 2009, at http://aboriginalsportcircle.ca/en/the_north_american_indigenous_games.
3. See CBC News, "PM Cites 'Sad Chapter' in Apology for Residential Schools," 11 June 2008, http://www.cbc.ca/news/canada/pm-cites-sad-chapter-in-apology-for-residential-schools-1.699389.
4. See CBC News, "First Nations Education Bill: Ottawa Won't Move Forward," 30 May 2014, http://www.cbc.ca/news/aboriginal/first-nations-education-bill-ottawa-won-t-move-forward-1.2659516.
5. See in particular Ronald Niezen's *Truth and Indignation* (2013). Researched and written during the TRC proceedings, Niezen's argument is that the cultivation of a grand narrative focused almost exclusively on the victim/survivor experience of Aboriginal children in Indian residential schools prevented many other stories from being told, including how the banal ways in which colonialism operated in the past continue to operate today.

1

Indigenous Eco-Technological Knowings Meet University Satellite Campus Teachings on the Rez

Peter Cole

ama7 sqit. nilhtsen skwatsits tsexox kukwstumlhkacw sawen tsecwa wa7lhkelapha ama7 ama7 s7atsxen tumulhana muta7 kalanwi

I raise my hands to the powers and spirits and beings of this place human non-human more-than-human spiritual intelligences and agencies stone and star people rivers and lakes of the water nations places of sky snow ice rain fog frost sleet and dew greetings lands baked by elder brother sun glaciers hued a spectral blue by grandmother moon's gaze greetings to the named and unnamed the many leggéd the slithering and finned the crawlers scurriers webmakers nesters burrowers swaddlers fliers and waders following your original instructions without the wisdom and providence of the unseen the invisible and unvisible including viruses bacteria archaea and rogue protein nations rna and dna tribes there would be no foundation nothing to frame with it is due to the ancestors' stewardship guidance and compassion that we are alive

wolf and grizzly bear are my protectors cousin frog dragonfly and snail care for the wetlands we are the younger relatives so visitors to the land we call home after our mother rebounded from the ice ages we returned to what had been our territory from southern harrison lake *qwáol'sa* our mocassin tracks run through the snowy sasquatch mountains the lost mines of the gold seekers the rushing glacier fed rivers deserts grasslands wetlands and the sheer high sierras and mountain meadows we have always been here longer than

Steve Courson

language can say we have always had language I am from the towns reserves and plots of land where people don't live anymore the animals and fish are gone the forests destroyed waters fouled burial places flooded the bones of our ancestors disinterred or removed from tree platforms by academics our home has been claimed and settled by those who claim religious royal legislative and legal rights to our land

in the short time since the newcomer arrived in our territories they have created social spiritual and environmental crises for us our survivance and regeneration are threats to mainstream socio-political legitimacy and epistemological supremacy with their own courts of law acknowledging that aboriginal title was not extinguished on or before contact successive settler governments have partnered with extractive industries seeking to limit our temporo-spatial tenure on the land not just today and in the future but in the past as well we became trespassers on our own land retroactively for a dozen generations mainstream educational narratives claim that we came to our traditional territories and wandered around our stories tell us we have always occupied the eternal now (before linguists added past and future tenses to our language) we have always been transitioning (present perfect progressive) we do not talk of roots unless we are making baskets our way has been seasonal migration navigating paddling portaging berry-picking my home is not one location described by a static locative noun not a district lot on a grid with fixed gps coordinates we construct homes for the seasons the weather and our rituals the wind tells us when another season is coming every cell in our bodies can feel it the stories that emerge from our allelic interfaces in particle-waves inform us it is time to dry fish and berries repair our winter gear prepare for leaner times make baskets arrowheads spear points fishing gear repair nets weirs and snares purify our intentions through prayer fasting ritual and being of good mind in the day to day

beginning in 1861 aboriginal children from the lower mainland of british columbia were forcibly made to attend residential school christian churches were used to undermine traditional aboriginal teachings belief systems and relationships and to assimilate the children into western ways (Cole, 2006; Olsen, 2003) families moved to the fraser valley to be near their incarcerated children the education the children received at st mary's made them un-prepared for life up home or in settler society they had forgotten how to be respectful to the living world including themselves their self esteem suffered from their treatment there their indigenous languages cultural knowings and practices were forbidden replaced with mainstream eurocentric teachings on leaving school many of our youth remained in settler communities marry-ing outside of tribal lines trying to adapt to the imposed values religions and economies but residential schooling worked against traditional indigenous relationalities of hand heart spirit and land

the time sequence of this story is spring 1999 to autumn 1995 like the hermit crab running backwards on the intertidal zone in the dark hours looking for a home a snail shell running forwards sideways in circles the quest is indigen-ous ecological knowings and practices eco-technologies and survivance stor-ies respectful research practices

this story of indigenous technologies and the land began in 1998–1999 when my partner pat and I were living and teaching in aotearoa new zealand a two-hour drive north of wellington the day we arrived all of the tv channels broad-cast the same rugby match so we walked out into the rain and found a warm place with great coffee near the central library it was cold and windy and the hotel chambermaids kept opening all the windows in our ground-level suite high winds off otaki gusted to 207 km/h peeling off metal roofs while the prime minister tried to peel off layers of memory culture and agency from the maori it didn't work if you know the maori you'll know that to be an under-statement though I don't want to essentialize maoriness I was honoured to guest lecture at massey u where my partner held a lectureship the maori stu-dents were key actors in their own education and most weren't interested in the western progress narrative on technology education maori and multicultural education and maori studies because they knew that their own cultures were progressive long before the incursion of modernity when I acted as an adjudicator in drama education at the end of my commentary the students rose up spontaneously and performed a powerful *haka* so sudden was the counter-narrative that I almost leapt from my chair it was clear from the first day of class the maori students were not going to swallow maori technology being the translation of the *pakeha* technology curriculum into maori so technology in class became the wonderful thing it was at home healing communication and honouring the spirit in all things

it was a privilege to be a guest speaker at *te hotaka whakapakari pouako hangarau* held in maori studies conducted entirely in maori except for my presentation everyone peeled a mattress from the stacks provided and created avenues and laneways a conference camp following this were workshops in maori technologies led by dr hirini melbourne (Melbourne, 1999) of tuhoe ngati kahungunu a professor at waikato university the technology workshops were about music as healing music as navigation music as spiritual renewal but it wasn't about sharps flats octaves resolving chord progressions or variations on a theme that was chucked it was about finding your voice your spirit recognizing the spirit of the land and the spirit of the *koauau* wooden flute or clay ocarina allowing them to enter you it was about harmonics connecting with land and sky and the spirits of them each of us had to connect with the instruments we were making of clay and of wood this transitioned into hirini speaking and playing a variety of mostly wind instruments his voice a spirit song ancestral voice he spoke passionately on maori technologies spiritual intelligences more-than-human agencies making instruments and playing them fitting the instrument to the body honouring ancestors using *taonga puoro* some instruments have two voices male and female including *putorino* made variously of maire (a hardwood) albatross bone stone and *matai* hirini says rhythm movement and connecting are essential to life the *hue puru hau* which is a large gourd *pakuru* a tapping stick *ku* a single-stringed instrument and a small gourd rattle that celebrates movement and life the *porotiti* is a small disc that creates sound when swung on a cord in earlier times it accompanied *karakia* prayers and set pitch for new compositions of *waiata koroua* in some areas it was used for healing purposes spun over the faces and chests of sleeping children who were suffering with colds or influenza the vibrations helped loosen the mucus it was also placed in the hands of those suffering from rheumatism and arthritis the vibrations created by manipulation of the instrument gave relief this family of instruments bade hirini farewell as he travelled to the spirit world

paddle paddle stroke paddle swooooooooosh paddle swoooooosh paddle elddap
suddenly without warning the text of my phd dissertation looms ahead
and above like a giant spiritbook as we walk homeward through *hokowhitu*
grove towards the bridge of coots ducks eels waterplants and canada geese
we are subsumed through this story into others by unbidden spontaneous
narratives

during the 1997–1998 academic year as a visiting scholar I co-taught educational technology and research methodology at a university in new jersey
where there were no self-declaring native american peoples in the college of
education except for the caretaker of the building a lenni lenape who had not
been told anything about his culture that had been invisiblized there weren't
any books in the library about his people and the students had never heard
of non-digital technologies and thought native americans were extinct some
students felt forests were better delivered on hypertext or by ups in the form
of furniture than in real time real space children asked (O'Riley, 2003) when
the grounds crew would clear the forest of the debris that was the forest part
of our job was to supervise student teachers throughout north central new
jersey there were metal detectors and armed guards at schools technologies
of control and surveillance most k–12 schools had one or two computers but
one "high-end" middle school near the northern border with new york had
400 computers all obsolete eight months later

january february 1997 melbourne australia we were invited lecturers for a
month at deakin university where we opened the school year and presented
to faculty and graduate students on indigenous education curriculum theory
technology discourses and research methodology we participated in sympo-
sia dealing with intercultural conversations and international distance education (privileging privileged foreign students) we met with koori graduate
students and learned that koori communities determined curriculum and
methodologies from pre-school to graduate school now that is a progressive
narrative two ideas stay with me from geelong both spoken by a yorta yorta
graduate student and grandmother we had been visiting the wool museum in
geelong and learning about the drover "boys" one comment was that her community had to get rid of tv and alcohol and the other that "when they get their
history straight they will be okay" (Patton, 1997) we met with members of the
marimbiak nations aboriginal corporation (mnac) and the victoria aboriginal
education association in the former a few handfuls of earth from each community were brought into the boardroom and set into a niche the length of the
boardroom table covered over by glass the director of mnac richard frankland
(1997) a gunditjmara man had recently won a national award for *no way to*

forget a film he wrote narrated and co-produced about the killing in custody of aboriginal youth malcolm smith which was screened at cannes here was a koori man using the technological savvy of the newcomer to open up spaces for indigenous voices and stories

as *st'at'imc* we have lived in our territory for thousands of years using stone wood and plant technologies none requiring electricity batteries the damming of rivers clear-cutting forests destroying the habitats of animals and birds or creating toxic effluents we have long used fire as a technology of renewal my earliest home memories are the smell and warmth of the wood stove the colour and shadows of light from kerosene lamps and candles and burning the grass every year going to bed and getting up with the sun we have always valued manual technologies tools and processes that promote judicious use of and respect for land and water knife axe chisel hammer saw pliers scythe shovel rake hoe nail horseshoe the planting stick using manual building skills and smithing that do not continually use energy from the earth and poison it with tailings as primary products sharing was valued above all and the potlatch allowed for wealth distribution as a community ceremony to the extent the giver would become poor yet wealthy in her/his generosity this runs counter to capitalism today the technologies of economic growth foreground cash crops monocrops genetically denatured crops that destroy the nutrients embedded in/as the very livingness of the earth digital technologies distance us from the land from our own bodies they limit our thinking and feeling and sense of belonging as part of the natural world there is a loss of a sense of individual and collective responsibility and interdependency with other earth beings aho

for more than a decade the research that pat and I have done with *st'at'imc* and other indigenous peoples has been about the regeneration of traditional ecological knowledges and practices including language the dissemination of results through the intermingling of poetic dramatic and storytelling voices we are concerned with the daily practices of orality and audition in our culture lifelong education for us has always been contiguous with the process of life survival and self-remembering before the coming of churches residential schools and prisons before we knew how we knew we knew

much teaching and administration of first nations education in k–12 and at post-secondary in british columbia in autumn 1995 is designed and taught by settler faculty many of whom are not aware of the complexities of and differentiations between various indigenous cultures knowledges and practices the use of present tense here keeps what is often relegated to the past from slipping away into forgotten stories dissolving referents universities continue the colonial policy of privileging mainstream western knowledges by flying in settler faculty to teach aboriginal students imperialism is normalized invisiblized as first nations students are liberated from local cultural narratives many *st'at'imc* see this practice of teaching modernist progress metanarratives and denatured reconstituted essentialized indigenous knowledges to indigenous peoples as cultural genocide *takem swat, tsitmusam ats7a kalanmints tsina sqweqwel cwis mitsaq lti zenka* we must attend to the spirits form a circle of protection healing and regeneration

lights fade to black voiceover announces a one-act play satellite campus scenario white teacher indigenous class (Cole, 2006) scene opens with a few bars of the *allegro* from mozart's serenade no 13 for strings in g major k525 spot on prologuist downstage centre speaking to audience in oral writing as in oral storytelling there is no pause for footnoting citation intertitles subtitles marginalia he says she says or stage directions it is up to the listener or reader to determine who is speaking from contextual clues for those not familiar with storytelling as a readerly writerly listenerly practice italics are used here to distinguish between teacher and student intertextual dialogic intervention takes place via migration of indigenous conversations from personal memory this class is called indigenous culture environment and technology the teacher speaks first in plain text crossfade to students a few bars from "indian reservation (the lament of the cherokee reservation indian)" with paul revere and the raiders crossfade into flashbacks sutures dream sequences shock cuts fragments visions tableaux montage lights gradually up on a classroom in a rural setting in the rainforest plateau on the west coast of british columbia

stupid indians cant they figure out how to give me references bibliography you'd think they never heard of apa scholarly citation how do they think they can get a half-decent mark using ideas that come out of a shoebox last week everything was working out not perfect anyway this indian guy after weeks of silence suddenly pipes up from the back row

hey teach'

I ignore his rude gesture as reverse patronizing and continue my lecture on plato

hey teach' he says *I got news for you*

you put your hand up if you want to talk in my class

not in my culture we only put our hands up if we're being robbed or arrested or when we hide food in the tree or to honour anyway I think you got your posses- sive adjectives mixed up it's "our" class we are a plurality and in our own way a collective singularity

very funny jimmy you have a way with words

I know when I talk I got great command so teach' if I'm so smart what's with the d you gave me am I that stupid or are you not sure how to "assess" my work

work huh it has no references shows no prior reading in the subject area it's self-indulgent subjective scribbling you don't even use a computer

I don't need a computer I got a pen and when that runs out I got a knife and lots of pencils my kids crayons charcoal slate lots of hardware anyway I got no 'lectricity in my shack like most of us here

are you trying to impress the rest of the class with your wit and repartee

no sir I'm just asking why the d why that's a favourite white person word we're not a hundred per cent sure what it means where it comes from how to use it it won't catch us fish or deer or help us find berries us indians don't have too much use for why and lots of other white words mostly those adverbs white people made up so the verbs wouldn't look so limp

we indians not us indians

we indians never heard of that tribe how about you teresano

subjective case not objective I was correcting your grammar

oh it's not mine mr t I don't own any part of the english language anyway most of the time us indians prefer the accusative case or the vocative locative dative ablative or instrumental because the nominative and genitive are not how we were taught to locate ourselves it's how we adapted to the imposed language and education system in my community we do not privilege reason metanarrative or abstraction over storying

as a faculty member I have professional standards set by the board of govern- ors the senate the ministry the faculty it's like ritual is to you people *kalanwi what do you know about our rituals you think you can container them by turning them into collective nouns you think you can understand what we do because you have the word "understand" in your language you think you can use reason as a prybar to surveil and control indigenous other no teach' my conversation continues long after yours ends ritual for us is not a time and place and action it is the ongoing spectrum of being doing and becoming self-remembering is not about self or about remembering but despite the division of the world into words events and sensations*

it seems we have a problem regarding acceptable academic style and validity

problem I don't think "we" have one of those all we got are a bunch of nouns stuck in traffic "problem" is part of binary thinking you think words join together no words from the academy join apart they are fences exclusionary barriers moats we indians got good languages too ucwalmicwts has worked for us for a long time especially before the linguists changed it to suit the languages they think in and understand

you are proving my point the education we provide allows you to argue with us

and you are proving mine that two people can have a conversation in which there is no exchange of anything but words you have mutated bakhtin from dialogic to parallel monologues in our community we reference our elders ancestors and the spirits

you refuse to let me teach you yet you invited me

you asked the boutique indians (Price, 2012) who run the education programs to invite you they have been whitewashed into believing we're only good for primary resource extraction training and employment now we are told the computer will save us we are told to trust that cyberspace is more fair more equitable less racist than downtown vancouver western education shows no respect for the land-based spiritual connection of first peoples with rivers and forests four-leggéds the wingéd ones fish nations the powers and spirits and beings moon and sun sky and earth stones and tree nations it is contrary to euro doctrine to pray to grandmother moon elder brother sun heretical to attribute divine power life and agency to stones visions dreams spiritual intelligences

does anybody know what the apa publication manual is edna

sure teach' I use it for a doorstop one time I threw it at a cub that was clawing my door it's good packs a real wollop you think you can just come up with these fictitious stories and that will make me change how I assess you

oh they're not fictitious no way indian truth is just more flexible than white truth

tell me what are the central tenets of your thesis

fade in overture of *le nozze di figaro* k492 in d major *presto tempo* fade out in out to accompany the conversation over the next four minutes adjust volume to suit

I do not subscribe to centre but to multiple loci conjuncted beaded concatenated decentred perimeter can be central the circle is important in my culture not as geometrical centre but as joining of hands coming together of minds hearts spirits the ovoid in our carvings have multiple foci as for tenets crabgrass and trickster discourse pi is important for us as the relationship between the seeming linearities of positional causality and the perimetral entanglement of community in our narratives perimeter is not conceptually geometrical a circle is not always round with non-dimensional points on it equidistant from an imagined centre for us the centre is everywhere

what are the underpinnings of your thesis

underpinnings have to do with foundations and structures our foundations are nomadic seasonal contextual not fixed static rigid ours must withstand violent seismic activity

what cultural understandings are you working with

cultural understandings are not authenticatable generalizable information bytes that can be synthesized from outside of our culture from outside of our language the assumption that others can find solutions for us is culturally insensitive we have been case studied action researched ethnographized to death we do not need empowering by others using western superstructures interfaces retrofittings subductions we must empower ourselves

who are your collaborators your subjects what is your research question

for us collaboration is communal consensual commensal we pass the stone or the stick or feather until everyone is of one mind my research does not employ the interrogative orality may have sufficed in pre-contact times it's time to move on you need to use academic discourses build from the shoulders of giants

western formats and genres have never been our way we do not want to talk about how white people talk about other people white or otherwise

precedence it is very important in our society it's how our courts operate

precedence you mean like who was here first if you're going to talk about precedence let's precede back to who was here before the captains and governors the surveyors the real estate speculators and railroads

precedence has to do with law not with prior residency

and it's colonizers who make up the laws that allow them to steal our homelands they are in a conflict of interest and should recuse themselves from negotiations where the appearance of bias is evident your democracy operates as tyranny of the majority

someone had to intervene you weren't making use of the land you had no knowledge of forest management the forests and potential hydropower were lying idle

the trees were growing the rivers were flowing the forest managed itself without chainsaws clear-cut log booms pulp mills heli-logging

you did not clear the land plant crops engage in commerce and economic growth

we ate locally we did not claw our mother with iron plows throw artificial fertilizers hormones radio-isotopes toxins onto her belly we have always had reciprocal relationships with salmon oolican berries the four-leggeds how is clear-cutting growth more money flowing does not mean economic growth only increased economic activity growth needs to be spoken of in context with economic growth comes the growth of poisons in food in water in furniture in carpets in clothing in the air everywhere where are these indicators on your economic graphs and flow charts where does the breach of the mount poley tailings pond and thousands like it in this country fit into your diagrams of growth growth is a euphemism for unregulated capitalism before euro settlement you had primitive ideas about religion and spirituality you prayed to trees fish birds and the sun made graven images of cedar

yes we carve masks totem poles house posts we speak with the creator with more than words give thanks by sharing feasting carving burning medicines brushing ourselves with cedar ceremony is always a verb and it is not confined to conceptual space

you had no science you knew nothing about the rotation of the earth or about distance or space and time you had no numbers

we had one two three and enough we did not need numbers we did not want to send space ships to the moon we can travel there in spirit without building anything we did not want to solve problems caused by the number systems we invented we prospered without logarithms derivatives square roots chi square medians and standard deviation

you are able to talk like this because we have taught you

I am able to translate from my language from the knowings of my community into the units of information I have harvested in your prisons residential schools and churches

you see you are richer metaphorically from us being here

the visitors came here in boats saw us on the shore in our longhouses living here content fishing picking berries roots bulbs clams seaweed now they want to virtualize us

you can't even tell me who your sources are

the forest and stones the sky the spirit beings the ancestors smile

we're talking about technology indigenous culture and environment

we got technology too teach' and we don't even have electricity they made us buy laptops those stupids at indian affairs and we got nowhere to plug them in or charge them they won't give us electricity because they say it costs too much for a transformer we got modems but the nearest phone line is two valleys over and nobody wants cellphone towers to fry their children's brains with wifi microwaves none of us wants the internet but we get pushed there pretty quick (parenthetical smile) we have entered a new millennium this is an age of global markets we need partnerships with industry better technologies interactive multimedia television documentaries

my people need to get rid of television and alcohol

who's stopping you

after six generations of residential schooling it takes time to reprogram to get back to how we have always lived we're each paying six grand for this degree we don't want to throw that money away learning to be white technologized in the margins we only want our children to have a better chance than we had to be st'at'imc not generic clones

then make your chances engage in modernist intellectual discourses

you mean like how traditional can never be modern how modernism as the empire's truth regime machine essentializes everything with capitalism the universal (dis)solvent how tribal can never be other than other how binary is the default position of mainstream western intellectual hegemony

you need to learn to think rationally see how the world really is not all your hocus-pocus

my grandmother showed me the fish wasn't where it looked like it was she said throw your spear where the fish is not where the water tells you it is it takes time to learn water when you can only think about reflection sometimes ideas and thinking and hearts need to bend with the natural world rather than controlling it with words numbers formulas refractive thinking is about realizing that numerical indices of refraction between different media is like seeing across through or between cultures the fish is where and how you have learned to see it value it relate to it

you are making students mistrust their own senses saying their perceptions are flawed you need reality therapy psychometric testing and assessment

I know about psychology how white experts analyze my community into discrete units quantize us tell us what is wrong with us tell us most of our children are special needs

where would we be without psychology who would assess children devise learning outcomes and provide quantitative structural analysis and code the unseen patterns *our community doesn't want or need your pre-emptive retroactive findings [that were better off lost] based on skewed presumptions about controls dependent and independent variables correlations binaries people-as-numbers and essentialist extrapolability my friend george told me this lakota saying "it's a good thing you're moving slow because you're going in the wrong direction"* (Charles, as cited in Cole, 2002)

what's that got to do with technology indigenous culture and environment

let's talk about environment starting with weather I see on tv weather people talking about meteorology some of us use a weather prediction drum to predict weather some use dogs we watch the animals plants birds insects george said that his elders speak of rain teachings how opening the window on the tundra at night is opening the window to the spirit world they are connected you won't get that in a textbook

not in my syllabus I'll tell you that

he speaks of our history being written on the tongues of our elders in the old days when there was no fixed meaning in the time when the earth's skin was thin

if you're trying to talk post-colonialism you're off track

there is no post when it comes to colonialism in case you haven't noticed you're the one standing at the front of the class telling us about ourselves and our land and cultures this is not why we are investing in post-secondary education to learn about ourselves second- or third-hand from a misinformed objective positioning we are in the margins to you but at least we got an aisle seat in case the architecture doesn't hold

you got a lot of smarts for a bush haida

I am not haida I am from this land that is enough the name of my people in your language has nothing to do with us we are not your words they are not from this land

I'm not interested in speculation or polemics I ask again who are your sources

all my relations

in particular

my friend laura (Tohe, as cited in Cole, 2002) *speaks lovingly about the land of the navajo o keo my feet below the land we belong to the land and james* (Riding In, as cited in Cole, 2002) *speaks of rain just hitting the desert that sound the dampness and this aroma happens*

what has this to do with technology indigeneity and environment

when n scott (Momaday, as cited in Cole, 2002) *was asked how long it took for a people to become indigenous he said he couldn't remember*

so much for orality

he spoke of identity being fixed in the earth the great matrix of the oral

orality is passé we've got writing tools everything else is anecdotal spurious

you expect me to transform my knowings into english words rhythms sounds

writing legitimizes english is a global language *ucwalmicwts is almost extinct*

some knowings are not in the form of words some are secret not to be shared writing is not always an option nor is speaking language is not separate from land or from body speaking involves movement not just of ideas or prayers but of the air that gives us life that gives life to the forest clouds are exhaled conversations forest breath

do you have any evidence do any of your sources have temporo-spatial locations

peter george (1998) speaks of "the successful navigation of the rapids" language has its turbulences back eddies whitewater time and space are turbulent creations transforming nature into formulas numbers equations following the lead of classical science modernist mainstream education needs to quantify turn everything into numbers

we are talking about environment indigeneity and technology not about language

they are entangled chris jocks (as cited in Cole, 2002) *speaks of "the relation of words land earth cultivation topography being rooted in ground there has always been a conversation in what the white man calls 'nature'" maybe we could become part of it*

speaking figuratively you mean

ines talamentez (as cited in Cole, 2002) from the apache nation speaks of spiritual homeland saying we must not cut into our mother even when you dig a pit for a sweat lodge it is with hands not a tool or implement you make an offering of perspiration

and what is your point

I do not speak in points or bullets or arrows we believe that land is a source of culture not a resource sue kidwell (as cited in Cole, 2002) talks about corn becoming skin skin becoming corn when I dance I am the corn

Figurative metaphors when extended lose their meaning how about using the scientific method analysis generalizability logic

what about common sense birgil kills straight (1998) speaks of rocks becoming of first world spirit of the sacred sites of the lakota and the songs

environment is not language they are separate this class is not about indigenous mythologies or cosmologies

this class is mostly "about" (smile) aboutness janice longboat (1998) says we must look after one another now that our health is at an all-time low we are out of balance harmony and respect with the earth and spirit keepers

harmony you mean osmotic isotonicity there is no harmony in nature except mathematically symbolically it's violent wild savage

I am not alluding to "in" nature it "is" nature there is no prepositional distantiation from indigenous medicine health-keeping is a way of life agenda not addenda janice talks about needing piece of mind medicine

we need antibiotics the canada food guide and medical models of health you're not going to correct anything with talk and romantic notions if there is no standard no standardization there is no surety of wellness any quack could practise *and does it seems including many admitted into medical schools and colleges of physicians and surgeons who kill people with unacceptable hygiene laziness and neglect chief jake thomas (1998) says that medicine friends are part of our healing we are told to look to our elders watch the animals seek beyond the words*

we don't have time to watch the animals we're too busy making a living nobody has time to garden anymore and learn about herbs we get what we need at the supermarket pharmacy and walk-in clinic

mohawk elder cecilia mitchell (1998) says she was told as a child you need medicines from where you live not from california you pick in the morning when the sun is coming up the power goes right into the plant first burn tobacco show respect for their lives

respect for food is a little over the top how does this relate to this course we need direct contact causal evidence not mumbo-jumbo

cecilia says that a plant has a spirit there are many warrior plants out there ready to give their lives for your body the creator's original breath is still here it is important to address everything as our relatives how we relate to others including plants and animals determines how we are responded to

nobody has time for any of that I am teaching you so you don't have to do manual work so you don't have to (pause)

what touch the land we need to alter the attitude and practice of accumulating wealth

we're all just trying to make a living

lee maracle talks about her relative joe capilano (Maracle, 1998) who said that if you eat like them you will live like them and die like them

we're a long way from the course readings our seminar topic is sustainable development

deb macgregor (1998) from whitefish river says there is no sustainable development only sustainable community sustainability would be giving back to the earth which already exists in communities it is not something they can be given every time a language is spoken a ceremony is done this is an act of sustainability we must live our knowledge we must protect the intellectual property rights of indigenous people

assuming they are under threat of seizure

they are continually poached look at the linguists who acknowledge indigenous speakers in their research but do not list them in their bibliography as primary sources my friend and colleague agnes mcfarland (1998) is a maori from tuhoi she wrote two master's theses both in maori one for the academy the other only for her tuhoe community written in an ancient maori dialect which she will not translate into english or to modern maori st'at'imc have knowings too before the white people came we taught our children without ministry of education prescribed curricula we had no special education needs education was for every person it was called living in the village

all good things flow into the city

if you are going to quote or paraphrase pericles teach' an acknowledgement in the form of a verbal citation is advised and you could be a bit more accurate

I was making a general statement responding to your paean on the village you have some interesting ideas but they are not mainstream epistemologies

the mainstream is made of tributaries my language and people are part of that stream tributaries are not greater or lesser than what they flow into

moving right along robert what is your project for this term

my project is to not have a project

fine one less paper to mark so you're not going to collect data no interviews

I will hold conversations with the land and the sky using participant observation

that's innovative but does the sky talk back does the land you need precedent

marie annharte baker michael marker pat o'riley tomson highway gerald vizenor bob lovelace bonita lawrence jason price are contemporary aboriginal writers who use the idea of respectful engagement and grassroots collaboration successfully if you just stick with the tried and true it'll be easier for everybody

we have been tried and found no truth just the metanarratives of empire

that's the history of colonialism victors and vanquished which side do you want to be on

mainstream white history is crooked filled with bent discovery stories prehistoricized indians essentialized assumptions assumpted essentialisms

marie what is your project I trust you'll be in line with academic norms

I am writing my dissertation so that my community and I are a unit an alliance a recognizable we rather than they and I

so your whole community is getting a master's degree that's nice what about you clarke

my project combines performance and collaboration in the creation and implementation of a series of related scripts which exemplify traditional and contemporary thought and social practices of first nations people

performance this isn't a drama class we're not doing installations I assume you'll use the interviewing mode

I will explore the narrative of our land and culture but not by subjecting my people to interrogation using the question and answer mode

where will you get answers if you have no questions

I will not investigate cross-section or situate my people in the space of ethnographic discourse

so where will the data come from will it rain down on you

I will speak with children parents elders who did not go to school and who went to residential school band school public school home school bush school downtown eastside school using conversation sharing stories you can't have a bunch of rambling narratives running off in all directions they have to be controlled organized analyzed coded

we decide together how the stories are to be told if we want to tell them we talk about what kind of education people in our community might need no coding just conversation

I assume you'll use a prior ethnography prelegitimized paradigms

the land and my people are not archaeological sites anthropological opportunities objects to be gazed at disinterred carbon-dated rediscovered or historiographically reframed we are not objects of otherness accusatives of grammatical extraterritoriality we will not anthropologize ourselves one another or seek legitimacy or acceptance from the colonizer

then what and where are you if you are not academically situated popular culture

we are our story our land is its story we are guardians and children of the land not its genitive agents my community is my sentence my phrase my word my ambience

sorry that won't do apa format is strictly enforced don't get me wrong we're not discriminatory we just want the same rules for everybody well that's it class I have a plane to catch see you next week

don't count on it teach' we're going fishing berry-picking harvesting seaweed and medicines graveyard cleaning fixing things up for the winter performing our ceremonies our responsibilities our original instructions kukwstum'c

2

All Our Relations: Aboriginal Perspectives on Environmental Issues in Canada

Deborah McGregor

The environment is fundamentally important to First Nation Peoples. It is the breadth of our spirituality, knowledge, languages and culture. It is not a commodity to be bartered with to maximize profit, nor should it be damaged by scientific experimentation.

The environment speaks of our history, our language and relationship to her. It provides us with nourishment, medicine and comfort. Our relationship and interaction was and is the basis and source of independence. We do not dominate her. We harmonize with her. (AFN, 1993: 39)

Métis people have a holistic view of the world that is based on the concept of integration with the natural environment. Métis people have a very close connection to the landscape and its ecosystems; the land and water are relied upon by the Métis for food, medicine, and spiritual fulfillment and livelihood. The interconnected, interdependent nature of ecosystems, of which the Métis people are a part, means that all aspects of the environment are connected in some way. (MNO, 2012: 3)

We, native people, have lived in our land since time immemorial. We know our lands, are experts in our environment. We do not study it for just a few years. It is a lifetime study. It is knowledge from the beginning passed on to us by our Ancestors. We have knowledge, true knowledge because it's our way of life. (Titi Kadluck, in McDonald et al., 1997: 1)

Ben Powless

Introduction

In Canada, it is commonly recognized that Aboriginal peoples (First Nations, Métis, and Inuit) tend to have close and intimate ties to the lands and environments they inhabit (RCAP, 1996). As the above quotations indicate, the health and well-being of Aboriginal people stem directly from these unique relationships.

To fully appreciate the relationships between Aboriginal peoples and the environment, it is important to have an understanding of Aboriginal world view, ontology, and epistemology. While the diverse languages, governance systems, laws, and practices of Aboriginal peoples shape their unique relationships with the environment, there are common environmental philosophies and shared values among the different nations evident in their interactions with the natural world. This is also true internationally, where many diverse nations from around the world have expressed common principles that reflect their values and experiences (Clarkson et al., 1992).

While Aboriginal people in Canada experience and express many of the same concerns relating to environmental challenges as other people in this country, the unique history, identity, culture, and constitutional status of Aboriginal peoples means that they experience such challenges in profoundly different ways. In particular, Aboriginal and treaty rights are front and centre in every discussion of the environmental challenges faced by Aboriginal peoples in Canada (AFN, 1993; MNO, 2012).

This chapter will provide an overview of a number of Aboriginal environmental perspectives and experiences and how these play out in the contemporary environmental governance landscape in Canada. Discussion will centre on the idea that *environment* is more than just the natural landscape, a home surrounding us. It includes aspects of the world that are tangible and intangible, physical and spiritual. Environment is not just the observed landscape; it is the relationship itself that Aboriginal peoples have with the land.

Three main strands form the basis of exploring Aboriginal environmental perspectives over time:

1. For thousands of years, Aboriginal peoples flourished on their territories by using their own knowledge systems to develop and maintain sustainable relationships. In this strand, Indigenous traditional environmental perspectives will be explored with a focus on Creation stories.
2. Aboriginal peoples' relationships to their environment/lands/territories have been severely disrupted through the colonial practices of Europeans. Understanding this history is essential to understanding the current situation Aboriginal people face in relation to environmental governance in Canada and the reasons behind their efforts to re-establish relationships with their territories.
3. After centuries of displacement and dispossession from their territories, Aboriginal peoples in Canada have increasingly sought to reconnect with their lands through various processes, including comprehensive land claims, self-government agreements, and other collaborative environmental initiatives. This strand explores the mechanisms in place that have the potential to lead to respectful coexistence between Aboriginal peoples and Canadian society.

Aboriginal Concepts of Environment: All of Creation

There are many different conceptions of the term "environment." The *Oxford English Dictionary* defines environment as a noun:

1. The surroundings or conditions in which a person, animal, or plant lives or operates.
2. The natural world, as a whole or in a particular geographical area, especially as affected by human activity.

Similarly, the Canadian Environmental Protection Act (1999) states that:

"environment" means the components of the Earth and includes
   (a) air, land and water;
   (b) all layers of the atmosphere;
   (c) all organic and inorganic matter and living organisms; and
   (d) interacting natural systems that include components referred to in
        paragraphs (*a*) to (*c*).

In these commonly applied definitions, the environment is seen as separate from people, despite the fact that we live immersed within it. The separation of humans from the rest of the environment is a key feature of the Western world view. Not everyone shares this view, or sees it as constructive in the move towards greater sustainability.

Louise Grenier (1998: 31) attempts to bridge the separation of people from the natural environment by discussing efforts to "treat people and the environment together as equally important." Grenier's work reflects a growing recognition globally that humans can no longer set themselves apart from the natural world. She uses the metaphor of an egg to describe human relationships to the environment whereby the yolk represents the people and the white represents the environmental ecosystem. Accordingly, the "egg of sustainability" expresses the human–ecosystem interrelationship and the need to assess human and ecosystem together—the whole system as well as the parts" (Grenier, 1998: 71). Although Grenier still views people and the environment as distinct, they are at least physically connected (the people are "inside" the environment).

The perspectives that Indigenous peoples have of the environment are significantly different from the views expressed above. Throughout this chapter I use the terms "environment," "the natural world," or "all of Creation" interchangeably since both tangible (material) and intangible features of the world, such as spiritual aspects, ancestors, and spiritual teachers, are equally important to Aboriginal peoples. The following section explores Aboriginal conceptions of "environment" through the lens of Indigenous Creation or origin stories.

Starting at the Beginning: Creation and Origin Stories

Origin stories say a great deal about how people understand their place in the universe and their relationship to other living things. Creation stories are the means by which cultural communities ground their identity in particular narratives and particular landscapes. (Johnston, 2005: 1)

Anishinaabe Creation stories inform us of our beginnings and provide the conceptual frameworks for an Indigenous understanding of our relationship to Creation and its many beings. Anishinaabe storytellers Basil Johnston (*Ojibway Heritage*, 1976) and Edward Benton-Banai (*The Mishomis Book*, 1988) both begin their books with Creation. Below is part of the story as told by Johnston (1976: 12):

> Kitche Manitou (The Great Spirit) beheld a vision. In this vision he saw a vast sky filled with stars, sun, moon, and earth. He saw an earth made of mountains and valleys, islands and lakes, plains and forests. He saw trees and flowers, grasses and vegetables. He saw walking, flying, swimming, and crawling beings. He witnessed the birth, growth and the end of things. At the same time he saw other things live on. Amidst change there was constancy. Kitche Manitou heard songs, wailings and stories. He touched wind and rain. He felt love and hate, fear and courage, joy, sadness. Kitche Manitou meditated to understand his vision. In his vision, Kitche Manitou understood that his vision had to be fulfilled. Kitche Manitou was to bring into being and existence what he had seen, heard and felt.

In the Anishinaabe world view, Creation comes originally from *vision* and people come originally from the spirit world. In addition to generating living beings, the Creation process begins to lay out the key ideas and principles that comprise the foundation for Indigenous laws and codes of conduct: how every being will relate to the Creator and all other beings in Creation. These laws do not just apply to people, but to all of Creation (sun, moon, stars, animals, etc.).[1] Jim Dumont, Anishinaabe scholar and Elder, adds, "The very first concept at the centre of everything is the spirit. If we can understand the place of Spirit in the Indigenous world view, that will define for us the starting place, the centre of our understanding" (Dumont, 2006: 4).

Richard Atleo, in his book *Tsawalk: A Nuu-chah nulth Worldview*, observes that many questions about life are answered in the origin stories since they reflect the interrelationship between the physical and spiritual realms, and that it has always been well understood "that all things come from the spiritual realm" (Atleo, 2004: 17). The origin stories, Atleo states, "consequently provide an orientation to the life and reality that, prior to colonialism, allowed the Nuu-chah-nulth to manage their lives and communities for millennia" (Atleo, 2004: 5).

Origin or Creation stories inform us of our relationships with the natural world and guide our conduct within it. They outline our duties as humans to ensure Creation continues. They lay out principles (often implicitly) for how humans are to coexist with non-human relatives and beings. The Haudenosaunee Creation story "tells us of the great relationships within this world and our relationships, as human beings, with the rest of Creation" (Williams in HETF, 1999: 2).

Further to this, origin stories illustrate how humans were fully integrated into the rest of Creation. John Petagumskum (in McDonald et al., 1997: 5) provides the following example:

> Everything created on this earth was put in its natural place. The Creator decided where everything, including all plant life, should be. . . . People have their place in the environment along with the animals. In the time when only Cree and Inuit were out on the land there was nothing to disturb the animals and plants. At that time, everything in the natural world spoke for itself. People were so connected with nature that they knew and read its signs. . . . The Elders watched and kept track of everything around them. They closely observed the animals in order to predict the weather.

People were simply part of Creation. The interactions between humans and other beings (animals) were guided by natural and spiritual processes that were understood and respected by humans and all other beings to ensure harmony. Indigenous origin stories point to the centrality of spirituality in how one conducts himself/herself appropriately and respectfully in relation to the natural world. The teachings and lessons embedded in Aboriginal peoples' stories that have provided them with guidance and key principles for living can thus be thought of as environmental principles.

Environmental Principles

Identifying basic Indigenous environmental principles embedded in the stories and the lived experiences of Indigenous peoples can help us develop a conceptual framework based on Indigenous world view and epistemology, though it is important to keep in mind that each Indigenous nation and culture developed its own conceptual frameworks (stories) for understanding relationships with the natural world based on where its people travelled and lived. Principles derived from such frameworks have persisted and continue to be applied despite historical attempts to eradicate them (HETF, 1999). Although Indigenous people who point to the ongoing relevance of Indigenous environmental principles are often criticized for wanting to "return to the past," such criticism indicates a narrowness of understanding and vision on the part of the critics. Such principles remain relevant today; in fact, they are essential to achieving what is now commonly referred to as "environmental sustainability."

The purpose of Aboriginal people developing a number of basic principles associated with environmental thought, perspectives, and values has been to ensure that all members of each community would understand their role and conduct themselves in a sustainable, ethical, and respectful way in relation to the environment. It was believed by many that ethical behaviour would follow if people understood their responsibilities to "all their relations."

Such an approach has been beautifully expressed in the text, *Words That Come Before All Else: Environmental Philosophies of the Haudenosaunee* (HETF, 1999), one of the few resources provided by Indigenous peoples that explicitly speaks to Indigenous environmental philosophies and values. In Haudenosaunee tradition, the Thanksgiving Address, *or Ohen:ton Karihwetehkwen*, is given before any gathering begins. It is aimed in part at building consensus and acknowledging "the power and duties of every part of the world, and joining our minds and determinations together to fulfill the obligations of humans beings in the web of life" (HETF, 1999: 1).

The principles outlined in the following pages are shown in artificially discrete categories and in no particular order. Their enumeration is simply intended to aid in following the flow of the text. In reality, the principles overlap. These principles and their application have always operated in an open, flexible way to allow for adaptation to changing circumstances. This will be evident in our examination of some of the similar and different ways that Aboriginal peoples have sought to gain control over environmental governance through self-government and comprehensive land claim processes.

Principle #1: The Earth Is Feminine

Many references made to the Earth (or environment) refer to the Earth as "our Mother." The Earth is feminine and she creates, as women do. Kim Anderson, Barbara Chow, and Margaret Haworth-Brockman (2013: 14) found a clearly gendered aspect to Aboriginal relationships with the Earth in their research on water and Aboriginal women. As they report:

> The feminine relationship with the spirit and life force of water is also present when it comes to the larger feminine body of Mother Earth (as the Earth is understood in many Aboriginal cultures). A number of the Grandmothers related the life-giving waters carried by women to the life-giving waters and cycles of the Great Mother.

The idea that the Earth is the mother of us all is a powerful one; it determines how one treats the Earth. If a society respects and values women and mother-hood, the Earth will be valued and treated accordingly. In many Aboriginal so-cieties, women were respected and regarded as powerful, especially in relation to their major life-giving ability—the power to give birth (Anderson, 2000). Just as our mothers nourish us, so does the Earth. Because the Earth is our mother, we have an intimate relationship with her, and we recognize our reliance upon her. Onondaga Elder and international Indigenous rights activist Oren Lyons (1980: 173) emphasizes the importance of this relationship: "Without the earth, without your mother, you could not be sitting here; without the sun, you would not be here." From an Aboriginal viewpoint, the Earth is to be treated gently and with loving care; she is not an entity that one would ever consider "con-quering" or exploiting for wealth and economic gain.

Even in death, there is life and rebirth. In death, we return to our mother. As community environmental activist Sally Benedict notes, "We have returned our People before us to Mother Earth. These are the resting places for our dead. It is their wish that their physical bodies return to the Earth, to be part of the system which encourages and promotes new life. That is to be respected throughout time" (HETF, 1999: 12).

Principle #2: The Earth Is Alive

The notion of the Earth as a life-giving entity is closely linked to the view that the Earth is alive and filled with spirit. "The Earth herself is a living, breathing, conscious being, complete with heart/feeling, soul/spirit, and physical and organic life, as it is with all the relatives of Creation" (Dumont, 2006: 12). The understanding that the Earth is alive results in even closer relationships between Aboriginal people and the Earth. As the late Sioux scholar, Vine Deloria Jr, wrote in *God Is Red,* Aboriginal identity is "virtually indistinguishable from the earth itself, the human being, as it were, is com-pletely in harmony with the Mother Earth and inseparable in every way" (1994: 149).

If our identity as people is inseparable from the Earth itself, we are likely to treat the Earth the way we treat our relatives. Just as we would not want to destroy ourselves or our relatives, we would not want to destroy Mother Earth. Doing so would ultimately mean that we harm ourselves.

Principle #3: All Living Things Are Equal

From an Aboriginal perspective, people should not view themselves as some-how above or separate from the other beings of the Earth, otherwise misfor-tune will occur (Clarkson et al., 1992). Instead, all living things are believed to be equal. Some beings may have greater power or more responsibilities than others, but all life is believed to be essential to the continuing work of Creation. Oren Lyons, in "An Iroquois Perspective" (1980: 171–3), expresses this idea of equality as follows:

> The history of my people, of the Ho-de-no-sau-ne, is a long history which deals in the principles of peace: basically peace and the power to keep the peace. Peace, equality and justice for people is given over into the hands of the chiefs, the welfare of all living things. In our perception all life is equal, and that includes the birds, animals, things that grow, things that swim. All life is equal in our perception. It is the Creator who prese s the reality, and as you read this singularly, by yourself in your sovere ty and in your being and in your completeness, you are a manifestatic f the creation. You are sovereign by the fact that you exist. And in this, relationship demands respect for the equality of life. These are the p ciples through which the council governs in their sense of duty. We a a government that is intertwined with spiritual guidance. The first du f the chiefs is to see that we conduct our ceremonies precisely. That i e first duty. Only after that do we sit in the council for the welfare of r people. So you can see that the separation of spiritual, religious ways n political ways does not exist within the structure of the Ho-de-no-sa e.

In this sense, every d ion is a spiritual and environmental decision, as decisions have always be made with concern for all living things.

Principle #4: The Seventh eneration

Closely related to the envi mental principle of equality is that of the seventh generation. Aboriginal pec s have long believed that they must consider how their actions will affect currently living things as well as those beings which will live in the future. cisions are made so as to ensure that generations to come will have the opportunity to "live life to its fullest." Aboriginal people thus look ahead seven generations in making decisions regarding the environment. Lyons (1980: 173) states that:

> We are looking ahead, as is one of the first mandates given to us as chiefs, to make sure and to make every decision that we make relate to the welfare and well-being of the seventh generation to come, and that is the basis by which we make decisions in council. We consider: will this be to the benefit of the seventh generation? That is a guideline.

According to Lyons, the abuses that Aboriginal people and Mother Earth face today are due to decision-making that has failed to consider the seventh generation and the welfare of all living things.

Principle #5: All Things Are Related: Interconnectedness and Interdependence

Integral to Aboriginal sacred traditions is the idea that all things depend on one another. Humanity holds a special place within nature, though it is fully interdependent upon and interconnected with every other aspect of nature. Dumont (2006: 12) writes:

> In the Indigenous mind, then, though humankind is of a "special creation event," the human person is *of the earth and from the earth*. Like all of the created world, the human being is part of the balance of nature and must find a special yet interconnected place within the created whole. The human person is a relative to all other persons of the Earth, and, along with all creatures calls the Earth, *Mother*.

The concept of interconnectedness is recognized and acknowledged in everyday activities both in personal prayer (often practised as a form of communication with the natural and spirit worlds, with the ancestors, etc.) and in communal activities such as ceremonies, feasts, and other celebrations. Communication between humanity and the rest of nature, however, is not only a one-way occurrence. Dreams are also considered an important way of communicating with the natural and spirit worlds, and it is often through dreams that these worlds communicate with people. The constant recognition that all things are related enables Aboriginal people to be acutely aware of how their actions will affect all other beings.

Principle #6: Natural Law

The natural law that many Aboriginal peoples speak of is quite simple, although it is expressed in a variety of ways. In simple terms, natural law is the requirement that we accept the way things (nature and environment) are, whether we fully understand them or not, and relate to all things in a respectful manner. Failure to adhere to this law could cause life as we know it to perish. This life-or-death aspect of natural law was much more immediate for societies in earlier times. As Clarkson et al. (1992: 4) state, "If they failed to consider what the environment had to offer, how much it could give, and at what times it was prepared to do this—they would simply die." In other words, there is nothing romantic about this view of our relationship to the Earth: it is based quite simply on the will to survive.

Understanding the natural law requires one to consider the seven generations principle. As Oren Lyons (1980: 174) describes, it is necessary to:

> Respect the proper manner so that the seventh generation will have a place to live in. Let us look at the large issues. We are concerned with all the children of this earth. We are concerned with the four colors of Man. Natural Law is very simple. You cannot change it: it prevails over all. There is not a tight rule, there is not a court, there is not a group of nations in this world that can change this Natural Law. You are subject and born to those Natural Laws. The Indians understood the Natural Laws. They built their laws to coincide with the Natural Laws. And that's how we survived.

Because the natural law is critical to survival, certain individuals in communities are responsible to ensure compliance. Delgam Uukw (Wa and Uukw, 1989: 7–8), Chief of the Gitksan people in British Columbia, relates the following:

> For us, the ownership of territory is a marriage of the Chief and the land. Each Chief has an ancestor who encountered and acknowledged the life of the land. From such encounters came power. The land, the plants, the animals and the people all have spirit—they all must be shown respect. That is the basis or our law.
>
> The Chief is responsible for ensuring that all the people in his House respect the spirit in the land and in all living things. When a Chief directs his House properly and the laws are followed, then that original power can be recreated....
>
> My power is carried in my House's histories, songs, dances and crests. It is recreated at the Feast when the histories are told, the songs and dances performed, and the crests displayed. With the wealth that comes from respectful use of the territory, the House feeds the name of the Chief in the Feast Hall. In this way, the law, the Chief, the territory, and the Feast become one. The unity of the Chief's authority and his House's ownership of the territory are witnessed and thus affirmed by the other Chiefs at the Feast.
>
> By following the law, the power flows from the land to the people through the Chief; by using the wealth of the territory, the House feasts its Chief so he can properly fulfill the law. This cycle has been repeated on my land for thousands of years.

Principle #7: Responsibility

Aboriginal conceptions of law are based on relationships and responsibilities to "all our relations" (McDermott and Wilson, 2010). Many of these laws found expression in ancient treaties among Indigenous peoples, such as that described by the *Dish With One Spoon Belt* (Corbiere, 2014). Such laws, treaties, and agreements also helped guide human conduct to ensure sustainable relationships with all of Creation.

Although most discourse regarding Aboriginal peoples and the environment currently centres on Aboriginal and treaty rights, all Aboriginal community members have a responsibility to care for the Earth (Walken, 2007). According to traditional teachings, every child would have been raised to assume some part, however small, in this life-giving endeavour. In turn, some people had more responsibility than others, such as those with specialized knowledge, including healers or ceremonial leaders.

Lessons on caring for the Earth and assuming responsibilities are often sought from animals and their spirits through various ceremonies and other practices, for it has long been recognized that careful observation of animals can teach people valuable lessons about the world. "For example, the tiny mouse teaches us to focus, to observe the world with all our energy and our being and to appreciate the wonder of our world" (Clarkson et al., 1992: 4).

In *Doing Things the Right Way: Dene Traditional Justice* (1995), Joan Ryan describes the Dene rules for stewardship and maintaining relationships among people, animals, plants, and spirits. Based on a number of interviews with Dene people, she writes that in the Dene traditional setting:

> Stewardship, that is the responsibility to maintain the balance of land-use, hunting and trapping with the availability of resources so as to ensure a viable environment for the future, was the key factor in the hunting and trapping economy. The basic rule was to take only what was needed, in a respectful way. Long before the Department of Renewable Resources was put in place, the Dené maintained their traditional territory well because they understood the fragile balance between the life cycle and the availability of food. The animals were not only game to be taken for food, fur, and hides, they also had a life force. (Ryan, 1995: 27)

For the Dene, all adults and children are responsible for helping maintain balance in the environment. The spiritual understanding that guided the type of relationship the Dene have with the natural world is expressed as responsibility. Ryan (1995: 28) describes this aspect of stewardship as "Every individual had a responsibility to behave 'the right way' with regard to animals and their spirits."

Many recent efforts by Aboriginal peoples in Canada to recover control over their environmental responsibilities have focused on gaining recognition of Aboriginal and treaty rights (AFN, 1993; MNO, 2012). Aboriginal culture teaches that with such rights come great responsibility. For example, while Aboriginal people may have the "right" to fish in certain territories, this does not mean that they are going to fish all the time and deplete the resource. With the right to fish comes responsibility, since obeying natural laws means that one is responsible to determine when, where, how, and for what to fish. In this way the fish stock never depletes; it is monitored and cared for.[2]

Aboriginal peoples' concern about water quality and its effects on human health is also tied to our responsibilities to protect water for all beings. As James Ransom (1999: 27) relates, "The Thanksgiving Address reminds us that it is our responsibility to take care of all life, including the Waters. We recognize that all life is interrelated. If the Waters are to fulfil their responsibilities, then we must ensure that they have the opportunity to do so."

Sometimes responsibilities can be gendered. In some traditional teachings women have a special relationship with water as a life-giving force. Anishinaabe Grandmother/Elder Josephine Mandamin (2003) relates her experience as a woman fulfilling this responsibility:

> The water we carried in our copper pail always reminded us of our womanly responsibilities as givers of life as Mother Earth gives us, her children, life. Without our mother the earth and her water, life would be arid and dead. The numerous, daily water songs that we sang for the water are now forever embedded in nature as we saw it and were welcomed by it. The words of the water songs made us ever humble as we walked with the copper pail of water. The copper reminded us of its element from the universe and how it formed to be a part of Mother Earth in her tender beginnings.

There are many examples of how Aboriginal people in Canada continue to take these responsibilities very seriously. One important example is the Great Lakes Mother Earth Walk led by Josephine Mandamin. As part of the process of assuming their responsibilities to water, the water walkers engage in epic journeys around the Great Lakes to raise awareness of water-related justice issues (Anderson et al., 2013). Routinely covering distances of over 1,000 kilometres, the goal of each walk is to raise awareness about water and to try and change the perception of water from that of a resource to be exploited for economic gain to that of a sacred entity that must be treated accordingly (Mandamin, 2012). Closely tied to the notion of responsibility is the idea of reciprocity.

Principle #8: Reciprocal Relations: Achieving Balance and Harmony

Aboriginal peoples have always had a close and intimate relationship with the Earth based on reciprocity rather than exploitation. One way that all relations within Creation are acknowledged is to ensure that when something is taken, something is given in return. For example, if one takes an animal's life, then that person is responsible to return something back to the animal or give something in exchange for that life. One must never take something and give nothing in return or imbalance will result. Anishinaabe environmental activist Winona LaDuke (1994: 128) explains that:

> reciprocal relations defines responsibilities and ways of relating between humans and the ecosystem. Simply stated, the resources of the economic system, whether they be wild rice or deer, are recognized as animate and, as such, gifts from the Creator. Within that context, one could not take life without a reciprocal offering, usually tobacco or some other recognition of the Anishinabeg's reliance on the Creator. There must always be this reciprocity.

If reciprocity is not adhered to, misfortune is likely to result. Adhering to reciprocal relations has long been recognized as essential to maintaining balance and harmony, and so Aboriginal societies and their governments were structured around trying to ensure and maintain such balance. Seeking to maintain balance brought about harmonious relations and helped support the cultivation of related values such as co-operation and sharing.

Principal #9: Cyclical Thinking

Thousands of years of observation and intimate interaction with the Earth have enabled Aboriginal people to develop an understanding of the world that envisions all parts of Creation as flowing in a cycle. LaDuke (1994: 128) observes that, "Within this understanding is a clear sense of birth and rebirth and a knowledge that what one does today will affect one in the future." Clarkson et al. (1992: 19) add:

> Through many years of experience, trial and error, hunger and hardship, our ancestors learned that the depletion of plant and animal life in their immediate environment meant starvation and death. The practical outcome of this was the movement of the people to match the changes of the

season and the cycle of the earth and its gifts. . . . Additionally, the patterns of life could be seen as a circular relationship. Everything that the people did today would have repercussions for tomorrow and for their own survival and the survival of future generations.

Instead of trying to make the world fit into linear or hierarchical patterns, Aboriginal people learned long ago to follow what came naturally, an approach that has enabled them to act in minimally disruptive ways in relation to the environment and that has helped them adapt to environmental changes when required.

Summary: All My Relations

The principles outlined above are not exhaustive, though they do constitute the foundation for an Aboriginal environmental ethic. It is important to keep in mind that all of these principles are interconnected and that it is therefore not possible to fully adhere to one principle without simultaneously following the others. Without practising respect, for example, it is difficult to act responsibly. Also, without a basic understanding of the reciprocal relationship between all beings in Creation it is difficult, if not impossible, to achieve and maintain harmony and balance. Caring for the seventh generation requires adherence to natural laws and taking responsibility, and so on.

The common strand that ties together various expressions of Indigenous environmental principles is Aboriginal people's holistic understanding of their spiritual and personal relationships with the environment. In her book *All My Relations: Native Struggles for Land and Life*, Winona LaDuke (1999: 2) writes:

Native American teachings describe the relations all around—animals, fish, trees, and rocks—as our brothers, sisters, uncles and grandpas. Our relations to each other, our prayers whispered across generations to our relatives, are what bind our cultures together. . . . These are our older relatives— the ones who came before and taught us how to live.

Indigenous perspectives of the land shape how environmental challenges are understood and experienced. Such understandings also speak to why Aboriginal peoples remain concerned about the impact of environmental degradation on people as well as on all other beings (relatives) and on Mother Earth herself. These are not merely concerns about "natural resources," for we are related to everything in nature. It is in this light that Aboriginal people in Canada understand why ongoing displacement and dispossession from their traditional territories has had, and continues to have, devastating impacts on their lives. A brief history of this displacement is the subject of the next section.

Historical Context: Dispossession of Lands and the Environmental Crisis

Various forms of environmental crisis have been a fact of life for Aboriginal peoples for centuries. Loss of land and/or access to their traditional lands since the arrival of Europeans in the Americas almost immediately resulted in life-threatening and even fatal situations. As discussed in the following section, current global environmental crises are intricately tied to the ongoing dispossession and exploitation of Aboriginal peoples' lands in Canada and many other parts of the world.

Dispossession of Lands and Resources

One of the most significant challenges that Aboriginal peoples in Canada have faced since the arrival of European colonizers is the systematic loss of their lands to make way for European settlement and resource development (RCAP, 1996).[3] Being dispossessed from their land has prevented Aboriginal people from being able to exercise their duties and responsibilities to "all their relations," and so it is hardly surprising that this issue continues to be a primary source of conflict between Aboriginal peoples and the rest of Canada (Linden, 2007).

Indigenous legal scholar John Borrows describes the connection between the dispossession of land and the impact of this dispossession on Aboriginal peoples:

> Aboriginal peoples have a pre-occupation. It is *of* land. They occupied land in North America prior to others arrival on its shores. Over the past two-hundred and fifty years Aboriginal peoples have been largely dispossessed of their lands and resources in Canada. This dispossession has led to another Aboriginal pre-occupation. It is *with* land. It is crucial to their survival as peoples. Its loss haunts their dreams. Its continuing occupation and/or reoccupation inspires their visions.
>
> Aboriginal peoples regard their traditional lands as sacred; it is integral to their culture and identity. They want to continue living on territories

that have sustained them for thousands of years. Yet the Crown now claims occupation of traditional Aboriginal lands. (Borrows, 2005: 3)

One key aspect of dispossession is exclusion from environmental decision-making, for Aboriginal jurisdiction and authority over decision-making have decreased as others have gained control over the lands. Traditional Indigenous governance structures and regimes were systematically undermined through various colonial interventions, including the ongoing imposition of the Indian Act (RCAP, 1996).

These two facets—dispossession from their territories and exclusion from decision-making—together have contributed to virtually every environmental challenge facing Aboriginal peoples today. For this reason, Aboriginal peoples have been seeking to reclaim their rightful place in environmental governance through a variety of means. Many Aboriginal leaders continue in their attempts to establish new forms of self-government and engage in land claims processes, though the experience of being excluded from decision-making or simply being ignored by environmental decision-makers has also resulted in leaders and/or other community members engaging in other kinds of action, including setting up blockades, various expressions of civil disobedience, and litigation (Borrows, 2005).

Aboriginal and Treaty Rights

One often misunderstood aspect of contemporary environmental discourse is the role of Aboriginal and treaty rights. Even policy-makers and environmental practitioners frequently lack appreciation of the importance of this issue. In Canada, Aboriginal and treaty rights are protected under section 35 of the Constitution Act of 1982 (Doyle-Bedwell and Cohen, 2001). Aboriginal people have increasingly asserted that for them to benefit fully from the constitutional protection these rights are meant to afford, the associated lands and environments must be healthy (Borrows, 2005; McClenaghan, 1999). For example, having the right to fish on traditional territories is virtually meaningless if the fish are too contaminated to consume.[4]

According to Linden (2007), the lack of recognition and respect for Aboriginal and treaty rights has been the main reason that Aboriginal people continue to experience being dispossessed from their lands. Such a separation has had profoundly negative social, cultural, spiritual, and emotional impacts on people that have resulted in the deplorable living conditions now present in many Aboriginal communities throughout Canada.

Environmental Injustice

Aboriginal peoples in Canada struggle every day against resource development initiatives that negatively impact their lands and communities (LaDuke, 1999). Many of the issues surrounding such development can be characterized as environmental injustice issues. While the Environmental Protection Agency of the United States (USEPA) developed an environmental justice policy in 1994 (USEPA, 2014),[5] Canada still has no such policy (Dhillon and Young, 2010). As a result, Aboriginal people do not have access to the kinds of resources and environmental protection supports necessary to address the environmental injustice issues that affect them (Edgar and Graham, 2008; O'Connor, 2002). Aboriginal peoples in Canada also continue to be denied opportunities to participate in the development of laws, policies, and processes that impact their environment and lands, often with devastating results (Dhillon and Young, 2010; RCAP, 1996).

Throughout Canada, as a consequence of pollution and other forms of degradation, Aboriginal peoples face social, cultural, economic, and spiritual change in their communities and environments, in ways that are generally not experienced by people in other communities. While people in non-Aboriginal communities tend to see the economic benefits from resource development, the same developments often result in high levels of toxins in water, air, land, and wildlife that Aboriginal peoples depend on for their subsistence and economic livelihood (Agyeman et al., 2009: 27–41).

The concept of environmental racism helps focus our analysis of why Aboriginal people in Canada are over-represented in incidences of environmental injustice (Dhillon and Young, 2010; Jacobs, 2010). Dhillon and Young (2010: 26) define environmental racism as "the deliberate or intentional siting of hazardous waste sites, landfills, incinerators, and polluting industries in communities inhabited by minorities and/or the poor." Peoples and communities subjected to this type of racism are often impoverished, marginalized, and excluded from dominant society in a variety of ways.

Beverley Jacobs (2010) analyzes two noteworthy examples of environmental racism relating to First Nations in Canada: the Kashechewan water crisis in northern Ontario and the effects of Alberta oil sands development on the Aboriginal people of Fort Chipewyan. In the case of Kashechewan, various levels of government had known for a number of years that the community had been experiencing water quality issues. In 2005, after the community had been under a boil-water advisory for two years due to e-coli contamination, the Ontario government finally declared the community to be in a state of emergency. This resulted in the evacuation of hundreds of people from the community, many of whom required medical attention (St Germain and

Sibbeston, 2007). Sadly, this is not an isolated event, as water quality issues continue to plague many First Nation communities across Canada (Dhillon and Young, 2010; Gelinas, 2005; McGregor, 2012). Fort Chipewyan is comprised of two First Nations as well as a Métis community, and water quality-related health issues have plagued the people living in the area for many years. Located downstream from the oil sands on the Athabasca River, which is the primary source of water for oil sands projects, the severely negative cumulative effects of industrial activity in the area have meant that Aboriginal people in Fort Chipewyan can no longer trust the environment they so closely depend on. The refusal by various levels of government to give credence to a recent medical examiner's report demonstrating higher than normal incidences of cancer and deaths in the Fort Chipewyan community is evidence of how government (in)actions have undermined the community's ability to realize environmental justice (Jacobs, 2010).

Exclusion from Environmental Decision-Making

Aboriginal people have been excluded from participation in decisions that impact their lives and lands throughout Canadian history (AFN, 1993; RCAP, 1996). In many cases where the interests of Aboriginal people have actually been considered, their input has been ignored or simply subsumed under that of other stakeholders.

The lack of contributions by Aboriginal people to Canadian environmental or natural resource discourse and policy has meant that much of the legislation and the regulations for environmental protection and conservation in this country do not reflect the unique concerns or perspectives of Aboriginal people. Current laws are inadequate for protecting Aboriginal peoples' traditional territories and rights since the knowledge that informs policies, laws, regulations, and programs for environmental and resource management is almost all based on Western scientific thinking (Berneshawi, 1997).

Despite the countless barriers and setbacks they have faced in having their voices heard, Aboriginal peoples continue to have a keen desire to be involved in environmental decision-making at various levels. Recent court decisions involving the Haida (2004), the Taku (2004), the Mikisew Cree (2005), and the Tsilhqot'in (2014) indicate that some progress has been made in gaining legal support for Aboriginal interests, although it has largely been achieved through lengthy, financially draining, and exhaustive legal processes. Another sign of hope occurred in November 2011, when Aboriginal Affairs and Northern Development Canada (AANDC) released official guidelines specifying that the Crown's unique and judicially recognized relationship with

Aboriginal peoples mandates consultation, and accommodation if appropriate, on matters that may adversely impact their rights under section 35 of the Constitution Act, 1982 (AANDC, 2011).

Environmental Degradation and Quality of Life

Aboriginal people assert that their cultural identity, their very survival as people, is threatened when the environment is degraded. The impact of environmental degradation on Aboriginal peoples can range from a change in diet (from "country food" to highly processed foods), to a decrease in drinking water quality, an increase in exposure to toxic chemicals from fish and game, and a decreased ability to exercise rights or practise ceremonies, to name just a few core effects (AFN, 1993; CIER, 2005). Efforts to restore environmental health therefore represent far more than a "cause" for Aboriginal people; it is a responsibility upon which the survival of their nations depends.

The Centre for Indigenous Environmental Resources (CIER) in Winnipeg conducted a comprehensive review of environmental challenges confronting First Nations in Canada. The numerous issues discussed at length in its *Environmental Issues Research Report* (CIER, 2005) are summarized in Table 2.1.

Lack of Recognition of Aboriginal Knowledge

The dispossession from one's land results not only in a people being unable to practise their cultural traditions, but also in the subsequent loss of knowledge about that land (CIER, 2005). While much traditional knowledge has been lost, fortunately, much still remains. Maintaining their traditional knowledge is one of the many reasons that Aboriginal people believe they should be included in environmental decision-making processes. In fact, increased interest around the world in Indigenous traditional knowledge (TK) and the role it can play in environmental decision-making gives credence to the view that Aboriginal people should be at the forefront of environmental discussions and decision-making in Canada. Only quite recently, Canadian governments and external agencies, such as ENGOs, NGOs, and academic institutions, have begun to acknowledge the legitimacy of Aboriginal world views, cultures, values, and traditional knowledge (AFN, 1993; Clarkson et al., 1992). In many instances, Aboriginal peoples are still prevented from having regular and meaningful involvement in environmental decision-making in this country (Bowie, 2013).

Table 2.1 | Some Environmental Issues Facing Aboriginal People in Canada

Environmental Issue	Cause	Effects on Environmental and Aboriginal Health
Overharvesting of traditional plants	Global increase in consumption of medicinal plants for herbal use	Reduced species diversity, with the potential extinction of indigenous plant species, threatens traditional ways of life, loss of food source, loss of plants for healing and ceremonial use.
Introduction of new species	Introduction of new species to North America	Indigenous species used for food, medicines, ceremonial use are threatened by invasive species.
Clear-cutting of forests	Inadequate forest management practices	Clear-cutting and other practices cause ecological disturbances (water quality, fisheries) affecting hunting, trapping, fishing, and gathering activities of Aboriginal peoples.
Loss of traditional foods	Contamination of food source by local industry or other industrial development	Health problems associated with eating alternative food (i.e., processed foods high in sugars and carbohydrates) occur when traditional foods cannot be consumed due to high levels of contamination. Loss of culture occurs when obtaining traditional foods is no longer practised.
Loss of land to industrial development	Industrial developments such as forestry, mining, oil and gas activities	Land, air, and water are contaminated due to industrial effluents, leading to loss of land and inability to pursue a traditional lifestyle (e.g., hunting, trapping, fishing, etc.).
Loss of access to traditional territories	Relocation, industrial development	Food, shelter, water, and ceremonial areas are lost. Cultural, social, and spiritual impacts result from loss of connection with land.
Poor water quality	Contamination of water sources due to point-source pollution, poor water and wastewater management, and poor infrastructure	Poor health results, including disease due to waterborne disease.

(Continued)

Table 2.1	(Continued)	
Environmental Issue	Cause	Effects on Environmental and Aboriginal Health
Climate change	Greenhouse gases, usually not produced in large amounts by Aboriginal communities, although they are disproportionately affected by them. Furthermore, there are disproportionate impacts on remote and northern communities.	Climate change impacts water, plants, and animals (e.g., migration patterns and behaviours), and affects infrastructure, especially in the North (e.g., ice roads, building foundations). Negative effects are seen in the traditional diet of Aboriginal peoples.
Loss of traditional activities; language	Industrial and urban encroachment on territories; relocation of communities	Sense of community and knowledge of nature/environment are lost through language loss.

Source: Adapted from CIER (2005).

Increasing Aboriginal Control in Environmental Governance

Over thousands of years, Aboriginal peoples developed intellectual traditions and knowledge systems that enabled sustainable relationships with all of Creation. These knowledge systems are rooted in the past, but also transform with time, incorporating new knowledge and insights to ensure that knowledge about how to relate properly with the natural world is maintained.

The three major groups of Aboriginal peoples in Canada—First Nations, Métis, and Inuit—have distinct conceptions of TK, although there is some commonality in their perspectives. Following are examples of how each group conceives of TK:

> Inuit Qaujimajatuqangit is a body of knowledge and unique cultural in-
> sights of Inuit into the workings of nature, humans and animals. Inuit
> Qaujimajatuqangit, then, has both practical and epistemological aspects that
> branch out from a fundamental principle that human beings are learning,
> rational beings with an infinite potential for problem-solving within the dic-
> tates of nature and technology. (Qikiqtani Inuit Association, 2007: para. 3)

Métis traditional environmental knowledge is built from community practices which form the foundation for understanding the natural world, building skills and behaviour adaptable and applicable to other facets of Métis life, maximizing use and benefit of natural resources within community accepted ethical boundaries, and contributing to personal and community spiritual, physical, intellectual and emotional health and development. While the phrase "traditional environmental knowledge" does not mention contemporary life, the purpose of understanding Métis traditional environmental knowledge is for adaptation and use in everyday life. Ancestral knowledge is an integral part of traditional environmental knowledge as it influences subsequent generations in understanding and interacting with the natural world. (MNC, 2011: 1)

The term Aboriginal Knowledge is understood to describe knowledge informed by aboriginal paradigms as applied to skills, understandings, expertise, facts, familiarities, beliefs, revelations and observations. Furthermore, AK is understood to include the customary ways in which aboriginal peoples have done or continue to do certain things, as well as the new ideas or ways of doing things that have been developed by Aboriginal peoples and which respect their traditions, cultures and practices. Many of these customary ways have been passed on from generation to generation and must be considered as sacred. (AFN, 2010: 4)

There has been a worldwide surge of interest in TK in recent decades, both in terms of understanding what it is as well as in recognizing its value in helping people move towards the establishment of more sustainable societies. This interest, in part, has provided many of the recent opportunities for Aboriginal people to become increasingly involved in resource management and other governance initiatives.

The degree to which Indigenous people are able to exert influence and control over environmental and resource management in Canada remains varied (Bowie, 2013). In the North, where a number of comprehensive land claims have been settled and self-government agreements negotiated, new institutions of governance have been established that specifically provide for Aboriginal involvement and the inclusion of TK (Natcher et al., 2007; Spak, 2005). In some parts of Canada, including Ontario, institution-building for the purposes of Aboriginal environmental and resource management has been more difficult to establish and is practically non-existent. The Indigenous environmental and resource management context in Ontario differs significantly from those areas in Canada where modern comprehensive land claims or modern-day treaties and other agreements have been concluded with the Crown. In Ontario, for example, nineteenth-century and early twentieth-century treaties dispossessed Aboriginal peoples of most of their traditional land base and set the "rules" for future relations with government to their disadvantage.

Where treaties do exist, it is the Crown's view that traditional Indigenous rights to lands and resources have historically been extinguished and that "the Crown now claims occupation of traditional Aboriginal lands" (Borrows, 2005: 3). As Métis scholar and activist Jean Telliet has observed, this view has resulted in environmental conservation and protection processes in Ontario being used as a means to deny Aboriginal people's authority and jurisdiction over their traditional territories. The natural resource regulatory regime in Ontario has historically sought to dispossess Aboriginal people of their lands, and "the dispossession is not finished" (Telliet, 2005: 4). Indigenous peoples in Ontario thus find themselves in the difficult position of striving to maintain ties to their territories through participation in Crown-led environmental and resource management regimes. However, the desire of Aboriginal peoples "to hold onto their lands and resources [and] to be more productive and preserve their ancient relationships" remains (Borrows, 2005: 3).

For Aboriginal knowledge and practices to flourish, Aboriginal peoples must be *part of the governance system*—they must, in fact, be decision-makers. Currently, the level of control of state-managed systems:

> continues to limit the extent to which First Nations are empowered to propose and implement change. . . . the pervasiveness of state management has in effect perpetuated historical conditions where First Nations governments have gained little autonomy in the management of lands and resources. (Natcher et al., 2007: 277)

As Aboriginal peoples begin to assert their own laws, values, knowledge, and traditions in environmental and resource management, state institutions must also reform to effectively accommodate Aboriginal interests.

Hundreds of recommendations put forward over the past two decades, including over 400 in the 1996 *Report of the Royal Commission on Aboriginal Peoples* (RCAP), reflect deep concern over the achievement of social and environmental justice for Aboriginal peoples in Canada. However, struggles are ongoing as Aboriginal peoples and the Canadian state continue to vie for control of lands and resources. James Anaya, the United Nations Special Rapporteur on the Rights of Indigenous Peoples, made the following observations in May 2014:

> One of the most dramatic contradictions indigenous peoples in Canada face is that so many live in abysmal conditions on traditional territories

that are full of valuable and plentiful natural resources. These resources are in many cases targeted for extraction and development by non-indigenous interests. While indigenous peoples potentially have much to gain from resource development within their territories, they also face the highest risks to their health, economy, and cultural identity from any associated environmental degradation. Perhaps more importantly, indigenous nations' efforts to protect their long term interests in lands and resources often fit uneasily into the efforts by private non-indigenous companies, with the backing of the federal and provincial governments, to move forward with resource projects. (Anaya, 2014: 19)

In spite of ongoing colonial tactics, many changes provide reason for optimism. International agreements and conventions, for example, have influenced the recognition of TK in environmental resource management in Canada (Butler, 2006; Higgins, 1998; Settee, 2000). Recent court decisions have also played a key role in steering policy and legislative frameworks towards greater support for the use of TK and one of its core transmission mechanisms: the oral tradition (Doyle-Bedwell and Cohen, 2001). Moreover, recognition of Aboriginal and treaty rights in the courts has begun to influence the development of land claims policy. In particular, modern-day treaty-making has entrenched TK as an integral part of many co-management regimes in northern Canada (Bocking, 2005; Spak, 2005; White, 2006).

In Canada, TK is therefore becoming more central to collaborative efforts that support increased Aboriginal control over lands and resources through self-government agreements, comprehensive land claims, and other mechanisms. This trend towards increasing Indigenous control represents a considerable opportunity for the expression of TK in environmental and resource management, as both Indigenous and non-Indigenous resource managers recognize a pressing need to incorporate TK as part of new and more progressive systems of management (Houde, 2007; Menzies, 2006; Sable et al., 2006). This growing support over the past three decades for the role of TK in environmental decision-making is reflected by governments in Canada agreeing to formally include TK in their environmental legislative and policy frameworks. For example, there is now reference to TK (or TEK, traditional ecological knowledge) in the Canadian Environmental Protection Act (CEPA), the Species at Risk Act (SARA), and the Canadian Environmental Assessment Act (CEAA). Supreme Court decisions ruling in favour of Aboriginal peoples as well as the enshrinement of Aboriginal and treaty rights in the Canadian Constitution have also influenced the recognition of TK in environmental governance (Doyle-Bedwell and Cohen, 2001;

Walken, 2007). Through their own endeavours, Aboriginal peoples have also pushed for more official recognition of TK in environmental governance in Canada (AFN, 1993; MNC, 2011).

Aboriginal peoples in Canada recognize that the incorporation of Aboriginal interests into environmental resource management must be much more than an add-on or an afterthought. Consequently, they have sought to develop "decolonizing" institutional frameworks that promote TK and Western science as equally valid ways of knowing. Most current institutions and programs are based on a Western framework, and so merely inserting components of Aboriginal knowledge at various convenient points will only serve to fragment TK and distort, and possibly destroy, its meaning (Stevenson, 2006). The voice of Indigenous peoples in environmental resource management systems can be adequately heard only if TK is given the opportunity to flourish *alongside* Western knowledge.

The dominance of Western-style environmental resource management regimes presents a significant challenge even to accommodating TK, let alone putting it on an equal footing with Western knowledge. It therefore seems that entirely new institutions and/or ways of envisioning new programs will have to be developed to meet this challenge in a way that supports Indigenous goals for self-determination. On Canada's east coast, the Unamak'ki Institute of Natural Resources (UINR) provides an excellent example of how Indigenous nations are incorporating TK into environmental and resource management work. UINR was established in 1999 to address the environmental concerns of the Mi'kmaq on Cape Breton Island, Nova Scotia. The goals of UINR include working co-operatively and collaboratively with others and ensuring Mi'kmaq traditions are maintained. The UINR incorporates the concept of Netukulimk, based on Mi'kmaq world view and environmental philosophy:

> Netukulimk is the use of the natural bounty provided by the Creator for the self-support and well-being of the individual and the community. Netukulimk is achieving adequate standards of community nutrition and economic well-being without jeopardizing the integrity, diversity, or productivity of our environment.
>
> As Mi'kmaq we have an inherent right to access and use our resources and we have a responsibility to use those resources in a sustainable way. The Mi'kmaq way of resource management includes a spiritual element that ties together people, plants, animals, and the environment. UINR's strength is in our ability to integrate scientific research with Mi'kmaq knowledge acquisition, utilization, and storage. (UINR, 2011)

The approach taken by UINR does not exclude the use of Western science or its tools. Instead, ensuring respect for Netukulimk is based on what the Mi'kmaq refer to as the "two-eyed seeing concept" or "Etuaptmumk." "Two-eyed seeing" is offered as a guiding principle from which two knowledge systems can be respected and used to address environmental concerns. In Canada, as Aboriginal peoples regain authority and jurisdiction over lands and resources, innovative collaborations based on Indigenous environmental philosophies can flourish, as UINR has shown.

Moving Forward: Nation-to-Nation Relationships

Environmental partnerships and collaborations between Aboriginal and non-Aboriginal people in Canada are becoming increasingly more important in the movement towards greater ecological and economic sustainability. The strength of such arrangements lies in the recognition that Indigenous peoples and TK have an essential role to play in the long-term resolution of environmental issues. In addition is the realization that from a social responsibility perspective, Canada cannot move ahead as a nation on these issues while a significant segment of the population, one that is in a very real sense "closer" to the issues than any other in this country, remains excluded from deliberative processes. The move towards increased inclusion of Indigenous people in such discussions and initiatives is therefore a welcome and long overdue step in addressing increasingly pressing environmental concerns.

Much remains to be achieved in terms of the overall impact of Aboriginal peoples' involvement in environmental governance in Canada. Self-government agreements and comprehensive land claims processes (modern-day treaty-making) offer important opportunities and provide reason for optimism in this area. There are numerous examples of successfully implemented Aboriginal environmental governance frameworks across Canada, including those developed by members of the Sechelt and West Bank First Nations in British Columbia (Wyatt et al., 2009). The comprehensive land claims process also offers opportunities for collaboration and co-management of institutionalized initiatives. For example, the Mackenzie Valley Resource Management Act (1998) established land and water co-management boards, including rigorous environmental assessment regimes and TK guidelines.

Another recent initiative outlined in the Chiefs of Ontario's (2008) *Water Declaration of Anishinabek, Mushkegowuk and Onkwehonwe in Ontario* calls for interested parties (governments, ENGOs, academic institutions, and others) to contribute to *First Nations-led* environmental governance discussions. This approach, which honours the unique status of Indigenous peoples and their ability to establish and maintain environmental partnerships, represents a departure from the Western paradigm that calls for First Nations to become involved in state-led environmental governance. As Smith (1995) argued over two decades ago, Indigenous peoples must not be treated as simply "another stakeholder" in environmental and resource management processes. As the voices of Aboriginal people and their many supporters demanded in the recent Canada-wide Idle No More protests, it is time for all environmental decisions impacting Aboriginal peoples in this country to be developed in the context of nation-to-nation relationships (RCAP, 1996).

Central to this discussion is the recognition that Aboriginal peoples have always developed and drawn upon their own intellectual traditions to adapt to changing environmental conditions and to develop or renew relationships with other peoples. It has also highlighted the ways in which over two decades of policy consultation, collaborative research, and inclusive grassroots activity in Canada clearly indicate growing support for alternative models of environmental governance in this country that embrace different and equally valuable ways of knowing. There is thus a degree of optimism among Aboriginal people and their supporters that "all our relations" will continue to benefit and hopefully begin to flourish, as Aboriginal peoples and the Canadian government learn how to coexist on a nation-to-nation basis.

Discussion Questions

1. The list of environmental principles in this chapter is not exhaustive. Describe other environmental principles or teachings you are familiar with that can be added to those included here. Describe stories you have heard that convey environmental messages.
2. Compare and contrast the two common definitions of "environment" that shape how the concept of "environment" is understood in Canada. What do you see as the main similarities and differences between the Aboriginal and Euro-Canadian perspectives?
3. Participants of Idle No More and other environmental movements and protests view their actions as a way to protect the environment, raise awareness of environmental problems, or express Aboriginal and treaty rights. Discuss any recent environmental protests you have read or heard about in the news or online in terms of the main issue, who was involved, how environmental concerns were expressed and ethics invoked

in the conflicts, whether or not the issue was resolved, and whether you think such protests and actions are effective in achieving environmental protection.

4. Describe some challenges or barriers that may exist for successfully incorporating traditional ecological knowledge (TEK) into environmental governance as well as what kinds of opportunities may exist with the recognition of TEK in environmental legislation in Canada.

5. Comprehensive land claims, self-government agreements, and recent court decisions that call for the recognition of Aboriginal rights and title all offer opportunities for increased Indigenous control of lands and resources (or environment) in Canada. Describe other opportunities that exist in Canada that can lead to greater co-operation and coexistence on environmental matters.

Further Reading

Crowshoe, C. 2005. *Sacred Ways of Life: Traditional Knowledge*. Prepared for the National Aboriginal Health Association. Ottawa. http://www.naho.ca/firstnations/english/documents/FNC-TraditionalknowledgeToolkit-Eng.pdf.

Haudenosaunee Environmental Task Force (HETF). 1999. *The Words That Come Before All Else: Environmental Philosophies of the Haudenosaunee*. Akwesasne, NY: Native North American Travelling College.

Kimmerer, R. 2013. *Braiding Sweetgrass: Indigenous Wisdom, Scientific Knowledge, and the Teachings of Plants*. Minneapolis: Milkweed Editions.

Kulnieks, A., D. Longboat, and K. Young, eds. 2013. *Contemporary Studies in Environmental and Indigenous Pedagogies: A Curricula of Stories and Place*. Rotterdam: Sense Publishers, esp. pp. 77–88.

Menzies, C., ed. 2006. *Traditional Ecological Knowledge and Natural Resource Management*. Lincoln: University of Nebraska Press.

Royal Commission on Aboriginal Peoples (RCAP). 1996. "Lands and Resources." In *Report of the Royal Commission on Aboriginal Peoples, Vol. 2: Restructuring the Relationship*, 421–685. Ottawa: Minister of Supply and Services Canada.

Notes

1. The Haudenosaunee, for example, acknowledge all aspects of the environment in their Thanksgiving Address, including (but not limited to) Mother Earth, the Moon, the Sun, the Thunderers, and Creation as well as the Creator (HETF, 1999).

2. Personal communication from Henry Lickers, Seneca, scientific director of the Mohawks of Akwesasne.

3. While the early colonization of the Americas was largely European in nature, the emergence of globalization now means that non-Western peoples, powers, and interests have become part of the "settlement and resource development problem" (and potential solution) for Aboriginal peoples in Canada.

4. The Berger Inquiry (Berger, 1977) was the first major inquiry to make explicit the link between Aboriginal rights, land claims, and resource development and exploitation, for it noted that Aboriginal concepts of environment and environmental health are inextricably linked to Aboriginal and treaty rights. See also Doyle-Bedwell and Cohen (2001); Walken (2007).

5. In addition, the US is developing a Tribal and Indigenous peoples environmental justice policy in recognition of the distinct ways that Aboriginal peoples experience environmental injustice.

3

The "Canada Problem" in Aboriginal Politics

David Newhouse and Yale Belanger

Introduction

It has been two decades since the Royal Commission on Aboriginal Peoples (RCAP) presented its final report in 1996 outlining the principles and proposing a way for achieving a new relationship between Aboriginal peoples and Canada. Grounded in the belief that Aboriginal peoples are full and equal partners in Confederation, the RCAP report presented a vision of a Canada encompassing 10 provinces, three territories, 40 to 60 Aboriginal Nations, and a parliamentary-embedded First Nations House, all confirmed and given expression by treaties. The vision was dismissed by governments as unworkable and costly, although, to be fair, the cost was mainly related to addressing the colonial legacy—i.e., cleaning up the past. As evidenced by the lukewarm response to the RCAP report, the conversation about Canada remains framed and dominated by the English and French, two ancient rivals whose transplanted-from-Europe rivalry eclipses alternative voices. Turtle Island's original peoples have nevertheless made some headway in having their role in Canada's foundation formally acknowledged even if those of French and British ancestry remain loyal to Canada's European roots. Nonetheless, Aboriginal and Canadian leaders agree that the politics surrounding Aboriginal peoples have yet to resolve the many contemporary issues that bear the mark of our country's long colonial history. It is with this brief overview in mind that this chapter examines Aboriginal politics through the lenses of the "Indian problem" and the "Canada problem."

Julie Oliver/Ottawa Citizen. Reprinted by permission

Aboriginal Peoples and Canada

John Ralston Saul, writing in *Reflections of a Siamese Twin: Canada at the Beginning of the Twenty-First Century* (1998), argues that Canada is founded on three pillars: English, French, and Aboriginal. Saul stresses that Canada has failed to recognize its Aboriginal people as a pillar or as a foundational group, let alone come to terms with most aspects of its Aboriginal heritage. Historians are identified as the key culprits in establishing the view that while Aboriginal peoples appeared as initial players in Canada's narrative, they largely vanished until their role in such "lively events" as the War of 1812 or those involving the Métis in 1869 and 1885 was needed to colour the storyline. History books in this case tend to gloss over Aboriginal peoples' ongoing presence in Canada's evolution. Saul's more recent book, *A Fair Country: Telling Truths about Canada* (2008), contends that Canada's foundational principles are Aboriginal in origin and that Canada should aptly be acknowledged as a Métis country. All concerns aside with how the term "Métis" is being used, Saul contends that the ideas of inclusivity and fairness that have been long associated with Canada's character are based not in European philosophy but in Indigenous political philosophy. If Saul's ideas are valid, then his is a unique contribution and represents a fundamental change in how Canadians might see themselves.

In a country where the century-old legacy of residential schools tends to catch most Canadians off guard, the general lack of public knowledge about the continuing role Aboriginal people have played in Canada's evolution is disappointing, though not surprising. Take Aboriginal constitutional recognition as an example. The British North America (BNA) Act of 1867 (now renamed the Constitution Act, 1867) assigned the responsibility for Indians and lands reserved to Indians to the federal government, thereby creating a guaranteed constitutional presence. Few people in Canada know about this, and those who do frequently interpret the word "responsibility" in much the same way as the early Europeans, which was that Canada needed to transform Indians into Europeans—more particularly, into either British or French people—and to ensure their absorption and assimilation into the body politic.

That Indians have continually resisted external efforts aimed at their cultural and social improvement—i.e., getting rid of the Indian problem—has been an enduring problem for Canada. Indeed, the government championed its assimilationist policy until it finally withdrew its *Statement of Indian Policy* (the iconic White Paper) in 1971 (Canada, 1969). Self-determination and self-government policies gradually replaced the official policy of assimilation during the next three decades, although many Aboriginal people argue that assimilationist attitudes implicitly inform Indian policy development to this day. Aboriginal peoples have nonetheless stood firm to their internally devised social, political, and economic principles throughout the history of their often turbulent relationship with Canada. As a result of their efforts, Aboriginal peoples today constitute distinct cultural and political communities with a set of Supreme Court–acknowledged rights that have been slowly evolving and expanding since the 1970s. This is a remarkable turn of events for a people who for so long have been seen through the lens of the "Indian problem" (Dyck, 1991).

For Aboriginal peoples, the "Canada problem" is about Canada's failure to transform into a territory that: (1) enables them to live as Aboriginal peoples in distinct communities; (2) recognizes the inherent right of Aboriginal peoples to make decisions on the important aspects of their lives; and (3) lives up to its many historic and contemporary promises. Some Aboriginal leaders have framed their work in light of a vision that honours the political distinctiveness of their peoples as well as their rightful inclusion in Confederation's great unfinished project. On the occasion of the territory of Nunavut being established as part of Confederation, some Inuit leaders referred to themselves as "Mothers and Fathers of Confederation." Joseph Gosnell, Chief of the Nisga'a Nation, remarked on the ratification of the Nisga'a Treaty in April 2000: "Today, the Nisga'a people become full-fledged Canadians as we step out from under the Indian Act" (www.newswire.ca, 13 April 2000). There was sign of hope from Canada expressed during the 3 July 2014 Ontario Speech from the Throne, which began with an acknowledgement of Aboriginal peoples' contributions to Ontario's development and of the provincial legislature at Queen's Park in Toronto being located on Mississauga traditional territory.

Aboriginal peoples were not part of the original discussions surrounding Confederation, nor were they consulted at the time. Consequently, their historic nation-to-nation relationships with their British and French colonial allies were initially defined as one of dependent wardship within the new country called Canada. Since that time, Aboriginal political objectives have revolved around correcting this mistake. Aboriginal peoples have developed remarkable allies for this project over the years, the most recent being the Supreme Court of Canada, which in *Tsilhqot'in Nation vs British Columbia* (2014 SCC 44) ruled that the doctrine of *terra nullius* (i.e., unoccupied or vacant land) never applied in Canada, thus signalling another milestone in Aboriginal attempts at correcting the historical record.

While Canada followed a consistent Indian policy until recent decades, Aboriginal peoples have been unwavering in their attempts to maintain historic political relationships as well as establish new ones based on a political philosophy rooted in the ideals of respect, co-operation, sharing, and harmonious relationships. Robert Williams (1997) contends that the early treaties between Aboriginal peoples and the rest of Canada are an excellent primary source for examining Indigenous political thought. He notes that successful relationships between peoples were based on a foundation of mutual reliance and trust that required visible signs of trust between diverse peoples. Signs of linking arms and creating a circle of security, peace, and happiness included sharing a peace pipe, exchanging hostages, and presenting one another with valuable gifts such as land and hunting grounds. Yale Belanger (2006) describes how these and similar processes informed both the pre- and the post-Confederation political organizing of Canada's Indigenous peoples (Mercredi and Turpel, 1993). The RCAP report likewise proposed an Aboriginal political vision of Canada based on ideas of mutual respect, mutual responsibility, and sharing, ideas further elaborated by the First Nations Leadership Council of British Columbia (2006). There is general agreement that the political vision of Aboriginal peoples since the early 1960s has focused on self-determination and self-government, which for most Aboriginal leaders means a return to the nation-to-nation relationship originally expressed in the Royal Proclamation of 1763.

Aboriginal peoples now occupy a unique place within Canadian history, the Canadian imagination, and Canadian citizenship.[1] The jurisprudence of the last century has clearly established a solid foundation of rights that accrue to Aboriginal peoples, both as individuals and as collectivities, and their unique legal status is defined in section 35.1 of the Constitution Act, 1982. International covenants have added moral authority to this position, and so by virtue of treaties, legislation, and jurisprudence Aboriginal peoples are now regarded as "citizens plus" and charter members of Canadian society. While this may not be politically accepted by all, the legal and constitutional acceptance of this unique status implies that a new approach is called for in discussions about the Canadian federation. As a first step, it is necessary to challenge (in order to replace) the dominant colonial paradigm of the "Indian problem" that has informed Aboriginal policy since Confederation. Even though it may appear that blatantly colonial language is no longer used in political circles, there is much evidence that its legacy lives on in the attitudes and actions of those who continue to try and solve the "Indian problem."

The Colonial Legacy

Since the European arrival to Turtle Island and the subsequent implementation of colonial governments after 1763, governing officials struggled with what to do with the original inhabitants. In their own ways, the French and English had a particular understanding of the "Indian problem." The problem would variously be framed by questions concerning Aboriginal humanity and whether they had souls; what was needed to turn them into good, civilized Christians; how to coexist alongside their communities while inducing them into military alliances; how to assimilate them or, more recently, how to promote their transformation into an ethnic group as part of Canada's self-proclaimed multicultural mosaic. Each of these views of the "Indian problem" has led to a range of proposed policy solutions by government officials. Informing their actions is the colonial belief in Indian inferiority and the need for the government to protect Indians from being exploited. Underlying this protected, special status was a civilizing ideology that sought to convert "the Indians" to Christianity and teach them to live and work in the manner of Europeans. It was believed that if they were to become civilized, Indians would be able to leave their old ways of life and assimilate into Canadian society. There is general consensus that this was the core government policy until the retraction of the White Paper in 1971.

The legacy of Canada's colonial Indian policy is manifest in Aboriginal people's historic and ongoing economic, social, and political marginality. Initially confined to reserves and remote areas as a result of original Indian policy, the majority of Aboriginal people in Canada now live in urban centres. Although Ontario has the largest Aboriginal population of any province, the vast majority of Aboriginal people are located in the western provinces.[2] Many studies[3] over the past two decades have clearly exposed the racism experienced by Aboriginal people within the Canadian justice system, while others[4] demonstrate the difficult relationship that many Canadians continue to have with the original inhabitants of this country. Despite Canada's Aboriginal people having constitutionally recognized special status, state representatives have consistently sought to exclude Aboriginal leaders from major political discussions and deliberations.

Canada's approach to developing Indian policy is ideologically and practically grounded in the Indian Act, which was originally adopted in 1876 as a consolidation of pre-colonial legislation and the policy ideas underlying it. While the Act has been amended from time to time, its underlying premises have not changed. John Tobias, a historian of Aboriginal peoples, argues that there has been a consistency to Canada's Indian policy over the past 100 years or so. He argues that the three policy pillars of protection, civilization, and assimilation in place by Confederation have always been the goals of Canada's Indian policy.[5] What has changed over time has been the relative emphasis placed on each.

Addressing the "Indian Problem" in the Second Half of the Twentieth Century

The Hawthorn-Tremblay Commission Report of 1966

There was a growing feeling during the 1950s that the integration of Indian people into greater Canadian society was progressing too slowly. Granting the franchise came to be viewed as one method of accelerating the assimilation process, and as a result the federal government extended the franchise and full citizenship to all Indian people nationally in 1960 without abolishing Indian status. In this light, Saul's (2008) contention that Canada is a Métis country is a remarkable idea that was clearly inconceivable prior to the 1960s. These steps at the time appeared to be a progressive shift towards the type of Indian political/societal participation Canadian politicians had long envisioned for Aboriginal peoples—Indians absorbed as citizens practising Euro-Canadian norms. A joint parliamentary report asserted in 1961 that most Canadians still considered Indians to be a racial minority, and that the time had come for them to "assume the responsibility and accept the benefit of full participation as Canadian citizens."[6]

Growing concern about the poor social and economic situation of the new citizens led the federal government to launch a number of studies, with Harry Hawthorn and Marc Tremblay preparing the most influential report. Appointed in 1963, Hawthorn and Tremblay presented their report to

Parliament in two volumes: Part I in 1966 and Part II in 1967. The "Hawthorn Report" in many ways laid the foundation for modern Indian policy, while provocatively suggesting that Indians ought to be "citizens plus." The authors rejected the idea of assimilation into mainstream society, suggesting instead that Indians had more rights than other citizens "by virtue of promises made to them and expectations they were encouraged to hold, and from the simple fact that they once used and occupied a country to which others came to gain enormous wealth in which the Indians shared little."[7] In short, Indians were now to be considered and included as "charter members of the Canadian community."[8] The commissioners stressed "a common citizenship as well as the reinforcement of difference."[9] The notion of "citizens plus" would prove exceptionally powerful, so much so that the Indian Chiefs of Alberta (1970) chose the term as the title for their response to the government's now infamous 1969 White Paper.

Hawthorn and Tremblay recognized the need for Indians to govern themselves and for Canada to accommodate Indian governments. Recommendations 67 and 68 of the Hawthorn Report state: "Continuing encouragement should be given to the development of Indian local government"[10] and "The problem of developing Indian local government should not be treated in the either/or terms of the Indian Act or the provincial framework of local government. A partial blending of the two frameworks within the context of an experimental approach which will provide an opportunity for knowledge to be gained by experience is desirable."[11] The Hawthorn Report proposed that Indian governments should be rooted in the Indian Act while blended into the provincial–municipal framework: a federal–provincial–Indian hybrid. Recommendation 72 states: "The integration of Indian communities into the provincial municipal framework should be deliberately and aggressively pursued while leaving the organization, legal and political structure of Indian communities rooted in the Indian Act."[12]

The White Paper[13] of 1969

The federal government's 1969 *Statement of Indian Policy* rejected the Hawthorn-Tremblay idea of Indians as "citizens plus." Guided by Pierre Trudeau's concept of a "just society," the 1969 White Paper envisioned Indians as ordinary citizens of Canada with neither special status nor any entitlement to different administrative arrangements or legal relationships. The central ideas of the proposed policy were the notions of "equality" and "equity," expressed in the overall goal of enabling Indian people "to be free to develop Indian cultures in an environment of legal, social and economic equality with other Canadians."[14] The White Paper went even further, proposing that programs and services be transferred to provincial jurisdiction and delivered accordingly. Indians would become the responsibility of the province in which they resided. It further recommended that Indians should receive government services from the same agencies as other Canadians.

Trudeau's government argued that it was the policy of a separate legal status for Indians that "kept the Indian people apart from and behind other Canadians," and that this "separate road could not lead to full participation, to better equality in practice as well as theory." The government proposed to repeal the Indian Act of 1876 since it supported the separate legal status of Indians. It also proposed to dismantle the Department of Indian Affairs within five years and appoint an Indian land claims commissioner to deal with issues resulting from treaties under a land claims policy. The treaties, described as "historic documents," were to be interpreted as containing only "limited and minimal promises" that had in most cases been fulfilled. Indian reserve lands would be turned over in fee simple to Indian bands, which could then determine ownership among their members. In other words, the White Paper proposed that Indians would assume the responsibilities and have the same legal status and rights as all other citizens, and that relations between the government and Canada's Indian people would move away from the policy regime of protection and special rights. In short, the solution to the Indian problem was to do away with Indian status.

Addressing the "Canada Problem"
The Red Paper of 1970

Most Indian leaders immediately opposed the White Paper. They argued that the government's proposals ignored or minimized treaties, dismissed separate legal status for Indians, and pointed to a future that envisioned Indians as a part of an emerging multicultural society. The Indian Chiefs of Alberta (ICA) presented their position in 1970 in a paper entitled *Citizens Plus*. This 1970 "Red Paper" presented an Indian political vision of the nature of the relationship between Indians and Canada, and while the vision acknowledged, along with Hawthorn, that Indians had special status within Canada, the Red Paper asserted that the Chiefs' notion of "citizens plus" was rooted in the treaties. The preamble to the Red Paper states: "To Us who are Treaty Indians there is nothing more important than our Treaties, our lands and the well being of our future generation." The statement argues for the continuation of Indian status, concluding that it is essential for justice and for their continuation as Indians: "The only way to maintain our culture is for us to remain as Indians. To preserve our culture it is necessary to preserve our status, rights, lands and traditions. Our treaties are the basis of our rights.... The intent and spirit of the treaties must be our guide, not the precise letter of a foreign language."[15]

On Indian lands, it reads: "The Indians are the beneficial (actual) owners of the lands. The legal title has been held for us by the Crown to prevent the sale and breaking up of our land. We are opposed to any system of allotment that would give individuals ownership with rights to sell." On services, the Red Paper concludes that:

> The federal government is bound by the BNA Act ... to accept legislative responsibility for Indians and Indian Lands. In exchange for the lands ... the treaties ensure the following benefits:
>
> a. to have and to hold certain lands called "reserves" for the sole use and benefit of the Indian people forever and assistance in the social, economic, and cultural development of the reserves; b. the provision of health services ... at the expense of the Federal government; c. the provision of education of all types and levels to all Indian people; d. the right of the Indian people to hunt, trap and fish for their livelihood free of governmental interference and regulation and subject only to the proviso that the exercise of this right must not interfere with the use and enjoyment of private property.

The Red Paper grounded the basic political philosophy used to guide Aboriginal leaders over the next 30 years. It was based on Indigenous notions of reciprocity and respect: we give you these lands in return for these rights and guarantees and services. These promises of reciprocity are set out in treaties and are based on the idea of a nation-to-nation relationship that confers a "citizenship plus" status for Aboriginal peoples. The Union of British Columbia Indian Chiefs issued *A Declaration of Indian Rights* the same year, and in 1971 the Association of Iroquois and Allied Indians in Ontario presented its position paper. Indeed, 30 years of reports and declarations by Aboriginal leaders expressed opposition to the views expressed in the White Paper and, more importantly, set out unique visions of the place of their people in Canadian society and the steps that needed to be taken to move relations between Aboriginal peoples and the rest of Canada forward.

While the Red Paper was foundational to the political reactions that Indian leaders had to the federal government's Indian policy proposal, the emerging Aboriginal vision was best captured by the response of the Manitoba Indian

Brotherhood (MIB) in its 1971 paper, *Wahbung: Our Tomorrows*. The preamble of the paper stated:

> The Indian Tribes of Manitoba are committed to the belief that our rights, both aboriginal and treaty, emanate from our sovereignty as a nation of people. Our relationships with the state have their roots in negotiation be-tween two sovereign peoples.... The Indian people enjoy special status conferred by recognition of our historic title that cannot be impaired, al-tered or compromised by federal–provincial collusion or consent.

Wahbung suggested an inclusive approach to development of Indian com-munities, both economically and as central to Indian life. Development should proceed not in bits and pieces but according to a comprehensive plan on sev-eral fronts. There were three elements to this plan: (1) helping individuals and communities recover from the pathological consequences of poverty and powerlessness; (2) protection of Indian interests in lands and resources; and (3) improved and sustained support for human resource and cultural develop-ment. The MIB plan rested on the idea that development and change needed to be directed by Indian people themselves so that Indians could address both individual and communal interests.

The government formally withdrew the White Paper in 1971, although it remains a potent symbol within Aboriginal politics of what governments have tried to do to solve the "Indian problem." Initial reactions by Indian leaders to the White Paper were informed by ideas expressed in the 1968 consulta-tions around revisions to the Indian Act. While there was no consensus among Indian leaders during the consultations about all the changes that were need-ed, there was consensus about the way forward: recognize the special rights of Indians, recognize the historical grievances over lands and treaties, deal with them in an equitable fashion, and give them direct and meaningful participa-tion in the making of policies that affect their future.

In 1973, a decision by the Supreme Court of Canada about Aboriginal land title involving the Nisga'a on the west coast of the country would alter the political landscape forever. In the *Calder* decision,[16] six of the seven Supreme Court justices determined that Aboriginal rights were in fact pre-existing, al-beit relegated to a lesser position in Canadian society.[17] This judgment en-trenched Aboriginal rights within the country's political legal landscape and laid the foundation for the renewal of the treaty process and the contempor-ary land claims policy. It also forced the government to reflect upon the pos-ition expressed in the Red Paper and *Wahbung* that not only did Aboriginal rights exist, but that these rights in certain cases entailed self-government. *Calder* also laid the foundation for changing the view of the history of Indians since it found that prior to the encroachment of settlers onto Native territories, "Indians were there, organized in societies occupying the land as their forefathers had for centuries."

The *Calder* case represented a turning point in addressing the "Canada problem" in that it clearly brought the judiciary and the law into the politics of Aboriginal peoples in a fundamental way. Aboriginal people began to use the courts to pursue land claims, redress past mistreatments, and further define their legal rights. Over the next two decades, the Supreme Court justices proved to be good allies, with landmark decisions handed down on Aboriginal fishing rights in *R. v. Sparrow* (1990) and *R. v. Marshall* (1999) and on land title and the validity of oral historical evidence in *Delgamuukw v. British Columbia* (1997).

Shortly before the *Calder* decision, the Council for Yukon Indians (CYI) presented its plan, *Together Today for Our Children Tomorrow*, for regaining control over lands and resources that included a comprehensive approach to development in its land claims statement to Prime Minister Trudeau. The CYI argued to "obtain a settlement in place of a treaty that will help us and our children learn to live in a changing world. We want to take part in the development of the Yukon and Canada, not stop it. But we can only participate as Indians. We will not sell our heritage for a quick buck or a temporary job."[18]

The CYI paper also promoted the importance of retaining a land base: "Without land Indian people have no soul—no life—no identity—no purpose. Control of our own land is necessary for our cultural and economic survival. For Yukon Indian People to join in the social and economic life of Yukon we must have specific rights to lands and natural resources that will be enough for both our present and future needs."[19] Land was seen not as a repository of resources awaiting exploitation but rather as a significant component of who Indians are and essential to any form of self-government.

The Push for Aboriginal Self-Government

Aboriginal self-government appears as part of the measures advanced to solve the "Canada problem" in the mid-1970s as the concept of self-determination morphed into self-government. The Federation of Saskatchewan Indians (FSI) (now the Federation of Saskatchewan Indian Nations [FSIN]) was the first Aboriginal organization to formally articulate the principles of Aboriginal self-government in a paper entitled *Indian Government* (1977). The principles advanced in this paper represent a position that has become familiar to public policy-makers throughout Canada.

Indian Government starts by articulating a foundational and immutable set of beliefs that cannot be refuted: "No one can change the Indian belief. We are Nations; we have Governments. Within the spirit and meaning of the Treaties, all Indians across Canada have the same fundamental and basic principles upon which to continue to build their Governments ever stronger." It also sets out eight fundamental principles: (1) Indian nations historically are self-governing; (2) section 91(24) of the BNA Act gives the federal government the authority to regulate relations with Indian nations but it does not authorize regulation of their internal affairs; (3) Indian government powers have been suppressed and eroded by legislative and administrative actions of Canada: Indian government is greater than what is recognized or now exercised and cannot be delegated; (4) treaties reserve a complete set of rights, including the right to be self-governing and to control Indian lands and resources without federal interference; (5) treaties take precedence over provincial and federal laws; (6) the trust relationship imposes fiduciary obligations on the trustee; (7) the federal government has mismanaged this relationship; and (8) Indians have inalienable rights, including the "inherent sovereignty of Indian Nations, the right to self-government, jurisdiction over their lands and citizens and the power to enforce the terms of the Treaties."

The FSI saw sovereignty as the right to self-government that has been inherited and comes from the people. The FSI asserted that sovereignty is both "inherent and absolute," and that Indians had neither surrendered this right nor had they ever been defeated militarily. They declared that Indian governments had traditionally exercised the powers of sovereign nations, and the most fundamental right of a sovereign nation is the right to govern its people and territory under its own laws and customs. "Inherent" means that Parliament or any other branch of any foreign government did not grant the right of self-government. Indians have always had that right, and the treaties reinforce this position.

The FSI further argued in their 1979 paper, *Indian Treaty Rights: The Spirit and Intent of Treaty*, that between 1817 and 1929 more than 20 major international treaties were signed between the Crown and the Indian nations. In return for these treaty rights, the Indian nations agreed to cede certain lands for use and settlement. The FSI advanced the view that treaties recognized the powers of Indian nations and established sovereign relationships between Indian nations and Canada.

Discussions surrounding Indian self-government broadened over the next few years to include Métis, non-status Indians, Inuit, and urban Aboriginal peoples as talks about repatriation of Canada's Constitution got underway, with the terminology changing from Indian to Aboriginal self-government.

The self-government discussion came to be dominated by the FSIN view of Aboriginal self-government, grounded in a view of Aboriginal peoples as self-governing nations with a broad and deep right to self-government guaranteed by treaty. This view resonated throughout the country and captured the political imagination of Aboriginal peoples far beyond those with treaties. Aboriginal peoples categorically rejected the idea of a universal citizenship[20] as articulated by the White Paper and firmly accepted and developed the idea of "citizens plus" articulated in the Hawthorn Report. What remained was to convince others of this position—in particular, the government of Canada.

In 1982, the Constitution of Canada was repatriated and recognized Aboriginal peoples as including[21] Indian, Inuit (formerly Eskimo), and Métis peoples. The Constitution also affirmed existing Aboriginal rights although it left them indeterminate. Section 37 of the Constitution Act, 1982 called for three constitutional conferences between Canada, the provinces, and Aboriginal peoples to try and determine what these rights were and what self-government meant.[22] These televised meetings brought the self-government discussions into the homes of Canadians and introduced them to contemporary Aboriginal leaders in conversation with members of the federal cabinet and the provincial premiers. The idea of self-government was hotly debated, its legitimacy and foundations questioned.

While the discussions were underway, the House of Commons established a special committee chaired by Keith Penner to deal with Indian self-government. The Penner Report (1983) advanced a view of Indian government as enhanced municipal-style government within a federal legislative framework, though with three important differences: (1) Indian government should be a "distinct order" of government within Canada with a set of negotiated jurisdictions and fiscal arrangements; (2) the right of Indian self-government should be constitutionally entrenched with enabling legislation to recognize Indian governments; and (3) the areas of authority for Indian governments could be education, child welfare, heath care, membership, social and cultural development, land and resource use, revenue-raising, economic and commercial development, justice and law enforcement, and intergovernmental relations.

The Penner Report argued for a new relationship with Aboriginal peoples based on Prime Minister Trudeau's comments at the First Ministers' Conference on Aboriginal Constitutional Matters (Ottawa, March 1983):

Clearly, our aboriginal peoples each occupied a special place in history. To my way of thinking, this entitles them to special recognition in the Constitution and to their own place in Canadian society, distinct from each other and distinct from other groups who, together with them comprise the Canadian citizenry. (Penner, 1983)

The report recommended that "the federal government establish a new relationship with Indian First Nations and that an essential element of this relationship be recognition of Indian self-government." It also recommended that:

> the right of Indian peoples to self-government be explicitly stated and entrenched in the Constitution of Canada. The surest way to achieve permanent and fundamental change in the relationship between Indian peoples and the federal government is by means of a constitutional amendment. Indian First Nations would form a distinct order of government in Canada, with their jurisdiction defined.

The report also indicated that "virtually the entire range of law-making, policy, program delivery, law enforcement and adjudication powers would be available to an Indian First Nation government within its territory."

The government of Canada accepted the Penner Report in March 1984 by stating that: "The Committee's recommendations have a special importance because they were unanimously supported by Committee members of all Parties." The government also agreed with the need to establish a new relationship with Indian peoples: "The effect ... is to call for the Government and Indian First Nations to enter into a new relationship.... Many of the details of the restructured relationship will have to be worked out after careful consideration and full consultation with Indian people." Importantly, the government response expressed agreement "with the argument put forth by the Committee that Indian communities were historically self-governing and that the gradual erosion of self-government over time has resulted in a situation which benefits neither Indian people nor Canadians in general."

The government did not initially accept the idea of constitutional entrenchment, though a decade later it would read the Constitution in such a way as to include the right to self-government within it:

> The Government of Canada recognizes the inherent right of self-government as an existing Aboriginal right under section 35 of the Constitution Act, 1982. It recognizes, as well, that the inherent right may find expression in treaties, and in the context of the Crown's relationship with treaty First Nations. Recognition of the inherent right is based on the view that the Aboriginal peoples of Canada have the right to govern themselves in relation to matters that are internal to their communities,

integral to their unique cultures, identities, traditions, languages and institutions, and with respect to their special relationship to their land and their resources. (Canada, 1995)

What makes the Penner Report important in the history of the development of Aboriginal government is that it was the first report by the Canadian government to present historical evidence that reinforced the FSIN argument that Indian nations have always been self-governing. The acceptance of the report in the House of Commons and the detailing of a plan for recognition of Aboriginal self-government represent the end of a phase in the debate about Aboriginal self-government. The first phase of the debate had focused on the question: Do Aboriginal peoples have the right to govern themselves? The second phase began when the federal government responded in 1984 by answering yes, though within the Canadian federation.[23]

Subsequent debates about Aboriginal self-government during the Meech Lake and Charlottetown constitutional talks in the late 1980s and early 1990s were thus concerned with the details of Aboriginal self-government rather than its validity. The Charlottetown Accord in particular, with its proposal of a distinct order of Aboriginal government, foreshadowed the recommendations of the Royal Commission on Aboriginal Peoples. These discussions involved federal, provincial, and municipal governments, and the role of provincial government representatives was crucial since it meant that the debates included not only questions surrounding government authority, jurisdiction, and funding in the areas of natural resources, social services, and education, but also issues of service delivery.

Due to the ongoing reluctance of state representatives to fully endorse Aboriginal self-government, Aboriginal leaders were unrelenting in their demand that self-government be recognized as inherent rather than granted, and that as such it could not be taken away. Discontent also resulted in a series of confrontations across the country. In response to a confrontation over Aboriginal lands at Oka, Quebec, the Conservative government of Brian Mulroney established the Royal Commission on Aboriginal Peoples (RCAP) in 1991 to investigate the evolution of the relationship between Aboriginal peoples, the government of Canada, and Canadian society as a whole. The 4,000-page, five-volume RCAP report tabled in 1996 recommended a restructuring of the relationship between Canada and Aboriginal peoples and set out the details of the "third pillar." It contained an Aboriginal political vision of Canada in which Aboriginal peoples comprise distinct political communities as Aboriginal nations that have a place within the governing structure of the country. It proposed that each nation would have a defined jurisdiction and authority as well as a role in relation to Parliament through a First Peoples House. Similar to the *Wahbung* recommendations, the report also called for a major effort to improve the social and economic conditions of Aboriginal peoples. Canada had agreed just prior to the release of the RCAP report to adopt Aboriginal people's view of self-government in the 1995 Inherent Right of Self-Government Policy, now known as the Inherent Rights Policy (IRP). Although there continues to be much debate about the implications of the term "inherent," the state's acceptance of the Aboriginal view of self-government meant that a key element of the "Canada problem" had been addressed.

The RCAP model of Aboriginal governments as "national governments" or "Aboriginal public governments" or "community of interest governments" goes far beyond the limited municipal-style governments first proposed by Hawthorn and subsequently endorsed by the Indian Chiefs of Alberta in the 1960s and early 1970s. The RCAP model envisions Aboriginal governments being informed by a distinct Aboriginal political culture rooted in local Aboriginal traditions of governance. It also envisions a continuing confederation of Canada with Aboriginal peoples occupying a distinct and constitutionally protected place within it. The RCAP embraced the notion of complexity in its vision and rejected a one-size-fits-all view of Aboriginal governance. It also called for a new round of treaty-making to give shape, form, and substance to it.

Aboriginal peoples' ideas of self-government were not developed in some abstract political philosophical vacuum, but arose through various land settlements and agreements over the previous two decades, including the Cree-Naskapi Act (1975), the Sechelt Indian Self-Government Act (1986), the Yukon Umbrella Final Agreement (1993), and the Nunavut Land Claims Agreement (1993). Post-RCAP agreements such as the Nisga'a Treaty (2000) and the Nunavik Inuit Land Claims Agreement (2005) lend further substance to the RCAP narrative. Numerous less sweeping agreements in areas such as health, education, child care, and economic development give some sense of how Aboriginal governance might proceed in program and service areas. The Centre for First Nations Governance (CFNG) also brought together a large body of experience and literature in contemporary Aboriginal governance for use by Aboriginal leaders to help educate the next generation of Aboriginal people. From 2001 to 2013, the CFNG was a national research and capacity-improving effort directed at the development of effective First Nations governance practices.

Contemporary treaty discussions have started in British Columbia and have been restarted in Saskatchewan. The process in British Columbia is being facilitated by the BC Treaty Commission and is a joint undertaking of

Canada and the First Nations Summit. The Commission is an independent agency overseeing the negotiation of new treaties in an area that was not part of the historic treaty process, which many thought had been dealt with when British Columbia entered Confederation in 1871. The treaty process in Saskatchewan is a joint federal–FSIN initiative, with the province as an official observer. This joint effort is developing a contemporary interpretation of Saskatchewan's four treaties in order to use them as the basis for building a new relationship with the federal and provincial governments. Discussions in this treaty process, which have arisen out of the land claim policy as well as the Royal Proclamation of 1763, include questions and issues involving not just lands and resources, but self-government as well.

In summary, the idea of self-government has broadened considerably over the past three decades. It has grown from an initial conception of local municipal-style government rooted in the Indian Act to a constitutionally protected inherent right, with its most recent expression in the idea of "Aboriginal national government" as a distinct order of government within the Canadian federation. The range of people affected by decisions regarding Aboriginal self-government has grown considerably as self-government talks have moved from focusing on status Indians residing on reserves to discussions that include Métis, Inuit, and urban Aboriginal people. The scope of authority and jurisdiction for self-government has thus enlarged considerably. Aboriginal governments are now seen as encompassing federal, provincial, and municipal authorities as well as some unique Aboriginal authorities. In the federal system, this means that the range of actors that need to be involved has also broadened significantly.

The debate over self-government has thus fundamentally changed. It is now about "how they will" rather than "whether they can" or "why they should." In the relatively short period of 26 years—from the White Paper of 1969 to the Inherent Right Policy of 1995—Canada moved from an official government policy of termination and assimilation to a reluctant acceptance of Aboriginal peoples' inherent right to self-government.

With growing legal and political recognition comes the issue of what to call the new Aboriginal political entities. The Indian Act created legal entities called "Indian bands," the RCAP recommended "Aboriginal Nations" and "Aboriginal governments," and the Charter of the Assembly of First Nations speaks of "Indian First Nations." Similar debates are occurring over what to call the members of these entities since the Indian Act-created "band member" is distinct from the legal category of person called "Indian." As a consequence, Indian bands can be comprised of members who may or may not be Indian. Most Indian bands have adopted the use of the term "First Nation" or

"Nation" along with a historic name in their ancestral language, though there is also disagreement over whether these new entities are comprised of "First Nations citizens" or "First Nations members."

Into the Twenty-First Century

The end of the twentieth century and the start of the twenty-first have seen Canada starting to come to terms with its colonial heritage. In particular, the Canadian government has begun to publicly acknowledge and atone for its past actions as well as promise that it will not engage in the same actions again.

On 7 January 1998, the minister of Indian affairs and northern development, Jane Stewart, stood up in the House of Commons and read a statement of reconciliation. There has been much debate over whether or not it was an apology and what the words meant. Many have also debated about whether or not she should have said it, whether it was sincere, whether it went far enough, and what its effect, if any, might be. While it's quite legitimate to debate and discuss these things, it is important to step back and look at the statement in another light, for it is the first statement by a government of the New World to acknowledge that it has been wrong in its treatment of the people that it encountered:

> The Government of Canada today formally expresses to all Aboriginal people in Canada our profound regret for past actions of the federal government which have contributed to these difficult pages in the history of our relationship together.

Prior to this, no other government in the New World—e.g., the United States, Mexico, Brazil, Argentina, Peru—or any government of the Old World— e.g., England, Spain, France, Portugal—had expressed such sentiments.

The statement also contained a profoundly different view of Aboriginal peoples and Canadian history. It said explicitly that Aboriginal peoples had lived here for thousands of years and that, along with having their own distinct forms of government and national cultures, they had made significant contributions to the development of Canada. It acknowledged that there had been deliberate and wrongful attempts based on attitudes of European racial and cultural superiority on the part of the Canadian government to both suppress Aboriginal cultures and values and to dispossess Aboriginal peoples of their lands/territories, and it vowed to change that. It also painted a picture of Aboriginal peoples as having remarkable strength, resilience, and endurance.

The statement goes on to say:

> Reconciliation is an ongoing process. In renewing our partnership, we must ensure that the mistakes, which marked our past relationship, are not repeated. The Government of Canada recognizes that policies that sought to assimilate Aboriginal people, women and men, were not the way to build a strong country. We must instead continue to find ways in which Aboriginal people can participate fully in the economic, political, cultural and social life of Canada in a manner which preserves and enhances the collective identities of Aboriginal communities and allows them to evolve and flourish in the future. Working together to achieve our shared goals will benefit all Canadians, Aboriginal and non-Aboriginal alike.

It is surely possible to be cynical about this statement, but it is important to acknowledge that in its ideas it conforms to the position held by many Aboriginal people. It is also important to acknowledge that it was primarily prepared by Aboriginal people who were working within one of Canada's major Aboriginal political organizations. It is a remarkable statement, yet it has been much ignored by Canadians as well as by Aboriginal people. Aboriginal people who chose to ignore it did so because they saw it as merely a statement of regret rather than a real apology. Many Canadians ignored it because they thought that the Indian problem was now on the way to a speedy and once-and-for-all resolution.

Even more remarkable was the statement of apology made a decade later by Prime Minister Stephen Harper. On 11 June 2008 the prime minister stood in the House of Commons to deliver a formal apology that stated in part:

> … In the 1870s, the federal government, partly in order to meet its obligation to educate Aboriginal children, began to play a role in the development and administration of these schools. Two primary objectives of the Residential Schools system were to remove and isolate children from the influence of their homes, families, traditions and cultures, and to assimilate them into the dominant culture. These objectives were based on the assumption Aboriginal cultures and spiritual beliefs were inferior and unequal. Indeed, some sought, as it was infamously said, "to kill the Indian in the child." Today, we recognize that this policy of assimilation was wrong, has caused great harm, and has no place in our country.
>
> … The government now recognizes that the consequences of the Indian Residential Schools policy were profoundly negative and that this policy

has had a lasting and damaging impact on Aboriginal culture, heritage and language....

The legacy of Indian Residential Schools has contributed to social problems that continue to exist in many communities today.

It has taken extraordinary courage for the thousands of survivors that have come forward to speak publicly about the abuse they suffered....

The government recognizes that the absence of an apology has been an impediment to healing and reconciliation. Therefore, on behalf of the Government of Canada and all Canadians, I stand before you, in this Chamber so central to our life as a country, to apologize to Aboriginal peoples for Canada's role in the Indian Residential Schools system.

... We now recognize that it was wrong to separate children from rich and vibrant cultures and traditions, that it created a void in many lives and communities, and we apologize for having done this....

The burden of this experience has been on your shoulders for far too long. The burden is properly ours as a Government, and as a country.... The Government of Canada sincerely apologizes and asks the forgiveness of the Aboriginal peoples of this country for failing them so profoundly.

We are sorry.

These are both extraordinary statements, and they begin to address the "Canada problem." They are in many respects the result of the unrelenting efforts of a confident, aggressive, savvy, educated, and experienced leadership that has emerged in Aboriginal communities over the past five decades. Behind the leadership is an ever-growing cadre: thousands of Aboriginal professionals who have gained post-secondary credentials and workplace experience in mainstream and Aboriginal communities. These professionals are slowly moving into decision-making positions and are effecting profound change at many different levels in a wide variety of economic, cultural, legal, and political contexts.

Behind them are thousands of Aboriginal students currently enrolled in post-secondary educational institutions across the country. Over the next few decades, these individuals will also be moving into leadership positions. As a whole, these people are determined, well-educated, and courageous; they want a better world for themselves and their children as well as the rest of Canada.

Many of the upcoming generation see Aboriginal self-government within their grasp. They have experienced aspects of self-government in education, health care, economic development, social work, housing, cultural programs, and language training.[24] They have also done much to ensure that federal and provincial policy, in particular, are consistent with Aboriginal principles and visions. For example, in 2003 they succeeded in getting the federal government to retract the First Nations Governance Act (FNGA), which the government had developed to provide a legislative basis for Indian band councils. The new generation of Aboriginal leaders showed that they were well-versed in their own political history and adept at crafting and putting forward a position that reflected their ideals in their condemnation of this Act, which they recognized as being incongruent with their principles and the foundations of Aboriginal self-government.

The members of this highly educated group also have an understanding of the world that is different from the understanding of those who came before them. They are imbued with an understanding of the fundamental condition of modern Aboriginal society that reflects and is cultivated by a post-colonial consciousness. The raising of this consciousness is resulting in more and more members of Aboriginal society being well aware that their society has been colonized in many ways, that there are clear implications of its colonization, and that they can choose deliberately, consciously, and systematically to deal with the ongoing legacy of colonization. It is a society of people who are coming to terms with what has happened to them and who are determined to overcome its colonial legacy. It is a society of people who are gathering strength and becoming increasingly determined to address the "Canada problem" using their new-found pride. Post-colonial consciousness will thus be the defining political and social force within Aboriginal society over the next generation as growing numbers of post-colonial Aboriginal people set about the task of renovating the master's house with their adapted versions of the master's tools so as to accommodate their desires more easily.

Over the past five decades, an Aboriginal modernity has emerged that forms the context and foundation of modern Aboriginal societies: confident, aggressive, assertive, insistent, desirous of creating a new world out of Aboriginal and Western ideas, and self-consciously as well as deliberately acting out of Aboriginal thought. Along with the profound effects the new Aboriginal society is having in the political realm, the emerging Aboriginal modernity is enabling Aboriginal and other Canadians to benefit from and celebrate the artistic values and skills as well as the entrepreneurial interests and visions of this country's Aboriginal people. In other words, Aboriginal people are changing Canada.

For example, Aboriginal art is now a recognized genre that includes Inuit soapstone carving, Iroquoian soapstone carving, Haida masks, Mi'kmaq baskets, Ojibway quill work (the quills belong to the porcupines), and postmodern Aboriginal expressionism in the work of artists like Kent Monkman.

The explosion in Aboriginal music was evident in 2013 when the Canadian Aboriginal Music Awards celebrated its tenth year as part of the 20-year-old Canada Aboriginal Arts Festival. The 2014 Aboriginal Peoples Choice Music Awards lists 100 nominees in 20 categories, and Canada's Juno Awards now honours the Aboriginal Album of the Year. Aboriginal literature has a wealth of celebrated writers that include Tomson Highway, Jeannette Armstrong, Drew Hayden Taylor, Thomas King, Eden Robinson, Joseph Boyden, and Richard Wagamese, to name a few of the more prominent authors. The national annual literary competition Canada Reads regularly features works by Aboriginal writers, and the 2014 winner was *The Orenda* by Joseph Boyden. Regular television series on CBC feature Aboriginal characters, and CBC Radio 2 and Thomas King produced an acclaimed weekly comedy show featuring Aboriginal actors called the *Dead Dog Café*. In September 1999 the CRTC approved the launching of the Aboriginal Peoples Television Network, which 15 years later is available on basic cable service across Canada. Indspire is an internationally recognized Aboriginal arts foundation that presents annual awards to Aboriginal people who have made outstanding contributions to their communities.

Profound changes in education have led to the creation of one Aboriginal university and 49 Aboriginal-controlled post-secondary institutions.[25] Virtually every public school on Indian reserves is now under First Nation control, and the curricula of the primary and secondary education systems of every province and territory now incorporate Aboriginal history and contemporary issues as well as Aboriginal language training. In 1991, the Arrowfax directory of Aboriginal organizations identified close to 6,000 Aboriginal organizations and businesses in Canada, split evenly between the profit and not-for-profit sectors. By 2014, this number had grown to approximately 14,000 businesses and 3,000 service organizations, with another 117 Aboriginal Friendship Centres serving urban populations across Canada.

An increasing number of Aboriginal people now choose mainstream careers in such areas as education, law, health care, social work, criminal justice, and business. They also serve as public servants in the federal, provincial, and Aboriginal sectors. Some academic studies point to the rise of an Aboriginal middle class.[26] A strong desire has emerged in the midst of these developments to bring forward and interpret traditional teachings and philosophies for a contemporary world. A new category of human knowledge, traditional Indigenous knowledge (TIK), has thus appeared on a broader stage and is beginning to be incorporated in mainstream school systems as well as in economic, legal, and even political contexts. One example of TIK being included in a formal educational context is Trent University's Ph.D. program, which is grounded in Indigenous knowledge and incorporates Elders and traditional Aboriginal teachers among its teaching faculty. In the political arena, the government of Nunavut has formally adopted a policy of incorporating Inuit Qaujimajatuqanit (Inuit traditional knowledge) into all aspects of its operations.

Aboriginal people from Canada have also worked collaboratively with Indigenous peoples around the world to foster a global movement focused on gaining recognition of Indigenous rights and improving the quality of Indigenous people's lives. For example, the World Council of Indigenous Peoples (1974–96) was founded by George Manuel, the former president of Canada's National Indian Brotherhood (now the Assembly of First Nations).[27] Canada's Aboriginal leaders also contributed significantly to the development and eventual adoption by the United Nations in 2007 of the Declaration of the Rights of Indigenous Peoples, which stated clearly that Indigenous peoples have the right to the recognition, observance, and enforcement of treaties concluded with states or their successors.

Unfortunately, these and many other remarkable political, artistic and entrepreneurial achievements of the past 40 years have not yet resulted in an overall improvement in the quality of life for Aboriginal people in this country. Growing post-colonial consciousness nonetheless means that more and more people are aware of a rather disparaging fact: while Canada is consistently ranked as one of the top five countries in the world in which to live according to the UNESCO measures of socio-economic development, First Nation reserves are consistently ranked near the bottom of these same measures. In their efforts to solve the socio-economic consequences of the "Canada problem," Aboriginal leaders, organizations, and academics, as well as grassroots community members and their supporters, have persisted in their efforts to advocate for additional resources to address the social and economic disparities experienced by Aboriginal people.[28] Many recognize that *Time* magazine's description in 1997 of the Canadian lands claim process as "one of the boldest experiments in social justice in Canada's history" can be read in any number of (at best) cautiously optimistic ways.[29]

Concluding Remarks on a Way Forward

Given the preceding discussion, what is a good way forward in relations between Aboriginal peoples and the rest of Canada? Two fundamental aspects of the "Canada problem" obviously need to be addressed. The first is overcoming poverty and its effects, which envelop many rural and urban Aboriginal communities. Despite positive political developments, many Aboriginal people still live in very difficult circumstances. That they remain so is the legacy of colonialism. The 2014 *Report of the United Nations Special Rapporteur on the Rights of Indigenous Peoples… in Canada* indicates that "daunting challenges" remain. The UN Special Rapporteur, James Anaya, concludes:

> the well-being gap between aboriginal and non-aboriginal people in Canada has not narrowed over the last several years, treaty and aboriginals [*sic*] claims remain persistently unresolved, indigenous women and girls remain vulnerable to abuse, and overall there appear to be high levels of distrust among indigenous peoples toward government at both the federal and provincial levels.

Meeting these challenges will require the state to develop an ethos of generosity towards Aboriginal peoples that will enable it to assist them in a variety of ways, including the sharing of resources. The reawakening of the entrepreneurial spirit among many Aboriginal people has been important, but the challenge is too great to leave it to the Aboriginal private sector. Continued development of an economic infrastructure that supports collaboration between Aboriginal and non-Aboriginal businesses is an important aspect of addressing this problem. It is also important for other Canadians to recognize that as Aboriginal people experience reduced poverty, increased education levels, improved housing, and increased employment levels, Canada will benefit as well.

The second set of challenges involves finding ways to change the governing structures and institutions of Canada to accommodate Aboriginal governance—to tackle the founding error in Confederation head on. At first glance this would seem to be a difficult and perhaps almost insurmountable challenge. Where to start? We start by recognizing that Aboriginal peoples have ideas about Canada, about how it ought to be governed, and about their place within the governance structure. We also start by recognizing that Aboriginal people have ideas about their own governments—the principles and ideas that ought to inform them. In many cases these ideas are based in traditional political thought that was grounded in experience.

The Guswenteh, or two-row wampum, has been put forward as one of the ways we can do this. The Guswenteh symbolizes two nations, separate and distinct, engaged in a relationship of mutual friendship and non-interference. The wampum depicts two solid blue or purple parallel lines separated by a row of white space. Much public discourse on Aboriginal self-government focuses on the ideas of separateness, distinctiveness, and non-interference.

What has largely been missing from the discourse is the idea of dialogue and learning. The spaces between the rows are not empty spaces. They are and can be places of conversation, dialogue, debate, discussion, and sharing. They are places where one can learn from the other. This is the place where diverse people can learn to use our "good minds." The dialogue in this space is not about cultural diversity, ethnocultural accommodation, or multiculturalism and how to support it. The dialogue is about how to recognize and embody Aboriginal governance within Canada in a meaningful and significant way.

In October 1983, the House of Commons Special Committee on Indian Self-Government (the Penner Committee) reported to the House that "contrary to the view held by non-Indians that political structures were unknown to Indian people prior to contact with Europeans, most First Nations have complex forms of government that go far back into history and have evolved over time." The Committee then recommended "that the federal government establish a new relationship with Indian First Nations and that an essential element of this new relationship be recognition of Indian self-government." Notably, the Penner Report was accepted by the House in a rare all-party agreement.

This event represented, in our view, the end of the philosophical debate about whether Indian people had a right to govern themselves: Aboriginal people, individually and collectively, had convinced Canadians and their government that they have this right. The first part of the debate lasted from 1867 until 1984: 117 years. The post-1984 debate moved on to details of implementation, which has proven to be challenging for both Aboriginal people and newcomers alike. The debate about details has now been fully engaged and currently rages passionately within Aboriginal communities, as well as between Aboriginal peoples and the rest of Canada. Though the second part of the debate may be with us forever, we should not be afraid of that. After all, European societies have been debating similar issues for at least the last few hundred years. And so Aboriginal people and the rest of Canada now join in a long tradition of debate about the origins, nature, structuring, uses, and limits of political authority.

It is also important that we turn our attention to examining the process of government development within Aboriginal communities and bring to bear the accumulated wisdom and understanding of both our own traditions and those of others. Aboriginal people bring their own political thought to the table and want to see it reflected in the governance of Canada. A major challenge is fostering the development of positive public attitudes towards Aboriginal peoples and their governments. A major RCAP recommendation involved the establishment of a significant public education effort aimed at educating Canadian citizens about Aboriginal aspirations, cultures, communities, and ways of living. An important part of this education will involve cultivating deeper awareness among Canadians of how the racism embedded in the colonial ways of the past is evident today. Fortunately, there is some indication of changing attitudes among Canadians, for while an Angus Reid poll commissioned by Indian and Northern Affairs Canada in 2000 indicated that only 25 per cent of Canadians believed Aboriginal peoples have a historic right to self-government,[30] only 16 per cent believed that Aboriginal people have "no claim to any more land in Canada" and a similar percentage believed that Indian land claims were "legitimate and should be fully compensated in land, money or both." Moreover, support for the honouring of treaties increased from 75 to 80 per cent between 2006 and 2008.[31]

Aboriginal peoples are transforming Canada as they work to address the "Canada problem." In seeking to solve this problem, the actions of Aboriginal leaders have been informed by Indigenous political philosophies based on collaboration and co-operation, accommodation and coexistence, and acceptance of diversity. These philosophies also inform contemporary expressions of reconciliation that were called for in the RCAP report. For example, the purpose of the Truth and Reconciliation Commission (2008) on residential schools was to "guide and inspire Aboriginal peoples and Canadians in a process of reconciliation and renewed relationships that are based on mutual understanding and respect." Similarly, the ongoing actions of the Idle No More movement that emerged in 2013 are grounded in Indigenous ideas of sharing and respect for Aboriginal sovereignty. Slowly but surely, Canada is transforming itself into a post-colonial state.[32] There is growing support for the idea that the foundations of our country lie in the political thought of its Indigenous inhabitants, which is inviting Aboriginal peoples and the rest of Canada to cultivate a shared vision for our country that will enable its original inhabitants to live with dignity and respect as Indigenous peoples.

Discussion Questions

1. Has the "Canada problem" changed over time? If so, what important elements have changed, and what are its current elements?
2. What do you see as elements of the solution to the "Canada problem"?
3. If your perspective of the "Indian problem" has changed over time, in what ways has it changed and what contributed to the change?
4. From the perspective of Canada, what are the contemporary aspects of the "Indian problem"?

5. If you were the prime minister of Canada, how would you address the "Indian problem"?

6. If you were an Aboriginal leader, how would you address the "Canada problem"? How might your response to this question differ depending on whether you were a First Nation, Métis, or Inuit leader?

Further Reading

Abley, Mark. 2013. *Conversations with a Dead Man: The Legacy of Duncan Campbell Scott*. Madeira Park, BC: Douglas &McIntyre,

Belanger, Yale D., ed. 2008. *Aboriginal Self-Government in Canada: Current Trends and Issues*, 3rd edn. Saskatoon: Purich.

Borrows, John. 2010. *Canada's Indigenous Constitution*. Toronto: University of Toronto Press.

Coulthard, Glen. 2007. "Subjects of Empire: Indigenous Peoples and the 'Politics of Recognition' in Canada." *Contemporary Political Theory* 6, 4: 437–60.

Irlbacher-Fox, Stephanie. 2009. *Finding Dahshaa: Self-Government, Social Suffering, and Aboriginal Policy in Canada*. Vancouver: University of British Columbia Press.

Newhouse, David, Cora Voyageur, and Dan Beavon. 2007 and 2010. *Hidden in Plain Sight: Aboriginal Contributions to Canada and Canadian Identity*, 2 vols. Toronto: University of Toronto Press.

Saul, John Ralston. 2008. *A Fair Country: Telling Truths about Canada*. Toronto: Viking Canada.

——. 2014. *The Comeback*. Toronto: Penguin Books Canada.

Notes

1. A literature on Aboriginal citizenship and its possible meanings within a nation-state has emerged over the past two decades. See, e.g., R. Maaka and A. Fleras, *The Politics of Indigeneity: Challenging the State in Canada and Aotearoa New Zealand* (Dunedin: University of Otago Press, 2005); Gerald Kernerman, *Multicultural Nationalism Civilizing Difference, Constituting Community* (Vancouver: University of British Columbia Press, 2005).

2. Statistics Canada. "Aboriginal Peoples in Canada in 2006: Inuit, Métis and First Nations, 2006 Census," online, Catalogue no. 97-558-X2006001.

3. See Royal Commission on Donald Marshall Jr, *Prosecution* (Halifax: Queen's Printer, Dec. 1989); Public Inquiry into the Administration of Justice and Aboriginal People, *Report of the Aboriginal Justice Inquiry of Manitoba* (Winnipeg: Queen's Printer, 1991); *Report of the Task Force on the Criminal Justice System and Its Impact on the Indian and Metis People of Alberta* (Edmonton, 1991); Commission of Inquiry into Matters Relating to the Death of Neil Stonechild (Regina, Sask.: Queen's Printer, 24 Sept. 2004).

4. *Report of the Ontario Task Force on Native People in the Urban Setting* (1981); *Urban Aboriginal Task Force Final Report (2007);* Debwewin, "Three City Anti-Racism Initiative," www.debwewin.ca (2005).

5. For a discussion of the historic origins of Canada's Indian policy, see John Tobias, "Protection, Civilization, Assimilation: An Outline History of Canada's Indian Policy," in Ian Getty and Antoine Lussier, eds, *As Long as the Sun Shines and Water Flows: A Reader in Canadian Native Studies* (Vancouver: University of British Columbia Press, 1983); John Milloy, *A Historical Overview of Indian–Government Relations, 1755–1940* (Ottawa: Indian and Northern Affairs Canada, 1992).

6. Canada, *The Report of the Joint Parliamentary–Senate Committee Hearings on Indian Affairs in Canada* (Ottawa: Queen's Printer, 1961), 605.

7. H.B. Hawthorn and M.-A. Tremblay, *A Survey of the Indians of Contemporary Canada: A Report on Economic, Political, and Educational Needs*, 2 vols (Ottawa: Queen's Printer, 1966, 1967).

8. Ibid.

9. Ibid.

10. Ibid.

11. Ibid.

12. Ibid.

13. A government white paper is a policy proposal released to invite comment and stimulate discussion. In this case, it did just that. In addition, the government proposal achieved lasting notoriety within Aboriginal communities by proposing that, for all intents and purposes, Indians become white.

14. Canada, "Statement of the Government of Canada on Indian Policy" (1969), www.fcpp.org/publications/worth_a_look/spr/native.html.

15. See, for instance, the Supreme Court's determination that the treaties must be interpreted in a liberal way so as not to harm or denigrate the Aboriginal interpretation of events. *R. v. Sparrow* (1990), 1 S.C.R. 1075.

16. See *Calder v. Attorney General of British Columbia* (1973). An excellent examination of the importance of the *Calder* decision is Hamar Foster, *Let Right Be Done: Aboriginal Title, the Calder Case, and the Future of Indigenous Rights* (Vancouver: University of British Columbia Press, 2008).

17. Mark S. Dockstator, "Toward an Understanding of Aboriginal Self-Government: A Proposed Theoretical Model and Illustrative Factual Analysis," Ph.D. dissertation (York University, 1993).

18. Council for Yukon Indians, *Together Today for Our Children Tomorrow: A Statement of Grievances and an Approach to Settlement by the Yukon Indian People* (Whitehorse: 1973), 18.

19. Ibid.

20. For a discussion on the concepts of universal versus differentiated citizenship, see Maaka and Fleras, *The Politics of Indigeneity*.

21. The word "includes" led to much speculation by Aboriginal leaders that perhaps there were other, yet undiscovered Aboriginal peoples.

22. The provinces have an interest in the discussion as it involves land, natural resources, and possible amendments to the Constitution, all issues that are within their purview. Over the next two decades, provinces became increasingly involved in Aboriginal affairs, in many cases establishing ministries and departments to deal with Aboriginal

peoples within their borders. Aboriginal leaders were initially reluctant to include provinces, since they saw their relationship as one with the Crown, refusing to accept the fanciful notion of the division of the Crown.

23. Yale D. Belanger and David R. Newhouse. "Emerging from the Shadows: The Pursuit of Aboriginal Self-Government to Promote Aboriginal Well-being," *Canadian Journal of Native Studies* 24, 1 (2004): 129–222.

24. Saul Alinksy, in *Rules for Radicals* (Toronto: Vintage Books, Random House of Canada, 1971), argues that the "have a little, want more" group leads societal change.

25. Aboriginal Institutes' Consortium, *Aboriginal Institutions of Higher Education: A Struggle for the Education of Aboriginal Students, Control of Indigenous Knowledge and Recognition of Aboriginal Institutions* (Toronto: Canada Race Relations Foundation, 2005).

26. *Report of the Ontario Task Force on Native People in the Urban Setting (1981); Urban Aboriginal Task Force Final Report* (2007); "Atlas of Urban Aboriginal People," online resource by Evelyn Peters, Department of Geography, University of Saskatchewan, http://gismap.usask.ca/website/Web_atlas/AOUAP.

27. For a good history of this effort, see Peter McFarlane, *Brotherhood to Nationhood: George Manuel and the Making of the Modern Indian Movement* (Toronto: Between the Lines, 1993).

28. Katherine Graham, Carolyn Dittburner, and Frances Abele, "Soliloquy and Dialogue: The Evolution of Public Policy Discourse on Aboriginal Issues since the Hawthorn Report," in *For Seven Generations: An Information Legacy of the Royal Commission on Aboriginal Peoples* (Ottawa: Canada Publications Group, 1996); Graham, Dittburner, and Abele, "Summaries of Reports by Federal Bodies and Aboriginal Organizations," in *For Seven Generations.*

29. Andrew Purvis, "Whose Home and Native Land?" *Time* (Canadian edn), 15 Feb. 1997, 18.

30. Quoted in Yale D. Belanger, *Aboriginal Self-Government in Canada: Current Trends and Issues,* 3rd edn (Saskatoon: Purich, 2008), 403.

31. Ibid.

32 For the emerging discussion on post-colonial states, see, e.g., Taiaiake Alfred, *Wasase: Indigenous Pathways of Action and Freedom* (Peterborough, Ont.: Broadview Press, 2005); John Borrows, *Recovering Canada: The Resurgence of Indigenous Law* (Toronto: University of Toronto Press, 2002); Gerald Kernerman, *Multicultural Nationalism: Civilizing Difference, Constituting Community* (Vancouver: University of British Columbia Press, 2005); James Tully, *Strange Multiplicity: Constitutionalism in an Age of Diversity* (Cambridge: Cambridge University Press, 1995); Dale Turner, *This Is Not a Peace Pipe: Towards a Critical Indigenous Philosophy* (Toronto: University of Toronto Press, 2006).

4

Elders' Teachings in the Twenty-First Century: A Personal Reflection

Marlene Brant Castellano

No one has the range and depth of knowledge that Jake had but there are many of us who carry some of his knowledge. If we work together we can do a lot to ensure that his teachings continue.

Paul Williams, on the passing of Chief Jake Thomas, 1998

The rapid decrease in the numbers of true Elders is most alarming. Who is to replace them? . . . The mantle will fall to those spiritual people, less evolved, of less ability and knowledge.

Joe Couture

The request from the editors of this fourth edition of *Visions of the Heart* to contribute an article on Elders prompted the response: "I'm not the person to write about Elders." While I have taken to heart teachings received first-hand or by report over the years from various Elders, I do not have the authority to speak of sacred knowledge. I count myself among those "less evolved" humans who are called upon to share what First Nations world view and knowledge have to contribute to well-being in the twenty-first century.

When I relay received wisdom, I carefully qualify my interpretations as coming out of the experience of a Mohawk woman and an academic, located in a particular context and generation, with no claim of authority to represent the real tradition. I know from reports of colleagues and friends that gifted individuals are engaged in the rigorous and lengthy process of formation to become "intermediaries between their respective cultural communities and the spiritual forces of the universe" (Couture, 2000: 42). This essay is not about those successors of "true Elders" described by Joe Couture (2011).

© Garth Lenz

The pages that follow map some of the ways that knowledge rooted in traditions as received from Elders is being shared, interpreted, applied, and transmitted outward to effect transformation in multiple domains and, perhaps, in society at large. Changes in modes of teaching are cited and, in particular, the concepts developed in written form.

In the last quarter of the twentieth century, a relatively small cadre of Elders firmly rooted in their respective Indigenous cultures and communities in Canada and the United States became magnets for knowledge-seekers from many regions. As stories of their power to awaken identity and restore balance to body and mind were told, as kernels of their teachings were shared, these Elders reached iconic status. I suggest that with the passing of many of that generation of Elders we have entered a period of transition characterized by uncertainty about the authenticity of new messengers and hence about the validity of the messages they bring.

Traditional ceremonies, Indigenous languages, and community validation are proposed as reference points to help navigate through uncharted waters, complemented always by personal responsibility of seekers to discern whether particular mentors are helping them move towards wholeness.

Viewing the Landscape from a Particular Place

I speak and write from the vantage point of a Mohawk woman and an academic who has been a witness and participant in the extraordinary process of reclaiming and affirming Indigenous ways of knowing that has engaged individuals and communities across Canada over the past 40 years. My direct experience with Elders, ceremonies, and cultural teachings has been centred in the Trent University community, where I have had the opportunity of extended association with Elders on faculty and periodic meetings with visiting Elders and traditional people. My understanding has been stimulated and enhanced by exchanges with colleagues and students who are on a similar path of learning, and I have been challenged in particular to translate my insights and apply them to the practice of research.

Selecting terminology to represent streams of knowledge is difficult. Ceremonies and instructions come from specific peoples—Cree, Ojibway, Mohawk—but their relevance is much broader. "Aboriginal" is a collective term including First Nations, Inuit, and Métis peoples in Canada, but use of the term may inappropriately gloss over the distinctiveness of peoples and their cultural heritage. "Indigenous knowledge" is used in international discourse to refer to the streams of knowledge from First Peoples around the world, but the term is not in common use in many communities. The adjective "traditional" acknowledges the ancient origins of teachings but obscures the dynamic nature of those teachings as they are experienced and adapted in contemporary settings. My perspectives have been greatly influenced by socialization in a Mohawk community, association predominantly with Iroquoian and Ojibway Elders, and interpretation through the medium of the English language.

I have learned from many people, but I am particularly indebted to Chief Jake Thomas, who was a colleague and mentor at Trent University for a decade and who shared many of the teachings introduced in this essay by way of illustration. Reflections and writing of Ross Hoffman and David Newhouse have contributed to articulating key ideas that frame the paper.

Uncovering Layers of Meaning

My first remembered encounter with traditional teaching was in the early 1970s at Trent University. Chief Jake Thomas had been invited to deliver a series of public lectures on Iroquois traditions. Jake was later to become a Condoled (Hereditary) Chief[1] of the Six Nations Confederacy. He was already a linguist fluent in five Iroquoian languages and English, a speaker in demand to lead ceremonies in Canadian and American traditional communities, a carver of masks that had been gifted to royalty on behalf of Canada, an artisan who had devoted years of his life to replicating symbols of traditional life—wampum belts, the ceremonial condolence cane, and rattles—and a teacher with a wealth of stories.

In a lecture on male and female roles, Jake talked about the protocol for gathering medicine:

> When you go out to gather medicine you must prepare yourself with prayer and cleansing, otherwise the medicine will hide from you. When you find the medicine it will be growing in families and you must leave the babies because they are the next generation. You must be careful to gather both the male and the female otherwise your medicine will have no power. When you collect water to prepare the medicine you must dip your bucket with the flow of the stream. Otherwise your medicine will have no power.[2]

Jake's words resounded deep within me. I had a sense of knowing that what he said was true, with meaning on multiple levels. He was providing a prescription for harvesting medicine plants, acknowledging the spirit of the plants and the conditions on which they would share their power. He was consciously presenting a metaphor for ordering respectful, complementary relationships between men and women. He was relating the particular human act of preparing medicine with a flow of power in the universe with which humans can align themselves. And he spoke with authority that was not his own but that of the law of life that he was conveying to us.

Jake subsequently joined the faculty of Native Studies at Trent and became a teacher of teachers as well as of students. After a lecture one day, when Jake was being bombarded with questions about traditional teachings, he chuckled: "Everyone has so many questions about culture, and it's so simple. It's all about respect and appreciation."

The words stayed with me but without any rich unfolding of meaning at the time. They came back powerfully in a dream. I was invited to lead a three-day workshop involving a class of social work students at the University of Manitoba, comprised of Aboriginal and non-Aboriginal practitioners. At the end of the first day of professionally organized content, the students informed me that this was not what they had come to the workshop to learn. They wanted to know how traditional culture could help them in their work. I went to sleep that night with the dilemma of what to do with the next two days unresolved.

At 3:00 a.m. I awoke with a visual image of computer paper unfolding (as it used to do) to reveal lecture notes, headed by the titles "Respect" and "Appreciation" in bright letters, sketching out how these Iroquoian principles correlated with good practices I had learned in social work training. At the workshop I announced that with reassurance in a dream I was ready to share some teachings from my own culture but I would need help in connecting them to the experience of the students who were working in Cree, Ojibway, Saulteaux, and Dakota settings. One of the participants revealed that she too had had a dream in which she was instructed to do what was asked of her that day. The seven or eight First Nations students, who had scarcely spoken the previous day, accepted my invitation and took seats on each side of me to become co-leaders for the rest of the workshop.

Learning from that experience has stayed with me. The meaning of a teaching may not be evident immediately, but it will come into focus when the time is right. We need to be ready to let go of our preconceived notions of what will work and take some risks. Help is available if we are willing to reveal our need. Teachings that we receive don't tell the whole story; we have to discover the sense that they make in new circumstances. Something that took hold in my own teaching was the approach of speaking from where I sit, without trying to project my insights into others' experience. Aboriginal people, especially those of older generations, are adept at lateral learning: absorbing messages embedded in a story and transferring them to their own context to make meaning.

When the capacity to listen deeply to stories has been disrupted by schooling that asks direct questions and demands direct answers, students of any age may need lengthy or abrupt reorientation to actually hear the teachings of Elders.

Sites of Learning

When Aboriginal people lived on the land, members of a community from childhood and throughout their lives were instructed in the laws of life through daily experience. Language that has evolved over many generations carries the code for interpreting reality. Language is learned within the family, and the world view embodied therein is reinforced by relationships and practices of the community. Public ceremonies and private rituals give shared expression to understandings that are implicit as well as explicit. In turn, communal experiences become incorporated in the language of family and community. The mutually reinforcing influence of each of these learning sites—language, family, community, and ceremony—is like a medicine wheel, always in motion, with each quadrant drawing from and enriching all the others.

A central feature of experience in traditional Mohawk society was the recital of the Thanksgiving Address, the words that come before all others, at the opening of any communal event. After acknowledging those who have come from different directions, the speaker invites all the assembly to put our minds together as one and give thanks to Mother Earth who supports our feet and brings forth all manner of life upon the Earth. The speaker then proceeds to give thanks to the waters that are essential to life; to the plants that give medicines, nourishment, and shelter to the people and all other life; to the birds that mark the passing of the seasons and please our ears with beautiful songs; to the animals of fields and forest who sacrifice their lives for our sustenance; to our elder brother the Sun who gives warmth and light to all creatures and marks the times upon the Earth; to our Grandmother the moon whose concern is for the faces of future generations coming to us from the Earth; to the stars and unseen forces of the four directions.

In each cycle of thanksgiving, the speaker affirms that all of those named have been faithful to the instructions given to them at the creation. The Thanksgiving Address concludes with the words: "So we look deep into our hearts and find the finest thoughts and the finest words, and we put all of these together as one and give thanks to the Creator of all."[3]

The Thanksgiving Address now figures centrally in language learning in communities where learners of multiple generations are engaged in recovering facility in the Mohawk language. Students are not only learning a mode of communication; they are gaining awareness of their place in an interdependent web of life; they are learning that, like all creatures, they have responsibilities and that they benefit from the responsibilities fulfilled by others; they are being reminded that "putting our minds together as one" is a sacred act; they are being affirmed as persons who have deep in their hearts "the finest thoughts and the finest words" that are worthy of offering up to the source of life. They are learning the deep meanings of respect and appreciation.

The devastating impact of colonialist interventions in Aboriginal lives is addressed elsewhere in this volume. Political structures, land-based economies, family cohesion, languages, and cultural transmission from one generation to another have been systematically undermined. Over the past 40 years, Aboriginal individuals across Canada have been returning to the teachings and ceremonies of their own ancestors or of related cultures.

The sites of learning extend beyond the family hearth and the village council of former times. Language instruction in elementary and secondary schools and oral history and culture courses in colleges and universities reinforce or reintroduce elements of cultural education to students. Skeptics say that such fragments of cultural education are only shadows of the real thing. Jake Thomas's response to critics of his taking traditional knowledge to the university, in classes open without discrimination to Aboriginal and non-Aboriginal students, was: "I can only give our own students a taste of the culture. It will be up to them to go back to the Longhouse to learn more. According to the Great Law of Peace[4] anyone of any nation is welcome to follow the White Roots of Peace to their source and take shelter."

For instruction situated in traditional contexts, adults and whole families from reserves and cities make pilgrimages to camps to take part in ceremonies, fasts, language immersion, and teaching sessions. Then they return to daily lives that may be quite distant from the tribal past. Whereas in the past Elders were reluctant to have their words recorded, oral histories and interpretations of symbols carved on rock and wood or etched on birchbark are now published. The texts of speeches are transcribed and studied. Knowledge deemed to be sacred, particularly knowledge of a ceremonial nature, is still not disclosed except to those who have been initiated in the sacred circle.

As teachings of Elders and the impact of ceremonies are carried outward from the traditional camp and integrated into contemporary lives, the shape of the knowledge and the means of transmission change, as anticipated by Joe Couture, referring to both Native and non-Native seekers:

[S]o many are not grounded in a sense of the real but mysterious power of nature in mountains, rivers, lakes, rocks, life-forms, all as enmeshed in the web of the universe. So, the legends and stories require pedagogical adaptation. The stories have to be retold, reshaped, and refitted to meet contemporary seekers' changed and changing needs. (Couture, 2000: 43)

Selected examples of the ways in which Elders' teachings are being adapted and applied are presented in the next section.

Teaching Methods and Key Concepts

In a traditional, land-based lifestyle, the student learns about reality by direct encounter with his or her environment and personal observation. Older relatives are available to model behaviour and to help make sense of perceptions. Stories recounted in the lodge present social and historical context and ethical imperatives.

When learners are immersed in an environment that lacks experiential reinforcements and tends to contradict the world view represented by Aboriginal traditions, teachers have to be more explicit in their approach to affirming Aboriginal ways. Formal learning in public schools is secular and directed to preparing students for social and economic participation in settler society. The disconnect between Aboriginal culture and formal education has been identified as an impediment to learning and to the development of positive

identity. In response, a number of urban and reserve communities have introduced "survival schools." The Joe Duquette High School in Saskatoon is one
these schools, which builds its program around the cosmology of the regional
culture, in this case, Plains Cree.

> The school's spiritual perspective is sustained by daily sweet grass cere-
> monies, feasts on special occasions, special ceremonies, and sweat lodges.
> Teachers conduct talking/healing circles to build trust so that students can
> speak about their feelings and lives. . . . Drumming and dancing circles
> introduce students to aesthetic dimensions of culture that unify psyches
> and social relations through celebration. Support circles for students gen-
> erate peer backing in dealing with abuse. (Regnier, 1995: 314)

Modifying and transferring selected practices from the traditional camp
and inviting Elders into the classroom are means of introducing successive
generations to the contemporary value of traditional teachings. Another adaptation is the articulation of key concepts and processes inherent in Indigenous
knowledge. David Newhouse of the Department of Indigenous Studies at Trent
University makes the point that learning *about Indigenous knowledge is not the
same as engaging experientially with* Indigenous ways of coming to knowledge
(Newhouse, 2008). Nevertheless, the discourse in the literature and seminars
and the introduction of structured field-based learning with Elders pave the
way for further direct engagement with Indigenous knowledge. A new generation of students and graduates is in the forefront of demonstrating that higher
education can open a path to deepening consciousness of Indigenous knowledge and identity.[5]

Joe Couture, a Cree/Métis trained as a psychologist, and Leroy Little Bear,
a Blackfoot scholar and lawyer, have been very influential in translating the
Indigenous world view into conceptual, philosophical language. Couture
quotes anonymous traditional sources as declaring: "There are only two things
you have to know about being Indian. One is that everything is alive, and two
is that we're all related" and "The centred and quartered Circle is the sign of
wholeness, of inclusiveness of all reality, of life, of balance and harmony between man and culture" (Couture, 2000: 36).

Little Bear sets out the axiom that "In Aboriginal philosophy, existence
consists of energy. All things are animate, imbued with spirit, and in constant
motion." He goes on to explain:

> The idea of all things being in constant motion or flux leads to a holis-
> tic and cyclical view of the world. If everything is constantly moving and

changing, then one has to look at the whole to begin to see patterns. For instance, the cosmic cycles are in constant motion, but they have regular patterns that result in recurrences such as the seasons of the year, the migration of the animals, renewal ceremonies, songs, and stories. Constant motion, as manifested in cyclical or repetitive patterns, emphasizes process as opposed to product. (Little Bear, 2000: 78)

Marie Battiste, a Mi'kmaq educator whose research has focused on the patterns of Mi'kmaw language, confirms the concept of constant flux reflected in verb-based linguistic forms that emphasizes the centrality of relationships, whether between humans or with other members of the natural order (Battiste and Henderson, 2000: 73–85).

A common feature of the knowledge systems of diverse Aboriginal peoples is the responsibility of humans to contribute to maintaining balance in the world. Little Bear explains:

Creation is a continuity. If creation is to continue it must be renewed. Renewal ceremonies, the telling and retelling of creation stories, the singing and re-singing of the songs, are all humans' part in the maintenance of creation. Hence the Sundance, societal ceremonies, the unbundling of medicine bundles at certain phases of the year—all of which are interrelated aspects of happenings that take place on and within Mother Earth. (Little Bear, 2000: 78)

In the field of Aboriginal health, the holistic understanding that well-being flows from a balance among physical, emotional, intellectual, and spiritual aspects of the whole person has become widely recognized, although biomedical treatment continues to focus on physical interventions. As in education, alternative, culture-based services give a place to spiritual dimensions of healing.

The medicine wheel, which brings together several key concepts of Aboriginal knowledge systems, has become probably the most recognized and widely used symbol in conveying traditional understandings. The centred and quartered circle can exemplify balanced awareness of wholeness that encompasses particulars, the holistic nature of well-being, the multiple domains of learning, the repeating cycle of life from infancy through youth, adulthood, and old age to a return to dependency and the spirit world.

Elders' teachings are concerned with personal development of apprentices as well as with knowledge acquisition. Moral precepts for personal behaviour and ethical precepts governing relationships are codified in principles such as kindness, honesty, sharing, and strength in Anishinaabe tradition (RCAP, 1996: vol. 1, 654) or the Good Mind that is fundamental to achieving peace, power, and righteousness in personal experience and community relations, as prescribed in the Iroquois Great Law of Peace (Newhouse, 2008). Unbundling the meaning of moral and ethical values encoded in ceremonies and traditional teachings is the lifetime pursuit of those who are destined to become Grandmother and Grandfather to the whole community, not just to their own kin.

Interpreters of Indigenous world view and ways of coming to knowledge consistently affirm that traditional teachings do not advocate an insular mind, shutting out alternative ways of perceiving reality and organizing perceptions. Battiste and Henderson encapsulate the tension involved in being open to new knowledge and maintaining the integrity of Indigenous knowledge:

> Indigenous educators . . . must balance traditional ways of knowing with the Eurocentric tradition. . . . They must embrace the paradox of subjective and objective ways of knowing that do not collapse into either inward or outward illusions, but bring us all into *a living dialogical relationship with the world* that our knowledge gives us. (Battiste and Henderson, 2000: 94, emphasis added)

David Newhouse uses the concept of "complex understanding" to elaborate how traditional knowledge fosters harmonious relationships in a social and physical universe in constant motion.

> Complex understanding occurs when we begin to see a phenomenon from various perspectives. Complex understanding doesn't seek to replace one view with another but to find a way of ensuring that all views are given due consideration. It doesn't work in an either-or fashion. A phenomenon is not one thing or another but all things at one time. Complex understanding allows for our understanding to change depending upon where we stand to see or upon the time that we look or who is doing the looking. Complex understanding is grounded in a view of a constantly changing reality that is capable of transformation at any time. (Newhouse, 2002)

As traditional teachings are carried outward from the tribal camp and village, across geographic space and generations, the modes of transmission are being adapted to the needs of learners who may not be grounded in an ecological consciousness, who need guidance in interpreting the stories and applying teachings to their life situation. Core concepts are being articulated in publications and integrated in teaching approaches and professional practice of Aboriginal professionals and non-Aboriginal colleagues. Symbols such as the medicine wheel, which were developed in specific contexts, are being shared and adopted across tribal and cultural boundaries. The content of traditional knowledge and the processes by which it is transmitted are becoming a focus of research by both Aboriginal and non-Aboriginal scholars.

Catalysts for Institutional Change

Ross Hoffman is an apprentice in traditional ways, of English and German origin. In his Ph.D. dissertation (Hoffman, 2006), Ross researched the impact of teaching and ceremonial guidance of a gifted Arapaho Elder and healer located in Wyoming. For more than a decade, from 1969 until his passing in 1981, Raymond Harris welcomed knowledge-seekers from Alberta and Saskatchewan, principally Cree individuals and families, to his camp. Hoffman documented how the first wave of apprentices became catalysts for reintroducing ceremonies that had been suppressed in their communities by prohibition in the Indian Act and aggressive resocialization of children in residential schools. These apprentices in traditional ways also became key figures in transforming the values and practices of Aboriginal organizations and services. A roster of Cree leaders in social change interviewed by Hoffman is not proposed as a representative sample. It is derived from personal contact pursued by the researcher. Nevertheless, their activities and recorded thoughts illustrate the rippling impact of Elders' teachings across geographical boundaries, institutions, and generations.

Harold Cardinal was a prominent figure in First Nations politics from the publication of his book *The Unjust Society* in 1969 until his passing in 2005. He was an advocate for the necessity of cultural and spiritual rebirth as a complement to the recovery of self-government and self-determination of First Nations. In interviews recorded by Hoffman, Cardinal recalled the influence of his encounter with tradition and ceremony under the guidance of Raymond Harris:

> I remember having a conversation with him one morning in Wyoming at the breakfast table, over morning coffee. Raymond said "I'm only giving you a start so you can go back and find out the ways of your people, because they exist there. I can't make you an Arapaho—you are a Cree. You must go back and talk with your own people, the traditionalists...."
>
> [T]he traditions were still alive. Some of the old people had kept them underground because of the pressure of the church and law. People had

kept them alive secretly. It was the generation, like my own who had been to residential school, the one or two generations who had been indoctrinated and who were Christians who felt that those traditions were evil because we had been separated from them, the culture, the spiritual traditions....

For many political leaders the Harris/Smallboy[6] influence was that it validated our core identity. It legitimated who we were. It validated that our direction was the right one—our political direction. Not only in this province, but nationally. (Hoffman, 2006: 114, 111, 145)

Others mentored by Raymond Harris had public impact. Eric Shirt, one of the founders and executive director of the Nechi Training Institute in Alberta, was a key figure in the movement breaking new ground in culture-based treatment for addictions. Douglas Cardinal, a Cree/Métis architect, has acknowledged that his vision for the Canadian Museum of Civilization was received in a sweat lodge and that ceremonial practice is an ongoing source of personal renewal. Pauline Shirt was a founder of Wandering Spirit Survival School in Toronto, one of the first urban-based survival schools in Canada.

Joe Couture, another member of the group journeying regularly to the Harris camp, was a towering figure, stimulating cultural awareness and renewal in post-secondary education, mental health, restorative justice, ceremonial practice, and philosophy over a period of 35 years. His influence continues after his passing in 2007. As chair of the Native Studies (now Indigenous Studies) Department at Trent University from 1975 to 1978, Joe encouraged faculty and students to explore culturally based experiential learning, which is now part of the department's academic approach, represented specifically in the vision and mission of the Ph.D. program. Joe's background in psychology and philosophy moved him to make connections in his writing with parallel streams of knowledge in contemporary philosophy and theology. His assertions that perceptions of reality opened up by traditional teaching are on a par with the great religious and intellectual traditions of the world have been taken up by younger scholars, providing a complement to the exploration of traditional environmental knowledge (TEK) that also gained recognition in the latter decades of the twentieth century.

The ongoing exploration of traditional perceptions of reality and application of these insights in contemporary life is evident in the work of scholars and teachers across Canada. Willie Ermine, a Cree from Saskatchewan who is an apprentice in traditional ways, wrote in 1995:

The being in relation to the cosmos possessed intriguing and mysterious qualities that provided insights into existence. In their quest to find meaning in the outer space, Aboriginal people turned to the inner space. This inner space is that universe of being within each person that is synonymous with the soul, the spirit, the self, or the being....

Aboriginal people found a wholeness that permeated inwardness and that also extended into the outer space. Their fundamental insight was that all existence was connected and the whole enmeshed the being in its inclusiveness.... The tribal ceremonies display with vivid multidimensional clarity the entries and pathways into this inner world of exciting mystery that has been touched by only the few who have become explorers of sacred knowing. Rituals and ceremonies are corporeal sacred acts that give rise to holy manifestations in the metaphysical world. Conversely, it is the metaphysical that constructs meaning in the corporeal. (Ermine, 1995: 103, 106)

Currently, as an ethicist and faculty member of the First Nations University of Canada, Ermine envisages the possibility of creative dialogue between Aboriginal knowledge systems and researchers operating from the perspectives of Western scientific culture. He proposes that a precondition for such exchanges is the creation of ethical space where the undercurrents that have disrupted reciprocal exchange are addressed by acknowledging differences in history, modes of thought, and values. In this ethical space the assumption that norms in Western society are appropriate models for knowledge creation in different cultural environments is deliberately suspended. Reorientation of ethics of engagement is essential, because "Western mind" incorporates images of Indigenous peoples that are rooted in oppressive historical relationships (Ermine, Sinclair, and Jeffery, 2004: 22–34; Ermine, 2008).

Gail Guthrie Valaskakis, a communications specialist of Chippewa and European background, elaborates on the implications of the identities constructed by outsider perceptions of Aboriginal peoples:

North Americans' representations of themselves and of Indians are linked in articulation to ways of knowing and experiencing otherness.... Drawn in literature and art, social imaginaries emerge and recede, inscribing Indians as primitive and pagan, heroic and hostile, exploited and defended. These politicized images are woven into policies—colonial and current—that isolate and identify Indians and also construct and position Indian identity, creating unsteady circles of insiders and outsiders. (Valaskakis, 2005: 213)

In his doctoral dissertation, John-Paul Restoule, an educator of Ojibway and French ancestry, explored identity formation by Aboriginal men in urban contexts. He documented the multiple identities of participants who juggled, negotiated, and adapted their presentation of self to themselves and to others as they moved from city to rural reserve, from private to public domains, and back again, fulfilling varied social roles (Restoule, 2004).

Communicating wisdom of the Elders requires at least two-pronged initiatives to affirm Aboriginal identity in an environment that offers fragmented and distorted images of Aboriginal people and devalues traditional ways of knowing. Engaging in discourse with the non-Aboriginal public can affect a shift in the mindset of the majority society and create a more hospitable environment for Aboriginal people struggling to give expression to their core identity. New formulations of Elders' teachings can also affirm for Aboriginal people the legitimacy of their exploration of language, tradition, and inner space.

In his research on the impact of Raymond Harris's work with the Plains Cree, Hoffman describes the core group of Cree traditional practitioners that he interviewed as "the first wave" who learned from "the Old Ones" and went on to become respected as Elders and mentors in their own right. Similar movements were emerging in other regions and Aboriginal communities across Canada. The social and institutional change initiated by the first wave of reborn traditionalists in the latter part of the twentieth century has been taken up by a second wave of knowledge-seekers and knowledge-holders who are animated by the conviction that Indigenous ways of knowing have intrinsic value for non-Aboriginal as well as Aboriginal peoples in Canada and around the globe. In discourse and practice in politics, health, education, the arts, and research in every domain, these new traditionalists are working to give Indigenous knowledge *visibility* as a way of being that is entirely relevant to the twenty-first century.

The necessity of giving expression to wisdom gained and the varied ways that it is communicated are underlined by Viviane Gray, a Mi'kmaq visual artist, citing Black Elk and Maria Campbell:

A human being who has a vision is not able to use the power of it until after they have performed the vision on earth for people to see. (Black Elk in Gray, 2008: 275)

[I]n the Plains Cree language, art is part of the mind or *mon tune ay chi kun* which translates to "the sacred place inside each one of us where no one else can go." It is [in] this place that each one of us can dream, fantasize, create and, yes, even talk to the grandfathers and grandmothers. . . . The thoughts and images that come from this place are called *mom tune ay kuna*, which mean wisdoms and they can be given to others in stories, songs, dances and art. (Campbell, 2005, in Gray, 2008: 268)

Preserving the Integrity of Traditional Knowledge

As traditional teachings become more widely diffused and incorporated in publications, practices, and statements of values in classrooms and organizations, applications of knowledge will become the responsibility of adherents who are physically and culturally distant from the "true Elders" who led the process of renewal. As many observe, true Elders were always rare, and they are passing away at an alarming rate. Who can be trusted to interpret the wisdom of the Elders? Joe Couture quotes an Elder's prediction that these times of emergence are to be marked by chaos and confusion before changing into a time of light and peace (Couture, 2000: 41).

While I have a sense that the quest for certainty in a universe characterized by constant change is doomed to fail, I suggest that there are touchstones that can help us avoid being tossed about by divergent and even competing interpretations of "the way." The touchstones are: ceremony, language, and community validation.

Ceremonies have stability over time. The reliability of oral tradition validated ceremonially has been recognized in Canadian law with the Delgamuukw decision of the Supreme Court in the face of arguments to the contrary. While particular features of protocol in a sweat lodge may differ from place to place, the core efficacy of sweat ceremonies to facilitate healing and transformation continues to be validated by participants. Jake Thomas, working as an oral historian of treaties and councils with ethnologist Michael Foster at the Museum of Civilization, demonstrated that his performance of council protocols illuminated what was recorded in colonial records reaching back close to 300 years (Foster, 1984: 183–207). Traditional ceremonies that reliably mediate connection to the Earth, to the community, and to one's own inner being are a critical counterbalance to the variability of concepts and interpretations that abound.

Indigenous languages reveal in their structure and content the values that have served the people over generations. Cardinal and Hildebrandt conducted research for the Treaty Commission of Saskatchewan on the language used by Cree, Saulteaux, Dene, and Assiniboine Elders in recalling and talking about the treaties. The researchers found a remarkable correspondence among the recollections, concepts, and terms of the different language groups. Based on collaborative interpretation with the Elders, they published a book exploring nine words or phrases that illuminated the view handed down in oral tradition of the sacredness of agreements undertaken, the means of securing good relations, and the commitments to respect future needs for a livelihood from the land. (Cardinal and Hildebrandt, 2000). Willie Ermine writes:

The idea of our progenitors was to try to gain understanding of many of the greatest mysteries of the universe. They sought to do this by exploring existence subjectively; that is, by placing themselves in the stream of consciousness. Our Aboriginal languages and culture contain the accumulated knowledge of our ancestors, and it is critical that we examine the inherent concepts in our lexicons to develop understandings of the self in relation to existence. The Cree word *mamatowisowin,* for example, describes the capability of tapping into the "life force" as a means of procreation. This Cree concept describes a capacity to be or do anything, to be creative. (Ermine, 1995: 104)

In quite personal terms, Caroline VanEvery-Albert describes her own journey of learning her ancestral language:

The Mohawk language is polysynthetic. This means that it is made up of small grammatical elements each of which has a specific meaning. These grammatical pieces are linked together to create words, which are equal to an entire sentence in English. Another interesting element of the language is that it is verb-based and nouns are incorporated. Below is an example of the complexity and beauty of the Mohawk language. [Gives an example of the elements making up a word.] This word, which when translated into English means I want or need something, literally means the earth will provide for me or give me benefit.... I was amazed by the relationship between the Mohawk language and Rotinonhsyon:ni world view. (VanEvery-Albert, 2008: 43)

Having the facility to consider a teaching as it is expressed in our ancestral language is a fundamental way of reflecting on its meaning and its consistency with the values inherent in the culture and the language.

The third touchstone I propose is community validation. While charismatic leaders and visionary holy men and women have existed in various cultures, Aboriginal societies value collective knowing rather than expert knowing. In another paper, congruent with Newhouse's description of "complex understanding," I wrote:

The personal nature of knowledge means that disparate and even contradictory perceptions can be accepted as valid because they are unique to the person. In a council or talking circle of Elders you will not find arguments as to whose perception is more valid and therefore whose judgement should prevail. In other words, people do not contest with one another to establish who is correct, who has the "truth." If a decision affecting the well-being of the community is required it will be arrived at through a process of discussion considering the several perspectives put forward and negotiating a consensus. (Castellano, 2000: 26)

Women speaking to the Royal Commission on Aboriginal Peoples warned of the dangers of naively putting trust in healers who lack community validation:

We have also come across many self-proclaimed healers who have abused and exploited traditional spirituality in their own Aboriginal people.... For controlling the spiritual malpractice, I guess it would be through all the Elders in each community. They would know the ones who are abusing the sweat lodge and abusing the medicines. (Lillian Sanderson in RCAP, 1996: vol. 3, 72)

Attachment to traditional lands formerly contributed to continuity of communities over generations. Mobility of individuals now makes the identification of persons and teachings that carry moral authority more complex, more dependent on effective communication networks.

Conclusion

Over the past two generations, First Nations, Inuit, and Métis people have been actively engaged in conserving and recovering our cultural heritage. Cultural renewal is not about going back to living in tipis and longhouses or returning to the hunting and gathering lifestyle, as critics would suggest. The goal is to uncover those deep life-affirming values that are part of our heritage and to reconstruct in contemporary form the relationships that give expression to those values. Resistance and reconstruction continue to be necessary to rebuild cohesive communities in which the stabilizing elements of language, family, community, and ceremony have been systematically undermined by colonizing forces.

Many of the Elders who gave vitality and guidance to the wave of renewal that gained momentum over the past 40 years are passing into the spirit world. It is not clear who will be their successors. Younger generations continue to look for "the wisdom of the Elders," which is repeated, reformulated, and interpreted at many sites, by many teachers. Young scholars are turning their attention to probing the depths of meaning embedded in the languages, ceremonial forms, and ethical instructions that have been passed on. Connections are being made with traditions of Indigenous peoples in other parts of the world. A small stream of non-Aboriginal people is seeking to learn from the wisdom of the Elders in matters as diverse as the environment, restorative justice, conflict resolution, and holistic healing.

There is much work to be done to restore wellness in our own communities and just relationships with the peoples with whom we share this land. This paper is an attempt to broaden the basis for dialogue within our communities and with our neighbours on how to realize *pimatziwin*, living well in Anishinaabe tradition, and *peace,* the ideal of respect and mutual responsibility valued in Iroquois tradition.

Nia:wen. Thank you for your attention.

Discussion Questions

1. Do Elders' teachings referred to in this chapter have relevance in the environment where you live, learn, and work?
2. Are there points of convergence between Indigenous world views and other philosophies or belief systems with which you are familiar? Elaborate.
3. Is oral communication necessary to the transmission of Elders' teachings? Why or why not?
4. Who are the legitimate teachers of Indigenous knowledge in contemporary times?
5. Do traditional teachings of particular Indigenous societies constitute an authoritative canon of knowledge? Provide a rationale for your view.

Notes

1. On the passing of a hereditary chief of the Six Nations Confederacy, a Condolence Ceremony for the clan of the deceased chief is held, and the candidate who has been endorsed in councils to assume the vacated title is then installed. Chiefs thus confirmed are called Condoled Chiefs. The condolence cane mentioned later is a symbol of the authority of the Confederacy Council. It is carved with mnemonic markings and "read" in the roll call of chiefs at the opening of council meetings.
2. As with other teachings attributed to Jake Thomas in this essay, this is my memory of what I heard. While I acknowledge and honour Jake as the source of the wisdom cited, any error in interpretation is my responsibility.
3. Ernie Benedict, Mohawk Elder, speaking at the opening of a meeting of the Canadian Psychiatric Association section on Native Mental Health on the Native Family: Traditions and Adaptations, London, Ontario, 1983. Transcribed with permission.

4. The Great Law of Peace is both the constitution of the Iroquois Confederacy and the formulation of how members of the Five (later Six) Nations should maintain peaceful relations. The centre of the Confederacy is symbolized by a great white pine tree whose roots, the white roots of peace, go out from the tree in the four directions.

5. See "Indigenous Knowledges and the University" (2008), special theme issue of the *Canadian Journal of Native Education* 31, 1.

6. Robert Smallboy was a Cree Elder in Alberta who led a return to tradition and life on the land around 1968.

5

Foundations: First Nation and Métis Families

Kim Anderson and Jessica Ball

We will raise a generation of First Nations, Inuit and Métis children and youth who do not have to recover from their childhoods. It starts now, with all our strength, courage, wisdom and commitment.

Declaration of a collective of national Aboriginal organizations,
quoted in Blackstock, Bruyere, and Moreau (2005: 1)

Teaching about the state of Indigenous[1] communities today, Cree/Métis Elder Maria Campbell (2008) often calls upon an image provided to her by the late Anishinaabe Elder Peter O'Chiese. O'Chiese likened colonization to someone dropping a complex and snugly fitting puzzle, causing it to shatter in a million pieces. This shattered puzzle evokes the impact of settler intrusion into the worlds of Indigenous peoples. O'Chiese used the image to encourage younger generations like Campbell and her students to go back and pick up the pieces of cultures, world views, families, and communities that were left scattered along the destructive path of colonial intrusions. Decolonization can thus be seen as a process of bringing those scattered pieces back together to rebuild Indigenous peoples and worlds and make them whole again. Where do Indigenous families fit in recreating the whole puzzle?

If we think about the puzzle as Indigenous America, one of the central components was relationships: relationships between individuals, families, and communities as well as relationships with the land and the ancestral and spirit worlds. Campbell talks about the teachings she received from O'Chiese regarding the shattering of Wahkohtowin, a Cree word that can be defined as kinship relative, relationships, or the act of being related to each other and all things in creation. Of all the abuses that Indigenous people experienced,

CP Images/Adrian Wyld

the attack on Indigenous relationships was perhaps the most devastating, because healthy Indigenous communities depended on how they managed relationships and systems of relations.

As we document later in this chapter, persisting high levels of crisis and poverty among Indigenous people in Canada are evidence of the collateral damage from ruptured relationships on a number of levels—social, environmental, and spiritual. But as many contributors to the Royal Commission on Aboriginal Peoples (RCAP, 1996) and the Truth and Reconciliation Commission (TRC, 2012) have observed, the strength of relationships endures in many families and communities, and many people are actively engaged in picking up the pieces of Indigenous families, communities, and cultures and putting them back together (Castellano, 2002). Family relations are a core element of *Wahkohtowin*, and the shattering and subsequent rebuilding of Aboriginal families are the subject of this chapter.

The authors acknowledge the challenge of writing broadly about "Indigenous families," since First Nation, Métis, and Inuit peoples are extremely diverse, both between and within these populations. For example, First Nation coastal cultures are often matriarchal and have very different spiritual beliefs, languages, and social structures from Plains cultures; and Métis people who come from different geographic and socio-historical locations differ greatly from one another and from other Indigenous groups. The various Inuit cultures in the Canadian North are distinctive in many ways from First Nations and Métis peoples. Some common values, practices, and histories can be called upon, however, to construct a cohesive portrayal of the past, present, and anticipated future of Indigenous families in Canada. A look at the shared characteristics of Indigenous family systems, therefore, can tell us a lot about some of the fundamental elements or foundations of Indigenous America, both past and present. In this chapter, we focus on First Nations and Métis examples. We have not described Inuit families because we are not personally familiar with their distinct family practices and systems. Some of our Inuit colleagues have explained to us that Inuit people do not relate to people of the "south" but live in a circumpolar world and have more in common with northern cultural groups living in various countries surrounding the North Pole. We thus begin by examining the family's historical function with a focus on First Nation and Métis cultures. We will then look at the shattering effect on family as a result of colonization before moving into a profile of contemporary Indigenous families and future directions.

Looking Back

Foundations: Kinship and Historical Indigenous Societies

Indigenous peoples have always believed that people thrive when they are embedded in a web of social relationships, with family being the core societal unit and source of belonging. Whereas these historical traditions, values, and approaches are still practised in the everyday lives of Indigenous peoples, we will start with a general overview of Indigenous families in land-based communities (i.e., Indian reserves or settlements) that were, until the second half of the twentieth century, strongly kinship-based.

Generally speaking, people lived in extended family groupings that allowed them to harvest and share resources through hunting, trapping, fishing, gathering, and agriculture. These groups often changed in size depending on the season and the resources available, as conveyed in this description of the Anishinaabek (Ojibway) prior to confinement on reserves:

> Ojibwa familial units would have looked rather different to an observer at different times of the year. In early autumn, in shallow water areas where wild rice grew, extended-family groups gathered canoes full of grain and processed it for winter use. After the rice harvest, Ojibwa groups both shrank in size and multiplied in number as people scattered to hunting and trapping areas inland from main bodies of water. The more northerly the environment, the smaller the winter camps tended to be, but no group could easily survive without at least two male hunters and two or more women to care for children, process food and furs, make clothing and moccasins, and net snowshoes, among other things. (Peers and Brown, 2000: 532)

Peers and Brown (2000: 532) point out that the family was "the primary unit of economic production within Ojibwa culture," as it was in other traditional Indigenous societies (Volo and Volo, 2007). Because so much of the economy depended on family well-being, marriages were decided based on how the extended family might ensure survival and well-being through resource procurement. Historians of the fur trade have demonstrated that the intermarriage of Indigenous women with traders was considered beneficial to Indigenous communities as well as to traders, since these unions consolidated alliances that served the trade (Brown, 1980; Van Kirk, 1980). Business was family business, and survival was a matter in which everyone in the family played a part.

Governance has always been managed through families and family alliances in First Nations and Métis communities—this is true even to some extent today. But the Indian Act significantly disrupted systems of governance based on family. In hunting societies such as many Plains communities, extended families were typically led by elder men, and often there were different types of "chiefs"—for hunting, warfare, and so on (Peers and Brown, 2000). Métis communities had chiefs and captains of the buffalo hunt, which were organized along family lines. In many west coast societies, hereditary chieftainships were passed to men or women. As leaders of the "house," Indigenous women also held political authority as clan mothers, through women's councils, or as leaders of extended families (Anderson, 2000). First Nation and Métis Elders talk about "head women" in their families, women who governed large extended families through the authority they had earned during their lifetime. This authority came from recognition that the elderly women made decisions based on the best interest of the family and future generations, a principle that is evident in a number of Indigenous societies (Anderson, 2000). Although elder women maintained some of this governing role in First Nation and Métis communities well into the twentieth century (Anderson, 2011; Fiske, 1993), their authority was greatly eroded by the introduction of patriarchal Western governing systems. Remarking on how women lost the "public function" of organizing the community that existed when his people were more migratory, Saulteaux Elder Danny Musqua has stated, "This damn Indian Act and the control they [government] put upon us, they destroyed the women's place among us!" (Anderson, 2011: 101).

First Nations peoples still organize to some extent according to clans, which represent broader kinship ties, both among humans and with the natural world (i.e., bear clan, eagle clan), but these systems have also been disrupted. Historically, clans were led by "head men" and "head women" who ensured adherence to community laws. One law was that people could not marry within their clan, which prevented marriage between "relatives." Aboriginal societies often also organized collective and community responsibilities according to clan—one clan might be responsible for overseeing health, others for negotiating with outsiders, and so on. The family and clan one was born into thus prescribed one's greater role in society and the way in which one built family and community into the future (Dickason with McNab, 2009).

In Aboriginal societies, child-rearing was typically shared in family groups; traditional Indigenous communities were the prototypical model of "it takes a village to raise a child." Children were raised by aunts and uncles, grandparents and great-grandparents, great-aunts and great-uncles. In spite of attempts to break these systems down, extended family models also continued to some extent into the twentieth century, as oral historians have noted (Anderson, 2011) and as evident in the statistical information we present later in this chapter. Up until recently, although children knew their biological siblings, parents, and grandparents, other members of the extended family could be equally considered a parent, grandparent, or sibling. The names people used to refer to one another are telling in this regard: a child might refer to any elderly person in his or her community simply as "grandmother," Kohkom, or "grandfather," Mosom (to use Cree as an example). Likewise, elders would refer to young people in the community as "grandchild," *Nosim*, and treat them accordingly. In Algonquian and Haudenosaunee societies, similar words could be used to address one's mother and her sisters (nikowi, "mother," and nikowis, "little mother" or "aunt" in Cree), and the offspring of one's mother's sister or father's brother would be considered a sibling. Thus, a child could have many mothers and fathers, grandparents, and sisters and brothers who played intimate roles in their upbringing. Roles relating to discipline, teaching, and play were divided up in a systematic way among kin so that children received comprehensive and balanced guidance as they moved towards adulthood.

Through ceremonies, children were both challenged and recognized as they moved through different life-stage milestones, and these events were grounded in community support. Babies were held and passed around at naming ceremonies, children were collectively celebrated at walking-out ceremonies (first steps), and youth were taught by various community members in puberty fasts and seclusions (Anderson, 2011).[2] These practices contributed to children's sense of belonging and responsibility, and are now being revived in many Indigenous communities.

It was considered vital to educate children about their roles and responsibilities in relationships because community survival depended on how well the family worked together and how well they managed their relationships with the animals and the land. Campbell has explained the significance of interconnecting roles within family and community by calling on a diagram shared by O'Chiese (see Figure 5.1). Within this system, as Campbell explains, children were at the heart of the community. Everyone worked together for the children's well-being because children represented the future and the survival of the people. Elders sat next to the children because they were their teachers and typically their caregivers. It was understood that elders and children had a special bond, since they were closest to the spirit world on either side. Women looked after the circle of home and community. It is important to note that women were not merely caregivers or servants within the family. Rather, it was women's job to manage the home and community in the most effective way. Men were charged with protecting and providing. They travelled outside the communities and brought in resources that women distributed and managed.

In this system, everyone was involved in ensuring the health and well-being of present and future generations. Responsibilities were organized according to gender and age so that everyone cared for relations and was also cared for. Reciprocity in relationships was important and can be seen, for example, in the relationships between elders and children: elders were teachers to children, who were expected in turn to help their elders. People also carried responsibilities to animals and plants, to the natural and spirit worlds, and were cared for in turn by these entities. These interconnecting responsibilities created a comprehensive web of relationships, and children were raised to know their responsibilities to this web (Anderson, 2011).

This brief overview emphasizes the ways that family and family systems underpinned everything from economics to politics, law, and social order, so the health of the family and family systems was paramount. "Family" meant life itself, as Nuu-chah-nulth hereditary chief Richard Atleo has expressed:

> In the Nuu-chah-nulth world view it is unnatural, and equivalent to death and destruction, for any person to be isolated from family or community. Nuu-chah-nulth life, therefore, is founded by creating and maintaining relationships. (Atleo, 2004: 27)

The following section will discuss how relationships, and thus life itself, were violated for Indigenous peoples.

Dismantling the Foundation

From the earliest encounters, Indigenous peoples were coerced and threatened by European newcomers to change the way they managed their families. This was not simply because the newcomers didn't like the way Indigenous peoples raised their children. Indigenous family systems came under attack because they stood in the way of colonization.

In seventeenth-century New France, the Jesuits complained that Indigenous children enjoyed the liberty of "wild ass colts" and noted an "excessive love of their offspring" among the peoples they encountered (Miller, 1996: 46, 55). This was problematic to the Jesuits because the autonomy and respect afforded to children in Indigenous societies made it difficult for them to "train" and assimilate children through the schools they were trying to establish. These early missionaries had ascertained that working with children held the most potential for converting populations to Christianity, but they were thwarted by the strength of these Indigenous families. Parents were reluctant to give up their children, and women were hostile to patriarchal family structures that would rob them of their power (Anderson, 1991; Miller, 1996).

Pressures to change Indigenous family systems intensified towards the end of the nineteenth century as Canada became a nation and settlers were encouraged to move west. Rose Stremlau connects the dismantling of kinship and removal from the land in the United States. She describes how reformers during the late nineteenth century campaigned for allotment, the subdivision of tribal lands into individual homesteads, as a way to dismantle "the kind of societies created by different systems of property ownership" (Stremlau, 2005: 276). Kinship systems supported Indigenous relationships with the land and vice versa, and all of these relationships would need to be dismantled to get rid of "the Indian problem." Stremlau writes:

> Reformers concluded that kinship systems, especially as they manifested in gender roles, prevented acculturation by undermining individualism and social order, and they turned to federal Indian policy to fracture these extended Indigenous families into male-dominant, nuclear families, modelled after middle-class Anglo-American households. (Stremlau, 2005: 265)

During this period, "field matrons" were sent out by the Office of Indian Affairs in the US to train Native American women in the ways of Victorian womanhood (Emmerich, 1991). Female missionaries in Canada took on a primary role in trying to convert Indigenous women to Euro-Canadian standards of conjugality and domesticity (Perry, 2005; Rutherdale, 2002), and in the early twentieth century, matrons in the United States used Indigenous women as domestic labour as part of their campaign to "civilize" (Jacobs, 2007). Indigenous mothers were infantilized through global colonial narratives and practices that positioned white women as superior in their mothering and thus in a position to oversee Indigenous women and their children (Jacobs, 2011). Indigenous motherhood, once widely understood as the foundation for governance and authority in Indigenous communities (Anderson, 2007), generally came under attack through public discourse in which Indigenous mothers and Indigenous women in general were cast as dirty, lax in discipline, and in need of training (Carter, 1997). Ongoing twentieth-century attacks on Indigenous mothering included subjection to eugenics and involuntary sterilization, which took place in Canada and the United States into the 1970s (Ralstin-Lewis, 2005; Stote, 2012; Torpy, 2000).

With these tools and pretexts, the heteropatriarchal nuclear family was forced upon Indigenous peoples across North America, as it was in other colonies—a project that caused disruption and damage to Indigenous men and fathers as well as to women and families (Innes and Anderson, 2015). Scholars have linked the imposition of a heteropatriachal order to violence on and within Indigenous communities (Driskill et al., 2011). In *Conquest: Sexual Violence and American Indian Genocide* (2005), Andrea Smith argues that the violent subjugation of Indigenous women was deemed necessary in order to colonize the "new world." Today, Indigenous communities suffer disproportionate levels of violence (RCMP, 2014), which has been linked to the dismantling of families and the violence of colonialism (Bourgeois, 2006).

All of these incursions were damaging to Indigenous families, but two twentieth-century strategies in particular caused an implosion that sent communities reeling: residential schools and the child welfare system. Beginning in 1879 and operating until 1996, residential schools took over the role of raising Indigenous children in Canada. Although they resisted, many communities lost whole generations of children; by 1930, almost 75 per cent of First Nation school-aged children were in residential schools (Fournier and Crey, 1997: 61). Many of these children were abused physically, sexually, emotionally, and spiritually. Some took their own lives. Many never returned to their communities. Those who did usually found themselves alienated from their families, lands, and cultures. When residential school survivors became parents, many struggled because they had lost their traditional family structures but also had not experienced positive parental role modelling in abusive institutions (Truth and Reconciliation Commission, 2012). Residential schools thus blew Wahkohtowin apart in a way that no earlier policy or practice had done. In the wake of this devastation, child welfare authorities removed the next generation of Aboriginal children from their homes in record numbers in what has come to be known as the "Sixties Scoop" (Miller, 1996). By the early 1980s, Native children represented less than 4 per cent of the population but made up 50, 60, and 70 per cent of the child welfare caseloads in Alberta, Manitoba, and Saskatchewan, respectively (Bennett and Blackstock, 1992).

O'Chiese and Campbell would link colonization, residential schools, and child welfare interference by referring to the aforementioned diagram of

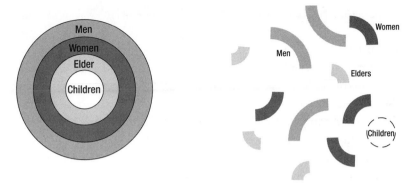

Figure 5.1 | Shattering of Family and Community Relations.

social relations (Figure 5.1). In this narrative, men were the frontline of resistance to colonization through warfare and negotiations, and when these lines broke down, women protected the culture and family by resisting change. In spite of these colonial inroads, strong kinship systems and relationships with the land persisted. State authorities thus came to the same conclusion the Jesuits had centuries earlier: the fastest way to overtake Indigenous communities, deal with "the Indian problem," and gain access to land was to assume the education and rearing of Indigenous children. Anishinaabe educator Sally Gaikezheyongai explains that the mass removal of children from Aboriginal communities was akin to ripping the heart and centre out of Indigenous worlds (Wemigwans, 2002). Once the heart was taken, everything else began to shatter and fall away: Elders had no one to teach, women had no one to care for, and men had nothing to protect and provide for. This created the conditions for an unravelling that communities struggle with to this day (see Figure 5.1).

The ongoing repercussions of these colonial interventions are evident in the challenges described in the next section.

First Nation and Métis Families Today

We begin this section with some basic demographic and socio-economic information about contemporary First Nation and Métis families, followed by a discussion of the current quality of life and emerging trends among Aboriginal families. (More extensive discussion of the demographic characteristics of Canada's Aboriginal peoples, and of their implications, is presented by Don Kerr and Roderic Beaujot in Chapter 8.)

Basic Characteristics of First Nation and Métis Families[3]

The most remarkable trend can be found in the increase in numbers of Aboriginal children and families. In 2011, the median age was 28 years, which is 13 years younger than the median of 41 years for the non-Aboriginal population. The median age of Inuit was 23, First Nations was 26, and Métis was 31 years old. Aboriginal children aged 14 and under make up 28 per cent of the Aboriginal population and 7 per cent of all children in Canada. Aboriginal youth aged 15 to 24 represent 18.2 per cent of the Aboriginal population and 5.9 per cent of all youth in Canada.

The population of First Nations people living in land-based communities (designated by the government as Indian reserves or settlements) is rapidly growing: of the 637,660 First Nations people who reported being registered Indians, nearly half (49.3 per cent) live on a reserve or settlement. Statistics Canada indicates that 40 per cent of First Nations people currently live on reserve, but First Nations and Métis people are also highly mobile. The last four censuses have shown a steady migration to urban centres, with more than half of First Nations and Métis people living in cities, predominantly Winnipeg, Edmonton, Vancouver, and Toronto. Alarmingly, a significant population of First Nations and Métis people is confined in correctional institutions.

Indigenous peoples also suffer disproportionately from poverty: the average household income of Aboriginal families in Canada in 2011 was little more than one-third of that of non-Aboriginal families. First Nations children living in land-based communities are particularly affected by extreme poverty: approximately 43 per cent of First Nations children live in a household with an annual household income of less than $20,000 (Statistics Canada, 2011).

Table 5.1	Aboriginal Populations in Canada, 2011		
	Number	% Aboriginal population	% Canadian population
First Nations	851,560	60.8	2.6
Métis	451,795	32.3	1.4
Inuit	59,445	4.2	0.2

Note: Several communities on reserves, including some with comparatively large populations such as the Mohawks of Akwesasne and Six Nations of the Grand River, did not participate in the 2006 census. The number of residents in Canada who report Aboriginal identity is considerably smaller than the number who report Aboriginal ancestry. Sources of population-level data about Aboriginal peoples are often conflicting and contested, and all are incomplete in terms of which populations of Aboriginal children have been surveyed. Sources: Statistics Canada (2013); National Household Survey (2011).

The 2011 census estimated that 41 to 52.1 per cent of Aboriginal children live below the poverty line, depending on criteria for defining poverty and whether estimates are for Aboriginal identity (a more exclusive criterion) or ancestry (a more inclusive criterion). One in four First Nations children in land-based communities lives in poverty, compared to one in six children in Canada as a whole. The gap between Aboriginal and non-Aboriginal adults in average annual incomes has increased over the past quarter-century (Cooke, Beavon, and McHardy, 2004). Aboriginal unemployment rates exceed the jobless rate of the population as a whole in every province, with rates in Saskatchewan and Manitoba more than triple the overall rate.

Related to employment and household income, average educational attainment among Aboriginal adults is lower than that among non-Aboriginal adults. However, the education gap is narrowing. In 2011, 60.2 per cent of First Nations adults aged 25 to 64 had earned at least a high school diploma, and 73.6 per cent of Métis adults aged 25 to 64 years had done so (Statistics Canada, 2011b). In the non-Aboriginal population, 89 per cent had received at least a high school diploma (Statistics Canada, 2011b). Educational attainment is improving especially among Aboriginal young adults: in 2011, 68 per cent of Aboriginal adults aged 35–45 years had completed at least high school compared to 58.7 per cent Aboriginal adults 55–64 years. In 2011, almost one-half (48.4 per cent) of Aboriginal adults had post-secondary qualification, including 14.4 per cent with a trades certificate, 20.6 per cent with a college diploma, 3.5 per cent with a university certificate or diploma below the bachelor level, and 9.8 per cent with a university degree. In comparison, almost two-thirds (64.7 per cent) of non-Aboriginal adults aged 25–64 had a post-secondary qualification.

Quality of Family Life

While some First Nation and Métis families are thriving, poverty and other socio-economic indicators show that a majority of Indigenous families are struggling. Indigenous leaders and scholars have asserted that the low quality of life for First Nation and Métis families is a direct consequence of the extent to which their parents and grandparents were negatively affected by colonialism (RCAP, 1996), pointing especially to the intergenerational repercussions of residential schooling.[4] Many of today's First Nation parents and grandparents did not learn parenting skills because they were institutionalized from a young age (Dion, Stout, and Kipling, 2003; Mussell, 2005). Many lost confidence in their capacity to engage in the kinds of nurturing social interactions with young children that promote attachment and intimate social interaction (Wesley-Esquimaux and Smolewski, 2003). These interactions are the primary vehicles for promoting self-esteem, positive cultural identity, empathy, language development, and curiosity about the world during infancy and childhood.

Child welfare involvement, for the most part, has exacerbated the disruption of Aboriginal families that began with the residential school debacle. Children removed from their homes and communities often suffer from a crippling loss of identity and sense of belonging because of being displaced from their homes, communities, lands, and cultures (Newhouse and Peters, 2003). In addition to these losses, Aboriginal families continue to experience trauma because of forced relocation of settlements, the dispersion of clans, and urbanization.

Indigenous peoples also suffer from the ongoing and pervasive influences of government policies and inequities in access to supports and services. First Nation and Métis family life is a function, in large part, of the quality of the environments in which they are embedded, including economic, political, physical, and social conditions. Risks and difficulties facing First Nation and Métis parents and their children are compounded by ongoing racism, political oppression, and social structural factors. The latter include poverty, environmental dispossession and degradation, and lack of community-based education, health, and family support programs that incorporate First Nation and Métis knowledge or that are relevant to local circumstances (Salee, 2006). These conditions produce a very different quality of life for most First Nation and Métis families compared to most non-Aboriginal families in Canada (Macdonald and Wilson, 2013).

Shattered Families and Lone-Parent Households

The shattering of Indigenous families caused by colonial government policies has reverberating effects on Indigenous families today. Residential schools, foster homes, racist peers and teachers in public schools, and biased health workers and child welfare workers have had an impact on the ability to sustain intimate family relationships—apparently especially for Aboriginal men (Anderson, Innes, and Swift, 2012). Today, half of Aboriginal children aged 14 and under (49.6 per cent) are living in a family with both their parents, either biological or adoptive, compared to three-quarters (76 per cent) of non-Aboriginal children living with both parents. Approximately one-third of Aboriginal children (34.4 per cent) live in a lone-parent family, mostly with their mother, compared with 17.4 per cent of non-Aboriginal children. Lone parenting is associated with a greater probability of living in poverty (Weitzman, 2003), a situation particularly likely for adolescent mothers.

The number of First Nation children born to adolescent women has remained high since 1986 at about 100 births per 1,000 women, a rate seven times higher than the rate for other Canadian adolescents and comparable to the adolescent fertility level in the world's least developed countries such as Nepal, Ethiopia, and Somalia (Guimond and Robitaille, 2008). On the other hand, national survey data possibly over-represent the numbers of children living in lone-parent households. Legal marriage is not an Indigenous tradition, and many Indigenous partners may not be married; many may be re-partnered with a co-resident adult who functions as a father or mother figure for a child; and some adults may report being a lone parent for financial reasons. As well, evidence suggests that many families still have extended and fluid family structures consistent with Wahkohtowin in traditional Indigenous cultures. For example, the 2011 census found that more Aboriginal (2.7 per cent) than non-Aboriginal children (0.4 per cent) live in skip-generation families—that is, with one or both grandparents where no parents are present. In addition, 9.1 per cent of Aboriginal children lived in multi-generational families with at least one of their parents and at least one of their grandparents, compared with 3.9 per cent of non-Aboriginal children. A further 1.2 per cent of Aboriginal children, compared to 0.2 per cent of non-Aboriginal children, lived with other relatives in arrangements that did not include at least one parent or grandparent. These relatives included extended family, such as aunts, uncles, or cousins (Statistics Canada, 2013).

Census and other survey findings, as well as anecdotal reports from First Nation and Métis communities and family-serving agencies, indicate that many First Nation and Métis fathers are elusive when it comes to family life. Increasing alarm about this pattern motivated an inaugural study involving interviews with 80 First Nation and Métis fathers of young children (Ball, 2010). Statistical data show that, compared to non-Indigenous men in Canada, First Nation and Métis men experience higher levels of poverty, homelessness, and unemployment (Statistics Canada, 2011), are nine times more likely to be incarcerated (Correctional Services Canada, 2006),[5] and evidence higher rates of suicide, mental and physical health problems, and injuries resulting in hospital admission (Health Canada, 2003). Combined with negative social stigma, media stories, and expectations for their roles as fathers, First Nation and Métis men face formidable obstacles to developing positive involvement as fathers. The vast majority of the 80 fathers interviewed reported that three or more of these problems create difficulties for connecting with their children, playing a positive role in family life, or sustaining connections with their children as their relationships with their children's mother or others change (Ball, 2010). Virtually all of the 80 men described past or current challenges with mental health or addictions, and most were struggling to generate a living wage and to secure adequate housing. Research about non-Indigenous fathers shows significant correlations between father involvement and developmental outcomes for children, mothers, and fathers (Palkovitz, 2002; Mahwah et al., 2012). Father absence is also associated with more negative developmental and health outcomes for children and fathers (Ball and Moselle, 2007). Grand Chief Edward John of the BC First Nations Summit contends that "Aboriginal fathers may well be the greatest untapped resource in the lives of Aboriginal children and youth" (John, 2003).

As Claes and Clifton (1998) and Mussell (2005) point out, the frequent lack of involvement of First Nation and Métis fathers in their children's lives tends to be interpreted as reflective of their indifferent attitudes. There is little acknowledgement in family support programs of the unique challenges faced by these men, most of whom have no memories of positive experiences with a father or father figure in their own lives as children and youth. While there is a trend towards increasing numbers of lone-father-headed households among First Nation and Métis men, no programs are specifically designed to help them learn how to effectively support their children's health and development (Ball and George, 2007).

Aboriginal Child Welfare

One of the dire consequences of the residential school experience and ongoing structural inequities confronting Aboriginal peoples is the growing over-representation of Aboriginal children in the care of the Canadian state. In 2011, almost half (48.1 per cent) of all children aged 14 and under in foster care were Aboriginal, representing 3.6 per cent of Aboriginal children aged 14 and under, compared with 0.3 per cent of non-Aboriginal children aged 14 and under (Statistics Canada, 2013). In some provinces, Aboriginal children in care outnumber non-Aboriginal children in care by a ratio of 8 to 1, and removals of Aboriginal children from home into child welfare custody appear to be increasing. The largest study of child welfare investigations involving First Nations children, conducted in 2008 and released in 2011, is the First Nations Component of the Canadian Incidence Study of Reported Child Abuse and Neglect (FNCIS, 2008). The study examined data from 89 provincial and territorial agencies and 22 First Nations and urban Aboriginal agencies. The rate of child maltreatment-related investigations involving First Nations children was 4.2 times the rate of investigations involving non-Aboriginal children: for every 1,000 First Nations children living in the geographic areas served by sampled agencies, there were 140.6 child maltreatment-related investigations in 2008, whereas for every 1,000 non-Aboriginal children living in the geographic areas served by sampled agencies, there were 33.5 investigations in 2008. Indeed, First Nations incidence rates for investigations are significantly higher than non-Aboriginal incidence rates for investigations in virtually every subcategory of investigation examined in the FNCIS study (Sinha et al., 2011).

The study also identified caregiver and household risk factors that contribute to First Nations over-representation, including wellness challenges, overcrowded housing, and poverty. These factors make it difficult for some families to provide adequately for their children's wellness. Child maltreatment has been shown in numerous studies not to be a leading precipitant of a child welfare investigation (Blackstock, Bruyere, and Moreau, 2005; Trocme et al., 2005).

The Assembly of First Nations (AFN) and the First Nations Child and Family Caring Society (FNCFCS) filed a human rights complaint in 2007, arguing that the federal government was discriminating against First Nations children by failing to provide equitable and culturally based services on reserve. The case is currently before the Canadian Human Rights Tribunal. When it was divulged that the government of Canada had withheld tens of thousands of documents it was obligated to disclose to the lawyers representing the AFN and the FNCFCS under the human rights commission rules, legal representatives for the government requested that the proceedings be put on hold so that it could gather together more than 50,000 outstanding documents. Discussions were undertaken on how to proceed given these revelations (Assembly of First Nations, 2013). The final arguments in the tribunal were heard in October 2014, and the results will be released some time in 2015.

The federal Indian Affairs ministry (now titled Aboriginal Affairs and Northern Development Canada or AANDC) also acknowledged shortfalls in funding for prevention and early intervention programs within child welfare services on reserves (Blackstock et al., 2005). No program within the department actively funds and monitors family support programs and early intervention services that are understood in Canada as important for promoting the transition to parenthood, effective parenting, and family stability—services that are available to First Nation children living off-reserve, Métis families, and all other Canadian families through provincial systems (Blackstock et al., 2005). Recommendations from the Truth and Reconciliation Commission *Interim Report* (2012) demonstrate the need for culturally appropriate parenting programs as well as health support services for today's generation of children in the areas of mental health and wellness, trauma, and long-term grief.

Health Consequences of Poverty and Shattered Families

On nearly every health indicator, poorer health has been found for Aboriginal adults (Adelson, 2005) and Aboriginal children (Canadian Institute for

Health Information, 2004; Smylie and Adomako, 2009) in comparison to the non-Aboriginal population. For example, children are more likely to be born prematurely, to be diagnosed with fetal alcohol spectrum disorder, to have a physical disability, or to suffer accidental injury. First Nation and Métis children have a 1.5 times greater probability of dying before their first birthday (Health Canada, 2005) and a higher rate of hospitalization for acute lung infections (Canadian Institute for Health Information, 2004). Oral health problems, especially baby bottle tooth decay, are one of the most prevalent problems for Aboriginal children (First Nations Information Governance Centre, 2012). The use of day surgery for dental caries was 8.6 times higher among children aged 1 to 4 years in neighbourhoods with high proportions of Aboriginal residents. Rates increased according to a Material Deprivation Index measuring household income, employment, and education (Canadian Institute for Health Information, 2013). In a survey of the self-reported wellness of First Nations living in land-based communities, poverty, lower levels of educational completion, household crowding, parent or grandparent residential school attendance, and living in a remote or isolated community all were positively associated with a higher prevalence of cigarette smoking among First Nations mothers (First Nation Information Governance Centre, 2012). Maternal smoking is associated with low infant birth weight and a plethora of child health problems associated with second-hand exposure to cigarette smoke.

Between 2007 and 2010, First Nations adults living in urban areas and Métis adults reported poor overall health and higher rates of chronic conditions compared with non-Aboriginal people (Gionet and Roshanafashar, 2013). Household food insecurity is much more prevalent in Métis (15 per cent), First Nations (22 per cent), and Inuit (27 per cent) households compared to non-Aboriginal households (7 per cent) (Gionet and Roshanafashar, 2013). Related in part to low availability of fresh foods, obesity is rapidly becoming the primary health concern among First Nations people living in urban areas (26.1 per cent) and in Aboriginal settlements and on reserves (36 per cent), as well as among Métis (26.4 per cent) and Inuit (23.9 per cent) (Public Health Agency of Canada, 2011). Mortality rates remain higher (and corresponding life expectancy remains lower) than they are among non-Aboriginal people (Tjepkama and Wilkins, 2011).

Frequent and often serious health problems experienced in Indigenous families cause a chronic sense of living with stress, in crisis, and with grief (Loppie and Wien, 2009). Family life is often destabilized by long absences of family members needing health care provided in cities far from home, frequent disruption of family routines in order to travel to health services, and accommodations within the home environment and household routines to meet the needs of a family member with a physical disability, psychiatric disorder, or chronic disease (Ball, 2008). Chronic disease, severe learning disabilities, frequent illness, and overall poor health of children place enormous burdens on their caregivers in terms of financial implications, time and effort, parents' sense of adequacy in being able to meet their child's needs, and parents' overall experience of stress. Coupled with a widely recognized lack of access to needed screening, diagnostic assessment, early intervention programs, treatment, and occupational therapy programs, particularly on reserves and in rural communities, many First Nation and Métis parents face enormous challenges on a daily basis with few resources (UNICEF Canada, 2009).

Families in Motion

A distinctive feature of life in First Nation and Métis families is their high mobility. First Nations living off-reserve and Métis families move nearly twice as often as non-Aboriginal families (Statistics Canada, 2006). In addition to the general trend towards moving to cities, First Nations people move in and out of reserves frequently in order to spend time with various family members, to go to school, or to access health and social services. Norris and Clatworthy (2006) refer to this high mobility as "churn":

> "Churn" refers to the very high rates of mobility and migration within urban areas, with high rates of in- and out-migration (to and from cities, between reserves and cities), and high rates of residential mobility within cities. These high rates of mobility and migration can impact in a number of ways, affecting the delivery of programs and services, and having disruptive effects on families and children. This is particularly relevant in the area of education, with indications that high mobility and change can negatively affect children's educational outcomes.

Additional negative impacts identified by Norris and Clatworthy include the potential for family instability and dissolution and weak social cohesion in First Nation and Métis communities and neighbourhoods. The National Council of Welfare (2007) asserts that the potential for these negative impacts is exacerbated when the family is headed by a lone parent and/or has low income and high needs, as do many First Nation and Métis families.

At the same time, First Nation and Métis parents often relocate as a strategy for gaining access to needed resources, including professional services and specialized programs for children with disabilities or health conditions, or education or employment for an adult family member (Ball, 2006). Another phenomenon that sometimes accounts for relocating is that the boundaries of First Nation and Métis family units tend to be permeable and family members often are in transition from one home or town to another, one set of relationships to another, or they divide their time among more than one place they call home. Sometimes an adult family member may leave the family unit temporarily or permanently because of difficulties in the primary-couple relationship. The remaining parent may welcome a new partner and one or more of his or her children or other relatives. Families may informally adopt a niece or nephew or even a neighbour. Families in urban centres may expand to include more distant relatives from rural or remote communities who come to the city for school, work, or special programs. The "open doors" found in many First Nation and Métis families may stem from the traditional extended family structures that were ubiquitous before colonization.

Putting the Pieces Back Together

As the previous section demonstrates, First Nation and Métis families suffer the consequences of shattered families and communities in their everyday lives, and there is plenty of work to be done. In addition to reinvigorating relationships to the animals and the land, rebuilding Wahkohtowin will need to include ways to rebuild our human relations through healing programs related to the residential school experience, education and support for mothers and fathers during the transition to parenthood, infant development programs, quality child care, family-strengthening initiatives, family literacy, community development, employment, and social justice. Efforts are being undertaken in all of these areas, but it will take time and resources to rebuild healthy communities. To use residential school healing initiatives as an example, Canadian government investments in the Aboriginal Healing Foundation (2006) enabled important programs, tailored to local community groups, to aid in the healing process. Yet, given the time needed to reconstitute strong cultural communities and family structures, federal government contributions to healing programs, administered by Indigenous organizations, need to be recommitted for some time to come. Unfortunately, in recent years, we have seen the elimination of health programs and supportive organizations in Canada, including the Aboriginal Healing Foundation, the National Aboriginal Health Organization, and the Network Environment for Aboriginal Health Research Centres. Indigenous peoples often assert that it took "seven generations" to erode their families, cultures, communities, and territories and it will take seven generations to rebuild their strength (Castellano, 2002).

This principle must be recognized in any dialogue around initiatives to re-build the human relationships within Wahkohtowin.

Although many initiatives could be highlighted to illustrate the good work of rebuilding Indigenous families and communities, this chapter will con-clude with examples that pertain specifically to children. If the dismantling of families, communities, and lives really set in when the heart—the children—was ripped from the core, perhaps one of the most effective ways of rebuild-ing Indigenous communities is to put the heart back in its place. A focus on children is particularly relevant considering the exponential increase in the numbers of children in Indigenous communities.

Early Childhood as a Strong Foundation for Family Strengthening

National organizations representing First Nation and Métis peoples have iden-tified early childhood care and development (ECCD) training and services as priorities within a holistic vision of social development, population health, and economic advancement (see Canada Council on Learning, 2007). In its seminal report, *The Circle of Care*, the Native Council of Canada (1990) con-ceptualized a direct link between culturally relevant child-care services that are controlled by First Nations and the preservation of First Nations cultures. First Nations scholar Margo Greenwood (2006: 20) underscored this link:

> Aboriginal early childhood development programming and policy must be anchored in Indigenous ways of knowing and being. In order to close the circle around Aboriginal children's care and development in Canada, all levels of government must in good faith begin to act on the recommen-dations which Indigenous peoples have been articulating for early child-hood for over 40 years.

Unlike most high-income countries, Canada lacks a national strategy to ensure access to quality programs to promote optimal early development and learning either for all children or for children in an identified risk category or equity group. Although the current "catch-as-catch-can" provision of ECCD programs is inadequate for all children in Canada, the situation is much more bleak for Aboriginal children: only about 20 per cent have access to any ECCD program (Ball, 2014). The number and distribution of spaces for Aboriginal children in out-of-home ECCD programs falls far short of demand. Yet, in many First Nation and Métis communities and community-based organiz-ations such as Friendship Centres, ECCD is seen as essential for protecting and enhancing the physical health, psychosocial well-being, and positive cultural identity of Indigenous children and their families. Consequently, many communities have created their own community-operated ECCD programs through their own fundraising initiatives (Preston, Cottrell, Pelletier, and Pearce, 2012).

Many of these programs reach out especially to families seen as needing extra support to provide adequate supervision, nutrition, and nurturance for their children to stop the cycle of recurrent removal of children by welfare agencies. Some programs reach out to children with health or developmental challenges. Some communities have initiated home visiting programs, nurseries, and preschools, creating culturally based program elements and drawing on curriculum found in early childhood programs, such as music and movement, storytelling, pre-literacy and pre-numeracy games, as well as parenting skills programs. A common objective of these programs is to reinforce the positive cultural identity of Aboriginal youngsters and their families by using culturally based pedagogy and service models (Preston, 2014). For example, program activities and materials often draw on traditional motifs in arts and crafts, drama, dance, and stories and provide opportunities to engage with positive Aboriginal role models in child care and teaching roles. Many communities integrate or co-locate resources and services that respond to particular local needs, such as parent education, counselling, speech and language services, dental care, and referrals (Ball, 2009).

Aboriginal Head Start

A significant contribution to family strengthening has come in the form of the federally funded Aboriginal Head Start (AHS) preschool programs, although only about 11 per cent of Aboriginal young children have access to these programs. AHS programs deliver culturally based, community-specific programs embodying six components: (1) parent/family involvement; (2) education and school readiness; (3) health promotion; (4) nutrition; (5) social support; and (6) culture and language. AHS programs have the flexibility to develop in ways that are family-centred, family-preserving, and delivered within a community development framework. The programs are informed by the communities' internally identified needs and vision for improving the quality of life of young children and their families (Mashford-Pringle, 2012).

AHS programs help to fill gaps in services to support families during the early stages of family formation, when parents—many of them very young and with few resources—need social support and practical assistance. Some AHS programs have the potential to reduce the high rates of removal of children from their families and communities. Anecdotal reports in the non-formal literature and at gatherings often describe how the programs help the families of participating children to gain access to food, warm clothing, income assistance, and health, mental health, and social services. This is a uniquely promising aspect of AHS because one challenge for ensuring Aboriginal children's access to needed supports and services is that they often do not make it as far as the entry point in mainstream service delivery systems set up to meet needs of children in middle-class families in urban centres (e.g., families with ready access to transportation as well as knowledge of how service systems work and of how to advocate to get their child's needs met). The potential for early childhood programs to become an entry point for young children and their caregivers, gradually introducing families to a range of other services and opportunities, has been documented in First Nations early childhood programs in BC (Ball, 2005). In view of a preponderance of lone-parent households, more investment is needed in quality, centre-based child care, both to provide stimulating, safe environments for infants and children and to enable parents to further their education and training and to generate income. AHS and similar programs that are family-centred, holistic, preventive, and community-driven are one way that Canada can act to promote the health and development of young children who are the next generation of parents. As well, while some steps have been taken to develop First Nation and Métis capacity in the ECCD sector through training of a short-term, non-accredited nature, accredited post-secondary education in ECCD remains an unmet but long-called-for need in Indigenous communities.

Reconnecting First Nation and Métis Children with Their Families and Cultures of Origin

Expanded investments also are needed in First Nation and Métis community economic development, child welfare programs such as family support and parent education, and education outreach to children as well as to adults. Significant numbers of First Nation and Métis children spend much of their childhood living in a series of foster homes or in adoptive families. Approximately one-quarter of children waiting for adoption in Canada are First Nation and Métis children (Adoption Council of Canada, 2009). Across Canada, child and family service agencies operated by First Nation and Métis councils are innovating programs to reconnect children with their families of origin and/or with their cultural communities. For example, in British Columbia, the Métis Community Services Society operates a "Roots" program to ensure that each Métis child and youth in government care has a plan that respects and preserves his or her Indigenous identity and ties to the individual's community and heritage. Another Métis program in BC is called "The

Circle of Life: Honouring the Spirit of the Family." This family preservation program works closely with families to provide education and support for Métis culture-based parenting, teachings from the medicine wheel, loss and grief counselling, family violence prevention, conflict resolution, life skills, and healing and spiritual growth. A third example is a program called *Nong Sila*, a Lekwungen term meaning "many grandparents, many grandchildren." This program arose in response to the fact that most First Nation and Métis children are placed with non-Aboriginal parents and these adoptees risk losing their cultural roots in their communities. The goal of *Nong Sila* is to promote adoption strategies grounded in the needs and cultural traditions of urban Indigenous peoples.

Child welfare policy reforms and expanded funding are needed to create effective systems of in-community placements for Aboriginal children needing temporary out-of-home care (e.g., kinship guardians and Aboriginal foster care) so that Aboriginal children and youth can maintain their identities and not be bereft of family, community, and the life that family and community provide, as described earlier in the quotation from Chief Atleo. The practice of "customary care," in which children are placed with relatives, continues to be promoted by Indigenous child welfare agencies as an effective practice (di Tomasso, de Finney, and Grzybowski, 2015).

Promising Initiatives

On the whole, programs that serve Indigenous children exist because Indigenous people have advocated and worked tirelessly to secure the supports they perceive as necessary for change. Their successes are tempered by the knowledge that much work remains. Although Canada has an Aboriginal Action Plan (Minister of Indian Affairs and Northern Development, 1997), no legal framework exists for implementing it and no mechanism is in place for monitoring the extent to which it is implemented (Assembly of First Nations, 2006b). Federal, provincial, and territorial governments have failed to mobilize a thoughtful and co-ordinated response to improve the quality of life of First Nation and Métis families, beyond the level of the apology offered by the Canadian government on 11 June 2008 (Office of the Prime Minister of Canada, 2008) for the multi-generational impacts of years of colonial interventions on First Nation and Métis children born into families today.

In terms of overall healing and support for adult caregivers, Anishinaabe investigator Chantelle Richmond and her colleagues (2008) find that First Nation and Métis adults report relatively high levels of social support. Yet it appears that colonial legacies have engendered some negative forms of social support in the form of relationship violence and peer pressure to engage in health-damaging behaviours (Richmond, 2009). Low social status, socio-cultural disruption, and the material deprivation of many First Nation and Métis families appear to combine to reduce their access to the kinds of social support and social networks shown to be health-promoting in research with non-Aboriginal peoples (Link and Phelan, 1995). It is imperative to find ways of providing supports to Aboriginal mothers and fathers to regain the strengths of their ancestors in raising children and youth and caring for elders. A program of action research involving First Nation and Métis community groups could explore effective components of culturally based initiatives to support Aboriginal women and men during the transition to parenting and early family formation.

Investments in programs to prepare Indigenous youth for parenthood are also imperative, given that many Indigenous men and women begin having children early and have more children than non-Aboriginal Canadians. The United Nations Population Fund and countries with high adolescent fertility such as the United States implement strategies to reduce adolescent fertility and to meet some of the unique needs of adolescent parents. Few programs in Canada specifically assist individuals and communities to address high adolescent pregnancy rates or meet the needs of First Nation and Métis adolescent parents and their children. Sustained investments are needed to promote the success of Indigenous youth in education, training, and transitions to the labour force, especially for girls. Research around the world has shown that employment that promotes social inclusion, a sense of purpose, and gender equality are the most effective measures to encourage young people to delay having children.

Among the efforts that First Nations and Métis organizations and communities are making to put the pieces of the family and community systems back together, many communities are forming their own agencies to serve children and families. The range of programs and the scope of delegated authority for child welfare varies among these new agencies, from cultural consultation to mainstream agencies to a full range of family support, prevention, and early intervention services, as well as foster and adoption placement (Bala et al., 2004). The issues facing this agenda and ways forward are beyond the scope of the current discussion. The challenges are especially acute for reserve communities, partly as a result of federal funding shortfalls, a lack of credentialed First Nation and Métis child welfare practitioners, and the difficulty of recruiting qualified practitioners to work in settings with few support services or alternatives for children (Blackstock et al., 2006).

Finally, rebuilding *Wahkohtowin* will only succeed if poverty among First Nation and Métis children and their families is adequately addressed.

The National Council of Welfare (2007: 26) links the impoverishment of many Aboriginal families to their tremendous programming needs, reliance on food banks, and cyclical poverty. Poverty makes the health and development problems of Aboriginal children both more prevalent and more entrenched. In turn, poverty and a lack of practical supports for families make it difficult for parents to meet children's needs, contributing to a continuation of the time-worn pattern of government apprehension of First Nation and Métis children and their placement in foster and adoptive homes.

Conclusion

Indigenous families will never look like they did in the past, when family was the foundation for Indigenous economies, governance, social systems, and law. But the notion of *Wahkohtowin* can be reconstructed so that strong families and kinship systems and healthy relations with the natural world will make Indigenous peoples strong again. There is evidence from the 2011 census that remnants of *Wahkohtowin* still hold. As Aboriginal peoples and their allies come together to reconstruct the puzzle, there are many strengths to build upon; new pieces will be added and others adapted to fit new circumstances. Maria Campbell teaches that rebuilding piece by piece can involve something as small as a song, a story, or a gesture, working with traditional ways to reconstruct families and communities into the centuries to come.

Many Indigenous children still have opportunities to be cared for by extended kin networks as they would have been in the past. But if we look at the structure of contemporary Indigenous families and communities, we can also see a creative and adaptive process happening in the absence of blood kin. Marlene Brant Castellano (2002: 1) notes that the extended family's traditional role is being assumed in many communities by Aboriginal agencies, many of which have borrowed from mainstream practice models and adapted them to reflect the community's culture. She describes how some Indigenous adults, working on recovery, are finding their way "home," not by returning to their original families but by knitting together connections in an urban environment with Aboriginal people who come from diverse nations, creating "families of the heart." This kinship model is evident in a story shared by Métis writer Joanne Arnott, who participated in a "traditional parenting skills" program in Vancouver that was facilitated by "Grandmother Harris." Arnott's experience was one of "home making" in which she was able to benefit from kinship support through the program's "family of the heart" (Arnott, 2006).

Another strength that will lend itself to rebuilding is the flexibility and accommodation to changing family configurations and new surroundings that many First Nation and Métis families have demonstrated over time. As was suggested by findings of the 2006 Aboriginal Children's Survey (Statistics Canada, 2009), First Nation and Métis children may enjoy the benefit of multiple caregivers, of being raised by a community rather than in the nuclear and patriarchal family model imposed by colonial authorities. Ball's research on Aboriginal fathers is evidence of the complex, fluid, and mobile nature of Aboriginal families. Although these features have often been cast in a negative light, they may also be seen as a strength to build on. Another strength is that Indigenous families continue to work together to face adversities such as poverty. As the daughter–mother team of D. Memee Lavell-Harvard and Jeannette Corbiere Lavell point out:

> Even in its contemporary manifestation, as opposed to the more historical notions of communal tribal living, for most members of the Aboriginal community everyday survival is still dependent on extensive networks of family and friends who support and reinforce one another. Unlike the non-aboriginal middle-class whose adult members can generally afford to pay others to assume their familial responsibilities, such as child and elder care, those who have almost no economic opportunity, much less actual economic security, must rely heavily upon the help of others. (Lavell-Harvard and Corbiere Lavell, 2006: 189)

Between extended families and "families of the heart," Aboriginal peoples have worked to meet the needs of children in their communities, and they call upon the genius of their cultures to do so. The Ontario Federation of Indigenous Friendship Centres (OFIFC, 2002), for example, demonstrates how families and communities work with children and youth on problems related to fetal alcohol spectrum disorder by tapping into kinship models, working with the land, using traditional parenting techniques, participating in ceremonies, and drawing on the Aboriginal family as medicine. A study expected to be released in 2015 of the OFIFC culture-based Akwe:go program for children 7–12 demonstrates how such programs can provide vital relationships, community, and a sense of belonging to children who may be marginalized or at risk (OFIFC, 2015). Individual families are holding onto or reclaiming practices to strengthen individuals and to rebuild families and communities. Naming ceremonies, walking-out ceremonies, puberty seclusions, fasts, and traditional infant care practices (e.g., using a cradle board) reinforce these vital relationships.

In closing, we share a story told by Lakota scholar John Red Horse:

> The Anishinaabe family drove its station wagon into a tight parking space at the Regional Native American Center in Minneapolis. Everyone in the family above the age of toddler joined in unloading suitcases, folding chairs and bustles. A celebratory dance was being held tonight—the Wild Rice Festival—and the family was there to dance, sing, and visit kin as well as old friends. Once in the building, those family members who would dance this evening went to the dressing area and changed from street clothes to regalia. One daughter carried her 3-year-old son back to the dance area; he was dressed in the regalia of a grass dancer. They got to their chairs, and the mother laid out a star quilt. She put her son on the quilt, and this was the first glimpse that any stranger had of the boy outside his mother's arms. These strangers looked at him with a sympathetic expression. The boy was disabled from the waist down.
>
> As the evening wore one, the strangers were taken aback with the circle of care and concern organized around the boy by family and friends. He was the centre of attention. Elders, including grandparents and older aunts; older brothers, sisters, and cousins; and a host of teenage and adult friends joined together to meet the boy's needs: holding him when he became restive, carrying him around to retail stands, entertaining him with play, and supervising him when his mother was dancing. The strangers beamed with pride because the boy danced in his own way—from the waist up, with head and shoulders keeping time to the beat of the drums. He participated in every inter-tribal dance and entered the dance contest for little boys. (Red Horse, 1997: 243)

Like all Indigenous stories, this one has many lessons and levels. The first observation might be that in many cases, extended family and community still work together, with children at the heart and centre. The significant presence of children in community gatherings comes across here; anyone who has spent time in an Indigenous community will know that children are always around, even in business venues that might be considered off-limits in a mainstream setting. As with stories of fetal alcohol spectrum disorder gathered by the Ontario Federation of Indigenous Friendship Centres, Red Horse's story demonstrates that Indigenous communities often recognize and honour children with different abilities and that cultural activities can be a way of providing them with a place and a way to participate. Red Horse's story, then, is the story of Indigenous families, now and into the future—one of strengths and challenges; of time-honoured systems and cultures; of modern settings, emergent tools and techniques; of children at the heart and a resolute *Wahkohtowin* falling into place.

Acknowledgements

For their helpful comments during the writing of this chapter, we are grateful to Sharla Peltier, Cathy Richardson, John Red Horse, and David Long. We thank Maria Campbell for permission to share her metaphor about the shattering of Aboriginal families and communities and John Red Horse for permission to share his story.

Discussion Questions

1. Why do you think family was identified as the most fundamental area of concern and the starting point for healing and hope in the report of the Royal Commission on Aboriginal Peoples?
2. Who took care of you as you grew up, and how did your experiences as a child contribute to how you view family now? In what ways is this similar to or different from the ways that Aboriginal peoples may have raised their children in the past?
3. What are Aboriginal and non-Aboriginal child and family social service agencies in your region doing to contribute to rebuilding the strength of First Nation and Métis families?
4. What challenges and opportunities do you see in your community or area of work that may affect the opportunities for First Nation and Métis families to a secure quality of life?
5. How might the growth of "families of the heart," as discussed by Marlene Brant Castellano, contribute to the development of new kinds of "kinship" networks and communities for Aboriginal peoples living in urban areas?

Further Reading

Ball, J. 2009. "Centring Community Services around Early Childhood Care and Development: Promising Practices in Indigenous Communities in Canada." *Child Health and Education* 1, 4: 183–206. http://www.journals.sfu.ca/che/index.php/english/index.

Blackstock, C., et al. 2005. *Wen:de: We Are Coming to the Light of Day*. Ottawa: First Nations Child and Family Caring Society of Canada.

Lavell-Harvard, M., and K. Anderson, eds. 2014. *Mothers of the Nations: Indigenous Mothering as Global Resistance, Reclaiming and Recovery.* Toronto: Demeter Press.

Siem'Smuneem Indigenous Child Wellbeing Research Network. 2011. *Honouring Our Caretaking Traditions: A Forum on Custom Indigenous Adoptions. Proceedings and Stories.* 18–19 Nov., University of Victoria. http://icwrn.uvic.ca/wp-content/uploads/2014/01/Honouring-Our-Caretaking-Traditions.pdf.

Notes

1. In this chapter, we are generally using "Indigenous" to refer to First Peoples in Canada, which include First Nations, Inuit, and Métis as recognized in section 35 of the Constitution Act, 1982.

2. These examples refer to Algonquian peoples.

3. Each source of data about Aboriginal peoples in Canada offers an incomplete set of information because of widely differing sampling opportunities and methods and different ways of asking questions, analyzing data, and reporting findings across data collecting agencies (e.g., Statistics Canada, Aboriginal Affairs and Northern Development Canada, Health Canada, National Aboriginal Health Organization). Thus, constructing a picture of First Nation and Métis families' quality of life and their health and development requires a synthetic process relying largely on proxies and anecdotal and non-formal reports, along with a handful of program evaluations that are far from conclusive.

4. To find bibliographies and literature on the impact of residential schools, visit the Truth and Reconciliation website: www.trc.ca.

5. Aboriginal offenders are increasingly over-represented in the Canadian justice system, with an increase of federal Aboriginal inmates of 43.5 per cent from 2005–6 to 2013, compared to a 9.6 per cent increase of non-Aboriginal inmates. While Aboriginal people, according to 2011 census figures, make up 4.3 per cent of the Canadian population, as of February 2013 they comprised 23.2 per cent of the federal inmate population. According to the Statistics Canada publication *Juristat*, "In 2010/2011, 41 per cent of females (and 25 per cent of males) in sentenced custody (provincially, territorially and federally) were Aboriginal" (Office of the Correctional Investigator, 2013).

6

First Nations Women in Canada

Cora J. Voyageur

Today, we women get placed in a "bicultural bind" where we vacillate between being strong and dependent, self-reliant and powerless, strongly motivated and hopelessly insecure.

Paula Gunn Allen (1992: 38)

They say that resilience is the key to survival. If this were the case, First Nations people, and particularly First Nations women,[1] should be applauded for their ability to adapt to the tremendous community upheaval they have experienced since European contact.

Since the "Indians" discovered Christopher Columbus on their shores more than 500 years ago, the roles, the lived experience, and the status of First Nations women have changed dramatically. According to Anita Olson Harper (2010: 176):

> The equality of men and women in pre-contact times was accepted as the voice of creation. Although their roles and responsibilities are different, men were not considered "better" or "more important" than women, or vice versa. The fulfillment of both roles together held a balance that was necessary for meeting both the physical livelihood and spiritual needs of the entire nation. These understandings were a continuing source of strength and peace for the society.

The newcomers employed colonialist ideologies to alter the foundation of Indigenous life in Canada. The subjugation of First Nations women began shortly after contact with Europeans. Cynthia Wesley-Esquimaux (2010) says that First Nations men began to adopt European notions of women's worth to win favour with the missionaries.

Reuters/Chris Wattie

Despite all of the changes endured by First Nations people, many aspects of the traditional women's roles have remained constant. They are still responsible for maintaining culture, stabilizing the community, and caring for future generations. They provide what Wesley-Esquimaux (2010: 24) calls "the stability and continuity of life."

Today, First Nations women share many of the concerns of women in general—child care, family commitments, education attainment, employment opportunities, personal safety, social equality, and political rights. However, unlike mainstream Canadian women, they must also contend with the restrictive policies of the Indian Act—patriarchal and colonial legislation that governs many aspects of First Nations life in Canada. In addition to this restrictive legislation, First Nations women find themselves in the dangerous position of more frequently falling victim to violence both within their own communities and in mainstream society.

First Nations women have had to fight many tough battles in their pursuit of social, economic, and political equality in Canadian society, and their many adversaries have come from government, mainstream society, and at times their own people. Sociologist Linda Gerber (1990: 72) argues that:

Native females suffer multiple jeopardy on the basis of a number of objective indicators of social and economic wellbeing. The fact that Indians as a group are disadvantaged and Indian females in particular suffer the greatest disadvantage suggests that Indian status, with its historical trappings of colonial dependency[,] does indeed create additional barriers to economic and social health. The position of Indian women with respect to labour force participation and income suggests that they are the most severely handicapped in their exchange relations with employers.

First Nations women's experience of multiple jeopardies manifests itself in many different ways and areas of their lives. For example, in the economic realm, the employment rate of First Nations women is relatively low, as is their income if they are employed. A 2012 Statistics Canada report, *Aboriginal Women in the Canadian Economy—The Links between Education, Employment, and Income*, shows that Aboriginal women constitute 59 per cent of the Aboriginal labour force compared to 62 per cent for non-Aboriginal women. They also are more likely than their non-Native counterparts to work in low-paying, low-status jobs in sales and service (Quinless, 2012). Although Aboriginal women's educational attainment level exceeds that of Aboriginal men, they still hold fewer educational credentials than non-Aboriginal women (Quinless, 2012).

In the political realm, First Nations women are significantly under-represented in elected positions in their communities. Even though they comprise 51 per cent of reserve populations (Quinless, 2012), only 20 per cent of elected community leaders are First Nations women (Voyageur, 2008). Being grossly under-represented in reserve politics means that many of the issues they are concerned about have a difficult time getting on the community's political agenda. As a result, it is extremely difficult for First Nations women to effect significant, positive changes in their communities.

In the social realm, First Nations women are among the most victimized groups in Canadian society. Currently, an estimated 1,200 Canadian Aboriginal women are missing, many of whom no doubt were murdered (RCMP, 2014). A proportional number of mainstream Canadian women would be nearly 18,000 missing or murdered (Leblanc, 2014). This number of victims would certainly cause alarm bells to go off across the country.

Although First Nations women have made tremendous strides in Canadian society, a number of social, economic, and political issues still must be addressed to achieve equity within mainstream society. This is no easy task, for First Nations women in Canada have been placed in the contradictory position of being both vulnerable and strong.

The oppression of First Nations women has a long history in Canada. Specific historical events such as the creation of the 1876 Indian Act and the passage of Bill C-31 in 1985 have affected First Nations women greatly. To fully understand the current position of First Nations women in Canadian society, one must examine their historical role.

First Nations Women: From Essential to Redundant

First Nations women were invaluable to the success of the early Canadian fur trade where their knowledge, skills, community connections, and economic linkages made them highly prized as wives for ambitious traders (Harper, 2010). Their affection, companionship, and child-bearing provided a comforting family environment for traders who lived far from their country of origin.

Once European women became part of fur trade society in the mid-1800s they were viewed as more civilized, respectable, and cultured than their Indian counterparts. They quickly supplanted First Nations women as the "preferred" spouses of aspiring traders. The once irreplaceable First Nations wife was rejected, reviled, deemed "less than," and summarily eliminated from "respectable" society (Harper, 2010: 178). European traders seemed to prefer the "glorified frailty" and dependence of settler women over the strength, endurance, and independence of First Nations women. As Robert Connell (2002) argues, men benefit when women are dependent upon them.

Although they were the more highly coveted wives of fur traders, white settler women had few rights and their value remained strictly in the private sphere. Their duties dealt primarily with the care for home and family. They prided themselves on their ability to aid the success of others by supporting their husband's ambitions and having a well-maintained home with clean and well-behaved children. A modern interpretation of this domestic role is Susan Faludi's (1991) assertion that women must sacrifice themselves for others for a society to work and that the advancement of women was bad for the family and the children.

That settler women were expected to remain virtuous at all times further alienated European men from First Nations women, as clergy and others spread rumours about First Nations women being promiscuous, "easily available," bad mothers, and poor housekeepers—basically lacking all the qualities of "decent" settler women (Harper, 2010: 177). They defined Indigenous women as domestically inept, and argued that they needed help to be raised to the moral, hygienic, and domestic standards of the more refined settler society. This damning indictment of First Nations women's domestic ability and degenerate morals has dogged them for centuries, and it could be argued that these attitudes contribute to the subordination that First Nations women suffer to this day.

Subordination of Indigenous Women

Many factors contributed to the, social, economic, and political situation experienced by First Nations women. These include the hegemonic view of European supremacy, patriarchy, the manipulation of the historical record, efforts to eliminate Indigenous people, and the creation of discriminatory legislation.

European Supremacy

With colonization, Europeans brought established opinions of their cultural, intellectual, and structural supremacy[2] over the Indigenous people they encountered in the new land. European ideology rested on the assumption that their civilization was superior to all others and carried with it the self-imposed burden of "civilizing the savages" (Dickason, 1992). In generalized terms, the European view of the world was simple: Indians were savages; women were socially and politically invisible; and individualism and patriarchy must prevail. These attitudes formed the foundation of the Eurocentric view that the newcomers must *fix* whatever they viewed as *unacceptable* in the social, economic, and political conditions of the New World.

Patriarchy: The Rule of the Father

History was and, some may argue, still is a man's world. In public affairs, women were invisible and viewed simply as their husband's possession. For example, a man was said to "take a wife" while a female's marriage was arranged by either her father or her brother. Ordinarily females had no social rights, and thus, European women had little or no political or economic power.

European men set standards for women's decorum and determined how a "cultured" woman should conduct herself. Restraint, modesty, submission, compliance, and piety all combined in the creation of a gender role for women (Boyer, 2009). Women were seen as psychologically unstable, physically fragile, and morally swayable, and it was assumed that they simply could not be trusted to make their own decisions. It is not surprising that European men brought these attitudes and standards to the New World and imposed them upon Indigenous women.

Prior to colonization, Indigenous women were a powerful force in that they controlled many of the economic, political, and social aspects of the societies in which they lived. Legal scholar Robert Williams (1990) states that traditionally women controlled the political realm in a number of North American

Indian tribes by selecting the male chiefs and other political leaders. They also held the power to initiate or call off war. In addition, women owned substantial property interests, including the marital home, and exercised exclusive dominion over the means of production and the products of major subsistence activities such as farming (Williams, 1990). Further, the Iroquois Confederacy was matriarchal prior to the arrival of the Europeans (Mann, 2000). Unlike patriarchy, this system was based on equality between genders. Iroquois women thus played a profoundly important role in the political and economic life of the community. Traditionally, they also contributed in significant ways to their communities as nurturers, educators, and providers (Mann, 2000).

The Manipulation of the Historical Record by the Literate

In Western society, the written word had long been considered the "true medium" of historical accuracy, while oral history was viewed as primitive, biased, and unreliable (Dickason, 1992). As a result, the content of the historical record was at the discretion of the literate and those with the ability and opportunity to put pen to paper, whatever their agenda, philosophy, or predisposition.

Early accounts of women's status in First Nations communities were largely written by men—European explorers, fur traders, and missionaries. These accounts tell us as much about the ideological perspectives of the authors as they do about the subjects of their accounts. These authors were also part of the patriarchal and hierarchical structure that benefited from the domination of women. As a result, early historical accounts most often do not acknowledge the contributions made by First Nations women to everyday life. Patricia Albers writes that recorded accounts either ignored or trivialized women's contributions, activities, and experiences since the writers dealt exclusively with Indian men and documented only the experiences and pursuits of males (Albers and Medicine, 1983).

Despite evidence of women's authority, it is clear that reporting of Indian activities has often been based on purely ethnocentric or Eurocentric interpretations. Anthropologist Alice Kehoe (1983) writes that late nineteenth- and early twentieth-century ethnographers were frustrated in their quest for data by the traditions of their discipline. However, since Indians were viewed as a "dying breed," it became important that details of their lifestyle be collected for posterity. This resulted in an urgency to gather Indian-related ethnographic information. For example, photographers Edward Sheriff Curtis and

Ernest Brown amassed voluminous photographic portfolios of Indigenous people from the nineteenth-century Canadian and American West.

Encounters between the recorder and the subject were limited in duration, frequency, and understanding. The resulting data and subsequent reports were often inaccurate and contained both gender and ethnocentric biases. One such common misinterpretation was the explanation given for an Indigenous woman walking behind her husband. The assumption that this practice reflects the female's inferior status clouds the real reason—that a man is responsible for protecting his wife because she is the giver of life and more powerful than he.

Data collection was guided by conventions that did not allow for accurate depictions of either the role or the contributions of First Nations women because of ingrained biases. One reason was that anthropologists predominantly were male and their scholarly custom was to speak exclusively to male subjects (Kehoe, 1983). Common practice dictated that the ethnographer and his male assistant interview a limited number of middle-aged and elderly men about life in the community. If and when Indigenous women were interviewed, the situation was uncomfortable for them since they were accustomed to being ignored by European men. In addition, it was culturally and socially inappropriate to discuss "women's matters" with men (Kehoe, 1983).

In contrast to what was written—or not written—about Indigenous women in the historical record, Indigenous customs held women in high regard; they were powerful, respected, and valuable within their communities. The view that Indigenous women were not important to their communities eventually was contradicted by later discoveries. For example, anthropologist Judith Brown states that older women in the Wabanaki, Algonquin, Delaware, Powhatan, and Iroquois tribes had authority over kinsmen and had the right to exert power over them to extract their labour (Brown, 1982). Wabanaki women achieved positions of leadership in both religious and political spheres when they reached middle age (Ezzo, 1988).

Eliminating the People of the *Terra Nullius*

First Nations people began to be subjugated almost immediately after the arrival of Europeans, whose actions were based on the idea that "savages" could not own the land. Europeans thus viewed the New World as *terra nullius* or vacant land and therefore free for the taking.

By the time of Canadian Confederation in 1867, missionary ideology and government policy held that the only way First Nations people could survive in the newly formed Canada was to give up everything that defined them as a people: religion, language, lifestyle, and identity. It was assumed that all First Nations people would naturally aspire to Canadian citizenship and would eventually embrace modernity—assumed to be the only way to evolve from a primitive society to an enlightened one. According to settler society, Indigenous tradition, culture, and identity presumably had no place in the lives of Indigenous peoples if they wanted to move forward.

Duncan Campbell Scott, assistant deputy superintendent of Indian Affairs, 1913–32, implemented an assimilation policy to rid Canadians and the government of the "Indian problem." The Parliamentary Subcommittee on Indian Women and the Indian Act (1982) noted that:

> Between 1913 and 1930 the administration of Indian Affairs followed a rigid policy of forced assimilation. Traditional practices such as the Sundance and the Potlatch were prohibited and traditional languages were suppressed. Duncan Campbell Scott in explaining the rationale for changes to the legislation in 1920 said "Our object is to continue until there is not a single Indian in Canada that has not been absorbed into the body politic. This is the whole object of this Bill." (McDonald, 1987: 30)

There were a number of means by which the settler population and its governments attempted to eliminate the "Indian problem." Many Euro-Canadians viewed education and religious training in European beliefs, values, and customs as an effective means of ensuring that every single Indian would be absorbed into the body politic. The residential school system was created with this idea in mind, for it was believed that "saving" the children would occur by means of transforming them from "savages" to "civilized" British citizens, and that this would result in the betterment of the Indian and of society as a whole (Voyageur, 1993). Separate legal Indian status was also conceived early on by white legislators as a temporary means of dealing with Canada's Indians, for they fully expected that all Indians would gradually abandon their Native identity to enjoy the "privilege" of full Canadian citizenship; a privileged status to which all would and should aspire (Francis, 1993).

When Indians met the minimal requirements for citizenship—literacy, education, and "acceptable" moral character—they were allowed the rights of full citizenship through voluntary enfranchisement. With citizenship came the right to vote, purchase alcohol, and obtain land under the homestead system with no further requirement that they live under the aegis of the repressive Indian Act. It is ironic that enfranchisement, the right of full citizenship in Canadian society, was used both as a reward and as a punishment for First Nations people. It was a defined as a reward (imposed by the state) for those who obtained a university degree, joined the military, or became a minister. But enfranchisement was a punishment for anyone caught in possession of alcohol or who raised the ire of the Indian agent. The Indian agent had absolute authority on the reserve and could delete whomever he chose from the band list, and that person would subsequently lose Indian status.

The Yoke of Oppression: The Indian Act

Section 91(24) of the British North American Act of 1867 granted the federal government the power of legislative control over Indians and their lands. Thus empowered, the Canadian Parliament began drafting provisions for what eventually was to become known as the Indian Act. The Indian Act was, and perhaps still is, the most oppressive legislation in Canadian history. Prior to the Indian Act, the statutory definition of Indians was all persons of Indian blood, their spouses, and their descendants. This definition was used to determine the right to possess or occupy lands. However, in 1869 the government passed the Gradual Enfranchisement Act, which determined the scope of the government's responsibilities for those with whom it had entered into the treaty process. It was also a deliberate attempt to reduce the number of First Nations people for whom the government would be responsible, although Dickason (1992) notes that this attempt was hardly successful, as very few Indians chose enfranchisement.

The first body of legislation to bear the official title "The Indian Act" was passed in 1876. This Act redefined "Indian" as:

> Firstly, any male person of Indian blood reputed to belong to a particular band;
> Secondly, any child of such person;
> Thirdly, any women who is or was lawfully married to such a person.
> (Paul, 1993: 19)

From its inception, the Indian Act encompassed virtually every aspect of Indian life. It is primarily social legislation, though its broad scope includes provisions for everything from liquor control to agriculture, education, mining, Indian lands, community bylaws, and band membership (Venne, 1981).

The Impact of Indian Act Legislation on First Nations Women

The measure that deprived an Indian woman of her status when she married a non-Indian was first legislated in the 1869 Act for the Gradual Enfranchisement of Indians. This Act was also the first piece of legislation that officially discriminated against Indian women by assigning them fewer fundamental rights than Indian men. Section 6 of the Act stated, "Provided, always that any Indian woman marrying any other than an Indian, shall cease to be an Indian within the meaning of this Act, nor shall the children issue of such marriage be considered as Indians within the meaning of this Act" (S.C. 1869, C6).

Numerous discriminatory provisions within the Indian Act limited Indian women's social and political rights and placed them in a subordinate position to men in their communities. The legal subordination of Indian women also contributed to cultural changes in many Indian tribes that had previously acknowledged the political power of their women. For example, the treaty process excluded women from discussions and required that "official" representatives be selected through an electoral system designed and imposed on First Nations by the Canadian government. Until 1951, the Indian Act denied First Nations women the right to vote in band elections. They were not allowed to hold elected office or to participate in public meetings that decided band business (Voyageur, 2008). The fact that Indian women lost the power they had in their pre-contact societies also meant that Indian men gained far more political power under the imposed system than they traditionally had possessed.

Furthermore, the 1876 Indian Act determined legal status by patrilineal affiliation. First Nations women were not legal entities and they had virtually no rights. Their assigned political status was inferior to that of their husbands, which was much like the political status accorded to women in European society. If an Indian man was enfranchised, then his wife and minor children were automatically enfranchised.

If an Indian woman married an Indian man from another reserve, then she became a member of her husband's band. The Act stated that a woman must follow her husband, but if her husband died or she divorced him then she was not allowed to return to her reserve. Another provision stated that upon the death of an Indian man, his estate passed to his children and not to his wife.

For women the most troublesome portion of the Indian Act was section 12(1)(b). It pertained specifically to Indian women losing their status by marrying non-Indian men:

12(1) The following persons are not entitled to be registered, namely...

(b) a woman who married a person who is not an Indian, unless that woman is subsequently the wife or widow of a person described in Section 11.[3] (Jamieson, 1978: 8)

According to section 12(1)(b), an Indian woman immediately lost her Indian status upon marrying a non-Indian man. She became one with her husband and therefore took on his identity under the patriarchal legislation. If her husband was non-First Nation then she became non-First Nation. Thus, she was stripped of her Indian status and not permitted to live on the reserve. Neither was she allowed to be buried on her home reserve upon her death. Unfortunately, many Indian women who married non-Indian men had no idea they had lost their Indian status until they attempted to return to their reserves following the breakup of their marriages.

What made this section so discriminatory is that if an Indian man married a non-Indian woman, he did not lose his status. To add insult to injury, a non-Indian woman who married an Indian man became an Indian in the eyes of the law. She was granted band membership and was allowed to live on the man's reserve. Lastly, a non-Indian woman who married an Indian man did not lose her Indian status if they divorced or if she became widowed; they and their children retained their band membership as well as the rights and privileges that followed from it.

It is ironic that Indian status became legislated by law rather than by blood, tradition, community ties, or heritage. Essentially, white women who married Indian men became Indians by legislation, while Indian females became "white" when they married non-Indian men. Under this legislation, these Indian women lost more than simply their identity and the possibility of reverting to their culture of origin; as non-legal entities they had no legal recourse and thus no way to remedy the situation.

The Beginning of Change

Government action to address the widely held views about First Nations women's "domestic limitations" would inadvertently serve as a catalyst for them to organize politically. In 1937, the Department of Indian Affairs encouraged First Nations women to gather regularly to acquire sound practices for better home and family care. The department also encouraged these women to form local chapters of the Native Homemakers Association on reserves across Canada (Voyageur, 2008).

This directive contravened Indian Act policy that stated that First Nations people could not meet in groups of more than four (Venne, 1981). Indian Act legislation, from 1885 to 1951, also placed a ban on travel outside the reserve without permission from the Indian agent (Venne, 1981). Still, First Nations women were encouraged to attend "home economics" conferences sponsored by the Native Homemakers Association (Voyageur, 2008). Little did officials at the Department of Indian Affairs know that these seemingly innocuous meetings of First Nations women would provide opportunities for them to organize dissent and strategize for change to their social and living conditions! In the context of government-sponsored "sewing groups," First Nations women began preparing for their official political involvement when legislative change finally came in the 1951 Indian Act amendments. As discussed in the following section, political activity that began in part with community-based "home economics" gatherings on Indian reserves throughout Canada eventually spawned a plethora of Aboriginal women's rights organizations (Voyageur, 2008).

The 1960s brought a number of legislative changes that greatly affected the political position of First Nations people in general and First Nations women in particular. As soon as changes to the Indian Act granted First Nations people the right to organize, they immediately began forming political organizations to fight for many needed changes. And as demands for Aboriginal and Treaty Rights grew, so, too, did the demands of First Nations women who chipped away at their discriminatory treatment by demanding legislative change in relation to the Bill of Rights in 1960, the Charter of Rights and Freedoms in 1982, and Bill C-31 in 1985.

The Bill of Rights

The Bill of Rights was enacted by the federal government in 1960. Unlike the Bill of Rights in the United States, which was added almost immediately to its Constitution, Canada's Constitution Act of 1867 did not include any such statement. It was not until after World War II that Canada joined other developed countries that had already understood the importance of protecting civil liberties (Hogg, 1992: 779). Section 1 of the Bill of Rights guaranteed equality under the law regardless of race or sex. Section 2 stated that any federal statutes or regulations that infringed any of the rights in the Bill would be addressed by Parliament. However, legal debate surrounding this provision focused on the question of whether section 2 rendered the infringing laws null and void or whether it was merely to be used as a guide. Court challenges addressing a variety of legal issues eventually contributed to amendments to the Indian Act.

The first important Indian case to challenge the Bill of Rights was *R. v. Drybones* [1970] S.C.R. 282. Joseph Drybones was an Indian man who was charged with possession of alcohol. At the time, the Indian Act stipulated that Indians were not permitted to possess alcohol (Hogg, 1992). The same rule did not apply to non-Indians, and so it was clear that this federal law discriminated against Indians. Furthermore, the case gave the Supreme Court of Canada an opportunity to determine the effect of section 2 of the Bill of Rights. The Court held that any federal law that infringed on the Bill of Rights would be inoperative, which meant that section 2 clearly was viewed as more than a guide.

Attorney General of Canada v. Lavell ([1973] S.C.R. 1349; known as the Lavell and Bedard case) dealt more specifically with Indian women. This case was the first in which plaintiffs attempted to win recognition for Indian women as "full persons" with the same rights and status as Indian men. Jeanette Corbiere Lavell, an Ojibway woman who had lost her status after marrying a non-Indian man, challenged the band administration's decision to strike her name from the band list. Yvonne Bedard, a Six Nations woman, had tried to return to her reserve to live in a house that had been left to her in her mother's will. However, her name had been removed from the band membership list after she married a non-Indian man, and so she and her children were ordered by band officials to leave the reserve (Atcheson, 1984).

Both Lavell and Bedard argued that because section 12(1)(b) of the Indian Act discriminated on the basis of sex, it directly contravened the Canadian Bill of Rights. The two cases were eventually heard together before the Supreme Court of Canada, and to the surprise of many the Court affirmed the validity of section 12(1)(b). The justices stated in their decision that the Canadian Bill of Rights meant equality only in the administration and enforcement of the law, and that the actual substance of the law could discriminate between men and women as long as the law was applied by its administrator in an even-handed way (Atcheson, 1984). Thus, the Supreme Court of Canada backtracked from the *Drybones* decision by refusing to declare this discriminatory section of the Indian Act inoperative.

The Lovelace case of 1981 was another important challenge to section 12(1)(b) of the Indian Act. Sandra Lovelace, a Maliseet woman originally from the Tobique Reserve in New Brunswick, had lost her status and band membership when she married a non-Indian man. She eventually took the Canadian government to an international court, the United Nations Committee on Human Rights, and argued that her rights as an Indian woman were denied by section 12(1)(b) (Stacey-Moore, 1993). She won her case, and as a result brought international shame to the Canadian government. The Human Rights Committee found the Canadian government in breach of Article 3 of the International Covenant on Civil and Political Rights, which guarantees freedom from sexual discrimination (Silman, 1987). The federal government delayed amending its discriminatory legislation for four years, though Indian women's groups across the country had already begun pressuring the government, national Native organizations, and local band administrations to deal with their concerns. For example, in 1979, 200 Tobique women and children marched from their New Brunswick reserve to Ottawa, a seven-day trek, to protest housing conditions in their community (Silman, 1987).

The Constitution and the Charter of Rights and Freedoms

The Bill of Rights—which had been framed as a simple federal statute, not as part the Constitution, and therefore applied only in federal cases—became much less significant after the adoption in 1982 of the Charter of Rights and Freedoms and its inclusion in the Constitution Act, 1982. The purpose of the Charter, which does have constitutional status and applies both federally and provincially, is to protect certain fundamental rights and freedoms, one of which is equality before the law. Aboriginal organizations nonetheless had to vigorously lobby members of Parliament to challenge the paternalistic attitude of the Canadian government and force them to acknowledge the rights of Canada's Aboriginal peoples.

Section 15(1) of the Charter of Rights and Freedoms states, "Every individual is equal before and under the law and has the right to the equal protection and equal benefit of the law without discrimination and, in particular, without discrimination based on race, national or ethnic origin, religion, sex, age or mental or physical ability." In addition, section 28 states, "Notwithstanding anything in this Charter, the rights and freedoms referred to in it are guaranteed equally to male and female persons." Although both sections state that discrimination on the basis of sex and race contravenes the Charter of Rights and Freedoms, the Indian Act did exactly that. It was not until three years after the adoption of the Charter of Rights and Freedoms that the discriminatory provisions of the Indian Act would be amended with the passage of Bill C31.

The entrenchment of Aboriginal and Treaty Rights in section 35 of the Constitution Act, 1982 was a major step towards honouring the rights of Indigenous women, and it greatly assisted them in their many fights against discrimination. As the Native Women's Association of Canada wrote about the process of entrenching Aboriginal rights into the Constitution, "These arrangements are required to provide an arrangement that gives Native women and their children a destiny that they can participate in fully and direct themselves" (Stacey-Moore, 1993: 21). Nonetheless, even though section 35 guaranteed Aboriginal and treaty rights to Indian people and section 27 of the Charter stated that these rights applied equally to men and women, women were not assured by the male leaders of First Nation governments that they would acknowledge, let alone support, their concerns. It was clear to many women that the fight for equality was not yet finished.

Bill C-31

Bill C-31 came into effect on 17 April 1985 and was intended to rectify section 12(1)(b) of the Indian Act. Bill C-31 also was meant to restore Indian status to people who previously had been enfranchised. Some have argued that Bill C-31 is an Indian issue rather than solely an Indian *women's* issue, since enfranchisement was granted for a number of reasons, such as obtaining a university degree, joining the military or the clergy, or voluntary enfranchisement (Voyageur, 2008). However, it is rightly seen as primarily a women's issue because Indian women were the most affected in that they lost their status after marrying non-Indian men. Joan Holmes (1987: 9) notes that 12,305 of 16,980 losses of status (72.5 per cent) involved women who had married non-Indian men. A United Nations Human Rights Committee Report noted that there were 510 marriages between Indian women and non-Indian men and 448 marriages between Indian men and non-Indian women in Canada between 1965 and 1978, though only the Indian women who married non-Indian men lost their Indian status (McDonald, 1987: 28).

The Indian Act requires that Indians be registered in a central registry and that applicants apply for Indian status to the registrar. Bill C-31 states that those eligible to be registered as status Indians include:

(i) women who lost status as result of marriage to non-status men;
(ii) individuals who lost status or were denied status through other discriminatory provisions of the Indian Act;
(iii) individuals who lost status through enfranchisement, a process that existed in the old Act whereby a person could voluntarily give up status; and
(iv) children of persons in any of the above categories. (Paul, 1993: 6)

In addition, Bill C-31 gives individual bands the authority to determine their own band membership. In other words, only First Nation governments are allowed to decide who their members are and what the rights and responsibilities of the governments are to those members. This is where much of the present-day contention between the federal government and self-governing bands lies.

Although Bill C-31 has helped to rectify some of the injustices of the Indian Act, it has also created new problems. For example, it supports a separation of status and band membership. The federal government determines status while the individual First Nation's administration (chief and council in most cases) determines band membership. Consequently, band councils, which are primarily comprised of men, still have the authority and power to determine whether an Indian woman who married a non-Indian man will be allowed to regain her band membership.

Bill C-31 has created new problems by allowing Indian status to be decided in three possible ways: Indian status (determined by Aboriginal Affairs in Ottawa); band membership (determined by chief and council); and both status and band membership (chief and council accept Aboriginal Affairs' decision to confer Indian status to an individual and subsequently confer band membership).

Taking Back Their Voices

The voices and concerns of Indigenous women in Canada have been heard strongly since the early 1970s through the efforts and determination of a number of Indigenous women's advocacy groups. These include the Native Women's Association of Canada (NWAC) (1974), the Ontario Native Women's Association (1972), and the Québec Native Women's Association (1975). These foundational Indigenous women's groups spawned additional advocacy organizations such as Pauktuutit, the Inuit Women's Association in 1984 and the Métis National Council of Women in 1992 (Voyageur, 2008). Through the efforts of the women in these organizations, Indigenous women were able to organize and find their own political voice. These organizations gave Indigenous women in Canada the support and strength they needed to speak for themselves individually and collectively for the first time since European contact.

Kenneth Lincoln, author of *Native American Renaissance*, refers to this articulation as a "rebirth" (Tsosie, 1988: 2). One of the first issues addressed by First Nations women was regaining the Indian status that many of them had lost as a result of marriage to non-Indian men. The tenacity of First Nations women such as Sandra Lovelace, Jeanette Corbiere Lavell, Yvonne Bedard, and the late Jenny Margetts won them recognition and respect as worthy adversaries. However, their political activism also brought threats, scorn, and even patronizing comments from the prime minister of Canada. Nellie Carlson, an activist who worked alongside Jenny Margetts in the Indian Rights for Indian Women advocacy group, recalled one exchange between members of their group and the prime minister during discussions about changing the sections of the Indian Act that blatantly discriminated against women for 16 years. Carlson stated that:

> This group of determined Indian women was not dissuaded when during a meeting the then Prime Minister Pierre Trudeau told us, "Go to [your] leaders. They will help you make the changes." To this remark, we retorted, "This legislation came from this building. What good can our leaders do about something that the government created? You must help us change it."[4]

The women's persistence paid off when the Bill C-31 amendment to the Indian Act was passed in April 1985, since the bill clearly stated that Indian status could not be gained or lost through marriage (Wherrett, 1996). No longer could First Nations women lose their status through intermarriage. Also gone was the opportunity for non-First Nation women to gain Indian status by marrying First Nation men.

Contemporary First Nations Women's Concerns

In her study of the link between political and social life on a British Columbia First Nation reserve, anthropologist Joanne Fiske writes that First Nation women's domestic responsibilities are undifferentiated from community obligations, "women are expected to share their surplus food, assist young people, and intervene in domestic disputes in an effort to restore harmony" (1990–1: 136). Fiske concludes that these women have never been able to fulfill their domestic goals without political action.

The First Nations world has always been a political world. First Nations women have been able to emerge from the purely domestic roles they were cast into to help rebuild their communities. A clear example of their movement from the private realm into the public sphere is the recent phenomenon of women being elected as chiefs. Women chiefs now lead more than 120 of Canada's 633 First Nations communities in Canada, and the number of elected female chiefs has more than doubled in the past 25 years. First Nations women's concerns for their families and community improvement are behind their tireless work and enduring advocacy efforts. In recent years, as discussed below, they have tackled such issues as matrimonial property issues and violence against Indigenous women.

However, First Nations women still encounter many obstacles in their pursuit of better communities. They must still contend with many archaic and racist notions that date back to first contact with Europeans. First Nations scholar Janice Acoose speaks of the myth of Indigenous women in the bifurcated role of either "Pocahontas" or "the squaw," as illustrated in a series of Hollywood movies (1995: 2). Although some of these stereotypical portrayals have diminished over time, the legacy of past attitudes is still being felt by Indigenous women to this day. The domination of male leaders in First Nations communities has contributed significantly to many of the problems that First Nations women continue to experience.

Community Conflict over Legislative Change

One of the consequences of male domination in many communities is conflict between First Nations men and women over the legislative changes described above. Challenges by First Nations women to the non-status issue have often been attacked by male-dominated First Nations political organizations, the largest being the National Indian Brotherhood (which later became the Assembly of First Nations, or AFN). The leaders of the NIB feared that if the Indian Act were to be struck down on the basis of discrimination, then all First Nations people might lose certain rights under the Indian Act. Specifically, they were concerned that the success of any equality argument would undermine the special protections provided under the Indian Act, and that the federal government's official statement on Indian policy (the government's infamous 1969 White Paper) would be implemented through the courts even though it had been defeated politically.

Many referred to reinstated Indians as "C-31s," and they were also sometimes scornfully called "paper Indians" or "new Indians" (Paul, 1993: 94). There continues to be much conflict between Bill C-31 First Nations people and other band members over the distribution of already scarce resources. Conflict over housing is one example. Reserves usually have long waiting lists for housing, and there has often been resentment towards "new" Indians who wanted to move back to the reserve, particularly among those who believed that Bill C-31 Indians did not have to wait as long for housing or that they were even placed at the top of the waiting list.

Some bands did not initially give band membership to people given status by the federal government because they did not have the desire, the resources, or the land base to do so. However, Supreme Court of Canada cases such as *R. v Corbiere* forced equal rights to be given to those who regained status through Bill C-31 and those who lived off-reserve. Since most reserves were already overcrowded, many felt that the conditions would only worsen if numerous reinstated Indians returned to the reserve. However, the feared influx of reinstated First Nations people to their home reserves has been unfounded to date. According to a report in 2000 by the Department of Indian and Northern Affairs, of the 114,512 First Nations people who regained Indian status under Bill C-31, only about 10 per cent had moved back to their reserves between 1985 and 1999. In addition, continued growth of First Nation populations has meant that the so-called "Bill-C-31s" made up only about 2 per cent of the total First Nations community in 2011. Moreover, many reinstated people have expressed little interest in returning to their reserve, in large part because they became established elsewhere and felt that their reserve had nothing to offer them as far as housing or employment was concerned (Paul, 1993: 108).

Unfortunately, a great deal of tension and conflict continues between reinstated members and band councils. In some cases, such as the Sawridge Band in Alberta, discriminatory practices have continued because the band implemented a rigorous and prying membership code so that few, if any, would qualify for membership. Indeed, many First Nations women have not been welcomed back to their communities in the traditional custom of open arms and warm hearts. Patriarchy cannot be solely blamed for this situation, for in most cases it has had more to do with an economic guarding of scarce resources by band leaders. Nonetheless, ongoing discrimination by band administrators has left many First Nations women skeptical about whether male-dominated organizations and band councils will ever be willing to affirm and support their rights.

Inequality

A third issue facing First Nations women is political inequality. Despite the impressive increase in the number of female chiefs, most elected leaders in the First Nations community are male. Although in the past many First Nations community leaders were male, they still sought women's input in their decision-making. Today, locally elected individuals serve as intermediaries between Aboriginal Affairs and Northern Development Canada (AANDC) and the people in their communities. AANDC makes all the important decisions, including fiscal ones. Sometimes the band is informed and consulted about these issues, and sometimes it is not. In most instances, band administrators simply carry out initiatives given to them by AANDC.

The chief and council members allocate resources to band members. They determine which band members receive limited band employment opportunities, education funding, occupational training, housing, housing repairs, and other band-administered services (Voyageur, 2008). This power, however limited, has a great impact on the day-to-day lives of band members. In some respects, the chief and council have taken over the powerful role that the Indian agent used to have as the intermediary between the government and members of the community. Band members recognize that it is therefore in their best interest to attempt to gain as well as to retain the favour of those with the power to allocate band resources.

Although women make up approximately 51 per cent of the Aboriginal population, they do not make up 51 per cent of the elected leadership. Even though there are growing numbers of women among the elected leadership across the country, there is no guarantee that women's concerns about child care, housing, education, family violence, and social programs will be heard and acted upon in every community. Part of the challenge is that a high percentage of First Nations women are single parents. According to Statistics Canada, approximately one-third of First Nations children under the age of 15 live with a lone parent, the vast majority of whom are women (Statistics Canada, 2008). This situation may lessen their influence with male-dominated councils since single mothers have less time to deal with community issues and are often viewed as having less influence in communities. Nonetheless, more women are increasingly holding decision-making positions in reserve communities. In the past, women in band offices would normally do the preparatory work on administrative tasks and would then have to receive approval from a superior, usually a male. However, this situation has been changing as more women than men have completed their post-secondary education and have opted to work in higher levels of band administration.

Advocacy

First Nations women have taken the initiative to protect their own rights and interests, since the past has shown them that First Nations men have not always acted in their best interests. Bold moves on the part of First Nations women have ruffled a few feathers in and beyond communities. For example, in the early 1990s the Native Women's Association of Canada (NWAC) attempted (unsuccessfully) to block the national referendum on the Charlottetown Accord, which proposed to substantially revise the Constitution, because they were excluded from negotiations involved in drafting the Accord. They charged that the consultation process used by male First Nations leaders infringed on their right to freedom of expression (Stacey-Moore, 1993). First Nations women demanded a seat at the constitutional table to ensure that their issues would be addressed and demanded a portion of the funds given to male-dominated political organizations.

This action publicly pitted First Nations men against First Nations women. The Native Women's Association of Canada was accused of placing individual rights over the rights of the collective and of going against tradition. It is ironic that the First Nations men who made these accusations were willing to abide by the rules of the wholly untraditional Indian Act. Women also became pitted against women as the NWAC was seen as dividing the First Nations community and wiping out the image of a "united front" cultivated by the Assembly of First Nations. In the end, the Charlottetown Accord was rejected in the 1992 national referendum, including by Aboriginal peoples, and two years later the NWAC lost its case before the Supreme Court.

By speaking on their own behalf, First Nations women have pursued their priorities and concerns. For example, matrimonial property rights were pursued by the Native Women's Association of Canada after the Supreme Court of Canada ruled that these rights did not apply on reserves. The NWAC (2007: 1) defined matrimonial real property as, "the house or land that a couple lives on or benefits from while they are married or in a common law relationship," and proposed solutions to the government to deal with the issue. Then Minister of Indian Affairs Chuck Strahl announced on 2 February 2009 that a Family Homes on Reserves and Matrimonial Interests or Rights Act was being developed that would protect individuals living on-reserve when the conjugal relationship breaks down (INAC, 2009). The Act received royal assent on 9 June 2013 and became law in Canada.

Violence against Indigenous Women

The problem of interpersonal violence, particularly violence against women and children, is another serious issue that Indigenous women have brought to the public's attention in recent years. Many women believe that male-dominated organizations and band councils have largely refused to give this issue priority because women and children are usually the victims and men are usually the perpetrators. As a result, Indigenous women have had to pursue justice in this area on a number of fronts. One was the Stolen Sisters Initiative of Amnesty International (2006), which investigated the circumstances surrounding the more than 500 Indigenous women in Canada who had been murdered or were still missing. The most sweeping recommendation from the

Amnesty International report called for the Canadian government and police to immediately implement measures to protect Indigenous women. The government finally responded with a major report in 2014 that was a call to action to address the concerns that had been raised by Amnesty International as well as by many other organizations (Ambler, 2014).

Unfortunately, the number of missing and murdered Indigenous women in Canada has increased substantially since 2006. The number of files on missing and murdered Indigenous women in Canada registered with the Royal Canadian Mounted Police stood at 1,200 in the summer of 2014 (RCMP, 2014). It seems clear that First Nations women and girls are seen as easy prey for violent men as there is a long history of brutalized and/or murdered Indigenous women across this country. The Robert Pickton case was particularly horrific, and it shocked Canadians when it was first discovered in the early 1990s. He had been linked to the disappearance of at least 26 women in Vancouver's Downtown Eastside. Agency and service workers who worked with these vulnerable populations in that area of Vancouver reported that women they had worked with were missing. These workers had expressed frustration for some time that little or no action was being taken by the Vancouver police about their concerns. The women, many of them Indigenous, were apparently viewed as a low priority due to their risky and transient lifestyles. Social service workers and many others expressed outrage that women were disappearing and that nobody, including the police, was concerned about them. Eventually, Pickton admitted to 49 murders, although he was tried only for some of them because the maximum possible sentence was passed on the first six murders.

Gilbert Paul Jordan (a.k.a. the Boozing Barber) was the first man in Canada to be charged with using alcohol as a weapon. His first victim died in 1965, but he was not charged with that death. Over the years he was found responsible for the deaths of between 8 and 10 Indigenous women who died of alcohol poisoning while in his presence (Justice Canada, 1995). It became evident that he had a perversion for drunken sex, and so he would encourage the Indigenous women he picked up in bars to drink large quantities of alcohol to the point where they suffered from alcohol poisoning. Court records state that he coaxed approximately 200 Indigenous women into drunken stupors over the years (R. v. Jordan, [1991] B.C.J. No. 2908). He was finally apprehended after a police sting operation was set up in a skid row hotel where he often found his victims. Police records indicate him saying, "have a drink, down the hatch baby, $20 if you can drink it right down" and "finish that drink, finish that drink, down the hatch hurry, you need another drink" (R. v. Jordan, [1991] B.C.J. No. 1927).

Violence against Indigenous women is not always at the hands of ordinary citizens; sometimes the ill treatment they receive is at the hands of the police. One such case is the sexual assault of a 14-year-old First Nations girl by an RCMP officer in Saskatchewan in the late 1960s (CBC News, 2000). This case came to light in the late 1990s when the victim finally came forward. The charge was based on an incident in which the youth had been questioned by a uniformed RCMP officer (and eventual member of Parliament), Jack Ramsay, at which time he had asked the girl to demonstrate her understanding of sexual intercourse (CBC News, 2000). Although Ramsay was convicted of attempted rape and sentenced to nine months in prison, he appealed the sentence and later pleaded guilty to a lesser charge of indecent assault, for which he received a year of probation and 120 hours of community service (CBC News, 2001).

Another report pointing to serious police neglect, this one by Human Rights Watch (2013) entitled *Those Who Take Us Away: Abusive Policing and Failures in Protection of Indigenous Women and Girls in Northern British Columbia, Canada*, found that dozens of girls and women have gone missing along what has been called "The Highway of Tears" in northern British Columbia. The report condemned the actions of the RCMP and police in British Columbia by asserting that law enforcement officials in that province had consistently refused to deal effectively or even take seriously the issue of missing and murdered Indigenous women in that province.

Conclusion

Indigenous women have reached a point in their political and individual growth where they will not sit helplessly by while others negotiate and in many instances simply ignore their future. They have recognized that waiting for others to address the many serious social issues in their lives has not worked for them in the past, and so they are increasingly pressing others to not only listen to their needs and concerns, but to take firm and positive action. First Nations women are also moving ahead, and are playing a large role in the education of their children and in the promotion of a healthy lifestyle. They continue to initiate and sustain many community programs and services, and they have made it clear that they are prepared to deal with problems facing their people in areas as diverse as family violence, child abuse, unemployment, alcohol abuse, loss of cultural identity, and the decrease in language retention. As a result, First Nations women are bringing about social, educational, and economic change through their relentless efforts and unwavering commitment to their families and communities.

In many respects, First Nations women still play the traditional role they played prior to European contact; they are still the caregivers, the transmitters of culture, and the nurturers. They are also working their way towards becoming the social and political equals of First Nations men that they once were. First Nations women are gradually earning the respect and recognition they deserve from First Nations men, the government, and society at large.

It is clear that First Nations women in Canada are taking control of many aspects of their lives. They are attaining the educational credentials that enable them to obtain better employment and are also starting businesses and entering band politics. Their determination and efforts show that they recognize they still are the ones who ultimately are responsible for the future of their families and communities, and that only time and the conditions of life for Indigenous peoples in Canada have changed their traditional role. As news stories and reports from advocacy groups and government clearly indicate, however, First Nations women in Canada continue to find themselves the victims of violence and of discrimination in many areas of their lives. The "bicultural bind" discussed by Paula Gunn Allen (1992: 38) remains, for First Nations women in Canada continue to alternate between "being strong and dependent, self-reliant and powerless; strongly motivated and hopelessly insecure." As is also evident, they continue to gather strength as they remain committed to working together and with others to ensure a good and hopeful future for their families, communities, and the rest of Canada.

Discussion Questions

1. How did European society subjugate its women?
2. How is the Canadian government responsible for the current situation of First Nations women?
3. What was the impetus for First Nations women to organize?
4. Why is it in First Nations men's best interests to maintain the status quo?
5. What are the benefits and drawbacks of Bill C-31 status?
6. What steps are First Nations women taking to ensure equality?

Further Reading

Amnesty International Canada. 2004. *Stolen Sisters: Discrimination and Violence against Indigenous Women in Canada*. Ottawa: Amnesty International.

Human Rights Watch. 2013. *Those Who Take Us Away: Abusive Policing and Failures in Protection of Indigenous Women and Girls in Northern British Columbia, Canada*. Toronto: Human Rights Watch.

Kelm, Mary Ellen, and Lorna Townsend. 2006. *In the Days of Our Grandmothers: A Reader in Aboriginal Women's History in Canada*. Toronto: University of Toronto Press.

Native Women's Association of Canada. 2009. *Voices of Our Sisters: A Report of Families and Communities*, 2nd edn. Ottawa: Native Women's Association of Canada.

Suzack, Cheryl, Sahri Huhndorf, Jeanne Perreault, and Jean Barman. 2010. *Indigenous Women and Feminism: Politics, Activism and Culture*. Vancouver: University of British Columbia Press.

Voyageur, Cora. 2008. *Firekeepers of the 21st Century: First Nation Women Chiefs*. Montreal and Kingston: McGill-Queen's University Press.

Notes

1. While the primary focus of this chapter is First Nations women, the use of other terminology, including "Indigenous," "Indian," "Native," "Aboriginal," and even "savage" acknowledges the varied ways and contexts in which these women have been "named." Most of these terms are political/legal designations, though the term "Indigenous" is used to convey the somewhat more universal idea of a people's identity being originally tied to particular lands. It is important to note that none of these labels are in Indigenous languages or reflect the identity of diverse Indigenous nations and communities in Canada. Rather, all of these terms were imposed by Europeans after their arrival for a variety of social, legal, and political purposes.

2. Structural supremacy means the hierarchical structure of European society at the time of contact, which was assumed by Europeans to be the best and only acceptable way in which to order society and its institutions.

3. Section 11 states:

   11(1) Subject to Section 12, a person is entitled to be registered if that person

   (a) on the 26th day of May 1874 was ... considered to be entitled to hold, use or enjoy the lands and other immovable property belonging to or appropriated to the use of the various bands or bodies of Indians in Canada:

   (b) is a member of a band

   (i) for whose use and benefit common lands have been set apart or since the 26th of May 1874 have been agreed by treaty to be set apart, or

   (ii) that has been declared by the Governor in Council to be a band for the purpose of the Act;

   (c) is a male person who is a direct descendent in the male line of the male person described in paragraph (a) or (b);

   (d) is the legitimate child of

   (i) a male person described in paragraph (a) or (b), or

   (ii) a person described in paragraph (c);

   (e) is the illegitimate child of a female person described in paragraph (a), (b) or (c)

   (f) is the wife or widow of a person who is entitled to be registered by virtue of paragraph (a), (b), (c), (d) or (e).

4. Personal interview with Nellie Carlson in Edmonton, June 2004.

7

Indigenous Men: Masculinity and Leadership

John Swift and Lee Maracle

Men have to have a deep love, appreciation, and connection to the land and for their nation before they can love their women.

Lee Maracle

Introduction

My name is John Swift and I am from Keeseekoose. My roots include Anishinaabek, Cree, and Métis (Scottish). When I started my academic career, I was interested in Indigenous governance issues and how Indigenous men dealt with having to lay down their arms in the battle against the theft of their homelands and the murder of their people. These themes have continued to interest me throughout my studies and influence this work you are about to read. They form part of my world view, and I am hopeful that you can glean something from this chapter that helps you in your journey in understanding Indigenous men, masculinity, and leadership.

Before I begin the more formal parts of this work, I would like to share how I experienced masculinity during my late teens and early twenties and the ways in which I was influenced by the Indigenous men who surrounded me and mentored me in my basketball and professional interests. While there were many other influences that contributed to my understandings of masculinity, the relationships I had with other Indigenous men formed the foundation of my learning about masculinity and leadership as a young man. The older men on my basketball team would get drunk regularly, do hard drugs, and if we were "lucky" enough they would let us tag along. In terms of relationships with women, I learned that domestic violence and having numerous sexual partners was the norm, and that women largely accepted that—or so it seemed. Violence between men was also the norm; it rarely escalated to

CP Images/Darryl Dyck

anything more than a fistfight but we kept each other in check with lateral violence. However, the violence we directed at ourselves was much more severe and deadly; encountering suicide and attempted suicide was a normal part of growing up, as were severe alcoholism, drug addiction, and drunk driving. Nevertheless, I also learned a lot of good things from these men. For example, I learned the importance of being there for each other when times were tough, whether on the basketball court or on the streets. I learned the importance of male friendship and the importance of listening when we shared sensitive parts of our lives with each other. I learned how important it is to laugh even when you don't feel like it.

Regarding my professional career, the early parts of it were spent flying around the country to serve on youth committees and to participate in provincial and national board meetings. Again, I found a culture that promoted partying, drugs, and having numerous partners for casual sex. Many of the male leaders would be out until four in the morning drinking and partying and then chairing meetings early the next day. In a few cases, the organizations' women would call them out for their behaviour and ask for an apology, but their doing so did little to curb this subculture. In retrospect, violence and its many nuances in those years seemed to be one of the main themes underpinning the relationships between men as well as relations between men and women. I am thankful to have made it through that dangerous and confusing part of my life, especially since many of my friends and family members did not. As a young man learning about masculinity and leadership in this environment, there seemed to be no boundaries to men's behaviour.

Contemporary Conversation on Indigenous Leadership

So, what does it mean to be an Indigenous leader in the neo-liberal landscape of this colony called Canada? What type of leader am I talking about? Does it really matter? What does "masculinity" mean? A lot of the old teachings speak to being good human beings, not to being a good man or a good woman, per se. Therefore, the concept of masculinity is a somewhat new way of describing and interpreting our experiences as gendered human beings. Taking note of this fact is important, especially when conducting research. Why? The old people may not recognize some of the academic jargon we use and we have a responsibility to navigate that contentious landscape as researchers and intellectuals. Therefore, for the purpose of this discussion, when I use the term "masculinity" I mean, "Masculinities, as socially constructed configurations of gender practice, [which] are also created through a historical process with a global dimension" (Connell, 2005: 1805). It is also important to note that the concepts of masculinity and leadership are in a constant state of flux due to internal expectations and external influences. For instance, I am still constructing what "leadership" means for me. As I grow older and more experienced, the meaning I apply to the concept keeps changing, not to mention the difficulties of working with language barriers between Indigenous and English dialects. I also wonder how I should relate my understandings of this subject in a manner that is not drenched in Western theory and academic jargon. Which audiences will "recognize" my words and experiences, and which ones will not? In contemplating these questions, the contributors to this chapter (myself included) realized that all we can share with you are our thoughts and feelings on what we have learned about Indigenous masculinity and leadership through our own journeys. In essence, what we are presenting here are small slices of our life stories, complemented by the insights of Indigenous and non-Indigenous scholars drawn from the academic literature.

I begin with a brief overview of contemporary Indigenous governance issues that are important to me and describe the background that has influenced my perspective on contemporary forms of Indigenous masculinity. These issues are not the only influences on my perspective, but they have been a major focus of my studies, so it makes sense to share what I have learned. I also asked two people who are experienced and knowledgeable in this area to assist me with this piece: Sto:lo member Lee Maracle shares her thoughts on the importance of land in the development of Indigenous leadership, and Mi'kmaq member Sakej Ward joins us in a conversation about his latest projects involving strategic planning with Sto:lo Elders and the rapid development (no pun intended) of the Rabbit Society. I also share some of my own journey towards unpacking male privilege and what that means in my personal life. Finally, Lee Maracle provides some closing thoughts.

Contemporary Governance Challenges for Indigenous Peoples

Before I delve into the interviews, I would first like to discuss my understandings of the theft of Indigenous homelands, the continuing acts of genocide against Indigenous peoples, and the inadequate and deceiving colonial pathways to reconciliation and justice in what is today called Canada. These issues provide the necessary context within which Indigenous masculinities can begin to be understood.

To be blunt, our homelands were stolen from us and their current occupation by settlers is maintained through institutional force justified by legislation and mythology, which boils down to Canada being an illegitimate state that maintains an iron grip on Indigenous lands and peoples through coercion and outright violence. These practices are partly based in the racial superiority ideology of *Manifest Destiny* and its partner in crime, *terra nullius*. Our ancestors did not agree to our current political, social, and economic reality, but rather wanted to share the land with our new guests. The stories I have heard about settlers arriving on our shores were always about starving people who were barely alive and who needed the help of Indigenous people to survive. I am proud to say that Indigenous people helped them, but I have also heard stories from Elders who say they wish we had not helped them, considering how their generosity was repaid. I am stating the obvious for the majority of my Indigenous audience, so let me move on to discuss the limitations of Indigenous people striving for justice through the court systems, treaty negotiations, and economic development. Why? Because these are the areas where the majority of our current leadership is pooled. Also, they form destinations towards which our young leaders are being directed, through academia and governmental programs that target some of our best and brightest young minds.

Regarding the legalist approach, a popular movement on behalf of Indigenous leadership constantly appeals to section 35 of the Canada's Constitution Act, 1982 for protection and affirmation of what has been coined "Aboriginal rights." I question this practice. Indigenous scholar John Borrows (2007: 116) raises an important issue in his analysis of the relationship between the Canadian Constitution, the Supreme Court of Canada, and the colonial state. He states, "Canadian courts do not respect the supremacy of the constitution's rule of law when they unquestionably support notions of underlying Crown title and exclusive sovereignty in the face of contradictory Aboriginal evidence."

In a similar vein, Taiaiake Alfred (2000: 5) asserts that without meaningful nation-to-nation treaties, "there cannot be any legitimate occupation of territory by subsequent authorities, only colonial imposition." While there are benefits to using legal mechanisms to promote Indigenous interests, Indigenous leadership must be realistic about the severe limitations of these processes as well. Starting from subordinate positions not only justifies the illegitimate power of the state, but it also severely limits what can be accomplished and what is *handed down* within those narrow legal colonial corridors. So, what are our options when we try to achieve a sense of justice and integrity through legal mechanisms, and the state and its court system can ignore the Constitution? One alternative pathway would be to start negotiating treaties and/or agreements with the state, but these options have their limitations as well. Alfred (2000: 1) provides this comment on the British Columbia treaty process:

> The emergent consensus of indigenous people involved with the British Columbia Treaty Commission (BCTC) is that the current process has failed. The shared rational and emotional foundation of this consensus is a realization that the Treaty Commission process is at its core morally bankrupt and driven by the twin objectives of placating natural resource industry lobbies and the coercive imposition of the federal and provincial governments' shared assimilationist agenda. It is a coherent and general conclusion among indigenous people that the failed attempt to negotiate a structural recognition of their constitutional rights to land and self-government within the BCTC is proof that the federal and provincial governments have neither the determination or sincere desire to resolve the fundamental sources of racial and political conflict that exist in British Columbia.

As Lee Maracle notes, while some may wish that assimilation was the shared objective, she doesn't believe it is since genocide is still the primary objective of the Canadian state. Article 1 of the 1948 United Nations Convention on the Prevention and Punishment of the Crime of Genocide states that it does not matter whether destructive intentions or actions are committed in wartime or peacetime, while Article 2 defines "genocide" as:

> Any of the following acts committed with intent to destroy, in whole or in part, a national, ethnical, racial or religious group, as such:
> (a) Killing members of the group;
> (b) Causing serious bodily or mental harm to members of the group;

(c) Deliberately inflicting on the group conditions of life calculated to bring about its physical destruction in whole or in part;

(d) Imposing measures intended to prevent births within the group;

(e) Forcibly transferring children of the group to another group.

Now consider how the current and recent experience of Indigenous peoples in Canada is reflected in the definition. The unsolved murder and disappearance of well over a thousand Indigenous women since 1980 has reached epidemic proportions, yet the federal government, despite frequent calls from a broad spectrum of Indigenous and Canadian society, has repeatedly refused to establish an inquiry. Indeed, Prime Minister Stephen Harper has insisted that such violence should be viewed as "crime" (many hundreds of isolated crimes!) but not as a "sociological phenomenon" (Kennedy, 2014). The complicity of the state is threefold: it has failed to prosecute; it has failed to protect; and it has prohibited Indigenous people from forming governance mechanisms to protect themselves.

As for causing serious bodily harm or mental harm to members of the group, Indigenous children are four times more likely to be bullied at school, suffer violence at public schools, and are tormented mentally by racial isolation and degradation without redress. In regard to "conditions of life calculated to bring about ... physical destruction," prohibiting Indigenous people from accessing the wealth from their territories is the deliberate infliction on the group of just these conditions. Indeed, the media in recent decades have repeatedly shown the abject impoverishment of many Indigenous peoples in the land now called Canada, a state of internal colonialism that Aboriginal activist, author, and theorist George Manuel termed "the Fourth World" more than 40 years ago (Manuel and Posluns, 1974).

The forcible transfer of Indigenous children to another group has a long history in Canada, from the residential schools, to the disappearance into white society of Inuit children sent to southern Canada for medical treatment, to the infamous "Sixties Scoop," when an estimated 15,000 Indigenous children were adopted into white families. This still goes on in the form of child apprehension and placement in foster care, with more children being removed from their birth families than ever were in the long era of residential schools. This is genocide and it is ongoing. Similarly, many of those who have volunteered themselves up for university have been "white-streamed" and this verifies and validates the genocide of their relations, particularly when they trivialize the genocidal intent and pick up on the state's rationale: assimilation.

According to Maracle, the conflict between Indigenous peoples and the Canadian state is not simply a conflict of race or politics. It is a national conflict—i.e., we are nations, this is our territory, and we can only cede it under conditions of free will. So long as the state is holding us hostage in an under-nourished, underfunded state of domination in which we are not permitted to resolve our condition by accessing the wealth in our territory, through such activities as oil extraction, timber harvesting, and mining, and others are not prohibited from pillaging that wealth, then it is a nation-to-nation colonial conflict. When we call it "assimilation," then we accept that Canada stole our territory fair and square and we must be willing to live with it. Maracle af-firms: "I may be the last woman standing who holds that we are nations, that national territoriality and access and control of that territory are what Canada is perpetrating against us, but I maintain that that is what it is. It is not that we should be included in their world, but they are in ours. They have moved into our house and usurped all of its wealth. As leaders, we must look at how we are to include them in our world and begin to struggle for that. That will make the struggle for liberation real."

For many Indigenous nations involved in the BCTC process, the critical insights of Alfred and Maracle not only ring true, but they force a consider-ation of what other options can be exercised by Indigenous peoples in their struggles to achieve a sense of justice. For the Nisga'a, they decided to nego-tiate an *agreement* with the state, which was finalized and implemented in May 2000. In discussing the limitations of contemporary Aboriginal rights discourse, Corntassel (2008: 106) draws attention to the analysis of political scientist Jim Tully, who states:

> As far as I am aware, this is the first time in the history of Great Turtle Island that an indigenous people, or at least 61 per cent of its eligible vot-ers, has voluntarily surrendered their rights as indigenous peoples, not to mention surrendering over 90 per cent of their territory, and accepted their status as a distinctive minority with group rights within Canada. This ap-pears to be the first success of strategies of extinguishment (release) and incorporation by agreement.

Maracle adds:

> This is not the first time: Sechelt caved in before the Nisga'a. But that is not my point. We need more than "a sense of justice." We need territoriality and nationhood. What makes the Nisga'a deal a capitulation is the submission of the nation to foreign taxation as a minority within Canada. This valid-ates the mother country as a legitimate state.

Alfred, Maracle, and Tully lead one to think that it is still the deep desire of the state to have Indigenous people sign away their lands and inherent roles and responsibilities willingly and with minimal cost attached, an idea I will elaborate later.

So far I have been speaking to governance issues and not linking them to Indigenous masculinity and identity, but I will address that now. While neo-liberal propaganda may suggest that gender and race play little role in the politics of the state, that assertion is seriously questioned by Australian sociologist Raewyn Connell, whose analysis of hegemonic masculinities in neo-liberal states is insightful. Connell states:

> Neoliberalism can function as a form of masculinity politics largely because of the powerful role of the state in the gender order. The state constitutes gender relations in multiple ways, and all of its gender policies affect men. Many mainstream policies (e.g., in economic and security affairs) are substantially about men without acknowledging this fact.... (Connell, 2005: 1816)

While Connell is, for the most part, discussing non-Indigenous masculinities, we can still glean valuable insights from the scholarly analysis of other colonial projects by non-Indigenous scholars. Within the political landscape of colonial Canada, Indigenous men often find themselves at the helm of colonial posts of political power. In fact, Anderson (2000) argues that settlers had to undermine the authority and power of Indigenous women if their efforts to colonize Turtle Island were going to be successful. Maracle sheds further light on this issue:

> This was done by removing the women from their home villages. For almost 100 years, women had to leave their villages to marry [whether they married on reserve or off]. Our positions of power in our original societies are connected to our families and clans. Once we are in the man's territory, it is his clan, his family, his village that holds original authority over the wife. Again, this is an act of genocide.

While the settlers were somewhat successful in their efforts, new political apparatuses had to be constructed to fill the power vacuum created by the removal of women from their governance roles, which meant Indigenous men assumed many of the political and familial decision-making roles and responsibilities. A prominent, contemporary example of the colonial extension of power that continues to funnel settler ideologies into Indigenous communities is the chief and council band governance system. The chief and council system is not Indigenous in any sense of the word and has been forced on Indigenous people through the Indian Act. Historically, there were war chiefs, peace chiefs, head men, sachems, sagamos, and the like who had considerable influence within and between nations, but all of these positions emerged from and were sustained by the communities they served. There have also been a number of loosely organized pan-Indian movements led by powerful and charismatic chiefs over the past few centuries, although these leaders had far more "operating autonomy" in their relations to the state than Indigenous leaders whose organized efforts have taken place in the context of the Indian Act. Collectively, the system today is called the Assembly of First Nations, a male-dominated organization that provides Indigenous men with a degree of power within this colonial apparatus, especially the National Chief. There are striking similarities between Connell's argument and the realities that Indigenous people experience in our everyday lives when we consider masculinity and leadership in the chief and council governance structure. For one, efforts to create contemporary forms of Indigenous governance that respect and honour the roles, responsibilities, and authority of Indigenous women in regard to community affairs and land stewardship are, at best, on the distant horizon. I should note, however, that I am not insinuating that Indigenous women have not played a critical role in the leadership throughout the country over the years, because they have. In fact, it is our women who have spearheaded, maintained, and continued to create space for Indigenous men to participate in imagining and creating a new future. Rather, what many find problematic (myself included) is the men who have benefited from assuming colonial roles and exercising oppressive power in ways that contribute to the genocide of Indigenous peoples and the oppression of women. Maracle comments:

> The chief-electoral system is completely dominated by the State, they have no authority whatsoever, their leadership amounts to kowtowing to programs designed to keep us in a hostage state, dependent and underfunded. AFN is a lobbying group that was formed to sweeten the pot by alleviating outright starvation. While we are not dying at the rate we were in the sixties, we are still unable to aggregate or access wealth from our territories and we are unable to wield power in them. Whatever rights we have are delineated by the needs of Canada; this is outright colonization.

Wealth? Power? How many times have Indigenous people been told the pathway to liberation is through capitalist means? Become business people and join Canadians in the capitalist project of exploiting and oppressing people and land in the name of profit. Within the neo-liberal landscape, new liberated futures can only be achieved through promises of economic development. What does "economic development" mean? What is a "global market"? What is "globalization"? How are the intricate relationships maintained between these structures? Again, I borrow from Connell, in her analysis of Antonio Negri's *Theory of Empire*. Connell (2011: 137) states, "Empire has become, in a certain sense, total. There is no 'outside' the system," and "the extreme expression of violence of the system has become endemic and indeed necessary to the functioning of the 'world market'." Is this violent mechanism what we, as Indigenous people, are hinging the futures of our children on? Is this the future we have been so patiently waiting for since our ancestors signed the first treaties? Who is this "violence" being projected against? What does Connell mean by "violence"? Are people being murdered, starved to death, and oppressed to ensure the Western world can continue to feed its voracious consumerist appetite, way of life, and world view? Is the planet being sacrificed in the process? Are some of our leaders supporting these actions through their leadership practices? The answer to all of these questions is YES. The bottom line of Connell's interpretation of Negri's work is that the neo-liberal landscape we are experiencing in colonial Canada is due to the failure of earlier capitalist strategies, and not an indication of a robust economic future from which we would all benefit. I therefore ask, what is the sense of investing so heavily in such a deadly system in the first place? Let's not fool ourselves, the only cusp we are on is admitting that many of our leaders have adopted oppressive colonial ideologies and practices and are willingly using their subordinate form of power against Indigenous peoples and their homelands, not to mention against Indigenous peoples and lands overseas. Maracle adds:

> The chiefs have accepted their role as plenipotentiaries of colonial authority on behalf of Canada. Economic development is not the same as national territoriality and access to and dominion over the wealth of that territory. Acceptance of domination in exchange for being a colonial functionary is a long way away from leadership. In order to lead, the leader must have a vision of the nation, a sense of the territoriality of that nation and a strategy for waging a successful struggle to achieve nationhood and independence.

We have to remember that colonialism, in theory and practice, is an age-old process. Much is to be learned from other groups of people who have been on the receiving end of such inhumane practices. In theorizing about the French and Algerian war of the mid-1950s to the early 1960s, Fanon (1964: 118) reminds us that, "Every colonized person who today accepts a governmental post must know clearly that he will sooner or later be called upon to sponsor a policy of repression, of massacres, of collective murders in one of the regions of 'the French Empire'." In Canada, then, how have we managed to escape this deadly contradiction? Sadly, we haven't. Indigenous participation in the business of empire has deadly consequences. What is even more disturbing is that the practice of colonization dehumanizes people, and at some level many of our Indigenous leaders have willingly accepted their genocidal role within the new colonial front of globalization, which is an indication that we have already begun to dehumanize ourselves. If Connell's assertion is correct that "Empire" is total (though I am not saying that I fully agree with this assertion), what does this mean for Indigenous people, more specifically men, who adopt and perpetuate colonial politics, practices, and beliefs? And what does it mean for the young men who are our next political leaders? Many of us have adopted these genocidal practices and are not honest about the consequences of such decisions. However, I am reminded that it is extremely challenging to step outside of the of empire of which Connell speaks. We are all guilty in some form or another. As my close friend and Wet'suwet'en member Ian Caplette reminds me, "We all have oil on the tips of our fingers. Just like a deadly addiction. We must have oil on the tips of our fingers at all times through our use of cell phones" (personal communication, 3 June 2014). In other words, we all have blood on our hands from the contemporary energy wars of empire, which are directed at both people and the planet and are taking place not just overseas (e.g., Iraq) but in our backyards (e.g., the tar sands). It is a disturbing thought.

Having discussed some aspects of the dirty business of colonization, I will now move on to the interviews I conducted with Lee Maracle and Sakej Ward, my personal thoughts on male privilege, and some concluding thoughts from Maracle.

Land, Love, and Leadership

In an effort to learn about and from the aforementioned issues, I have sought to understand the complexities involved through my own and others' life experiences. My Uncle Andrew once said, "Who knows more about what it's like to be an Indian than an Indian person? If you want to know about these ways, then surround yourself with Indian people" (personal communication, August 2009). Thus, the following conversation with Lee Maracle comprises part of my effort to understand what constitutes Indigenous masculinity and leadership in contemporary times. Our discussion speaks to the importance of land, love, and leadership from Indigenous perspectives.

John Swift: Lee, the last time I saw you in Toronto you made a comment to me that really struck me. You said, "Men have to have a deep love, appreciation, and connection to the land and for their nation before they can love their women." The power of that statement seemed to paralyze me. It stuck in my mind and heart, and I have revisited it over the last few months to try and work out what it meant for me. I had never looked at relationships and leadership development in that manner before, but it makes perfect sense.

In the work I have done with the Sto:lo community of Cheam (Swift, 2011), I have learned that the women of the community are the holders of the law. A facet of that responsibility extends to taking care of hunting and fishing grounds. In other words, one main source of power for Sto:lo women is their relationships with the land and all the living energies within it. I remember my good friend from Union Bar, Freddie Quipp, saying of his wife, June: "The reason I moved to Cheam, June's territory, is because that is where her power is. That is where her medicines are. That is where her fishing grounds are. That is where her people are." What are your thoughts on this?

Lee Maracle: The marriage laws of 1888 altered the power women had that Fred Quipp speaks of until Lovelace won her case.[1] My aunt was removed from our community for marrying a Cheam man. Her authority, her power, her place, her people were suddenly gone. She spent the first two decades of her adult life in a blur, drinking, depressed and powerless. This removal also removed her children. None of her children grew up in the village of her family of origin. They all belong to Cheam. In a sense, she has progeny.

John S.: Yes, this issue of colonial interference in governing who is a status Indian through membership and marriage laws and thus, who has rights to the scant resources allocated to these subjects, continues to be an issue in contemporary times. As Palmater (2011) discusses, the state's genocidal policies and practices are strategically aimed at controlling Indigenous identities in efforts to save money and extinguish status Indians through policy. By telling her own story, Palmater brings into view how the genocidal policies of the state have restricted her family's ability to live on reserve, be surrounded by her people, and benefit from agreements meant to help the people. It is a frustrating conundrum that many Indigenous people find themselves in. Consequences that are not a far leap from what you are saying with your aunt.

In contemplating Freddie's response, I think he was saying something very similar to your statement. I question, then, what happens when men do not have a deep love for their land and nation? What does this mean for the governing authority of women? Also, what are potential consequences for the land?

Lee M.: For men I deliberately use "the land" while Freddie uses "her land." It is the reason that men went to live with their wives, first, her power is there, her medicine, her land, her very language, reference posts, historical markers, sense of development, continuity, and history are all in her homeland. Our stories are connected to the land, our responsibilities are connected to the land, and they are site-specific, and it is the women who are the carriers of that knowledge, that sense of being. Although I am a member of the Sto:lo nation I was born at Ts'leil Waututh or [Inlet] and "Sto:lo" means river, so my sense of the world is oceanic, and sound-based [as in Howe Sound and Puget Sound]. I was born at the end of an inlet that is connected to the deepest sound in North America, home of the giant octopus who gave us the turquoise used to paint our poles. I participated in the ceremony that called the baby octopus to shore, where they roll over and the women pick the ink sacks, and then they return to the ocean. This ceremony, this agreement, exists among the women of oceanic Salish peoples and the octopus. It is also part of our medicine ways as turquoise is a healing colour. Wellness is paramount in the raising of sons. Our sons are diplomats; it takes deep thought to create the diplomacy of Salish man, and the women [aunts, grammas, older cousins, and the mother] must raise sons that are ready to go and become part of a woman's family, village, land, and power once they have become men. And the women must let go of the sons almost daily from birth. When we talk about "selflessness," this is what we mean. The sound gives me depth; the inlet, place, position, and ceremonial relations with the beings of the sea that we need to be who we are and will always want to be.

John S.: When I think about how I was raised, I was adopted out to a non-Native family, and the values and practices they taught me were much different from what you speak about. First, there was no importance attached to the spiritual connection to land. There were no sites that we visited on a regular basis that contributed to my notion of identity, nor did we practise the types of ceremony you speak of with the octopus. My experience was very different from that of my biological mother. I remember her telling me stories of how our family would escape the racist practices of the local settler community (Kamsack, Saskatchewan) by living in Pee Paw plains in Saskatchewan with her parents and siblings in a small log cabin in the warmer months. My grandmother would build wigwams for them to sleep in and they lived off the land for the most part. Today, my brother, sister, and I go back to that place to visit and reminisce. There was a critical break in my connection to place and culture as a result of being adopted out, but thankfully I still found my way back.

Lee M.: I wonder what this removal has done to your vision. I know the Crees of Saskatchewan can differentiate the colour in the grasses as they walk across the land, the clarity of the sight, insight, and foresight are steeled in the relationship to the great grasslands of the prairies. What happens when you are removed? How does your vision change?

John S.: These are great questions, Lee. The words you shared with me at my kitchen table regarding the links between my adoption and genocide have had a profound impact on me. The non-Native woman who adopted me was a friend of my biological mother, and for some reason I had constructed my experience as being different from "other" Indigenous people who had been adopted out due to the state-sanctioned genocidal policies and attitudes of the "Sixties Scoop." In talking about my adoption you said, "Ahhhhhh . . . tell me more about that." I shared my story and you responded, "That is the genocide I am talking about. You have lived it. What does it feel like?" I was shocked and felt like you had punched me right in the heart. I denied your assertion and quickly tried to intellectually manoeuvre through the discussion. It was in that discussion with you that I began to see my experience differently. One of the most profound insights I had was linked to my sense of belonging. You asked, "Did you ever feel like you were part of the family? Did you want to be part of the family?" My answer to both questions was no. For the first time in 40 years I had come to understand what was deep in my heart. Wow! I continue to unpack that conversation each and every day. As freeing as the conversation was, it still comes with facets of confusion that I do not fully understand.

It is important to note that I feel this confusion in my heart, mind, body, and spirit. This confusion is mostly due to the fact that I love many of the members of my adopted family and continue to have meaningful relationships with them. When I first started unpacking this mess, I was reminded of Maria Campbell's poem, "Jacob" (1998), and the importance of understanding how an individual's links to culture are broken through colonial policy and practice. What does it feel like to be a subject of assimilative policy? What does it feel like to live the genocidal theory and practice of empire? What does it feel like to lose your ability to consent? In short, I felt like puking.

I share this part of my story with you to stress the importance of the psychological, spiritual, bodily, and emotional damage that colonialization causes in people. I am fascinated and at times in disbelief about how deeply colonial ideologies have saturated my mind, body, spirit, and heart. Even when I think I have washed it off, I can at times still feel the oily, grimy residue on my skin. For me, to become an effective leader that my ancestors will recognize, I must unpack these pains and put them back where they belong. Understanding these complex colonial relationships is no easy task. Most mainstream wellness services seem more geared towards bandaging a bleeding wound in efforts to get you back out producing for the dominant economy as soon as possible, rather than getting at the root of the problem. It wasn't until I was introduced to Indigenous and African scholars such as Alfred (2005), Memmi (1965), Fanon (1963), Maracle (1996), and Anderson (2011) that I was able to get glimpses of the larger picture. These writers helped me to gain a better understanding of the deadliness of colonialism and potential pathways to liberation, which have to be considered when discussing notions of Indigenous masculinity and leadership in a contemporary context.

Lee M.: One of the weaknesses of understanding the nature of colonialism is that we are literally surrounded by the mother country, overwhelmed by it and held hostage by it: the wealth from the land is in fact generated by the colonial relations and the destruction is also driven by colonial needs, and men shoulder the responsibility of caretaking the land just as women do. The land is our mother and as such is a woman, but the Canadian state has her in its grip. The trick is to keep the illegitimacy of the state in the forefront of our minds, never for a moment abdicating our duty to the land.

John S.: Hmmm . . . when I hear that about the mother country having a grip on Turtle Island, I wonder how this relates to some of the feminist literature I have been reading, especially a piece by Paula Gunn Allen (1992) that speaks to the deicide of femininity. In short, the author suggests that cultural symbols that were once identified as being feminine are being overwritten with notions of the masculine. I never recognized the significance of this practice until I started seeing the larger war being waged against women by men on an international level. To a large degree, the industrialized world we live in is very masculine in nature. To erase the feminine makes the practices of the masculine seem normal and, thus, the destruction of the land becomes part of that damaging process. What are your thoughts on this?

Lee M.: Cities themselves disconnect people from land and constitute the first "defeminization of cultures" across the globe. How are we going re-matriate our cultures, our thinking, and our being in these cities? There is evidence of Indigenous cities here in North America that were abandoned, and I believe they were abandoned partly for environmental reasons [destruction of farmlands] and partly because we could not resolve the burgeoning unsettling of our co-lineal [male–female balanced leadership] world within these cities. Cities seem to require institutions, organs of power, and the moment that you create institutions then you are a step removed from the feminine sources of power such as family, clan, etc. There is already a degree of distance, alienation, disconnect in the very formation of institutions. We have been struggling with this for some time without knowing it. In the Women, Memory and Power project[2] we interviewed a number of women who created institutions and tried to maintain the original belief systems, goals, etc., inside them. Although we have not been successful, this is a good direction. If we can build institutions that are not disconnected, alienated, and distanced from our original systems, then we can transform the cities. I believe connection to the land is at the heart. Our longhouses were managed by women. All the organizations in the country were founded by a dozen women and one or two men. The defeminization of these institutions occurred over time, but the women did not recognize it at first until it was almost a fait accompli. These are the sorts of things that men need to be studying, re-looking at, and asking, "How do I feminize my council?"

John S.: Yes, I agree with you. The Indigenous leaders in colonial positions of power are often looking for what Taiaiake Alfred (2005: 41) calls the "path of least resistance" in issues related to governance and economic development. In many cases these pathways require adopting and perpetuating the same oppressive ideologies that we are trying to root out of our communities. In the process, Indigenous men often find themselves in these contradictory positions. Some are there out of ignorance and others simply choose to bow down to colonial power to reap the minuscule scraps of colonial political power. One of the authors that helped me understand this is the Maori scholar Brendan Hokowhitu (2012: 46), who says:

> the challenge indigenous peoples face is to realise that traditionalised elite indigenous masculinities have now become an encumbrance, and that often we are left holding on to false traditions, which only serve to exclude and limit indigenous men to hetero-patriarchal, hyper-masculine, stoical, staunch, violent, and often destructive behaviours.

While Hokowhitu is talking about Maori leadership, there are striking similarities to what he is saying when we look at contemporary Indigenous male leadership within Canada. It is important to note that I am not just speaking about administrative structures such as AFN and band councils, but also men in positions of power within the academy and social service agencies and those who are ceremonial leaders. The colonial ideological saturation that Alfred and Hokowhitu speak of has even leaked into our homes. Locating it, exposing it, and rooting it out are key in our efforts to reimagining and rebuilding our Indigenous Nationhood.

Speaking of rooting out empire, I wanted to get your thoughts on the proposed Northern Gateway pipeline from Alberta to Kitimat, BC, as well as the proposed Keystone XL pipeline from Alberta to the US Gulf coast. From a historical perspective, the practices of colonialization always involve power imbalances and domination of certain groups, and the rape of people and land seem to be the norm. I believe the Canadian state attempting to push through the Northern Gateway and Keystone XL pipelines is an extension of this ideology—dominating and raping the land and the Indigenous people is part of this process. What are your thoughts?

Lee M.: The rape of the land is the first step towards rape of women; it is followed by the complete erasure of the people whose oil it is. But it is more than that, for Canada needs the development of the North in order to save itself from the recurring recessions. It stands to gain $6 billion a year. It needs this money to repair the aging infrastructures of its cities, relieve itself of debt, and beef up its military, which contributes further to the rape of the people whose oil it is and to their ongoing inability to sustain their lives, as hunting, gathering, and fishing grounds in the area are damaged and destroyed by industrial development. In order to desecrate the earth, one needs to be completely alienated from the land. In order to desecrate a people one needs to be completely alienated from them. Dominance of any kind precludes and eliminates any affection; love is impossible under corporate rape.

John S.: It's interesting that you bring love into the conversation. As a young man, I was in Yuquot (Friendly Cove) and had the opportunity to learn from the late Mowachaht/Muchalaht Elders, Sam and Violet Johnson. In discussing the importance of Indigenous languages, Violet asked me, "What is your definition of love?" I gave her my definition, which, in retrospect, probably sounded like something out of an English dictionary. I can't remember my exact words, but I knew it sounded narrow and limited. She responded, "Yes! It does mean that, but it means so much more too. I can't tell you what else it means because there are no English words for the translation and you are not a language speaker." From that day on, I have felt like I am missing out on a richness that I cannot yet see due to my language limitations.

I have only recently begun to grasp an understanding of the importance of love within the context of Indigenous liberation and nation-building. Ten or fifteen years ago I would have choked on the words I am about to say, due to where I was in my personal journey as a younger man. I was angry that we live on run-down reserves, angry that we have to beg for money for programming, and angry that we are burdened with educating our guests on their own genocidal and privileged histories. Thankfully, there is something in the wisdom of our old people that I am beginning to see.

My interest in the field of cymatics has helped me to make some of the critical links to better understand what the old people mean when they tell me that love is more powerful than anger and fear. In short, sound resonation is a practice that Indigenous people have weaved throughout our cultures and ceremonies. We begin our life with a song, as you have reminded me. We cry. To expand on the importance of sound resonation, loving environments produce sound resonations and frequencies that are beneficial to the energies within our body. To produce these environments we used song, chants, ceremonies, drumming, meditation, and gentleness with each other. In contrast, fear-based environments produce an energy that is detrimental to the well-being of our bodies, for it often "sticks" to us and has to be brushed off or we become sick. This is an area that I am looking forward to learning more about. Thank you for sharing that.

Lee M.: In order to create leaders, we need thinking children. Thinking children are difficult. I have met so many people that used to tell me, "Your children are wild, they get away with murder." No, I would answer, they would never kill anybody, they are kind. Being a good parent is about restraining the desire to dominate them, instructing them mercilessly, and pushing up the desire for young leaders, men and women. As parents, we need to use language in ways that do not cut into the natural desire of our sons and daughters to lead themselves. Look at any toddler, they do what they want to do, then we step in confining, containing, curtailing, and instructing them how to be not thinking. That forces them to follow adults and carries on into their school years; soon they believe that adults are everything and children are next to nothing. They dominate your grandchildren who then grow up spiritless. That is not the kind of children I wanted. On the other hand, they need a foundation. Story, art, song, and dance are their foundations. Their community and their land are their foundations.

My children are leaders, both my sons and my daughters. Their grandmothers took them onto the land, and they scampered in our mountains, along the sto:lo [river], in the sea and in the inlet. They began mountain climbing at four and five years old. When they began learning to read, they wrote poems about our mountains and "learning the ways of the mountains and the rivers." I knew they would be young leaders loyal to the land and the children. It was such a key. Whenever they fell off the path, off we would go, hiking in the mountains, or crawling around the river's edge, fishing in the canyon, so that they never strayed far from "home." Home was not vested in me or their dad, but in their grandmothers and their land. We didn't have to teach them to be anti-colonial; they came to that themselves during the Oka crisis. They jumped into it full throttle. They formed their own youth groups; they organized themselves, and now they work with youth. They use the same non-instructional, non-dominating, non-oppressive style of working with the youth, connecting them to the land, to the Elders and through art, imagining the good life—Bimaadziwin—and so they create young leaders. They watch the children, see their interests, and encourage stepping up and realizing their dreams.

My sons teach their sons to respect and honour the Earth and women by example. If they love the land, they will protect it, caretake it. If they love the Earth, they will love one another. You teach children to lead by being a leader yourself. I led the way in writing; my children lead the way for other children in the arts too. I led the way in my engagement of politics and activism; my children lead the way in the same way. You cannot love fracking if you love the land. You cannot love the Enbridge pipelines if you love the land. We get back our positions as women by stepping up and men need to step aside when we do. It really is that simple. My son went to live on his wife's reserve. She wanted a studio, my son stepped up to build, but he first had to step aside and say yes to the studio, not argue about how can we afford it, isn't it going to invade our family? etc. etc. He just had to say ok, now let's figure out how we can make it happen, and that helps to develop his leadership skills. Women need to know that their sons belong with their wives. Sons leave, but daughters are forever. We need to restore as much of our systems as possible, keep as many relations within the community alive as is possible, so we are not isolated couples with a few children trying to fulfill ourselves through a small group of people. We will fail. We are community-based, so we need to build a community within which we can interact, find our own sense of leadership. Otherwise we struggle to overpower each other.

Weaving New Webs

My Uncle Andrew always told me, "No man has the right to tell another man how to live his life. That is between that man and the Great Spirit." He added, "I can lay down roles and responsibilities in front of you, nephew, and it is up to you if you pick them up—or not. I cannot force you. You may pick up all of the bundle, you may pick up only part of it, or you may leave it there, but the choice is yours" (personal communication, August 2009).

This next section highlights past and present work with men and young boys undertaken by Sakej Ward and myself in relation to Indigenous masculinities and leadership development. In the spirit of my Uncle Andrew, take what you need and leave the rest.

Sakej Ward: Strategic Planning with Sto:lo Elders and the Rabbit Society

I first met Sakej Ward at a presentation on traditional leadership that he facilitated for the Indigenous Governance program at the University of Victoria in 2009. Over the years since then, we have kept in touch and have learned from each other how to approach our shared interest in working with men to contribute to the reimagining and rebuilding of Indigenous nations.

As a younger man, Ward served in the special forces for both the Canadian and United States militaries. After departing these male-dominated institutions, he spent the next 21 years working with Indigenous men's societies, which are recognized in more contemporary times as warrior societies. His motivation and his long-term goal are to see the liberation of Indigenous people from colonial control through the rebuilding of both men's societies and other Indigenous institutions. Taking an intergenerational approach, his latest projects include strategic-planning sessions with Sto:lo Elders and recruiting youth for the Rabbit Society. Ward complements his work with a master's degree in Indigenous governance. The following interview explores his latest projects.

John Swift: Sakej, Mīkwēc for taking the time to have this important discussion with me. I am interested in learning about the work you are doing with the Sto:lo Elders and youth. What do you have going on, brother?

Sakej Ward: Yeah, I am working with Sto:lo Elders and young children. The work with the Elders involves strategic planning around regenerating traditional roles and responsibilities. It is really a strategic visioning process. When we arrive at the vision and identify strategic goals, then we will start planning outcomes. You know, where are we going? Recruitment and/or community networking?

The Rabbit Society is for the young children where we teach them cultural skills to live out in the bush. It is based on a Lakota model. Really, it is to build them up in becoming young men and women. The Rabbit Society is built upon traditional values, with the intent of skill development to allow them to survive in the bush. We do shelter-building, water collection and purification, and fire-building. Once the individuals have these skills down, then we work into more communal responsibilities such as trapping, hunting, fishing. These are group activities to stress the importance of community.

John S.: Why do you do this type of work?

Sakej W.: It comes from the role that I have as a warrior. Pursuing that path means I am helping our communities recover from colonization. This is a long-term strategy around nation-building. For example, the Elders group and Rabbit Society—I see them as traditional institutions that need to be built up. We need to build up from the bottom—families, communities, then governance.

John S.: Right on, man. Love it! Why is this work important in the larger context of Indigenous liberation efforts?

Sakej W.: Coming from the warrior perspective, it is about confronting and resisting colonialism. Hopefully, my efforts play a role in restoring our way of life. The cultural and spiritual aspects are what are really important to me.

John S.: One of the strengths I see in your work is that you're not dependent on governmental funding. Why is that?

Sakej W.: Yeah, any true Indigenous governance rebuilding is not going to be funded by the state to begin with. Even if there was funding, that money would come with so many limitations that we couldn't really do the kind of work that is necessary with re-establishing traditional Indigenous governments. I would also say that to do this on our own is self-determination in action, when you cut the ties and dependency relationship with the government. We get no resources to do this work. Some may see this as limiting, but it opens new doors and we have freedom of choice. That is what I mean by self-determination. We have control over how we are going to build. Finally, and most importantly, it is about service to your community and people. Regardless of the fact that there is no funding, this is all volunteer work on behalf of my wife and me. It's about trying to give back.

John S.: That is very cool, man. Is there a thirst within the community for this type of work?

Sakej W.: Interestingly, I am starting to see it more and more. In the strategic planning the Elders want to get more involved and stay involved and we are still in the early stages. In regards to the Rabbit Society, we started out with four or five kids and it has quadrupled.

John S.: That's hopeful and reassuring. Have you met any resistance at the community level to your work and ideas?

Sakej W.: Not a structured or active resistance, but I think we could say assimilated mentalities pose passive resistance. What I mean by that is we would probably have higher participation rates if people didn't have assimilated mentalities that hinder them from valuing traditional institutions and rebuilding them. If the people started to revalue the skills, teachings, and knowledge that underpin traditional governance institutions, then I think we would see much more participation.

John S.: Yeah, I agree. One of the problems I have with critics of your type of work is that they say it is essentialist in nature. I would strongly disagree. When I say "essentialist in nature" I mean feeding that notion that we are nothing more than our past and we are always striving to return to some kind of romanticized view of that image and identity. It takes imagination, networking, ceremony, and learning in different ways to re-imagine and rebuild Indigenous communities in contemporary times. What I mean by that is we have to employ numerous ways of knowing in this journey. We have to draw on intergenerational knowledge, observation based ways of knowing, and revealed knowledge, which comes from the land and the other side. There is a bit of room to escape this conundrum through articulation theory (Tengan, 2008), which situates "cultural authenticity" secondary to the people's freedom to make, unmake, and remake culture as they see fit, but it is still frustrating when critics try to box this type of work in by framing it in terms of an essentialist argument. Anyway, I am getting off topic here. Share a bit more with me about your Rabbit Society. How does your Rabbit Society relate to Indigenous liberation efforts?

Sakej W.: If we can really develop the youth while they are young by connecting them back to the land, then that is a definite strength. As we know, colonization strategy is to disconnect us from our land and culture. Therefore, efforts to reconnect are vital in assuming our role of taking care of the land. When our youth get older, then mobilizing them to protect the land won't be as hard. Right now there is such a deep disconnect that when you start to talk about protecting the land it is hard for them to understand. Get them young and instill these values and hopefully they will protect the land as they get older.

John S.: Yeah, like Lee says, "Men have to have a deep love, appreciation, and connection to the land and for their nation before they can love their women." What have you seen come out of your efforts and where do we need to go from here?

Sakej W.: The Rabbit Society has grown and the skill development has progressed, which is great. Also, I'm seeing attitude and language changing with the younger generation. With the work I'm doing with Elders, it is all about relationship-building. I used to walk by Elders and say "Hi," but now I have a deeper relationship with them, which makes future work more meaningful.

John S.: Let's get to a really important part of this discussion. What about gender? How do women influence the work that you do?

Sakej W.: Personally, I have five females in my home and they are constantly guiding me. They tell me when I have a stupid idea. Also, my wife (Melody) helps out so much when I am working with the Elders. She also helps out with the Rabbit Society. She parallels the work I am doing by developing women's groups in the community. My wife and mother-in-law constantly remind me of how to conduct myself in the community.

John S.: You're a lucky man, Sakej. They must love you a lot. Also, I respect your ability to humble yourself in a way that allows the relationships between you and the women of your family to grow in a nurturing and empowering manner. It sounds like they are contributing to your sense of identity, which brings me to my next question. What role do women play in reconstructing men's identity? You have mentioned the roles that your children as well as your mother-in-law and your wife play in your life, but if we were looking at this from a larger theoretical perspective it almost seems that some men, we are not there yet. What I mean by that is many men are not ready to accept or look at the role our women play in our identity formation. What are your thoughts?

Sakej W.: I think there is a certain fear among men and we don't recognize it as misogyny or patriarchy. There is a fear that we will be seen as weaker or inferior to other men if we let a female guide and influence our decision-making and thought processes. I remember being in my early twenties and really having this patriarchal, dominant male mentality. The army didn't do anything to tame that view. In fact, it did everything it could to empower it. In many colonial institutions, prisons included, there is a deliberate effort to foster the dominant male mentality partly by demeaning females. Males are taught that anything associated with female traits, let's say emotion, for instance, is wrong. More disturbingly, you have to do everything to eradicate it and become almost stoic. The only emotion you are allowed to feel as a male is anger. This creates the barriers in our young men to not let any woman have any form of influence in their decision-making or actions. It is this Western world view of the dominant male that really becomes a hindrance in our development as men.

John S.: Yeah, I agree with you. Society is constantly bombarding men with messages of the hegemonic and marginal masculinities (Connell, 2005), which has very real consequences for women and men outside of these narrow and damaging concepts.

I want to thank you for taking the time to share your story with me. I respect the work you are doing and learn a lot each time we speak.

Sakej W.: Thank you.

John Swift: Questioning Male Privilege

I was having lunch with a female classmate while in graduate school and we were discussing the jobs we had held as much younger professionals. I shared that I was the program director of an Indigenous organization at 19 years of age. She responded, "That was due to your male privilege," adding, "there is no way I could have held that type of position as a 19-year-old Indigenous woman." Her comments made me think about the whole process I went through to get that job, and in the end, I knew there was something to what she was saying, but I had to delve into the matter more deeply.

I was a young man with no formal training or experience developing programs and supervising staff, but I did have a gift for working with people. I had no idea how to manage a budget, never mind making five-year funding projections tied to proposal writing, but I applied. I needed a job and I liked the organization. My competition was a mature, non-Native woman who had direct experience in this field from working in a local non-Indigenous organization. For some reason, I was awarded the job. I knew that my Indigenous ancestry and affirmative action may have played a role in my getting the position, but I never considered that the privilege associated with my gender may have also factored into that equation. As I unpacked that experience, I saw links that supported my friend's comments. For example, there were males in leadership positions who participated in promoting chauvinistic and sexist attitudes and behaviours in the workplace, which often went unchallenged by both male and female staff members. In short, the allowances granted to men's behaviour within this atmosphere privileged men at the expense of women, which makes my friend's comments on my being hired for the job all the more valid. However, I should also note that changing attitudes about workplace behaviours and increased opportunities for women to advance in this and other workplaces are enabling women to feel safer and more hopeful about succeeding than previous generations could.

My second insight came when I started thinking about my educational career and how male privilege has played a role in my being able to attend school for so long and in my being a parent. Over the last 15 years that I have been pursuing post-secondary education, my partner has assumed the role of primary child-care provider. While she also had aspirations of post-secondary education, it never happened (for a multitude of reasons), but that is not the point. The point is that my role as a male within my family came with certain privileges of which I was not entirely aware as a younger man, especially during my late teens and twenties. For the most part, I made the decisions in my household. Regardless of how awful it tastes to have those words come out of my mouth, I have to acknowledge that I perpetuated the patriarchal world of male privilege within my own family, and that ensured my academic success while limiting the potential success of my female partner. It is a disgusting truth and one largely influenced by the privileges given to me as a result of being male within this colonial project called Canada.

Once I began looking at how male privilege plays out in my daily life, I began to see imbalances everywhere. My female friends jog with their phones and keys in hand. They park in well-lit areas and they don't put themselves in situations where they have to trust men they don't know. They feel they have to choose their wardrobes carefully to ensure they are not *putting themselves* at risk. They have to be careful of the areas they enter because these spaces have differing levels of what is considered appropriate male behaviour. I don't feel I have to do these things. I leave my phone in the car when I jog around the lake. In other words, I don't experience the world in the same way that some women do. Because of my gender, I experience a sense of assumed safety that not all women get to enjoy. It is a disgusting reality. In work meetings, it is not uncommon for the men to dominate the dialogue and/or to cut off female speakers. It usually doesn't take long before the conversation becomes one-sided, mirroring an old boys' club. And we haven't even begun to touch on consent, rape, sexual violence, domestic violence, and the murdering of Indigenous women. If we Indigenous men are serious about being effective leaders in rebuilding our nations, we have a serious amount of work ahead of us in unpacking the disgusting truths of male privilege.

Lee Maracle: Conclusion

Working through this article has been such a labour of love. For so long, women have had to struggle to be heard in a political vacuum. Some men have even objected to women having meetings apart from men. Some women have made comments about how women need to remember "men are sacred too." I only know 5,000 Indigenous women, but I have not heard one of them state that men are not sacred. It is women who are bearing the burden of raising families without fathers, raising grandchildren without grandfathers, defending themselves against assault, murder, rape, and so forth without the defence of the men in their families. In short, the world seems to have forgotten that Indigenous women are sacred, but it begins with the land. The truth is those men who are connected to the land respect all life, particularly women. Women who are respected, love. It seems to me that for Indigenous men to have the courage to step out and lead, to volunteer to assist in the rearing of children (like Sakej), they need to be loved by women and love the land. Genuine leadership will guide us to who we are and will always want to be. Outside of being ourselves, we will forever be hungry for something we have difficulty naming: connection to the land. Picking up our bundles as caretakers transforms us from aggressive, angry individuals to loving and respectful human beings. Once we learn to love one another, we will realize that we also wish to cherish the world and all humans, animals, birds.... We will become leaders calling everyone to the good life, the good mind, rather than trying to get more from government. When we move towards the good life, suicide ceases to be an option.

Discussion Questions

1. What does it mean to have an intimate relationship with land, and how do you think this is tied to Indigenous male leadership?
2. Do you think intimate relationships with land are important? Why or why not?
3. What role should women play in revitalizing traditional notions of Indigenous masculinity and identity, and in revisioning what Indigenous male leadership may mean in our time?
4. Besides the "pathways of least resistance," what can Indigenous peoples do to protect their homelands from further encroachment and environmental damage?
5. What does it mean to be an Indigenous male leader today?

Further Reading

Alfred, T., and J. Corntassel. 2005. "Being Indigenous: Resurgences against Contemporary Colonialism." *Government and Opposition* 40, 4: 597–614.

Ball, J. 2013. "Indigenous Men's Journeys to Become Meaningfully Involved Fathers in Canada." In J. Pattnaik, ed., *Father Involvement in Young Children's Lives: A Global Analysis*, 201–24. New York: Springer.

Innes, R.A., and K. Anderson, eds. 2015. *Indigenous Men and Masculinities: Legacies, Identities, Regeneration*. Winnipeg: University of Manitoba Press.

Maracle, S., M. Smolewski, K. Minich, I. Logan-Keye, J. Danforth, W. Campbell, K. Anderson, R. Innes, and J. Swift. 2013. *Bidwewidam: Indigenous Masculinities, Identities and mino-bimaadiziwin*. Toronto: Ontario Federation of Indian Friendship Centres.

McKegney, S. 2014. *Masculindians: Conversations about Indigenous Manhood*. Winnipeg: University of Manitoba Press.

Notes

1. Sandra Lovelace Nicholas, a Maliseet woman from the Tobique Reserve in New Brunswick, married a non-Indian man, which meant she lost her "Indian status" and "band membership." When the marriage ended she returned to the reserve but experienced discrimination for herself and her child because they were denied the housing,

education, and health care afforded to "registered Indians": according to the Indian Act, she was no longer an "Indian." She filed a complaint with the United Nations Human Rights Committee, which ruled in 1981 that Canada's Indian Act was in breach of human rights. Finally, four years later, in 1985, Bill C-31 amended the Indian Act to allow Indigenous women and their children to retain Indian status and to end federal control over who could or could not be a band member. In 2005 Sandra Lovelace Nicholas was appointed to the Canadian Senate by Prime Minister Paul Martin, where she has been a steadfast voice for Indigenous rights.

2. The Indigenous Women, Memory and Power project was begun by a collective of Indigenous women at the University of Toronto and the Native Canadian Centre of Toronto and was funded by the Aboriginal Peoples Program of the federal Department of Canadian Heritage. The project, from September 2013 to March 2014, brought forth Indigenous women activists from the past half-century, creating an "oratorical continuum" across generations that involved the sharing of oral storytelling and experiences through interviews and public presentations. See https://firststoryblog.wordpress.com/2014/06/05/indigenous-women-memory-power.

8

Aboriginal Demography

Don Kerr and Roderic Beaujot

It is clear that despite declining fertility rates, Aboriginal people will be a continuing presence in Canadian society; indeed, their population share is projected to increase. Demographic projections thus reinforce the assertion of Aboriginal people that they will continue as distinct peoples whose presence requires a renewed relationship with the rest of Canadian society.

Report of the Royal Commission on Aboriginal Peoples (1996)

Introduction

Canada has witnessed some remarkable demographic developments during the past 20 years. In 2010, very few countries in the world had as high a life expectancy and as low a fertility rate as Canada. International comparisons suggest that Canada ranks among the healthiest countries in the world, with an estimated life expectancy at birth for 2010–11 of about 81.5 years (Martel, 2013). As for the birth rate, Canada entered the twenty-first century with its total fertility rate falling to a historic low—at only about 1.5 children per woman in 2005—prior to rebounding somewhat more recently, up to 1.6 in 2011 (Statistics Canada, 2012a).

Continuing improvements in Canada's social and economic development have contributed significantly to these changes. Indeed, the United Nations Development Program (UNDP) has consistently placed Canada near the top of its annual ranking of countries according to its Human Development Index. Meant to capture differences in life expectancy, per capita gross domestic product, and level of education, this ranking has been widely portrayed to the Canadian public as suggesting that Canada is "one of the best countries in the world to live in." While Canada's ranking relative to other countries has recently slipped somewhat (at least partially due to greater "progress" being

CP Images/Darryl Dyck

made in other countries), its rank has remained "very high" on this index. In 2011 Canada was listed as sixth out of 185 countries (UNDP, 2012).

An innovative application of this index to the Indigenous peoples of Canada clearly indicates that Aboriginal Canadians have not shared equally in this affluence. Cooke and Beavon (2007) rank Canada's First Nations forty-eighth on the list, which is only slightly above countries like Uruguay and Mexico. While they note that living conditions are better "off-reserve" than "on-reserve," these authors rightfully highlight the general frustration of First Nations political leaders who point out that Canada is certainly not among the "best countries in the world" to live for First Nation peoples (Mercredi, 1997). While Cooke and Guimond (2009) report modest progress since the 1980s in reducing the gap between Aboriginal and non-Aboriginal Canadians on this index, unemployment remains very high, housing conditions are often substandard, and health care and educational services are often inadequate.

In this context, it is not surprising that the demographic dynamics of the Aboriginal population are also quite different from those of Canada as a whole. In particular, mortality continues to be significantly higher, with major challenges in terms of population health. Birth rates also tend to be relatively high, with child-bearing often beginning at a younger age relative to other Canadians. In turn, the growth rate of the Aboriginal population continues to outpace that of the overall population, resulting in a younger age/sex structure. This leads to a somewhat unique set of challenges compared to those of the broader society.

Understanding the unique demography of Aboriginal peoples in Canada requires that we view it in broad historical context. In reviewing Canada's history, the National Chief of the AFN, Shawn Atleo (2009), highlighted a few facts that are often neglected or downplayed by the broader society, including "the well documented theft of Indian lands and forced relocations of First Nations communities; the criminalization and suppression of First Nation languages and cultural practices; the chronic under-funding of First Nations communities and programs; and the denial of Treaty and Aboriginal rights." The demographic situation that characterizes the present is best understood by beginning with this colonial past, as the legacy of colonization continues to reverberate throughout the lives of First Nations and other Aboriginal peoples in Canada.

We begin this chapter with a brief overview of the demographic history of Aboriginal peoples in Canada—from the period before contact with Europeans through to the depopulation and excessive mortality that occurred during the eighteenth and nineteenth centuries. From here, we broadly sketch the dramatic demographic recovery of Aboriginal Canadians from the late nineteenth century onward. Given that much confusion and inadequate information characterize public discussions of Aboriginal peoples, we then clarify the terms used to identify Aboriginal peoples in the Canadian census.

The discussion of definitions is followed by an overview of what is currently known of present-day population size, fertility, and mortality, as well as some of the implications of recent trends for population structure and composition. This will all be related to evidence on the evolving social and economic conditions of Aboriginal Canadians, as well to Canada's overall demographic development.

Pre-Contact Demography

Most accounts of Canada's demographic history begin with European contact. Historical research largely relies on historical records and documents, and for that reason there have been large obstacles to documenting the early history of the peoples of the Americas. Nonetheless, demographic evidence of North America before European contact has been pieced together through the efforts of archaeologists, physical anthropologists, and ethnohistorians. Physical anthropologists make estimates of the living conditions, diet, fertility, morbidity, and mortality of pre-contact peoples through the systematic study of skeletal remains and burial sites. Archaeologists provide insight into settlement patterns and technology use before contact. Ethnohistorians piece together the meaning of scattered and incomplete documents left behind as the first Europeans came into contact with the Aboriginal population. Information drawn together from these and other sources enables us to make a number of inferences about the demography of the original inhabitants of

Canada both before and immediately after contact with Europeans (Dickason and Newbigging, 2015).

When the Portuguese, the Basques, and the French were first navigating the waters off Newfoundland, approximately 50 distinct languages (as opposed to dialects) were spoken within the boundaries of modern-day Canada. This rather conservative estimate includes only those that have been relatively well documented and classified (Goddard, 1996; Sturtevant, 2006). Decades of exhaustive historical study have enabled historians and linguists to approximate the locations and distributions of these languages at the time of contact as well as categorize them according to their structure (Sturtevant, 2006). Linguists have classified them into 11 major linguistic families, further indicating the high level of linguistic diversity (Figure 8.1).[1]

Although it is challenging to reconstruct population distribution in the distant past, there is consensus that the most densely populated region in the country at this time was along the west coast of British Columbia. Approximately one-half of the 50 languages spoken in Canada were located within present-day British Columbia. Thanks to the abundance of food and the mild climate, population densities were higher there than in any other region, including the Iroquoian territories of southern Ontario and Quebec. What is clear is that Canada's west coast pre-contact peoples depended largely on the sea for subsistence, as aquatic foragers, whalers, and fishermen. In addition, this part of North America is noted for a greater supply of flora and fauna than other parts of Canada (Muckle, 2007).

With this sedentary way of life, the peoples of the west coast of Canada were among the most densely populated "non-agricultural" peoples ever documented by anthropologists (Boyd, 1990). The second-most densely populated region of Canada before the arrival of the Europeans was the territories of the Iroquoians of the St Lawrence River and Great Lakes. Unlike the peoples of British Columbia, these farmer-hunters mostly practised slash-and-burn (swidden) agriculture. The "typical" pre-contact Iroquoian village was occupied year-round and usually lasted a few decades, or until the land was no longer fertile (Saunders et al., 1992). The length of habitation resulted in a good deal of physical evidence of the various settlement patterns in this region during the pre-contact period, as well as of early regional trade routes and likely socio-economic and political alliances (Waldram et al., 2006).

As we look farther north, population densities declined. The northern boreal forest, also called the taiga, is spread across much of modern-day Canada and is noted for its particularly long and severe winters. Populations in northern Quebec and Ontario were quite low, and there is little evidence of permanent settlements among the Algonquin, Montagnais, Ojibwa, and Cree

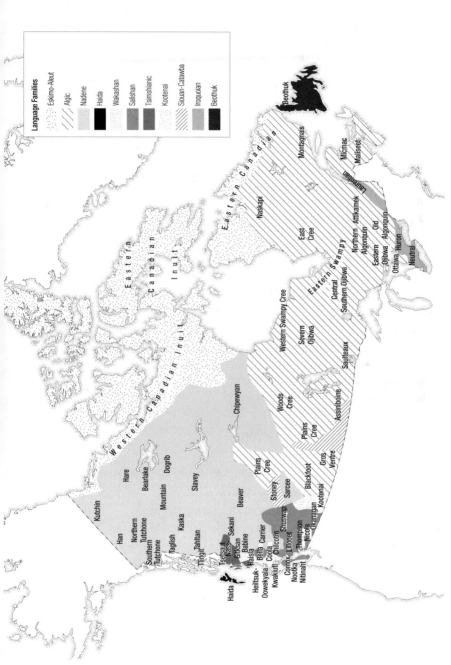

Figure 8.1 | Native Languages and Language Families of North America: Pre-Contact Canada.

Source: Roderic Beaujot and Don Kerr, *Population Change in Canada*, Figure 2.1 "Native Languages and Language Families of North America". Based on Goddard (1996).

before the arrival of the Europeans. Unlike agricultural peoples, members of these tribes adapted to an often difficult environment by acquiring an intimate knowledge of the food to be found in the boreal forest and by hunting and trapping the many mammals and birds over a wide area (Dickason and Newbigging, 2015). Both the fauna and flora of the boreal forest are much less rich than those found in the deciduous forests farther south, and scholars agree that the scarcity of food undoubtedly limited population densities in the northern regions. Demographers and physical anthropologists studying non-agricultural peoples refer to the "carrying capacity" of a specific region, which specifies the number of people that can be supported in an area given the available physical resources and the way the people use those resources (Boserup, 1965; Harris and Ross, 1987). Obviously, the carrying capacity of the northern regions was relatively low, which explains the higher concentration of populations in the south regions of the country.

In the western provinces of today's Canada, the northern Great Plains were thinly populated with smaller communities whose main source of food was bison and other game. In the Arctic, the Inuit were spread extremely sparsely across an enormous land mass from Greenland to present-day Alaska. Owing to their remote location, some isolated bands of Copper and Netsilik Inuit were unknown to the Canadian government until the 1920s (Morrison, 1984). Whereas the Beothuk of Newfoundland encountered Europeans in the sixteenth century, some isolated Inuit bands did not encounter people of European descent until 400 years after Europeans set foot on this land.

Health and Mortality Conditions

Although some historians have portrayed pre-contact America as a "disease-free paradise" (Stewart, 1973; Dobyns, 1983), more recent research by physical anthropologists has shown that description to be inaccurate (Waldram et al., 2006; Williamson and Pfeiffer, 2003). In fact, pre-contact North American samples of skeletal remains suggest that mortality was high (by modern standards), particularly among the young. Evidence indicates there were various contagious diseases, gastrointestinal illnesses, and anemia (at least partially related to meat-borne parasitic infection and burden), deaths due to trauma and accidents (fractures and broken bones), respiratory illnesses, and malnutrition and periodic starvation (Ubelaker, 2000).[2]

This situation was by no means unique to North America, for similar patterns of illness and mortality were evident at the same time in Europe and all other major world regions. There is general consensus that life expectancy across the world and throughout most of human history fluctuated anywhere between 25 and 35 years (Wiess, 1973; Angel, 1984). Nonetheless, it is clear that the high level of mortality in the Americas was greatly exacerbated by the introduction of diseases of European origin (Waldram et al., 2006). Still, it is important to note that many populations in pre-contact Canada likely were healthier than their contemporaries in Europe. For example, while much of fifteenth-century Europe's population was deeply impoverished and ate a low protein diet based almost exclusively on wheat, rye, oats, and barley (Singman, 1999), the rich diet of fish, sea and land mammals, seaweed, and plant foods in British Columbia provided a diversity of nutrients and protein for those who lived there. There is also clear historical evidence of recurrent famine throughout medieval Europe, conditions made even more difficult by several major pandemics and warfare.

In populations with high mortality, the risk of death is highest among infants and young children. In addition, childbirth has always been a risky event in pre-modern populations, with an elevated risk for both infant and mother (Van Lerberghe and Brouwere, 2001). The scattered evidence available suggests that before European contact in Canada, child-bearing started early in a woman's life and continued until menarche (Charbonneau, 1984). Involuntary infertility was more common than it is today, owing to untreated disease as well as lower levels of nutrition and the periodic shortage of food (Romaniuc, 2000). Most women breast-fed their children for as long as two years, which lowered fertility but enhanced the survival chances of the young by widening the spacing of births (Jain and Bongaarts, 1981).

European Contact, Excessive Mortality, and Population Decline

Romaniuc (2000) describes the pre-contact stage as being most likely a quasi-stationary demographic state characterized by high mortality offset by moderately high fertility. After contact, the Aboriginal population of Canada underwent an almost three-centuries-long depopulation.

A recurrent theme in the study of pre-modern populations is the so-called *crise de mortalité*—that is, a sudden and pronounced rise in the death rate, with devastating consequences for populations of local areas or even of broader regions (Meuvret, 1965; Charbonneau and Larose, 1979). The extent to which Canada was depopulated as a result of European colonization is certainly open to debate, but by all accounts this was an enormous disaster in both physical and cultural terms. As we note below, it was not until the late nineteenth century that population numbers among the Aboriginal population finally stabilized and began slowly to recover (Charbonneau, 1984),

Though there is little disputing this population decline, there is less agreement about the extent of the decline. Estimates vary widely, largely because of differences of opinion as to the accuracy and completeness of the earliest population figures recorded by colonial administrators (Daniels, 1992; Thornston, 2000; Ubelaker, 2000). The obvious difficulty faced by ethnohistorians in trying to piece together the pre-contact situation is that in many of the earliest accounts, some communities were already in a state of social disorganization and epidemic, whereas others had remained intact and largely isolated from European influence. Even today, in the modern census in Canada, the undercount has been estimated to be several times higher among Aboriginal people than among the population in general. Consequently, all efforts at demographic reconstruction continue to be somewhat speculative and open to debate.

Dickason (1992) proposed that "the most widely accepted estimate is about 500,000" for pre-contact Canada, a figure later adopted by the Royal Commission on Aboriginal Peoples (1996) in its brief appraisal of the demographic history of Canada. In contrast, Mooney (1928) provided a very conservative approximation of just under 200,000 based on a systematic review of what are admittedly partial and imprecise early written accounts, while Charbonneau (1984) estimated the pre-contact population to be about 300,000. At the opposite extreme, a few estimates suggest that the pre-contact population may have been many times higher than Dickason's figure of 500,000, perhaps as high as 1.5 million, on the assumption of major depopulation that could not possibly be detected from early colonial records (Dobyns, 1983; Thornston, 1987).

Population Decline and Recovery

If we accept Dickason's pre-contact estimate of 500,000, it would take another 250 years after Jacques Cartier first sailed into the Gulf of St Lawrence before a comparable number of Europeans were living in the territories of modern-day Canada. Charbonneau (1984: 24) notes that this basic observation is far too often overlooked in historical accounts of the demography of Canada. For instance, Charbonneau points out that historian L.E. Hamelin's observation that it took many decades for the population of Canada to establish itself after the founding of the city of Quebec completely ignores the original inhabitants of the land.

In contrast to Dickason's estimate of 500,000 Aboriginal inhabitants living in pre-contact Canada, the 1871 census accounted for only about 103,000 Aboriginal persons (see Figure 8.2). While this latter figure is in all likelihood

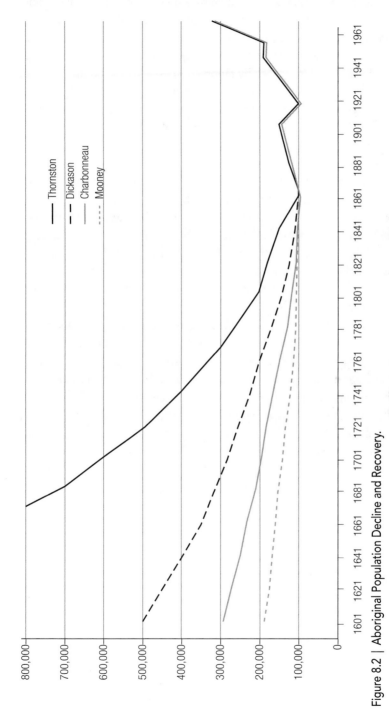

Figure 8.2 | Aboriginal Population Decline and Recovery.

Sources: Dickason (1992); Royal Commission on Aboriginal Peoples (1996); Mooney (1928); Charbonneau (1984); Thornston (1987).

an undercount—for reasons outlined below—it no doubt represents a demographic disaster. Figure 8.2 portrays impressionistically the wide range of estimates that have been published on the size of Canada's pre-contact population, from Dickason's (1992) mid-range estimate through to the more conservative numbers proposed by Mooney (1928) and Charbonneau (1984). Thornston's (1987) pre-contact population estimate of about 1.5 million is also included merely as an extreme example in the opposite direction. In this context, Dickason's mid-range estimate implies a depopulation ratio of about 5:1, with the pre-contact population of 500,000 down to only about 100,000 by 1871.

In the demographic evolution of Aboriginal peoples in Canada, the late nineteenth century can be regarded as the beginning of a period of demographic stabilization and recovery. Although mortality remained very high, the most serious of epidemics were subsiding and the total number of Aboriginal deaths was less than total births. As a result, it is estimated that the Aboriginal population grew from its nadir of about 100,000 in 1871 to 200,000 by mid-twentieth century, and to roughly 300,000 by the 1971 census (Goldmann and Siggner, 1995).

While the Aboriginal population has experienced major reductions in both fertility and mortality during the past 100 years, demographers disagree about why the timing and pace of these changes departed significantly from that of other Canadians (Young, 1994; Trovato, 2000, 2001). For example, there is still much uncertainty about the extent to which Canada's Aboriginal population has evolved in isolation (or in demographic terms, as a "closed" population) and how population numbers have been affected by intermarriage and assimilation to the larger society.

We suggest that the Canadian census likely understated the actual size of Canada's Aboriginal population as defined by ancestry in the latter nineteenth and early twentieth centuries. The nadir of only about 100,000 persons in the 1871 census was likely an undercount, as many persons of Aboriginal descent, for a variety of reasons, were not reporting their ancestry. Similarly, the low figures as documented throughout the first half of the twentieth century were in all likelihood a serious understatement, a situation that has only recently been somewhat corrected. The number of Canadians reporting Aboriginal ancestry over recent censuses has climbed dramatically. As we note below, this growth is beyond what is possible through natural increase, and for this reason, we shift our attention to issues relating to how people identify themselves on a census and the associated difficulties of shifting cultural affiliation.

The Contemporary Situation

Defining the Aboriginal Population: Difficulties due to Changing Identities

Most demographic research focuses on countries or on populations defined in terms of political boundaries and place of residence. Consequently, the definition of who is to be included in the target population is typically straightforward, relying on rules relating to citizenship or usual place of residence. In the study of Aboriginal peoples, it is much more complicated to define exactly who is to be included. Aboriginal peoples are spread throughout Canada, across provincial and territorial boundaries, and live in both rural and urban regions of the country. There are no clear residency rules that can be used in identifying this specific population, nor is there a clear legal status that can be used in identifying *all* Aboriginal people.

At one point in Canada's history, the Aboriginal population could be defined easily on the basis of ancestry and way of life. In spite of the great variety among Aboriginal languages, customs, and material culture, there were recognizable common elements of culture and biology. Today, however, the situation has become far more complicated—owing to several centuries of cultural exchange, assimilation, intermarriage, and births of mixed ancestry. Though it may have been obvious to the seventeenth- or eighteenth-century observer who was Cree or Mi'kmaq, as opposed to British or French, today it is often far from obvious.

As an example of some of the difficulties involved, the question must be addressed as to how one classifies persons of mixed ancestry. This issue is not of minor consequence, since the majority of Canadians who currently report Aboriginal ancestry do so as part of a reported mixed ancestry. Of the 1,836,035 people (about 5.6 per cent of Canada's population) who reported Aboriginal ancestry in the 2011 National Household Survey (NHS), well over half (1,207,575) also reported other, non-Aboriginal origins (Statistics Canada, 2013a). Similarly, some people of Aboriginal ancestry report no specific affiliation or identification with a given Aboriginal ancestry or culture (Siggner et al., 2001). The question is, is it enough to rely on the reported ancestry in the identification of this population, and if not, what are some of the other criteria that have been proposed?

The Canadian Census as a Source of Demographic Data

The Canadian census has historically been the most comprehensive source of demographic data on Aboriginal peoples in Canada, and has long been the exclusive source of demographic data for many Aboriginal groups. Historically, the census has estimated the number of Aboriginal people in Canada by asking respondents about their ancestry (as obtained through the "ethnic or cultural origin" question). In the 2006 census, for example, respondents were asked "to which ethnic or cultural group(s)" they belonged, with an encouragement to report as many origins as deemed appropriate. Whereas some respondents have answered that question with very specific responses (such as Objiway, Mohawk, or Cree), others have simply identified themselves as First Nations, North American Indian, Métis, or Inuit.

Although the census is the most comprehensive source of demographic data on Aboriginal peoples in Canada, several difficulties are associated with the information it provides. One problem is the fundamental issue of data comparability over time. For example, while the definition of "Aboriginal" has relied on the ethnic or cultural origin question in the census, the wording to this question has changed frequently, and important changes in methodology and in the way people answer these questions have occurred over time. Until the 1971 census, the ethnic origin followed only the male line of descent. Before 1986, multiple responses to the ethnic origin question were either disallowed or at least discouraged, a situation that has been completely reversed since 1986. In addition, the long-form census questionnaire of the Canadian census was replaced in 2011 by the National Household Survey (NHS), a voluntary survey that, unlike the census, was not mandatory. This produced an uncertain level of bias, for the final response rate for the 2011 NHS of 68.6 per cent was considerably lower than the 93.5 per cent response rate of the 2006 census long form (Statistics Canada, 2012b).

Encouragement to indicate multiple identity origins has led to more people reporting Aboriginal ancestry. As demonstrated in Figure 8.3, the number of people reporting Aboriginal ancestry has increased dramatically over recent years—from only 496,500 in 1981, up to 1,678,235 in the 2006 census, and up further to 1,836,035 in the 2011 NHS (Statistics Canada, 2013a). In just 30 years the size of this "ancestry-based" population has dramatically increased by over 250 per cent. Underlying this change was an increase in the number of people who reported Aboriginal ancestry as part of a multiple response, increasing from 79,085 in 1981 to 997,715 in 2006, and up further to 1,207,575 in 2011. As Canada's overall population growth was about 1 per cent a year over this same period (with about half of this growth due to international migration), it is clear that the growth of the Aboriginal population was obviously due to much more than pure demographic change.

Nevertheless, it would be quite wrong to suggest that all of this growth was merely the result of the change in census methodology. There have also been important shifts in the propensity of Canadians to report Aboriginal

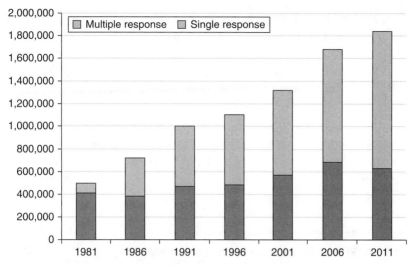

Figure 8.3 | Census Counts of Aboriginal Populations, Based on Ancestry, 1981–2011.

Sources: Statistics Canada, *Census of Canada*, 1981–2006; 2011 National Household Survey.

ancestry. Passel (1997) has noted a similar change in the US, and argues that a new-found political awareness and self-confidence has contributed to a rise in North American Indian consciousness (Passel, 1997).

It has been argued that most racial and ethnic identities in societies such as Canada and the United States are in a state of flux (Eschbach, 1995; Hout and Goldstein, 1994; Lieberson and Waters, 1988). Among many Canadians of mixed ancestry, for example, respondents to the census often change their declared ethnic affiliation from one census to the next in a manner that is often very difficult to predict. The result is that the sizes of ethnic groups appear to change independently of natural increase and migration (Goldmann, 1998; Guimond, 2003). With recent shifts in declared ethnic affiliation, Canadians appear to be far more likely to report their Aboriginal ancestry than was the case historically. Whenever subjectivity and choice enter into how populations report on their ancestry, it becomes very difficult to compare demographic data over time.

Aboriginal Populations

According to section 35(2) of the Constitution Act, 1982, the three major groups of Aboriginal peoples in Canada are "the Indian, Inuit and Métis peoples." While some suggest that such a classification obscures a virtual "kaleidoscope of cultures and traditions" (Frideres and Gadacz, 2012), most demographers accept it despite its "obscuring effects." Although the corresponding populations in these three major groups are not carefully defined, many researchers have tended to rely on information collected through the census on ancestry or cultural origins when classifying people into one of the above categories.

A further subdivision into two additional groups is provided for in the Indian Act: North American Indians (First Nations peoples) who hold legal Indian status and those that do not (non-status). Although the Indian Act has undergone many revisions since the nineteenth century (Savard and Proulx, 1982), it did establish certain legal criteria for identifying who had status as an "Indian" and who did not. As suggested by Romaniuc (2000: 123), the "status population" can almost be thought of as "de jure" members (or citizens, if you like) of Canada's First Nations.

According to the 2011 NHS, which also asked Canadians whether they are "registered under the Indian Act," only about one-third (34.7 per cent) of the Aboriginal ancestry population reported being status Indians (637,660 people out of 1,836,035). In reality, this percentage is probably higher, as past census-based estimates have understated the true size of this population owing to difficulties of data collection. This is also likely true with the 2011 NHS. There are many other Canadians with Aboriginal ancestry beyond the status population, often with similar social and cultural traits, yet they are without the same bundle of legal rights as those who are formally recognized by the federal government (that is, they are "non-status"). For a wide variety of reasons, most Canadians with Aboriginal ancestry are not on the register maintained by Aboriginal Affairs and Northern Development Canada (AANDC). The 2011 NHS reports, for example, that 1,198,375 persons with Aboriginal ancestry are not currently registered under the Indian Act (Statistics Canada, 2013a, 2013b). Some merely have ancestors who either refused or were not allowed to establish treaties or agreements with the Crown, while others lost their status through enfranchisement. In addition, much of the rapid growth of the Aboriginal population recorded in recent censuses has occurred among the "non-status" and Métis populations.

The original inhabitants of Canada's Arctic regions, the Inuit, are clearly the least numerous of the three major groups. Responses to the question on ancestry in the 2011 NHS revealed 72,615 people of Inuit ancestry in Canada. That figure is based on both single and multiple replies regarding ancestry (Statistics Canada, 2013a). In Canada the word "Eskimo" has gradually been replaced by "Inuit," the Inuktitut word that the Inuit use to refer to themselves. Largely situated in Nunavut, Yukon, and the Northwest Territories, as well as in northern Quebec and Labrador, Inuit of Canada's Arctic have much in common, historically and culturally, with many of the original inhabitants of Alaska and Greenland, not to mention the Chukotka of the northern regions of Russia.

The third major Aboriginal group is the Métis, and in the 2011 NHS 447,655 people reported Métis ancestry (Statistics Canada, 2013a). While the word "Métis" has two different meanings ("métis" just means "mixed" in French), its more common use denotes a hybrid culture that developed primarily in western Canada from the marriages of Cree, Ojibwa, and Salteaux women to French and Scottish fur traders. Whereas most people in the western provinces who describe themselves as Métis in the census do so in reference to these origins, an unknown number continue to use other meanings. As defined by the Métis National Council: "Métis means a person who self-identifies as Métis, is distinct from other Aboriginal peoples, is of historic Métis Nation Ancestry and who is accepted by the Métis nation" (Teillet, 2010). Consequently, there are Aboriginal persons reporting Métis ancestry in all provinces of the country, including areas far removed from the traditional Métis homeland in the Prairie provinces.

Aboriginal Identity

To further complicate matters, Statistics Canada has evolved an additional definition of the Aboriginal population based on "identity" rather than "ancestry." As mentioned above, the use of "ancestry" to define the Aboriginal population results in a total population count in 2011 of 1,836,035 (or about 5.6 per cent of Canada's population). Alternatively, the identity-based definition produced a smaller total of 1,400,685 persons in 2011, i.e., roughly 4.3 per cent of Canada's population (Statistics Canada, 2013b). This more restrictive definition has subsequently been used by Statistics Canada in most of its 2011 NHS releases.

Efforts to establish time-series data on Aboriginal populations will always be hindered by the "fluid or situational character" of such concepts as ancestry, cultural origins, and identity (Boxhill, 1984; Lieberson and Waters, 1993). Some people of Aboriginal ancestry may deny their origins, others may have a passionate commitment to these origins, and still others may be indifferent or simply unaware. It was in direct response to some of these difficulties that Statistics Canada introduced a new question on Aboriginal identity in 1996 in order to more narrowly focus on Canada's First Nations. This new question, which was also used in 2001 and 2006, specifically asked Canadians whether or not they "consider themselves as being Aboriginal—that is, North American Indian, Métis or Inuit" (Statistics Canada, 2008a). Whereas one might argue that a count based on ancestry is more objective, the question on identity is arguably more meaningful since it indicates whether or not individuals feel an allegiance to or association with Aboriginal culture. Not surprisingly, the numbers are somewhat smaller, as about 76 per cent of persons reporting Aboriginal ancestry state that they "consider themselves" to be Aboriginal.

If we use this narrower definition of the Aboriginal population, about 62.2 per cent of people with First Nations ancestry report that they "identify" themselves as First Nations people (or 851,560 people out of 1,369,115), whereas 81.9 per cent of those with Inuit ancestry identify themselves as Inuit (or 59,445 people out of 72,615). Among the Métis, the figure of 451,795 people "identifying" themselves as Métis was slightly greater than the 447,655 who reported Métis "ancestry" (Statistics Canada, 2013b). Despite the rather striking "fluidity" of this reporting over time, Statistics Canada documents major growth for all major Aboriginal identity populations over time (Table 8.1). Since 1996 when this information was first collected in the census, this population has grown by roughly 75 per cent overall, an increase that could not possibly be the result of only demographic factors. Particularly striking in this context is the phenomenal growth in the numbers identifying as Métis, more than doubling (+121.3 per cent) in only 15 years since 1996. Closer to expectations, the Inuit population grew by 47.8 per cent over 15 years, which implies a very high rate of demographic increase that is equivalent to a rate of slightly greater than 2.5 per cent annually.

As Statistics Canada has subsequently used this "identity population" in most of its data releases from all censuses since 1996 and in the 2011 NHS, the implication is that this more accurately captures the essence of what one might define as a core Aboriginal population. Canadians of Aboriginal ancestry who do not report Aboriginal identity are far less likely to speak an Aboriginal language, to live in rural or more remote regions of the country, and to be registered Indians or live in a First Nations community (Norris, 2000; Frideres and Gadacz, 2012). Furthermore, while virtually all people in the status population identify with their ancestry, this is far less likely to be the case among persons who are non-status.

Table 8.1 | Size and Percentage Increase in the Population with Aboriginal Identity, Canada 1996–2011

	1996	2011	% change
Total Canadian population	28,528,125	33,476,688	17.3
Aboriginal identity population	799,005	1,400,685	75.3
First Nations (N. American Indian)	529,040	851,560	61.0
Métis	204,115	451,795	121.3
Inuit	40,220	59,445	47.8
Multiple and other Aboriginal responses	25,640	37,885	47.8
Non-Aboriginal population	27,729,120	32,076,003	15.7

Sources: Statistics Canada, *Census of Canada* (1996); 2011 National Household Survey.

The growth of the Aboriginal population in Canada remains dramatic, and there are problems of reliability in our numbers, whether we are working with the "identity"-based or "ancestry"-based figures. As a result, it remains difficult to discern how much of the apparent change in the socio-economic characteristics of either population is due to real economic changes in the lives of Aboriginal Canadians and how much is due to changes in how Aboriginal people officially identify themselves. This contributes to major problems when documenting changes in the socio-economic characteristics of the Aboriginal population over time, let alone making sense of the demographic changes associated with fertility, mortality, and migration.

The Dynamics of Population Change

The demographic transition of Canada's population has moved through stages of high mortality and fertility in the eighteenth and nineteenth centuries through to the relatively low birth and death rates of the present. As we note in the following sections, while Canadian mortality and fertility have dropped quite noticeably overall, the demographic history of Canada's Aboriginal population is quite distinct and demonstrates the heterogeneity of experience that has characterized Canada's overall demographic history.

Mortality

In an overview of mortality patterns among Aboriginal peoples in both Canada and the United States, Trovato (2001) points to a number of common problems. While there have clearly been long-term gains in both life expectancy and infant mortality, Aboriginal North Americans continue to experience mortality conditions that are worse than that of the whole population. Canada is among the world leaders in the health of its population, but epidemiological patterns in Aboriginal mortality and morbidity are clearly different from this overall situation.

The information currently available on mortality is unfortunately less than complete. Part of the reason for this is that Canada's system of vital statistics, which should document all births and deaths in the country (including cause of death), has never collected information on ancestry or cultural origins. The best source of information available on the mortality of Aboriginal people has historically been the Indian Register, the population register maintained by AANDC (2013). This register, which includes information exclusively on the status population, has been continuously updated in documenting births and deaths as far back as the nineteenth century. In addition, there is the lesser known population register on the Inuit of northern Quebec, which has documented births and deaths as far back as the 1940s (Robitaille and Choinière, 1985). For the non-status and Métis populations, without access to a population register, more recent efforts have been made at both indirect estimation (Norris et al., 1995) and data linkage to the information collected on deaths, as documented in vital statistics, with ancestry and identity information, as recorded in the Canadian census (Wilkins et al., 2008; Peters, 2013; Tjepkema et al., 2009).

Canada as a whole has witnessed some dramatic reductions in mortality, with average life expectancy at the end of the twentieth century being about 30 years longer than at its beginning. In 1901, male life expectancy at birth was roughly 47 years while female life expectancy stood at roughly 50 years (Statistics Canada, 1999). In comparison, Romaniuc (1981) has estimated a life expectancy at birth in 1900 for First Nations of only 33 years, more than 15 years lower than the Canadian average at this same date (see Table 8.2).

Among Inuit, evidence collected in the 1940s indicated a life expectancy at birth of only about 35 years (Robitaille and Choinière, 1985). This was a very high level of mortality even by the standards of that time; the overall Canadian life expectancy at the time was almost 30 years longer (66 years for females and 63 years for males). The situation was not much better for First Nations people: by 1941 the status Indian population had an estimated life expectancy of only 38 years.

By 2001, the life expectancy of First Nations people (status Indians) in Canada, at 70.4 years for First Nations males and 75.5 years for females, was still noticeably shorter than Canada's overall average. Among Inuit, Tjepkema et al. (2009) estimate a 2006 life expectancy of slightly less than 70 (67.6 years for males and 72.8 for females). For the Métis, Tjepkema et al. (2009) estimate a life expectancy somewhere between that of the non-Aboriginal population and other Aboriginal groups (about 73 for males and 76 for females).[3] Relative to the total Canadian population, the longevity disadvantage of the Métis can be estimated to be about 5 years, while it is approximately 6–7 years for the First Nations and 10 years for Inuit. Stated differently, the estimated longevity for the Métis in 2001 was roughly comparable to the longevity of other Canadians in the late 1970s, while First Nations longevity was comparable to that of other Canadians in the early 1970s. For Inuit, mortality rates in 2006 were comparable to what other Canadians faced in the 1950s.

Particularly striking among the changes during the post-war period has been the reduction in infant mortality. As late as the 1940s, the infant mortality rate among First Nations was as high as 200 deaths per 1,000 live births

Table 8.2 | Estimated Life Expectancy at Birth for Status First Nations, Inuit, and Total Canadian Populations, Selected Periods and Years, Canada, 1900–2006

Year or Period	Status First Nations, Both Sexes	Inuit					
		Year	Northern Quebec	Northwest Territories	Inuit Nunangat	Year	Total Canada
1900	33					1901	47.0M/50.0F
						1921	58.8M/60.6F
1940	38	1941–51	35	29		1941	63.0M/66.3F
		1951–61	39	37			
1960	56	1961–71	59	51		1961	68.4M/74.2F
1960–4	59.7M/63.5F	1971–81					
1965–8	60.5M/65.6F					1966	68.7M/75.2F
1976	59.8M/66.3F		62			1976	70.2M/77.5F
1981	62.4M/68.9F					1981	71.9M/79.0F
1982–5	64.0M/72.8F					1984–6	73.0M/79.8F
1991	66.9M/74.0F	1991	58M/69F		63.5M/71.1F		
1995	68.0M/75.7F				64.7M/71.6F		
2001	70.4M/75.5F	2001			65.0M/70.0F	2001	77.1M/82.2F
2006		2006			67.7M/72.8F	2006	78.2M/82.3F

Sources: INAC (2005); Wilkins et al. (2008b); Romaniuc (1981); Medical Services Branch, Health and Welfare Canada (1976); Nault et al. (1993); Loh et al. (1998); Robitaille and Choinière (1985); Norris (2000); Statistics Canada (2008b); Peters (2013).

(Romaniuc, 2000), a rate that was to drop dramatically to about 40 deaths per 1,000 by the 1970s and to only about 12 deaths per 1,000 by the 1990s (Loh et al., 1998). Similar reductions have been documented among Inuit, from at least 200 deaths per 1,000 births down to about 28 deaths per 1,000 by the early 1990s (Frideres, 1998). Again, this decline lagged behind that of other Canadians; for example, the infant mortality rate for Canada overall has fallen to only about 5 deaths per 1,000 (Statistics Canada, 2008b). According to Health Canada (2003), this rate has also continued to converge among First Nations towards the rate observed nationally, which is approximately 6.5 deaths per 1,000 births. Among Inuit, the rate was about 15 deaths per 1,000 by 2001, or roughly three times what was observed among other Canadians (Department of Health and Social Services, Nunavut, 2004).

Causes of Death

The epidemiological transition in Canada has involved important shifts in the pattern of disease dominance, particularly a decline in mortality associated with infectious disease. Currently, the big killers in Canada are degenerative diseases, in particular cancer and heart and cardiovascular diseases. To a large extent this shift in the pattern of disease dominance in Canada has been the result of success in reducing the risk of premature death, thanks in large part to the gradual introduction of various public health measures, an improved standard of living, and the intervention of modern medicine and antibiotics.

Yet, while this is true for the Canadian population overall, this is less the case for the Aboriginal population, for which the mortality profile continues to be somewhat distinct. From birth to old age, mortality rates are consistently higher for Aboriginal Canadians across most causes of death, and there are some particularly striking differences.

The 1991 to 2001 Canadian census mortality follow-up study (which linked information from vital statistics with the census) provided comprehensive information on the mortality of Canada's Aboriginal population, including information on cause of death (Tjepkema et al., 2009). Working with a 15 per cent sample of the national population (aged 25 and older), Wilkins et al. (2008) followed the mortality experience of a very large representative sample of Canadian adults over a 10-year period (1991–2001), including a representative sample of persons who self-identified as Aboriginal in the census and/or reported that they held status under the Indian Act. Their research confirmed that First Nations and Métis peoples have a shorter life expectancy than other Canadians, though the Métis are slightly lesser disadvantaged than First Nations. Wilkins et al. (2009) found that Aboriginal persons, and status Indians in particular, continue to be more likely to die prematurely across a wide range of causes (see Figure 8.4).

Since the age structure of the Aboriginal population is relatively young, it is useful to standardize death rates prior to comparing populations, i.e., to explicitly adjust for differences in age structure across populations before comparing the risk. For example, as the First Nations group has a much higher proportion of population at younger ages, one would expect they would proportionately have a higher number of deaths due to accidents. Similarly, one would expect that they would have a smaller proportion of deaths due to diseases typically associated with old age, such as cancer or heart disease. This is merely due to age structure, or the proportion of a population at risk to a specific type of death (i.e., younger people in general tend to be at much greater risk of injuries and accidental death whereas older persons are at much greater risk of death due to degenerative causes).

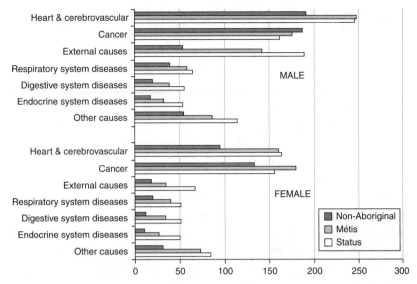

Figure 8.4 | Age-Standardized Mortality Rates (per 100,000 Person Years) by Leading Causes of Death, First Nations, Métis, and Non-Aboriginal Population, Aged 25 or Older at Baseline, 1991–2001.

After standardizing for difference in age structure, Figure 8.4 lists the six leading causes of death for the Aboriginal population, with systematic comparisons across population groups. In so doing, it demonstrates that First Nations male and female death rates are typically higher than those of non-Aboriginal Canadians—with the exception of the age-standardized cancer rate among Aboriginal men. The Métis also experience higher rates, albeit to a lesser extent than the First Nations population (Tjepkema et al., 2009).

Particularly striking in this context is the importance of "external causes" of deaths, such as motor vehicle accidents, suicide, falls, and drowning. Among First Nations (status) men, deaths due to external causes are second only to deaths due to heart and cerebrovascular disease, whereas among Métis men external causes comprise the third most prevalent cause of death behind heart/cerebrovascular disease and cancer. The standardized rates of external causes for both First Nations men and women are roughly three times those of the non-Aboriginal population, whereas for the Métis the standardized rates are roughly twice as high. The disadvantage in terms of heart and cerebrovascular disease is particularly pronounced for both First Nations and Métis. Here the age-standardized rates are approximately 25 per cent higher for men and 50 per cent for women relative to the non-Aboriginal population.

With regard to the additional causes of death shown in Figure 8.4 (respiratory system, digestive system, and endocrine system diseases), without exception the status Indian group remains the most disadvantaged for both men and women, while the Métis also consistently report higher age-standardized rates. The remaining category of "other causes" serves as a residual category that includes deaths resulting from musculoskeletal system disease, genitourinary system disease, mental disorders, nervous system diseases, infectious diseases, and ill-defined conditions. Across all of these major categories the Aboriginal population experienced a higher age-standardized rate, with the status Indian population typically experiencing the highest rates.

As estimated by Tjepkema et al. (2009) almost two-thirds of the difference in terms of excess mortality between Aboriginal men and the general population can be traced to heart disease/circulatory system diseases and external causes (accidents); for women, differences across a wider range of factors are responsible, including cancer and endocrine system diseases (diabetes). These authors further note that the mortality of First Nations has many similarities with other Canadians who experience serious socio-economic disadvantage; in other words, much of the disparity in terms of public health and mortality can be explained by disparities in terms of socio-economic factors. To the extent that Aboriginal Canadians make gains in terms of education, income, and occupation, one can anticipate continued gains in population health and reduced mortality.[4]

Fertility

The evidence available on the child-bearing behaviour of Aboriginal peoples early into the twentieth century suggests that fertility was high—although nowhere close to the theoretical maximum that could occur if a population had absolutely no constraints on fertility. As was the case in most pre-modern societies, a number of factors explain a fertility level below the theoretical maximum. For example, involuntary infertility was likely much more common than in present-day populations, owing to untreated disease as well as the nutritional constraints imposed by often difficult ecological conditions. In addition, overall fertility levels were reduced by the practice of prolonged breast-feeding, often for as long as two years. While prolonged breast-feeding widened the spacing of births, it also maximized the chances of infant survival.

As with the epidemiological transition, relatively little evidence suggests that fertility levels changed significantly for Aboriginal peoples until the post-war period of the twentieth century. Estimates of crude birth rates (the number of births per 1,000 persons) for First Nations peoples from 1900 to the 1940s suggest that the birth rate was about 40 births per 1,000 (Norris, 2000). Among the Inuit, the crude birthrate was about 30 to 35 births per 1,000 in 1941, somewhat lower than one might expect for a pre-transitional population (Robitaille and

Choinière, 1985). This level of fertility combined with high mortality thus contributed to moderate population growth. Among First Nations, the crude birth rate fell to about 22 births per 1,000 by the 1990s (Frideres, 1998), compared to the overall birth rate in Canada of 11 births per 1,000 (Statistics Canada, 2009).

While mortality declined in quite a pronounced and steady manner from the post-war period on, fertility did not. Evidence indicates that rather than dropping in the 1950s and 1960s, Aboriginal fertility actually increased somewhat over this period. For example, the crude birth rate among First Nations climbed to about 50 births per 1,000 during the 1950s and 1960s, while some evidence suggests that fertility among Inuit may have approached the phenomenal rate of almost 60 births per 1,000 at that time. Romaniuc (1981, 2000) has argued that the "natural rise in fertility" among these Aboriginal populations was due to rapid social change and modernization, a view that is contrary to classical "demographic transition theory," which asserts that modernization introduces a period of decline in both fertility and mortality.

Although the birth rate went up in the 1950s, this situation was relatively short-lived, and more recently, fertility among Aboriginal peoples has dropped in quite a pronounced manner (see Figure 8.5). From the early 1960s onward, the fertility of Aboriginal Canadians has been on a downward trajectory. While the available time series on First Nations and the Inuit indicate

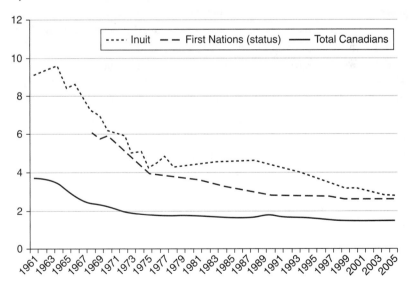

Figure 8.5 | Total Fertility Rates for Inuit, First Nations (Status), and Total Canadian Population, Canada, 1961–2005.

Sources: Statistics Canada (2008a); Nault et al. (1993); Loh et al. (1998); Robitaille and Choiniére (1985); Norris et al. (1995); Norris (2000); Ram (2004); Clatworthy (2009); Malenfant and Morency (2011).

that fertility has not fallen to levels as low as the below-replacement fertility of Canadians overall, by 2005, fertility rates had declined to levels of 2.6 and 2.7 births per woman respectively, as measured by the total fertility rate (TFR). In many ways, both in terms of the timing and level of childbearing, the gap in fertility outcomes between Aboriginal and other Canadians has lessened. While rates have stabilized somewhat over recent years, it is possible that Aboriginal fertility could continue its downward trajectory into the future.

Demographic Differences by Aboriginal Group

Fertility and Mortality

In light of the distinctive histories and characteristics of Canada's four major Aboriginal population groups—status and non-status First Nations, Inuit, and Métis—we should not be surprised that some important differences in mortality and fertility are found across these populations. Although all four groups have witnessed both mortality and fertility decline, the evidence suggests that this is true to a lesser extent among the Inuit and the status Indian populations.

Since non-status and Métis populations have the highest level of intermarriage with other Canadians, it makes sense that their demographic characteristics more closely resemble those of the larger population. Census data indicate that along a whole range of socio-economic variables, from education, labour force participation, and language used to place of residence, the non-status population and the Métis have much more in common with other Canadians than do either status First Nations people or Inuit. This is undoubtedly due to the fact that a majority of Inuit continue to live in remote northern regions and a significant proportion of status First Nations people continue to live on reserves and in some of Canada's more remote settlements. In contrast, both the non-status population and the Métis are more likely to live in urban areas or in non-Aboriginal communities, which means that they do not experience the same level of geographic and social segregation as First Nations and Inuit peoples.

Past estimates of mortality and fertility have consistently ranked Inuit as having the highest fertility and mortality. In turn, they are followed by the status population, who have higher fertility and mortality than either the Métis or the non-status population (Norris et al., 1995). According to a series of indirect estimates of fertility for 2001, the total fertility rate was about 3.21 children per woman for Inuit, 2.68 for status First Nations, and 2.15 for the Métis (Ram, 2004). A similar ranking is suggested by the limited information available on the state of population health, where Inuit and the status population are much more likely to be suffering from a serious illness, disability, or chronic disease.

Census data also indicate that fertility is lower among Inuit who live in southern Canada than among those in the North (Robitaille and Choinière, 1985). Similarly, the mortality and fertility of First Nations people living on reserves is higher than among those living elsewhere (Loh et al., 1998). Clearly, important differences exist in the demographic dynamics of the Aboriginal populations, not only varying by Aboriginal group but also by place of residence. In general, the demographic experience and behaviour of Inuit and First Nations people who have migrated from their home communities and more remote settlements into Canada's larger cities and towns more closely resemble that of the non-status and Métis populations.

Population Structure

In keeping with the differences in fertility, the age structure of Canada's Aboriginal population continues to be much younger than that of other Canadians. This implies a distinctive set of challenges and priorities. Age and sex influence the working of society in important ways, and Canadian society overall has witnessed important changes over recent decades as its population pyramid has become increasingly "top-heavy" due to the aging of the population. This is in contrast with the structure of the Aboriginal population, which has a large proportion of children and young adults (see Figure 8.6).

According to Statistics Canada's Population Estimates program, the median age[5] in Canada in 2011 was 40 years, which is 12.3 years older than the median age of 27.7 years among the Aboriginal identity population (Statistics Canada, 2013c). Furthermore, the median age of both First Nations people and Inuit is even younger: approximately 26 among the First Nations and 23 among Inuit (Statistics Canada, 2013b). The median age of the Métis is slightly higher at 31, though this is still almost a decade younger than for Canada overall. It is not an exaggeration to suggest that this situation has a profound impact on the health and social fabric of Aboriginal communities. A very young age structure (and a very high proportion of children) has important implications for living conditions and many societal institutions, and also represents a potential major force for social change into the future.

Specifically, while only 16.3 per cent of Canadians are under the age of 15, 28 per cent of the Aboriginal identity population is under 15. The highest percentage of population under 15 is found among Inuit, with 33.9 per cent of this population under the age of 15. At the other end of the age spectrum, it is

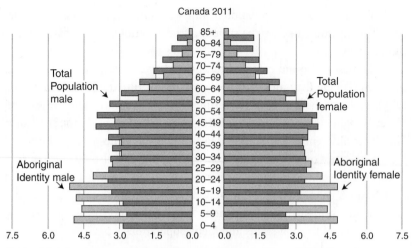

Canada 2011

Figure 8.6 | Percentage Distribution by Age Group and Sex of Total Canadian and Aboriginal Identity Populations, Canada, 2011.

Sources: Statistics Canada, 2011 National Household Survey; Statistics Canada (2013a, 2013b).

noteworthy that while about 1 in 7 Canadians (14.4 per cent) was 65 or older in 2011, about 1 in 17 (5.9 per cent) of Aboriginal Canadians were in this age group. The percentage of Inuit over 65 was 4.1 (Statistics Canada, 2013b).

In public policy debates surrounding the impact of age structure in the Canadian context, the issue of population aging is typically highlighted. The significant differences between the overall population structure of Canada and the population structures of Aboriginal peoples suggest why many issues of broader public concern in Canada are often completely out of line with the needs of Canada's Aboriginal peoples. The age structure of Aboriginal Canadians indicates a whole different set of priorities, from meeting the educational requirements of the young to assisting young adults and families as they attempt to establish themselves in the labour market or seek affordable housing. What is clear is that the role of the welfare state and government is very different in a young population than in a rapidly aging population. An acknowledgement of the underlying demographic situation of Aboriginal Canadians can assist in the development of informed policy that is fair to everyone living in this country.

Legislative Change as a Non-Conventional Growth Factor

The relatively recent development of higher-than-average fertility rates has contributed to rapid growth of the Aboriginal population in Canada. As was pointed out above, this rapid growth is due to a wide range of factors beyond simply high natural increase. For example, since populations are defined according to their cultural origins, the fact that people have become much more willing to report Aboriginal ancestry has had a direct effect on population numbers. Addressing the needs of these increasing numbers of Aboriginal persons, due to their changing and/or clarifying their identity, calls for consideration of a non-conventional growth factor—legislative reform.

Revisions to the Indian Act by the federal government have at times had an appreciable influence on the size and rate of growth of the First Nations population. A legislative change of some importance in this regard was made in 1985, when the Act was amended through Bill C-31 to restore Indian status to people (and their children) who had lost their status under certain provisions of previous legislation.[6] Bill C-31 has had a dramatic impact as 117,000 people were reinstated as "status Indians" between 1985 and 2007 (INAC, 2009). Since the total population of the status population is about 868,206 persons, according to 2011 figures, acknowledging the impact of this legislative change is fundamental if we are to understand the rate of growth and composition of this population. Moreover, a 2013 amendment to the Indian Act through Bill C-3 allows for the potential reinstatement of not only the children but also the grandchildren of women who had previously lost status (AANDC, 2013). The federal government has estimated that somewhere between 20,000 to 40,000 additional persons may become newly entitled to registration under this provision (INAC, 2009)

Clatworthy (2003) has argued that it is quite possible these legislative changes will actually reduce the total number of persons who qualify to be registered under the Indian Act over the long term, compared to what the situation would have been without such changes. This is in part because Bill C-31 has reformed the status-inheritance rules. Specifically, section 6 of Bill C-31 contains descent rules that specify two separate ways one can acquire status under the revised Indian Act: under either section 6(1) or section 6(2). Children born to parents who were both status Indians acquired entitlement under section 6(1). Children with one parent registered under section 6(1) and a non-registered parent acquired entitlement under section 6(2). But people with one non-registered parent and one parent registered under section 6(2) have not been entitled to Indian status from 1985 onward. In other words, the children and/or grandchildren of status Indians can lose status if there are two consecutive generations of out-marriage to non-status persons. To the extent that status Indians have children with persons without status, we can expect an increase in the number of children registered under section 6(2). Moreover, over the long term there will undoubtedly be an increase in the proportion of Aboriginal people who will not be eligible for Indian status at all, despite their Aboriginal ancestry and self-identity.

According to research projections by INAC (2000) on the effects of out-marriage, it was estimated that up to a quarter of all children born to status Indians living off-reserve would no longer be eligible for Indian status by as early as 2010. INAC also projected an increase in the proportion of all children in each subsequent generation who acquire entitlement under section 6(2) as opposed to section 6(1), which also means that a growing proportion of Aboriginal children will not qualify as status Indians. Without further amendments to the Indian Act, it is possible that the majority of Aboriginal children soon will not be recognized as having official Indian status.

Conclusion

We began this chapter by observing that Aboriginal Canadians have not shared equally in the affluence of Canadian society. Unemployment remains very high, housing is often substandard, and health care and education are often inadequate. This chapter then charted the demography of Aboriginal Canadians in terms of population size, fertility, and mortality, as well as some of the implications of recent trends. As other chapters of this book have examined the socio-economic conditions of Aboriginal peoples, our attention here has been focused on the demography of Canada's Aboriginal population.

Paying careful attention to the demographic dynamics of the Aboriginal population of Canada highlights a few important differences compared to the overall Canadian population. One is that the demographic behaviour and experience of Canadians is not the same for all segments of the population. Whereas fertility and mortality in Canada have fallen to unprecedented low levels with a steadily declining rate of natural increase, Aboriginal peoples continue to have above-replacement fertility and relatively high mortality along with a relatively high rate of natural increase. As a consequence, the age structure of Aboriginal peoples is dramatically different from that of other Canadians. As we noted above, this has important implications for the internal dynamics of Aboriginal communities and for the broader realm of public policy.

In addition, we have pointed out the enormous definitional challenges that demographers often face in conducting research. The conventional practice by most users of census or demographic data is to accept the census definitions and categories and then to make sense of whatever data or time series are available. Nonetheless, it should be appreciated that most classifications used in the census and the federal statistical system are in fact socially constructed composites that have arisen from a variety of historical and contemporary influences. Definitions of what it means to be Aboriginal have been incorporated into the legal infrastructure of Canadian society and have largely been imposed on Aboriginal peoples.

As Frideres and Gadacz (2012) note, the Indian Act granted the federal government of Canada the power to legally define who had Indian status. This continues to have significant economic and political consequences in the lives of Aboriginal people in Canada since some Aboriginal people consider themselves well represented by this definition while others do not. Consequently, there is much uncertainty in the demographic future of the Aboriginal peoples since it depends not only on demographic trends but also on various non-conventional growth factors such as legislative reform, intermarriage, identification with cultural origins, and the degree to which cultural continuity is maintained from one generation to the next. Various socio-economic, cultural, and political unknowns will have a direct impact on how people identify in the future, perhaps an even larger impact than strictly demographic factors. This observation is certainly of concern to many Aboriginal Elders, teachers, and political leaders who have an interest in maintaining symbols of culture and group identity.

While there are grounds for both optimism and pessimism, taking a longer-term view of the demographic development of Aboriginal peoples during the last half-century might be best understood as a period of demographic recovery with profound developments looming close on the horizon.

Discussion Questions

1. We reported that the Aboriginal population is very young relative to Canada as a whole. What are some of the public policy implications of this basic demographic reality?

2. As the Aboriginal population shifts from youth into working-age groups over the next 15 years, what impact do you think this will have on the issues facing Aboriginal people?

3. How does the population health of the Aboriginal population differ from that of other Canadians? Why is this the case, and what can be done about this problem?

4. It is projected that as First Nations people have children with persons who are not registered, a growing proportion of children of Aboriginal ancestry will eventually not be able to qualify for Indian status. How is this possible, and what effects do you think it will have on First Nations in Canada?

Further Reading

Andersen, Chris. 2014. *"Métis" Race, Recognition, and the Struggle for Indigenous Peoplehood*. Vancouver: University of British Columbia Press.

Kerr, Don, and Roderic Beaujot. 2015. *Population Change in Canada*, 3rd edn. Toronto: Oxford University Press.

Romaniuc, Anatole. 2000. "Aboriginal Population of Canada: Growth Dynamics under Conditions of Encounter of Civilizations." *Canadian Journal of Native Studies* 20: 95–137.

Trovato, Frank, and Anatole Romaniuk, eds. 2014. *Aboriginal Populations: Social, Demographic, and Epidemiological Perspectives*. Edmonton: University of Alberta Press.

White, J.P., J. Peters, D. Beavon, and P. Dinsdale, eds. 2010. *Aboriginal Policy Research*, vol. 10: *Voting, Governance, and Research Methodology*. Toronto: Thompson Educational Publishing.

Notes

1. In fact, most of those languages would have had less in common with each other than did the European languages that were establishing themselves on the eastern coast of North America at this time, all of which belonged to the same major linguistic family (Indo-European) with the exception of the linguistically isolated Basque language.

2. See Chapter 12 by Cooke and Long for a more extended discussion of pre- and post-contact health conditions.

3. These estimates of life expectancy (at birth) for the Métis are the authors', as roughly based on Tjepkema et al. (2009). While Tjepkema et al. estimated Métis life expectancy at age 25, it is possible to use indirect estimation procedures to roughly convert these estimates to life expectancy at birth (using available model life tables).

4. See Chapter 12 by Cooke and Long for a more extended discussion of population health.

5. "Median age" refers to the middle point of the total population at which half the population is older and half is younger, whereas average age is the sum of the ages of all persons in a population divided by the number of people in the population.

6. See Chapter 6 by Voyageur for a more extended discussion of how Bill-C-31 has affected Aboriginal women in particular.

9

Aboriginal Languages in Canada: Generational and Community Perspectives on Language Maintenance, Loss, and Revitalization

Mary Jane Norris

Ultimately it is through language that we not only preserve what we have but create and re-create that which is to come. And if we can ignite the fire of everyday life back into the language, we will no longer be racing against the clock, but instead trying to outrun the sun: the former quest is finite, the latter eternal.

Fillerup, 2000: 33, from Tompkins et al. (2013: 143)

Introduction

Ruptures from generation to generation in the maintenance and transmission of traditional languages have resulted in many of Canada's Indigenous languages being endangered today. Certainly Canada's Aboriginal communities differ widely, particularly in relation to the levels of vitality and endangerment of their languages. Some communities have focused their resources and efforts during the past 20 years to revitalize the use of traditional languages, though the languages of many other communities are currently endangered and even close to extinction. From a long-term and more international perspective, even the largest and most viable of Canada's Indigenous languages can be considered potentially "unsafe" or vulnerable (Norris, 2010).

Understanding why many Aboriginal languages in Canada have become endangered—or extinct—is a complex problem requiring examination of a wide variety of factors that affect the dynamics of language survival. These factors range from the historical pressures associated with the forces of colonization and the legacy of Canada's residential school system, to more recent developments involving urbanization, globalization, and the changing

demographic, socio-economic, geographic, cultural, and residential characteristics of Canada's Aboriginal populations over the past 50 years (Norris, 1998, 2010, 2011a, 2011b). As I argue in this chapter, generational and community perspectives are useful when studying the loss and revitalization of Aboriginal languages, particularly when these perspectives engage a people's history, the relationship between their identity and culture, and the health and well-being of their families and communities in reserve, rural, urban, and northern settings across Canada.

The following analysis of Aboriginal languages in Canada is comprised of roughly four parts. We begin with a general overview of the relationship between culture and language, paying particular attention to the relationship between European colonization and the loss of traditional Indigenous languages. We then consider the current state and diversity of Aboriginal languages in Canada as well as demographic analysis of patterns and trends of language acquisition and learning. We also examine some of the more pressing challenges facing those who are committed to the revitalization of Aboriginal languages across generations and communities. In the third and largest part of the chapter, a number of initiatives and ongoing developments supporting Aboriginal language revitalization in Canada are considered. We focus on initiatives that acknowledge the vital importance of Indigenous language in Aboriginal communities, culture, and identity, as well as those that seek to cultivate appreciation for the ways that Indigenous knowledge and language in education can contribute to the health and well-being of individuals, families, and whole communities. Included in this section is discussion of Perley's (2011) concept of "alternative vitalities," which highlights the development and use of alternative means of communication such as texts, recordings, historical accounts, and new media. This section also presents descriptions of a number of community-based language immersion programs and culturally based teaching programs that promote language survival and revitalization. The chapter concludes with thoughts on the outlook and prospects for the survival and revitalization Aboriginal languages in Canada, including the implications this revitalization has for cultural continuity and the health and well-being of future generations of Aboriginal peoples and their communities.

Factors Endangering Aboriginal Languages in Canada: From Colonization to Globalization

The current state of Aboriginal languages in Canada and the prospects for their revitalization vary considerably. Recent (Norris, 2013b) updates of UNESCO's *Atlas of the World's Languages in Danger* (Moseley, 2010) suggest that 90 different languages are currently spoken in Canada by First Nations, Inuit, and Métis peoples and that, in addition, three other languages, having recently become extinct, are no longer spoken as first languages. The many Aboriginal languages in Canada reflect a diversity of distinctive histories, cultures, and identities linked to family, community, the land, and traditional knowledge. While there is much evidence of Aboriginal language and cultural revitalization efforts across Canada (Norris, 2011a; Norris et al., 2013), those involved face the daunting task of addressing the continuing legacy of colonization and the challenges the larger mainstream society can pose for Aboriginal individuals, families, and communities in the survival of their languages, cultures, and identities. Furthermore, unlike other heritage languages in Canada, Aboriginal languages are generally indigenous to the country and cannot rely on immigration to maintain or increase their populations of speakers; hence their survival and maintenance depend on their transmission from generation to generation, since Aboriginal children are the future speakers of their languages (Norris, 1998).

A major consideration in understanding the devastating effects that language loss can have on Aboriginal cultures and identities for individuals, their families, and communities is that language is not just about speaking. All languages represent a way of thinking and perceiving the world that is interwoven with the knowledge, culture, and identity of a people. Language is a critical component in maintaining and transmitting cultural integrity and identity from generation to generation, and reflects a unique world view specific to the culture to which it is linked (Crystal, 2000; Norris 1998, 2000). Losing a language is thus not just losing a way of communicating: it is like losing a world. As Hale (1992) noted, "language embodies the intellectual wealth of the people who use it" (cited in Abley, 2003). Although loss of language does not necessarily lead to the death of a culture, it can severely handicap transmission of that culture. According to Fishman (1996: 81), "if you take language away from a culture, . . . you take away its greetings, its curses, its praises, its laws, its literature, its songs, its riddles, its proverbs, its cures, its wisdom, its prayers." Moreover, "you are losing all those things that essentially are the way of life. The way of thought, the way of valuing, and the human reality that you are talking about" (from Blair, 2013: 146).

Canada's formal education system has not been at all conducive to the maintenance of Aboriginal languages and cultures in this country. While the general approach to formal education in Canada has been based since its inception on a number of myths that cultivate highly individualistic attitudes among students (Carl and Belanger, 2012), government-sponsored residential schools have had a particularly devastating effect on Aboriginal children and their families and communities. Along with separating Aboriginal children from their families and denigrating the Indigenous knowledge embedded within traditional cultural practices, values, and ways of living, Aboriginal students were regularly and often severely punished for speaking their languages (Wesley-Esquimaux and Smolewski, 2004). Consequently, the residential school experience has had profound and lasting effects on the expression and transmission of Indigenous identity, culture, and traditional knowledge across generations of Aboriginal peoples (Hare, 2011).[1]

Scholars agree that the loss of Indigenous languages is a global phenomenon, and the causes and factors underlying the endangered state of these languages are numerous and complex. As Mosely (2010) notes, "it would be naïve and oversimplifying to say that the big ex-colonial languages, English or French or Spanish, are the killers and all smaller languages are the victims. . . . There is a subtle interplay of forces." Indeed, a multiplicity of forces—historical, societal, economic, geographic, and demographic—underlies the state of Indigenous languages. In this respect, while many in Canada point to the devastating consequences of colonization and the residential school system in relation to Aboriginal languages, other influences are also at play. For example, the fact that most Aboriginal languages were predominantly oral may also have diminished, in an already difficult environment, their chances of survival (Norris, 1998). The present-day force of mainstream languages, coupled with globalization and urbanization and their pervasiveness and un-relenting influence in everyday life, can significantly affect less widely used languages and their prospects for survival.

The continual exposure of Aboriginal people to the more dominant lan-guages and the pressure to use them in everyday life in school, work, and the marketplace has been a powerful catalyst in the decline of Aboriginal languages (Norris, 1998, 2007, 2008, 2011b). Furthermore, the challenges of language maintenance and survival can be exacerbated in an urban environ-ment, outside of Aboriginal communities. Over the past 30 years, many of Canada's Aboriginal languages have seen long-term declines in their inter-generational transmission as a mother tongue (or first language).

It is important to stress that many of the underlying factors affecting the transmission of an Aboriginal mother tongue from one generation to the next are related to its continued use as a major home language, especially on a daily basis—ideally, as one "spoken most often" in the home, as recommended by the Royal Commission on Aboriginal Peoples (RCAP, 1996). Yet within families and communities, various dynamics can affect home language use, such as: the life-cycle transition from youth into adulthood; residence within or outside Aboriginal communities, on reserves, or in urban areas; migration to and from reserves, Aboriginal communities, and urban areas; family forma-tion and linguistic out-marriage (exogamy) or parenting; and entry into the labour force (Norris, 1998).

Understanding Language Endangerment and Revitalization: From Conceptual Explanation to Demographic and Geographic Analysis

The UNESCO *Atlas of the World's Languages in Danger* regards intergenera-tional language transmission as the major factor in determining degrees of lan-guage endangerment. For most of Canada's Aboriginal languages in the *Atlas*, the level of intergenerational transmission is generally derived from census data based on estimates of the average age (in years) of the language's mother-tongue population (first-language speakers) in combination with the size of the given language's mother-tongue population (Moseley, 2010; Norris, 2009a).

The six categories of intergenerational transmission include:

i. Safe: The language is used by all ages, from children up, in all domains; intergenerational transmission is uninterrupted. (This category is not included in the *Atlas*, and none of Canada's Aboriginal languages fall in this category.)

ii. Vulnerable/unsafe (viable, but potentially endangered): The language is used by some children in all domains; but it may be restricted to certain domains (e.g., home).

iii. Definitively endangered: Children no longer learn the language as a mother tongue. The language is used mostly by the parental generation and up.

iv. Severely endangered: The language is used mostly by the grandparental generation and up; while the parental generation may understand it, they do not speak it to children or among themselves.

v. Critically endangered: The language is used mostly by very few speakers, of the great-grandparental generation, and they speak the language partially and infrequently.

vi. Extinct: No speaker of the language exists. (Languages in this category are included in the *Atlas* if they presumably have become extinct since the 1950s.) (Moseley, 2010)

Three main language variables from the Canadian census used to assess Aboriginal language vitality and endangerment include mother tongue, home language (spoken most often), and knowledge of, or ability to speak, an Aboriginal language. Four main demographic indicators developed from these variables for analysis include: (a) the size of the population with an Aboriginal mother tongue; (b) the index of continuity, as an indicator of intergenerational transmission based on home language spoken most often; (c) the average age of the mother-tongue population, an important indicator of the viability of a language; and (d) the index of second-language acquisition based on the ability to speak an Aboriginal language. This last indicator provides clues as to how the language was learned, either at home as a mother tongue or later in life as a second language.

On the whole, the 28 per cent of Aboriginal languages in Canada classified as vulnerable are still relatively healthy or viable since they are spoken as first languages by young as well as older generations of Aboriginal speakers. However, the other 72 per cent are endangered, which means that most Aboriginal children are no longer learning the traditional languages of their parents, grandparents, or great-grandparents as their mother tongues. As a result of long-term declines in home language use and mother-tongue transmission, an estimated 16 per cent of Aboriginal languages are now definitely endangered, another 19 per cent are severely endangered, and 37 per cent are critically endangered since they are only spoken partially or infrequently by a few in the older generations (Norris, 2010, 2011a).

The impact of the long-term erosion of Aboriginal languages from generation to generation is evident today as approximately 220,000 (19 per cent) of Canada's 1.2 million Aboriginal people who self-identified as First Nation, Métis, or Inuit in the 2006 census reported an Aboriginal language as their mother tongue. That more, 252,000 (21 per cent) of Aboriginal people, reported being able to converse in an Aboriginal language strongly suggests that other speakers had learned their traditional language as a second language. Five years later, the 2011 National Household Survey (NHS)[2] yielded somewhat similar contrasts, though with lower percentages: approximately 202,500 persons (14.5 per cent) of Canada's 1.4 million Aboriginal identity population reported an Aboriginal mother tongue, while approximately 241,500 (17.5 per cent) said they could converse in an Aboriginal language.

Also, just 12 per cent of Aboriginal people reported in the 2006 census that an Aboriginal language was the language they used most often at home, compared to the 19 per cent reporting an Aboriginal mother tongue. Similarly, 8.5 per cent of Aboriginal people reported in the 2011 NHS that they spoke an Aboriginal language most often at home, compared to 19 per cent reporting an Aboriginal mother tongue. Still, in other homes where an Aboriginal language is not spoken on a "most often" basis, an Aboriginal language can nevertheless still be spoken on a "regular" basis. For example, in 2006 an additional 5 per cent of Aboriginal people reported speaking an Aboriginal language on a regular basis at home, while that number almost doubled to 9.5 per cent in the 2011 NHS (Norris, 2013a). While regular home use of an Aboriginal language can contribute to its being learned and surviving, it is generally acknowledged that continued use as a major home language, especially on a daily basis, is critical to intergenerational language transmission (RCAP, 1996).

Children are obviously the major source of growth for the Aboriginal mother-tongue population in Canada, thanks in large part to relatively high fertility rates among the Aboriginal population in combination with intergenerational transmission.[3] Yet, the decreased use of Aboriginal languages in the home has significantly lowered the chances of children acquiring their traditional language as a mother tongue. This has resulted in long-term declines in intergenerational transmission and, for many endangered languages, declining mother-tongue populations. The index of continuity measures the prospects of transmitting a language as a mother tongue from one generation to the next by comparing the number of persons speaking the language "most often" at home to the number that have the language as their mother tongue (based on either

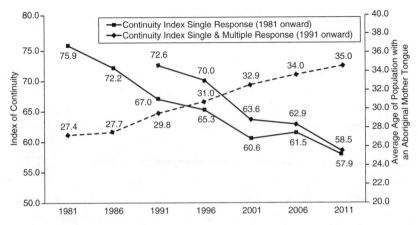

Figure 9.1 | Continuity of Aboriginal Languages and Average Age of Population with an Aboriginal Mother Tongue, 1981–2011.

Source: *Census of Canada*, 1981–2006, author's calculations from Norris and Snider (2008); 2011 NHS, author's calculations from Norris (2013a).

"single" or "single and multiple" responses to mother tongue and home language).[4] Data from the 2006 census and the 2011 National Household Survey included in Figure 9.1 indicate long-term erosion in major home language use. There was an overall decline in the index of continuity (single response) from a ratio of 76 persons speaking an Aboriginal language most often at home per 100 with an Aboriginal mother tongue in 1981 to 61 persons by 2006 (Norris and Snider, 2008). This was followed by a further decrease to 58 persons per 100 in 2011 (Norris, 2013a). Similar trends in the index of "single and multiple" responses saw declines from an index of 73 in 1991 to 63 in 2006 and 58.5 in 2011. Over the same period, data in Figure 9.1 illustrate an inverse trend of rising ages for the Aboriginal mother-tongue population, from an average age of 27.4 years in 1981 to 34 years by 2006 and 35 years in 2011.

Age composition trends in Figure 9.2 demonstrate an aging Aboriginal mother-tongue population with an ever-rising share of older people and a declining share of children and youth. Between 1986 and 2006, the share of older adults (age 55 and over) in the mother-tongue population increased from 12 per cent to 17 and 18 per cent in 2001 and 2006, respectively, while the share of children and youth (ages 0–19) fell from 41 per cent to just 32 per cent in 2006 (Norris and Snider, 2008). Data from the 2011 NHS suggest a continuation of these trends, with children and youth accounting for 30 per cent, and older adults 21 per cent, of the mother-tongue population.

As a result of long-term declines in major home use of Aboriginal languages, today's Aboriginal youth are much less likely than their elders to

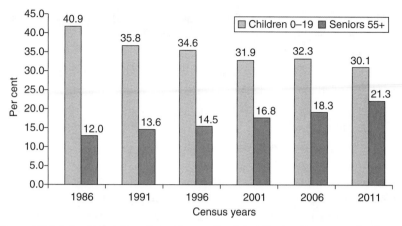

Figure 9.2 | Aging Populations Reporting an Aboriginal Mother Tongue, as the Shares of Children and Youth Decline.

Source: *Census of Canada,* 1981–2006, author's calculations from Norris and Snider (2008); 2011 NHS, author's calculations.

have an Aboriginal language as a mother tongue. In 2006, 33 per cent of Aboriginal people aged 65 and over reported an Aboriginal language as their mother tongue compared to just 15 per cent of children and youth. The 2011 NHS reveals similar contrasts but with even lower corresponding shares of 24 and 12 per cent, respectively. The relatively low proportion of mother-tongue/first-language speakers among Aboriginal children and youth in Canada means that the viability of many Indigenous languages in this country is in danger, for in general a language is considered endangered if it is not learned by at least 30 per cent of the children in a community (UNESCO, 1996: 23).

Differences between Endangered and Viable Languages in Their Home Language Use

Aboriginal languages vary significantly across Canada in their home language use and continuity. Intergenerational transmission and continuity are still relatively strong for viable languages such as Inuktitut,[5] which had a continuity index in 2011 of about 78 persons speaking Inuktitut at home for every 100 persons with an Inuktitut mother tongue. In contrast, many of the much smaller endangered languages, especially those in British Columbia such as Tlingit, Haida, and Wakashan, have an extremely low chance of being passed on to the younger generation as a first language. On the other hand, some small languages such as Attikamek and Montagnais-Naskapi show good prospects for intergenerational transmission with continuity indexes of around 90 (Norris, 1998; 2008, 2011a, 2011b).

Endangered and viable Aboriginal languages also differ in their demographic and geographic characteristics and patterns of home use. Mother-tongue populations of endangered languages are older than those of viable languages, and speakers of endangered languages are more likely than viable language speakers to be more urbanized and to marry or parent with people who do not speak an Aboriginal language (Norris, 2003). In homes where an endangered language is spoken, the language is more likely to be used on a "regular" basis but with a mainstream language (e.g., English or French) being spoken most often. In 2001, for example, only 10 per cent of those who spoke the endangered Haida language at home used it on a "most often" basis. In contrast, the more viable languages of Inuktitut and Cree were spoken most often by 82 per cent and 69 per cent, respectively, of their home language users (Norris and Jantzen, 2002; Norris, 2008).

Age is obviously an important indicator of the state and viability or endangerment of any language since the younger first-language speakers are, the healthier is their language. Figure 9.3 illustrates both the significant range in the state of the many different viable and endangered Aboriginal languages

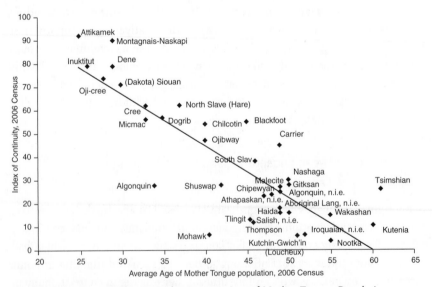

Figure 9.3 | Language Continuity by Average Age of Mother-Tongue Population, by Aboriginal Languages, Canada.

Note: n.i.e. = not included elsewhere

Source: 2006 Census, Statistics Canada, author's calculations from Norris (2011b: Table 1, 24).

and the strong relationship between language continuity and average age of the mother-tongue population.

High language continuity is associated with young mother-tongue populations, whereas low continuity is associated with old mother-tongue populations (Norris and Snider, 2008; Norris, 2011a, 2011b). Languages such as Inuktitut and Attikamek have average ages of mother-tongue populations of about 25 years and correspondingly high indexes of continuity. In contrast, Figure 9.3 indicates that more severely and critically endangered languages such as Haida and Wakashan, of which first-language speakers are of the grandparental and great-grandparental generations, respectively, have average ages around 50 years or older combined with very low continuity indexes (Norris, 2011a, 2011b).

Challenges in Revitalizing Aboriginal Cultures and Languages across Generations

Grenoble (2013) identifies attitudes as a key component of language vitality. In other words, positive commitment to language revival among youth, families, and communities can contribute to new connections across generations. Crystal (2000) notes that attitudes across generations about language ability and activities that may appear old-fashioned to youth or that involve a lowering of standards among older generations can result in internal conflict within a community. Crystal identified two attitudes towards the role of language in relation to cultural identity. One is that language is an obligatory feature of ethnicity and culture and the other is that it is an optional feature. Those who view language as obligatory see it as a necessary means by which a people express their history and cultural identity; that is, without language it is not possible to be a member of the community. In contrast, those who view language as optional and who see far more elements in culture than language affirm that it is possible for people to be community members and to contribute to the culture of their community even if they do not speak its language. Crystal argues that the former position tends to be held by those who speak the Indigenous language, while the latter view is supported by those who do not. Communities that adopt the obligatory view concentrate their revitalization activities on language itself; that is, on teaching and learning as well as training and resources. In contrast, language revitalization activities of communities that adopt the optional view tend to have a culture-first view. Community approaches towards language revitalization range between these two perspectives depending on the state of the language, available resources, and support.

In his study of the challenges in revitalizing the Maliseet language, Bernard Perley (2011) asked, "If Maliseet is no longer spoken, are we still Maliseet?" Perley explored his question by gathering accounts and narratives from different generations of Tobique community members, and his findings are consistent with Crystal's views on the obligatory and optional positions of the role of language in culture and identity. Specifically, Perley found that supporters of the obligatory stance in the community were more likely to be speakers of the Maliseet language, whereas those taking the optional position were more likely to be non-speakers. Perley (2011: 9) points to a problem with any definition of language that focuses on speaking in his assertion that "the simple definition of language death restricted to the spoken language precludes any possible alternatives that may contribute to the language revitalization (either in the present or as deferred to a future generation)." He further argues that "aboriginality, as a process of self-determination, will provide Maliseet language and identity advocates the opening to create alternative vitalities to ensure that future generations of Maliseet children will survive as Maliseet" (Perley, 2011: 183). As described in the following sections, a wide variety of initiatives across Canada indicate that many communities are committed to maintaining or revitalizing the language and culture of their people.

Generational and Community Perspectives on Language Learning among Aboriginal Youth

Trends indicating renewed interest in revitalizing Aboriginal languages among Aboriginal youth (Norris et al., 2013; Norris, 2008, 2011a) are good news not only for the survival of endangered languages, but also for bridging the connections across generations. Children and youth learning the endangered languages of their elders, particularly when these languages are severely or critically endangered, are often learning languages their own parents have never learned or do not speak. Yet, the ability to speak their endangered language also affords youth opportunities to communicate with grandparents and great-grandparents in their traditional language.

Aboriginal youth in general are considerably less likely than their elders to speak an Aboriginal language, and among youth who can speak, they are more likely than their elders to be second-language learners (Norris, 2003, 2007, 2008). In 2001, Aboriginal people under the age of 25 represented 38 per cent of the total Aboriginal mother-tongue population in Canada and approximately 45 per cent of second-language speakers. Consistent with this pattern, a much higher proportion of children and youth learned their traditional languages as a second language compared to speakers 65 years of age or over (Norris, 2006, 2007, 2008; Norris and Jantzen, 2002). Children most likely to learn an Aboriginal language as a second language tend to be from linguistically mixed families living in urban areas (Norris, 2003, 2007, 2008, 2011b; Norris and Jantzen, 2003). Young people in urban areas are significantly more likely to be second-language learners in contexts where intergenerational transmission is much less likely compared to their counterparts within Aboriginal communities, reserves, and settlements (Norris, 2011b; Norris and Jantzen, 2003).

From a demographic perspective, second-language learning is a critical counterbalance to mother-tongue decline and a necessary response for the revival of endangered languages. Unfortunately, many mother-tongue populations are aging beyond child-bearing years, and the ideal family and community conditions for mother-tongue transmission, that is, living within Aboriginal communities in families where both parents have an Aboriginal mother tongue, are becoming more the exception than the norm. In 2001, just over 10 per cent of Aboriginal children and youth lived in such "ideal" conditions (Norris, 2008, 2011a).

For this reason, many Aboriginal communities across Canada have been striving to preserve their traditional culture and languages by involving all generations of their members, as well as educators, teachers, and language planners and co-ordinators, in a variety of language activities and school programs. Second-language learning and language revitalization efforts appear to be a response to mother-tongue decline in those communities with waning intergenerational language transmission and aging mother-tongue populations (Norris, 2006, 2011a). Between 1996 and 2001, the proportion of communities where most Aboriginal speakers had learned the language as their mother tongue dropped from two-thirds to less than half, whereas the proportion of communities where most speakers had acquired it as their second language doubled from 8.5 to 17 per cent. Fully one-third of communities enumerated in 2001 could be classified as being in transition from a mother-tongue to a second-language population (Norris, 2006, 2007).[6]

Second-Language Learning of Endangered Languages

Viable and endangered languages are similar in their patterns of younger second-language learners and older first-language learners, with second-language learners accounting for higher proportions of speakers in the younger age groups. However, these generational contrasts are much more pronounced with endangered languages, as illustrated in Figure 9.4. Second-language learners constitute the majority of endangered language speakers,

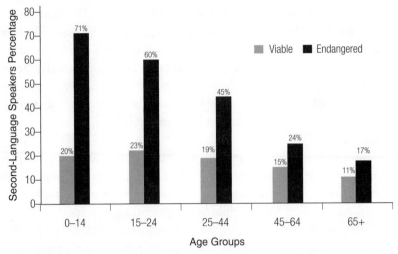

Figure 9.4 | Second-Language Learners in Younger Age Groups: The Majority of Those Who Speak Endangered Languages, Total Aboriginal Languages, Canada, 2001.

Source: *Census of Canada*, 2001, author's calculations from Norris (2007).

with 71 per cent of children under the age of 15 being able to speak an endangered language in 2001. This is in contrast to the 20 per cent of children who could speak a viable language. On the other hand, contrasts in second-language learning between viable and endangered languages are much less pronounced among older generations since older speakers of both viable and endangered languages are more likely to have learned their language as a mother tongue (Norris, 2007, 2008, 2011a).

The language development of today's Aboriginal youth has significant implications for the future prospects of Canada's Aboriginal languages, particularly endangered ones. The rise in second-language acquisition among the growing youth population is promising, given the long-term decline in language continuity and natural transmission of endangered languages. Young second-language learners are also an increasingly important segment of those who speak an endangered language, and their contribution is critical to the growth and long-term viability of many endangered languages (Norris, 2011a, 2007).

Secondarily Surviving Languages

In the event that second-language learning contributes to the survival of a language with no first-language speakers, such languages are best described as "secondarily surviving" languages rather than extinct. Second-language learning has special relevance to the future prospects of critically endangered languages, in both Canada and the United States because "most efforts among North American Indians to preserve some knowledge of their traditional languages have focused on second language learning.... Since many of the North American languages that are on the verge of extinction as first languages are often associated with (often vigorous) heritage communities it can be anticipated that the number of secondarily surviving languages will grow considerably in the next few decades" (Hinton, 2001, from Golla in Moseley, 2007). Current trends in revitalization and second-language learning of endangered Aboriginal languages in Canada suggest that even as the few remaining elderly first-language speakers of critically endangered languages pass away, many of these languages may not necessarily become extinct but rather be sustained as secondarily surviving languages through younger generations of second-language speakers (Norris, 2011a).[7]

The more critically endangered the language, the greater the likelihood that its continuation will rely on second-language learning as a secondarily surviving language. Similarly, in communities where traditional languages are endangered, the greater the degree of endangerment, the greater is the necessity to learn the language as a second language, as illustrated in Figure 9.5. In communities where traditional languages are not endangered,

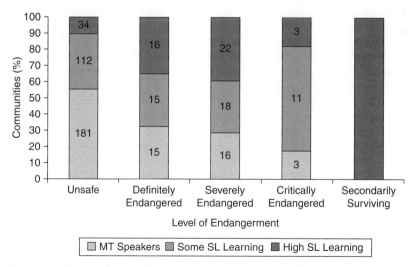

Figure 9.5 | First- and Second-Language Learning in Communities with Speakers, by Degree of Endangerment.

Source: *Census of Canada*, 2001, author's calculations, adapted from Moseley (2010) and Norris (2009b).

second-language learning accounts for less than 45 per cent of the main form of language acquisition; on the other hand, it represents an increasingly larger share of language learning in endangered language communities, where rates rose from 56 per cent in communities with languages that are "definitely endangered" to 71 and 83 per cent of "severely endangered" and "critically endangered" communities, respectively (Norris, 2011a).

Aboriginal Language Revitalization in Canada: Attitudes, Benefits, Initiatives, and Ongoing Developments

Intergenerational and Community Attitudes and Approaches to Learning and Maintaining Aboriginal Languages

Findings from the Aboriginal Peoples Survey (APS) conducted since 1991 suggest that the survival and maintenance of traditional languages is important to all generations of Aboriginal people. In 1991, nine in 10 Aboriginal adults stated that they wanted to relearn the Aboriginal language they once knew, while the great majority of Aboriginal adults and nearly three-quarters of urban residents who never spoke an Aboriginal language stated that they wanted to learn one. The 2001 APS also indicated that speaking an Aboriginal language was important to all generations of Aboriginal people (Norris, 2007; Statistics Canada, 2003: 32).

Second-language acquisition by today's Aboriginal youth reflects their increasing interest and desire in learning their traditional languages and in having opportunities for renewal and support. Even in the case of relatively strong languages like Inuktitut, Inuit youth say they do not want to lose their ability to speak Inuktitut well, and that they recognize the importance of receiving support through family and community members as well as those involved in their formal education (Cloutier, 2013; Tulloch, 2005, 2008). Relatedly, Morris and Mackenzie's (2013) study of three Innu communities in Labrador demonstrated the importance of raising awareness of language loss within a community. These researchers helped implement a program involving the dual language assessment of Innu children, and they found that in terms of contributing positively to school success, simply conducting tests in both Innu and French led to more collaboration and exchange between Innu and non-Innu staff in all three communities. Awareness and interest about the Innu language and its degree of endangerment was heightened; and, as well Innu speakers became trained in testing and test development. The researchers expressed hope that such outcomes would "ensure sustainability in the future" (Morris and Mackenzie, 2013: 175).

Family and community play a critical role in the transmission of language from parent to child, affecting whether a child learns the Aboriginal language as a mother tongue or as a second language. On their own, neither family capacity nor community support is sufficient to ensure the adequate transmission of an Aboriginal mother tongue. Many Aboriginal children, particularly those living in urban areas or with an endangered linguistic heritage, have generally not experienced ideal conditions for learning an Aboriginal mother tongue—i.e., they have not lived within an Aboriginal community or in a family where both parents have an Aboriginal mother tongue (Norris, 2011a, 2011b).

Fortunately, it appears that there is strong interest in revitalization among all generations, even if a language is endangered with almost no possibility of intergenerational transmission. Parent–child patterns of language transmission from the 2001 census suggest that many Aboriginal parents want to ensure their children have at least some knowledge of their endangered ancestral language. For example, while 70 per cent of children with Salish-language parentage could speak their endangered language, 90 per cent had learned it as a second language and the remaining 10 per cent had acquired it as a mother tongue (Norris and MacCon, 2003).

To foster language learning, whether as a mother tongue or as a second language, it is important that youth have access to sources of learning in various domains such as home, school, and work. In addition, opportunities and supports to use their language are important whether they live in an Aboriginal community on a reserve or a settlement or even in an urban area. While APS results reinforce the importance of parents and home use of languages, they also point to other important sources of learning for children, including their extended families of aunts, uncles, and grandparents as well as schoolteachers and other community members. Generally the more sources children have for help in learning their Aboriginal language, the better they fare in terms of the degree of difficulty they experience in understanding the language. According to the 2001 APS, in Aboriginal communities where children receive help from only one major source, 80 per cent have difficulty understanding the language. In communities where children receive help from many different sources (parents, grandparents, aunts and uncles, teachers, and other persons), on average just under 30 per cent have low proficiency in understanding the language (Norris, 2011a).

Also, while children most often learn Aboriginal languages from parents and grandparents, their influence and that of others vary considerably depending on place of residence and the language ability of their older family members. For example, Winnipeg has the largest number of people with an

Aboriginal mother tongue of any Canadian city and the largest proportion of Aboriginal adults with the ability to speak an Aboriginal language very well or relatively well; on the other hand, only a minority of Toronto's Aboriginal adults in the parental and grandparental generations can speak an Aboriginal language. These contrasts in language ability are reflected in the cities' different learning sources for children in 2001. In Winnipeg, 52 and 54 per cent of children received help from parents and grandparents respectively, whereas only 6 per cent received help from teachers and 18 per cent from other persons. In sharp contrast, 39 per cent of children learning an Aboriginal language in Toronto received help from teachers and a full 62 per cent received language support from other persons (Norris, 2011a, 2011b).

Benefits of Language Revitalization: Contributions to Health and Well-Being of Individuals, Families, and Communities

Studies suggest that the very process of learning an Aboriginal language may also contribute to increased self-esteem among youth, community healing and well-being, and cultural continuity (Ball, Moselle, and Moselle, 2013; Ball, 2009; Chandler, 2006; Chandler and Lalonde, 2008; Canadian Heritage, 2005; Tulloch, 2008). Children, parents, grandparents, and great-grandparents who are working together to preserve and revitalize their language understand that they are also strengthening relations across the generations throughout their communities and contributing to the health and well-being of individuals, their families, and communities.

Ongoing initiatives in Aboriginal language revitalization are not unique to Canada, as noted by Sarkar et al. in their Mi'gmaq language revitalization initiative, which is "a local manifestation of a worldwide movement among Indigenous peoples to reclaim aspects of their 'ways of knowing, being and doing' brought under threat by centuries of colonization" (Sarkar et al., 2013: 40; see also Grenoble and Whaley, 1998; Hinton and Hale, 2001; Martin, 2003).

A review of the literature on language education and cultural identity in Tompkins et al. (2013) also illustrates the positive impact of Indigenous language education on the "cultural and ethnic self-affirmation" and the identity of young people. Francis and Reyhner (2002: 13) observe that by "taking on the task of learning and perfecting one's indigenous language, young people resist *the externally imposed conditions for integration into the broader society.*" Further to this, Andrea Bear Nicholas (2001) claims that communities who engage mother-tongue or Aboriginal language instruction "are engaging in the single most important act of self-determination possible, since language, culture and identity are inextricably interwoven." Wright and Taylor (1995) also found a positive effect on the personal and collective self-esteem of Inuit students from early ancestral language education, while "Ball and Simpkins (2004) suggest that such self-knowledge and pride can even counter the effects of racism" (from Tompkins et al., 2013: 139–40).

Language Revitalization Initiatives within Communities: Links with Culture, Identity, Traditional Knowledge, and Well-Being

Aboriginal communities across Canada are attempting to address the challenges of reviving their endangered languages in a number of ways, including community-led language immersion programs in conjunction with university–First Nation collaborations (Norris et al., 2013). Others are incorporating such "alternative vitalities" as stories, texts, recordings, historical accounts, and new communication technologies (Perley, 2011). Here we focus on initiatives within a few communities that have sought to preserve and revitalize their traditional languages, cultures, and identities. In the process, they have bridged connections across generations and enhanced community well-being. As in Canada overall, the communities and their languages highlighted here vary in terms of the degree of language endangerment as well as their experience of language loss, maintenance, and revitalization.

Case #1: The Halkomelen (Hul'qumi'num) Community of Cowichan: Generations Preserving Their Traditional Language, Culture, Identity, and Traditional Knowledge

The reserve community of Quw'utsun, which is part of the Cowichan First Nation in British Columbia, is striving to preserve and revive its severely endangered Salish language of Halkomelen (hul'qumi'num). The average age of the population that speaks Halkomelen as a first language is 50 years.

Statistics from the 2006 census suggest that second-language learning among Cowichan youth is well underway in this community. In both 2001 and 2006, more people could speak Halkomelen than had it as a mother tongue, whereas in 1996 those who knew their language were all older first-language speakers. While Halkomelen was the mother tongue of 18 per cent of youth by 2006,[8] nearly 25 per cent had the ability to carry on a conversation in that language. This is a significant development, for youth are playing an increasingly significant role in the revitalization of the community's language. Although youth represented almost half of the community's population of 1,800, they accounted for almost 70 per cent of the community's second-language speakers in 2006.[9] Clearly, both young and old Cowichan members recognize that preserving a traditional Indigenous language is more than just preserving words. Rather, it is about maintaining the links between language, identity, and the land (Blythe and McKenna Brown, 2003) in ways that enable older generations to share their knowledge of the land and community history.

Both the community Elder Arvid Charlie and his nephew Chuck Seymour, the language co-ordinator for the Cowichan Tribes, agree on the importance and salience of language in shaping and maintaining culture, identity, and traditional knowledge. As noted by Norris (2011a), while Elder Arvid Charlie believes that learning the language of one's people through Elders' teachings is essential to maintain one's culture and identity, his younger nephew emphasizes the value of language as indispensable to correctly interpret and maintain traditions, teachings, and traditional knowledge:

> If you don't know your language, you lose your culture and your identity. We need to keep our identity.... I hope one day that our language will come back and, along with it, our culture and teachings. This is my dream that one day we'll be speaking fluently and that all our teachings, all our sacred values will come back and be alive. (Arvid Charlie, community Elder)
>
> Our traditions are maintained through the use of our language. I heard another uncle of mine say younger people misinterpret teachings because we don't understand the language, and I say "we" because I am of the same age of a number of people who don't understand the language. So it has to be driven home, and that's where we need to focus is with some of the young adults. Kids, they pick it up, no problem. (Chuck Seymour, language co-ordinator for the Cowichan Tribes)

In the case of severely or critically endangered languages, members of the parental generation either have not learned their language as children or do not generally speak their traditional language due to past discouragement from learning or using their languages, or, in the case of residential school survivors, they were prohibited from or punished for speaking their languages. Thus, parents whose children learn their ancestral language often feel a great sense of pride and hope for the future (Norris, 2008). The sentiments expressed in the following comment by a Cowichan parent and shared by many in the community reinforce findings noted earlier: that the revitalization of Aboriginal languages contributes to family and community well-being and bonding (Norris, 2011a).

> We've lost so much, so much of that has been taken away from us with residential schools that this feels like a complete circle in that our youth now can learn the language of our elders and carry that on because there are whole generations that have lost out on that, that's been stripped from

them and stolen from them. So to have our young ones starting to learn that and be fluent in that, it's just wonderful to see, and it's healing for our community. (Comment of Cowichan parent in Norris, 2011a: 139)

Case #2: Maliseet Community of Tobique: Generations of "Being"
Maliseet—The Roles of Language, Culture, and Identity
In his ethnographic study of the Maliseet people, anthropologist Bernard Perley (2011) explored the relationship between the traditional Maliseet language and Maliseet identity among members of his own community, the Tobique First Nation in New Brunswick. According to the UNESCO *Atlas*, the Maliseet language (also known as Malecite, Wolostokwiok, or Wolastoqi) is considered to be definitely endangered with an average age of almost 40 years for its mother-tongue population.

Perley grouped his community interviewees into four broad generational categories: elders who are in their mid-sixties and up; older adults in their forties to mid-sixties; young adults in their twenties and thirties; and school-age youngsters in elementary and high school. Perley assessed the extent of the skills, knowledge, and use of the Maliseet language of each generation relative to the three factors of their Maliseet identity: language, blood, and Aboriginality. These aspects of Maliseet identity incorporate Maliseet language and world view, Aboriginal identity formation as a process promoting self-determination, and the politics of mixed-blood and "blood quantum." Maliseet identity is complicated by the impact of "Indian Act" legislative amendments on band membership rules, which, as for most First Nations, require entitlement to Indian registration (though a minority adopt other rules, such as "blood quantum" (Clatworthy, 2003)).

While a complete summary of Perley's findings is beyond the scope of this chapter, some key points highlight the complexity of the relationship between language and identity as well as some of the implications of language loss and revival across generations.

Elders: While elders varied in their language skills, knowledge, and use and their degree of language involvement, all contribute to the preservation of Maliseet in different ways. Some elders collect stories, attempt translations, and produce textual materials for community use. Although most elders, some now in their sixties, can still use the language for communication and have successfully transferred it to their own children, they recognize the necessity of often shifting between Maliseet and English in their conversations with younger generations to ensure effective communication.

Older Adults: While all adults in this study spoke Maliseet as their first language, they tended to speak with varying degrees of proficiency. While as children they witnessed language use in all social domains, being the generation that experienced language shift they experienced fewer and fewer contexts as adults in which Maliseet was the preferred language of communication. Perley regards this generation as the one most likely to experience the "tip" towards the demise of the Maliseet language, and with that, complications in the relationship among language, world view, blood, and identity, as well as diminished intergenerational transmission of Maliseet to their own children. Their offspring, now the community's young adults who were more likely to have acquired English as their first language, offer a differing view on the role of language in Maliseet identity.

Young Adults: The young adults of the community had limited knowledge of the Maliseet language. While they were familiar with some phrases and vocabulary, they could not speak the language for communicative purposes. For this generation, language tended to be "the common weakness in their Maliseet identity options" such that living in community on the reserve was a more important factor for one's Maliseet identity than being able to speak the Maliseet language.

Youngsters: The first language of children on the reserve is English. Although children living on reserve are taught their traditional language in the community's elementary school, downtown schools provide fewer opportunities for children to learn their language. Perley found that divisions were created between children with different school experiences when some of the young girls who had learned the Maliseet language used it as an identity marker that left the other girls unresponsive and excluded. He noted the increasing presence of Aboriginality through the social and cultural domains of both home and school settings, where children, with the help of parents, teachers, and friends, were learning to work together in creative ways to (re)define what it meant to be Maliseet.

Perley makes the point that "alternative vitalities" apart from the speaking aspect of languages, such as texts, recordings, and historical accounts, can be important tools for the revitalization of endangered languages. In his discussion of emergent vitalities of language, culture, and identity, he stresses how and why the Maliseet language needs to be reintegrated into the lives of community members:

> The life of the Maliseet language depends upon its reintegration into the lives of the Maliseet people. If the Maliseet language is reinstated in its role as the mediator for Maliseet culture, Maliseet identity, and everyday conversations, then we can celebrate the life of the Maliseet language and the survival of Maliseet identity for generations to come. (Perley, 2011: 200)

Case #3: Wolastoqi (or Maliseet) Community of Tobique and the
Mi'kmaw Community of Eskasoni: Language Immersion Programs
and Student Identities

Another example of current language developments within communities are language immersion programs for the Mi'kmaw and Wolastoqi (or Maliseet) languages within the two Atlantic Canada First Nation communities of Tobique, New Brunswick, and Eskasoni, Nova Scotia. According to the UNESCO *Atlas*, Mi'kmaw is a vulnerable language while Malecite (or Maliseet Wolostokwiok) is considered to be definitely endangered. On average, mother-tongue speakers of Mi'kmaw are much younger than those of Wolastoqi (or Maliseet), with average ages of 31 and almost 40 years, respectively.

In their research, the team of university and First Nation researchers and teachers—authors Joanne Tompkins, Anne Murray-Orr, Sherise Paul-Gould, Starr Sock Roseanne Clark, and Darcie Pirie—assessed the impacts of immersion on students by exploring the links between language and identity, educational success, career opportunities, lifelong learning, and contributions to community among the youth. They found that significant positive change was achieved through a model of education that incorporates Indigenous knowledge, language, and culture:

> The programs at Eskasoni and Tobique demonstrate the capacity of schools, which have for too long been vehicles of assimilation and cultural loss, to become places where Aboriginal identities and languages can flourish. The results of this study support the claim that Indigenous immersion programs are an obvious choice for communities wishing to stabilize and revitalize the Indigenous languages. (Tompkins et al., 2013: 143)

Tompkins et al. explored the impacts of the community-implemented immersion programs in three key areas: students' fluency in the Aboriginal language, student identities as Mi'kmaw or Wolastoqi, and academic achievement in other subjects. The researchers found strong evidence of links between language and identity, educational success, career opportunities, lifelong learning, and community contributions, even for students who were up to five years out of the program. Their findings reflected growing recognition of the importance of traditional languages in the educational success and well-being of Aboriginal children (Ball, Moselle, and Moselle, 2013; McIvor, 2013; Guèvremont and Kohen, 2012; Ball, 2009).

Language is significant for cultural identity and belonging and in securing children's long-term academic, economic, and social success. As noted by

Demmert (in Ball, Moselle, and Moselle, 2013: 3): "Aboriginal language and cultural programs, and student identification with such programs, are associated with improved academic performance, decreased dropout rates, improved school attendance rates, decreased clinical symptoms, and improved personal behaviour of children."

Ball stresses that children who experience culturally appropriate language learning programs are more able to communicate well across generations in their families and communities. She notes: "Programs that help Aboriginal children learn their heritage language, rather than treating European-heritage language skills as normative, can support their cultural identity formation, cultural knowledge and connectedness with their cultural community" (Ball, 2009: 39). Consequently, Ball recommends that a national strategy for supporting Aboriginal early language development should support the "implementation and evaluation of culturally grounded approaches developed in consultation with families and communities as demonstration projects" (Ball, 2009: 41). In a discussion on the critical role women play in the continuity and revitalization of Aboriginal cultures and languages within families and communities, Norris (2009b) points to the increasing recognition within Aboriginal education of the need for an education that acknowledges the importance of language and cultures, the strengthening of Aboriginal identity and the participation of elders and women.[10]

Case #4: Mi'gmaq Community of Listuguj: Language Revitalization Initiative Using Generation-based Indigenous Research Paradigm
Our last example of community-based language developments is the revitalization of the Mi'gmaq language in the community of Listuguj, Quebec. In an innovative initiative by the Listuguj Education Directorate (LED), a team of local instructors, native speakers, and researchers from McGill University—Mela Sarkar, Janine Metallic, Beverly Baker, Constance Lavoie, and Teresa Strong-Wilson—is working to revive the community's language, which appears to be more endangered in Listuguj than in Eskasoni. "The proportion of fluent speakers of Mi'gmaq in the community of Listuguj is less than 20 per cent and dropping" (Sarkar et al., 2013: 39). They note that they found only a few fluent speakers under the age of 60. Sarkar et al. used a participatory action research orientation, with Listuguj community members taking the lead in their language revitalization initiatives, including an early-years Mi'gmaq immersion project, a teacher education program for adult learner-speakers of an Indigenous language who wish to start learning circles in their own communities, and a participatory evaluation component for the adult language classes to help generate new community-based assessment practices.

Sarker et al. report that all participants in their project learned to combine Indigenous and Western ways of knowing, being, and doing through their discussions with members of the Listuguj community. Their application of the traditional Mi'gmaq eight-pointed star design gave appropriate direction for each new phase of the project, and incorporating a generational perspective in the community's Language Revitalization Initiative highlighted the important and ongoing role played by all community members in the revitalization of the Mi'kmaq language. The researchers noted that collaboration in multi-literacies pedagogy and language assessment practices was especially critical since it honoured the place of Indigenous knowledges and practices within Listuguj's Mi'gmaq culture.

Practically everyone in the community of Listuguj is committed to helping to create new speakers of Mi'gmaq. According to one community member, "The ultimate goal of our initiative is to create younger second-language speakers of Mi'gmaq, who will then also be able to help ... pass on the language to future generations as teachers, parents or both" (Sarkar et al., 2013: 40). Another community member stated that their hope over the next five years of working together was that it would "be possible to report that substantial numbers of new speakers of Mi'gmaq are carrying the language forward to community language status in Listuguj" (Sarkar et al., 2013: 44).

Alternative Vitalities; Cultural Approaches; New Technologies and Media

Aboriginal people of all ages and from all locations are embracing the use of new technologies, media, and curricula in the preservation and revitalization of their endangered languages. Proceedings from the 2013 Foundation for Endangered Languages (FEL) conference held in Ottawa (Norris, Anonby, Junker, Ostler, and Patrick, 2013) highlighted a wide variety of community connections, collaborative approaches, intergenerational initiatives, cultural, technological, and social media-related innovations, and community–researcher alliances, both within Canada (some of which have already been discussed here) and internationally. One group of researchers noted that using new language technologies to secure the usability of minority languages over the Internet would raise the profile of endangered languages in the eyes of the younger, digitally oriented generation. They also noted increased use of a variety of mother-tongue languages in social media, on YouTube, and in text messaging and various other technologies and blogs by members of the younger generations (Soria, Zoli, and Mariani, 2013).

Various Aboriginal language and cultural organizations throughout Canada, such as British Columbia's First Peoples Cultural Council (FPCC), are also working directly with First Nation communities to preserve and revitalize

Indigenous languages. As part of developing strategies that help communities recover and sustain their languages and cultural heritage, the FPCC encourages the development and use of a wide range of alternative vitalities as well as language-specific developments. Some examples of FPCC initiatives and collaborations include:

- *FirstVoices* (http://www.fpcc.ca/language/FirstVoices) is an online Indigenous language archiving and teaching resource (e.g., dictionaries, alphabets, songs, stories, words, and phrases as well as audio and video) developed by Elders and youth to enable Indigenous communities to document their language for future generations.
- *Endangered Languages Project* (www.endangeredlanguages.com), an online resource for accessing, recording, and sharing samples of and research about endangered languages across the globe, also provides advice and best practices for those working to document or strengthen Indigenous languages.
- *Our Living Languages Exhibition* (http://royalbcmuseum.bc.ca/our-living-languages/), a three-year exhibition, opened on Aboriginal Day, 21 June 2014. In this exhibition, the FPCC and the Royal BC Museum are showcasing the diversity of the 34 First Nations languages in British Columbia, celebrating the communities who are working hard to ensure these languages continue to be vital, and providing support and encouragement to efforts by increasing understanding of the complexities of language revitalization.

Beck and Hess (2014) discuss another major west coast initiative that blends alternative vitalities and traditional stories of Elders. *Tellings from Our Elders* is a compilation of the recording and transcription of the stories of the Coast Salish people in Snohomish, which is a dialect of Lushootseed,[11] the language of the Indigenous peoples who live on the southern and eastern shores of Puget Sound. The stories of the Elders, who are members of the last generation to claim the language as their mother tongue, provide a wealth of cultural and linguistic information and crucial resources that are essential to cultural revitalization and for creating strategies for language use.

Generations Preparing for the Future

Many communities trying to preserve and revitalize their traditional languages are confronted not only with the task of preserving the words of the traditional language but also with the challenge of creating new vocabulary so that the language can be used in the day-to-day world of home, school, work, and the marketplace. The processes of language preservation, maintenance, and revitalization also require the application of new technology in documentation, development, and delivery of language references and school curricula. Often, the challenges of these language activities require the input of both the oral traditions of the older generations and the skills of everyone in the community. This was demonstrated in the Cowichan community, which saw all generations collaborate in the development of a variety of resources to learn traditional language vocabulary (Norris, 2011a).

School and community initiatives that invite Aboriginal children to learn their traditional language as a second language at school will encourage them to take responsibility to pass on their traditional language to the next generation. This task will certainly not be without its challenges given the various factors that can erode home use of their traditional language, such as migration from Aboriginal communities, linguistic intermarriage, and the prevailing influence of English and French in daily life (Norris, 2007). Furthermore, the nature of the challenges they will face as parents in transmitting their traditional language will also depend on various factors: how they themselves learned their language, whether as a mother tongue or second language; their degree of fluency; whether they speak their language in the home and whether they speak it as a "major home language" or just on a "regular" basis; as well as opportunities to speak the language within the community (Norris and Jantzen, 2003; Norris, 2008).

Given the prevailing influence of English and French throughout mainstream mass media, popular culture, and other aspects of their daily lives in school or work, Aboriginal youth of today must understand and speak at least one of these languages. At the same time, learning their traditional language can help ground their identity by fostering family ties, strengthening community relationships, and preserving historical links (Crystal, 2000; Norris, 2007, 2008). In her study of Inuit youth and their language, Tulloch (2008) explains that "language brings and binds community members together. Without it some Inuit feel disconnected; they miss acceptance and the opportunity to participate fully in their community." In the case of language loss or declining fluency, "Breakdowns in language competence are linked to interruptions in the social network," while in the case of revitalization, "increased language competence can result in increased opportunities for community engagement. Learning their traditional language is not a luxury for youth any more than communicating with one's parents and grandparents, knowing where one comes from and being able to gain the kind of education one values" (Tulloch, 2008: 73–5). As Fonda (2009: 76) notes, youth learning their traditional language is an essential contributor to social capital and cohesion.

Further evidence of the significance of Indigenous language and culture in Aboriginal children's wellness, education, and opportunities for quality of life is also found in results from the First Nations Regional Health Surveys (FNRHS). In summarizing their findings, the FNRHS authors make it clear "that strategies aimed at improving community wellness for First Nations youth must be tied to First Nations identity, self-esteem, and cultural continuity and that they must emphasize family and social cohesion within First Nations communities" (cited in Ball, Moselle, and Moselle, 2013: 14).

The need for culturally grounded language learning initiatives and the contribution of all generations in preserving and revitalizing traditional languages raises a number of important and challenging questions, particularly given the pressure in a socially mediated age to know and communicate almost exclusively in English. For example, how appropriate is the application of a technology for language learning that has been developed outside of the cultural context or setting in which it is implemented, particularly if it has been developed without the input of Aboriginal teachers or Elders? What are the consequences of children attempting to learn a language in isolation from its particular culture, traditions, and community of origin? Can culturally appropriate and/or land-based knowledge be properly acquired within urban and/or socially mediated settings? And, to what extent can secondarily surviving endangered languages contribute to cultural continuity, identity, and traditional knowledge?

Concluding Remarks

Indigenous languages matter to Indigenous people. They matter spiritually, culturally, socially and economically. (Tompkins et al., 2013: 139)

It is becomingly increasingly clear that Indigenous language learning is vital to the health and well-being of individuals, families, and communities as a whole. It is also evident that culturally based curricula contribute in significant ways to the overall well-being and educational success of Aboriginal students. Current curricular initiatives in schools are giving hope to many that language revitalization and maintenance will continue for generations to come. At Koksilah Elementary school, for example, Cowichan children are taught their language by members of the community for 30 minutes every day using a curriculum developed by the First Nation. Nearly 800 students are now part of the program. People in the community recognize that their children are the future, and that it is critical for them to learn the language well enough, especially as second-language speakers, to ensure a healthy future for their language and their community.

> The people here know that if hul'qumi'num is to survive, this generation of learners will have to pass on their knowledge to the next. For that to happen successfully, a lot more effort is required. Some here dream of a hul'qumi'num immersion program in the schools. That means developing advanced curriculum and more language instructors. (Duncan McCue, CBC reporter, in Norris, 2011a: 139)

Information from interviews with Elders, teachers, parents, and other community members in Eskasoni and Tobique highlights how and why they view Mi'kmaw and Wolastoqi language learning among the children in their communities as vitally important (Tompkins et al., 2013). Elders spoke about the sacredness of the language and their moral obligation to pass it on to the next generation as an integral part of their Mi'kmaw identity. As an Elder in the community named Jennie noted, "Speaking Mi'kmaw is important to our culture and how we are. Like how we are and how we act as Mi'kmaw. If our language is gone, then our culture is gone" (interview, 29 April 2010, in Tompkins et al., 2013: 141). The appreciation that many teachers talked about in relation to the confidence, leadership qualities, and other identity traits in their former immersion students was well expressed by a teacher from Eskasoni, who stated that "They have the pride and the ability to be potential leaders in our community, not just within our school" (interview, 11 March 2010, in Tompkins et al., 2013: 141).

Parents in communities across the country have echoed these observations, and a growing body of research, within Canada and also the United States,[12] shows that both students and educators are understanding that learning to speak their language is essential not only to their own health and well-being but, more importantly, to the future health and well-being of their families and communities.

Generational and community perspectives are critical to understanding the dynamics and demographics of Aboriginal language maintenance, loss, and revitalization, as well as to appreciating their broader implications with respect to cultural continuity, identity, family, and community. Members of Aboriginal communities across Canada are becoming increasingly aware that keeping their languages alive for generations to come depends on the contributions of each and every member of their community. They recognize that efforts to preserve, maintain, and revitalize traditional languages can significantly contribute to the cultural continuity and identity of their people, to connections across their generations, to the well-being of their families and communities, and ultimately to the hopeful vision that they are indeed "here to stay."

Discussion Questions

1. What language do you communicate with in most social contexts and in what ways does your language reflect a unique world view that is specific to the culture that supports it?
2. What does it mean to say that losing a language is like losing a world? How do you think it would affect you if almost no one you knew spoke the language you had grown up with from birth?
3. What types of family and geographical location characteristics are most conducive to children acquiring an Aboriginal language as their mother tongue or first language?
4. Why is second-language learning often the only option for today's younger generations, and what are some of the ways in which different generations are working together as participants, teachers, and/or learners to preserve their languages and cultures?
5. How would you explain the prospect of "secondarily surviving" languages in Canada (i.e., these languages have no first-language speakers), and what kinds of challenges do you think this will pose to communities that seek to cultivate healthy individual and community identities as well as ensure cultural continuity through the passing of traditional knowledge to future generations?

Further Reading

Ball, Jessica, Ken Moselle, and Sarah Moselle. 2013. *Contributions of Culture and Language in Aboriginal Head Start in Urban and Northern Communities to Children's Health Outcomes: A Review of Theory and Research.* Prepared for Division of Children, Seniors and Healthy Development, Health Promotion and Chronic Disease Prevention Branch. Ottawa: Public Health Agency of Canada.

First Peoples' Cultural Council. 2014. *Report on the Status of B.C. First Nations Languages 2014. Second Edition* http://www.fpcc.ca/files/PDF/Language/FPCC-LanguageReport-141016-WEB.pdf

Moseley, Christopher. 2010. *Atlas of the World's Languages in Danger*, 3rd edn. Paris: UNESCO. http://www.unesco.org/culture/en/endangeredlanguages/atlas.

Norris, Mary Jane, Erik Anonby, Marie-Odile Junker, Nicholas Ostler, and Donna Patrick, eds. *Endangered Languages beyond Boundaries/Langues en péril au-delà des frontières: Community Connections, Collaborative Approaches and Cross-Disciplinary Research*. Proceedings of the 17th FEL Conference, Ottawa, 1–4 Oct. 2013. Bath, UK: Foundation for Endangered Languages.

Perley, Bernard C. 2011. *Defying Maliseet Language Death: Emergent Vitalities of Language, Culture, and Identity in Eastern Canada*. Lincoln: University of Nebraska Press.

UNESCO Ad Hoc Expert Group on Endangered Languages. 2003. "Language Vitality and Endangerment." Paper submitted to the International Expert Meeting on UNESCO Programme Safeguarding of Endangered Languages. Paris: UNESCO, Mar. www.unesco.org/culture/ich/doc/src/00120-EN.pdf.

Notes

1. For more extended discussions of how residential schools have affected individuals, families, and communities, see Chapter 11 by Jonathan Dewar, Chapter 10 by Jan Hare and Sara Davidson, and Chapter 5 by Kim Anderson and Jessica Ball.

2. With respect to the most recent 2006–11 period, it is important to note the caution from Statistics Canada regarding comparability of 2011 NHS data with the 2006 census data. The 2011 NHS data are derived from a voluntary survey and are therefore subject to potentially higher non-response error than those derived from the 2006 census long-form data (Norris, 2013a). For further detail and related publications, see Statistics Canada at http://www.statcan.gc.ca/start-debut-eng.html.

3. To a lesser extent, adults relearning their mother tongue and more people reporting their Aboriginal mother tongue can also contribute to growth (Harrison and Norris, 2012).

4. The index is expressed as the number of people who speak the language "most often" at home for every 100 persons who speak it as their mother tongue. A high measure of 80 to 100 indicates high continuity, while a measure below 30 indicates very low continuity and that the language is not likely to be transmitted to the next generation.

5. Inuktitut is viable overall but some of the different Inuit dialects/languages are considered to be endangered (Norris, 2009a, 2013a, 2013b).

6. Apparent signs of increased second-language learning between censuses must be interpreted with some caution. In the case of critically endangered languages, for example, the index of second-language acquisition could reflect more a decline in the numbers of aging first-language speakers relative to the numbers of second-language speakers rather than an increase in second-language learners (Norris, 2013a)

7. In Canada, Huron is an example of a secondarily surviving language. While Huron-Wendat is extinct in the sense that the last Aboriginal speakers died in the first half of the twentieth century, there are efforts to bring the language back to life (John Steckley, professor, Humber College, personal communication, July 2002, in Norris and Jantzen, 2002).

8. Some caution in interpretation of changes over the 1996, 2001, and 2006 censuses is advised given data were not adjusted for complete comparability across all three censuses. Furthermore, some changes in language ability of community members may not be due solely to language-specific activities, but might also reflect effects of migration of speakers and non-speakers to and from a community.

9. The ongoing efforts to save the Cowichan community's ancestral language of Halkomelen were originally profiled on CBC's *The National* on 19 June 2009. See www.cbc.ca/national/blog/video/aboriginal_issues/saving_aboriginal_languages.html. See Norris (2011a) for a more detailed account of the Cowichan experience in reviving its Halkomelen language.

10. See Chapter 6 by Cora Voyageur for a more extended discussion of the place of Aboriginal women in families and communities.

11. Lushootseed is a member of the Salish language family, of which approximately 20 surviving languages are spoken from northern Oregon to central British Columbia, and from the Pacific coast eastward into Montana and along the British Columbia–Alberta border.

12. Recent (June 2014) American developments in Native language immersion and education legislation also recognize the importance of culture-based education and Native language acquisition for student achievement, education outcomes, and well-being within Native communities. "The Senate Committee on Indian Affairs found strong support for...Native American language programs...[which] provide...huge benefits to students....Place-based and cultural-based education keeps students engaged and increases student achievement....In Rural Alaska our communities are plagued with high suicide rates, and high dropout rates, which correlate directly with a loss in culture and language." *Indian Country Today*, at http://indiancountrytodaymedianetwork.com/2014/06/21/speaking-languages-educators-back-native-american-language-bills-155398?page=0%2C0.

10

Learning from Indigenous Knowledge in Education

Jan Hare and Sara Florence Davidson

Put simply, each and every learning experience that affirms Indigenous knowledge systems enhances the quality of life for Aboriginal people.

(Hare, 2011)

The educational landscape for Aboriginal children and families in Canada has undergone many changes since Europeans first settled in our country. But no matter how the educational landscape has been transformed, the transmission and continuity of Indigenous knowledge has been the foundation for learning that Aboriginal families, communities, and nations have always maintained for their children. It has been our knowledge systems, cultural traditions and values, and ancestral languages that have ensured the survival of Aboriginal people since time immemorial and that have affirmed our place within the Canadian context. They are the sources of strength Aboriginal children and youth draw upon as they navigate the educational challenges they face, whether they attend schools on-reserve or in rural or urban communities. Aboriginal families and communities are well aware that navigating the educational terrain of community-controlled, public, and independent schooling requires their children to experience Western forms of knowledge, but they have always asserted that educational approaches should never be to the exclusion of our own knowledge systems. In addition, Indigenous perspectives on learning do not see Indigenous and Western knowledge traditions in opposition to one another (Battiste, 2002). Rather, Indigenous peoples' ability to thrive is a testament to the ways they can accommodate, and choose from, changing traditions, including Western educational approaches.

Make a Future

We know that our future generations of Aboriginal children will walk in "two worlds" and need to be armed with a strong sense of who they are as Aboriginal people, contributing to their families and communities, while at the same time ensuring our participation in the social, economic, and political fabric of Canadian society. This chapter describes the role of Indigenous knowledge in education, examining how Canadian educational policies and practices have moved from the denigration of Indigenous knowledge in learning institutions to finding spaces in learning settings where Indigenous knowledge as a foundation for learning is having a positive impact on the educational outcomes of Aboriginal children and youth, leading to hope and healing for Aboriginal people. Just as important are the new learning opportunities that Indigenous knowledge and Aboriginal approaches to education provide for all learners.

Aboriginal children and youth do not experience the same success with schooling as their non-Aboriginal counterparts. The Programme for the International Assessment of Adult Competencies (PIAAC) reports literacy scores as generally lower for Aboriginal populations than for non-Aboriginal populations, with disparities between the two groups less marked for urban Aboriginal people than for Aboriginal people living on reserves and in more rural contexts (Statistics Canada, 2013). These lower levels of literacy are also observed in young Aboriginal children (Cowley and Easton, 2004). In 2012, 72 per cent of First Nations people, 42 per cent of Inuit, and 77 per cent of Métis (18–44 years old) had earned a high school diploma or equivalent (Bougie, Kelly-Scott, and Arriagada, 2013). Of the First Nations youth living on reserve in 2006, only 39 per cent had completed high school or the equivalent compared to the Canadian average of more than 87 per cent (Aboriginal Affairs and Northern Development Canada, 2011). While Aboriginal enrolment in post-secondary education is increasing, entrance and completion rates remain relatively low compared to those of non-Aboriginal students enrolled in university and college (Mendelson, 2006).

Too often, Aboriginal learners and their families bear the blame for their failure to achieve in educational systems that do little to recognize the systematic and valued forms of learning in their cultures, values, languages, and ways of knowing. The education of Aboriginal people must therefore be understood within the larger colonial enterprise that has long sought to eliminate the "Indian problem" in this country. Aboriginal education also must be viewed in the context of the systemic barriers and inequalities inherent in the current education system that marginalize Indigenous knowledge systems and result in significant challenges to the educational success of Aboriginal children and youth. The historical legacy and current circumstances of schooling for Aboriginal people must be understood by all Canadians if we hope to attain equality and mutual respect for all learners in our schools today, as well as strengthen relations between Aboriginal peoples and the rest of Canada.

Long-standing local, national, and international policy statements convincingly argue that improved educational outcomes for Aboriginal learners are critical to enhancing more general social, health, and economic indicators for Aboriginal people in Canada. *Indian Control of Indian Education* (NIB, 1972), the final *Report of the Royal Commission on Aboriginal Peoples* (RCAP, 1996), and the United Nations Declaration on the Rights of Indigenous Peoples (United Nations, 2008) all affirm that education is the means by which Aboriginal people in Canada will strengthen their identities, families, communities, and economies, and that they have the right to an education that reflects the cultures, histories, traditions, languages, and aspirations of their peoples. Along with asserting that Aboriginal people will find meaning and relevance in educational opportunities through the inclusion of Indigenous knowledge in school curricula, they note the many ways that paying respectful attention to Indigenous knowledge will benefit Canada's ability to address a wide variety of economic, environmental, social, and educational issues.

An increasingly urgent need for creative dialogue and for change exists in relation to the educational landscape of Canada. The Aboriginal population in this country continues to steadily increase, and half of the 1.4 million people who identify as First Nations, Inuit, or Métis are under 25 years of age. Moreover, Aboriginal youth ages 16–24 now represent the fastest-growing

segment not only of the Aboriginal population but of the Canadian population overall (Statistics Canada and Council of Ministers of Education, 2006).[1]
The sense of urgency surrounding the need for fully collaborative and creative dialogue in education in Canada is partly based on the recognition that
increasing numbers of young Aboriginal people in this country are now and
will continue to seek economic and social opportunities at a much greater rate
than their non-Aboriginal counterparts. The following discussion is, however,
much more than a call for open dialogue about the need to effect positive educational change on behalf of Aboriginal peoples in Canada. Our hope is that it
will be part of a growing dialogue through which more and more people come
to understand the many ways that such change can benefit all of Canada.

The Role of Indigenous Knowledge in Traditional Education

Indigenous knowledge represents the local and culturally specific knowledge
of a people that is dynamic, adapting over time and place (Battiste, 2005).
The knowledges of Indigenous people are derived from their ways of living,
knowing, and being in this world. Indigenous knowledge emerges from the
values, beliefs, and practices associated with their world views (Barnhardt and
Kawagley, 2005). Mi'kmaq scholar Marie Battiste (2005: 8) tells us that:

> Indigenous peoples have their own methods for classifying and transmit-
> ting knowledge, just as they have Indigenous ways of deriving a livelihood
> from their environment. Information, insight, and techniques are passed
> down and improved from one generation to another.

Indigenous knowledge is intimately connected to land (Barnhardt and
Kawagley, 2005; Battiste, 2002; Cajete, 2000), where meaning and identity are
constructed through landscapes, territory, and relationships with place and
the natural world. For example, it is increasingly customary to acknowledge
the traditional territory of Indigenous peoples as part of events, gatherings,
and lifelong living and learning. This not only demonstrates respect for the
traditional custodians of the land, but it speaks to the personal and communal
relationship of Indigenous peoples to land and place. It acknowledges our
long-standing presence on the lands, our spiritual and relational connections
to place, and how land is an intimate part of identity.

As Indigenous peoples, our knowledge systems include processes that are
intergenerational, experiential, and tied to narrative and relational ways of
ensuring the continuity and relevance of our knowledge systems. Indigenous

scholars Barnhardt and Kawagley (2005: 10) tell us that traditional education practices:

> were carefully constructed around observing natural processes, adapting modes of survival, obtaining sustenance from the plant and animal world, and using natural materials to make their tools and implements. All of this was made understandable through demonstration and observation accompanied by thoughtful stories in which the lessons were embedded.

The emphasis on learning by watching, listening, and then doing is underscored by many Aboriginal Elders reflecting on their childhoods. In recalling her Kwakwakewak childhood on the northwest coast of British Columbia, Agnes Alfred (2004: 83–5) recounts:

> I watched my grandmother in her daily activities, whether cooking, preparing fish, digging roots or clams, weaving baskets or making rope. . . . I also followed my grandmother around when she was stripping bark off the trees so I would know how to do it myself.

Innu Elder Elizabeth Penashue shares her parents' hands-on approach to learning: "When I was old enough as a little girl my mother encouraged me to work, cleaning beaver and other animals. My mother would perform and the children would sit around and watch, so that they can learn" (Kulchyski, McCaskill, and Newhouse, 1999: 200).

Storytelling has always provided Aboriginal children with valuable teachings about how things came to be and how to live in this world in a "good way." Pueblo poet and writer Simon Oritz (1992: 7) tells us:

> Oral tradition of Native American people is based upon spoken language, but it is more than that too. Oral tradition is inclusive. It is the actions, behaviors, relationships, practices throughout the whole social, economic, and spiritual life process of a people. In this respect, the oral tradition is the consciousness of a people.

Storytelling was always a part of children's daily living, as shared by Mary Lou Andrew in her interview with Sto:lo scholar Jo-ann Archibald (2008: 73):

> Stories were told when children were being taught how to sew, how to do laundry... in my childhood, my grandmother, my grandfather, always had stories... [when] walking through the fields or if you went to gather fruit or

food, or just going from point A to point B, there was a story to be told.... You got not only the history about the place, the land; you were taught [other] lessons.... You got social studies ... sometimes even science was thrown in, when you had to deal with herbs and medicines. You learned the importance of why you do something.

Anishinaabe children learn that they came to the world by being lowered from above after a union of Mother Earth's four elements, wind, air, fire, and water. When the Earth was flooded, it was Nanaboozho and other animals floating on a log that searched below the waters for any sign of Earth. It was Muskrat who was successful in the animals' attempts to bring up the dirt from the depths below. And it is Turtle who bears the weight of Earth, which expands on the turtle's shell to form what we know today as Turtle Island or, more familiar to non-Aboriginal people, North America. It is through the amusing, and sometimes serious, antics of the trickster that Aboriginal children learn important life lessons. Known as Raven or Coyote among First Nations communities in British Columbia, Glooskap among the Mi'kmaq, Nanaboozho to the Anishinaabe, Wesakechak in Cree oral traditions, or identified as a shape-shifter within specific language traditions, this character provides us with new understandings of the world by taking on many transformations.

Other practices for communicating knowledge have accompanied the oral tradition. Drumming, dance, and song have always been part of celebration and ceremony. Whether the hand-held drums played among the Cree, the water drums used by the Anishinaabe, or the wide and light hand-held drums of the Innu, their beat and rhythm go together with song, story, and dance. Aboriginal dances tell stories whereby the movements, style, and regalia of the dancer come together to give meaning. Some dances are considered prayers to give thanks. Some are shared at powwows or feasts. Other dances are more sacred, such as spirit dancing among the Northwest Coast groups in British Columbia or curing dances among the Haudenosaunee of southern Ontario and Quebec, which remain private as to when and where they are danced. These private expressions are not for others to know about as they are shared with specific people and follow careful protocols. House posts and totem poles are another kind of narrative "text" that may honour a family or clan or tell us a story. These texts are as fully committed to meaning-making for their communities as the written word privileged in schools (Hare, 2005). Aboriginal children learn to read these alternative texts and to know the protocols and teachings associated with them. Just as important to the knowledge gained through story, place, ceremony, and other cultural expressions are the systematic rules that guide the use of Indigenous knowledges.

Honouring traditional protocols contributes to the continuity and protection of Indigenous peoples' cultural and intellectual traditions.

Ancestral languages are intimately connected to the world views of Aboriginal peoples (Battiste, 2000). As the very means by which the oral content of Indigenous knowledge is contained and transmitted, ancestral languages may convey cultural values, shape thought and identity, and describe relationships to people and place. Odawa Elder Liza Mosher explains the visceral connection to the thought and feelings that ancestral languages provide:

> Native language is very important because our teachings are in the language. You miss out on the meaning when you talk about it in English.... What I understand is when I hear the teachings in the Lodge, how beautiful and sacred it is when it reaches people in the language I can't even describe how it feels. But when you talk about it in English, it is not the same, you don't have that feeling as you have in the language. (Quoted in Kulchyski, McCaskill, and Newhouse, 1999: 160)

The languages of Aboriginal people express their distinct relationship with land (Task Force on Aboriginal Languages and Culture, 2005).[2] Place names, land-based experiences, custodial responsibilities to landscapes, and traditional territories and identity all are given expression and meaning through ancestral languages. Moreover, the transmission of language from one generation to another ensures the continuity of Indigenous knowledge.

Living and learning have always been interwoven for Aboriginal people. Family and community were responsible for making sure that children learned the necessary skills and knowledge to ensure their survival. Elders and other traditional people in the community such as traditional healers, two-spirited and medicine people, and knowledge carriers also had specific roles and have always been important sources of Indigenous knowledge. For example, Elders are revered for their role as holders of traditional knowledge and for the responsibility they carry for sharing that knowledge.[3] Elders are leaders among their people who help guide, teach, and care for children and families. Traditional healers took a holistic approach to helping the mind, body, and spirit. They drew on the natural world of plants and medicines, as well as on the guidance of prayer and ceremony and the wisdom of the Elders to provide healing. Extended family has always been highly valued, and it was not unusual for children to live with grandparents, aunties, and cousins who shared responsibilities to care for children.

Indigenous knowledge has always been at the heart of traditional educational approaches. Children acquired knowledge and skills through looking, listening, and experiential learning (Miller, 1996). They came to understand who they were and their place in this world through the stories inscribed in landscape and other narrative texts in their lives (Hare, 2005). Learning took place in meaningful contexts such as on the land, in specific places, or within celebration and ceremony. Family and community members were teachers and caregivers to children, and ancestral languages were the mode of communication for transmitting our knowledge through the generations. The many sources of Indigenous knowledge not only prepared children for a sustenance lifestyle, they also served to enrich families, communities, and nations. It is our ways of knowing and being in this world that have made us strong, vibrant nations, and wherever our knowledge systems thrived they gave rise to proud, prosperous children and families.

Colonizing Indigenous Knowledge in Education

Missionaries were the first outsiders to take on the task of providing a formal education system for Aboriginal people, with the primary goal of civilizing "Indians" to Christian and settler ways. Schooling options offered by missionaries included day and boarding schools, early integration experiments, and schooling for alliances (Hare, 2003). Missionaries in New France set up day schools and boarding schools where Aboriginal children could attend daily or live for a certain length of time. These schools were established as early as the 1600s, with the first known boarding school set up by the Recollects in 1620 (Miller, 1996). The Jesuits followed shortly thereafter, and residential schools eventually became the norm across Canada as settlement expanded westward. Most of these early schooling arrangements allowed people to carry on with their seasonal living and maintain their cultural practices and traditions. Initially, missionaries gained knowledge of ancestral languages in the locales where they established their missions to Aboriginal peoples, who, for the most part, accepted missionaries for their own purposes in their changing world. These purposes included developing literacy skills through Bible reading and aligning with specific missionaries, who sometimes served as conduits to government officials (Hare and Barman, 2007). Development of these and other new skills demonstrate Indigenous peoples' ability to learn from others and to accommodate their traditions.

When Aboriginal people came to be viewed as a threat to the plans of the government of Canada they were construed as a problem and a hindrance to the formation of the Canadian state and the settlement of a new European-founded nation (Hare and Barman, 2000). The government deemed the assimilation of Aboriginal people into the settler society as a necessary means of gaining access to their land and resources that would benefit settlers and newcomers. Assimilation also was seen as a way of ridding themselves of the "Indian problem." Government officials believed that if Aboriginal people gave up their seasonal lifestyle and "lost" their cultural practices, values, and languages, they could be persuaded to take up sedentary pursuits among white settlers in towns and villages and on farms. As historian John Milloy (1999: 4–5) notes in his comprehensive review of the residential school system in Canada, "Aboriginal knowledge and skills were neither necessary nor desirable in a land that was to be dominated by European industry and, therefore, by Europeans and their culture."

Since European newcomers deemed Aboriginal people to be inferior (Dickason, 1984), they assumed that these people needed to be assimilated through strict indoctrination into Christian ways in the most expedient and aggressive manner. Day and boarding schools had proven to be ineffective means of assimilation because they allowed children to remain with their families, clans, and villages. This kept Indigenous knowledges intact and gave Aboriginal people choices about their children's schooling, including whether or not they would even allow them to take part.

The government soon recognized that to "do away with the tribal system and assimilate the Indian people in all respects with the inhabitants of the Dominion" (Sir John A. Macdonald, as cited in Milloy, 1999: 6), it was necessary to remove Aboriginal children and youth from their families. This, officials determined, would help prevent the intergenerational transmission of Indigenous knowledge. Motivated by Indian policy in the United States that saw Native American children confined to segregated residential institutions, Canada soon adopted a similar approach based on the recommendations put forward by Nicholas Davin in his report to the government. By 1880, residential schools had become the model of schooling for Aboriginal children and youth across Canada, and the government decided that Aboriginal people would be required by law to send their children to these schools. As Métis Elder Grace Zoldy (as cited in Logan, 2012: 82) describes:

> We never said anything 'cause we thought it was normal. We thought it was normal in the white system. We didn't know they were coming here to use us and abuse us in any way possible. We didn't know that. Our parents didn't know that.

The number of residential schools in Canada exceeded 80 by the 1930s (Dickason and Newbigging, 2015: 238), and there is now widespread agreement, thanks in large part to the many stories told by residential school survivors and others to Canada's Truth and Reconciliation Commission (TRC), that the entire history of residential schools has left a painful legacy that belongs to all Canadians.

From the beginning, the government gave responsibility for "civilizing" Aboriginal children and youth to various Christian denominations and ecclesiastical traditions. Government and religious representatives were convinced that full transformation of the Indian child called for indoctrination into Christianity alongside a basic education. Institutional routines included giving children a number associated with their Christian name, having children wear school uniforms and follow strict rules that governed all behaviour inside as well as outside of the classroom, a rigorous program of prayer, and a combination of labour and very rudimentary in-class learning. Recalling her early mornings at Kamloops Indian Residential School in the 1930s, Sophie shared that:

> We marched from there down to the chapel and we spent over an hour in the chapel every morning, every blessed morning. And there they interrogated us on what it was all about being an Indian.... He [the priest] would get so carried away; he was punching away at the old altar rail ... to hammer it into our heads that we were not to think or act or speak like an Indian. And that we would go to hell and burn for eternity if we did not listen to their way of teaching. (Quoted in Haig Brown, 1988: 59)

Although manual labour was not viewed as a necessary part of the educational curriculum, school administrators deemed it necessary because of the minimal funding the government provided to run the schools. Children were needed to help with the daily operation of schools as well as to provide paid services for businesses and individuals in neighbouring towns. Children and youth would attend classes for part of the day and provide labour for the school in another portion of the day.[4] Clara Campbell, who attended the St Mary's Mission located on Sto:lo territory in British Columbia, recalls:

> I think we maybe only had two hours of school in the morning. We didn't have much school. The bigger girls sort of were working. They did two or three hours of work, and then in the afternoon they had two or three out of school. That's the way it was when I was there. (Quoted in Glavin, 2002: 30)

There is widespread agreement in personal accounts as well as in comprehensive reviews of residential schooling in Canada (AFN, 1994; Fournier and

Crey, 1997; Furniss, 1995; Glavin, 2002; Grant, 2004; Haig-Brown, 1988; Ing, 1991; Jaine, 1993; Knockwood, 1992; Miller, 1996; Milloy, 1999; Nuu-chah-nulth Tribal Council, 1996; Secwepemc Cultural Education Society, 2000) that the most destructive feature of residential schools was the denigration of Indigenous knowledges that were embedded within ancestral languages, traditional cultural practices, and ways of living. Upon their arrival at school, Aboriginal children were immediately forbidden to speak their ancestral languages and were expected to take up English, or French in Quebec. The fact that children only spoke an Aboriginal language upon their arrival at school made it extremely difficult for them to learn in the classroom and to adjust to the expectations of teachers and administrators. A member of the Nuu-chah-nulth Nation, Ambrose Maquina, recalls just how difficult it was when he came to Old Christie Residential School (at what is now Tofino, BC): "We ended up in a school room. I didn't know what A.B.C. was. I never spoke English. I didn't understand English…I couldn't even speak English…I felt really lost! Yeah, really, really, lost" (quoted in Nuu-chah-nulth Tribal Council, 1996: 45).

What stands out most for survivors of residential schools was the abuse they experienced as punishment whenever they were caught speaking their languages. Children were hit, strapped, whipped, and beaten by teachers and administrators who refused to accept their languages as valid. In her memoir of her time at Shubenacadie Residential School in Nova Scotia, Isabelle Knockwood (1992: 98) observed, "when little children first arrived at school we would see bruises on their throats and cheeks that told us they had been caught speaking Mi'kmaw." One Aboriginal woman's unsettling recollection reveals the extent of the punishment:

> Today I understand quite a few words in my language. But every time I try and talk it, my tongue hurts. I didn't know why. I ran into another woman who went to residential school with me and we were talking about it. She asked me if I remembered how they would stick a needle in our tongue if we got caught talking our language.… Maybe that's why my tongue hurts whenever I try to talk my language. (Quoted in Assembly of First Nations, 1994: 25)

The widespread prohibition against speaking one's ancestral language was devastating. As noted previously, ancestral languages are at the very heart of Aboriginal peoples' culture and are the primary means by which Indigenous knowledge is expressed, cultivated, and learned. The loss of Aboriginal languages by the majority of students who attended these institutions was inevitable, and it continues to have devastating consequences in the lives of Aboriginal individuals, families, and communities throughout Canada. Knockwood (1992: 99) explains: "The punishment of speaking Mi'kmaw began on our first day at school, but the punishment has continued all our lives as we try to piece together who we are and what the world means to us with a language many of us had to re-learn as adults."

Expressions of Indigenous knowledge in the form of social practices, cultural traditions, and values also suffered irreparable damage as a result of assimilation policies and practices of residential schools. Outward appearance was altered by way of dress and grooming. Girls had their hair cut to "respectable" lengths, and boys had their heads shorn, which ignored the fact that many young Aboriginal children had been raised to understand the sacredness and the status associated with how their hair was kept. For example, among the Anishinaabe, a braid in the hair was a symbol of strength and unity whereby mind, body, and spirit, represented in the three strands of the braid, are woven together. In other words, Aboriginal children had their pride and dignity taken away when their hair was cut. The consequences for those who attempted to maintain aspects of their culture were the same as for speaking the language. Recalling her time at Kamloops Indian Residential School in the interior of British Columbia, one woman explained just what could happen if children attempted to maintain any of their traditional ways:

> We were not allowed to speak our language; we weren't allowed to dance, sing because they told us it was evil. It was evil for us to practice any of our cultural ways.... Some of the girls would get some Indian food... they'd take it away from us and just to be mean they'd destroy it right in front of us. (Quoted in Haig-Brown, 1988: 58)

The forced separation of children and youth from families and members of their communities also prevented the passing on of Indigenous knowledge from one generation to another. Whereas parents, Elders, extended family, and community members shared the collective responsibility of helping children make sense of their world and how to live in it, residential schools prevented their involvement in the schools and ultimately in their children's lives during their formative years into young adulthood. The schools provided an environment devoid of family interactions as children were separated from their siblings. The result of this was that many children never returned to their families after attending a residential school. The former National Chief of the Assembly of First Nations, Phil Fontaine, attended the Fort Alexander Residential School north of Winnipeg. He describes how even his most basic emotional needs were not met in the 10 years he attended:

At home I learned certain things about love and how it was expressed, but that was cast aside when I went to residential school. There, I was completely cut off from my parents and I lost a lot. I lost my sense of family. I didn't develop the kind of love one should experience in a family. (Jaine, 1993: 53)

Remembering his time with his family, another residential school survivor shared that "I learned my language from my dad, I learned about the medicine, I learned about the land, some of the old stories" (quoted in Secwepemc Cultural Education Society, 2000: 167). The connections to family and community were intentionally severed by law so that children and youth could be under the complete control of government and church. By preventing Aboriginal children and youth from maintaining the traditional ways of their people, the government, through school administrators, ensured that they would be unable to return to them after they left school.

There is clear evidence that Aboriginal families and communities have suffered greatly from the disparaging of Indigenous knowledge at these institutions. Our traditional approaches to living and learning were eroded as the policies and practices of these schools emphasized preparing children and youth for agricultural, industrial, and domestic pursuits patterned on white ways and denying the importance of land-based relationships and learning. The banning of cultural practices such as ceremonies, singing, smudging, and drumming meant that children were unable to carry their meaning forward to future generations. The emotional and spiritual toll on children and their families from being punished whenever they attempted to express Indigenous knowledge has left their identities in a fragile state. As one Aboriginal survivor of the Kamloops Indian Residential School shared:

They took away my belongings, they took away everything from me. Everything that's important to me, mother, father, culture.... And they put what they wanted in us, made us ashamed of who we are. Even right to this day, it still affects me. Like I really want to get in to Indian things and I just can't because of them telling us it was of the devil. Every time I try, something blocks me. I can't, because I am afraid. (Quoted in Secwepemc Cultural Education Society, 2000: 29)

The Intergenerational Legacy of Residential Schooling

What cannot go untold is the fact that the abuse that children and youth suffered at these institutions resulted in intergenerational trauma for individuals, families, and communities. The personal recollections of those who attended these schools reveal dehumanizing experiences marked by isolation, hunger, humiliation, hypocrisy, shame, and fear, all carried out through spiritual, emotional, physical, and mental abuse (Hare, 2007). Residential school survivors have revealed that sexual abuse was rampant in these institutions. The abusive practices of many adults who ran these schools also turned many of the youth into aggressors against their fellow students. The tragic results of this legacy have spilled back into Aboriginal families and communities and into Canadian society generally.

Recent court proceedings, in which many former students brought criminal charges against school administrators and teachers, provided an opportunity for school survivors to share their experiences and for healing to begin. Following the public disclosure in the 1980s of abuse against former students, churches began to publicly apologize for their role in the schools. The Royal Commission on Aboriginal Peoples (1996) called for a public inquiry to investigate and document the totally devastating impact that residential schools had on Aboriginal peoples. The federal government responded, first in 1998 when the Indian affairs minister, Jane Stewart, issued an apology. As residential school survivors continued to seek redress through the courts, the government and churches eventually signed a settlement agreement that promised to provide compensation to residential school survivors. Part of this process involved Prime Minister Stephen Harper making a formal apology on behalf of the government in the House of Commons in June 2008 (see Chapters 3 and 11). The prime minister's statement expressed profound regret for past actions of the government and announced a healing fund to support community initiatives that would provide aid to residential school survivors and their families. The Assembly of First Nations assisted survivors throughout the compensation process. A key component of the Indian Residential Schools Settlement Agreement was the establishment of the Truth and Reconciliation Commission (TRC, 2008–14), whose mandate was to document and witness survivor testimonies with the goal of creating a complete historical record of the system and its legacy, and to promote education and awareness among all Canadians about the residential school system and its impacts. This Commission was expected to present its final report in 2015.

Many Aboriginal people expressed hope that the prime minister's apology would enable them to move forward in their relationship with Canada in a positive and concrete way. However, there have since been varying responses to Canada's apology (Aboriginal Healing Foundation, 2009). For example, as Inuit Elder John Amagalik (2012: 38) indicates:

Because there has been no harmonious relationship [between Aboriginal people and Europeans], we have to start with *conciliation*. We have to overcome the distrust and hostility, make things compatible, and become agreeable. For this to happen, many things need to be considered [emphasis in original].

Following the apology, it has been the important work of the TRC to acknowledge that the colonial history shared by all Canadians has resulted in very different outcomes for Aboriginal and non-Aboriginal peoples. While many are seeking reconciliation between Aboriginal and non-Aboriginal people, a number of scholars argue that certain processes must form any reconciliation efforts. For example, Cherokee scholar Jeff Corntassel and colleagues (2009) tell us that reconciliation is not an Indigenous concept. They take issue with government attempts at reconciliation that focus solely on historical injustices of the past. Mohawk scholar Taiaiake Alfred (2009) is deeply concerned about current conceptions of reconciliation that are framed within the rhetoric of empathy and nation-building. He argues that colonization is linked to the contemporary realities of Aboriginal peoples and claims that reconciliation must be fundamentally concerned with a process of restitution that includes Aboriginal peoples' rights to land as both an economic and a spiritual base for their well-being.

Euro-Canadian Paulette Regan (2010) outlines how Canadians can begin to participate meaningfully in reconciliation. She challenges all non-Aboriginal people, whether they were born and raised in Canada or are recent immigrants to this country, to examine the histories that have been constructed and that they hold onto about their place and privilege in this country. This sentiment is echoed by Indigenous scholar Martin Canon (2012), who points out that because all settlers in Canada have derived some degree of privilege from colonialism, they can only begin to make reparations by confronting their largely taken for granted investment in colonial dominance.

Creating Space for Indigenous Knowledge in Education Today

Residential schools began to fade from the Canadian educational landscape in the early 1950s, which is when educational policy started to promote Aboriginal children attending schools alongside non-Aboriginal students. There was increasing support for educational options for Aboriginal children, including providing schools under government control on reserves as well as opportunities to attend public schools off-reserve. Nonetheless, every schooling option failed to accommodate Indigenous knowledge into curriculum and teaching approaches. Schools relied on provincial curricula, which did not reflect the histories, experiences, or perspectives of Aboriginal people. Families and communities remained on the margins of their children's education, since on-reserve schools were governed by policies set out by the Department of Indian Affairs. Moreover, provincial school boards did not consider the participation of Aboriginal parents as necessary or valuable. As a result, early efforts to integrate Aboriginal children with their non-Aboriginal peers failed to enhance Aboriginal student success. This was evidenced in a high incidence of school-leaving, low parental participation, streaming of Aboriginal children and youth into special education, and age–grade lags.

Despite attempts to provide a wider range of educational opportunities for Aboriginal students, efforts to assimilate Aboriginal peoples through federal government policies continued throughout the 1960s. Then, in 1969, the federal government attempted to do away with the Indian Act by passing responsibility for Aboriginal affairs to provincial governments through its infamous White Paper. In a varied set of political responses exemplified in the Indian Chiefs of Alberta's 1970 Red Paper and the Union of British Columbia Indian Chiefs' Brown Paper, Aboriginal groups overwhelmingly rejected the proposed policy on the grounds that it would see their political and legal rights to self-determination relegated to the status of other Canadians. A clear Aboriginal response came from the National Indian Brotherhood in a policy focused on education for self-determination and fostering a positive Aboriginal identity. Their document, *Indian Control of Indian Education*, remains a landmark in Aboriginal education in Canada. It proposed that Aboriginal peoples had the right to determine how best to meet their educational goals. While providing a vision for the future of Aboriginal education in this country, the policy document was highly critical of educational facilities for Aboriginal students, of the quality of teacher training, and of the limited way school curricula included Aboriginal perspectives, pedagogies, and histories. In effect, it insisted that Indigenous knowledge must be at the core of all learning experiences for Aboriginal children and youth.

In 2012, the government of Canada proposed Bill C-33, otherwise known as the First Nations Control of First Nations Education Act. This legislation was intended to provide First Nations students with educational opportunities that met acceptable standards, provided culturally and developmentally appropriate forms of learning and support, and would lead to equitable educational experiences for Indigenous students across the country. Bill C-33 emphasized development of a core curriculum for First Nations schools that would enable students to transfer between schools on- and off-reserve as well as to improve school attendance and the quality of teaching. Government representatives argued that their bill met the conditions set out by the Assembly of First Nations and fulfilled the previous promise made to move towards Indian control of Indian education. They pointed out that Bill C-33 promised positive changes in the curriculum of on-reserve schools serving First Nations students and the promotion of accountability on the part of everyone involved in First Nations education.

Bill C-33 was nonetheless strongly criticized and eventually led to the resignation of AFN national chief Shawn A-in-chut Atleo, who had worked closely with the Harper government and supported the proposed legislation, after its overwhelming rejection by other First Nations leaders. They objected to Bill C-33 for a number of reasons, most notably that it would continue to undermine First Nations control of First Nations education by maintaining existing governing structures and regulating standards. In addition, they argued that it did not address the many challenges that exist due to the lack of adequate funding for First Nations education in Canada. First Nations leaders also asserted that there had been inadequate consultation throughout the development of Bill C-33, and that the government thus had not honoured the movement towards reconciliation. Much like earlier responses by Aboriginal leaders to various government attempts to maintain control of "Indian education," the rejection of Bill C-33 by First Nations leaders clearly demonstrated their agency and commitment to resisting continued government efforts to maintain colonial arrangements.

Aboriginal peoples across Canada are increasingly asserting that the responsibility rests with all Canadians to create space for Indigenous knowledge in formal learning settings. They note that if education in Canada is to benefit all students, this will require all Canadians opening their minds as well as their hearts to the different ways that knowledge is constructed, shared, and valued. Their vision, which has been articulated in the national Accord on Indigenous Education (Archibald, Lundy, Reynolds, and Williams, 2010), has been supported by the Association of Canadian Deans of Education. The Accord recognizes that Indigenous ways of knowing should flourish at all educational levels and that engaging Indigenous world views and ways of knowing will benefit all learners in Canada. In other words, the Accord asserts that Indigenous knowledge systems should be central to education policy, curriculum, and pedagogy, and that will be of benefit to all Canadians.

Current educational trends that support Indigenous knowledge in the learning experiences of Aboriginal and in some cases of non-Aboriginal children and youth are encouraging. One of the most promising initiatives for Aboriginal children is Aboriginal Head Start (AHS),[5] a nationally funded early childhood education intervention program begun in 1995 that enables on-reserve and urban Aboriginal communities to design and deliver pre-educational programming for their children. The program takes a holistic approach to helping families prepare young Aboriginal children (up to six years of age) for schooling by nurturing their emotional, social, cognitive, and spiritual development. Family and community work together to help realize the operating principles of the program, which include family involvement, health promotion, nutrition, social support, culture and language, and school readiness. A Public Health Agency of Canada (2012) evaluation of the urban and northern communities program of AHS found that children participating in the program experienced significant gains in their use of language as well as in their motor skills and in academic development overall as compared to non-participating Aboriginal children. Moreover, the age comparison of Aboriginal and non-Aboriginal children found that the scores for Aboriginal children were similar to those of non-Aboriginal children by the end of the school year (Public Health Agency of Canada, 2012). In their analysis of literature examining early childhood education for Aboriginal children, Preston et al. (2012) found that Aboriginal pedagogy was one of five features of effective early childhood learning environments.

Increasingly across Canada, conversations are occurring about incorporating Indigenous knowledge in mainstream education (Brayboy and Maughn, 2009). In British Columbia, efforts to enhance the academic performance of Aboriginal children and youth have brought together Aboriginal communities, provincial school districts/boards, and the Ministry of Education to develop goals and strategies that will serve the educational needs of Aboriginal learners (Morin, 2004). These Aboriginal Education Enhancement Agreements seek to emphasize the role of Indigenous knowledge by incorporating Aboriginal culture, language, history, and perspectives into the learning experiences of Aboriginal students enrolled in public schools. In Manitoba, a full-credit course for Aboriginal and non-Aboriginal Grade 12 students, "Current Topics in First Nations, Métis, and Inuit Studies: A Foundation for Implementation," has been introduced. The goal of the course, which examines Indigenous perspectives, knowledge, and traditions, is to encourage all students to become more informed and actively engaged members of Canadian society (Manitoba Education, 2011).

Elsewhere in Canada, public school boards have been gradually incorporating Indigenous knowledge as well as the specific histories and cultures of Canada's Aboriginal peoples into their curricula. In 2007, for instance, the Ontario Ministry of Education implemented an Aboriginal Education strategy in its First Nations, Métis, and Inuit Education Policy Framework (Ontario Ministry of Education, 2007). The policy framework describes a number of strategies based on a holistic and integrated approach to improving Aboriginal student learning outcomes. The policy framework also placed the onus on the province's Ministry of Education, school boards, and individual schools to create space for Indigenous knowledge, recognizing that "factors that contribute to student success include teaching strategies that are appropriate to Aboriginal learner needs, curriculum that reflects First Nations, Métis, and Inuit cultures and perspectives, effective counseling and outreach, and a school environment that encourages Aboriginal student and parent engagement" (Ontario Ministry of Education, 2007: 6). A recent evaluation of the program indicates that the implementation of the strategy resulted in significant improvements for Aboriginal students across a number of performance measures, including higher province-wide assessment scores, greater participation of Aboriginal parents, and increased graduation rates (Ontario Ministry of Education, 2013).

Post-secondary institutions in Canada are also making efforts to accommodate Indigenous knowledge and approaches to learning. In December 2014, Colleges and Institutes Canada announced the launch of its Indigenous Education Protocol for Colleges and Institutes. Developed by its Indigenous Education Committee, the document outlines a number of principles that signing institutions agree to adopt, including: ensuring that Indigenous knowledge and education are respected and given proper priority; increasing Indigenous content and approaches to learning; and building understanding and relationships among Indigenous and non-Indigenous peoples (Colleges and Institutes Canada, 2014).

Initiatives such as the Indigenous Education Protocol, which are designed to support the learning needs and self-determination of Aboriginal people, are not new as several post-secondary institutions across Canada have been offering Indigenous teacher education programs for years. For example, the Native Indian Teacher Education Program at the University of British Columbia celebrated its fortieth anniversary in 2014. From its inception, this program has integrated traditional Indigenous values in a way that prepares graduates to teach in public, band-operated, and independent schools. Furthermore, the program provides opportunities for students to start their program in field centres located in rural areas, thus allowing them to remain closely connected to their communities (Teacher Education Office, University of British Columbia, n.d.). Program developers believe that equipping Aboriginal students to teach in a variety of contexts would enhance appreciation for Aboriginal perspectives in schools, which in the end is of benefit to all students.

Language revitalization efforts are closely linked with Aboriginal education goals.[6] Hermes (2007) asserts that Aboriginal language immersion programs offer the greatest promise in Indigenous language revitalization, while others describe them as the most effective means of ensuring the intergenerational transmission of Indigenous knowledge (McCarty, 2003; Reyhner et al., 2003). In their research with Mi'kmaq language programs, Usborne et al. (2011) determined that Aboriginal language immersion programs not only supported the learning of the Mi'kmaq language, but that students enrolled in such programs also demonstrated as much success in English-language proficiency as students in classrooms where the instruction was primarily in English. Across Canada, immersion language programming is taking hold slowly as communities struggle with loss of language speakers and communities and governments offer staggered support for language revitalization initiatives. There are, however, some hopeful signs of success. Immersion programs exist from preschool to Grade 3 in Onion Lake, Saskatchewan, and Kahnawake, Quebec. The Adams Lake Indian Band in British Columbia hosts a "language nest" for preschool as well as a full language immersion program from kindergarten to Grade 7 in its community school (McIvor, 2009). The University of Victoria offers a Bachelor of Education in Indigenous Language Revitalization that operates in partnership with First Nations communities interested in developing immersion and other language revitalization programs.

The benefits of language revitalization may go well beyond educational achievement and success. Hallet, Chandler, and Lalonde (2007) report that First Nations communities in British Columbia with higher knowledge of ancestral languages among their members have fewer incidents of suicide compared to First Nations communities with lower levels of ancestral language fluency. These findings suggest that ancestral language may be not only a prime expression for Indigenous knowledge, but may support the efforts of Aboriginal people who are committed to cultivating a shared sense of identity and hope.

The Way Ahead

Once the foundation of the learning experience of Aboriginal children and youth, the sharing of Indigenous knowledge was severely disrupted by assimilationist schooling policies and practices that aimed to rid Aboriginal people of their Indigenous identity. For well over a century, residential schools were the primary means by which governmental and religious bodies attempted to systematically eradicate Aboriginal languages, cultures, and values from the lives of Aboriginal children. In short, they sought to fully alter the way Aboriginal children and youth came to understand and live within their world. The legacies of residential schooling persist, and as a result Aboriginal children and youth continue to face many challenges and barriers to success in their schooling.

Evidently, as Indigenous knowledge and approaches to learning find their way into school curricula, pedagogical approaches, and policies, Aboriginal children and youth increasingly are able to experience meaningful educational success. Indigenous knowledge is concerned with issues of power, place, and relationship, and thus promises to offer support to children and to bring hope to Aboriginal people and communities (Villegas, Neugebauer, and Venegas, 2008). The educational initiatives discussed in this chapter recognize that efforts to support Indigenous knowledge in student learning provide hope to many Aboriginal people in this country, for they are helping them to develop Indigenous solutions to the challenge of living in twenty-first-century Canada. Put simply, they illustrate that every learning experience that affirms Indigenous knowledge systems enhances the quality of life for Aboriginal people (Hare, 2011).

The future benefits of Indigenous knowledge systems to Canadian society as a whole should not be underestimated. It is clear that the inclusion of Aboriginal world views, values, languages, culture, and approaches to learning in mainstream school curricula significantly broaden the learning experience of all students. This is important, for reconciliation between Aboriginal people and the rest of Canada requires widespread awareness and understanding of a shared colonial history that has produced very different outcomes for Aboriginal and non-Aboriginal people. It is only through an Indigenous understanding of this colonial history that Canadians will be able to acknowledge their role in keeping Aboriginal peoples on the social, economic, and educational margins of the places where we live and learn. As Barnhardt and Kawagley (2005) note, "Our challenge now is to devise a system of education for all people that respects the epistemological and pedagogical foundations provided by both Indigenous and Western cultural traditions." Increasing respect and understanding for other cultures and their knowledge systems offer hope and healing to all of us.

Discussion Questions

1. How do traditional Indigenous approaches to education relate to current practices and policies in Aboriginal education?
2. Compare Aboriginal peoples' sources of knowledge and the kinds of knowledge they value with the sources and kinds of knowledge that you learned to value in school. How are they similar? How are they different?

3. What have you learned about Indigenous knowledge and the history of Aboriginal peoples in school? How do you think your experience of school might have been different if Indigenous knowledge and approaches to learning had been an integral part of your education?
4. How do you see yourself participating in reconciliation processes that ask you to consider how you have benefited from colonial relations?
5. What might the future of education in Canada look like if Aboriginal peoples' vision of education is embraced by the rest of Canada?

Further Reading

Battiste, Marie. 2013. *Decolonizing Education: Nourishing the Learning Spirit*. Saskatoon: Purich Publishing.

Canadian Council on Learning. 2007. *Redefining How Success Is Measured in First Nations, Inuit and Métis Learning*. Ottawa: Canadian Council on Learning.

Castellano, M. Brant, L. Davis, and L. Lahache. 2001. *Aboriginal Education: Fulfilling the Promise*. Vancouver: University of British Columbia Press.

Highway, T. 1999. *Kiss of the Fir Queen*. Toronto: Anchor Canada.

Kirkness, Verna J. 2013. *Creating Space: My Life and Work in Indigenous Education*. Winnipeg: University of Manitoba Press

Miller, J.R. 1996. *Shingwauk's Vision: A History of Native Residential Schools*. Toronto: University of Toronto Press.

Notes

1. See Chapter 8 by Don Kerr and Roderic Beaujot for a more detailed discussion of the implications of current demographic developments.
2. See Chapter 9 by Mary Jane Norris and Chapter 2 by Deborah McGregor for more extended discussions on the relationship between Aboriginal languages and the land and identity.
3. Further discussion of Elders is in Chapter 4 by Marlene Brant Castellano.
4. This practice was the origin of the "half-day" schooling system.
5. For information on Aboriginal Head Start, see www.hc-sc.gc.ca/fniah-spnia/famil/develop/ahsor-papa_intro-eng.php (retrieved 21 Dec. 2014).
6. See Norris, Chapter 9, for an in-depth analysis of the challenges facing those engaged in language revitalization as well as recent positive developments in this area.

11

Art and Reconciliation

Jonathan Dewar

I've always believed that the art object itself cannot heal. For me, the process of creating art is a process of healing for myself. The object itself, the result, is not a healer, but it could be a trigger, a trigger for somebody else to consider their own situation, in their own context.

Adrian Stimson, interview with author, 2015

Introduction

Charles Hauss (2003: 1) wrote that in the last few years, "reconciliation has become one of the 'hottest topics' in the increasingly 'hot' field of conflict resolution." To be sure, one need only to conduct a simple Google search of scholarly works that feature "reconciliation" and "Canada" as principal keywords to discover the proliferation of new works focusing on reconciliation in the Canadian context. But how did we get *here* and what exactly are we doing *here*? I ask the latter question in a discussion of art because in the world of art it is the *doing* that is essential—and Canadian artists and art theorists are at the forefront of engaging with both the theory and, much more importantly, the practice of reconciliation. This is not to say that the arts offer definitive answers; rather, artists highlight the complexities of asking how one practises reconciliation, since many, including Boer (2004) and Gaertner (2011), argue that reconciliation is difficult—if not impossible—to define.

This chapter is based on a five-year study I began in 2009 on the role that First Nations, Inuit, and Métis artists and art play in reconciliation generally and, more specifically, within the context of the Indian Residential Schools Truth and Reconciliation Commission (TRC). The purpose of the discussion is to explore how artists and art scholars are challenging the very definition

The Tyee

of "reconciliation" as well as inviting others to reflect critically on the meanings of and relationships between art and healing, commemoration, and memorialization. While the following discussion engages the literature on the
relationship between art and reconciliation, it centres on the perspectives,
questions, and insights I gleaned from one-on-one interviews and comments
made at public events by artists, curators, and art scholars in relation to
Canada's Truth and Reconciliation Commission.

Where Are We?

During the last decade of the twentieth century, an intensifying spotlight was
directed at the history and tremendously damaging legacy of Indian residential schools in the lives of Canada's Indigenous peoples.[1] Trudy Govier (2003:
78) observes that Canada has tended to turn away from residential schools
and other events of our colonial history because the stories "are unpleasant
and incompatible with the favored picture we have of ourselves, and they

imply a need for restitution and redress, threatening our rather comfortable way of life." Her point is that all Canadians must acknowledge that "through patterns of colonization, land use, racism, disregard for treaties, and the residential school system, we are linked significantly to the institutions that are responsible . . . we share responsibility for these things" and we "are beneficiaries of the injustices" (Govier, 2003: 78–9).

The legacy of the residential schools was first meaningfully illuminated at the grassroots level during the late 1970s and early 1980s. During this time, former students, or as they have come to be known, "survivors," came together in support of health and healing. Since then, much broader social movement support has grown as Aboriginal communities across the country have demanded apologies from the government and churches involved in running particular schools. Emma LaRocque (2010) notes that while engagement with issues surrounding residential schools in the arts, literature, and scholarship became increasingly prominent from the 1980s on, concepts of healing and reconciliation began to develop and evolve during this time alongside political and personal activism. Healing, in particular, became well defined in grassroots efforts as well as government initiatives. Needless to say, healing initiatives and movements have become inextricably woven into the experiences of individuals as well as community, institutional, and societal efforts to address the legacy of residential schools. In fact, one may argue that while healing initiatives and movements represent the positive outcomes of residential schools, they are often overshadowed by the many more painful and destructive legacies they left behind.

Residential schools came to unprecedented national prominence in 1996 with the release of the final *Report of the Royal Commission on Aboriginal Peoples* (RCAP), an inquiry that raised a number of deeply troubling questions about the past and present experiences and realities of Canada's Aboriginal peoples. The negative impacts of residential schools for survivors and their descendants loomed large throughout the RCAP report, and the many shocking details revealed in the report led to a federal policy document, *Gathering Strength: Canada's Aboriginal Action Plan* (Government of Canada, 1997). A key recommendation in *Gathering Strength* resulted in the creation of the Aboriginal Healing Foundation (AHF), a national, not-for-profit organization managed by Aboriginal people. The AHF was established in 1998 through a government grant of $350 million and was given an 11-year mandate to help cultivate community-based, Aboriginal-directed healing initiatives that addressed the legacy of physical and sexual abuse suffered in the residential school system and its intergenerational impacts (Castellano, Archibald, and DeGagné, 2008).

By 2005, survivors and groups representing their interests were taking legal action to force the federal government to offer an "official" apology beyond the statement made by Indian affairs minister Jane Stewart in 1998, and to financially compensate survivors. Individual lawsuits against government, churches, and perpetrators grew in number, as did class action lawsuits. This wave of activity led to negotiations that culminated in 2007 with a finalized agreement for the multi-billion dollar Indian Residential Schools Settlement Agreement (IRSSA). The two components of the IRSSA that received significant (and often negative) mainstream attention were compensation[2] and the creation of a Truth and Reconciliation Commission (TRC).[3] Two major sources of funding were intended to address the issue of compensation within the IRSSA: the Commemoration Fund ($40 million), which was distributed through a process of proposal adjudication by the TRC and Aboriginal Affairs and Northern Development Canada, and the Healing Fund, which provided an additional $125 million to fund existing projects until 31 March 2012.[4] Despite these positive developments, it was not until Canadian prime minister Stephen Harper delivered an official apology in the House of Commons on 11 June 2008 that the legacy of Canada's residential schools rose to national prominence. In his unprecedented speech, the prime minister noted that:

> For more than a century, Indian Residential Schools separated over 150,000 Aboriginal children from their families and communities. . . . Tragically, some of these children died while attending residential schools, and others never returned home. . . . The burden of this experience has been on your shoulders for far too long. The burden is properly ours as a Government, and as a country. There is no place in Canada for the attitudes that inspired the Indian Residential Schools system to ever prevail again. You have been working on recovering from this experience for a long time, and in a very real sense we are now joining you on this journey. The Government of Canada sincerely apologizes and asks the forgiveness of the Aboriginal peoples of this country for failing them so profoundly.[5]

Many people in Canada immediately viewed the prime minister's speech as a sign of profound hope for future relations between Aboriginal peoples and the rest of Canada. Still, many survivors, artists, and scholars continue to note that the silences with regard to residential schools have also been profound, and that the breaking of these silences is a very recent phenomenon. For survivors and those affected intergenerationally, the silences surrounding residential schools are deeply personal as well as communal since they have been felt not only across and within families and Aboriginal communities, but throughout their relations with the rest of Canada for over 100 years. For many others, ignorance and deliberate silences around residential schools continue to exist, albeit in the unaddressed backgrounds of their everyday lives.

It is particularly obvious as we look back at the 1970s and 1980s that residential schools remained in the proverbial shadows, even as artists were lauded for their frank depictions of so-called "Native life" and their works were described as seminal and influential, words often associated with Maria Campbell's *Half-Breed* (1973) and Jeannette Armstrong's *Slash* (1985). Tomson Highway's plays *The Rez Sisters* (1988) and *Dry Lips Oughta Move to Kapuskasing* (1989) also received national prominence. We are now certain that residential schools and related realities such as day schools, the "Sixties Scoop,"[6] and off-reserve as well as urban struggles lurk in the background of these works. Visual artists also began to address the many social issues experienced by Indigenous peoples in Canada during this time, although most of their work provided the same kind of subtle and coded messages found in literary works. Norval Morrisseau's 1975 canvas, *The Gift*, for example, is not overtly about residential schools but rather about the "gift" of Christianity and smallpox. It was not until Joanne Cardinal Shubert's 1989 installation, *The Lesson*, and Jim Logan's early 1990s acrylic on canvas series on residential school abuse, *A Requiem for Our Children*, that the mould of subtle and coded art was shattered in a purposefully shocking way.

Despite the fact that artists have not addressed issues surrounding residential schools until very recently, more and more Aboriginal artists are now doing so. It is clear that watershed "moments" concerned with health and healing such as the RCAP (1993–6) and the TRC (2008–15) provided the kind of direction and support that both challenged and enabled Indigenous authors, poets, playwrights, and scholars to begin exploring the legacy of residential schools in and through their work.[7]

Certainly the concept of reconciliation, that of "restoring good will in relations that have been disrupted" (Castellano, Archibald, and DeGagné, 2008: 3), existed long before the TRC and will exist well beyond its five-year mandate. It is thus important for people to learn to pay attention to the role in reconciliation of Aboriginal artists and their art prior to the TRC and outside of the context of residential schools. Nonetheless, a particularly bright and historic spotlight is currently being shone on issues involving Aboriginal peoples in Canada: a truth and reconciliation process in the form of a commission. The TRC is a landmark opportunity for Canadians to begin to meaningfully reconcile the difficult aspects of their history, for it represents an important step forward for a country that has embarked on a path of truth and reconciliation in response to the problem of colonialism in general and the legacies of residential schools in particular.

I note in more detail below that the TRC presented a clear and open invitation to Aboriginal artists to engage issues surrounding residential schools in their work, and as an art scholar I find Gayatri Spivak's (1988) notion of *speaking to* particularly helpful when talking about art that has been produced, is in production, or is being envisioned. Linda Alcoff, in her 1995 article "The Problem of Speaking for Others," nicely describes the concept of *speaking to* after deconstructing the academic postures of *listening to* and *speaking for*:

> to promote *listening to* as opposed to *speaking for* essentializes the oppressed as non-ideologically constructed subjects. But Spivak is also critical of *speaking for* which engages in dangerous re-presentations. In the end Spivak prefers a *speaking to* in which the intellectual neither abnegates his or her discursive role nor presumes an authenticity of the oppressed but still allows for the possibility that the oppressed will produce a *counter-sentence* that can then suggest a new historical narrative. (Alcoff, 1995: 244)

Just as there is now broad-based support for Aboriginal peoples in Canada to fully participate in research involving their people and communities, Aboriginal artists also rightly expect that "others" will help them create the kind of spaces that will enable them to speak for themselves both in their art and through research that seeks to engage their art. Further, to understand Aboriginal perspectives on art and reconciliation we must respect traditional ways of knowing. I seek to honour these ways in my study by including knowledge that is personal, oral, experiential, holistic, and conveyed through narrative expression (Castellano, 2000).

Allan J. Ryan (1999: xi) noted that the artists in his study "constitute a loose alliance of socially active, politically aware, and professionally trained individuals ... who have ... exhibited with one another, written about one another, lectured on one another, curated exhibitions for one another, and to varying degrees influenced one another." I engage the artists and art explored in my study in a similar fashion, for I seek to make sense of how networks and/or communities of artists engage and interact with each other within the particular policy framework presented by the IRSSA and TRC—or in resistance to it.

The TRC organized seven mandated national events as well as numerous community events between 2008 and 2015, and included such prominent authors as Basil Johnston, Beatrice Mosionier, and Joseph Boyden in their artistic programming. While the TRC initially placed its open call for artist submissions firmly on the testimony side of its mandate, it eventually provided a much more refined description of how they envisioned the contributions of artists in the work of the Commission. It did so by affirming that the TRC:

> believes that artists have a profound contribution to make in expressing both truth and reconciliation. The TRC invites all artists to submit works that relate to experiences at Indian Residential Schools or that relate to the legacy and impact of those experiences on former students, parents, future generations, communities, and on relationships within families and between communities. In addition, the TRC invites artists to submit works relating to apology, truth, cultural oppression, cultural genocide, resistance, resilience, spirituality, remembrance, reconciliation, rejuvenation and restoration of Aboriginal culture and pride. Why is the Truth and Reconciliation Commission of Canada gathering artistic works? The TRC believes that collecting artistic works is an important and meaningful way to express the truth, impact and legacy of the Residential School experience and to assist with reconciliation. (TRC, n.d.)

Community and Responsibility

The work of the TRC in many ways highlights that the convergence of truth-telling, reconciliation efforts, and commemoration can present artists and scholars with a unique opportunity to test and build critically upon the notion that Aboriginal peoples have a responsibility to build their own communities. In this light, I appreciate Jace Weaver's (1997) theory of "communitism" (a combination of *community and activism*), for it reflects the ways I have sought to position my scholarly and professional efforts that address Aboriginal issues in ways that honour and serve Aboriginal communities.

Communitism is a theory that supports the artist's "proactive commitment to native community" (Weaver, 1997: 43). There are many related theories about the importance of community to Aboriginal artists and their obligations to their community. For example, Jeannette Armstrong (1999: 3) has written and spoken at length about *En'owkin*: "[T]his idea of community, as understood by my ancestors, encompassed a complex holistic view of interconnectedness that demands our responsibility to everything we are connected to." Interestingly, En'owkin is the name given to the Indigenous cultural, educational, and creative arts institution Armstrong has long been affiliated with in Penticton, BC. Armstrong defines the concept as an "Okanagan conceptual metaphor which describes a process of clarification, conflict resolution and group commitment. We focus on coming to the best solutions possible, through respectful dialogue literally through consensus."[8] She explains that her concern:

> has mostly been about the broader effects to our Indigenous Nations (as opposed to the heinous effects on individuals which other experts are engaged in) in regard to the decline and extinctions of original languages and cultures as a result of the subtractive (to Indigenous culture) and submersion (in colonial culture) education process that the schools were about. The loss of language is a loss of a way to see and experience the world from within an Indigenous perspective unique to each specific place each language and culture is indigenous to. The concept has been the subject at the centre of all of my arts, my writing, my activism in arts and culture as well as Indigenous rights, and my work in culture and language revitalization, for living Indigenous language renewal, for authentic Indigenous arts practice recovery, for the revival in education pedagogy, of Indigenous philosophy . . . and science perspectives. I believe that the role of reconciliation in a broader sense must provide ways and means to assist in the remedy of what has been destroyed. . . . Truth, from the perspective above, must not just include personal testimonials of abuse and loss, but attempt to display the depth and breadth of effects to all strata of Indigenous nations—social, psychological, intellectual, economic, and so on, as well as to attempt to display the truth about the depth and breadth of the meaning to the rest of world of the loss of even a single language and a single way of perceiving life. Understanding the whole picture is the first step to reconciliation. It seems to me, only an artist might attempt to make these visible whether through formal or informal response as artist. (Dewar interview)

Reconciliation, for both Weaver and Armstrong, is arguably about the larger Canadian community. Thus, their view that an Aboriginal person is obliged to serve the needs of his/her community also encompasses efforts that are part of a much broader healing or breach-repairing paradigm since they acknowledge that a healthy community—that is, the artist's community—requires healthy contexts and relations.

While reconciliation is an effort that may be essential to communitism, it is also related to Armstrong's (1997) concept of *people without hearts*,[9] which refers to a people having "lost the capacity to experience the deep generational bond to other humans and to their surroundings. It refers to a people's collective disharmony and alienation from their land. It refers to those whose emotion is narrowly focused on their individual sense of well-being without regard to the well-being of others in the collective." While it may seem as though Armstrong is speaking about the disharmony within Aboriginal communities that has resulted from the many disruptions caused by residential schools, she is in fact relating an anecdote involving her father's use of the term to characterize the neighbouring non-Aboriginal Penticton community of her childhood. She uses the Okanagan term deliberately to include her neighbours in her world view and may, in this sense, be said to be characterizing "the collective" as the broader Canadian community.

It is clear that efforts to address the legacy of residential schools have significantly influenced the reconciliation conversation in Canada. As I embarked on my journey to interview artists across the country, I wondered whether art that engaged the legacies of residential schools prior to the IRSSA would be markedly different from post-IRSSA art, particularly given the exclusive, legal nature of the Agreement and the emotional and social impacts of its components.

I also wondered how to address the concept of "community" when my intent was to interview a diverse and potentially disparate group of individuals who self-identify as both Aboriginal and artist. The question this raised for me throughout my study was which "community" people were talking about—Aboriginal or artist? There are problems with strictly using the first conception of community because of the diversity across and within First Nations, Inuit, and Métis. The problems with emphasizing the latter conception are that while the concept of *artistic community* is broadly accepted among those involved in the arts, that understanding of community is not addressed in generally accepted research guidelines. Further, Aboriginal artists understand that their responsibility to the community—to "give back"—refers to each individual's specific Aboriginal community. My study thus presented an opportunity to explore notions of community from the perspectives of individual Aboriginal artists as well as to examine the intersections and/or barriers between their First Nation, Inuk, Métis, or other identities and their identities as artists. It also provided a significant opportunity to explore not only the sense of responsibility that each artist had of what it means to "give back" to their various communities, but also what it meant for me to give back to the communities I am part of through my own work.

Maria Campbell has helped me begin to find answers to my "wonderings." She says, "I am familiar with concepts of truth and reconciliation from the place of a community activist because I work with community and I work with families in community, so I see them on the front lines, so to speak. And I'm an artist on the front lines" (Dewar interview). She adds:

It's always been my work, because of my own background. In order for myself to heal and to find some semblance of sanity in my life, I went to work with other people who were going through what I had gone through.

So most of my work for the last 40 some years has been with women and children in crisis, so I work a lot with youth and with families. And that's even in my teaching; when I was teaching at university it was geared to that. And my work as a writer and as a playwright, you know, it's all about healing family, because I feel if families are not healed and helped, then we don't have anything; we don't have any kind of future, no matter how many apologies, no matter what, we have nothing if we can't.

But not all artists understand and express the special responsibility they feel to community in the same way. Alex Janvier's 2001 canvas, *Blood Tears*, has been featured prominently in the last few years, on the cover of the 2008 Aboriginal Healing Foundation's volume *From Truth to Reconciliation: Transforming the Legacy of Residential Schools*, and in the major 2013 exhibition *Witnesses: Art and Canada's Indian Residential Schools*. When Janvier was asked if he considered himself an activist or an activator, he said, "None of those two descriptions. We were just acting as people who wanted to move forward as artists and wanted to be recognized as artists, not as curio-makers. I didn't want to be qualified as a curio-maker, I was doing serious work and the others were doing serious work in their own style" (Dewar interview). Nonetheless, Janvier did mention that painting residential school-themed or -inspired works was important to him personally: "I had to heal too. I'm a sick person from all that [and if others] could see that [work], then they could chime into it on their own terms." Moreover, Janvier's *Blood Tears* invites others to join him in his journey by including on the back of the canvas his own terms of loss:

- Language of Denesu'line targeted, forbidden to speak was to be strapped, and severely punished!
- Loss of culture, custom
- Loss of parenthood, parents and extended families
- Loss of grandparents
- Loss of Elder's knowledge
- Loss of traditional belief, told that it was evil
- Told the Indian ways was the work of the devil . . .
- Many, many dies of broken bodies, of twisted conflicting mental difference
- Most dies with "Broken spirit"
- Some lived to tell about it
- The rest are permanently, "Live in fear"
- The rest will take their silence to their graves as many have to this day

Defining/Defying Reconciliation

As noted previously, the last few decades have seen a considerable amount of scholarship as well as theoretical and practical focus on reconciliation[10] between aggrieved parties within nation-states. Due in large part to the response by scholars and other writers to South Africa's Truth and Reconciliation Commission, there is now a large body of international literature concerning the role of art and artists in truth and reconciliation processes that have often involved formal commissions. A similarly expansive body of literature concerns the role of art and artists in commemoration, another core component of the IRSSA and one that will be administered by the TRC following its final report. And a considerable body of literature, including a growing literature specific to Canada and Aboriginal North America, focuses on the role of art in healing and the therapeutic nature of art. The notion of "art as witness" is of considerable importance here and provides a fascinating way to explore the relationship between art and reconciliation.

We can begin our discussion of reconciliation with a simple dictionary definition. *Webster's Revised Unabridged Dictionary* (2009) defines "reconciliation" as: "1. the act of reconciling, or the state of being reconciled; reconcilement; restoration to harmony; renewal of friendship. 2. Reduction to congruence or consistency; removal of inconsistency; harmony."

In contrast, Brian Rice and Anna Snyder (2008: 46) understand reconciliation in the context of truth and reconciliation commissions, and so they define it in terms of the five general aims of TRCs, which are to: "1) discover, clarify, and formally acknowledge past abuses; 2) respond to specific needs of victims; 3) contribute to justice and accountability; 4) outline institutional responsibility and recommend reforms; and 5) promote reconciliation and reduce conflict over the past."

Similarly, the mandate of Canada's Indian Residential Schools Truth and Reconciliation Commission defines reconciliation as: "an ongoing individual and collective process [that] will require commitment from all those affected including First Nations, Inuit and Métis former Indian Residential School (IRS) students, their families, communities, religious entities, former school employees, government and the people of Canada. Reconciliation may occur between any of the above groups" (Castellano, Archibald, and DeGagné, 2008: 413). Of course, reconciliation between peoples in the context of wrongs done in a colonial past (and present) is much more complicated. While it is not possible to capture all of the complexity in one study, the following are some key areas of focus.

Jennifer Llewellyn (2008: 185) nicely encapsulates the task of Canada's TRC, saying that it is:

> well positioned to paint a comprehensive picture of the residential school system and its legacy. This will provide the necessary context to give meaning and legitimacy to the common experience payments and independent assessment process parts of the settlement. From this picture of the past, the commission will be able to recommend the way through to a future marked by new, reconciled relationships within Aboriginal communities and between Aboriginal and non-Aboriginal peoples.

Llewellyn (2008: 186) also highlights the key challenge to TRCs in Canada and elsewhere: "As the TRC [in Canada] begins its journey, it must figure out how to navigate the complex and difficult road of 'truth' and map a course toward reconciliation. In doing so, it will face the substantial challenge that others who have travelled this path before have encountered: bridging the gap between truth and reconciliation." She uses the example of the South African Truth and Reconciliation Commission to illustrate how the challenges involved in bridging this gap can be addressed:

> The South African slogan ["Truth. The road to reconciliation."] does serve as an important and necessary temper on unrealistic expectations. It cautions that truth and reconciliation are not one and the same. Distinguishing the two also makes clear that while truth may be necessary for reconciliation, it alone is not sufficient. There is a road toward reconciliation, and truth is a fundamental part of the journey, but there are other steps to be taken along the way. The lesson of this slogan for the South African commission was clear. They could not promise nor be expected to produce reconciliation. Indeed, no one process or institution could achieve this goal. This same conviction underpins the description of reconciliation in the Indian Residential Schools TRC's mandate as an ongoing process. (Llewellyn, 2008: 187)

Llewellyn makes an essential point here; there is no generally applicable road map to reconciliation—and certainly not one that can be copied from other commissions. Since reconciliation involves truth-telling along with many other steps, I wondered whether art itself is a form of truth-telling and/or whether it is some other step on the path of truth and reconciliation. To explore these questions in depth, it is important that we listen carefully to what Aboriginal art scholars and artists have to say about reconciliation.

Taiaiake Alfred and Jeff Corntassel (2005: 598) argue that the reconciliation discourse is flawed at its very roots: "Far from reflecting any true history
or honest reconciliation with the past or present agreements and treaties that
form an authentic basis for Indigenous–state relations in the Canadian context, 'aboriginalism'[11] is a legal, political and cultural discourse designed to
serve an agenda of silent surrender to an inherently unjust relation at the
root of the colonial state itself." Alfred (2005: 152) further calls reconciliation an "emasculating concept," saying that "[r]econciliation as a concept or
process is not as compelling, factually or logically speaking, as resurgence
because, being so embedded in the supposedly progressive discourses on
Onkwehonwe–Settler [Aboriginal–non-Aboriginal] relations . . . it is almost
unassailable from within established legal and political discourses, thus presenting a huge obstacle to justice and real peacemaking." Without "massive
restitution . . . for past harms and continuing injustices committed against
our peoples," he writes, "reconciliation would permanently enshrine colonial injustices and is itself a further injustice." He argues that we must place
the discourse within the broader colonial context of Canada's history and
present; otherwise, Indigenous–settler relations will continue to be built on
a foundation of "false decolonization" (Alfred, 2005: 112), a foundation he
sees as fundamentally immoral. He also challenges the notion of Indigenous
peoples being "victims of history" by arguing that the discourse has been too
conciliatory on the Indigenous side, with Indigenous people seeking only to
"*recover* from the past" (emphasis in original) and settling for Euro-Canadian
notions of reconciliation. This is not resistance or "*survivance.*"[12] Rather,
it is acquiescence to "a *resolution* that is acceptable to and non-disruptive
for the state and society that we have come to embrace and identify with"
(Alfred, 2005: 130).

John Paul Lederach also writes about conflict and the challenges of
bringing about positive transformation and resolution at interpersonal,
group, and societal levels in the context of persistent and ongoing violence.
His concept of moral imagination is "the capacity to imagine and generate constructive responses and initiatives that, while rooted in the day-to-
day challenges of violent settings, transcend and ultimately break the grips
of those destructive patterns and cycles" (Lederach, 2005: 29). His use of
the word "moral" is key, for it refers to integrity and allowing for the use
of imagination where dogmatic, ideological positioning cannot: "*moral* . . .
appeals to something great . . . beckon[ing] us to rise toward something
beyond those things that are immediately apparent and visible. The quality of this phrase I most wish to embrace reverberates in this potential to

find a way to transcend, to move beyond what exists while still living in it" (Lederach, 2005: 27–8, emphasis in original). Lederach also offers a strategy for moral action:

> This is the challenge of restorying: It continuously requires a creative act. To restory is not to repeat the past, attempt to recreate it exactly as it was, nor act as if it did not exist. It does not ignore the generational future nor does it position itself to control it. Embracing the paradox of relationship in the present, the capacity to restory imagines both the past and the future and provides space for the narrative voice to create. (Lederach, 2005: 149)

Lederach (2005: 159) writes: "The real challenge of authenticity and the moral imagination is how to transcend what has been and is now, while still living in it. For the moral imagination to make the journey across this terrain it will need to address complexity and support change over time." It is perhaps the journey into this moral space that Alfred (2005: 77) may be arguing for when he challenges Indigenous peoples to:

> us[e] words, symbols and direct non-violent action as the offensive weapons of our fight ... [and] seek to contend, to inform our agitating direct actions with ideas, and to use the effects of this contention to defeat colonialism by convincing people of the need to abandon the cycle of subjugation and conflict and join us in a relationship of respect and sharing.

Alfred's call for "words" and "symbols" may well be a call for art, as both Martha Minnow (1998) and Jill Bennett (2005) allow. Minnow highlights a number of elements that truth commissions cannot offer, including vengeance and closure through prosecution. She writes: "Disappointments with truth commissions are likely to erupt over the reliability and completeness of the reported facts, over interpretations, and over the apparent trade of truth for punishment" (Minnow, 1998: 129). Outside of the reports that relay such information, Minnow sees other avenues that efforts at reconciliation can take, including memorials that often accompany or are integral to the formal reporting of commissions. She notes that unlike formal reports, "[m]ore literal and concrete forms of commemoration and monuments use sculptures and paintings, museums, plays, and poems" (Minnow, 1998: 138). Minnow believes that art can help a people move well beyond commemoration, since "the Art of the unthinkable should disturb as well as commemorate" (1998: 142). Bennett (2005) follows this line of thought, though she examines it within the context of "trauma art," which she deconstructs along with notions of political art and the political in art.

Dian Lynn Million (2004: 73) follows yet another direction in placing reconciliation dialogue within a healing paradigm:

> *Healing* from trauma and historical trauma is now an international discourse on social "collateral damage" among those who have suffered the fate of History as the subjugated, linked to demands for justice from the perpetrators of their distress. Across a spectrum, at the level of the International, community and individual, *healing* is the reaffirmation of boundary; of holism from fragmentation.
>
> Canada has attempted to handle the material/physical outcome of its colonialism in Native communities through institutionalization, and now increasingly through therapeutic interventions that are often self-administered bureaucracies. (emphasis in original)

Million (2004: 74) also places reconciliation dialogue in a larger colonial context: "The residential school survivor's abuse discourse continuously struggles to articulate a something else larger. It is the struggle to make Canada hear: that Canada recognize not only their past acts but their present ones; acts whose resonance and material outcome are a continuation of their colonization, 'not a psychological problem to be defused in a therapist's room.'"

According to these and other authors, the healing paradigm and the movements of healing that take place within its ethos, which may or may not include or lead into reconciliation, are intimately connected to trauma. For example, Marlene Brant Castellano (2006: 160) writes about historic trauma in the context of the multiple assaults suffered by Aboriginal people: "Memories of family networks and whole communities reach back through generations, repeating themes of loss and powerlessness, relocation, epidemics and residential school."

When I interviewed Métis artist, curator, and scholar David Garneau in November 2011, he initially said of the concepts of truth and reconciliation that "I haven't been deeply involved but I've been paying attention, reading, puzzling over things" (Dewar interview). And he would go on to puzzle deeply, however, at the time, he said:

> I remember when South Africa Truth and Reconciliation was going on, there was one leader, a flower painter, who was a great speaker. When asked why he made such beautiful and political innocuous works in this time of crisis, he said that he did not draw to make work about the inequities and horrors but about the good things in life; after all, they were fighting for a change, to move away from those horrors and toward what, well, toward the sort of

things he was painting. Bob Boyer also said, "The people I hang out with, non-artists, they like beautiful things, that's why I want to make my things beautiful." He did make very agitated things at certain times, and then he did very personal work. It was all coded though, sometimes very hard to read, the titles usually helped. But there's some people who want to make their way through the world, and be healthy people. How long can you be angry? How long can you be damaged and make that? You know, imagine being in a room like this and making unhappy art all the time. I mean that's gotta be part of it. Part of it too is that, [if an artist is] making a living off his work, he's got to make some things that people can live with.

Garneau increasingly found that he could not live with the concept of reconciliation as defined by the TRC. By the summer of 2012, he had more clearly defined the landscape he found himself operating within. He writes:

[t]he colonial attitude, including its academic branch, is characterized by a drive to see, to traverse, to know, to exploit, to translate (to make equivalent), to own, and to exploit. It is based on the belief that everything should be accessible, is ultimately comprehensible, and a potential commodity or resource, or at least something that can be recorded or otherwise saved. Primary sites of resistance, then, are not the occasional open battles between the minoritized, oppressed, or colonized and the dominant culture, but the perpetual, active refusal of complete engagement: to speak with one's own in one's own way; to refuse translation and full explanations; to create trade goods that imitate core culture without violating it; to not be a Native informant. (Garneau, 2012: 32)

Garneau thus challenges the very word "reconciliation" by calling for "irreconcilable spaces of Aboriginality," which he sees as:

a synonym [of conciliation] with a difference. Re-conciliation (emphasis in original) refers to the repair of a previously existing harmonious relationship. This word choice imposes the fiction that equanimity is the status quo between Aboriginal peoples and Canada. [However], initial conciliation was tragically disrupted and will be painfully restored through the current process. In this context, the social imaginary that the word describes is limited to post-contact narratives. This construction anaesthetizes knowledge of the existence of pre-contact Aboriginal sovereignty. It narrates halcyon moments of co-operation before things went wrong as the seamless source of harmonious origin. And it sees the residential school era, for example, as an unfortunate deviation rather than just one aspect of the perpetual colonial struggle to contain and control Aboriginal people, territories, and resources. (Garneau, 2012: 35, emphasis in original)

Art and Healing

Many survivors and others impacted by the legacy of Canada's residential schools have submitted artworks to the TRC. It goes without saying that Aboriginal writers have been exploring the above themes for decades, and that a call by the TRC in 2009 was not the only catalyst for residential school-related writings and other forms of art. It was, however, a significant catalyst. Funding from the Aboriginal Healing Foundation was certainly a major incentive for poet and playwright Armand Garnet Ruffo, who used an early call put out by the AHF to begin work on the screenplay that would eventually become his award-winning film *A Windigo Tale* (released in 2010). Ruffo comments about silence when he notes that in the 1960s, 1970s, and 1980s "nobody talked about it.... We played right by the residential school. When I'd ask my mother what's that building, she'd say, don't worry about that and then eventually it was torn down" (Dewar interview). In contrast, he reveals that *A Windigo Tale* is very much about healing:

[W]hat struck me is that [Armstrong and Highway] were dealing with [residential schools] in an oblique way, not hitting it dead on. But really talking about the impact of it more, and that's what I was interested in, as well, loss of culture . . . and language. So that became a big issue and of course residential schools did come up, because that's why most of us have lost [our culture], either directly or indirectly, because of that. So I wanted to talk about those issues as well, like we were all doing [at the En'owkin Centre in Penticton, British Columbia, in the 1980s and early 1990s].

While *A Windigo Tale* and many other works of art are concerned to bring about healing, it is important to keep in mind LaRocque's cautionary note about an "aesthetic of healing":

As constructive as [it may sound], we must be careful not to squeeze the life out of native literature by making it serve, yet again, another utilitarian function. Poets, playwrights, and novelists, among others, must also write for the love of words. Healing is fast becoming the new cultural marker by which we define or judge Aboriginal literature. (LaRocque, 2010: 168)

Jill Bennett's (2005) view that the TRC allows for a unique opportunity to test her theories about art and healing suggests that there is a much larger but obviously related field that Aboriginal artists may be engaged in—or may be resisting: art therapy and its use in healing and reconciliation in Canada.

Art therapy and the expressive arts exist within the healing landscape in Canada, and recent literature that focuses on or acknowledges its use by and for Aboriginal peoples notes a natural relationship between art therapy and Aboriginal culture, particularly traditional healing and shamanism. As Stephen K. Levine (1997: 11) says, "Shamen are the prototype of the artist as therapist."

Shaun McNiff (2004: 186) describes the shaman as an archetype and includes a useful discussion of the similarities between art therapy and shamanism: "The parallels between shamanism and the field of art therapy seem to lie in the commitment of both to work with psychological conflict and struggle through creative action and enactment." In contrast, Levine delves into Western and Indigenous philosophical traditions in the search for a theoretical basis to explain why and how creative processes contribute to healing. He writes:

> In turning to the arts for healing, we are re-discovering an ancient tradition. In early societies and in indigenous cultures, all healing takes place through ceremonial means. Music, dance, song, story-telling, mask-making, the creation of visual imagery and the ritual re-enactment of myth are all components of a communal process in which suffering is given form. (Levine, 1997: 10)

Levine (1997: 188) goes on to note that many professionals now do what shamans once tended to in traditional healing: "Today, the various roles of the shaman are divided among different professional groups—physicians, psychotherapists, artists, and priests. With regard to the creative transformation of emotional conflict, this role fragmentation has diffused the shaman's source of power, which lay in the integration of body, mind, spirit, and art" (ibid, 188).

Along with healing, there is also resistance in art. Linda Tuhiwai Smith writes in *Decolonizing Methodologies: Research and Indigenous Peoples* that "for indigenous people, the critique of history is not unfamiliar, although it has now been claimed by postmodern theories." She explains that the "idea of contested stories and multiple discourses about the past, by different communities, is closely linked to the politics of everyday contemporary indigenous life.... These contested accounts are stored within genealogies, within the landscape, within weavings and carvings" (Smith, 1999:33).

While Charlotte Townsend-Gault (1999: 113) acknowledges that Western notions of "art" may for some Aboriginal peoples be "a colonizer's term, a restriction and distortion of the cultural expressions of the past which fails to do justice to the visual culture of the present," she wonders whether "the conflict between Aboriginal and Euro-American aesthetics [may have] been both productive and extending." She writes that since at least the mid-1980s, many Aboriginal artists have been concerned in their work "to remember, to condemn, to overturn, to instruct, to translate across cultural boundaries, and yet to withhold translation, to make beautiful things, according to various ideas of beauty and, sometimes, riotously and discomfitingly, to entertain."

Commemoration

And how do we remember? As with art therapy, some artists are involved formally or informally in efforts to commemorate and memorialize, others are resistant to engaging these through their art, and still others simply do not focus on commemoration and memorialization. A key question is what role, if any, does reconciliation play in commemorative art and vice versa?

Because the Commemoration Fund exists within a settlement agreement, we can also ask whether commemorative art is necessarily bound to what John Torpey (2003) calls "reparations politics,"[13] which encompasses all those things we do to address historical wrongs and misdeeds such as apologies, monetary compensation, revising historical narratives, and commemoration. If so, this may well be ground upon which resistance might be built. As Govier (2003: 79) writes, "Collective acknowledgement is especially important because strategies such as the construction of museums and memorials and the amending of educational policy are more available to collectives that to individuals." However, doing so cultivates certain kinds of processes and relationships. As Brian Osborne (2001: 41–2) has postulated:

national mythologies and symbols are manipulated to encourage identification with the state and reinforce its continuity and ubiquity. Through various means and circumstances, otherwise detached individuals are implored to recognize one another as being members of a larger group sharing a common historical metanarrative ... on the foundations of a "should have been" past, rather than an actual history.

There is certainly already ground for resistance apart from recent political responses to residential schools, for it is now common knowledge that residential schools were a mass atrocity that the Canadian state committed in concert with Christian denominations against fellow citizens (Chrisjohn and Young, 1997; Haig-Brown, 1988; Milloy, 1999). It thus seems clear that memories of the schools are not held by Aboriginal people alone, and that all Canadians share the burden of recollecting and responding to the history of residential schools.

Not surprisingly, the meanings of commemoration and the way commemoration is expressed vary greatly between communities and individuals as well as among and between Aboriginal and non-Aboriginal peoples. Cultural and spiritual or religious beliefs about grieving, for instance, inform how people choose to commemorate. Similarly, world view shapes what people remember, how we remember, and how that remembering impacts our physical, spiritual, emotional, and mental well-being. In *Lakota Grieving*, Stephen Huffstetter (1998: 28) writes about a rudimentary exchange between Lakota and non-Aboriginal grieving practices:

> A Lakota world view questions why western culture tries to dichotomize civil and religious practice anyway. Both are a part of life. . . . An elderly Lakota woman recounted the first time she went to a "white" funeral. After the rosary, the altar society served cake and coffee. Just as she was settling into conversation, people started leaving and sons and daughters of the woman being waked started gathering their belongings to leave. "I could not believe they were going to leave their mother alone by herself in the church all night! Didn't they know how lonely she would feel and how much she needed them around to help her through this hard time of death?" Her relationship with the spirit of her dead friend was still very real and tangible for her.

Moreover, Aboriginal communities have unique, sacred ceremonies, customs, and spiritual connections to their dead. Commemorative practices for honouring the dead and the missing are entered into Aboriginal collective memory in specific and sacred ways. For example, Huffstetter (1998: 29) notes how an oral culture of memorialization is cultivated at Lakota wakes since the "real work of the wake went on with the gathering, the sharing of the meal, renewing family ties and remembering. People use the time to talk and tell stories about the one who had died, as a way of beginning to memorialize them."

Clearly, national commemoration of residential schools cannot presume to replace community customs. At best, such efforts can seek to expand the collective memory of those who will be remembered. If residential schools are placed within a broader Canadian context—a colonial history—the history may be rationalized as a shared Canadian history in which most people in Canada are former students, perpetrators, bystanders, or descendants of one or more of those identities. But as John Gillis (1994: 3) has written, each of those experiences spawns its own memories or forgettings: "National memory is shared by people who have never seen or heard of one another, yet who regard themselves as having a common history. They are bound together as much by forgetting as by remembering." This is particularly true if the forgetting is in response to trauma. In this light, Joachim Wolschke-Bulmahn (2001: 2) links identity and memory:

> Identity and memory are not stable and objective things, but representations or constructions of reality. The members of a particular nation, for example, share a specific history, but do they necessarily have the same identity? The way humans see themselves as a member of a particular group depends also on their own interpretation of history, their own ideas about the future, and their political, moral and other ideals. Identity and memory have to do with particular interests, such as class, gender, or power relations.

Gillis (1994: 3) also notes that "[t]he concepts of memory and identity are related to each other" and that identity is "inconceivable without history and without the remembrance and commemoration of history, however much such remembrance may distort historical events and facts." Even though "memory and identity are two of the most frequently used terms in contemporary public and private discourse," Gillis reminds us that:

> [t]he parallel lives of these two terms alert us to the fact that the notion of identity depends on the idea of memory and vice versa. The core meaning of any individual or group identity, namely, a sense of sameness over time and space, is sustained by remembering; and what is remembered is defined by the assumed identity.

Gillis (1994: 5) also says that "[a]t this particular historical moment, it is all the more apparent that both identity and memory are political and social constructs, and should be treated as such."

Richard Handler (1994: 29) does just that when he argues that "cultures are not individuated entities existing as natural objects with neat temporal and spatial boundaries." "Who we are," he writes, "is a communicative process, that includes many voices and varying degrees of understanding and, importantly, misunderstanding." He argues that in order to combat the reproduction of hegemonic and oppressive ideologies, "our critiques of identity [must] focus on those mainstream claims that too often go unchallenged . . . rather than writing exclusively about the 'invention' of minority identities, traditions, and cultures."

Gillis (1994: 5) affirms this view when he asserts that "memories and identities are not fixed things, but representations or constructions of reality," and that "we are constantly revising our memories to suit our current identities." He also argues that memory and identity operate within a social framework, noting that "'memory work' is like any other kind of physical or mental labour, embedded in complex class, gender and power relations that determine what is remembered (or forgotten), by whom, and for what end."

While Gillis focuses in part on "collective amnesia" in writing that "[n]ew memories require concerted forgettings," Maurice Halbwachs (1992: 182) places all collective memory in particular social contexts. Halbwachs writes that the "individuals call recollections to mind by relying on the frameworks of social memory," which means that social groups influence individual identity and memory. While "the various groups that compose society are capable at every moment of reconstructing their past . . . they most frequently distort that past in reconstructing it." He also says that "a remembrance is in very large measure a reconstruction of the past achieved with data borrowed from the present, a reconstruction prepared, furthermore, by reconstructions of earlier periods wherein past images had already been altered" (Halbwachs, 1992: 69).

Noa Gedi and Yigal Elam (1996) go so far as to question the usefulness of the term "collective memory" by arguing that so-called experts, which they refer to as "memoriologists," have simply reinvented an old, familiar term. They note that for historians, collective memory is useful metaphorically in that it stands in for myth. They reject Halbwachs's (1992: 40) argument that "there is really no room for history as a science, that is, as a methodological effort aimed at reconstructing actual past events by means of conventional methods of verification . . . and finally, proposing theoretical models which would explain them." Claiming that Halbwachs's "notion of history writing . . . is rather an intentional formation of the past without any obligation to 'historical truth,'" Gedi and Elam write that such a view results in history becoming a tool for the ideological and moralistic needs of society:

> Collective memory has become the predominant notion which replaces real (factual) history . . . and real (personal) memory. . . . Indeed, "collective memory" has become the all-pervading concept which in effect stands for all sorts of human cognitive products generally. . . . What is lost . . . is the dialectical tension between the old simple personal memory as a questionable

source of evidence, and history as a corroborated version of past events. Instead we now have history as "collective memory," that is, as a fabricated narrative (once called "myth") either in the service of social-ideological needs, or even expressing the creative whim of a particular historian.

Not all of those who have adopted "collective memory" and use it profusely necessarily embrace the theory behind the term. (Gedi and Elam, 1996: 40–1)

Like Halbwachs, Pierre Nora (1989: 8) places collective memory in a social context but argues that it changes due to changes in social structures. He asserts that:

The conquest and eradication of memory by history, then, confronts us with the brutal realization of the difference between real memory—social and unviolated, exemplified in but also retained as the secret of so-called primitive or archaic societies—and history, which is how our hopelessly forgetful modern societies, propelled by change, organize the past. On the one hand, we find an integrated, dictatorial memory—unself-conscious, commanding, all-powerful, spontaneously actualizing, a memory without a past that ceaselessly reinvents tradition, linking the history of its ancestors to the undifferentiated time of heroes, origins, and myth—and on the other hand, our memory, [is] nothing more in fact than sifted and sorted historical traces.

According to Nora, what was once a much more holistic environment of memory becomes an artificial archival form of memory. Where memory "is life, borne by living societies ... in permanent evolution, open to the dialectic of remembering and forgetting, unconscious of its successive deformations, vulnerable to manipulation and appropriation," history is "the reconstruction, always problematic and incomplete, of what is no longer."

Essentially, we have moved away from living with and experiencing memory to letting static sites of memory, like museums and monuments, do all the work. Gedi and Elam (1996: 49) call Nora's view "radical," and argue that he "substitute[s] the monument for living memory, thereby turning it into the actual location of 'collective memory.' The end result is that because history and memory stand in opposition to one another, he has to declare *lieux de memoire* as 'another history.' We thus no longer deal with events but with sites."

Kirk Savage (1994: 146) notes that "all shared memory requires mediating devices to sustain itself." Archives and monuments thus represent mediating devices, and when they are combined with rituals of remembering they help cultivate a certain collective memory and identity, since "the public monument represents a kind of collective recognition—in short, legitimacy—deposited there" (Savage, 1994: 135–6). Relatedly, Brian Osborne (1998: 431) states that every monument can become a "dynamic site of meaning," and that monuments can thus be seen as "spatial and temporal landmarks; they were loaded with memory; they performed a didactic function; they were signs of national progress; they were heroic figures (men, of course!) who represented the anonymous masses; symbols of rights and liberties" (Osborne, 2001: 50).

Gillis presents a wide-ranging overview of the historical phases of commemoration in the West, from the pre-national through the national to the present post-national phase. He notes that in the pre-national phase only the elites of society institutionalized memory, which was separate from the popular, living memory that existed among regular people. While he views the national phase of commemoration as more democratic, he suggests that it is highly institutionalized and controlled by agents of the state, who almost always venerate men of "historical significance." In contrast, the post-national phase embodies a "tendency toward the personalization of memory," away from the collective and towards a "plurality of pasts" (Gillis, 1994: 14, 18). Osborne (1998: 54) agrees with Gillis that collective memory and identity represent contested terrain in noting that "each group [has] its own lists of heroes and villains," and that "rather than being sites of consensus building, public space and its population of carefully selected monuments and statuary become contested terrains."

Gillis (1994: 5) also writes that patterns in the historical relationship between memory and identity can be traced through various forms of commemoration, since commemorative activity is "by definition social and political, for it involves the coordination of individual and group memories, whose results may appear consensual when they are in fact the product of processes of intense contest, struggle, and, in some instances, annihilation." Daniel Levy (1999: 65) further recognizes that commemorative activity can involve conscious and unconscious decisions to include and exclude at the national level, and that the "histories of nations are increasingly problematized and have become a realm of commemorative combat," or what I would call competing memories. After asking what version of history and what image of a nation's past prevail in the public sphere, he concludes that the "contested nature of the nation and the multiplication of other identity options are thus reflected in the proliferation of struggles over collective memory."

Alan Gordon (2001) defines "public memory" as "conceptions of history enshrined in historic sites and public monuments in the streets, parks, and squares of a city." Although Gordon regards public memory as contested terrain, he argues that all collective memory includes rather nebulous, non-material cultural expressions such as customs and traditional practices. The choice of who is commemorated and how they are to be commemorated through monuments thus "reveal[s] much about the sense of history of the men and women who select them, and in this respect, commemoration is closely related to power: it reveals an ongoing contest for hegemony. Public memory, then, works to turn history into a shared experience in the interest of broadly and loosely defined political goals."

The notion of "teaching" is therefore of critical importance, says Roger Simon (2004: 197), "particularly if we take public memory as a sphere for developing a historical consciousness—not as an individual awareness and attitude but as a commitment to and participation in a critical practice of remembrance and learning . . . to remember anew." Similarly, Osborne (1998: 72) concludes by asking, "Is there a need for a new paradigm of heritage commemoration? . . . The classical allegorical forms of didactic statuary and monuments no longer resonate with the modern world. Rather than being declarative sites of conceptual closure, perhaps they should be ambiguous sites of pondering and reflection."

As with the truth-telling component of the TRC, commemoration initiatives face the challenge of reaching those who may find it difficult to hear or listen to the stories of others. Just as there is diversity across First Nations, Inuit, and Métis experiences with residential schools, so too will there be diversity across the non-Aboriginal public that will listen to these stories. In this light, Simon (2004) proposes that we should see commemoration initiatives as part of a transformational process involving those who are willing to listen, view, and ponder.

This is precisely what Métis artist Christi Belcourt asks of viewers of the stained glass window *Giniigaaniimenaaning (Looking Ahead)* she was commissioned to design for the Centre Block on Parliament Hill in 2011. She describes the experience she hopes viewers of *Giniigaaniimenaaning* will have:

> The story begins in the bottom left corner of the glass, with your eye moving upwards in the left panel to the top window, and flowing down the right window to the bottom right corner. The glass design tells a story. It is a story of Aboriginal people, with our ceremonies, languages, and cultural knowledge intact; through the darkness of the residential school era; to an awakening sounded by a drum; an apology that spoke to the heart; hope for reconciliation; transformation and healing through dance, ceremony, language; and resilience into the present day. The title of the piece is

"Giniigaaniimenaaning," [which] translated into English means, "Looking Ahead." The title is in Anishinaabemowin (Ojibway) and includes, within the deeper meaning of the word, the idea that everyone is included and we are all looking ahead for the ones "unborn."

Belcourt invites viewers of *Giniigaaniimenaaning* on a journey from a pre-contact history where traditions are intact, through the 150 years of Indian residential schools, culminating with survivors breaking their silence. At its peak, the window includes a banner referencing 2008, the year of Prime Minister Stephen Harper's official apology. The right panel depicts dancing and drumming, healing activities, a mother holding a baby, and the words "I love you" in Cree, Anishinaabemowin, Inuktitut, and Mi'kmaw. And then the circle is complete, with a return to the earth, to the lodge, and to traditional ways.

The unique journey of every survivor is often very powerful, which Belcourt explains is why it is important for listeners and viewers to hear and understand the stories behind such pieces. That each survivor has a specific message to convey is evident in the words of a survivor Belcourt went to for advice before beginning her piece.

So I offered tobacco and I said, "What do you think about this, should I do it? And if I do it, what should be in there?" And that's when she told me, "Yes, do it." She said, "Make it about hope." ... She said, "I don't have hope because I've been affected so badly ... but I want to have hope for the future generations. I want them to have hope." She said, "I can't, but I want them to have it." (Dewar interview)

Discussion Questions

1. How does the legacy of Indian residential schools—and its larger colonial context—affect survivors, those impacted intergenerationally, and the general public at large?
2. What are some of the different ways that Aboriginal and non-Aboriginal artists, curators, and scholars define "reconciliation," and why do they define it differently?
3. In what ways is art or art-making an avenue for healing? Has art been an avenue for healing in your own life or in the life of someone you know?
4. What does it mean to say that people remember, commemorate, and/or memorialize in different ways?

Further Reading

Castellano, Marlene Brant, Linda Archibald, and Mike DeGagné, eds. 2008. *From Truth to Reconciliation: Transforming the Legacy of Residential Schools*. Ottawa: Aboriginal Healing Foundation.

Dewar, Jonathan, and Ayumi Goto, eds. 2012. *West Coast Line #74: Reconcile This!* (special issue) 46, 2 (Summer).

Gillis, John R., ed. 1994. *Commemorations: The Politics of National Identity*. Princeton, NJ: Princeton University Press.

Milloy, John. S. 1999 *A National Crime*. Winnipeg: University of Manitoba Press.

Weaver, Jace. 1997. *That the People Might Live: Native American Literatures and Native American Community*. New York: Oxford University Press.

Notes

1. "Indian residential schools" is the term used by the government of Canada, with some variants, including the inclusion of Inuit as a descriptor. "Residential schools" refers to all government-funded, church-run schools where children were in residence, including industrial schools, boarding schools, student residences, hostels, billets, and even Inuit tent camps in the North. First Nations, Inuit, and Métis children were all subject to the assimilatory goals of the government and the proselytizing efforts of the various churches through schooling. While the government of Canada has formally apologized for the residential school experience, the "day schools," which affected some First Nations and Inuit but proportionally many more Métis students, have not been formally addressed.

2. The United Church of Canada offered the first apology in 1986. Other apologies and statements followed: the Oblate Missionaries of Mary Immaculate (Roman Catholic) in 1991, the Anglican Church in 1993, and the Presbyterian Church in 1994 (Castellano, Archibald, and DeGagné, 2008: 64–5).

3. An interim executive director was appointed in September 2007 to set up the TRC secretariat in advance of the process that eventually named Harry LaForme as Commission chair and Claudette Dumont-Smith and Jane Brewin Morley as the other two commissioners. The TRC began its work on 1 June 2008, but on 20 October of that year LaForme resigned due to irreconcilable differences between himself and the other commissioners. Dumont-Smith and Brewin Morley resigned from the TRC shortly thereafter. The TRC was reconstituted on 10 June 2009 with the appointment of Justice Murray Sinclair as chair and Marie Wilson and Wilton Littlechild as commissioners.

4. There are two compensation elements: (1) the Common Experience Payment (CEP), a process through which all former students who can prove their residency at a school on the government-approved list could apply for compensation based on a formula of $10,000 for the first year of attendance and $3,000 for each additional year; and (2) the Independent Assessment Process for specific abuse claims. The AHF published two studies exploring issues surrounding compensation: *Lump Sum Compensation Payments Research Project: The Circle Rechecks Itself* (2007) and *The Indian Residential Schools Settlement Agreement's Common Experience Payment and Healing: A Qualitative*

Study Exploring Impacts on Recipients (2010). The AHF had also received $40 million in 2005 from the federal government, bringing the total of funds received by the AHF through the two mandates to $515 million. The AHF's mandate under the IRSSA officially ended on 31 March 2012. However, it has continued since then with a small operational staff managing monies from the Catholic entities, parties to the IRSSA, which chose to commit a portion of their obligated financial commitment within the IRSSA to the Healing Fund.

5. A lengthier excerpt from Prime Minister Harper's apology is included in Chapter 3 of this book. The full text of this apology, as well as the statements of apology from the other federal party leaders in the House of Commons (note especially that of NDP leader Jack Layton, who was instrumental in getting the government to issue the formal apology), and the responses by the leaders of national Aboriginal organizations (see especially those of AFN National Chief Phil Fontaine and of Beverley Jacobs, President of the Native Women's Association of Canada), are all available in Hansard, the official verbatim record of parliamentary sessions in Canada. See http://www.parl.gc.ca/HousePublications/Publication.aspx?DocId=3568890.

6. The "Sixties Scoop" refers to the alarming number of Indigenous children removed from their homes by various Children's Aid or social services bodies during this decade and beyond.

7. Dickason and McNab (2009) have noted that Aboriginal peoples have been passing on their storied life lessons through many forms of cultural expressions from time immemorial.

8. Accessed 15 Nov. 2014 at: http://www.enowkincentre.ca/about.html.

9. Armstrong translates this from the original Okanagan, which is not reproduced in print.

10. It is important to note that artistic and scholarly concepts of "reconciliation" engaged in this chapter and elsewhere may or may not have been influenced by Canada's Truth and Reconciliation Commission. The focus of the TRC is specific to residential schools in Canada, and given that the settlement agreement is somewhat exclusive by virtue of its attachment to an "approved" list of schools, it is also exclusive in that it has defined an approved "membership" to the experience.

11. Alfred and Corntassel reject the term "aboriginal" outright in favour of "Indigenous," arguing that "this identity is purely a state construction that is instrumental to the state's own attempt to gradually subsume Indigenous existences into its own constitutional system and body politic."

12. This concept was introduced by Gerald Vizenor (1999) and blends notions of survival and resistance.

13. Torpey (2003: 3) defines "reparations" narrowly to mean "a response to past injustices" and "reparations politics" as "a broader field encompassing 'transitional justice,' 'apologies,' and efforts at 'reconciliation' as well."

12

A Way Forward in Efforts to Support the Health and Well-Being of Canada's Aboriginal Peoples

Martin Cooke and David Long

The Commission recommends that . . . Governments, in formulating policy in social, economic or political spheres, give foremost consideration to the impact of such policies on the physical, social, emotional and spiritual health of Aboriginal citizens, and on their capacity to participate in the life of their communities and Canadian society as a whole. (RCAP, 1996: section 3.3.4)

Introduction

While announcements of extraordinary discoveries and advancements in modern medicine are now relatively common, we also regularly hear about the outbreak of diseases that had presumably been "cured" as well as serious health problems experienced among particular populations. Moreover, users of Facebook, Twitter, or other social media are inundated with appeals for financial support to help fight new and old wars against every imaginable disease and illness. Marketing campaigns by pharmaceutical companies as well as health promotion advocates regularly "remind" us through mass and social media about widespread problems with depression and other non-physical health issues, though such campaigns often stress that successful treatments depend on properly identifying and managing the symptoms of individual patients. Given the attitudes expressed in these and countless other health-related messages, it should hardly be surprising that many people in Canada view illness and health in largely medical terms and primarily as a matter of individual behaviour and treatment of their physical symptoms. As is evident in the following discussion, however, there is a different—and we would

© Isabelle Dubois/ArcticNet

argue much more hopeful—way of viewing illness and health in the lives of Aboriginal people in Canada.

We follow the Royal Commission on Aboriginal Peoples (RCAP) in view-ing illness and health in the lives of Aboriginal individuals and communities in Canada from the social determinants of health (SDH) perspective. Along with engaging the physical, emotional, and spiritual dimensions of illness and health, SDH seeks to understand how and why illness and health in different populations are related to people's social characteristics and circumstances. The SDH model also takes into account that illness/health are affected by the material and social capital of Aboriginal individuals and communities as well as by cultural attitudes and practices surrounding illness/health within specif-ic communities and in the broader society. Consequently, while application of the SDH model can provide a very broad and even national-level understand-ing of illness/health in Canada, it can also provide insight into illness, health, and well-being at the community level.

Understanding illness, health, and well-being in the lives of Aboriginal individuals and communities in Canada from the perspective of commun-ity members is, of course, no simple task. As Peter Cole and other contribu-tors to this collection note, it is challenging to honour traditional Indigenous knowledge (TIK) without essentializing the experience and perspective of Indigenous peoples. While aspects of the TIK worldview apply to all peoples, countless traditional teachings are passed down in quite specific ways by Elders from generation to generation. In other words, TIK embodies the unique experiences, relationships, and perspectives of members of particu-lar communities as well as the experiences and wisdom of ancestors and all their relations. Respecting and understanding TIK in this way is essential if we hope to meaningfully address issues surrounding the illness, health, and well-being of Aboriginal people, whether we are focusing on conditions in specific communities or on the national average.

We begin this chapter with a brief socio-historical analysis of the development and implementation of Aboriginal health legislation, policies, and programs in Canada. This is followed by a detailed discussion of the two perspectives on illness, health, and well-being mentioned above. After noting certain contrasts between the holistic, Indigenous approach to health/well-being and its Western scientific, biomedical counterpart, we discuss the ways that the SDH perspective contributes to our understanding of illness, health, and well-being in the lives of Aboriginal peoples in Canada. We conclude with a discussion of initiatives that seek to bring Indigenous and Western ways of seeing and being together in the world of Aboriginal health. Before we begin our discussion of a number of key developments in Aboriginal health legislation and policy, a few introductory comments on how the RCAP framed the relationship between health and healing are in order.

The RCAP: Clarifying a Vision for Aboriginal Health and Healing

While the history of commissions and inquiries into issues involving Aboriginal peoples in Canada indicates ongoing concern to understand and address inequity and injustice, the fundamental goal of the RCAP was to move relations between Aboriginal peoples and Canadian institutions forward in a good way (RCAP, 1996). One of the critical areas the Commission identified as being in need of change was health. Indeed, the "Health and Healing" chapter in the RCAP report comprehensively addressed the physical, social, emotional, spiritual, and environmental elements of Aboriginal people's health. Not surprisingly, the report highlighted that the average health of Aboriginal people in Canada was much poorer than that of other Canadians.

European colonization affected the lives of Canada's Aboriginal peoples in countless ways. Testimony presented to the RCAP indicated that it had not only affected their individual health and well-being, but that it had also torn apart the interpersonal, cultural, structural, and spiritual fabric of practically every family and community. The final report of the RCAP detailed these negative impacts. Loss of traditions and languages, family and community disruption, political corruption among community leaders, serious economic disparity and unemployment in many communities, addiction, suicide, disease, disability, and shorter lifespans were clearly linked to hundreds of years of colonizing attitudes, Indian Act legislation and policies, and every-day practices of Europeans (RCAP, 1996). Although the Indian Act initially was only applicable to status (treaty) First Nations, colonization profoundly affected the Inuit as well as Métis and non-status Aboriginal people in many negative ways (Long, 2014). Despite this fact, the final RCAP report is anything but a litany of horrific experiences and harsh criticisms. Rather, the report em-bodies a vision of reconciliation and hope intended to bring healing to past, present, and future generations of Aboriginal peoples through the establish-ment of a new relationship with the rest of Canada (RCAP, 1996; Long, 2004).

Many of the RCAP recommendations related to health and well-being were wide-ranging and sought to address fundamentally systemic problems. For ex-ample, they supported strengthening community control over health service delivery and training sufficient numbers of Aboriginal health professionals to reduce reliance on non-Aboriginal experts (Long, 2009). They also focused on the need to empower communities to define the content of their own health care services, in part to honour and maintain culturally specific conceptions of illness, disease, healing, and wellness. While the report acknowledged that Western science and medicine provide invaluable assistance in understand-ing and addressing many health-related issues affecting Aboriginal people, it also specified that the findings of scientific research and the application of any medical advancement must be controlled by and be of direct benefit to the individuals and communities involved in their development. Moreover, the report called for Aboriginal people and the rest of Canada to work cre-atively together to address the legacy of colonialism in every area of life, in-cluding its impact on illness and health. As we note in the following section, the RCAP followed roughly 150 years of often intense "negotiations" between Aboriginal peoples and representatives of the Canadian state, and it is clear that illness and health have always been a central issue in the relationship.

Jurisdiction and Responsibility for Aboriginal Health

A significant issue in the long-standing debate over the role of the state in supporting Aboriginal health has been a lack of clear understanding regard-ing the administration and delivery of Aboriginal health services. While sec-tion 94 of the 1867 Constitution Act assigned full legislative authority over "Indians and lands reserved for Indians" to the federal government, provincial and territorial governments remained responsible for administering health and social services to their people. In other words, although provincial and territorial governments were to be responsible for providing health care to those living within their geopolitical boundaries, the federal government assumed responsibility for providing administrative oversight of First Nations and Inuit health care. Métis as well as First Nations people who had lost status either through out-marriage or because they did not belong to an officially recognized band would remain the responsibility of the provinces. In this way, the federal and provincial governments of Canada have responded to the health care and social service needs of Aboriginal peoples in Canada by dividing them into two distinct groups.

Even for those whose health and well-being clearly falls under federal jurisdiction, the question of what kind of services and resources the federal government should provide has long been the subject of much discussion and debate. Only Treaty 6, signed in 1876 by the government of Canada and the Cree of central Alberta and Saskatchewan, mentions government provision of health care in its terms:

> In the event hereafter of the Indians . . . being overtaken by any pestilence or by general famine, the Queen . . . will grant to the Indians assistance . . . sufficient to relieve them from the calamity that shall have befallen them. . . . A medicine chest shall be kept at the house of each Indian Agent for the use and benefit of the Indians at the direction of such agent. (AANDC, 1964)

There continues to be much dispute over the meaning of the "medicine chest." According to many First Nations leaders, treaty agreements include comprehensive health care to all descendants of the original Indigenous signatories (RCAP, 1993: 42; Littlechild and Littlechild, 2009). In contrast, governments in Canada have historically argued that the government is responsible only to Aboriginal people who have proper legal status and who live on First Nation reserves or in distinct Aboriginal communities.[1]

Care and concern for Aboriginal health have been shifted between levels of government and from department to department since Canada's very beginning. Although the Department of Indian Affairs (DIA) was originally charged with the administrative responsibility to provide health services for on-reserve Aboriginal people, this changed in 1945, the year after Parliament passed the National Health and Welfare Act and Indian health services were transferred to the newly established Department of Health and Welfare.[2] While there may have been some wisdom in transferring Aboriginal health into this ministerial portfolio, doing so nonetheless contributed to a fragmentation of Aboriginal health policy and program initiatives since the DIA retained authority over health-related areas such as housing, education, welfare, and even sewage, sanitation, and safe drinking water.

A 1979 federal Indian health policy paper was the beginning of the end of full federal control over health care for Aboriginal peoples in Canada. In much the same way that the 1969 White Paper had served as a catalyst for the building of coalitions by Aboriginal people and their supporters to engage in large-scale resistance, the 1979 health policy paper generated heated debate over who should control Aboriginal health care in Canada. By the mid-1980s, negotiations between Aboriginal leaders and government representatives resulted in the development of a health transfer agreement model that enabled First Nations and Inuit communities to have greater control over their own health-related services. By 2002, roughly 47 per cent of eligible communities had signed such an agreement. These communities, combined with 151 others that had established community-based health services agreements and 41 that were involved in the pre-transfer phase, added up to more than 80 per cent of all eligible Aboriginal communities in Canada (Waldram, Herring, and Young, 2006: 270). The tide had clearly turned in relation to Aboriginal people having control over their own health and well-being.

The long-standing distinction between federal services for status First Nations and Inuit and provincial services for Métis and non-status First Nations people also appears to be breaking down in other ways. Although the federal government pays for services to status First Nations and those Inuit who are beneficiaries of an Inuit land claim agreement, similar services in cities and other off-reserve areas typically are provided at provincially funded clinics or hospitals. Both provincial and federal governments have funded Aboriginal health promotion or screening programs in urban and other off-reserve areas, many of which operate on a "status-blind" basis. Provinces have also recently abandoned their reluctance to be involved in the health of on-reserve First Nations. For example, the Ontario government is currently funding a variety of services to Ontario First Nations, including a network of Aboriginal Health Access Centres both on and off First Nations reserves. In British Columbia, a tripartite accord between the provincial and federal governments and BC First Nations organizations transferred responsibility for the delivery of health care services across the province to a new First Nations Health Authority. The 2013 decision of the Federal Court of Appeal to uphold the ruling in *Daniels v. Canada*—that Métis (but not non-status First Nations) should be considered "Indians" for the purposes of the Indian Act—may further erode the distinctions between Aboriginal peoples in terms of the provision of health services (Long, 2014).

Clearly, the health status of the Aboriginal population in Canada cannot be separated from the history of colonialism and the relationships between Aboriginal peoples and the Canadian state. As a result, while there appears to be growing recognition of the benefits of Aboriginal control over Aboriginal health, the question of how to move forward in a good way is a complex question. As we note in the following section, the deep cultural differences between Aboriginal and non-Aboriginal peoples' understandings of and responses to illness and health are among the more significant challenges in addressing this question.

Perspectives on Health: Western and Indigenous

Part of the historical dispute about Aboriginal health in Canada is rooted in different conceptions of illness and health. In very basic terms, the Western, "allopathic" approach to human health is based on a biomedical model that views the human body as an organic system of interrelated physical parts. Given that the "ideal state" of this system is for all body parts to function smoothly and in well-co-ordinated fashion, human health is a matter of whether or not the parts of our bodies function properly, individually and within complex systems. Physicians and other health professionals involved in research and diagnosis are thus essentially responsible for identifying what is wrong with the parts that are not working so they can properly intervene and treat, remove, or replace the diseased or improperly functioning part. Health practitioners and policy-makers who operate from this perspective tend to conceptualize health as mainly a physical state, characterized by the absence of physical disease. Even mental illnesses such as depression tend to be considered from within a "physical framework" of malfunctioning neurotransmitters, receptors, and parts of the brain itself. The result is that treatment of sickness and disease is primarily focused on physical interventions aimed at sick individuals, who for the most part are seen in isolation from their relationships in families, communities, or society at large.

In contrast, Aboriginal peoples' conception of illness and health emphasizes that the life of each human being is deeply connected to all of "creation" in the past, the present, and the future.

> Health is the core of the well-being that must lie at the centre of each healthy person and the vitality that must animate healthy communities and cultures. Where there is good health in this sense, it reverberates through every strand of life. (RCAP, 1993: 51)

Physical manifestations of illness are important, but this much broader and holistic perspective on health assumes that the emotional and spiritual dimensions of life must also be given consideration when "diagnosing" the potential causes of empirically measurable ailments.

Although there is a great deal of diversity in health and healing practices among Aboriginal peoples, "healing" is generally focused not only on the body but more fundamentally on restoring good relations between the whole self and others, and with honouring one's relation to all of creation—past, present, and future—through tradition and ceremony. From this perspective, health is more than the absence of physical disease in an individual. Rather, it is the measure of the spiritual, mental, emotional, and physical well-being of individuals, communities, and "all their relations."

The holistic perspective understands many of the health problems experienced by Aboriginal people to be directly related to the profound disruption and destruction of their cultures and communities. As noted throughout this edition of *Visions of the Heart*, the long history of colonialism and its (continued) devaluation of Aboriginal experiences and world views are at the root of such destruction. Many agree with Cindy Blackstock (2003) that minor tinkering with health legislation and/or social policies and programs will continue to remain largely ineffective since they do little to address the root causes of exclusion and racism that have become normalized through the Indian Act and hundreds of years of colonialism. For example, as representatives of the Nechi Institute (1988: 4) noted:

> Attempting to heal isolated Aboriginal individuals apart from their family and their community cannot heal abuse and other imbalances of life. To get to the root cause of abuse and neglect, the entire system that allowed it to occur must be restored to balance. This means that the accumulated hurt of generations, carried to our families and our communities, needs to be released through a healing process.

What this healing process ought to look like in relation to Aboriginal health continues to be open to much discussion and debate. A common idea expressed in statements to the RCAP was that resources and social change efforts should be directed towards community-based TIK programs and initiatives that are responsive to the diversity of experiences and circumstances between as well as within Aboriginal communities (Ferris et al., 2005; Saulis, 2003). Still, public health developments in Canada and elsewhere since the early 1990shave indicated that there is some complementarity between allopathic and Indigenous initiatives, even though they may appear to be grounded in two very different worlds.

The Changing View of (Public) Health in Canada

Indeed, the establishment of the RCAP occurred during a significant time in the history of public health in Canada and elsewhere. Two significant shifts in health policy that had become entrenched by the early 1990s reflected the radically new approach to public health that had emerged during the 1960s and 1970s in Canada and other wealthy countries in the West. The first was a move towards general disease prevention and away from a primary concern with those who were already ill or who were most at risk of becoming ill. It was recognized that although it would always be a primary role of the health care system to treat the sick and those likely to become sick, there needed to be much greater emphasis on disease prevention in the broader population. As social epidemiologist Geoffrey Rose (1985) noted, it had become increasingly clear that greater overall reduction in the "burden of illness" for many types of health problems could be achieved by focusing on the health of the population as a whole rather than on only those at "high risk."

The second shift was that health researchers began to pay greater attention to the social and economic determinants of health and well-being. It had long been recognized that those with lower education, income, and social standing tended to be in poorer health and to live shorter lives (Raphael, 2006). However, early health researchers had focused on the direct, or what they referred to as the "proximal," causes of illness such as poor food and water quality, smoking and excessive drinking, and poor housing. This changed during the late 1960s and early 1970s as population health researchers began to focus on the broader relationships between social, economic, and political contexts and poor health. The landmark Whitehall studies in the UK identified a reliable "status gradient in health," meaning that researchers had found a direct relationship between lower social status and higher mortality, regardless of the adequacy of diet or other physical conditions (Marmot et al., 1984). The Whitehall studies were influential in highlighting the benefits of understanding the *social* determinants of health in communities and societies, which helped shift academic and policy attention away from a strictly biological and clinical focus on individual illness and health.

Canada also contributed significantly to the new public health initiative during this time through the publication of two documents. The first was the

Lalonde Report (Lalonde, 1972), which is widely cited as the first government articulation of the SDH approach to public health. A decade later, the World Health Organization's First International Conference on Health Promotion resulted in the publication of the *Ottawa Charter for Health Promotion* (WHO, 1986). The *Charter* stated that the prerequisites for health were peace, shelter, education, food, income, stable ecosystem, sustainable resources, social justice, and equity. Population health researchers soon added such critical health determinants as healthy child development; adequate incomes; a small gap between rich and poor; the absence of discrimination based on gender, culture, race, and sexual orientation; lifelong learning opportunities; healthy lifestyles; meaningful work opportunities with some control over decision-making; social relationships that respect diversity; freedom from violence or its threat; freedom from exposure to infectious disease; protection of humans from environmental hazards and protection of the environment from human hazards. A number of fundamental values informed the *Charter*, including that:

- Individuals are treated with dignity, and their innate self-worth, intelligence, and capacity of choice are respected.
- Individual liberties are respected, but priority is given to the common good when conflict arises.
- Participation is supported in policy decision-making to identify what constitutes the common good.
- Priority is given to people whose living conditions, especially a lack of wealth and power, place them at greater risk.
- Social justice is pursued to prevent systemic discrimination and to reduce health inequities.
- Health of the present generation is not purchased at the expense of future generations.

The strategic principles articulated in the *Charter* further specified that:

1. Health promotion addresses health issues in context. It recognizes that many individual, social, and environmental factors interact to influence health. It searches for ways to explain how these factors interact in order to plan and act for the greatest health gain.
2. Health promotion supports a holistic approach that recognizes and includes the physical, mental, social, ecological, cultural, and spiritual aspects of health.

3. Health promotion requires a long-term perspective. It takes time to create awareness and build understanding of health determinants. This is true for organizations as well as for individuals.

4. Health promotion supports a balance between centralized and decentralized decision-making on policies that affect people where they live, work, and play.

5. Health promotion is multi-sectoral. While program initiatives often originate in the health sector, little can be done to change unhealthy living conditions and improve lifestyles without the support of other people, organizations, and policy sectors.

6. Health promotion draws on knowledge from a variety of sources. It depends on formal knowledge from the social, economic, political, medical, and environmental sciences. It also depends on the experiential knowledge of people.

7. Health promotion emphasizes public accountability. Those providing health promotion activities need to be accountable and to expect the same commitment from other individuals and organizations.

The SDH approach promoted through the Lalonde Report and the *Ottawa Charter* gained much support over the next three decades, and became institutionalized in 2005 through the creation of the Public Health Agency of Canada (PHAC) as well as the position of the Chief Medical Officer for Canada. Given that the RCAP pursued its mandate during the early and mid-1990s, it is not surprising that many of those involved were familiar with and sympathetic to the values and principles that informed the new public health perspective. What may be surprising to some is that the final RCAP report noted that the fundamental principles underlying the "newly discovered" public health perspective had been part of Indigenous wisdom and teachings for millennia, and that it invited representatives of Aboriginal, federal, provincial, and territorial governments to endorse the principles of:

- holism—that is, attention to whole persons in their total environment;
- equity—that is, equitable access to the means of achieving health and rough equality of outcomes in health status;
- control—by Aboriginal people of their lifestyle choices, institutional services, and environmental conditions that support health;
- diversity—that is, accommodation of the cultures and histories of First Nations, Inuit, and Métis people that make them distinctive within Canadian society and that distinguish them from one another. (RCAP, 1996: section 3.3.1)

From this broad perspective, recommendations directed at improving the health of Aboriginal populations focused on better education and income, as well as on reducing social and economic inequality between Aboriginal people and non-Aboriginal Canadians. Other initiatives within public health and health research since the 1990s have reinforced some of the recommendations of the RCAP. These include an increased focus on the relationship between community and neighbourhood characteristics and individual health as well as increased attention to culture, notably the movement from "cultural awareness" to "cultural competence" in the delivery and design of health care programs. In all, these developments embodied support for a much more socially inclusive perspective on public health initiatives.

The RCAP also helped to advance a more socially inclusive approach to Aboriginal health by promoting a new kind of dialogue between Western and Aboriginal health researchers and policy-makers. It challenged those with a fairly narrow, empirically scientific approach to engage an Indigenous perspective that supported a more holistic, locally based, and culturally relevant approach to the gaining of new knowledge. Along with highlighting the benefits of "participatory action research" for those engaged in community-based health research (Episkenew and Wheeler, 2002), the RCAP sought to change the dynamics of power between researchers and the Aboriginal subjects of research so that research findings would be seen as simply one of the outcomes in an ongoing relationship between health researchers and Aboriginal communities (Flicker et al., 2008; McCaulay et al., 1999). Whereas most Aboriginal health research had involved non-Aboriginal researchers studying the health status of Aboriginal peoples, Aboriginal organizations and communities increasingly began to demand control over the way research was conceived, conducted, reported, and used by potential stakeholders (Long and LaFrance, 2004; McNaughton and Rock, 2004; O'Riley, 2004). By 1996, many non-Aboriginal stakeholders interested in Aboriginal health clearly were in agreement with the principles and vision of the RCAP. At the same time as the final report of the RCAP was released, the Canadian Public Health Association expressed support for both increased collaboration between government and those involved in community-based research and for the promotion and development of research projects that combined different methodologies (Canadian Public Health Association, 1996).

Much research conducted since the publication of the final report of the RCAP has helped to bridge two ways of thinking about the health and well-being of Aboriginal peoples in Canada. The resulting new knowledge has contributed to the development of a wide variety of initiatives that have directly benefited Aboriginal communities. This is not to say that those involved are ignoring a number of fundamental, and perhaps even irreconcilable, differences between the perspectives of scientifically grounded health researchers and researchers who seek to honour Elder wisdom and TIK in community contexts. Indeed, the recent case of Makayla Sault, an 11-year-old girl who was a member of the New Credit First Nation, brought national attention to both the profound differences between Western and traditional medicine as well as complex questions surrounding the right of First Nations parents and children to decide what is in their best interest in the face of life-threatening illnesses.[3] This case also highlights the highly contentious and political nature of issues surrounding illness and health in the lives of Canada's Aboriginal peoples.

Notwithstanding the challenges that these differences and tensions present, the following sections illustrate how interactions and collaborations between health scientists, social epidemiologists, and community-based researchers appear to be contributing to a more holistic understanding of health and well-being in the lives of Aboriginal peoples in Canada.

The Demography and Social Epidemiology of Aboriginal Health

One way the SDH perspective changed the Aboriginal health research landscape was to open up new research areas and topics. In contrast to research that had focused almost solely on the physical health (problems) of individuals, SDH researchers sought to understand the ways that social circumstances contributed in positive or negative ways to the physical health and well-being of individuals, families, and whole communities. In academic and medical research circles, this approach is often referred to as "social epidemiology" (Berkman and Kawachi, 2000). As is evident below, this perspective is useful when studying trends in mortality and self-rated health[4] as well as more specific aspects of physical health, including the diseases to which Aboriginal people are particularly at risk.

According to Caldwell (2006), the theory of demographic transition argues that societies tend to move through several stages of population growth. While most populations initially remain fairly constant, with high birth rates roughly balanced by high mortality rates, improved conditions contribute to lower mortality and higher population growth. That Aboriginal populations in Canada have grown much more rapidly than the general population of Canada since World War II suggests that they are experiencing this kind of transition (Waldram, Herring, and Young, 2006; Guimond, Kerr, and

Beaujot, 2004). The rapid growth of Aboriginal populations in Canada has also involved changing patterns of mortality and fertility (Caldwell, 2006). As is evident in Table 12.1, life expectancy at birth in 1980 for registered Indian males and females was, respectively, 60.9 and 68.0, which was roughly 10 years lower than life expectancy rates for the Canadian population as a whole (Indian and Northern Affairs Canada, 2005). However, while the life expectancy of the general population had risen to 77 years for men and 82.1 years for women by 2001, the gap between the general and registered Indian populations had decreased to less than 7 years by this time (Verma, Michalowski, and Gauvin, 2003). Although life expectancy estimates are difficult to arrive at for Métis and Inuit, it appears that life expectancy among the Métis was higher in 2001 than among the registered Indian population. The same cannot be said for Inuit, for as Wilkins et al. (2008) note, Inuit life expectancy at birth was approximately 10 years lower than that of Canadians in 1991. As Inuit life expectancy appears to have *decreased* between 1991 and 2001, Table 12.1 indicates that this gap had actually widened to 12 years by 2001.

Falling mortality and high fertility rates have clearly contributed to significant growth of Aboriginal populations in Canada over the past 50 years. The infant mortality rate began to decline rapidly in the 1960s when the fertility rate of Aboriginal peoples was high. Since its peak around 1967, when Aboriginal fertility was more than four times that of the general Canadian

Table 12.1 | Estimated Life Expectancy at Birth (Years) for Aboriginal Populations and Canada, 1981, 1991, 2001

	1981 (1980)		1991 (1990)		2001	
	Male	Female	Male	Female	Male	Female
Registered Indians*	60.9	68.0	66.9	74.0	70.4	75.5
Métis**	–	–	–	–	72.4	79.9
Inuit	–	–	66.0	69.6	64.4	69.8
Canada	72.0	79.2	74.6	80.9	77.0	82.1

*Registered Indian life expectancies estimated for 1980, 1990, and 2001.
**Estimates calculated using geographic areas with high concentrations of Aboriginal peoples rather than ethnic identifiers on mortality data.
Source: Registered Indians: INAC (2005); Métis: Wilkins et al. (2008); Inuit: Wilkins et al. (2006); Canada: Statistics Canada (2009).

population, the fertility of Aboriginal populations has declined to about one-and-a-half times the Canadian rate (Statistics Canada, 2003). Still, First Nations, Inuit, and Métis populations have a considerably higher proportion of young people relative to the general Canadian population, and it appears that this will continue to be the case for years to come (Steffler, 2008).

An Aboriginal Epidemiological Transition?
The Changing Causes of Mortality

As noted previously, mortality in most pre-modern contexts tends to be caused by epidemics of contagious disease that are often the result of poor sanitation and lack of nutrition. Some demographers argue that the mortality rates of Western populations have passed through the "stage of receding pandemics" into the stage in which mortality is largely a result of chronic diseases such as cardiovascular diseases and cancer. In contrast, others have proposed that many Western populations have moved into a fourth stage in which these degenerative diseases occur later in life (Olshansky and Ault, 1986). Demographers refer to this change in the age at which populations are likely to die as the "compression of mortality." Essentially, the risk of dying becomes considerably lower in youth and young adult years, and mortality therefore becomes "compressed" into the later years of life. This seems to have happened in Canadian Aboriginal populations in recent decades, or at least among those registered under the Indian Act (Go et al., 1995).

Still, it is not entirely clear that the changing birth, mortality, and health patterns among Aboriginal populations in Canada are following the same patterns that the general Canadian population have followed. Three things are worth pointing out in order to make sense of the differences between the causes of death for Aboriginal and non-Aboriginal populations in Canada (Table 12.2). First, although Canadians in general may have passed through the "age of receding pandemics," Aboriginal people continue to be at high risk for communicable diseases causing death such as pneumonia and influenza. Second, rates of cancer and other chronic degenerative diseases such as heart disease have risen among Aboriginal people to the point that their risk of mortality due to these causes is now close to that of non-Aboriginal peoples. Third, many are concerned that "lifestyle" diseases such as diabetes are having far more serious effects on Aboriginal people than for the Canadian population as a whole. Moreover, the rates of death by accidents, violence (including suicide), and poisonings continue to be much higher than they are for other Western populations (Table 12.2) or for Indigenous populations in other countries (Trovato, 2001).

Table 12.2 | Age-Standardized* Mortality Rates (per 100,000) by Primary Cause of Death, Aboriginal and Non-Aboriginal Canadians, 1990

	Aboriginal	Non-Aboriginal	Risk Ratio**
Malignant neoplasms (cancer)	98.9	143.0	0.7
Ischemic heart disease	83.8	89.6	0.9
Cerebrovascular disease	28.1	30.9	0.9
Other chronic pulmonary disease	10.8	16.1	0.7
Pneumonia and influenza	24.4	17.7	1.4
Diabetes mellitus	19.5	13.3	1.5
Assault	8.1	1.5	4.5
Intentional self-harm	27.8	12.2	2.3

*Age-standardization accounts for the fact that the two populations have different age structures and makes the rates directly comparable.
**The ratio of the Aboriginal rate to the non-Aboriginal rate. This can be interpreted as the relative risk of mortality. For example, the risk of death due to cancer for Aboriginal people is 0.7 times that of non-Aboriginal people.
Source: Bramley et al. (2004).

It is clear that Aboriginal populations in Canada are not simply following the general Canadian population through the four stages of the epidemiologic transition. In fact, Aboriginal peoples in Canada appear to be experiencing relatively high rates of all of the major causes of death—infectious, chronic, and lifestyle diseases—simultaneously. Moreover, if we include illnesses and diseases that do not necessarily cause death, Aboriginal populations experience much higher rates of most chronic and infectious diseases than the non-Aboriginal population (Young, 1994). Understanding these differences and the reasons behind them is of critical importance, though making sense of different patterns of disease and the overall health status of Aboriginal peoples in Canada is a complex task. As is evident in the following section, health researchers offer a number of different explanations for these phenomena.

Explanations for Health Inequalities: Biology, Behaviour, and Society

There have generally been two emphases in health researchon the possible causes of disease and poor health in Aboriginal populations. One is "risk

factor" epidemiological research that focuses on how various personal behaviours, characteristics, or life conditions contribute to the health status of
Aboriginal individuals (McDowell, 2008; Susser, 1998). The risk factor that has
received the most attention from academic and policy researchers is the lack
of health care, especially on remote reserves or in other Aboriginal communities (MacMillan et al., 2003; Newbold, 1998; Shah, Gunraj, and Hux, 2003).

There has also been some interest in the role of genetic differences between Aboriginal populations and the general Canadian population, especially with regard to the role these may play in the very high rates of diabetes in
Aboriginal populations (Dyck, Klomp, and Tan, 2001; Young et al., 2000; Neel,
1962). However, genetic predisposition theory has been challenged on empirical grounds as well as on the basis of it reintroducing the concept of "race,"
which many now argue is a socially constructed concept with little actual
relationship to genetic diversity (Fee, 2006). For example, while Aboriginal
people exhibit higher rates of smoking and alcohol use than other Canadians
(Retnakaran et al., 2005), research indicates that the prevalence of diabetes
in Aboriginal populations is related more to levels of physical activity and
percentage of body fat rather than to a genetic propensity to obesity (Liu et al.,
2006). In other words, it seems clear that social and economic circumstances
rather than genetic makeup contribute to Aboriginal peoples' relatively high
rates of diabetes and other major health issues.

Social Determinants of Health

Although health researchers have continued to examine the more immediate and obvious factors affecting health, support for SDH research in Canada
has increased over the past two decades. The SDH perspective encompasses
a broad range of theories and models that focus on how the social and economic contexts in which people live directly and indirectly produce certain
health outcomes. And because SDH research seeks to examine the relationships between health and the social conditions of people's lives rather than
the characteristics of individuals, it is much more broadly focused than research on the behavioural or biomedical factors that contribute to disease,
illness, and death.

The SDH frameworks developed by Raphael (2006) and the Public Health
Agency of Canada (2003) are reproduced in Table 12.3. Although these two
frameworks include many similar determinants, the inclusion of Aboriginal
identity as a determinant of health by Raphael somewhat obscures that the
health of Aboriginal people is negatively affected by other determinants.
For example, Aboriginal children may be subject to a variety of conditions

in early life, such as poor maternal nutrition, that put them at higher risk of poor health at older ages. Aboriginal youth are also more likely to engage in risky behaviours such as smoking and alcohol use earlier in life than their non-Aboriginal counterparts (Munro, 2004). It is also the case that Aboriginal people continue to have lower educational attainment than other Canadians (Clement, 2008). In addition, the health status of Aboriginal people is affected by food insecurity, which indicates an unreliable supply of nutritious and culturally acceptable food. Willows and colleagues (2009) found that Aboriginal households are more than five times as likely to experience food insecurity as non-Aboriginal households. Moreover, this finding merely refers to those living off-reserve and does not include those living in remote or northern communities where fresh fruits and vegetables or other healthy foods are often very expensive, and many traditional food sources have become threatened by environmental change or the loss of knowledge of traditional food, harvesting, and preparation (Willows, 2009). Housing has also been a long-standing issue in urban areas as well as in First Nations and Inuit communities (Walker, 2008), and poor housing conditions have been linked to the spread of a variety of infectious diseases, including tuberculosis (Clark, Riben, and Nowgesic, 2002; Rosenberg et al., 1997).

Although environmental health might not be strictly seen as a *social* determinant of health, some SDH frameworks have included a clean and healthy environment as a key determinant, partly on the grounds that environmental degradation is an outcome of social processes and also because the risk of living in unhealthy environments is unevenly distributed. For example, many Aboriginal communities, and First Nations in particular, have had long-standing issues related to poor water quality and sanitation that have put them at risk to serious infections such as E. coli and Helicobacter pylori (Eggertson, 2006; Sinha et al., 2004). Although federal Aboriginal Affairs officials have repeatedly stated that providing adequate and safe water supplies to First Nations is a priority, 97 First Nations communities were still under boil-water advisories or "do not consume" orders as recently as September 2013 (Health Canada, 2014).

SDH research clearly indicates that many serious health issues are related directly or indirectly to low income and poverty, which continue to disproportionately affect Aboriginal people in Canada. The role of income and income inequality in relation to population health is nonetheless a complex and much-contested area of research. Psychosocial explanations focus on the distribution of income and the physical effects of low social status (Wilkinson, 1999). Epidemiological approaches that focus on the implications of social resources such as social capital in relation to health note, for example, that low-income individuals or communities may have social networks that are less able to deliver the kind of social or material support that can lead to better health outcomes (Hawe and Shiell, 2000). Still other social epidemiologists note that health is directly affected by income since it improves access to services, better housing, better food, and other goods (Muntaner and Lynch, 1999; Muntaner, Lynch, and Smith, 2001).

There have also been some attempts to develop SDH frameworks that apply specifically to Aboriginal health (see Anderson, 2007). Whereas Raphael (2006) included Aboriginal identity itself as a determinant of health, others have suggested that other important determinants may be unique to Aboriginal peoples (Table 12.3). For example, Wilson and Rosenberg (2002) suggest that participation in traditional activities such as hunting or fishing as

Table 12.3 | Social Determinants of Health Frameworks

Social Determinants of Health (Raphael)	Key Determinants of Health (Public Health Agency of Canada)	Aboriginal-Specific Determinants of Health (Wilson and Rosenberg; Richmond and Ross)
• Aboriginal status	• Healthy child development	• Participation in traditional activities
• Early life	• Education and literacy	• Balance
• Education	• Employment/working conditions	• Life control
• Employment and working conditions	• Health services	• (Environmental) education
• Unemployment and employment security	• Physical environments	• Material resources
• Health care services	• Income and social status	• Social resources
• Housing	• Social support networks	• Environmental/cultural connections
• Income and income distribution	• Social environments	
• Social safety net	• Personal health practices and behaviours	
• Social exclusion	• Biology and genetic endowment	
• Food security	• Gender	

Sources: Raphael (2006); PHAC (2003); Wilson and Rosenberg (2002); Richmond and Ross (2009).

well as ceremonies and other cultural activities may have independent effects on health. Richmond and Ross (2009) identify six determinants related to the experience of environmental dispossession, or the separation of First Nations and Inuit from their natural environments. The sacred connection Aboriginal peoples have to their lands means that these factors are unique determinants of their health.[5]

Sorting out causal links in the health of different populations has been a challenge for SDH researchers. Although Raphael (2006) claims that the SDH approach enables researchers to focus beyond behaviour and risk factors, McDowell (2008) argues that much SDH research has been of the "risk-factor" variety. Susser (1998) has also argued that examining correlations between various conditions and health does not provide clear understanding of the actual processes that produce inequalities in health. While some SDH researchers are using increasingly complex models to explore contextual factors and longitudinal data, others have been developing more "process-sensitive" approaches in order to provide an alternative to strictly quantitative, epidemiological research on Aboriginal health.

Indigenous and Community-Based Health Research

Although there is no clear definition of Indigenous research methodology, it is in general part of a movement to regain control over the production of knowledge by those whose lives are most directly affected by the research (Newhouse, 2004). Support for Indigenous research is based on the recognition that Aboriginal research in general and Aboriginal health research in particular have often been used to build and maintain colonial relations (Tuhiwai Smith, 1999). For both Aboriginal and non-Aboriginal peoples and organizations in Canada, control over Aboriginal research has become an important political priority (Episkenew and Wheeler, 2002; McNaughton and Rock, 2004; McPherson, 2005; O'Riley, 2004).

Increasingly, much Aboriginal health research has taken the form of community-based, participatory action research (PAR). The popularity of PAR has been due in large part to the fact that it seeks to invert traditional power relations between "researchers" and "researched" by engaging members of studied communities in all stages of research (Flicker et al., 2008; Macaulay et al., 1999). Whereas academic research has often been criticized for being of little practical value to participating individuals and communities, every effort is made during the design and implementation of PAR projects to keep the needs of participating communities in mind (Steenbeck, 2004).

Some proponents of Indigenous methodologies claim that Western scientific research processes are inherently incompatible with Indigenous world views, and that only Aboriginal communities can legitimately engage in research involving members of their communities (Tuhiwai Smith, 1999; McPherson, 2005). Quantitative statistical research is sometimes singled out as particularly at odds with an Indigenous approach to research since it reduces the complexity of people's lives and situations to numbers, and also because it has often been linked to government attempts to define and control Indigenous peoples (O'Neil, Reading, and Leader, 1998; Rowse, 2009). The main criticism of quantitative health research is that it does not serve the interests of Aboriginal peoples, in part because it isolates individuals from their local, cultural, and historical contexts and also because it frames health in terms of a narrow, Western definition of health and well-being (Michelle and Lemyra, 2006; Salée, 2006).

Whereas traditional risk-factor epidemiology examines statistical correlations between various predictors and morbidity or mortality, community-based Indigenous health research tends to focus on understanding processes associated with the progress of disease or with healing within particular communities. Cammer's (2006) studies on the experiences of older northern First Nations adults with mainstream dementia care is an example of research that was able to incorporate aspects of local geography and cultural factors into the research design, while Richmond and Ross (2009) developed the Aboriginal determinants of health framework listed in Table 12.3 in order to outline how Aboriginal conceptions of health could be integrated into mainstream health research.

Both Cammer (2006) and Richmond and Ross (2009) found from their interviews with First Nations and Inuit community health representatives that the historical dispossession of these people from their traditional environments had had an enormous negative impact on their health. As a result, Richmond and Ross proposed that a social determinants framework for Aboriginal health should include balance, life control, education, access to material resources, and social resources, as well as the maintenance of environmental and cultural connections. Similarly, Adelson (1998) found that ideas of well-being among the Cree in northern Quebec were intimately tied to their access to traditional foods, land, hunting, and lifestyles. In all, this type of research suggests that support for traditional ways and the ability to resist threats posed by settler culture and political domination are essential if Aboriginal people are to regain control over their own health.

It is clear that both past and present Aboriginal health in Canada must be understood in the context of colonial domination and oppression.

Articulating an Indigenous health research paradigm to better understand how relations of domination have affected Aboriginal peoples' health was one of the primary goals of the RCAP, and has remained of central concern to many Aboriginal and non-Aboriginal health researchers since that time. Fortunately, much evidence indicates that attitudes and perspectives on Aboriginal research have significantly changed since the publication of the final report of the RCAP. A particularly important document in this regard is the second edition of the *Tri-Council Policy Statement (TCPS)* on research ethics, which is a set of guidelines for university research ethics boards across Canada (Interagency Advisory Panel on Research Ethics, 2011). Chapter 9 of the revised *TCPS* deals exclusively with research involving First Nations, Inuit, and Métis, and demands that researchers consult with Aboriginal stakeholder organizations and communities prior to engaging in research involving Aboriginal people. The *TCPS* honours the principles of "ownership," "control," "access," and "possession" (OCAP) that were developed to govern the First Nations Regional Longitudinal Health Survey. This survey was the first major source of health-related quantitative data produced through an Aboriginal-directed process, and the OCAP guidelines were developed to ensure that the communities participating in that survey controlled how their data would be used (National Aboriginal Health Organization, 2006; O'Neil, Reading, and Leader, 1998). Although the health status of Aboriginal peoples continues to be much poorer on average than non-Aboriginal people in Canada, these and many other developments indicate that there are signs of hope in the relations between Aboriginal peoples and the rest of Canada.

Changing Relationships and Continuing Tensions

Admittedly, however, Aboriginal health research is a messy business, and those committed to addressing the health needs of Aboriginal communities through their research face a number of challenges. First, Aboriginal communities have long been characterized by a high degree of mobility and permeability. Furthermore, as FitzMaurice and McCaskill (Chapter 13) note in their discussion of urban issues, for some time now the majority of the Aboriginal population in Canada has lived in urban settings. If defining the membership of a discrete First Nation or other Aboriginal community is difficult, defining a "community" in an urban setting is even more so.

It is also the case that Aboriginal communities in Canada are comprised of groups and individuals with often quite divergent perspectives and interests (Fox and Long, 2000). Every community includes groups or individuals who feel poorly represented or even marginalized and oppressed by the formal or informal power structures of relations in their community. For community-based researchers, it may well be unclear how to best define "community" and whose particular interests are being addressed in any given project. Indeed, the complexity of Aboriginal communities presents a significant challenge to those who seek to understand and address the health and well-being of Aboriginal peoples, whether they are engaged in a PAR project or research projects that seek to understand illness and health in the context of a people's social characteristics and circumstances.

Despite the various sources of tension between the different approaches to Aboriginal health research discussed above, we are convinced that there are numerous reasons to support their use and coexistence. Although research that focuses on the lived realities of individuals is important and necessary, we are of the mind that population-level statistics and epidemiological approaches are critical to understanding overall patterns of disease and whether conditions are improving or getting worse. While the standard epidemiological approach to research may not produce immediate results for communities or individuals, it provides very useful information and direction to policy developers and service providers. As important as it is to honour a distinctly Aboriginal conception of health and well-being, objective measures of life expectancy and prevalence of particular diseases and other health-related problems provide invaluable information about the relationship between health and the particular social, economic, and political circumstances of Aboriginal people in Canada.

Ultimately, the tension between an Indigenous approach to health research and an epidemiological approach reflects the interests and "worlds of experience and responsibility" of those who have a stake in Aboriginal health. For example, academics and other professional researchers are often constrained by occupational pressures such as publishing the findings of their work in peer-reviewed academic publications or limiting the time they spend developing relationships with community members. Divergent perspectives and interests exist among as well as between members of specific Aboriginal organizations, communities, and nations. It seems obvious that while the tensions and politics of Aboriginal health research have much to do with divergent world views, they also reflect the very concrete struggles for power and control between everyone who has a stake in the health and well-being of Aboriginal communities (Long and Fox, 2000).

Conclusion: Living with Contradictions

Throughout this chapter we have sought to address two key themes that inform the health of Aboriginal peoples in Canada. The first is understanding the current health situation of Aboriginal people in this country and the factors that contribute to disparities in the status of their health. We have noted that while the health status of Aboriginal people in this country has not significantly improved in the ways called for in the final RCAP report, it is clear that there have been significant and positive changes to health promotion and health research involving Aboriginal peoples in Canada over the past 20 years. The second theme we explored addressed the ways that health knowledge is produced and used, which includes how illness and health are defined and measured, who controls the research process, and what people do with the information they gather or that they have access to.[6] We noted that the politics of Aboriginal health research reflects differential power relations at many levels and in many different contexts. We also noted that the question of what counts as evidence is vitally important for the production of policy and, ultimately, for improving the health of Aboriginal people in this country.

It is important to recognize that discussions regarding control over the research process, including who "owns" the data it generates, are not limited to Aboriginal health in Canada since they are part of a broader discourse regarding the relationship between research and power. In general, this discourse has drawn attention to how and why those who privilege Western, scientific ways of knowing have maintained power and conditions of inequality by systematically discounting and/or erasing the perspectives of racialized and colonized peoples from the accepted evidence (Bonilla-Silva and Zuberi, 2008; Tuhiwai Smith, 1999). Although there are important arguments about the legitimate role of statistical methods in reproducing these relations (e.g., Zuberi, 2008), discussions surrounding the "legitimacy" of Indigenous methodologies are in this respect less about the type of research conducted and more about the relations between peoples involved in the research.

This is not to say that there is consensus in discussions about the legitimacy of different methodological approaches in Aboriginal health research. For example, while most Western scientific researchers used to support behavioural and genetic explanations for patterns of disease and premature mortality, the findings of such research as well as the legitimacy of these approaches have increasingly come under fire by their Western colleagues. Moreover, although the RCAP (1996) argued for the fundamental importance of honouring local knowledge and supporting community control over research projects that required their participation in any way, it also recognized the many ways that certain Western, scientific approaches that meaningfully contextualize illness and health can benefit and even complement more traditional and holistic ways of understanding and addressing Aboriginal health issues in Canada. Research highlighting the social determinants of health is one of the best examples of this, for it indicates that Aboriginal people in Canada continue to be significantly at risk to poor social, economic, and environmental conditions, and that these conditions negatively affect their health and well-being in many different ways. SDH research has helped us to understand that the significantly lower than average levels of education and income experienced by Canada's Aboriginal peoples are directly related to their poor living conditions, and that their impoverished living conditions are directly related to a wide variety of health and social problems.[7]

It is perhaps tempting to conclude from our discussion that we think the "best" way forward is to invite the use of multiple approaches to understanding Aboriginal health, since it is evident that each contributes an important part of the total picture of Aboriginal health in Canada. However, to accept this middle position ignores profound ontological and epistemological differences between traditional, wisdom-based perspectives that understand Aboriginal health and well-being in the context of all our spiritual and material relations[8] and the empirically focused perspective of Western medical science that understands illness and health in quantitatively and qualitatively measurable ways. According to those who support TIK, epidemiological research results in rather narrow and even potentially misleading pictures of the whole of our lives. Moreover, they note that statistical techniques and the data they generate do not necessarily improve our understanding of processes that relate social conditions to health outcomes. As well, the supporters of TIK point out that these techniques and data in fact cloud our understanding whenever these processes are different for Aboriginal peoples and other Canadians. Lastly, TIK advocates remind us that depending solely on empirical data to tell stories of Aboriginal health contributes in many ways to the ongoing reproduction of colonial relations.

On the other hand, it seems to us that it is equally narrow and limiting to assume that all health-related experiences and processes that affect Aboriginal peoples are unique and can only be understood in traditional ways, since doing so would mean discarding decades of fruitful theoretical and empirical work that bears directly on the health and well-being of Aboriginal people in Canada. Moreover, ignoring disproportionately high rates of particular illnesses and morbidity across the lifespan and discounting the effects of living in diverse places and social circumstances would severely limit our understanding of the ways that colonization continues to make its presence felt in the lives of Aboriginal people throughout this country.

Rather than suggesting that we therefore simply adopt a multiplicity of world views and research practices, we have another suggestion: that Aboriginal and non-Aboriginal peoples learn to live somewhat *uncomfortably* with the coexistence of paradigms that are "other" than their own. This would mean accepting that research as a fundamentally human endeavour is constantly changing, and that it would be wise to be respectful as well as honest and skeptical about the foundations of any research practice. Although we recognize that this might not be the most satisfying position to take regarding Aboriginal health research, our sense is that it is the most respectful and honest, and that it will therefore bear the most useful and hopeful results.

All of this suggests that, in the end, illness, health, and healing have everything to do with people being in right relationship, and that all stakeholder relationships must be based on dignity and respect for research of any kind to serve a healthy and healing purpose. Until relations between Aboriginal and non-Aboriginal peoples in Canada are based on a shared commitment to treat each other in this good way, we perhaps have little choice but to remain open to the challenges and possibilities of walking "uncomfortably" together on the path of healing.

Discussion Questions

1. The chapter suggests that traditional Indigenous approaches and Western medical approaches to health have some fundamental differences. Briefly describe these differences.

2. What do you think are currently the most important healing and health-related issues facing Aboriginal people in Canada? In what ways might these be similar to and different from the health-related issues facing non-Aboriginal people in this country?

3. While Aboriginal people in Canada currently have shorter life expectancy than other Canadians, some have suggested that it is inappropriate to focus research only on reducing the gaps between Aboriginal and non-Aboriginal Canadians, arguing that it inappropriately sets the non-Aboriginal standard as the benchmark and the goal to which Aboriginal peoples should aspire. What do you think about this argument?

4. The social determinants of health perspective focuses attention on the "upstream" factors that affect health, such as the distribution of income in society, rather than on the "downstream" factors, such as individual behaviour or genetics. Does this correspond with the way you generally think about health and health policy?
5. The authors of this chapter state that the two different perspectives on health and health research can coexist, although uncomfortably. What do you think are the prospects for this coexistence?

Further Reading

Browne, Annette J., Victoria L. Smye, and Colleen Varcoe. 2005. "The Relevance of Post-Colonial Theoretical Perspectives to Research in Aboriginal Health." *Canadian Journal of Nursing Research* 37, 4: 16–37.

Vasiliki, Douglas. 2013. *Introduction to Aboriginal Health and Health Care in Canada: Bridging Health and Healing.* New York: Springer.

Menzies, Peter, and Lynn F. Lavallee, eds. 2014. *Journey to Healing: Aboriginal People with Addiction and Mental Health Issues.* Toronto: Centre for Addiction and Mental Health.

Salée, Daniel. 2006. "Quality of Life of Aboriginal People in Canada: An Analysis of Current Research." *IRPP Choices* 12, 6.

Waldram, James B., D. Ann Herring, and T. Kue Young. 2006. *Aboriginal Health in Canada: Historical, Cultural, and Epidemiological Perspectives.* Toronto: University of Toronto Press.

Notes

1. This claim of less federal responsibility is despite the fact that nearly two-thirds of Aboriginal people in this country now live in urban areas or other non-reserve communities, and that fewer than half of Aboriginal people in Canada have "status" (FitzMaurice and McCaskill, Chapter 13, this volume). As Wilson and Young (2008) note, a significant consequence of this arrangement has been that much of the research on Aboriginal health has focused on First Nations reserves and Inuit communities, which has resulted in a serious lack of information about the health of non-status First Nations, Métis, and other Aboriginal people.
2. This department is now known as Health Canada.
3. "Makayla Sault's Parents Speak Out about Daughter's Death," CBC News, 26 Feb. 2015, http://www.cbc.ca/news/aboriginal/makayla-sault-s-parents-speak-out-about-daughter-s-death-1.2973938.
4. Although more recent mortality data on certain Aboriginal population groups are available, wherever possible we have used data that include all Aboriginal population groups.
5. See Deborah McGregor's contribution in Chapter 2 for an extended discussion of Aboriginal peoples' relation to the land.

6. There is a certain irony to how colonial power is perpetuated in much research involving Aboriginal peoples. As TIK becomes legitimized in scientific circles, many Western researchers receive government funding for research and travel to gather stories and insights from Elders and other wisdom keepers. Although *TCPS* guidelines now specify that Aboriginal communities are granted the right to "own" the findings of any and all research involving their people, communities that seek government funding and other resources depend on researchers being allowed to translate their findings/stories for academic and government audiences. Consequently, Western researchers become more and more entrenched as "experts," which allows (or forces) other knowledge seekers as well as politicians to remain at arm's length from Aboriginal community members.

7. Cooke et al. (2007) and Stephens et al. (2005) note that the legacy of colonization is evident in the poorer health outcomes of Indigenous populations the world over, and that progress in virtually every locale has been almost universally slow.

8. We invite readers to carefully (re)read the opening two paragraphs of Peter Cole's contribution to this collection (Chapter 1).

13

Aboriginal Communities in the City: Reflections along the Path to Self-Government

Kevin FitzMaurice and Don McCaskill

Crossing the city limits does not transform Aboriginal People into non-Aboriginal People; they go on being the particular kind of person they have always been—Cree, Dene, Mohawk, Haida.

(RCAP, 1996: 538)

Aboriginal cultural identity in the city is a blend of ancestry, language, shared urban history, networks of relationships, Elders, urban Aboriginal organizations, community participation, and the potential role of urban self-government to reinforce all of these things.

(Urban Aboriginal Task Force, 2007: 79)

The title of my story would be "Power to the People." That's what I am part of, "the people," and we do have power when we are focussed and targeted. In the city we have gotten together and moved mountains and it is only through people coming together that we have that power.

(McCaskill and FitzMaurice, 2014: 134)

The majority of Aboriginal people in Canada now consider the city as home. The 1951 census recorded that only 6.7 per cent of the Aboriginal population resided in Canadian cities; by 2011 this number had increased to 56 per cent. In spite of popular stereotypes and misconceptions of Aboriginal people living primarily on remote reserves far beyond the pale of urban civilization, actually Aboriginal people have a long-standing connection to Canadian cities. Former Aboriginal settlements and gathering places have been transformed over time into cities, and many continue to be contested under outstanding land claims.[1]

Urban Aboriginal communities today are extremely complex; they are generally young, culturally diverse, highly mobile, and home to an increasing

TML Daily

number of "newcomers." Many members of urban Aboriginal communities experience varying degrees of poverty, while an emerging minority is increasingly affluent. Recent statistical trends have pointed to improvements in educational levels, income, and employment rates. However, when compared to the overall population, urban Aboriginal residents trail behind the overall population on most indicators of community health. As well, urban Aboriginal communities are engaging in diverse practices of community and organizational development and governance, processes that present many opportunities as well as challenges.

Organized into two major sections, this chapter provides an overview of some of the major trends in urban Aboriginal communities and governance in Canada. Beginning with a demographic overview, we move on to discuss the implications of these findings in relation to issues of urban Aboriginal communities and governance in Canada. The second half of the chapter explores questions relating to urban Aboriginal identity politics, culture and community, Aboriginal rights in the city, organizational development, and the present challenges to political representation. Finally, we point to areas most in need of further research in urban centres, including:

- the crisis of Aboriginal language loss;
- the phasing out of geared-to-income urban Native social housing;

- the place of Aboriginal-ancestry-only populations in community development;
- the impact of urban Aboriginal "newcomers" or "ethnic drifters" on demographic outcomes for all urban Aboriginal people;
- the unmet needs of the Aboriginal middle class and their role in community-building;
- the application of an Aboriginal rights framework in the city; and
- the work of urban Aboriginal councils as an expression of Aboriginal self-government in the city.

Part 1: Urban Aboriginal Community Profiles in Canada

In spite of some limitations to census data,[2] it is nonetheless useful to understand some demographic facts regarding the complex and dynamic nature of urban Aboriginal communities in Canada. In excess of 1 million people (1,400,685) now self-identify as Aboriginal persons, comprising 4.3 per cent of the total Canadian population (see Box 13.1 for Statistics Canada definitions of the terms of Aboriginal identity). Notably, of those who identify[3] as Aboriginal in Canada, a minority (23 per cent) live on a reserve, while the remaining 77 per cent live off-reserve in both rural (21 per cent) and urban (56 per cent) settings. The on-reserve population is comprised primarily

Table 13.1 | Location of Residence, Aboriginal Identity Population, 2011 Census

Category of Aboriginal Identity	Total	On-Reserve	Rural	Urban
Total Aboriginal identity	1,400,685	326,254 (23%)	287,333 (21%)	287,333 (56%)
Registered Indian	697,510	313,880 (45%)	83,701 (12%)	292,954 (42%)
Métis	418,380	4,184 (1%)	121,330 (29%)	297,050 (71%)
Inuit	59,115	1,773 (3%)	33,104 (56%)	25,419 (43%)
Non-status Indian	213,900	6,417 (3%)	49,197 (23%)	160,425 (75%)

Note: See Box 13.1 for definitions of the different Aboriginal identity categories.
Source: Figures generated from AANDC (2014).

Box 13.1 | Statistics Canada Definitions: Aboriginal Identity,
Registered or Treaty Indian Status, and Non-Status Indians

"Aboriginal identity" refers to whether the person reported being an
Aboriginal person, that is, First Nations (North American Indian), Métis or Inuk
(Inuit) and/or being a Registered or Treaty Indian (that is, registered under
the Indian Act of Canada) and/or being a member of a First Nation or Indian
band. Aboriginal peoples of Canada are defined in the Constitution Act, 1982,
section 35(2) as including the Indian, Inuit, and Métis peoples of Canada.

"Registered or Treaty Indian Status" refers to whether or not a person reported
being a Registered or Treaty Indian. Registered Indian refers to persons who
are registered under the Indian Act of Canada. Treaty Indians are persons who
belong to a First Nation or Indian band that signed a treaty with the Crown.
Registered or Treaty Indians are sometimes also called Status Indians.

"Non-status Indians" commonly refers to people who identify themselves as
Indians but who are not entitled to registration on the Indian Register pursuant
to the Indian Act. Some of them may be members of a First Nation.

Source: Statistics Canada, 2011 National Household Survey. Reproduced and
distributed on an "as is" basis with the permission of Statistics Canada.

(96 per cent) of registered Indians, while they account for only 50 per cent of
the urban Aboriginal population, with Métis, Inuit, and non-status populations making up 30, 5, and 15 per cent, respectively.

Focusing on the 11 census metropolitan areas (CMAs)[4] across Canada in
which significant numbers of people who indicated having an Aboriginal
identity reside, we see from Figure 13.1 a considerable and sustained growth
of Aboriginal people in urban areas over the past 30 years. Moreover, the western cities of Winnipeg, Vancouver, and Edmonton have the highest Aboriginal
identity populations in Canada. In eastern Canada, Toronto is home to the largest number of Aboriginal people, followed by Ottawa–Gatineau, Montreal,
and Sudbury.

Since 1996, the census has also provided for the possibility of someone
indicating Aboriginal ancestry/origins as something distinct from a corresponding Aboriginal identity. In other words, a person may indicate having
an Aboriginal ancestor (perhaps distant) without feeling that she or he is in
fact an Aboriginal person with an Aboriginal identity. Although focused on
the Aboriginal identity population of 1,400,685 in its reporting and analysis,

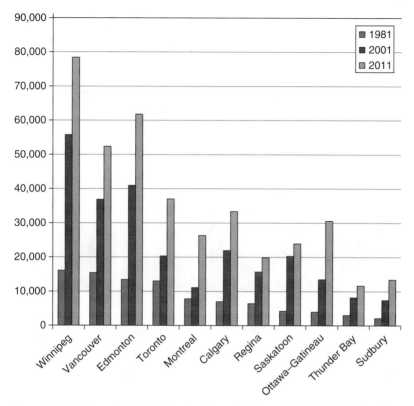

Figure 13.1 | Urban Aboriginal Identity Counts in Selected CMAs 1981, 2001, 2011.

Source: Statistics Canada, 2011 National Household Survey.

the 2011 census nonetheless indicates the Aboriginal-ancestry-only population as being 435,315 persons; thus making the total Aboriginal population in Canada 1,836,000 persons (AADNC, 2013).[5]

If we include the Aboriginal ancestry-only[6] population figures across CMAs, Figure 13.2 shows us a dramatic redistribution of population rankings whereby the three eastern CMAs of Montreal, Ottawa–Gatineau, and Toronto become much more prominent, having the highest percentage of Aboriginal ancestry-only populations (73, 51, and 42 per cent, respectively), while the western cities of Regina, Thunder Bay, and Winnipeg have the lowest (3, 4, and 5 per cent, respectively).

However, as published census data tabulations focus exclusively on those reporting Aboriginal identity, it is this population (1,400,685) of urban Aboriginal people upon which we have based this initial community demographic profile. Table 13.2 indicates that in the cities of Winnipeg, Thunder

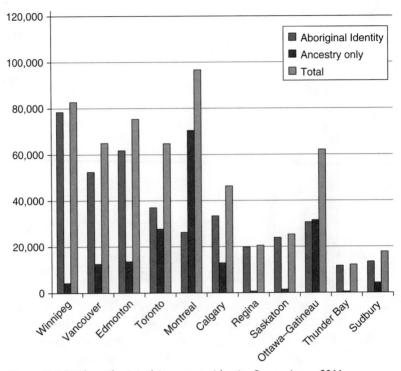

Figure 13.2 | Urban Aboriginal Ancestry to Identity Comparisons, 2011.

Source: Statistics Canada, 2011 National Household Survey.

Table 13.2 | Aboriginal Identity Population Characteristics per CMA, 2011

CMA	Aboriginal Identity Population	% of City Population	% of Métis	% of Registered Indians	% Increase 1981–2011
Winnipeg	78,420	11.0	59	33	388
Vancouver	52,375	2.3	35	34	241
Edmonton	61,765	5.4	52	34	360
Toronto	36,995	0.7	27	26	184
Montreal	26,285	0.7	34	16	236
Calgary	33,370	2.8	51	31	377
Regina	19,785	9.5	42	49	210
Saskatoon	23,895	9.3	48	42	468
Ottawa–Gatineau	30,570	2.5	40	19	667
Thunder Bay	11,670	9.8	21	64	287
Sudbury	13,405	8.5	48	32	526

Source: Statistics Canada, 2011, National Housing Survey.

Bay, Regina, and Saskatoon, Aboriginal people now make up between 9 and 11 per cent of the total population. Moreover, Winnipeg, Edmonton, and each of Saskatoon and Sudbury have the highest proportions of Métis people among their Aboriginal populations, at 59, 52, and 48 per cent, respectively, while Thunder Bay and Regina have the highest proportion of registered Indians. Notably, Montreal and Ottawa–Gatineau have the lowest proportion of registered Indians at 16 and 19 per cent, respectively. All of the selected cities have experienced significant percentage increases in Aboriginal population numbers over the past 30 years, with the least increase being 184 per cent in Toronto. From Table 13.2 we see that the cities experiencing the most significant growth in Aboriginal identity populations are Ottawa–Gatineau, Sudbury, Saskatoon, and Winnipeg.

What is particularly interesting about these exceptionally high levels of growth in the urban Aboriginal population over the past 30 years is that in contrast to the early years—or what demographers refer to as the "first wave" of movement from reserves to urban centres between 1951 and 1971—these increases are not the result of the emigration of Aboriginal people from reserves to cities,[7] nor are they a result of natural increases relating to birth rates of a younger Aboriginal population already living in the city (Norris, 2003b: 62). Rather, the overall phenomenon of "ethnic mobility" or "new arrivals" is the result of legislative changes within Indian Act definitions of status Indians as well as of a notable change in the politics of identity. In response to the effective political activism of Aboriginal women in the late 1970s and early 1980s and the subsequent legal challenge of Sharon McIvor in the early 2000s, the rules governing entitlement to Indian status (section 12 of the Indian Act) were amended in 1985 with the passing of Bill C-31, and later in 2011 with Bill C-3.[8] The number of people registered under Bill C-31 from 1985 to 1999 resulted in the growth of the urban Aboriginal population to roughly 114,700 people, which accounted for a 35 per cent increase in the national population of registered Indians at that time (Clatworthy, 2003: 86). As the previous loss of Indian status under the old section 12 provision often meant a corresponding loss of on-reserve housing, the vast majority of these reinstated status Indian women, children, and grandchildren lived in urban centres (Peters, 2006: 319). The initial 2012 projection for Indian status reinstatement resulting from Bill C-3 is 45,000 individuals, and approximately 96 per cent of these are expected to live in urban areas.[9]

In addition to these legislative amendments, there has also been a significant upward trend in intergenerational ethnic mobility such that, for a diversity of personal reasons, individuals are increasingly choosing to change their ethnic identity over time. Between 1986 and 1996, this particular form of ethnic mobility accounted for 41 per cent and 56 per cent of the proportional population growth of the North American Indian and Métis, respectively (Guimond, 2003: 43).

A second type of intergenerational ethnic mobility occurs in families of mixed Aboriginal and non-Aboriginal parents whereby the Métis identity of one or more of the children comes to be acknowledged only later in their life (Guimond, 2003: 43). Recent increases in the Métis population indicate that the majority of Métis people, 71 per cent of whom lived in cities in 2011, is on the rise and is surpassing the growth of all other Aboriginal groups. In 2011, 451,795 people reported that they are Métis. This number is more than double the 1996 population, which means there was an astounding 115 per cent increase in the Métis population between 1996 and 2011. The phenomenon of Aboriginal people marrying non-Aboriginal people is not new. A study of Aboriginal people in four major cities in the 1970s found that 50 per cent of respondents in Toronto and 39 per cent in Edmonton had brothers or sisters married to non-Aboriginal people (McCaskill, 1981: 85).

Important to note, however, is that Aboriginal population growth due to ethnic mobility does not affect all cities with the same degree of intensity. In the western cities of Regina, Saskatoon, Winnipeg, and Edmonton, population growth is largely a consequence of natural (net birth rate) increases. In Vancouver and Calgary, as well as in the cities of eastern Canada, on the other hand, ethnic mobility plays a much larger role in the recent grow of the Aboriginal population (Siggner and Costa, 2005: 14). Given the possible socio-economic differences between those recently deciding to identify as Aboriginal and those who have always identified as such, questions have become increasingly complex regarding the longer-term demographic trends of the total urban Aboriginal community. The marked increase in the census numbers of newly identifying Aboriginal people has been more significantly affected by changing social definitions than it has by the natural growth of the urban Aboriginal population.[10]

Similar trends of upward movement are evident in the area of education. In their long-term (1981 to 2001) study of census data, Siggner and Costa (2005) indicate that high school completion rates for urban Aboriginal youth have increased, as have post-secondary completion rates for young urban Aboriginal adults. These increases, however, did not correspond equally across gender. Aboriginal females had higher completion rates both for high school and for post-secondary education (Siggner and Costa, 2005: 6). Significant increases in levels of education among urban Aboriginal people also were found by researchers in two recent studies in Ontario. A 2007 study by McCaskill and FitzMaurice discovered that 35 per cent of Aboriginal respondents in Ottawa had graduated from a post-secondary institution. Similarly, McCaskill and FitzMaurice (2011) found in their study of urban Aboriginal people in Toronto that 47 per cent of respondents had completed a college diploma or university degree and that 7 per cent possessed a graduate degree.

Employment rates for urban Aboriginal people in most major cities also improved between 1981 and 2001, with Regina being the exception. However, the gap in employment rates between Aboriginal and non-Aboriginal people did not improve significantly over this time except in Winnipeg, Edmonton, and Sudbury, where the difference narrowed by 7 to 10 per cent (Siggner and Costa, 2005: 7). According to this study, the discrepancy narrowed in most cities over the 20-year period between Aboriginal and non-Aboriginal people in terms of median income derived from employment.

According to 2011 census data presented in Table 13.3, we can see that when compared to the total population in each of the selected CMAs (except Ottawa–Gatineau and Montreal), the urban Aboriginal population has lower employment rates, percentages of university degrees, and median incomes. The differences between median incomes for urban Aboriginal people and the general population are lowest in Ottawa–Gatineau, Toronto, and Montreal. The Table 13.3 figures further show that the relatively high earnings of Aboriginal people living in Ottawa–Gatineau, Toronto, and Montreal relate

Table 13.3 | Selected Demographics: Comparing Aboriginal and Overall Populations per CMA, 2011

CMAs	Ages: 0–17 % Difference	Employment Rate % Difference	Median Income Aboriginal as % of Overall	University Degree % Difference	5-Year Mobility % Difference
Winnipeg	14	3.6	76	13	10
Vancouver	12	5.6	78	17	8
Edmonton	9	8.1	80	14	12
Toronto	5	1.4	93	14	8
Montreal	11	–0.4	87	11	4
Calgary	17	3.1	79	18	11
Regina	4	8.4	72	10	16
Saskatoon	3	10.2	66	11	14
Ottawa–Gatineau	21	–1.3	100	15	7
Thunder Bay	15	11.2	60	8.2	22
Sudbury	8	1.5	80	7.3	9

Source: Statistics Canada, 2011 National Household Survey.

closely to stable employment and living circumstances, university education, and an older population. It is quite striking to note that Aboriginal people have higher employment rates than the overall population in both Ottawa–Gatineau and Montreal, and that the median income of Aboriginal people in Ottawa–Gatineau is now equal to the general population in that city. The 2011 Toronto Aboriginal Research Project (TARP) also revealed a significant number of Aboriginal individuals with relatively high incomes. Thirty-seven per cent of respondents in the TARP study earned over $40,000 and women had higher incomes, on average, than men (McCaskill and FitzMaurice, 2011: 93).

In contrast, Table 13.3 shows us that the Aboriginal populations living in Thunder Bay, Saskatoon, Regina, and Winnipeg have the lowest relative median incomes, employment rates, and university completion rates and the highest relative mobility rates.

Mirroring national income distribution trends in Canada, the 20-year period from 1981 to 2001 studied by Siggner and Costa marked the movement towards economic polarization within urban Aboriginal communities (Heisz, 2007: 6). During this time, there was a 281 per cent growth in the number of Aboriginal employment income earners making $40,000 or more. At the same time, however, those employed and making less than $15,000 grew by 550 per cent (Siggner and Costa, 2005: 39). We see in Figure 13.3 that in 2011, compared to the total population, Aboriginal people in large urban areas were significantly more likely to either not have an income or to earn less than $20,000 a year than to earn more than $40,000 a year. Similar to the Siggner and Costa study from 1981 to 2001, Figure 13.3 reveals a clear pattern of economic polarization in that the majority of city residents (70 per cent of the Aboriginal population and 62 per cent of total population) were either without an income or were part of the working poor, meaning that they earned less than $40,000 per year. The middle class—those earning between $40,000 and $80,000 per year—occupied a minority position (23 per cent of Aboriginal population and 26 per cent of total population).[11]

Moreover, it is within cities with the greatest relative economic disparity and disadvantage that we see Aboriginal people continue to be involved with the criminal justice system. La Prairie (2003: 182) has noted that young, less educated, poor, and unemployed Aboriginal males are significantly over-represented in correctional institutions in Canada. Thunder Bay, Saskatoon, and Regina have some of the largest discrepancies between the Aboriginal and overall populations (see Table 13.3) and also have the largest percentage of Aboriginal people living in extremely poor neighbourhoods. Indeed, the greatest proportion of Aboriginal people in Canada's prisons come from these cities as well as from Winnipeg (La Prairie, 2002: 197). But even Aboriginal people living in cities with higher rates of education and

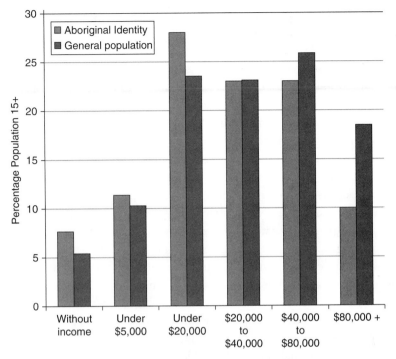

Figure 13.3 | Employment Income Distribution across 11 CMAs, 2011.

Source: Statistics Canada, 2011 National Household Survey.

income disproportionately experience contact with the law. For example, 21 per cent of respondents from Toronto involved in the TARP study reported having been involved with the criminal justice system either as a victim, offender, or both (McCaskill and FitzMaurice, 2011: 319).

Five additional demographic considerations relevant to the study of urban Aboriginal people in Canada are: access to affordable housing, language use and transmission, high rates of population mobility, links to communities of origin, and an increasing understanding of the city as home. Across all CMAs in Canada, and most acutely felt in cities with the greatest relative disadvantage as well as the largest percentage of Aboriginal people living in extremely poor neighbourhoods, there is a significant unmet need for supportive, geared-to-income social housing for Aboriginal people in urban contexts. In its 2009 report, the National Aboriginal Housing Association indicated that the incidence of housing need among the non-reserve Aboriginal population is long-standing and is presently over 20 per cent compared to 12.4 per cent among non-Aboriginal people, with a total of just over 10,000 Aboriginal housing units nationally.[12]

The federal government, through the Canada Mortgage and Housing Corporation (CMHC), sought to address urban Aboriginal housing problems by developing the Urban Native Housing Program (UNHP) in the 1970s, although the government discontinued construction of new homes under this program in 1993.[13] Most of the long-term mortgages in the UNHP operating agreements between the CMHC and urban Aboriginal housing organizations across the country are coming to an end. This means that many of the properties will no longer be affordable to the Aboriginal population since the agreements to provide geared-to-income rent subsidies for these properties are also coming to an end. This dire situation will lead both to an increase in the number of evictions and to homelessness experienced by Aboriginal people living in the city; furthermore, given that most agreements are ending, it is a problem that is sure to intensify nationally over the next 5 to 10 years. Urban Aboriginal housing organizations are consequently calling for the immediate renewal of operating agreements and further investment by the government in capital improvements and additional housing units to preserve and expand on affordable housing programs for Aboriginal people living in urban settings.

Another recent trend involving urban Aboriginal youth is increased interest in learning an Aboriginal language as a second language.[14] The challenges to learning and revitalizing Aboriginal languages in urban centres are great, however, for many Aboriginal languages in Canada have become endangered as a consequence of the long-term effects of the residential school system and other factors. Already low rates of Aboriginal language use by Aboriginal people in general, combined with increased ethnic mobility, growing cultural diversity (Aboriginal as well as non-Aboriginal), and living as minority populations in urban centres populated by a majority of non-Aboriginal residents all are factors having a significant downward effect on already low rates of Aboriginal language use in Canadian cities.

The use of a language at home is essential to its transmission to the next generation as a mother tongue. In their work on protecting languages under threat, UNESCO suggests that languages that are not learned by at least 30 per cent of the children in that community are endangered (Norris, 2003a: 95). Overall, from 1996 to 2011 there has been a significant decline in already low language levels across the country. In Figure 13.4, we see that in the total Aboriginal population there has been a significant decline in the ability to speak an Aboriginal language, from 29 per cent in 1996 to 17 per cent in 2011. This trend is intensified in urban centres, signalling an Aboriginal language crisis in Canadian cities.

In spite of a growing trend in learning Aboriginal languages as a second language,[15] we see in Figure 13.5 that in Vancouver, Toronto, Montreal, and Ottawa–Gatineau the percentage of urban Aboriginal community members

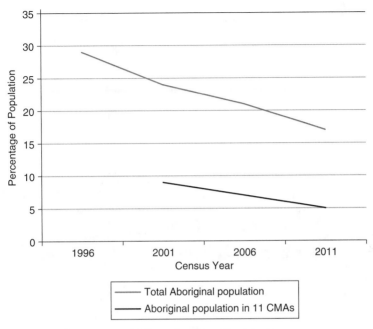

Figure 13.4 | Comparing Ability to Speak an Aboriginal Language.

Source: Statistics Ca nada, 2011 National Household Survey.

able to speak their language has declined from 2001 to 2011 to under 3 per cent (2.6 per cent average).

Given the higher percentages of Aboriginal language use within reserve communities, it is perhaps not surprising that those with the ability to speak an Aboriginal language are much more likely to move between reserve and urban areas, which has contributed to the "churn effect" where there are high rates of Aboriginal mobility (Norris, 2003a).

High rates of mobility between urban centres and reserves and within and between urban centres are unique to urban Aboriginal populations. Table 13.3 points to a higher rate of mobility for urban Aboriginal people relative to the overall population across all selected CMAs, with the most significant rates occurring in Regina, Thunder Bay, Saskatoon, and Edmonton. Registered Indians are more likely to move, and they also account for the majority of Aboriginal people who move between reserves and urban centres (Norris, 2003b: 64). Moreover, although some of the larger cities have experienced slight increases in "net migration" over recent years, this movement is generally understood as reciprocal (Norris, 2003b: 63).

Another important characteristic of urban Aboriginal people that has remained consistent over time is their continued connection to their

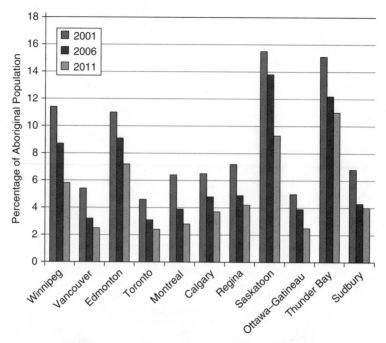

Figure 13.5 | Ability to Speak an Aboriginal Language across 11 CMAs.

Source: Statistics Canada, 2011 National Household Survey.

community of origin, particularly among First Nations and Métis peoples. A study conducted in Vancouver, Edmonton, Winnipeg, and Toronto in the 1970s found that more than two-thirds of Aboriginal people annually returned home "sometimes" or "often" (McCaskill, 1981: 88). Similarly, the 2007 Urban Aboriginal Task Force (UATF), the 2010 National Aboriginal Peoples Study, and the 2011 Toronto Aboriginal People's Study all found that a significant number of urban Aboriginal residents have maintained a strong relationship to their community of origin.[16] In all three studies, the most common reasons for visiting the community of origin were to visit family and friends and for cultural reasons such as attending powwows, socials, or ceremonies. The maintenance of links with the community of origin is a reflection of such factors as the proximity of First Nations and Métis communities to cities, the history of mobility among Aboriginal people, the fact that the land is such a fundamental source of traditional and contemporary Aboriginal culture, and the continuance of strong family and social ties.

The complex relationship between the city and community of origin is reflected in the comments of participants in a life history study in Toronto where, on the one hand, a long-term resident of Toronto extolled the virtues of her community of origin:

> Birch Island (Wiigwaaskingaa) will always be my home. It left an impression on me because it was such a wonderful place to grow up in. The air was clean and at night you could see a wonderful light show of stars in the sky.... It is so different in the city, children are stuck inside the house and there is bumper-to-bumper traffic. Everyone seems to be rushing to their destinations. (McCaskill and FitzMaurice, 2014: 40)

On the other hand, a different Toronto resident who visits her community of origin frequently suggests that the city is her home:

> When it gets stressful here, I think about moving back to the reserve, even retiring there.... Then I think my grandkids are down here, my kids are down here. My sisters are down here, my life is down here, and it's cold up there in the winter.... The difference here is that you can always get a pizza, there's theatres, art galleries, shows, and my volunteer work. (McCaskill and FitzMaurice, 2014: 120)

The understanding of the city as home in spite of continued links to communities of origin is an important finding in the national Aboriginal Peoples Study (2010), which found that the vast majority (71 per cent) of urban Aboriginal residents from across Canada felt that their city is their home (Environics, 2010: 36). The city as home was also an important theme that emerged from the 2014 Toronto life history study: the majority of respondents understood the city as home, and the connection to their communities of origin is often two-way in that friends and family will also visit Toronto and establish connections with the urban Aboriginal community in the city (McCaskill and FitzMaurice, 2014: 17).

Part 2: Urban Aboriginal Identities, Community, and Governance

Structural Prospects of Urban Aboriginal Governance

The possibility of urban Aboriginal governance raises a diversity of theoretical questions surrounding identity, culture, and community and practical questions concerning rights, jurisdiction, and Aboriginal–non-Aboriginal governmental relations. Developing urban self-government agreements for land shared by Aboriginal and non-Aboriginal residents requires a different approach from the land-based models most often associated with First Nations and modern-day treaty governments established through land claim settlements. In a commentary provided to the Royal Commission on Aboriginal Peoples (RCAP), Dan Smith, then president of the United Native Nations of British Columbia, argued for the need to:

> emphasize that there is an urgent need for non-reserve Aboriginal people to be treated equally and fairly. After all, we are working toward the same end … whether [we] reside on- or off-reserve. The majority of bands, tribal councils, and treaty areas do not have the capacity or infrastructure to address off-reserve Aboriginal issues and concerns.… Historically, off-reserve Aboriginal people have had to look after themselves individually, and then over a period of time to organize into groups for mutual support. Self-determination for individuals and families is the foundation of Aboriginal people both on- and off-reserve. (RCAP, 1996: 580)

In response to submissions from Aboriginal people across the country, the RCAP proposed two possible models of urban Aboriginal governance. The "reform of urban government and public authorities" model called for greater involvement of urban Aboriginal people in mainstream urban governments through the establishment of permanent Aboriginal political representation on municipal councils and related political bodies and the co-management of urban programs and services.

Alternatively, and with the understanding that enhanced Aboriginal participation in mainstream urban governance structures would fall short of community expectations for greater autonomy through meaningful self-government, urban Aboriginal governance could emanate out of a "community of interest" model. Broadly stated, urban Aboriginal governance based on a community of interest would entail the voluntary association of a diversity of urban Aboriginal organizations. Governance in this way could take the form of a specific service sector arrangement and/or it could operate through an array of agencies and institutions that would establish a larger city-wide politically representative body (RCAP, 1996).

The Basis of Governance: Identity, Community, and Culture

In helping us to understand the aspirations for urban Aboriginal governance and some of the related questions of race, power, jurisdiction, and rights, it is important to begin with a brief exploration of the fundamental ideas of identity, community, and culture. At the core of our identity (the self) is a desire to exist as an individual as well as a member of a group, whether a family, clan, community, nation, and/or nation-state. Through our ever-changing relationships with others we are able to find meaning as part of an ongoing process of defining our individual and collective identities. How we live our lives personally, intimately, and reflexively to some degree relates to how we choose to organize and govern ourselves collectively/politically. Critical to this process, however, is the power to be able to decide for oneself who one is in relation to others. In a collective sense, it is the power to establish and maintain the boundaries that define who "a people" is in relation to other peoples. Having organized and created the collective agency to define and maintain the parameters of our associations—the boundaries of our communities—we can begin the process of self-governance, but always in relation to those "others" understood as being on the outside of one's own community. To some degree, the collective identity of community members is expressed through institutions designed by members to protect, maintain, and enhance solidarity and express the community's culture and identity. For example, communities develop a network of organizations and informal social relationships that permit and encourage their members to support and sustain their communities. The degree to which a community develops its own institutions varies. In some communities, individuals can meet all of their needs within the institutional structures of the community. On the other hand, some communities, including some Aboriginal communities in urban settings, consist primarily of a network of interpersonal relationships with no supporting formal institutions.

Within the context of individual and collective identities, culture may be thought of as the medium of understanding through which all of this can happen. It is what provides community members with "meaningful ways of life across the full range of human activities, including social, educational, spiritual, recreational, and economic life, encompassing both the private and public spheres" (Schouls, 2003: 5). Moreover, it is when we acknowledge the need for recognition and respect from others that we come together into larger groups and communities. Communities provide opportunities for individuals to live and work together with others to create multiple, dynamic, and interwoven individual and group identities and cultures. They involve an ongoing and complex process of negotiating power that enables members to define the boundaries of where each person belongs as well as to clarify for each person where and how they can find meaning and how they fit, and thus whether they are strangers or not.

Colonial Racism: A Background to Contemporary Urban Aboriginal Governance

As a fundamental way in which culture is expressed, language plays a critical role in individual and collective identity formation and the negotiation of power. As stated previously, low levels of use of Aboriginal languages among urban Aboriginal people is a major source of concern and has stimulated significant attempts to revitalize language usage in all cities in Canada. For example, virtually all friendship centres and many schools, colleges, and universities offer Aboriginal language courses. In her submission to the Royal Commission on Aboriginal Peoples, Dawna Le Blanc of the Anishinaabe Language Teachers Association stated:

> Languages reflect fundamental differences in culture in ways that specific language groups perceive their world, their family relationships, kinship structure, relationship to other cultures, and to the land. Language impacts on our cultural, educational, social, economic, and political life, therefore language has a direct bearing on how we see ourselves as a people and our role in self-government, on land claims and our claim to a distinct society. (RCAP, 1996: 534)

Different languages, therefore, can be significant markers/boundaries of cultural distinctiveness and community.

Within the same language, however, cultural as well as political differences can still be negotiated through the reproduction of specific discourses but not others. The meaning of Aboriginal rights and in particular the Aboriginal right to self-government are central sites of Aboriginal and state discursive struggles that can be understood as part of a critical engagement with the power relations that have shaped, and continue to shape, the politics of urban Aboriginal identity and community governance.

For example, it can be argued that in limiting Aboriginal identity questions in the census to ancestry, identity, registered status, and First Nations membership and by defining all related demographic topics of interest, Statistics Canada has a significant degree of influence in shaping how Canada understands urban Aboriginal identity, community, and governance. Most scholarly and governmental reports and publications (including this one) that engage urban Aboriginal issues from a demographic perspective draws almost exclusively on census data provided by Statistics Canada. Significantly, the census can be seen as an attempt by the federal government to define the boundaries of urban Aboriginal identities and communities for Aboriginal people and to establish the parameters of what can be discussed in terms of urban Aboriginal governance. As noted earlier in this chapter, increasing numbers of Aboriginal individuals and communities are recognizing this (ab)use of power and are choosing to resist the process altogether. Nonetheless, Statistics Canada has attempted to develop consensus with Aboriginal people since 2001 as to the nature of the questions to be asked on the census and in the Aboriginal Peoples Survey through a series of consultative workshops involving a wide range of Aboriginal people.

Although Statistics Canada functions to reproduce and consolidate the categories of Aboriginal identity for Aboriginal people, it did not independently create these categories. Rather, current Statistics Canada definitions are the result of a long-standing and ongoing legal discourse about the jurisdictional powers of the federal and provincial governments under sections 91 and 92 of the Constitution Act, 1867.[17] In the eyes of the newly configured nation-state of Canada, former nation-to-nation relations between numerous Aboriginal peoples and the British Crown became domestic affairs of colonial control.[18] Informed by the popularized, racist notions of Aboriginal cultural inferiority,[19] section 91(24) transformed diverse nations of Aboriginal allies and trading partners and their lands into uniformly defined "Indians"[20] and "Indian lands" within the sphere of federal jurisdictional authority (Carter, 2007: 101–31). Section 91(24) has had profound implications for Aboriginal people since it provided the legal (in fact, constitutional) basis behind early policy and programs designed to assimilate Aboriginal peoples and their lands into the Canadian body politic. After the 1969 White Paper's blatant attempt to assimilate status Indians met with widespread Aboriginal resistance, the federal government formally repudiated its assimilationist policy in favour of increased consultation and the establishment of self-government and land claim initiatives. Nonetheless, many Aboriginal people continue to suspect that more subtle forms of colonial policy continue to inform contemporary government programming.

Although many of the features of early colonial relations are beyond the scope of this chapter, it is important to mention here that in spite of (or perhaps because of) the early attempts by the federal government to assimilate Aboriginal people through legislation and policy, many Aboriginal nations sought to negotiate what was considered, to be nation-to-nation treaty relations with the Canadian government from 1871 to 1921. During this time the reserve system was created as a means of isolating "Indians" away from urban centres and separating them from members of mainstream society. Moreover, this post-Confederation time of assimilation marked the passage of the Indian Act of 1876, a law that severely repressed almost all aspects of

Aboriginal cultural, spiritual, and political life. It also marked the beginning of the residential school system, which is now widely recognized as the source of large-scale devastation[21] and, thus, of personal as well as collective hardship in many of today's reserve and urban Aboriginal communities.

After many generations of colonial repression, the Indian Act was significantly amended in 1951 to allow increased civil rights. One significant change was the ability to move freely off reserves; as a result, many Indians soon began to move to urban centres to seek new opportunities for education, employment, and housing. In the process they began creating new identities, families, communities, and formal associations and institutions. Beginning as Indian and Métis clubs during the 1950s, friendship centres started out as Aboriginal community-building organizations and developed into social services organizations. Since these early years, the number of friendship centres and related urban Aboriginal agencies has grown in step with an expanding urban Aboriginal population that has increasingly participated in the creation of Aboriginal community life in the city (Newhouse, 2003: 252).

The history of Aboriginal urban institutions in Canada is quite distinct from one city to the other. Each major city has more than 50 Aboriginal organizations. Many organizations emerged initially from friendship centres and have grown significantly in numbers and size. For example, in Toronto one of the largest Aboriginal organizations, Native Child and Family Services of Toronto, has 180 staff and a budget of over $20 million (FitzMaurice and McCaskill, 2013: 88). The vast majority of urban Aboriginal organizations are involved in health and social services, focusing on providing services in such fields as health, justice and corrections, policing, poverty, child welfare, social housing, homelessness, troubled youth, family counselling, education and training, alcohol and drug counselling, shelters, drop-in centres, and street patrols in order to meet the substantial needs of the urban Aboriginal population. These organizations often function in ways that are significantly different from non-Aboriginal social service agencies in that they attempt to provide services and structure in a culturally based manner (McCaskill and FitzMaurice, 2007: 87). There are other types of Aboriginal organizations in cities as well, such as arts and business organizations, and a number of more informal programs and activities such as powwows, socials, Elders' conferences, and sports events.

Many urban Aboriginal organizations have developed creative culturally based structures, programs, and services over the years to meet the needs of their clients, often developing a common cultural ethos of care, helpfulness, and dedication within a non-hierarchical human resource management structure. A 2013 case study of six urban Aboriginal organizations in Toronto discovered that the inclusion of Elders, traditional teachings, ceremonies, medicines, and cultural events has enabled these organizations to contribute to the healing of individuals as well as to help develop vibrant Aboriginal cultural identities and communities in an urban setting (FitzMaurice and McCaskill, 2013: 12). The work of many Aboriginal social service agencies often involves addressing the many significant challenges surrounding mental health problems, addictions, cultural loss, and identity confusion, all of which are related to Aboriginal experiences of intergenerational trauma. At the same time, these organizations often face major funding challenges as they typically rely on government funding, which is increasingly short term and unstable. It has always been very rare for urban Aboriginal organizations to receive core administrative funding. Moreover, despite their complex and challenging caseloads, social service workers face unrelenting bureaucratic challenges such as steady evaluation and reporting requirements, having to reapply annually for grants, and having to continually search for new funding sources. For example, Native Child and Family Services of Toronto currently has close to 60 different sources of funding (2013: 91).

The predominance of social service organizations has fed the negative stereotype that the majority of urban Aboriginal people are poor and possess a number of negative social traits. Aboriginal individuals who have attained economic success in cities may sometimes feel that there is little institutional support for their Aboriginal identity and, thus, they may not conceive of themselves as part of the urban Aboriginal community as it currently exists. Research in Ontario cities suggests that factors such as negative stereotypes, the lack of relevant programs and facilities to meet their needs, and divisions within the urban Aboriginal community contribute to an alienation of the emerging urban Aboriginal middle class (McCaskill and FitzMaurice, 2007: 171). In Toronto, for example, despite the fact that their Aboriginal culture was important to them, only 18 per cent of those respondents who earned over $40,000 annually indicated that they were involved with the Toronto Aboriginal community and only 29 per cent participated in cultural events in the city (McCaskill and FitzMaurice, 2011: 227). Many reasons were given for the lack of involvement in activities and events, including the lack of Aboriginal organizations that meet their needs, a lack of Aboriginal people living in proximity to one another, and substantial divisions among Aboriginal people in the city. These factors have significant implications for urban Aboriginal community development and for any broad-based participation in urban Aboriginal governance. Indeed, an important challenge for urban Aboriginal people will be to create organizations and facilities that more adequately meet the needs of the emerging middle class if an inclusive, self-governing, urban Aboriginal community is to be sustained in the long run.

The broader context for understanding urban Aboriginal governance, however, has its roots in the early period of colonization when Aboriginal identities and communities were systematically created, segregated, and oppressed. Much of the legal and ideological infrastructure that emerged during this early period persists today. Indians and their lands continue to be both a federal responsibility in accordance with section 91(24) of the Constitution Act, 1867 and heavily regulated by the Indian Act. Racism thus plays a significant role in disadvantaging urban Aboriginal people, for they experience it in ways both personal and systemic that discriminate and that exclude them from positions of power and privilege (McCaskill and FitzMaurice, 2007: 103). Moreover, conceiving of Aboriginal culture in a racialized way—as static, exclusively traditional, and reserve-based—makes it irreconcilable with urban modernity. According to this view, one cannot be both urban and Aboriginal; moving to the city is regarded as a process of shedding of one's Aboriginal identity and cultural distinctiveness through which one eventually becomes fully integrated into the urban Canadian culture and lifestyle.

At the same time, it is important to recognize the agency of urban Aboriginal people. They have not simply been passive recipients of racialized, legal structures and policy initiatives, for they have worked together to create a "boards of directors" governance structure that allows for full representation of diverse peoples and interests within the larger urban Aboriginal community. Indeed, many Aboriginal organizations believe that the most effective model of urban Aboriginal governance is one that formally recognizes their role in representing and addressing diverse needs and interests within the urban Aboriginal population and that also allows for the expansion of their reach into the broader urban Aboriginal community. In most Canadian cities, Aboriginal organizations have come together to form varying types of governing councils designed to represent Aboriginal people.

Jurisdictional Uncertainty in Urban Areas

A major impediment to the development of vibrant and supportive urban Aboriginal communities is policy and programming uncertainty and confusion stemming from disagreements between federal and provincial governments over legislative authority for urban Aboriginal people. Driving the racialized view of Aboriginal culture as static and reserve-based is the federal government's position that the Indian Act legislates its only responsibility, which is for Indians who live within reserve boundaries (Hanselmann and Gibbins, 2002: 3). According to this view, Indians stop being Indians once they leave the reserve. As a result, the federal government has tended to focus on reserve-based policy development and programming for status Indians at the expense of urban Aboriginal people.

The recent formation of some administrative and funding links between the federal government and the urban Aboriginal community suggests that the federal government's view towards urban Aboriginal peoples may be changing. Post-secondary education funding, some social services programming, and the provision of non-insured health benefits are examples of continued off-reserve federal support of status Indians. Moreover, the federal government has initiated the Office of the Federal Interlocutor within Aboriginal Affairs and Northern Development Canada (AANDC), which is mandated to implement the Urban Aboriginal Strategy, "an approach based on problem-solving partnerships with provincial governments, urban Aboriginal organizations, municipalities and other federal departments."[22]

The provinces, for their part, have consistently put forward a position that Aboriginal people are legally the same as other urban people. Government representatives argue that once Aboriginal people take up residence in urban areas, provincial responsibilities towards them parallel those for non-Aboriginal residents, which means that services and programs are "needs-based" rather than contingent upon a unique legal or cultural status. Aboriginal units in all provincial government, in some cases ministries, focus on Aboriginal communities and on the co-ordination of provincial policies and programs towards all Aboriginal people, including those in urban centres (Malloy, 2001: 134–6). Nonetheless, all provincial governments in Canada maintain that any specific policy or programming development relating to urban Aboriginal people should be under the jurisdiction of the federal government (Hanselmann and Gibbins, 2002: 4).

The existence of ambivalent positions within and between governments in Canada contributes to urban Aboriginal "policy confusion," which has resulted in a great deal of inconsistency and inequity in the provision of programs and services. Since most urban Aboriginal agencies experience chronic underfunding, program planning is a challenging and uncertain process. The consequence of chronic underfunding is that much-needed programs and services provided by urban Aboriginal organizations are often short-term and highly unpredictable (FitzMaurice and McCaskill, 2013: 12).

As a representative of an urban Aboriginal organization noted in a presentation to the RCAP:

> Most of us are always fighting over dollars, to keep our administration going, to house ourselves, and look after our administration costs, whether we're Métis, Treaty, whatever.... [W]e give people the runaround now when they come into the city. Well, you're Treaty and you've not been here one year so you go to this place. But, oh no, you've been here a year already so you go to this place. Well, you're Métis, you have to go somewhere else. It's too confusing for people. (RCAP, 1996: 538)

Missing from both federal and provincial discourses on urban Aboriginal people and their institutions is any mention of the inherent right to urban Aboriginal self-government and of the provision of programs and services as a function of that right.

First Nations Land Claims and the Urban Reserve

In many respects, a static, pre-contact understanding of Aboriginal culture is evident in much common-law discourse over the past 30 years that has sought to restrict Aboriginal rights to guidelines on hunting and fishing access, a *sui generis* title to the land, and, most recently, a duty to consult.[23]

The much more dynamic view that Aboriginal peoples have of their cultures was legally bolstered with the inclusion of section 35 in the Constitution Act, 1982. Section 35 recognizes and affirms existing Aboriginal and treaty rights for Aboriginal people and acknowledges that Indians, Inuit, and Métis are Aboriginal peoples of Canada. Moreover, since 1995 the federal government has recognized that the inherent right to Aboriginal self-government is enshrined in section 35. Consequently, the inherent right of Aboriginal peoples to govern themselves has been acknowledged by government representatives during negotiations of land claim agreements with First Nations communities as well as throughout the process of creating Nunavut as an Inuit homeland and public government.

An important development in land claim discussions that directly affects urban Aboriginal communities has been the creation of the "urban reserve." In accordance with the federal "Additions to Reserves" and "Treaty Land Entitlement" policy, several land claim negotiations (primarily in Saskatchewan) have included the creation of reserve land within city limits. Governed as part of rural-based First Nations reserve lands, albeit situated within city limits, urban reserves have thus far been developed primarily as economic development initiatives for First Nations members.[24] While many of these initiatives are still in relatively early stages of development, they appear to represent a growing trend in First Nations governance within urban communities (Loxely and Wien, 2003: 222).

Emerging Questions and Challenges: Urban Aboriginal Governance, Aboriginal Rights, and Cultural Diversity

Competing discourses on Aboriginal rights, whether these include the Aboriginal assertion of full political sovereignty or the state's more restricted view, have focused almost exclusively on land, natural resources, and governance arrangements for First Nations communities outside of urban-based organizations and communities. There are many examples in urban centres across Canada of Aboriginal agencies seeking to co-ordinate their efforts through local governance structures.[25] Nonetheless, representatives of urban Aboriginal organizations continue to be uncertain about how (and even whether or not) the concept of Aboriginal rights is applicable and useful in their efforts to meet the diverse needs and interests of the members of urban Aboriginal communities. In response to discussions at a recent Prime Minister's Roundtable on Aboriginal People that focused on Aboriginal rights, Peter Dinsdale (then president of the National Association of Friendship Centres [NAFC]) commented on the concerns his organization had about an Aboriginal rights-based focus:

> rights are necessarily nation-based, focusing on nations and governments. But what about those who fall through the cracks? The NAFC would prefer that the discussion centered more on needs. This may not be as politically exciting or as persuasive as the rights-based approach, but it is what is needed to ensure that all are included. The NAFC operates on a "status blind" basis, is pan Aboriginal, and focuses on needs. So far, the NAFC has not had great success in advocating a needs-based approach to Aboriginal issues. But there is tremendous need for homeless services, and to deal with kids who have dropped out of school. Talk about rights will not solve these issues. (Institute on Governance, 2005: 9)

One of the key outstanding questions relating to urban Aboriginal community development, service delivery, and governance in Canadian cities is whether pursuing an Aboriginal rights discourse would be more productive than the proposed "needs-based" approach. In other words, would advocating for an urban Aboriginal rights agenda as a more dynamic and inclusive view of section 35 lead to greater self-government and control by urban Aboriginal organizations and more stable and equitable funding as a function of that right?

As noted above, jurisdictional inconsistency and funding uncertainty have largely resulted in a volatile and patchwork approach to social service program delivery. The demographic profile of the urban Aboriginal population outlined in Part 1 of this paper documented a community that experiences significantly lower levels of education, income, and labour force participation and higher levels of instability and criminalization than the overall urban population. Urban Aboriginal people are also more likely to live in lone-parent families, have poorer health status, higher rates of homelessness, and greater housing needs, and are more likely to experience domestic violence than their non-Aboriginal counterparts (Hanselmann and Gibbins, 2002: 2).

Advocates of urban Aboriginal rights are also asking whether Aboriginal political representation within municipal governing bodies should be mandatory as an Aboriginal right of governance? This opens up the much larger question of whether an urban Aboriginal rights agenda that affirms diverse Aboriginal identities (Indian, Inuit, and Métis) as well as the authority of section 35 could provide the foundation for consistent and supportive urban Aboriginal–state relations and comprehensive political representation within a "community of interest" political framework.

The complexity of current urban Aboriginal political relationships poses some significant challenges to those who are committed to developing a strong and vibrant urban Aboriginal community. Almost every effort to develop a viable urban Aboriginal governance structure has involved a struggle to clarify who should decide on community membership and the meaning of "Indian," "Inuit," and "Métis." Uncertainty remains over whether "Indian" should refer to status Indians only and thereby exclude all those who have lost their status, or whether it should be an inclusive term that includes everyone of Indian/Aboriginal ancestry.[26] There is also a great deal of uncertainty and disagreement over the question of political representation and who within the urban community should be empowered to participate in this process. Will it be exclusively those with a long family history of identifying as Aboriginal people, or will members of the new ethnically mobile Aboriginal population also be included?

As noted earlier, the answer to these questions has significant implications for Aboriginal residents living in many urban centres in Canada. For example, the Aboriginal ancestry-only population in Montreal, Ottawa, and Toronto is a significant percentage of the total Aboriginal population in these urban centres, as is true for a growing number of other centres. The question remains as to whether those with Aboriginal ancestry and not Aboriginal identity ought to be included in the urban Aboriginal rights paradigm. Affirming that

Aboriginal ancestry members are covered under section 35 of the Constitution Act, 1982 would mean that they would become equally empowered members of the urban Aboriginal community and therefore equally entitled to the same rights and privileges as their urban Aboriginal identity counterparts.

Although in many ways urban Aboriginal organizations have established an Aboriginal governance presence within individual social service sectors such as law and justice, housing, health, and child and family services, a number of structural divisions within most urban Aboriginal communities inhibit the broadly based movement towards the establishment of formal political associations (Carli, 2012: 11). As noted throughout the RCAP report, existing urban Aboriginal social service agencies are a key part of any future urban Aboriginal "community of interest" governance structure because they could work together to form a larger city-wide, politically representative body. However, the vast majority of urban Aboriginal organizations are not politically accountable by design. In spite of having boards of directors based within the community, most of these organizations are structured around a non-political, client–worker relationship. The primary goal of most urban Aboriginal organizations is not to retain clients in order to ensure their long-term support for the organization, but rather to help and provide clients with services until they are no longer in need of assistance. In other words, the purpose of the client–worker relationship is to provide professional, confidential support rather than to cultivate public, political relations. Indeed, social service workers often do not publicly acknowledge or associate with their clients in order to ensure and preserve confidentiality outside the workplace. This bureaucratic "professionalization" of Aboriginal social service workers thus enables them to maintain a degree of distance between themselves and their clients. However, the existence of professional distance makes it challenging for those who are committed to developing broadly based, non-service organizations that properly represent the diverse interests of members of the urban Aboriginal community, particularly since some members of that community feel disenfranchised and socially isolated.

As previously discussed, culture plays an important role in the formation of identity, community, and governance. Although culture is ever-changing across relationships and time, cultural differences can signify the boundaries between community members and non-members at any given moment. For example, the significant decline in use of Aboriginal languages in urban centres is an important marker of declining cultural meaning and distinctiveness. Moreover, the mixing of diverse Aboriginal and non-Aboriginal cultures in urban centres presents a challenge to urban Aboriginal governance advocates who are committed to building strong and vibrant urban Aboriginal communities.

A number of other factors also make it challenging for those who have a vision to develop culturally inclusive, politically effective urban Aboriginal communities that provide equitable employment opportunities for all members. These include the predominance of relatively apolitical urban Aboriginal social service organizations as well as a lack of sustained activity and overall coherent purpose and direction on the part of cultural and political Aboriginal organizations in urban areas. Although new identities, communities, and hybrid Aboriginal cultures are developing around many urban Aboriginal social services agencies that intentionally incorporate aspects of Aboriginal culture into their services, it is clear that not all urban Aboriginal people are committed to this approach to community-building. Research in Ontario indicates that although many urban Aboriginal social services staff members are part of the emerging middle class, a significant segment of this population has moved away from the Aboriginal social service community. While they still consider themselves Aboriginal, for various reasons they do not participate in Aboriginal agency-sponsored cultural events and do not feel that they belong to the urban Aboriginal community per se (McCaskill and FitzMaurice, 2007: 193).

Finally, relatively high Aboriginal mobility within urban areas presents an important challenge to the development of strong and vibrant urban Aboriginal communities characterized by culturally inclusive and politically representative governing structures. This population mobility, or "churn," within and between urban centres and between First Nation and urban communities hinders the construction of a common urban Aboriginal identity, the sharing of meaningful cultural experiences, and the working together of different peoples to establish and maintain strong and stable forms of political association and governance. It appears that the effects of churn may lessen over time as the emerging urban Aboriginal middle class expands, for as we noted earlier, mobility rates decrease proportionally as income, education levels, and labour force participation increase. Ultimately, however, creatively imagining and fostering urban Aboriginal communities in Canada that are culturally inclusive and that provide equitable socio-economic opportunities for urban Aboriginal residents will require the commitment to develop governance structures that honour Aboriginal peoples' inherent rights as well as cultivate new kinds of social, economic, and political relations between Aboriginal peoples living in urban settings.

Recommended Areas for Further Research

As a broad review of urban Aboriginal demographics and questions of community development and governance, this chapter has highlighted a number of pressing topics for further research and analysis.

- Given that already low rates of Aboriginal language use continue to decline dramatically in Canadian cities such that in Vancouver, Toronto, Montreal, and Ottawa the average percentage of those able to speak their language is presently 2.6 per cent, research urgently is needed on best practices for language revitalization strategies for Aboriginal youth in urban centres.
- Given the significant need for supportive, geared-to-income urban Aboriginal social housing and the increasing finalization of Urban Native Housing Program (UNHP) operating agreements, there is a growing affordable housing crisis for Aboriginal people in most Canadian cities. As the agreements end over the next 5 to 10 years, many of these UNHP properties will no longer be affordable to a majority of Aboriginal people, resulting in evictions and possible homelessness. There is a pressing need for research that documents this growing challenge and explores the renewal of operating agreements and the further investment in capital improvements and additional housing units to preserve and expand on long-term affordability.
- Given the very high population counts of the Aboriginal ancestry-only populations in the three eastern census metropolitan areas of Montreal, Ottawa–Gatineau, and Toronto and that Statistics Canada excludes this population in its analysis and reporting, there is a need to better understand this population in terms of its demographic profile, its membership in urban Aboriginal communities, and its possible role in community development and governance.
- The impact of urban Aboriginal "newcomers" or "ethnic drifters" in enhancing demographic outcomes for all urban Aboriginal people is also an important area that requires further research. Given the importance of ethnic mobility to the recent growth of the Aboriginal population, particularly in Vancouver, Calgary, and the cities of eastern Canada, research is needed into the relationship between newcomers and recent upward trends in urban Aboriginal census data, the emergence of an urban Aboriginal middle class, and the experiences and needs of the middle class and its role in community-building and governance.
- Lastly, the development of urban Aboriginal community councils in most cities in Canada is an area that requires further research with particular attention to the application of an Aboriginal rights framework in the city and as a model of representative urban Aboriginal self-government.

Discussion Questions

1. What does it mean to be part of a community? In what ways do you think urban Aboriginal communities are similar to other communities in Canada, but also unique?
2. What are some of the challenges to the recognition and respect of Aboriginal rights, particularly the section 35 right to self-government, in urban centres in Canada?
3. Explain the difference between "needs-based" and "rights-based" approaches to Aboriginal policy and programming? Does this distinction matter in urban centres?
4. What do you feel might be the reasons that some members of the emerging Aboriginal middle class are moving away from social service–based urban Aboriginal communities? What are the implications of this trend for urban Aboriginal identity, community, and governance?
5. What are the implications of Aboriginal language loss in cities across Canada?

Further Reading

Anderson, C., and E. Peters. 2013. *Indigenous in the City: Contemporary Identities and Cultural Innovation.* Vancouver: University of British Columbia Press.

McCaskill, D., and K. FitzMaurice. 2007. *Urban Aboriginal Task Force: Final Report.* Toronto: Ontario Federation of Indian Friendship Centres, Ontario Métis and Aboriginal Association, and Ontario Native Women's Association. At: http://ofifc.agiledudes. com/publication/urban-aboriginal-task-force-ontario-final-report. In addition to the Ontario-wide final report, five Urban Aboriginal Task Force (UATF) reports have been completed for Sudbury, Ottawa, Thunder Bay, Kenora, and Barrie–Midland. All UATF reports can be found in pdf format at http://www.ofifc.org/ofifchome/page/ index.htm.

———, ———, and J. Cidro. 2011. *Toronto Aboriginal Research Project: Final Report.* Toronto: Toronto Aboriginal Support Services Council. At: http://www.councilfire.ca/Acrobat/ tarp-final-report2011.pdf.

Newhouse, D., and E. Peters, eds. 2003. *Not Strangers in These Parts: Urban Aboriginal Peoples.* Ottawa: Policy Research Initiative.

———, K. FitzMaurice, et al. 2012. *Well-Being in the Urban Aboriginal Community: Fostering Biimaadiziwin.* National Research Conference on Urban Aboriginal People. Toronto: Thompson Educational Publishing.

Peters, E. 2006. "We Do Not Lose Our Treaty Rights outside the... Reserve: Challenging the Scales of Social Service Provision for First Nations Women in Canadian Cities." *GeoJournal* 65: 315–27.

Notes

1. Including areas within and/or adjacent to the cities of Vancouver, Edmonton, Saskatoon, Thunder Bay, Sudbury, and Ottawa. The Mississaugas of New Credit land claim covering much of the Greater Toronto Area (GTA) was signed in 2010.

2. In terms of comparability of data from the last census, changes were introduced to the terminology of the identity questions for the 2011 NHS questionnaires (N1 and N2). "North American Indian" was replaced by "First Nations (North American Indian)" and "Inuit (Eskimo)" was replaced by "Inuk (Inuit)" in both the question and the response categories.

3. For consistency in meaning across the demographic profile and analysis sections of this chapter, we have adhered to the 2011 Statistics Canada definitions of Aboriginal identity.

4. CMAs, per the Statistics Canada definition, have an urban core population of 50,000 or more with a total population of 100,000 or more.

5. For further reading, see AANDC (2013: Figure 6).

6. Although not included in the data outlined in Table 13.1, this population is generally understood as being predominantly urban (75 per cent urban in the 2006 census).

7. The Aboriginal population living on reserve had an average positive annual growth rate of 1.8 per cent from 1996 to 2011. See AANDC (2013: Figure 8).

8. See Chapter 6 by Cora Voyageur on Aboriginal women for a more detailed discussion of the development and implications of changing definitions in legislation and policy.

9. See *Report to Parliament: Gender Equity in Indian Registration Act*, https://www.aadnc-aandc.gc.ca/eng/1360010156151/1360010230864#chp3.

10. The impact of ethnic mobility on the emergence of an urban Aboriginal middle class should also be taken into account in any analysis of recent census data, for although it is difficult to measure, the emergence of an urban Aboriginal middle class does indicate significant improvements in the general well-being of urban Aboriginal people in Canada.

11. For further reading on Canada's diminishing "middle class," see Heisz (2007).

12. The city of Toronto waiting list for affordable social housing is approximately 79,000 individuals. See National Aboriginal Housing Association (2009). Also see McCaskill, FitzMaurice, and Cidro (2011: 239); Walker (2008).

13. The federal government (CMHC) initiated the Affordable Housing Initiative in 2001 by providing one-time capital subsidies for the building of new homes, but this did not include an ongoing subsidy program geared to income.

14. See Mary Jane Norris, Chapter 9, for a more extended discussion of language loss and revitalization.

15. The desire among Aboriginal youth in Toronto to learn an Aboriginal language as a second language was a key finding of the Toronto Aboriginal Research Project. See McCaskill, FitzMaurice, and Cidro (2011). Also see: 2011 Census Report, "Aboriginal People and Language," http://www12.statcan.gc.ca/nhs-enm/2011/as-sa/99-011-x/99-011-x2011003_1-eng.cfm.

16. For further reading, see McCaskill and FitzMaurice (2007: 88); Environics (2010: 33); McCaskill, FitzMaurice, and Cidro (2011).

17. Broadly speaking, the federal government maintained authority for matters of national concern while the provincial jurisdiction revolves around matters of social policy for its residents.

18. See Newhouse and Belanger, Chapter 3, for a more in-depth discussion of political relations between Aboriginal people and the rest of Canada.

19. For further reading on the many dimensions of stereotypes of Aboriginal people, see Francis (1992) and Berkhofer (1979).

20. A Supreme Court decision in 1939 (*In re Eskimos*) also brought Inuit within federal responsibility. Métis, with the exception of those living in Métis settlements in Alberta, were not subject to special federal or provincial legislation.

21. For further reading on the residential schools, see John Milloy, "A National Crime," in RCAP (1996: vol. 1, ch. 10); Chrisjohn, Young, and Maraun (2006).

22. For more information, see AANDC, https://www.aadnc-andc.gc.ca/eng/1100100010447/1100100010448.

23. The recent 2014 Supreme Court decision in *Tsilhqot'in Nation v. British Columbia* strengthens the discourse on Aboriginal rights and calls for greater co-operation and sharing of power between federal and provincial governments and Indigenous communities with Aboriginal title to the land. See http://scc-csc.lexum.com/scc-csc/scc-csc/en/item/14246/index.do.

24. For further reading on Treaty Land Entitlement Policy, see AANDC, https://www.aadnc-aandc.gc.ca/eng/1100100034819/1100100034820.

25. Some prominent examples include Toronto Aboriginal Support Services Association, Aboriginal People's Council in Vancouver, Ottawa Aboriginal Coalition, the Aboriginal Council of Winnipeg, Barrie Area Native Advisory Circle, and Aboriginal Council of Lethbridge.

26. See Chapter 8 on demography by Don Kerr and Roderic Beaujot and Chapter 9 on Aboriginal languages by Mary Jane Norris for more detailed discussion of issues and questions surrounding Aboriginal identity and ancestry.

14

The Failed Foreign System of Criminal Justice and the Problem with Canada

Lisa Monchalin

Before our white brothers came to civilize us we had no jails. Therefore we had no criminals. You can't have criminals without a jail. We had no lock or keys, and so we had no thieves. If a man was so poor that he had no horse, tipi, or blanket, someone gave him these things. We were too uncivilized to set much value on personal belongings. We wanted to have things only in order to give them away. We had no money, and therefore a man's worth couldn't be measured by it. We had no written law, no attorneys or politicians, therefore we couldn't cheat. . . . I don't know how we managed to get along without the basic things which, we are told, are absolutely necessary to make a civilized society. But now visible progress is everywhere—jails all over the place, and we know these jails are for us Indians. What a pity that so many of us don't appreciate them!

John (Fire) Lame Deer (1994: 70–1)

Introduction: The Continued Failure of the Canadian Criminal Justice System

In his opening remarks to delegates at the 1975 National Conference and Federal–Provincial Conference on Native Peoples and the Criminal Justice System, then Solicitor General of Canada Warren Allmand stated:

> we said that we came here to solve some serious problems and I hope that we can move that along today. Some of these problems have been with us for a long time and have been ignored for a long time and we are trying to do something about them. . . . I hope we can set up continuing mechanisms to make sure that what we start here will be carried forward. (Solicitor General Canada, 1975: 35)

The Solicitor General noted in his final report of the conference that: "concern over the jailing of a disproportionate number of Canada's native people promoted calling a national conference to consider issues of prime importance not only to native peoples but also to the governments under which they live" (Solicitor General Canada, 1975: 3).

The government of Canada's Correctional Investigator observed in 2012 that very little had changed since 1975, and that four decades of inquiries into the state of criminal justice in Canada had repeatedly identified the over-representation of Aboriginal people as a significant problem for all of Canada (Office of the Correctional Investigator, 2012). Major reports examining the many injustices Aboriginal people have experienced at the hands of the Canadian criminal justice system include the 1983 report by the Ontario Native Council on Justice entitled *Warehousing Indians,* as well as the 1988 report of the Canadian Bar Association, *Locking up Natives in Canada.* Serious problems were also clearly identified in a 1989 report, which asserted that Canada's criminal justice system had not only "failed Donald Marshall, Jr. at virtually every turn from his arrest and wrongful conviction for murder...to... his eventual acquittal by the Court of Appeal," but that Donald Marshall had been treated this way because he was Native (Hickman, Poitras, and Evans, 1989: 1). The "utter failure" of the Canadian criminal justice system was also named in the 1991 report by the Law Reform Commission of Canada, which noted that Aboriginal participants in the study had identified that "virtually all of the primary actors in the process (police, lawyers, judges, correctional personnel) patronize them and consistently fail to explain adequately what the process requires of them or what is going to happen to them" (Law Reform Commission of Canada, 1991: 5). Similar comments by Aboriginal people can be found throughout the interim report from the Royal Commission on Aboriginal Peoples (RCAP), *Bridging the Cultural Divide: A Report on Aboriginal People and Criminal Justice in Canada* (RCAP, 1995). Four years later, the opening statements in the Aboriginal Justice Implementation Commission's *Report of the Aboriginal Justice Inquiry of Manitoba* (1999) asserted that: "The justice system has failed Manitoba's Aboriginal people on a massive scale. It has been insensitive and inaccessible, and has arrested and imprisoned Aboriginal people in grossly disproportionate numbers."

Fast forward to today and it is clear that the Canadian criminal justice system continues to fail Aboriginal people in this country. In October 2012, the Office of the Correctional Investigator noted that over-representation of Aboriginal peoples in the federal prison system was still "pervasive and growing." Moreover, an independent reviewer asserted in 2013 that First Nations' under-representation on Ontario juries was a symptom of a much larger problem within the criminal justice system, stating that "the justice system generally as applied to First Nations peoples, particularly in the North, is quite frankly a crisis" (Iacobucci, 2013: 1). Thus, we begin our discussion with a brief overview of disproportionate rates of incarceration and victimization involving Aboriginal people in Canada. We then examine the roots of this crisis of (in)justice in Canada as well as a number of its more serious consequences in the lives of Aboriginal people. This is followed by a brief outline of Aboriginal peoples' understandings of justice as well as a vision of a good way forward in relations between Aboriginal peoples and Canada. We conclude by highlighting some of the efforts by Aboriginal people and their supporters to bring hope as well as justice to Aboriginal peoples in all their relations.

Incarceration and Victimization of Aboriginal Peoples

Mohawk scholar Patricia Monture (2011) pointed out that crime involving Aboriginal people in Canada had not decreased during the previous 40 years despite many national and provincial inquiries and reports. In comparison to other Canadians, Aboriginal people continue to have much greater contact with the criminal justice system as victims, offenders, witnesses, and many times all three (Environics Institute, 2010: 97). In 2011, Aboriginal people made up 4.3 per cent of Canada's total population, yet Aboriginal adults (over 18 years of age) accounted for 28 per cent of admissions to sentenced custody, 25 per cent of admissions to remand, and 21 per cent of admissions to probation and conditional sentences (Perreault, 2014). Moreover, Aboriginal males accounted for 27 per cent of the admissions to provincial/territorial sentenced custody and 23 per cent of admissions to remand centres during the same time period. Proportional representation was even greater for Aboriginal women, who accounted for 43 per cent of all female admissions to provincial/ territorial sentenced custody and 37 per cent of female admissions to remand (Perreault, 2014).

Disparities in over-representation are even higher in the Prairie region. For instance, in 2005 Aboriginal people in Saskatchewan accounted for 81 per cent of adults admitted to provincial custody and 76 per cent of youth custody admissions even though they accounted for only 14.9 per cent of the province's total population (Office of the Correctional Investigator, 2012: 11). Certain prisons in the Prairie region also reveal acute levels of Aboriginal over-representation, such as the Stony Mountain Penitentiary in Manitoba (approximately 11 kilometres from Winnipeg), where more than 60 per cent of those incarcerated are Aboriginal.

From 1998 to 2008, the proportion of Aboriginal people admitted to provincial and territorial sentenced custody increased from 13 per cent to 18 per cent. The proportional increase was even higher for Aboriginal females, whose admissions rates rose from 17 per cent to 24 per cent during this time (Perreault, 2014: 20). In terms of incarceration rates in federal prisons, there was a 35 per cent increase in the federal male Aboriginal incarcerated population from 2001 to 2010. Once again, the numbers are much higher for Aboriginal women, as their incarceration numbers increased by 85.7 per cent during the same 10-year period (Public Safety Canada, 2011: 61). That the criminal justice system in Canada continues to treat Aboriginal people in fundamentally unjust ways is clearly evident in comparative rates of incarceration between 2001 and 2011, for while there was a 7 per cent overall increase in the non-Aboriginal incarcerated population under federal jurisdiction during this time, the percentage of Aboriginal people incarcerated in federal prisons rose by over 37 per cent (Public Safety Canada, 2011: 35, 61).

Aboriginal people in Canada are also disproportionately represented as crime victims, being three times more likely than non-Aboriginal persons to be victims of violent crime, which includes sexual assault, robbery, and physical assaults (Brzozowski, Taylor-Butts, and Johnson, 2006). The 2009 General Social Survey on Victimization revealed that 37 per cent of Aboriginal people reported being victims of crime in the 12 months preceding their survey, compared to 26 per cent for non-Aboriginal people (Perreault, 2014: 7). This is equivalent to almost 322,000 Aboriginal people aged 15 years or older who were victims of crime in the preceding 12 months, which is a daily average of approximately 882 victimizations.

In 2009, 13 per cent of all Aboriginal women (aged 15 and over) living in the provinces had been violently victimized. Put another way, in that year alone approximately 67,000 Aboriginal women experienced some sort of violent encounter, and over a third of these women were victimized on two or more occasions (Brennan, 2011: 7). Amnesty International (2004) reported that Aboriginal women in Canada aged 25–44 were five times more likely than non-Aboriginal women in the same age group to die of violence. Little has changed since then according to a Human Rights Watch report (2013), which noted that Aboriginal women and girls are still much more likely than the general population of Canadian women and girls to be violently victimized and to die as a result.

As of 31 March 2010, the Native Women's Association of Canada's Sisters in Spirit Initiative had identified 582 documented cases of Aboriginal women who had gone missing or who had been murdered (Native Women's Association of Canada, 2010). Most of these cases are quite recent, with 56 per cent of them occurring between the mid-1990s and 2010. In a database of missing and murdered women in Canada covering the time period of 1946 to 2013, Maryanne Pearce (2013) found 824 cases of missing or murdered Aboriginal women. Of those who were identified as Aboriginal, 258 were First Nations, 29 were Inuit, and 10 were identified as Métis. In the majority of the cases (510), there was no documented information on whether the women were First Nations, Inuit, or Métis (Pearce, 2013: 25, 24). There was also conflicting information as some sources listed nine women as being of Aboriginal ancestry while others listed them as non-Aboriginal. Another eight cases involved unidentified human remains, although, according to Pearce, a number of analysts indicated that the women were of Aboriginal heritage. A 2014 report by the Royal Canadian Mounted Police (RCMP) revealed 1,181 cases of missing and murdered Aboriginal women between 1980 and 2012. Overall, 1,017 of these were identified as murders and the other 164 were classified as missing. The report also states that while Aboriginal women only represent 4.3 per cent of the total female population in Canada, they represent 16 per cent of female homicides (RCMP, 2014: 7–9).

The crisis of missing and murdered Aboriginal women has persisted. Acute levels of victimization and offending have been known for decades, and the responses by government have remained largely the same. As noted in the following section, the Canadian criminal justice system has primarily addressed all aspects of crime involving Aboriginal people through its three institutional arenas: police, the courts, and corrections.

The Standard Response to Aboriginal Criminal Justice: Police, the Courts, and Corrections

Anthropologist Rémi Savard (2003) contends that the Canadian criminal justice system lacks credibility in the eyes of many Aboriginal people largely because of the way it has contributed to the systematic dismantling of Aboriginal systems of justice. Interviews with 2,614[1] urban Aboriginal people in 11 Canadian cities[2] during 2009 showed that over half (55 per cent) of the respondents reported little or no confidence in the Canadian criminal justice system (Environics Institute, 2010: 99). The same survey also found that urban Aboriginal people were more than twice as likely as Canadians in general to have low confidence in the Canadian criminal justice system. In general, members of all three major Aboriginal population groups lack confidence in the criminal justice system, with 57 per cent of First Nations people, 55 per cent of Métis people, and 39 per cent of Inuit reporting little or no confidence in any aspect of the system.

Not surprisingly, the Environics study also found that urban Aboriginal people strongly supported the desire for an Aboriginal justice system that would be separate from the mainstream criminal justice system. This was especially the case among respondents who had little or no confidence in the criminal justice system. Support for a separate system was highest among First Nations respondents at 63 per cent and Inuit at 62 per cent. While 51 per cent of Métis respondents did not fully oppose a separate criminal justice system for Aboriginal peoples, 32 per cent were somewhat opposed and 19 per cent were undecided (Environics Institute, 2010: 100).

Criminologist Jeffery Reiman has pointed out that instead of trying to eliminate crime, criminal justice systems are designed to protect the interests of those who are wealthy and powerful and punish those who are poor. Those who are in positions to change policy thus tend to support only those changes that serve their own particular interests (Reiman, 2007: 4). As Mohawk scholar Taiaiake Alfred and Tsalagi scholar Jeff Corntassel point out, "contemporary settlers follow the mandate provided for them by their imperial forefathers' colonial legacy" (Alfred and Corntassel, 2005: 598). While the words used by the early colonizers to describe Aboriginal peoples may have changed, the fundamental attitudes of the colonizers still pervade Euro-Canadian institutions, political systems, and discourses. In other words, the original colonial concern to establish and maintain control over Aboriginal people in this country is clearly evident in the policies and practices of those who maintain positions of power in Canada's criminal justice system.

According to Reiman (2007: 4), the government is more than capable of changing policies to reduce crime. Instead, it has implemented a "get tough on crime" agenda that includes hiring more police, tinkering with the colonial court system, and "enhancing" prison systems. The government continues to support this agenda in the face of large amounts of empirical evidence indicating that such an approach will do nothing to actually reduce levels of crime (Waller, 2008, 2014). Sociologist David Garland (2001: 26) argues that crime control strategies are not implemented by governments simply because they are viewed as insightful and possibly effective. Rather, governments tend to adopt strategies because they identify certain ways of addressing crime-related problems that "fit with the dominant culture and the power structure upon which it rests." In other words, most government-supported crime reduction ideas and initiatives support the dominant interests and institutions in a given society by assigning responsibility to those who are already in positions of power.

Crime prevention experts have known for decades that simply increasing the number of police officers to engage in the standard practice of "reactive policing" does nothing to reduce levels of crime. This understanding goes back at least four decades, when Kelling et al. (1974) ran a field experiment to test the effects of increasing the number of police officers on routine patrol in marked cars. The researchers found little effect in doing so and concluded that increasing the number of officers on the streets was not an effective way to achieve reductions in crime. Despite current widespread understanding among crime prevention experts that having more police officers on the streets does not reduce crime, Irvin Waller (2014: 36) notes that "a larger and larger portion of police budgets goes for more and more cars to respond to calls for service, thereby reinforcing isolated, reactive policing."

Since the beginnings of policing in Canada, the state's crime prevention strategy has remained essentially the same—that is, to react punitively to whatever they (i.e., the police and the courts, with some legislative direction) deem to be criminal. One of the primary reasons the North West Mounted Police (which would later become the RCMP) was formed in 1873 was to address the "problem" of Aboriginal resistance to settler colonization (Fleming et al., 2008: 99). Current approaches by Canadian criminal justice representatives clearly indicate that that they continue to deem it to be criminal for Aboriginal peoples to assert our inherent rights in our homelands. Relatively recent instances of this happening include (to name a select few): the infamous Oka crisis during the summer of 1990 involving the Mohawk people of Kahnawake and the Canadian military; the 1995 land dispute protest by members of the Stony and Kettle Point First Nation near Sarnia, Ontario; the protests by the Six Nations in Caledonia, Ontario, against the development of properties on their lands in 2006; and over two years of protests by First Nations people and their supporters, beginning in 2012, against shale gas exploration on the traditional lands of the Elsipogtog First Nation in Rexton, New Brunswick. There have also been reports of government officials spying on those involved in the recent Idle No More movement (Ling, 2013), which is now an international grassroots movement based on Aboriginal inherent rights and the peace and friendship foundations of the treaties. Amnesty International (2013) has also reported government surveillance on Gitxsan activist Dr Cindy Blackstock, who has spoken out strongly in support of equal rights for Aboriginal children in Canada's child welfare system.

The standard approach to policing has also largely continued, which for Aboriginal people typically has meant being policed by non-Aboriginal people. There are currently some Aboriginal police officers in Canada and there are also Aboriginal people employed in various police service roles. The hiring of Aboriginal people by police agencies has largely been purposeful, and the practice largely began with the introduction of the Band Constable Program in 1969, which allowed band councils to hire band members to administer bylaws in their First Nation communities (Cummins and Steckley, 2003: 20). This program was expanded in 1971 to create "special constables" whose purpose was to supplement senior police forces at the local level. However, the status and authority of special constables were significantly less than those of regular police officers since they were not permitted to carry firearms, they received a minimal salary, they were expected to use their own cars, and in some cases they did not even receive uniforms (Cummins and Steckley, 2003: 20–1).

The Special Constable Program was soon expanded to the federal police service, which resulted in a slight increase in the authority given to Aboriginal police officers (Cummins and Steckley, 2003: 24). Similar to the special constables program that operated in Aboriginal communities, the federal program had a number of problems. As well as receiving smaller salaries, Aboriginal special constables received less training than their non-Aboriginal counterparts. Special constables also reported being treated with hostility by community members and in general experienced feelings of social isolation. The Special Constable Program was replaced in 1990 with the Aboriginal Constable Development Program; instead of being "special" adjunct officers, this program sought to increase the number of Aboriginal people who were qualified to become regular RCMP members. This practice has large-ly remained intact to the present day in that police agencies across Canada continue to actively recruit Aboriginal people. One can go to powwows or Aboriginal Day celebrations and see policing agencies (as well as other crim-inal justice agencies) setting up tables and engaging in impressive marketing campaigns to recruit Aboriginal people.

While Canadian government representatives have presented the ac-tive recruitment of Aboriginal people by policing agencies as a positive de-velopment in Canadian criminal justice, others view it as a means by which Aboriginal people have become active participants in our own colonization since it involves our people being recruited to become agents of the colonial state responsible to enforce colonial laws. According to Jane Dickson-Gilmore and Carol La Prairie (2005: 71), most Aboriginal policing initiatives represent an attempt to "Indigenize" or "Indianize" the white colonial system. Room is made for Aboriginal people to be slotted into various roles within the justice system, though the system itself stays the same. Doing so gives the appear-ance that the system is fundamentally "good" and that it is only necessary to make minor changes for the system to be "good" for all citizens of Canada (Dickson-Gilmore and La Prairie, 2005: 68).

In an attempt to reduce the incarceration rates of Aboriginal people, the courts and the government have tinkered with the laws. They have also at times supported the diversion of Aboriginal people who have been con-victed of a crime away from prisons through alternative programs. Parliament amended the Criminal Code in 1996 to include section 718.2(e), which made specific reference to Aboriginal people in its wording:

> All available sanctions other than imprisonment that are reasonable in the circumstances should be considered for all offenders, with particular attention to the circumstances of Aboriginal Offenders.

Much like hiring special constables, amending the laws represents another attempt to Indigenize or Indianize the colonial justice system in ways that are supposedly a better "fit" for Aboriginal people.

In the case of *R. v. Gladue* (1999), the Supreme Court interpreted the amend-ed section 718.2(e) to mean that "the jail term for an Aboriginal offender may in some circumstances be less than the term imposed on a non-Aboriginal offender for the same offence" (*R. v. Gladue*, 1999). The Court further ruled that "Aboriginal offenders must always be sentenced in a manner which gives greatest weight to the principles of restorative justice, and less weight to goals such as deterrence, denunciation and separation."

In her examination of whether the amendment had been successful in reducing the incarceration levels of Aboriginal offenders, Fennig (2002: iii) found that "Aboriginal over-incarceration levels had actually *increased*" since the introduction of section 718.2(e). According to Fennig, law reform alone clearly does not address the root cause of Aboriginal over-incarceration, and disproportional incarceration rates are a symptom of a much larger issue related to political, social, and economic disadvantage.

Not surprisingly, authorities in Canada's corrections system also have tried to adjust part of the system to "fit" Aboriginal peoples. According to Martel, Brassard, and Jaccoud (2011: 237), "Canada is a forerunner in the Indigenization of its correctional apparatus." For example, Correctional Services Canada (CSC) established a national healing program for Aboriginal offenders in all federal prisons and facilities after an extensive review of the system in 2009. It also introduced Aboriginal-specific provisions into the Corrections and Conditional Release Act, including sections 81 and 84. Section 81 provides CSC the ability to "enter into an agreement with an Aboriginal community for the provision of correctional services to Aboriginal offenders," while section 84 allows incarcerated Aboriginal people to be "released into an Aboriginal community" if the community and the incarcerated person express an interest in this happening.

Under section 81, two types of healing lodges have been established: CSC-operated lodges, and lodges run in agreement with CSC but operated by Aboriginal communities. Currently, there are four healing lodges operated in Canada by Aboriginal communities and four CSC-run lodges (CSC, 2013). CSC (2013) outlines the purpose of its healing lodges as places:

> where we use Aboriginal values, traditions and beliefs to design services and programs for offenders. We include Aboriginal concepts of justice and reconciliation. The approach to corrections is holistic and spiritual. Programs include guidance and support from Elders and Aboriginal communities.

According to the Office of the Correctional Investigator, several problems with the implementation of sections 81 and 84 of the Corrections and Conditional Release Act include major discrepancies between funding support for healing lodges operated by Aboriginal communities and those operated by CSC. In 2009–10, the yearly allocation per incarcerated individual at CSC-run healing lodges was $113,450, whereas Aboriginal-operated lodges received only $70,845 per incarcerated individual. Moreover, employee salaries at Aboriginal healing lodges were 50 per cent lower than those of employees who were doing similar work at CSC-run lodges (Office of the Correctional Investigator, 2012: 4).

Corrections Canada officials have stated that section 84 was intended to facilitate the process of Aboriginal communities setting conditions for offenders who wanted to be released back to their home communities. In practice, however, the Office of the Correctional Investigator admitted that the process had become "cumbersome, time-consuming and misunderstood." The deeper problem, according to Martel et al. (2011), is that although numerous attempts have been made over the past two decades to bring aspects of Aboriginal spirituality inside Canada's prison walls, the structures and processes of Canada's entire corrections system continue to be informed by deeply entrenched colonial attitudes.

Healing lodges are supposed to be places that incorporate Aboriginal values, traditions, and beliefs; that include Aboriginal concepts of justice and reconciliation; and that have a holistic and spiritual approach to life. In an analysis of initiatives intended to support Aboriginal peoples, however, the Office of the Correctional Investigator (2012) found limited understanding and awareness within CSC of Aboriginal peoples, cultures, spirituality, and approaches to healing. Problems of under-funding also limited the number of Elders available to provide support, guidance, and ceremonies to incarcerated Aboriginal peoples. The Correctional Investigator also found the response to urban Aboriginal peoples to be inadequate, for while corrections employees typically assumed that incarcerated Aboriginal peoples would be returning to a First Nation community after release, many in fact had no plans to do so.

Beyond the many problems and limitations the Office of the Correctional Investigator found within Canada's corrections system, it is important to acknowledge that the integration of Aboriginal cultures and perspectives into prison-based healing initiatives have benefited many Aboriginal people who have been pulled into the system of incarceration. For example, Heckbert and Turkington (2001) found that Aboriginal programs had helped turn around the lives of 65 per cent of the 68 Aboriginal ex-incarcerated individuals they interviewed. In many respects the success of programs and supports for incarcerated people based on Aboriginal traditions shows how impactful and effective our cultures can be, even within the confines of colonial structures. Our cultures and traditions helped us thrive for thousands and thousands of years. Since the arrival of Europeans in the Americas, they have been the key to our survival in the face of European attempts at physical as well as cultural genocide.

Despite the apparently good intentions of some CSC officials, the incorporation of Aboriginal peoples' traditions or cultures into the operation of

CSC represents an attempt to "fit" or adapt Aboriginal peoples into a colonial-based system. Even Canada's Correctional Investigator (2012: 12) noted that "the findings from various task forces and commissions all point to the *failure to adapt* correctional systems to meet the needs of the growing Aboriginal offender population" (emphasis added). The Correctional Investigator then followed the well-worn colonial path in proposing that certain adjustments, modifications, and adaptations needed to be made within the current systems and structures. A select number of recommendations included: more funding for healing lodges and beds; more Aboriginal awareness training for CSC staff; addressing funding shortages as well as service issues affecting the number and role of Elders working within prisons; appointment of a Deputy Commissioner of Aboriginal Corrections; and reducing the red tape that hindered the successful implementation of section 84 in the Corrections and Conditional Release Act. It is clear that these and many other recommendations propose changes within a colonial system rather than aim to effect much broader and more beneficial changes for Aboriginal people outside the Eurocentric boundaries of the systems and structures of CSC.

According to Story and Yalkin (2013), federal and provincial government departments spent $20.3 billion on the criminal justice system in Canada in 2011–12 to support the police, the courts (youth justice, legal aid, prosecutors, and judges), and corrections (including parole). They also note that national criminal justice expenditures steadily increased from 2002 to 2013. The problem, as Garland (2001: 65) notes, is that it is "notoriously difficult to overcome the inertia of an institutional system once it has become established." Such institutional inertia is particularly hard to overcome when those in positions of power are able to cloud people's awareness of problems within the system through the rhetoric of benevolence (Cohen, 1985: 20). Despite the Canadian government's apparently strategic, political commitment to "get tough on crime," there is not a shred of empirical evidence that increasing the number of police, tinkering with colonial laws, or locking Aboriginal people into prisons will stop the next generation of Aboriginal people from being engaged with the criminal justice system as (accused or convicted) offenders or victims.

The Canadian criminal justice system has not provided justice for Aboriginal people in this country, and increased spending over the years has done nothing to reduce crime involving Aboriginal people. In many respects this is because most proposed solutions to their over-representation in Canada's prisons assume the legitimacy of the *Canadian* criminal justice system. If all the problems Aboriginal people experience with the justice system continue to be framed from a colonial-centric stance, then all explanations for and responses to "their problems" will continue to be addressed in the context of the workings of a colonializing state. As official inquiries and reports continue to identify ways that Canada's justice system is "failing" Aboriginal peoples, there will be ongoing calls for better policing practices, increasingly flexible court procedures and decisions, and more culturally sensitive programs in CSC.

Rather than continuing to ask what should be done about Aboriginal over-representation in the *Canadian* criminal justice system, perhaps it is time to ask the question of how we can reduce harm and victimization affecting Aboriginal peoples in occupied Canada. And rather than framing the current situation in terms of the "problem" of over-representation of Aboriginal people—which places blame on Aboriginal peoples for not conforming to a foreign system—over-representation should be framed as the "problem" of a colonial system that continues to impose foreign structures, institutions, discourses, laws, and cultures in the territories of Indigenous peoples. As Waziyatawin and Yellow Bird (2012: 4) have pointed out, "our uncritical participation in this colonial system undoubtedly increases the rate at which we are failing and failing."

"The Roots of Injustice Lie in Our History"

In his introduction to the final report of the RCAP in 1996, Dene leader and RCAP co-chair Georges Erasmus stated that "the roots of injustice lie in history." Mohawk scholar Patricia Monture (2007: 207) elaborates on this idea when she notes that "the past impacts on the present, and today's place of Aboriginal peoples in Canadian society cannot be understood without a well-developed historical understanding of colonialism and the present-day trajectories of those old relationships." Put another way, to understand the present and plan well for our future, we must first engage honestly with our past.

The first peace and friendship treaties between Aboriginal peoples and Europeans acknowledged Aboriginal peoples' sovereignty. Algonquin Anishinaabe-kwe researcher and activist Lynn Gehl (2014: 55) notes that the early treaties were established "in the interest of establishing or renewing friendship, peace, trade and sharing." Many peace and friendship agreements were codified in wampum belts. The first treaty agreement involving Aboriginal people and Europeans was the Two-Row Wampum Belt agreement of 1613 between the Haudenosaunee and Dutch peoples (Lyons, 1997: 308). Treaty agreements such as the Two-Row Wampum represented "the codification of a non-interference relationship, meaning that each nation would respect the internal governance and jurisdiction of the other" (Gehl, 2014: 55).

The relationship was symbolized by two rows of purple beads on a background of white beads. One purple line represented the Aboriginal people's canoe, laws, traditions, and customs while the other purple line represented the Europeans' ship, laws, traditions, and customs (Lyons, 1997: 308; Williams, 1986: 291). The three rows of white beads between the two purple rows represented the binding of relations between sovereign peoples based on respect, peace, and friendship between independent nations (Mohawk Council of Akwesasne, 2014).

Unfortunately for Aboriginal peoples, the British approach to treaty relations soon began to focus on displacing Aboriginal people by procuring their land (Gehl, 2014) as well as legislating most every aspect of Aboriginal peoples' lives (Dickason, 2002). Aboriginal peoples thus went from being sovereign allies to wards of a colonial state living on lands "reserved" for them as Indians. And it was soon clear that the colonizers would waste little time implementing their agenda to "get rid of the Indian" by attacking the heart of Aboriginal communities in a number of ways. Many sacred rituals as well as everyday behaviours were soon prohibited—i.e., criminalized—with the passage of the Indian Act in 1876. For example, Indian Act amendments in 1884 stated that anyone found engaging in the potlatches of the Northwest Coast, the Indian dance known as the Tamanawas, or other ceremonies would face imprisonment (Dickason, 2002). In 1920, amendments to the Indian Act outlawed traditional hereditary forms of leadership and replaced them with the European-designed structure of band elections. In certain areas in the prairie West, Aboriginal people were not allowed to leave their reserve without a pass that had been approved by an agent of the government, otherwise known as the Indian agent (Barron, 1988). In 1920, the Canadian government also made it mandatory for Aboriginal children to attend church-run "Indian" residential schools. Refusal to send children to these schools would result in parents or other relatives being fined or imprisoned (Furniss, 1995: 108). Children who did attend were prevented from speaking their traditional languages, and any who did were often severely punished (Chrisjohn, Young, and Mauran, 2006: 61). The loss of traditional languages has been devastating for Aboriginal peoples, for as anthropologist W.E.H. Stanner notes, "no English words are good enough to give a sense of the links between an Aboriginal group and its homeland" (Chamberlin, 2004: 79).

We cannot understand the crime, victimization, and harm experienced by Aboriginal peoples today without acknowledging the colonial history of relations between Aboriginal peoples and the Europeans who established and settled in Canada. As Waziyatawin and Yellow Bird (2012: 3) point out, "most of our contemporary daily struggles are also a direct consequence of colonization."

In its 2012 ruling in *R v. Ipeelee*, the Supreme Court of Canada similarly stated that: "The overwhelming message of the various reports and commissions on Aboriginal peoples' involvement in the criminal justice system is that current levels of criminality are intimately tied to the legacy of colonialism."

Crime prevention research has shown that negative childhood and youth experiences are closely linked to crime and associated risk factors (see Farrington and Welsh, 2007). Gabor Maté (2012) explains that the environment an individual is raised in plays a role in shaping the neurological patterns in the brain that affect behaviour later in life. Those who are raised with violence and abuse have a neurological predisposition to acting in angry or violent ways, many times turning to drugs and alcohol, as well as other self-harming behaviours, to cope with or "bury" the emotional pain. In a review of research on victimization and offending, Siegfried, Ko, and Kelley (2004: 8) conclude that while there is no single risk factor or experience that causes one to turn to violence or crime, chances of becoming an offender are drastically increased if an individual experiences violent trauma as a youth. Along with noting that violent victimization is a "warning signal for future violent offending as well as a precursor to being a repeat victim of violence," Siegfried et al. (2004: 4, 7) note that "numerous studies over the past 10 years have shown a clear relationship between youth victimization and a variety of problems in later life, including mental health problems, substance abuse, impaired social relationships, suicide, and delinquency."

After completing over 2,000 consultations and public hearings in Aboriginal communities across Canada, the RCAP identified that many problems, including intergenerational abuse among Aboriginal peoples, are the consequence of their traumatic experiences in residential schools. As noted in the final RCAP report:

> The survivors of the Indian residential school system have, in many cases, continued to have their lives shaped by the experiences in these schools. Persons who attended these schools continue to struggle with their identity after years of being taught to hate themselves and their culture. The residential schools led to a disruption in the transference of parenting skills from one generation to the next. Without these skills, many survivors have had difficulty in raising their own children. In residential schools, they learned that adults often exert power and control through abuse. The lessons learned in childhood are often repeated in adulthood with the result that many survivors of the residential school system often inflict abuse on their own children. These children in turn use the same tools on their children. (RCAP, 1996: 379)

Lakota Sioux youth-care expert Martin Brokenleg (2013) argues that Aboriginal people are completely normal people who have lived through an abnormal history. Trauma and violence expert Judy Atkinson notes that traumatic symptoms are "the natural and predictable reactions of normal people...to abnormal experiences" (Atkinson, 2002: 52). Thus, turning to alcohol or acting out violently must not be viewed as "signs of personal weakness or mental illness," but rather as natural human responses to tragedies, adversities, or other disasters (Atkinson, 2002: 52, quoted in Comack et al., 2013: 38).

The abnormal colonial experiences of Aboriginal people in Canada have also contributed to a number of risk factors in their lives that are associated with crime. Some of the more common risk factors include lower levels and less access to formal education, overcrowded living conditions, inner-city living, poverty, social exclusion, racism and discrimination, lack of cultural identity, addictions, family violence, and living in single-parent families. Although the presence of multiple risk factors in someone's life does not necessarily mean they will offend or be victimized, the risks for both increase dramatically if one is exposed to such factors. Thus, of the crimes Aboriginal people might commit or become victim to, risk factors can explain potential reasons for this. Yet it must be recognized that rates of over-representation in incarceration are not a result of Aboriginal people simply committing more crimes, but rather are due to entrenched structural racism. The criminal justice system operates to sustain existing colonial power structures. Policies and practices that uphold Euro-Canadian world views and values—passed down from the colonial forefathers—remain embedded within the criminal justice system.

The Way Forward: Re-establishing Peace, Friendship, and Indigenous Systems of Justice

It is clear that Aboriginal people's experiences with the Canadian criminal justice system are in many respects a consequence of centuries of colonial policies and practices designed to "get rid of the Indian problem." While it can be argued that the current treatment of Aboriginal people in Canada is not as overtly racist as that of the early colonizers, there is clear evidence that representatives of Canada's criminal justice system continue to propose colonial-based solutions designed to enhance and/or adapt the Euro-Canadian structures of police, courts, and corrections to the needs of Aboriginal people. It is also clear that this needs to change, and that the changes must be radical if justice is to be realized for all peoples in Canada.

Taiaiake Alfred (2005: 152) has asserted that "without massive restitution, including land, financial transfers, and other forms of assistance to compensate for past harms and continuing injustices committed against our peoples, reconciliation would permanently enshrine colonial injustices and is itself a further injustice." But just as there is more to justice than punishing accused offenders, true reconciliation is based on much more than material compensation. As the history of colonial relations has taught us, relationships that lack a shared commitment to pursue peace by treating one another with respect and dignity are doomed to failure. It is in this light that Aboriginal peoples and their supporters have called for a radical (re)visioning of justice and reconciliation in Canada.

Haida Elder Woody Morrison (2014) explains that the Euro-Canadian justice system views justice "being served" when one is found guilty of a crime and has been successfully convicted in a court of law. Justice is therefore only achieved when one is convicted and not when one is acquitted. Any ruling from the courts is also commonly viewed as both absolute and final, and holds an authoritative claim to "truth" (Smart, 1989). Furthermore, the Euro-Canadian system demands that justice-related problems be addressed according to the colonial ways and means of the Canadian state.

In contrast, Aboriginal people's views of justice are informed by a vision of right relations between all aspects of creation. Accordingly, justice is much more than something to be achieved within the narrow confines of the *Canadian* criminal justice system; it is a way of relating with all others that is based on a commitment to peace and to treating all our relations with respect. Ojibway author Richard Wagamese (2013) explains that:

> "All my relations" means all. When a speaker makes this statement it's meant as recognition of the principles of harmony, unity and equality. It's a way of saying that you recognize your place in the universe and that you recognize the place of others and of other things in the realm of the real and the living. In that it is a powerful evocation of truth.
>
> Because when you say those words you mean everything that you are kin to. Not just those people who look like you, talk like you, act like you, sing, dance, celebrate, worship or pray like you. Everyone. You also mean everything that relies on air, water, sunlight and the power of the Earth and the universe itself for sustenance and perpetuation. It's recognition of the fact that we are all one body moving through time and space together.

Those who call for reconciliation as a way for Aboriginal peoples and the rest of Canada to heal the legacy of colonialism in our relations recognize that it will not be an easy journey. As Seema Ahluwalia (2009: 9) has noted, "while reflecting on our rather shameful history will be painful for Canadians, continuing along a path of denial, hypocrisy, and historical amnesia will serve no one." Nishnaabeg writer and scholar Leanne Simpson (2011: 21) also points out that Aboriginal people's desire for reconciliation with Europeans is anything but new, for many treaty negotiations with Europeans over the past 400 years have involved attempts to reconcile.

Colonization is fundamentally based on a lack of respect for all others, and so treaty agreements between Aboriginal peoples and Canada in practice have never provided true commitment to peace and full reconciliation from the state. Recent apologies by government representatives for the past actions of Canada towards Aboriginal people expressed a desire for reconciliation, although these same officials have never publicly acknowledged the colonial attitudes and practices of their own government (Simpson, 2011: 21–2). Indeed, some have attempted to completely deny that colonialism ever existed. The most blatant example of this occurred just over a year after Prime Minister Stephen Harper presented his apology in Parliament to residential school survivors in June of 2008 when, in September 2009, he proclaimed in front of world leaders at the G20 Summit in Pittsburgh that Canada "has no history of colonialism" (Cannon and Sunseri, 2011: 263).

For Leanne Simpson (2011: 22), true reconciliation requires real action and support for First Nations to revitalize their cultures, languages, families, traditional forms of governance, economies, and everything else that colonialism has destroyed. She also asserts that reconciliation must involve re-educating Canadians through a process of decolonization, which, according to Waziyatawin and Yellow Bird (2012: 3) involves "the meaningful and active resistance to the forces of colonialism that perpetrate the subjugation and/or exploitation of our minds, bodies, and lands." In other words, the radical purpose of decolonization is to overturn colonial systems and liberate Indigenous peoples.

This was unnecessary in the early relations between Aboriginal peoples and Europeans, for many of them were based on peace and friendship. That the basis of our current relations has significantly diverged from these principles is evident in the highly disproportional involvement of Aboriginal people with the Canadian criminal justice system. The more storied perspective of our Aboriginal people views this as the time for Euro-Canadians to get back in their ship and be supportive partners in peace and friendship rather than interfering with Aboriginal nations as we steer our own canoes. As the Two-Row Wampum conveys, we will both travel down the river of life side by side in our own respective boats, remaining independent and not trying to steer the other's vessel (Morito, 1999: 276; Williams, 1986: 291).

The vision of non-Aboriginal Canadians walking beside rather than in front and going down the river of life in tandem with Aboriginal peoples based on peace, friendship, and respect is a good way forward. Similar visions were expressed when the British and Great Lakes Covenant Chain Confederacy Wampum Belt was presented in 1764 by the superintendent of Indian affairs to members of over 24 Nations and approximately 2,000 chiefs. This wampum agreement reiterated that our relationships often tarnish—like silver—over time, so they also at times require polishing and re-polishing (Borrows, 2002: 163; Gehl, 2011).

Re-polishing our relationships depends in part on every Canadian acknowledging that Aboriginal nations in Canada were thriving before the arrival of Europeans. Although there were vast differences among the many nations, each with different languages, customs, and governance structures, they held in common a belief in the sacredness of women and children. Traditional teacher and visionary Black Elk (Oglala Lakota) acknowledged the importance and influence of women when he said, "when the women are defeated then we as a nation are truly defeated" (cited in Hansen, 2012: 6). The colonial project stripped away the central roles that women held in their communities, particularly as residential schools tore families apart by replacing children's caring, loving environments with relations characterized by abuse, violence, and at times genocidal intent. Addressing injustice in the lives of Canada's Aboriginal people thus requires that Aboriginal and non-Aboriginal peoples in Canada commit to honouring the sacredness of Aboriginal women and children.

The Idle No More (INM) movement, which was initiated by three Aboriginal women and one non-Aboriginal woman, is another means by which our relations can be re-polished since it calls for recognition of our original peace and friendship agreements. Begun in November 2012, INM is a peaceful grassroots movement taking a stand against "ongoing colonial assaults by the Canadian state and corporations" (Lilley and Shantz, 2013: 113). The initial purpose of INM was to stop Bill C-45, the second of the Conservative government's two omnibus budget bills in 2012, which, among other things, potentially gutted environmental impact assessment, limited the reach of impact assessment in regard to fisheries and navigable waters, and made subtle but significant changes to the Indian Act to make it easier for resource companies to trespass on Aboriginal lands. The vision for change among movement supporters quickly grew. As INM pioneer Sheelah McLean stated, "When we started the rallies and the petitions, the central goal was to stop Bill C-45. Since our first rally in Saskatoon on November 10, 2012 we have framed that goal within a long-standing history of colonial attacks on Indigenous lands and bodies" (Lilley and Shantz, 2013:115). INM activists were unsuccessful in their fight to stop the passing of Bill C-45, though since that time their vision has expanded to include Aboriginal human rights, equal treatment of Aboriginal peoples, honouring the treaty relationship as well as Aboriginal sovereignty, and protecting the Earth's resources.

In many respects, INM represents both an ongoing demand for justice as well as a vision of peace, friendship, and respect in relations between Aboriginal peoples and the rest of Canada. In fact, it is common for INM supporters to reaffirm original peace and friendship treaty agreements at their rallies. For instance, Six Nations activist Beverley Jacobs, the former president of the Native Women's Association of Canada, spoke about the treaty relationship with a Two-Row Wampum belt in hand at an INM rally at the Vancouver Art Gallery on 23 December 2012. During the INM National Day of Action on 7 October 2013, which marked the 250th anniversary of the Royal Proclamation of 1763, Cayuga hip hop artist Sino General spoke in reference to the Two-Row Wampum when he stated that "we need to get off their ship and back in our canoe." General was cautioning others against taking their colonial "citizenship" since that would mean agreeing to be a "citizen" in their "ship." In all, the INM movement is positioned as both a site of resistance as well as a site of solidarity for those who are committed to justice and to promoting a good way forward in relations between Aboriginal peoples and the rest of Canada.

While individuals within the INM movement share a passion and vision for Aboriginal justice, there is a tremendous amount of diversity among INM supporters. People within the INM movement thus provide us with an important reminder of the uniqueness of every Aboriginal nation and community, both past and present. In the past, the methods developed by many traditional communities to deal with wrongdoing were framed within the world view of each community. Simpson (2011: 23) notes that Nishnaabeg legal systems focus on restoration and the rebalancing of relationships. Similarly, Opaskwayak Cree Nation scholar John Hansen explains that traditional justice processes in Cree communities involve the full restoration of all community members. The Cree system of justice involves accountability whereby offenders acknowledge their wrongdoing and must learn about the consequences of the pain they have caused (Hansen, 2012: 4). According to Mi'kmaq Elder Daniel Paul, achieving justice in traditional Mi'kmaq societies involved bringing together disputing parties "for mediation and reconciliation" until everyone reached an agreement "based on justice and fairness." Any final agreement had to address all main "concerns of the individuals, groups or governments involved" (Paul, 2006: 9). Despite the diversity of world views and traditional systems of justice, most Aboriginal peoples past and present have shared a commitment to the principles of respect and maintaining balance within their communities. INM supporters and many others envision a time in which all peoples in Canada share the same commitment.

Concluding Remarks

It is time for Aboriginal approaches to justice to play a major role in reconciliation. A people's approach to justice reflects their world view and world views are embedded in the language a people use to frame their legal system. It is in this light that an important way forward for Canada's approach to justice is envisioned; that is, to support the reinvigoration of traditional Indigenous languages, legal systems, and governance structures that rightly focus not only on reducing harm but also on cultivating peaceful relations between all peoples. As Hansen (2012: 15) notes:

> Indigenous justice systems have been dismissed or marginalized while our overrepresentation in the prisons increases. An Omushkegowuk response to wrongdoing encourages accountability, repairs harm, restores relationships, forgives wrongdoers and advocates peace. This is what our ancestors did, and this is what we should continue to do. The struggle for restoring justice and accountability should expand and develop in all policies concerning Indigenous justice.

We must continue to direct our efforts to rebuilding the heart of our communities that the colonial project sought to destroy. This means (re)committing ourselves to honour the roles and sacredness of our women and children, reclaiming our traditional lands, and dedicating ourselves to reinvigorate our cultures and traditional languages. Rebuilding our communities will also include learning to walk with our non-Aboriginal sisters and brothers. As a community member involved in a recent study of Aboriginal crime prevention programming in Winnipeg stated in response to the question of whether non-Aboriginal people should be partners with Aboriginal people: "Well to the extent that if it's perpetuating the dialogue of colonization and if there's racist undertones then no, but if it's about ... basing this on human rights and walking beside people not in front, then yes" (Monchalin, 2012: 305).

This is a just and good way forward.

Discussion Questions

1. In what ways has Canada's criminal justice system been set up to "fail" Aboriginal people in this country?
2. Why are Aboriginal people over-represented within the criminal justice system as both victims and offenders?
3. What has your experience been with the Canadian criminal justice system, and in what ways does your experience support the view that the system works to support the interests and positions of dominant people in society?
4. How might harm and victimization affecting Aboriginal people in Canada be reduced?
5. What does it mean to "Indigenize" or "Indianize" the Canadian criminal justice system, and why would this not provide a long-term solution to reducing harm and victimization affecting Aboriginal people?
6. What role can all Canadians play in achieving a good way forward towards justice?

Further Reading

Borrows, John. 2002. "Wampum at Niagara: The Royal Proclamation, Canadian Legal History, and Self-Government." In Michael Asch, ed., *Aboriginal Treaty Rights in Canada*. Vancouver: University of British Columbia Press, 155–72.

Chrisjohn, Roland, and Sherri Young, with Michael Maraun. 2006. *The Circle Game: Shadows and Substance in the Indian Residential School Experience in Canada*, rev. edn. Penticton, BC: Theytus Books.

Comack, Elizabeth. 2012. *Racialized Policing: Aboriginal People's Encounters with the Police*. Black Point, NS: Fernwood.

———, Lawrence Deane, Larry Morrissette, and Jim Silver. 2013. *"Indians Wear Red": Colonialism, Resistance, and Aboriginal Street Gangs*. Black Point, NS: Fernwood.

Human Rights Watch. 2013. *Those Who Take Us Away: Abusive Policing and Failures in Protection of Indigenous Women and Girls in Northern British Columbia, Canada*. New York: Human Rights Watch.

LaRocque, Emma. 1997. "Re-examining Culturally Appropriate Models in Criminal Justice Applications." In Michael Asch, ed., *Aboriginal Treaty Rights in Canada*. Vancouver: University of British Columbia Press, 1997.

O'Connor, L.J., and Morgan O'Neal, with Lloyd Dolha and Jim Ada. 2010. *Dark Legacy: Systemic Discrimination against Canada's First Peoples*. Vancouver: Totem Pole Books.

Office of the Correctional Investigator. 2012. *Spirit Matters: Aboriginal People and the Corrections and Conditional Release Act*. Ottawa: Office of the Correctional Investigator.

Notes

1. These interviews took place between March and October 2009 (Environics Institute, 2010: 7).
2. These cities were Vancouver, Edmonton, Calgary, Regina, Saskatoon, Winnipeg, Thunder Bay, Montreal, Toronto, Halifax, and Ottawa (Environics Institute, 2010: 7).

15

Reconciliation and a Way Forward: A Concluding Dialogue

David Newhouse and David Long

Reconciliation

It is our hope that readers of the fourth edition of *Visions of the Heart* will appreciate the challenges involved in trying to capture the *life* of ongoing dialogue in writing. We also hope they will recognize that the contributions to this collection embody a particular way forward in relations involving Aboriginal and non-Aboriginal people in Canada, a way that reflects a commitment to walk together on a post-colonial[1] path that seeks truthfulness, healing, and reconciliation. Those who walk this path understand that telling the truth, experiencing healing, and becoming/being reconciled are anything but abstract, unadorned principles or points of view. Rather, we understand them to be the essence of healthy, whole relationships. And while sincere commitment to truthful dialogue and action may be challenging to all involved, it is our conviction that such commitment is both a sign as well as a means of ongoing healing and reconciliation for those who seek a positive way forward in our relations with one another. As many other contributors to this collection have noted, reconciliation is a process that requires ongoing commitment to dialogue and action, and is therefore always in the process of becoming.

This is not to say that the post-colonial way forward is clear and straight, for the commitment to engage in truthful dialogue—which we believe involves listening in humility and openness as well as speaking with respect and honesty—can lead us down many unexpected paths and bring healing and reconciliation to all our relations in sudden and at times unsettling ways. Such dialogue inevitably shifts and even jars taken-for-granted thought and

Giibwanisi Dizhnikaaz & Steve da Silva / BASICS Community News Service

behaviour, and it affects most everyone who is involved very differently. The goal of post-colonial dialogue and action is therefore not simply to become the same. It reflects an attitude of heart and mind that honours the wisdom that informs our different ways of being and doing. Consequently, although moving forward is no easy task, we are confident that it will become more inviting and hopeful to the extent that those involved are as committed to *listening humbly* as they are to *speaking truthfully* and *acting wisely* as we learn to treat ourselves and all our relations with dignity, honesty, and respect. In the words of then National Chief of the Assembly of First Nations Phil Fontaine (2008):

> We need to try and create the same kind of transformative change when it comes to First Nations and Aboriginal people so all Canadians can be proud of us, so all Canadians can know that we are being treated fairly and that all Canadians will know that we are being treated with respect. Here I come to you this evening; I am the National Chief for the Assembly of First Nations, representing First Nations people, distinct peoples with rights that are unique to us. We are the only peoples in this land that have treaties with the federal Crown, yet I have to convince the federal government year after year of the legitimacy of the community I represent, the legitimacy and validity of this organization to represent all First Nations people. If I speak out of turn, I will get punished.

David Long: I am growing to appreciate that many others have taught me to know the wisdom of treating others with respect, dignity, and kindness. But as I read the comments by National Chief Phil Fontaine, I am struck not only by the difference between my world of experience and that of many Aboriginal people in Canada, but also how little I know of your experience and perspective. Perhaps you could begin our "way forward" dialogue by sharing your understanding of how Aboriginal peoples experience and make sense of life.

David Newhouse: For Aboriginal peoples, educated in historical and traditional understandings and experiences, the world is in a state of constant flux and change. Movement is the central aspect of life. Things change constantly; new understandings emerge; new relationships need to be formed and old relationships renewed or discarded. Living in a world of contingencies and negotiated spaces requires a constant attention to the big picture as well as a mindfulness of the details of relationship. While one may have a desire for stability and certainty, it is rare for these to be achieved for any lengthy period of time. The stability that one desires emanates from inside rather than outside. Spirituality provides a groundedness that allows one to successfully live in an ever-changing world. We live in the world as the last created, dependent upon the lives of others for continued existence and as the least powerful in a web of beings.

We live our lives in relationship. We are defined through relationship. A good life is one that is filled with good relationships. We are expected to create good relationships, to cultivate them, to find ways of accommodating those who enter into one's life. We give our lives meaning through the relationships we create. We uphold the world through relationship. The idea of living in relationship to all of creation is a central theme of Indigenous philosophies throughout the world. Surrounding this idea is a moral imperative that speaks to the requirement to accommodate one's existence to those who enter one's world and to find ways to live harmoniously together, to find mutual benefit in the world and to help each other to achieve them.

David L.: While I was raised as a second-generation Canadian of Irish–British descent to live in the way you mention, my world of experience has undoubtedly been quite different from yours. My everyday involvements with school, media, church, sports, work, and countless leisure pursuits have socialized me to take "living dominantly" for granted. Apart from very superficial social studies lessons I had on the value of multiculturalism, I cannot honestly say that I have been encouraged to "invite" others into my life who are not part of my privileged, dominant world. It seems to me that those who are socialized to move "comfortably" within and around the dominant culture are taught that Canada is *our people's* world, and that even if we don't really know who *our people* are, we can rest assured that the way things are organized means that most of life should go well for us. Dominant living has taught me that working towards any kind of justice (social, environmental, etc.) is my individual prerogative, and that there are many privileged opportunities at my disposal if I want to take advantage of them. Many current circumstances and public conversations often subtly reinforce the "dangers" of engaging in post-colonial dialogue and action by reminding me that doing so may very well result in having to give up certain privileges and opportunities that I, along with many "dominant others," have learned to take for granted.

I am reminded here of Offred, the main character in Margaret Atwood's (1985) *The Handmaid's Tale* whose life as a handmaid had taught her that "the slave always understands the master better than the master understands the slave, since for the slave such understanding is a matter of survival." It seems to me that in many ways, dominant and disadvantaged people living in Canada face very different challenges in coming to terms with where "we" go from here. I know from our discussions that you and I are both committed to moving forward together in a good way, though I wonder what that means to you.

David N.: I am reminded of the concept of "double consciousness" as set out by W.E.B. DuBois (1903) in the early twentieth-century sociological classic, *The Souls of Black Folk*. He writes, "It is a peculiar sensation, this double-consciousness, this sense of always looking at one's self through the eyes of others, of measuring one's soul by the tape of a world that looks on in amused contempt and pity. One ever feels his two-ness—an American, a Negro; two souls, two thoughts, two unreconciled strivings; two warring ideals in one dark body, whose dogged strength alone keeps it from being torn asunder."

As an Aboriginal person, I am profoundly aware that I am different. I am also deeply aware that my difference is seen as problematic to many non-Aboriginal Canadians whose government has had an official policy of attempting to transform my people into Europeans for a century and a half. The desire to live well as an Aboriginal person has been what has sustained my ancestors through this long and often arduous journey. Indigenous philosophies, which are profoundly optimistic and practical, have been part of that sustenance. I and I think all Aboriginal peoples in Canada live with this double consciousness every day of our lives.

Fortunately, Indigenous philosophies are profoundly transformative, for they assume, among other things, that all human beings are capable of change and want to live well together, that all human beings desire peace and are capable of working to create peace, and that a destructive relationship can be transformed. We are aware that harmony, while not the natural order of things, requires effort and attention, not just to one's own existence but to the existence of others; it requires an acknowledgement that others have a right to live and to pursue their idea of a good life. Achieving harmony may require that one help others to live in ways that one does not agree with.

These are some of the ideas that we as Indigenous peoples come to the table with. We come always with a sense of profound hope and goodwill because we believe in this idea of transformation. We have much experience in living with beings more powerful than us.

In the early part of the twenty-first century, as Aboriginal peoples, the public discourse has centred on healing and reconciliation in the context of the post-colonial. We talk of the need to move forward, away from the colonial legacy that continues to define the existence of many Aboriginal peoples. The question of how to move forward raises a series of questions: What are we moving forward to? What does moving forward entail? Will healing get us there? How will we know when we are healed and when we are reconciled? And what is the desired state of affairs that we wish to create for ourselves, as Aboriginal and otherwise[2] peoples in this nation-state we call Canada? This process of imagining a desired future, then interrogating the present to see how we might move towards it, and then engaging in actions designed to move us towards it is what I call reconciliation. It is a process directed towards creating new relationships and ultimately is intended to foster good lives.

We have been made to feel uncomfortable in our own land. To continue to live in our traditional territories, to use its resources to sustain us in this new world, we have to launch a land claim; we have to prove to the satisfaction of the state that we have lived here since time immemorial, that we have had effective control and stewardship over the land, and that we never gave it up voluntarily. This state of existence, of being exiles in one's own house, so to speak, confined in a sense to a small space, has profound effects upon one's psyche. Many Aboriginal people feel caged, imprisoned forever in the past, reluctant participants in the contemporary world. We begin to long for the past, for a world that no longer exists and that can no longer be. It can be a dispiriting existence.

However, I can see signs of positive change. The movement to cities, the reclamation of language and cultural practices, a growing pride in self-identification as Aboriginal persons, and a growing creative community are all cultivating a new sense of optimism that we have survived and perhaps can now thrive.

David L.: I too see much positive change, and although I admit there continue to be aspects of my life that remain, as Paulette Regan (2011) would say, quite "unsettled," I honestly can't begin to fathom what it means to live a "dispiriting existence." I recognize there is wisdom in acknowledging that we all share the human condition, though being sociologically mindful has taught me that the relationships and circumstances in my life have contributed to the particular—and relatively privileged—ways I have experienced poverty, addiction, abuse, and at times despair in my family and community relationships.

I have always identified closely with Indigenous ways of knowing and being, and with a deeply spiritual connection to "our land." I experience "the land" as a sacred gift, and it pains me when others treat any aspect of creation as a resource to be exploited or simply a hindrance to their particular definition of comfort. We are all part of creation, and so I see and feel and know all my relations to other humans, the land, and all else as sacred. I thus don't see any of us as "strangers in a strange land"; we are inhabitants of the same land with diverse experiences, perspectives, and relationships with it. However, since being *of* a particular land involves both timeless spiritual connections as well as the chronological time a people spends inhabiting it, it seems to me that the length of time Aboriginal people have inhabited this particular land has provided opportunity to cultivate a much deeper and more intimate and respectful relationship with it.

While I am not Aboriginal (though as an aside, neither have I ever viewed myself as merely "otherwise"), I have long been committed to walking humbly, treating others charitably and with fairness, as well as to honour, embrace, and celebrate difference. I was raised to understand that human beings flourish individually and collectively when we treat our own people as well as "others" with respect, dignity, and love. As a sociologist who has long been fascinated and occasionally confused by the ways that humans engage and express social difference, I have explored the past and present by examining statistical as well as countless personal stories told by people whose circumstances, experiences, and opportunities are not only different from but also far more colonially disadvantaged than mine. There is what I would call a mirage of difference expressed in almost every mass media and even social media context, but underneath the surface they perpetuate a fairly privileged and self-centred, capitalist storyline about being and becoming dominant. Messages and stories that assume and that deep down even celebrate dominance reflect both the unwillingness and the inability to understand how to include social difference in a vision that seeks to move forward in a good way. This makes me wonder how you see difference both among as well as between peoples, and what that would mean for how you understand reconciliation as a process that involves imagining a desired future, interrogating the present to see how we might move towards it, and then engaging in actions designed to move us towards it.

David N.: We have, I think, moved beyond the point where the questions of how to move forward can be answered only by the Canadian state and "otherwise" peoples within it. Our common conception of Canada is that it is a state that can accommodate many within a tent held up by common values. We have lived with the English–French dialogue on this for many years and have learned that the set of relationships that comprise Canada does not fall apart when the distinctiveness is recognized. In fact, English Canadians have begun to learn that Canada is strengthened when distinctiveness is recognized and celebrated, a finding that the founders of the Iroquoian confederacy encountered half a millennium ago. The newcomers to our land, while technologically and materially advanced in many ways, have yet to learn how to accommodate themselves to their new landscape and to learn from it. The writings of John Ralston Saul are important in this regard, for he is dedicated to changing how Canadians see Aboriginal peoples. His *A Fair Country* (2009) and *The Comeback* (2014) both present Aboriginal peoples as important contributors to Canada, which we know is a view that was not possible a half-century ago.

David L.: I agree, though I wonder how you envision the transformation of our relations in Canada in light of some of the deep divides cultivated by colonialism that affect Aboriginal people in Canada as well as many disadvantaged "others." I am particularly interested in how you envision transformation and reconciliation in the context of relations between and among Aboriginal people. As contributors to this edition and many others note, colonialism has far more devastating effects than merely contributing to material and social inequality. Much has been written on the ways that internal colonialism has benefited some Aboriginal people at the expense of others in their families and communities. In what ways do you think reconciliation between and among Aboriginal people is an important part of reconciliation between Aboriginal peoples and the rest of Canada, and what might that process look like? And in what ways might "others" in Canada be involved in the process of moving forward?

David N.: I am glad that the question of reconciliation in my own mind is no longer a question of whether but when and how. Let me explain why I'm optimistic about the outcome of this project and offer some cautions and concerns.

In my half-century of life, I have seen incredible changes in how we think about Canada and Aboriginal peoples. The thesis of two founding nations, French and English, is receding, and emerging to take its place is a more complex thesis involving pillars and influences. The three pillars (Aboriginal, French, and English) are seen as contributory, influential, and interactive. The idea of Aboriginal peoples as a burden on the state, as represented by the assignment of constitutional responsibility for Indians to the federal government rather than to the provincial governments, is waning. State action regarding Aboriginal peoples is more likely to be seen through the lens of accommodation and investment rather than as responsibility and expense, although there has emerged in jurisprudence over the past three decades a set of "Aboriginal rights" that occupies a unique place in Canada constitutionalism. The state itself has moved, somewhat reluctantly and slowly, to accommodate Aboriginal interests particularly around self-government. Canada has apologized, twice, for an official state policy of assimilation and has taken some, albeit limited, steps to make reparations for this century-long policy. The Truth and Reconciliation Commission has continued the good work of the RCAP and many other inquiries, initiatives, and movements that have contributed to healing and moving forward. On the economic front, the land claims policies and treaty process are concrete efforts that can do much to assist in improving the economic status of some Aboriginal peoples.

We have also seen incredible changes in the way in which we see ourselves as Indigenous peoples living within nation-states. Canada itself has been transforming itself to accommodate Aboriginal peoples. There is now constitutional recognition, a set of rights arising from this, and a record of jurisprudence, as well as a sense that something more needs to be done. The issue is no longer whether change will come, but when it will come.

At the same time as these incredible changes are occurring at the state level, overall living conditions of Aboriginal peoples have not improved much. Some would argue that Aboriginal peoples are having a tough time holding their own in the modern capitalist, pluralistic society that Canada has become. There is considerable evidence that this view may turn out to be wrong. Witness the incredible explosion of Aboriginal entrepreneurial activity over the past decade, the care with which land claims settlements are being implemented, and the debate about the role of Aboriginal governments in fostering good business and economic climates. What we tend to forget is that overcoming the colonial legacy is a long, multi-stage, complex process. We cannot consider the post-colonial project complete but only in its early stages.

The colonial legacy is more than its material effects. We are familiar with the colonial marginalization and dispossession that has resulted in lower levels of education, low incomes, poor housing, and poor health, both physical and mental. These are real problems that need to be addressed. As you note, the effects of colonialism go much further and deeper. Colonialism steals the spirit of a people as it seeks to replace an Indigenous sense of self with a different one: one premised on the idea of inferiority. Colonialism creates a sense of boundary, limitedness, and powerlessness. It robs one of the ability to imagine a transformative future consistent with one's own cultural teachings. It forces one to live in an eternal present with no future other than that which is imagined by the colonial masters. The psychological and spiritual effects are the most long-lasting and require the most effort to overcome.

When I look around for signs of post-colonial activity, I see tremendous effort underway at addressing this central aspect of the colonial legacy. Let me explain what I see and why I am optimistic about the reconciliation project.

What is new and different from the situation four decades ago is the emergence of what I call "post-colonial consciousness," not just within Aboriginal peoples in Canada and elsewhere but within some Canadians. This consciousness is an important foundation for what is to come. What I mean by this particular type of consciousness is a keen awareness of the history and effects of colonization visited upon Aboriginal peoples, a strong desire to take steps to ensure that the policies and actions of the past are not repeated, the gathering of skills and knowledge to deal with its contemporary effects and inoculate society as much as possible against any future recurrence. It is also desirous of creating a world out of Indigenous thought and Western thought. Central to Indigenous post-colonial consciousness is this desire, and it has led to a set of actions across all levels of society: local, regional, provincial and national, class. We can understand the establishment of National Aboriginal Day at the national level or the various Treaty Days as concrete examples of positive change that came about because of post-colonial consciousness. Similarly, I see examples in the land claims process, although some would view the process as the continued exercise of power by a colonial state. I think we have to allow for multiple interpretations of actions, acknowledging that decolonization is a complex task, not prone to simplicity.

However we see the changes that are happening, post-colonial consciousness is driving much of the Aboriginal effort at reconciliation.

Reconciliation fosters a deeper sense of belonging to the Canadian nation among Aboriginal people by demonstrating a willingness to accommodate their interests. Accommodation at the present time is a nonetheless a reluctant act that is not carried out with any sense of enthusiasm or joy, and accommodation continues to be arrived at only after a long and arduous confrontational process that often involves litigation. Post-colonial consciousness helps us to understand why it is fundamentally wrong for the land claims process to continue to place the onus on Aboriginal peoples to justify the right they have to their own lands.

Reconciliation is changing the founding myth of the country, for we are learning to recognize that Canada is founded upon three primary pillars and that it's political and cultural institutions have some Aboriginal aspects to them. Making these elements visible in the ceremonial life of the country is an important element in creating a sense of inclusion.

Reconciliation is healing the wounds resulting from past actions. There is also a sense of loss that has not been addressed and needs to be addressed. Often, loss is expressed as "anger"; we are only beginning to recognize the emotional aspects of the relationship.

We are doing some of these things, but most of it is out of the sight of ordinary Canadians. Many who frequent Tim Hortons or Walmart or Holt Renfrew all share a basic lack of understanding of this aspect of the reality of Canadian–Aboriginal relationships; whether they are liberal or conservative, those who give thought to issues involving Aboriginal peoples at best frame them in social justice terms. For them, the issues are far away and of little consequence. Aboriginal peoples are part of the past or a people who have not been able to adjust to modern times. I spent a year sitting in coffee shops listening to conversations about Aboriginal peoples. It was an interesting exercise to discover just how much is not known and how much blame people place on Aboriginal peoples themselves for the current state of affairs. "If only they would become like us" was a constant theme of these conversations.

I am heartened by the efforts underway in many parts of the country to change this situation through the public school curriculum. Perhaps in a generation the coffee shop conversations will be different, and more things will be in plain sight.

Moving Forward

David N.: How do we move forward, or perhaps we should ask an even more basic question: What does it mean to move forward? What are we moving forward to? It is clear what we are trying to move away from, though it is simple to say that we are moving from a colonized world to a decolonized world. But what does a decolonized world or, to be more specific, a decolonized Canada look like?

Talking about moving forward is difficult because of the wide range of things that could be talked about and the dominance of the legal political framework in public discourse. It might be easy to describe a bureaucratic framework and process that we could say, if followed, would lead us to a reconciled state. I'm going to resist this easy route, because I think that while frameworks and process are important aspects of moving forward, they can only take us so far. They have the air of panacea and promise that are important to keep us going through the difficult times, though they are not the answer.

Moving forward means that we turn our eyes from the past to the future. I think this means we have to let go of the past. What I mean by this is that we cannot let the past dominate our lives and trap us. We can use the past to guide our actions, to learn what not to do, and to remember what we are moving away from. It can become our moral compass, a way to gauge our actions. I am reminded of a *Star Trek: The Next Generation* episode in which the *Enterprise* crew become caught in a time warp and can only get out of it by learning what had happened and then finding ways to not do what had gotten them into the fix in the first place. Not knowing their past kept them trapped in an endless loop. But letting go of the past can be a fearful act, for we can forget completely. Moving forward is finding ways to collectively re-member what has happened and to remind us regularly of what not to do to recreate the iniquitous world that we currently inhabit as Aboriginal peoples and Canadians.

Moving forward requires that we articulate a vision of a future state of affairs, that we imagine a future that we can work towards, that we articulate a set of principles for our relationship on this land, how we will share, how we will live next to each other and among each other, and how we will treat each other. I am reminded of the vision of Canada put forward by Aboriginal peoples in the RCAP final report and the negative reaction by the Canadian government that chose to ignore it. I am reminded of the story of the Peacemaker in bringing the Great Law to Atatarho, lead Chief of the Onondagas. Each time he presented the ideas Atatarho says, "It is not yet." The story concludes with his acceptance of the Great Law and his transformation from a twisted mind to a good mind.

Moving forward requires conversation and dialogue between Aboriginal peoples and the Canadian state, between Aboriginal peoples and their neigh-bours, and between Aboriginal individuals and their friends. Conversation and dialogue identify commonalities, bring out differences, and can help us find ways to live together with mutual respect. Conversation and dialogue can prevent problems from becoming larger and perhaps even from starting. Conversation and dialogue can be both structured and formal and unstructured and informal, occurring in both the expected and the unexpected places.

Each time I think about these questions and issues I am reminded of a conversation I had a few years ago with a colleague when we were working on a report on Aboriginal policy. We had concluded our review of the literature and were talking about how to approach the "Indian problem." He remarked at one point in the conversation: "I have thought about these issues using all of the intellectual tools of my profession as a political scientist. I cannot find a solution to them using these tools. Perhaps we need new tools."

Moving forward means that we have to start from the place that states, "we are all here to stay." We have to find ways that foster and nurture our collective selves, that foster a sense of connectedness and belonging, that honour our histories and engage us in creating a collective future of mutual benefit. I am reminded of the Iroquoian ideal of the good mind. Perhaps this idea could help us to move forward. A good mind is one that is balanced of reason and passion and that is filled with a yearning for peace between peoples. I am also reminded of the Guswentah, the two-row wampum that sets out a relationship between peoples and allows for a way for them to conduct a dialogue that fosters a sense of joint enterprise. And the spaces between the two rows are spaces we create that enable us to learn from one another. Perhaps if we conceive of Canada as a huge Guswentah space we might be able to move forward differently. Bringing Indigenous ideas to the discussion may be the tools that we need. We are all here to stay, which means that we need to recognize the legitimacy of all those who speak.

David L.: We are of the same mind.

I have a few final comments and related questions. Along with characterizing colonialism as a fundamentally exploitive and profoundly destructive human endeavour, the tendency of most post-colonial critics is to condemn the entire culture of colonizing peoples. While I agree there is nothing redemptive in colonial thinking and arrangements, I think it is important that we guard against essentializing as well as idealizing any people's culture. This is particularly true now, as Aboriginal and European peoples need to learn how to share and cultivate many basic and hopeful human qualities in our relations, including the desire and ability to explore, adapt, trust, and love.

Also, in the chapter you wrote with Yale Belanger on Aboriginal politics you state: "Over the past five decades, an Aboriginal modernity has emerged that forms the context and foundation of modern Aboriginal societies: confident, aggressive, assertive, insistent, desirous of creating a new world out of Aboriginal and Western ideas, and self-consciously as well as deliberately acting out of Aboriginal thought." I am pleased that the spirit you call "Aboriginal modernity" is expressed in the words of practically every contributor to this fourth edition, particularly those written by our new contributors, including Peter Cole, Lisa Monchalin, Jonathan Dewar, and Deborah MacGregor, as well as John Swift and Lee Maracle. Each of them reminds us in new and at times rather stark and challenging ways how the colonial legacy continues to live on in the pain, suffering, and despair of many Aboriginal people in Canada, and that a good deal of their pain, suffering, and despair is a result of the colonial attitudes and arrangements that have been adopted and continue to be sustained by their colonially co-opted Aboriginal brothers and sisters.

They also assert in their own ways that only a truly radical re-visioning and implementation of traditional teachings and social arrangements will enable Aboriginal peoples—and presumably the rest of Canada—to move forward in good and hopeful ways. I am wondering what you think of this view, particularly in light of the very diverse expressions of Aboriginal modernity evident in everything from highly educated Aboriginal individuals assuming high-profile leadership roles in contexts that are "other" than Aboriginal, to economic development partnerships between First Nations and multinational corporations, to community-based language revitalization initiatives, to national Aboriginal Achievement Awards, to face-to-face sharing of personal accounts by Truth and Reconciliation Commission participants, to the global reach of Idle No More activities. What is the relationship between these and many other current expressions of Aboriginal modernity, and what do you think reconciliation between all peoples in a post-colonial Canada will look like?

In more simple terms, how will we know when we are reconciled?

David N.: As I mentioned earlier, I think it is important to see reconciliation as an ongoing process rather than an end-state. Reconciliation is the process by which we mutually accommodate our own disparate ideas about how to live well together. This means that we will always be involved in reconciliation in some way or another; to a large extent, this is the essence of Canada: negotiation and accommodation and reconciliation.

One way that expressions of Aboriginal modernity are contributing to reconciliation is that they are challenging and helping Canadians to think differently about their country and come to terms with a continuing significant presence of Aboriginal peoples as distinct peoples with a distinct legal status confirmed in jurisprudence. This has meant that Aboriginal peoples have had to find new ways to present ourselves as part of Canada. This is challenging, for while it is important that we honour and express our differences, it is also important for Aboriginal people to learn how to do so in ways that do not lead Canadians to openly question the reconciliation project. It is important for all of us to learn to recognize and honour the differences within each group. We cannot present ourselves to each other with so many incommensurable differences that we cannot find common ground.

As Supreme Court Justice Antonio Lamer remarked in *Delgamuukw* (1997): "Let's face it. We are all here to stay." This makes reconciliation an important and central part of moving forward. The Leadership Council of British Columbia in 2006 defined reconciliation as building a positive, enduring relationship based on trust and mutual respect. A decade earlier, the RCAP report used similar terms to define the characteristics of a reconciled relationship between Aboriginal peoples and other Canadians. Indeed, for over a century Aboriginal peoples have been laying out how they view the nature of the relationship they wish to establish with Canadians and with the new Canadian state. Expressions of Aboriginal modernity are showing how new voices see this relationship unfolding and how they would like it to move forward.

We continue to learn in new ways that reconciliation is always a difficult political project because it involves power and accommodation. Canada as a state has almost unlimited power to influence the political and social reality of Aboriginal peoples. There is a long history of the use of this power in ways that have not been beneficial to Aboriginal peoples, that have created mistrust, and we now live with its consequence. Part of reconciliation means agreeing not to use the power of the state against Aboriginal people, but to use it to support Aboriginal initiatives as well as create spaces of dignity and respect that enable Aboriginal and other peoples to live well with each other. Many new voices are helping us to see what this should look like in many different places.

Reconciliation involves dealing with the sense of grievance and unfairness that has dominated Aboriginal–state relations over the past few decades, particularly since 1969. As Grand Chief Phil Fontaine stated in the quotation at the beginning of our dialogue, the land claims process requires one to negotiate with Canada for a share of what were once homelands and to use its methods to prove historic use and ownership. Getting Canada to live up to the terms of its treaties without litigation has long caused a sense of real grievance, for it exhibits a grudging reluctance on the part of the government to fulfill its responsibilities towards Aboriginal peoples. Many young Aboriginal scholars, Idle No More round dancers, and residential school survivors are giving voice to long-held grievances in new ways.

Canadians are learning that reconciliation is dealing with the sense of inequity that continues to exist: economic, social, and political. There are real inequities, with serious consequences, that continue to fuel this sense. Part of reconciliation must therefore also continue to help Canadians understand the roots of these inequities, that the inequities do not have origins in Aboriginal moral character, and that they are the result of a centuries-long assault on Aboriginal lands and livelihoods. Many new voices are joining with those who have been speaking the truth for a long time about the roots of the inequities experienced by many Aboriginal people in Canada.

Certainly I think that a commitment to truth is important, as is a commitment to speak truths. These are the foundations of moving forward. A commitment to act upon these truths so that the colonial past is not repeated is also critical. Our good words have to be translated into political action that changes the present and future. This is the difficult challenge. We live in a world of *realpolitik* where those who have power get to make the rules and need to be reminded or forced to think about and act for others. Witness the Kelowna Accord, agreed to in 2005 by Aboriginal peoples, provincial premiers, and the government of Canada after an 18-month set of negotiations and then simply cancelled by a new federal government without discussion or consultation with any of the partners. Similarly, the New Relationship approach started by British Columbia in 2005, which culminated in the proposed Recognition and Reconciliation Act in 2009, has now stalled. Despite good intentions, the New Relationship is at a standstill because those involved cannot agree on the legal or political meanings of these terms. It appears that the New Relationship may be too threatening to certain powerful interests. The treaty processes underway in Saskatchewan and British Columbia are also examples of the difficulty of reconciliation. We have difficulty in translating truths into action.

We have, however, been able to translate truths into action in many hopeful ways. We have seen the establishment of the territory of Nunavut and the creation of the Nisga'a Nation and Treaty, as well as various land claims and self-government agreements around the country. Much of our history involves hard, painful, and unjust experiences. But we also know that our history shows us that positive, transformative change is possible. Our history together shows us that Canada does not fall apart when Aboriginal peoples come into the body politic in substantive and meaningful ways. In fact, if we look closely we can see that we are all better off as a result. Am I hopeful? Yes, at times. I am occasionally overwhelmed by the enormous scale of the task that looms ahead: the transformation of Canada and this land into a place where Aboriginal peoples live with respect and dignity again. We sustain ourselves through continually renewing our commitment to these lands and their spirits.

Notes

1. We are using "post-colonial" in the sense of an awareness of the facts of colonialism and an expressed desire to, as Neal McLeod (2001) says, "fix what went wrong."
2. We encounter at the very start this problem of how to speak of the collectives that we are part of. The use of "non" doesn't sit well with me, nor does "ROC" (rest of Canada) as it evokes the English–French rivalry. I like Sherman Alexie's term "Native American or otherwise" and have adjusted it here for a Canadian context. Even this is not ideal, since "othering" can result in a loss of human characteristics.

Glossary

Glossaries are comprised of particular definitions of terms specified by the author(s) of a given text. It is therefore important to recognize that each definition contained in this (or any other) glossary reflects the particular perspective and focus of its contributors and that definitions of many terms often change over time as they are informed by new experiences, attitudes, and understandings. It is also important to note that the following definitions were arrived at through dialogue among various contributors to this as well as previous editions of *Visions of the Heart* and that, in the end, the definitions that follow are those that appealed most to the majority of discussants.

Aboriginal people (also Indigenous peoples): Descendents of the original occupants of the land. Aboriginal people remain a fundamentally autonomous and self-determining political community that continues to possess a special relationship with the colonizers, together with the rights and entitlements that flow from their unique relational status. Legal categories for Aboriginal people in Canada include registered or status Indians, Métis, Inuit, and non-status Indians. However many Aboriginal people prefer to identify themselves by their cultural community of origin (e.g. Gwitchin, Cree, Métis, Nisga'a).

Aboriginal Peoples Survey (APS): Statistics Canada has conducted this national survey every 5 years since 1991. Survey results reflect the responses of individuals who identify themselves as Aboriginal people, in contrast to general census data comprised of responses from individuals who have Aboriginal ancestry but may or may not identify themselves as Aboriginal people. The APS is a national survey of Aboriginal peoples (First Nations peoples living off-reserve, Métis and Inuit) living in urban, rural and northern locations throughout Canada. The purpose of the survey is to identity the needs of Aboriginal people and focus on issues such as health, language, employment, income, education, housing and mobility.

Aboriginal revitalization: Growing support for Aboriginal spirituality and cultural traditions in a wide variety of modern social and political contexts.

Aboriginal rights (also indigenous rights): By virtue of their status as the descendents of the original occupants, Aboriginal peoples possess both inherent and collective claims (rights) over those jurisdictions related to land, identity, and political voice that have never been extinguished but continue to serve as a basis for entitlement and engagement.

Aboriginal self-government: The ideal of parity between Aboriginal, provincial, and federal political authorities and powers.

Aboriginality (also indigeneity): A nominalization of the adjective "Aboriginal" in the same way that ethnicity nominalizes the adjective "ethnic." Aboriginality refers to a shared awareness of original occupancy as a catalyst for challenging the status quo with respect to who gets what and why.

Age Specific Suicide Mortality Rates (ASSMR): Statistical measure of suicide rates according to the age of the deceased.

Alberta Métis Settlements Accord: An agreement between the Métis Settlements Councils and the Alberta provincial government that was formally legislated in November 1990. The agreement established Métis land ownership rights (fee simple ownership of 1.28 million acres) and a reorganized form of governance for the Métis of the eight Alberta settlements. The Alberta government also agreed to pay $310 million over 17 years and to establish the Transition Commission, which consisted of a membership tribunal, a revenue trust fund, and other groups to work with provincial government and settlement representatives to assist in implementation and maintenance.

American Indian Movement (AIM): Organization initiated and controlled by American Indian people, dedicated to grassroots, social, and political revitalization of Indian people.

Amerindian: Inclusive term that denotes individuals from all groups of indigenous peoples of North America.

Assembly of First Nations (AFN): National organization established in 1982 to represent the perspectives and interests of status Indians in Canada.

Assimilation: Process through which a dominant group seeks to undermine the cultural distinctiveness of a subordinate group by subjecting them to the rules, values, and sanctions of the dominant group and by then absorbing the "de-cultured" minority into the mainstream.

Band council: Elected body of representatives including a chief and band councillors, which is responsible to administer the affairs of a First Nation band.

Band councillor: Member of a First Nation band elected (every two years) by fellow band members to develop band-related policies and administer community resources.

Band members: First Nations people who belong to a particular band. Before 1985, all registered Indians belonged to a band. Since Bill C-31 was passed, status and band membership were separated, and bands were given jurisdiction over band membership. Only band members have rights to live on the reserve held in trust for a band, run for band council, vote in band elections, or participate in decision-making about how band resources are to be dispersed.

Biculturalism: Two nations with two distinct cultures existing within the context of a single, overarching political/legal framework.

Bicultural bind: The experience of First Nations women in Canada who continue to alternate between being strong and dependent, self-reliant and powerless, strongly motivated and hopelessly insecure.

Bilingualism: Government policy that grants equal, official status to two distinct languages.

Bill C-31: In June 1985, Parliament enacted a series of amendments to the Indian Act, known as Bill C-31: Act to Amend the Indian Act. The legislation brought the Indian Act into line with the provisions of the Canadian Charter of Rights and Freedoms. The three principles that guided the amendments were: the removal of sex discrimination; restoring Indian status and membership to women; and increasing the control Indian bands have over their own affairs.

Blood quantum: a highly contentious, and some argue racializing concept referring to the "measure or degree" of one's ancestral blood. Similar terms used in Canadian political circles (Aboriginal as well as Federal and Provincial government) include: genealogical proximity; degree of "North American Indian" parentage, genealogical connection, or genealogical standard (e.g. some First Nations specify "blood quantum" rules for band membership) though all of these are part of current discourses engaging the spiritual, personal and collective meanings of the relative "amount of Indian blood" in an individual.

Burden of illness: Also known as "burden of disease," refers to the impact a disease or illness has on a population, based on a series of indicators of mortality and morbidity.

Bureaucratic paternalism: Formalized, ideologically grounded relationship between super ordinate and subordinate peoples, which controls all aspects of the subordinate peoples' lives.

Charter of Rights and Freedoms: The Charter adopted when the Canadian Constitution Act, 1982, terminated the United Kingdom's imperial rule over Canada. The Charter protects certain fundamental rights and freedoms of Canadian citizens such as equality before the law.

Churn: A demographic term that refers to the high rates of mobility and migration by First Nations people within urban areas, with high rates of in- and out-migration occurring to and from cities as well as between reserves and cities. The reason for churn is that First Nations people move in and out of reserves in order to spend time with various family members, to go to school, or to access health and social services.

Clans: Extended family groups related by blood or marriage.

Colonization: The establishing of imperial rule over foreign territories and peoples through economic, social, and political policies. Colonizing policies and practices are often informed by racist and ethnocentric beliefs and attitudes.

Comprehensive land claims: Process of clarifying Aboriginal peoples' legal relationship with the land as a basis for cultural renewal, economic development, and political control.

Compression of mortality: A pattern in which deaths in a population occur over an increasingly narrower range of years, typically in older ages.

Constitutionalism: The political and moral framework (or first principles) that govern a society or country and provide a blueprint for defining internal relationships among the governed.

Constructive engagement: The process by which central authorities such as the Crown and Aboriginal peoples establish a non-dominating, co-determining relationship in a spirit of cooperative coexistence.

Cooptation: Process through which socially, organizationally, and/or politically powerless people come to support the perspectives of those who have power and control over them.

Council of Elders: A group that provides direction to the Assembly of First Nations by developing the rules and procedures for members and by overseeing the individual and collective activities of AFN members.

Counter-hegemony: Ideas and practices designed to challenge and/or subvert processes and structures that support those in positions of power and dominance.

Crown sovereignty: The power and right of a monarch to rule over people and resources in a given territory.

Cultural genocide: Destruction of a people's cultural ways and means, often through colonial policies, legislation, and practices.

Cultural awareness: An understanding of how an individual's culture may influence their values, beliefs, and behaviour.

Cultural competence: The ability to communicate effectively with individuals from other cultures. Competence entails ones attitude toward and knowledge and awareness of different cultural practices and beliefs.

Curriculum: Contents, sequence, and scope of material taught in formal educational contexts.

Decolonization: Process of restructuring relations between indigenous and colonizing peoples, often through efforts to establish Aboriginal right to ownership of land and control by Aboriginal people over social and economic development.

Demographic transition: A model that helps explain how a country with high birth and death rates has transitioned to low birth and death rates as a result of economic developments in that country. The model consists of three stages, with stage 1 and 2 often representing developing countries and stage 3 representing developed countries.

Department of Indian Affairs and Northern Development (DIAND): Federal government department established in 1966. Also referred to as Department of Indian Affairs (DIA), Department of Indian and Northern Affairs (DINA), and Indian and Northern Affairs Canada (INAC). Previous Indian affairs branches had resided in the Secretary of State, Department of the Interior, Department of Health and Welfare, and Department of Citizenship and Immigration.

Devolution: Colonial governmental policies and practices designed to decrease governmental responsibility and simultaneously increase indigenous peoples' responsibility for the administration of their people's own affairs.

Distal causes of illness: Factors indirectly related to the causal pathways of a specified health outcome. For example, while smoking can be defined as a proximal or direct cause of lung cancer, education or employment can be a distal or indirect cause.

Dualism: The view that the world consists of fundamental entities. In the case of human existence, it is the view that human life is comprised of two distinct entities: the soul and the body.

Environmental racism: The deliberate or intentional siting of hazardous waste sites, landfills, incinerators, and polluting industries in communities inhabited by minorities and/or the poor.

Epidemiologic transition: A generalized pattern of historical changes in the major causes of death in populations. These changes are thought to have occurred as a result of demographic, economic, and sociological factors, as well as technological change.

Ethnocentrism: The view that a people's cultural and institutional ways are superior to those of other peoples.

Ethno history: Use of written historical materials and/or a people's oral literature or memory to reconstruct a people's cultural history.

Existentialism: Philosophical perspective that asserts that human experience is the ultimate reality and that humans are ultimately both free to act as they choose and responsible for the actions they take.

Families of the heart: Marlene Brant Castellano describes a growing trend, especially in urban areas, whereby families are formed and grow based on choice, reaching out to and incorporating individuals who may or may not be related biologically or through legal unions.

Food insecurity: The availability of food and an individual's access to it. Food security is considered to exist when an individual does not live in hunger or fear of starvation.

Fourth World: Concept describing the phenomenon that emerges as a people develop customs and practices that wed them uniquely to their own land.

Global cultural pathology: Set of perspectives, attitudes, and actions that are contributing to the destruction of the Earth's ecology.

Guswenteh (also two-row wampum): Symbolizes two nations, separate and distinct, engaged in a relationship of mutual friendship and non-interference. The wampum depicts two solid blue or purple parallel lines separated by a row of white space. The spaces between the rows are and can be places of conversation, dialogue, debate, discussion, sharing, listening and learning.

Hegemony: Ideological as well as political processes and structures through which one class or people achieve domination over others.

Holism: The perspective that the inner and outer states of existence are profoundly connected and that the purpose of all of life is harmony and balance between all aspects and dimensions of reality.

Holistic healing: The view that healing involves the harmonious restoration of physical, psychological, emotional, and spiritual dimensions of human life.

Indian Act Indian: Any male person of Indian blood reputed to belong to a particular band; any child of such person; or any woman who is or was lawfully married to such a person.

Indian Acts (1876, 1951): Bodies of federal legislation that specified who, legally, was an Indian, what Indian peoples were entitled to under the government's legal obligation, who could qualify for enfranchisement, what could be done with Indian lands and resources, and how Indian peoples were to be governed (through Indian agents and elected band councils).

Indian control of Indian education: Policy initiated by the National Indian Brotherhood in 1972 that sought to shift control of First Nations education into the hands of First Nations people, including increasing the involvement of Aboriginal parents in the education of their children.

Indian Register: A list of all Indians registered according to the Indian Act. The register carries information about the name,

date of birth, gender, marital status, and place of residence (on- or off-reserve) of all registered Indians. The Indian Register was centralized in 1951. Previously, individual Indian agents were responsible for lists of individuals eligible for registration.

Indian reserve: Land, the legal title to which is vested in the Crown, that has been set apart for the use and benefit of an Indian band and that is subject to the terms of the Indian Act.

Indigenization: Process through which colonial laws, policies, and organizational practices are reformulated according to indigenous peoples' perspectives and interests.

Indigenous: People who were born in or are natural to a specified territory or land.

Indigenous people's movement: Global effort dedicated to protecting the rights of indigenous people by seeking to redress injustices committed against them and ensuring their social, economic, and political well-being.

Indigenous (or Aboriginal) **sovereignty:** Based on the principle that (a) Aboriginal peoples are sovereign in their own right regardless of formal recognition, (b) they possess a right of sovereignty if not necessarily the right to sovereignty, and (c) Crown sovereignty can be shared by way of multiple yet joint jurisdictions.

Indoctrination: Process through which individuals are socialized to see and act in exclusive, narrowly defined ways.

Internal colonialism: Context and process through which: one ethnic group or coalition rules the affairs of others living within the state; there is territorial separation of the subordinate ethnic groups in "homelands," "native reserves," and the like; land tenure rights for subordinate groups are different from those of members of the dominant group; an internal "government within the government" is established by the dominant group to rule the subordinate groups; unique legal status is granted to the subordinate group and its members, who are then considered to have a corporate status that takes precedence over their individual status; members of the ruling ethnic groups are considered individuals in the eyes of the state; economic inequality is ensured, since subordinate peoples are relegated to positions of dependency and inferiority in the division of labour and the relations of production.

Inuit: Relatively recent Aboriginal immigrants who share genetic similarities with certain Asian peoples and who are the majority inhabitants of Canada's northern regions.

Jurisdictions: The right of authority to have final say or control over a territory, its inhabitants, and activities within that domain. Implies some degree of non-interference from external authorities.

Land claims: Process of negotiating agreements that specify the rights of occupation in relation to a particular territory, as well as arrangements between governments, private enterprises, and Aboriginal peoples to control the resources available on lands or other places designated sacred by Aboriginal groups.

Marginality: Personal experiences and social designation of those with subordinate social, economic, and political status.

Métis: Individuals who identify themselves as being Métis. The history of the Métis is complex, but many people who identify with this Aboriginal group trace their origins to combined Indian and non-Indian parentage. Distinct Métis and "mixed-blood" cultures emerged in various areas of Canada, the community at Red River being probably the best

known. In 1982, the repatriated Canadian Constitution identified the Métis as one of the three Aboriginal groups officially recognized by the government of Canada.

Morbidity: An epidemiological term referring to the experience of disease or illness.

Multiple jeopardy: The fact that Aboriginal women are disadvantaged in relation to both their social and their economic well-being.

Mysticism: The belief that becoming/being are rooted or grounded in one's relationship to all immanent and transcendent aspects or dimensions of reality.

National Indian Brotherhood (NIB): National organization established in 1968 by Aboriginal people to represent the perspectives and interests of status Indians.

Nations: A people whose shared awareness of their distinctiveness in history, culture, and homeland provides a catalyst for collective action to preserve or enhance self-determination over their lives, destiny, and life chances.

Native Council of Canada (NCC): National organization established in 1968 by Aboriginal people to represent the perspectives and interests of the Métis and non-status Indians.

Native Women's Association of Canada (NWAC): National organization established in 1973 by Aboriginal women to represent the perspectives and interests of non-status Indian, status Indian, Métis, and Inuit women.

Natural law: The requirement that we accept the way things (nature and environment) are, whether we fully understand them or not, and relate to all things in a respectful manner.

Nepotism: Context in which those in positions of power use their position to provide social, political, and/or material benefits primarily to their own relatives or close friends.

New Public Health: Concept encompassing two new approaches in public health. One is the shift from treating to preventing illness or disease. The second is the development of social and economical determinants in addition to biological factors in order to better understand health outcomes.

New traditionalists: Aboriginal people committed to combining traditional Aboriginal and modern Western ways of thinking and acting.

Non-status Indian: Individuals who identify culturally as Indian but who do not have legal status as such either because they or their ancestors gave up that status or because their ancestors were never registered initially.

Nunavut: Canada's third territory, stretching from Hudson Bay to the northernmost parts of Ellesmere Island. Under the terms of the Nunavut land claim settlement agreement, signed on 25 May 1993, the government of Nunavut has powers like those of other territorial governments, established and maintained in the context of a very close working relationship with the federal government. The basic land claim settlement gives the Inuit outright ownership of about 18 per cent of the land—353,610 square kilometres, including 36,257 square kilometres of subsurface mineral rights. The remaining 82 per cent of Nunavut remains Crown land, although the Inuit keep the right to hunt, fish, and trap throughout Nunavut. The federal government also agreed to pay Nunavut $1.15 billion, intended for economic development and social revival.

Organized dissent: Strategically organized social activity focused on challenging status quo arrangements and practices.

Participatory Action Research: A research approach that includes community members and researchers as collaborators and that usually has the goal of producing some concrete outcomes for the community, perhaps in addition to research reports. Participatory Action Research is now often referred to as Community-Based Participatory Research and is a popular method within minority populations because of its ability to empower communities while research is being conducted.

Paternalism: A "father knows best" ideology that views those who maintain power and control over the affairs of others as legitimately deserving of their authority and power and that has served to perpetuate inequality and the oppression of Aboriginal people in Canada.

Patriarchy: A social system marked by the supremacy of the father, the reckoning of descent and inheritance according to male lineage, and the dependent legal status of wives and children.

Pedagogy: Methods of teaching based on one's perspective of how and why humans learn.

Plausibility structures: Organized set of beliefs and practices that explain and legitimize a particular way of thinking about one's place in the world and one's relationship to other human beings.

Population health: An approach to public health and epidemiology that considers the health of the entire population rather than individuals already ill or most "at risk" to disease.

Post-colonialism: Deconstructing analysis/critique of the social ideas, policies, everyday practices, and organizational structures that perpetuate the subordination of indigenous and other marginalized peoples. In Canada, the most egregious forms of colonialism have been addressed, though systemic aspects of colonialism such as Crown authority have yet to be explored or explained. A post-colonizing constitutionalism privileges the idea of Aboriginal models of self-determination over land, identity, and political voice.

Power brokers: The role played by the chief and council members on some First Nations reserves, since they have the power to determine who receives the limited band resources such as band employment opportunities, educational funding, occupational training, housing allocation, housing repairs, and other band-administered benefits and services.

Primordial experience: The connection of Elders (as well as shamans and others) to the pervasive, all-encompassing reality of the life force, which reveals to them the oneness of all that has been, is, and is to come.

Proximal causes of illness: Factors that are closely related to a specified health outcome. For example, genetic makeup can be a direct causal pathway in developing diabetes.

Racism: Assumption that psycho-cultural traits and capacities are determined by biological race, coupled with the belief in the inherent superiority of a particular race and the right of its people to have domination over others.

Reconciliation: A process through which people express their commitment to restoring respect and good will in relations that have been disrupted.

Residential schools: Government-established facilities, often run by religious groups, that housed Aboriginal children for the purposes of providing them with a European education.

Resolution 18: A resolution introduced by Premier Peter Lougheed of Alberta in 1982 that represented a formal commitment by the government to negotiate a renewed relationship between the province and the eight Métis settlements in Alberta. It eventually led to the Métis Settlements Accord and to land ownership for the Métis.

Resource mobilization: Processes through which individuals and organizations bring human and material resources together to achieve collective goals.

Self-determination: Essentially a political and politicized assertion about autonomy and control, the right of a people to exercise control over political, cultural, economic, and social issues that are of concern to them.

Self-government: Predicated on the premise that a people have the authority to create and maintain the organizational structures necessary for administering the daily affairs of their community.

Shaman: Intermediary to the spirit world. Includes individual men and women who, because of dreams, visions, illness, or some inborn sensitivity or need, directly experience the presence of spirits and who therefore may receive sacred knowledge and/or possess special power to guide and cure others.

Social capital: A resource of individuals or communities that is hypothesized to affect health. Aspects of social capital can include social networks, trust, and reciprocity between community members and links to various institutions.

Social determinants of health: Social and economic factors that influence an individual's health and well-being. These factors include, but are not limited to, income, employment, education, housing, gender, age, culture, and social support networks. They can influence health outcomes either collectively or independently.

Social epidemiology: The branch of epidemiology that looks at social factors such as education, employment, and housing and their effects on health outcomes within a population.

Social infrastructures: Groups, organizations, policies, legislation, and practices established to address the diverse cultural, health, justice, and education-related needs of individuals living in a given community.

Social movement ideology: Set of beliefs that inform the experiences as well as legitimize the actions of a diverse body of people committed to reorganizing society or any of its major components.

Specific land claims: Land claims based on perceived violations by federal authorities of their treaty obligations.

State: A set of politically dominant institutions that has a monopoly on the legitimate use of violence and that is formally comprised of the legislature, executive, central and local administration, judiciary, police, and armed forces.

Status: The relative position of a person on a publicly recognized scale or hierarchy of social worth.

Status Indians: First Nation individuals whose membership in a First Nation band is formally recognized by the federal government.

Structural supremacy: The hierarchical structure of European society at the time of contact between First Nation and European peoples.

Tradition: Any human practice, belief, institution, or artifact regarded as the common inheritance of a social group.

Traditional: Anderson and Ball (Chapter 4) use "traditional" to signify communities that live in close relationship with the land and with the wisdom of the ancestors of their particular cultural group. It is important to note that traditions and traditional

ways are not static and that many of the values, principles, and practices that come from "traditional" Aboriginal ways still operate in contemporary communities. Many traditional ways are also now being reclaimed to suit current generations.

Traditional knowledge (TK): Knowledge informed by the paradigms that Aboriginal people apply to skills, understandings, expertise, facts, familiarities, beliefs, revelations, and observations. TK includes the customary ways that Aboriginal people have done or continue to do certain things, as well as the new ideas or ways of doing things they develop which respect their traditions, cultures and practices.

Treaties (numbered): Written documents signed by representatives of the Crown, the federal government, and First Nation leaders, which outline the conditions of the formal relationship between the sovereign peoples designated in the document.

Truth and Reconciliation Commission (TRC): A component of the Indian Residential Schools Settlement Agreement established to inform all Canadians about what happened in Indian Residential Schools (IRS). The TRC was given a five-year mandate to document the truth of survivors, families, communities and anyone personally affected by the IRS experience, including First Nations, Inuit and Métis former Indian Residential School students, their families, communities, the Churches, former school employees, Government and other Canadians.

Unemployment rate: Percentage of the total labour force (individuals 15 or older) who were, during the week prior to enumeration: (a) without work, actively looked for work in the past four weeks, and were available for work; or (b) were on lay-off and expected to return to their job and were available for work; or (c) had definite arrangements to start a new job in four weeks or less and were available for work.

Wahkohtowin: A word defined as "the act of being related to each other" in the *Alberta Elder's Cree Dictionary* (LeClaire and Cardinal 1998). However, it carries a bigger bundle than the definition implies, since it speaks to a world view in which everything is understood to be interrelated: humans, animals, plants, the land, and the spirit world. The health and well-being of one is thus dependent on the other.

Welfare dependency: Social, economic, and political conditions cultivate an apparently inescapable cycle of poverty in which individuals and communities become dependent on regular government handouts.

White Paper (1969): Federal government policy designed to phase out federal responsibilities towards First Nations people and to eventually remove the special status of "Indian" peoples in Canada.

Wisdom: A holistic understanding of what is true, right, and lasting.

Women's issues: Issues of concern to Aboriginal women, including, to name a few of the more prominent ones, child care, housing, education, family violence, social programs, spirituality, political representation, and legal status.

World view: A particular social group's set of beliefs, which constitute their outlook on humanity and the world.

References

Introduction

Dickason, Olive Patricia. 1997. *Canada's First Nations: A History of Founding Peoples from Earliest Times, 2nd edn.* Toronto: Oxford University Press.

Niezen, Ronald. 2013. *Truth and Indignation: Canada's Truth and Reconciliation Commission on Indian Residential Schools.* Toronto: University of Toronto Press.

Report of the Royal Commission on Aboriginal Peoples. 1996. http://www.collectionscanada.gc.ca/webarchives/20071115053257; http://www.ainc-inac.gc.ca/ch/rcap/sg/sgmm_e.html.

Saskatchewan Indian Federated College. *A Brief to Propose a National Indigenous Research Agenda.* Submitted to the Social Sciences and Humanities Research Council.

Chapter 1

Cole, P. 2006. *Coyote and Raven Go Canoeing: Coming Home to the Village.* Montreal and Kingston: McGill-Queen's University Press (Native and Northern Series).

Cole, P. 2002. "land and language: translating aboriginal cultures." *Canadian Journal of Environmental Education* 7, 1: 67–84.

Frankland, R. 1997. Personal communication, Mirimbiak Nations Corporation, Melbourne, Australia.

George, P. 1998. "Opening Address." Indigenous Knowings Conference, McMaster University/Six Nations Grand River Polytechnic. Hamilton and Six Nations, Ont.

Kidwell, S. 1998. Translating Native American Cultures: A Conference on Representation, Aesthetics, and Translation. New Haven, Conn., 8 Feb.

Kills Straight, B. 1998. Panel Discussion. Indigenous Knowings Conference, McMaster University/Six Nations Grand River Polytechnic. Hamilton and Six Nations, Ont.

Longboat, J. 1998. Panel Discussion. Indigenous Knowings Conference, McMaster University/Six Nations Grand River Polytechnic. Hamilton and Six Nations, Ont.

Maracle, L. 1998. Reading. Indigenous Knowings Conference, McMaster University/Six Nations Grand River Polytechnic. Hamilton and Six Nations, Ont.

McFarland, A. 1998. Personal communication, Palmerston North, New Zealand.

McGregor, D. 1998. Indigenous Knowings Conference, McMaster University/Six Nations Grand River Polytechnic. Hamilton and Six Nations, Ont.

Melbourne, H. 1999. Te Hotaka Whakapakari Pouako Hangarau Conference, Massey University, New Zealand.

Mitchell, C. 1998. Indigenous Knowings Conference, McMaster University/Six Nations Grand River Polytechnic. Hamilton and Six Nations, Ont.

Olsen, S. 2003. *No Time to Say Goodbye: Children's Stories of Kuper Island Residential School.* Winlaw, BC: Sono Nis Press.

O'Riley, P. 2003. *Technology, Culture, and Socioeconomics: A Rhizoanalysis of Educational Discourses.* New York: Peter Lang.

Patton, R. 1997. Personal communication, Deakin University, Geelong campus, Australia.

Price, J. 2012. Personal communication, Vancouver.

Thomas, J. 1998. Indigenous Knowings Conference, McMaster University/Six Nations Grand River Polytechnic. Hamilton and Six Nations, Ont.

Chapter 2

Aboriginal Affairs and Northern Development Canada (AANDC). 2011. *Updated Aboriginal Consultation and Accommodation Guidelines for Federal Officials to Fulfill the Duty to Consult.* Ottawa: Public Works and Government Services of Canada, Minister of the Department of Aboriginal Affairs and Northern Development Canada. http://www.aadnc-aandc.gc.ca/DAM/DAM-INTER-HQ/STAGING/texte-text/intgui_1100100014665_eng.pdf.

Anaya, J. 2014. *Report of the Special Rapporteur on the Rights of Indigenous Peoples, James Anaya, on the Situation of Indigenous Peoples in Canada.* Advance unedited version. New York: United Nations Human Rights Council. http://unsr.jamesanaya.org/docs/countries/2014-report-canada-a-hrc-27-52-add-2-en-auversion.pdf.

Anderson, K. 2000. *A Recognition of Being: Reconstructing Native Womanhood.* Toronto: Second Story Press.

——, B. Clow, and M. Haworth-Brockman. 2013. "Carriers of Water: Aboriginal Women's Experiences, Relationships, and Reflections." *Journal of Cleaner Production* 60: 11–17.

Agyeman, J., R. Haluza-Delay, C. Peter, and P. O'Riley, eds. 2009. *Speaking for Ourselves: Constructions of Environmental Justice in Canada.* Vancouver: University of British Columbia Press.

Assembly of First Nations (AFN). 2010. *First Nations Ethics Guide on Research and Aboriginal Traditional Knowledge.* Ottawa: AFN.

Atleo, R. 2004. *Tsawalk: A Nuu-chah-nulth Worldview.* Vancouver: University of British Columbia Press.

Benton-Banai, E. 1988. *The Mishomis Book: The Voice of the Ojibway.* Hayward, Wis.: Indian Country Communications.

Berneshawi, S. 1997. "Resource Management and the Mi'kmaq Nation." *Canadian Journal of Native Studies* 1: 115–48.

Berger, T. 1977. *Northern Frontier, Northern Homeland: The Report of the Mackenzie Valley Pipeline Inquiry,* vol. 1, *Social, Economic and Environmental Impact.* Ottawa: Minister of Supply and Services Canada.

Bocking, S. 2005. "Scientists and Evolving Perceptions of Indigenous Knowledge in Northern Canada." In U. Lischke and D. McNab, eds, *Walking a Tightrope: Aboriginal Peoples and Their Representation.* Waterloo, Ont.: Wilfrid Laurier University Press.

Borrows, J. 2005. *Crown Occupations of Land: A History and Comparison.* Prepared for the Ipperwash Inquiry. Toronto: Office of the Attorney General, Government of Ontario. http://www.attorneygeneral.jus.gov.on.ca/inquiries/ipperwash/policy_part/research/index.htm.

——. 2010. *Canada's Indigenous Constitution.* Toronto: University of Toronto Press.

Bowie, R. 2013. "Indigenous Self-Governance and the Deployment of Knowledge in Collaborative Environmental Management in Canada." *Journal of Canadian Studies* 47, 1: 91–256.

Butler, C. 2006. "Historicizing Indigenous Knowledge: Practical and Political Issues." In C. Menzies, ed., *Traditional Ecological Knowledge and Natural*

Resource Management. Lincoln: University of Nebraska Press.

Canadian Environmental Protection Act. SC 1999. c. 33, s. 3.

Chiefs of Ontario. 2008. *Water Declaration of Anishinabek, Mushkegowuk and Onkwehonwe in Ontario.* Toronto: Chiefs of Ontario. www.coo.org.

Centre for Indigenous Environmental Resources (CIER). 2005. *Environmental Issues Report.* Winnipeg: CIER. http://www.cier.ca/information-and-resources/publications-and-products.

Clarkson, L., V. Morrrissette, and G. Regallet. 1992. *Our Responsibility to the Seventh Generation: Indigenous Peoples and Sustainable Development.* Winnipeg: International Institute for Sustainable Development.

Corbiere, A. 2014. "'Their Own Forms of Which They Take the Most Notice': Diplomatic Metaphors and Symbolism on Wampum Belts." In A. Corbiere, M.A. Corbiere, D. McGregor, and C. Migwans, eds, *Anishinaabewin Niiwin: Four Rising Winds,* 47–64. M'Chigeeng, Ont.: Ojibwe Cultural Foundation.

Deloria, V., Jr. 1994. *God is Red: A Native View of Religion.* Golden, Colo.: Fulcrum.

———. 1999. "If You Think About It, You Will See That It Is True." In B. Deloria, K. Foehner, and S. Scinta, eds, *Spirit and Reason,* 40–60. Golden, Colo.: Fulcrum.

Dhillon, C., and M. Young. 2010. "Environmental Racism and First Nations: A Call for Socially Just Public Policy Development." *Canadian Journal of Humanities and Social Science* 1, 1: 25–39. http://cjhss.org/_cjhss/pubData/v_1/i_1/contentsFrame.php.

Doyle-Bedwell, P., and F. Cohen. 2001. "Aboriginal People in Canada: Their Role in Shaping Environmental Trends in the Twenty First Century." In E. Parson, ed., *Governing the Environment: Persistent Challenges, Uncertain*

Innovations, 169–206 Toronto: University of Toronto Press.

Dumont, J. 2006. *Indigenous Intelligence.* Sudbury, Ont.: University of Sudbury.

Edgar, L., and J. Graham. 2008. *Environmental Protection: Challenges and Prospects for First Nations under the First Nations Land Management Act.* Ottawa: Institute on Governance. http://iog.ca/sites/iog/files/2008_fn_land_mgt_act.pdf.

Gelinas, J. 2005. *Report of the Commissioner of the Environment and Sustainable Development to the House of Commons,* Chapter 5: "Drinking Water in First Nations Communities." Ottawa: Office of the Auditor General of Canada.

Grenier, L. 1998. *Working with Indigenous Knowledge: A Guide for Researchers.* Ottawa: International Development Research Centre.

Haudenosaunee Environmental Task Force (HETF). 1999. *Words That Come Before All Else: Environmental Philosophies of the Haudenosaunee.* Cornwall Island, Ont.: Native North American Travelling College.

Higgins, C. 1998. "The Role of Traditional Ecological Knowledge in Managing for Biodiversity." *Forestry Chronicle* 7, 3: 323–6.

Jacobs, B. 2010. "Environmental Racism on Indigenous Lands and Territories." http://www.cpsa-acsp.ca/papers-2010/Jacobs.pdf.

Johnston, B. 1976. *Ojibway Heritage.* Toronto: McClelland & Stewart.

LaDuke. W. 1994. "Traditional Ecological Knowledge and Environmental Futures." *Colorado Journal of International Environmental Law and Policy*: 126–48.

———. 1999. *All Our Relations: Native Struggles for Land and Life.* Cambridge, Mass.: South End Press.

Linden, S. 2007. *Report of the Ipperwash Inquiry: Volume 4: Executive Summary.* Toronto: Office of the Attorney

General. http://www.attorneygeneral.jus.gov.on.ca/inquiries/ipperwash/index.html.

Lyons, O. 1980. "An Iroquois Perspective." In C. Vecsey and R. Venables, eds, *American Indian Environments: Ecological Issues in Native American History*, 171–4. Syracuse, NY: Syracuse University Press.

McClenaghan, T. 1999. *Molested and Disturbed: Environmental Protection by Aboriginal Peoples through Section 35 of the Constitution Act, 1982*. Toronto: Canadian Environmental Law Association. http://www.cela.ca/publications/molested-and-disturbed-environmental-protection-aboriginal-peoples-through-section-35-c.

McDermott, L., and P. Wilson. 2010. "Ginawaydaganuk: Algonquin Law on Access and Benefit Sharing." *Policy Matters* 17: 205–14.

McDonald, M., L. Arragutainaq, and Z. Novalinga. 1997. *Voices from the Bay: Traditional Ecological Knowledge of Inuit and Cree in the Hudson Bay Bioregion*. Ottawa: Canadian Arctic Resources Committee and Environmental Committee of the Muncipality of Sanikiluaq.

McGregor, D. 2012. "Traditional Knowledge: Considerations for Protecting Water in Ontario." *International Indigenous Policy Journal* (Special Issue on Water and Indigenous Peoples) 3, 3. http://www.iipj.org/.

Mandamin, J. 2003. "Mother Earth Walk: Lake Superior." http://www.motherearthwaterwalk.com/aboutus.html.

———. 2012. "N'guh izhi chigaye, nibi onji: I Will Do It for the Water." In A. Corbiere, D. McGregor, and C. Migwans, eds, *Anishinaabewin Niizh: Culture Movements, Critical Moments*, 12–23. M'Chigeeng, Ont.: Ojibwe Cultural Foundation.

Métis National Council (MNC). 2011. *Métis Traditional Knowledge*. Ottawa: Métis National Environment Committee. http://www.Métisnation.ca/wp-content/uploads/2011/05/Métis-Traditional-Knowledge.pdf.

Métis Nation of Ontario (MNO). 2012. *Special Impacts Report: Lands, Resources and Consultations*. Ottawa: Métis Nation of Ontario. http://www.Métisnation.org/media/354499/special_impacts_report-screen.pdf.

Menzies, C. 2006. *Traditional Ecological Knowledge and Natural Resource Management*. Lincoln: University of Nebraska Press.

Natcher, D., and S. Davis. 2007. "Rethinking Devolution: Challenges for Aboriginal Resource Management in the Yukon Territory." *Society and Natural Resources* 20, 3: 271–9.

O'Connor, D. 2002. "First Nations." Chapter 15 in: *Part Two. Report of the Walkerton Inquiry: A Strategy for Safe Drinking Water*, 485–97 Toronto: Queen's Printer for Ontario.

Oxford On-Line Dictionary. "Environment." http://www.oxforddictionaries.com/definition/english/environment.

Qikiqtani Inuit Association. 2007. "Inuit Qaujimajatuqangit." http://www.qia.ca/i18n/english/iq.shtm.

Ransom, R., and K. Ettenger. 2001. "Polishing the Kaswetha': A Haudenosaunee View of Environmental Cooperation." *Environmental Science and Policy* 4: 219–28.

Ransom, J. 1999. "The Waters." In Haudenosaunee Environmental Task Force, *Words that Come Before All Else: Environmental Philosophies of the Haudenosaunee*, 25–43. Cornwall Island, Ont.: Native North American Travelling College.

Royal Commission on Aboriginal Peoples (RCAP). 1996. *People to People, Nation to Nation: Highlights from the Report of the Royal Commission on Aboriginal Peoples*. Ottawa: Minister of Supply and Services.

Ryan, J. 1995. *Doing Things the Right Way: Dené Traditional Justice in Lac La Martre, N.W.T.* Calgary: University of Calgary Press.

Sable, T., G. Howell, D. Wilson, and P. Penashue. 2006. "The Ashkui Project: Linking Western Science and Environmental Knowledge in Creating a Sustainable Environment." In P. Silltoe, ed., *Local Science vs. Global Science: Approaches to Indigenous Knowledges in International Development*, 109–27. Oxford, NY: Berghahn Books.

Settee, P. 2000. "The Issue of Biodiversity, Intellectual Property Rights, and Indigenous Rights." In R. Laliberte, P. Settee, J. Waldram, R. Innes, B. Macdougall, L. McBain, and F. Barron, eds, *Expressions in Canadian Native Studies*. Saskatoon: University of Saskatchewan Extension Press.

Smith, P. 1995. *Aboriginal Participation in Forest Management: Not Just Another Stakeholder*. Ottawa: National Aboriginal Forestry Association.

Spak, S. 2005. "The Position of Indigenous Knowledge in Canadian Co-management Organizations." *Anthropologica* 47, 2: 233–46.

St Germain, G., and N. Sibbeston. 2007. *Safe Drinking Water for First Nations. Final Report of the Standing Senate Committee on Aboriginal Peoples*. Ottawa: Senate Committees Directorate.

Stevenson, M. 2006. "The Possibility of Difference: Rethinking Co-management." *Human Organization* 65, 2: 167–80.

Teillet, J. 2005. *The Role of the Natural Resources Regulatory Regime in Aboriginal Rights Disputes in Ontario*. Toronto: Ipperwash Inquiry, Office of the Attorney General.

United States Environmental Protection Agency (USEPA). 2014. "Environmental Justice." http://www.epa.gov/environmentaljustice.

Unamak'ki Institute of Natural Resources. 2011. "Mi'kmaq Sustainable Resources." http://www.uinr.ca.

Wa, G., and D. Uukw. 1989. *The Spirit in the Land: The Opening Statement of the Gitksan and Wet'suwet'en Hereditary Chiefs in the Supreme Court of Canada*. Gabriola, BC: Reflections.

Walken, A. 2007. "The Land Is Dry: Indigenous Peoples, Water, and Environmental Justice." In K. Bakker, ed., *Eau Canada: The Future of Canada's Water*, 303–20. Vancouver: University of British Columbia Press.

White, G. 2006. "Cultures in Collision: Traditional Knowledge and Euro-Canadian Governance Processes in Northern Land-Claim Boards." *Arctic* 59, 4: 401–14.

Williams, P. 1999. "Creation". In Haudenosaunee Environmental Task Force, *Words That Come Before All Else: Environmental Philosophies of the Haudenosaunee*, 1–7 Cornwall Island, Ont.: Native North American Travelling College.

World Commission on Environment and Development (WCED). 1987. *Our Common Future*. Oxford: Oxford University Press.

Wyatt, S., J. Fortier, and M. Hebert. 2009. "Multiple Forms of Engagement: Classifying Aboriginal Roles in Contemporary Canadian Forestry." In M. Stevenson, and D. Natcher. *Changing the Culture of Forestry in Canada: Building Effective Institutions for Aboriginal Engagement in Sustainable Forest Management*, 163–80. Edmonton: CCI Press and Sustainable Forest Management Network.

Chapter 3

Belanger, Yale D. 2006. "Seeking a Seat at the Table: A Brief History of Indian Political Organizing in Canada, 1870–1951." Ph.D. dissertation, Trent University.

Calder v. Attorney General of British Columbia (1973), 34 D.L.R. (3d) 145.

Canada. 1961. *The Report of the Joint Parliamentary–Senate Committee Hearings on Indian Affairs in Canada.* Ottawa: Queen's Printer.

———. 1969. *Statement of Indian Policy of the Government of Canada.* Honourable Jean Chrétien, Minister of Indian Affairs and Northern Development. Ottawa: Queen's Printer.

———. 1995. *Federal Policy Guide Aboriginal Self Government: The Government of Canada's Approach to Implementation of the Inherent Right and the Negotiation of Aboriginal Self Government.* Ottawa: Queen's Printer.

———. 1996. *Report of the Royal Commission on Aboriginal Peoples.* Ottawa: Canada Communications Group.

Centre for First Nations Governance. http://www.fngovernance.org.

Delgamuukw v. British Columbia (1997), 3 S.C.R. 1010.

Dyck, Noel. 1991. *What Is the Indian Problem? Tutelage and Resistance in Canadian Indian Administration.* St. John's: Institute of Social and Economic Research.

Federation of Saskatchewan Indians. 1977. *Indian Government.* Saskatoon: Federation of Saskatchewan Indians.

———. 1979. *Indian Treaty Rights: The Spirit and Intent of Treaty.* Saskatoon: Federation of Saskatchewan Indians.

Environics Institute. 2010. *Urban Aboriginal Peoples Study: Main Report.* Toronto: Environics Institute.

First Nations Leadership Council. 2006. *Progress Report,* vol. 1, issue 1 (Apr.). Vancouver: First Nations Leadership Council.

Henderson, James Sakej. 1994. "Empowering Treaty Federalism." *Saskatchewan Law Review* 58: 241–329.

Historica Canada. 2014. "Fathers of Confederation." *The Canadian Encyclopedia.* Accessed 24 June 2014. http://www.thecanadianencyclopedia.ca/en/article/fathers-of-confederation.

Indian Chiefs of Alberta. 1970. *Citizens Plus.* Edmonton: Indian–Eskimo Association of Canada.

Manitoba Indian Brotherhood. 1971. *Wahbung: Our Tomorrows.* Winnipeg: Manitoba Indian Brotherhood. www.manitobachiefs.com/amc/history/Wahbung.pdf.

Mercredi, Ovide, and Mary Ellen Turpel. 1994. *In the Rapids: Navigating the Future of First Nations.* Toronto: Penguin.

Penner, Keith. 1983. *Special Committee on Indian Self-Government in Canada.* Report of the Special Parliamentary Committee on Indian Self-Government. Ottawa: Queen's Printer.

R. v. Marshall (1999), 3 S.C.R. 533.

R. v. Sparrow (1990), 1 S.C.R. 1075.

Saul, John Ralston. 1998. *Reflections of a Siamese Twin: Canada at the Beginning of the Twenty-First Century.* Toronto: Penguin Group Canada.

———. 2008. *A Fair Country: Telling Truths about Canada.* Toronto: Viking Canada.

Toronto Aboriginal Support Services Council. 2011. *Toronto Aboriginal Research Project: Final Report,* by Don McCaskill, Kevin Fitzmaurice, and Jaime Cidro. Toronto: Mukawa Associates.

Tshilhqot'in Nation v. British Columbia (2014), S.C.C. 44

Williams, Robert A. 1997. *Linking Arms Together: American Indian Treaty Visions of Law and Peace, 1600–1800.* New York: Oxford University Press.

Chapter 4

Battiste, Marie, and James (Sa'ke'j) Youngblood Henderson. 2000. *Protecting Indigenous Knowledge and Heritage.* Saskatoon: Purich.

Campbell, Maria. 2005 [1985]. *Achimoona.* Saskatoon: Fifth House.

Cardinal, Harold, and Walter Hildebrandt. 2000. *Treaty Elders of Saskatchewan*. Calgary: University of Calgary Press.

Castellano, Marlene Brant. 2000. "Updating Aboriginal Traditions of Knowledge." In George Sefa Dei, Budd Hall, and Dorothy Goldin Rosenberg, eds, *Indigenous Knowledges in Global Contexts: Multiple Readings of Our World*, 195–210. Toronto: University of Toronto Press.

Couture, Joseph. 2011. "The Role of Native Elders: Emergent Issues." In David Long and Olive Dickason, eds, *Visions of the Heart: Canadian Aboriginal Issues*, 3rd edn, 18–34. Toronto: Oxford University Press.

Delgamuukw v. British Columbia, [1997] 3 S.C.R. 1010.

Ermine, Willie. 1995. "Aboriginal Epistemology." In Marie Battiste and Jean Barman, eds, *First Nations Education in Canada: The Circle Unfolds*, 101–12. Vancouver: University of British Columbia Press.

——. 2008. PowerPoint presentation on Ethical Space at the Ninth Global Forum on Bioethics in Research, 3–5 Dec., Auckland, Aotearoa/New Zealand. http://gfbr9.hrc.govt.nz/index.php/presentations.

——, Raven Sinclair, and Bonnie Jeffery. 2004. *The Ethics of Research Involving Indigenous Peoples*. Report of the Indigenous Peoples' Health Research Centre to the Interagency Advisory Panel on Research Ethics. http://www.iphrc.ca/Upload/ethics_review_iphrc.pdf.

Foster, Michael. 1984. "On Who Spoke First at Iroquois–White Councils: An Exercise in the Method of Upstreaming." In Michael K. Foster, Jack Campisi, and Marianne Mithun, eds, *Extending the Rafters: Interdisciplinary Approaches to Iroquoian Studies*. Albany: State University of New York Press.

Gray, Viviane. 2008. "A Culture of Art: Profiles of Contemporary First Nations Women Artists." In Gail Guthrie Valaskakis, Madeleine Dion Stout, and Eric Guimond, eds, *Restoring the Balance: First Nations Women, Community and Culture*, 267–81. Winnipeg: University of Manitoba Press.

Hoffman, Ross. 2006. "Rekindling the Fire: The Impact of Raymond Harris's Work with the Plains Cree." Ph.D. dissertation, Trent University.

Little Bear, Leroy. 2000. "Jagged Worldviews Colliding." In Marie Battiste, ed., *Reclaiming Indigenous Voice and Vision*, 77–85. Vancouver: University of British Columbia Press.

Newhouse, David. 2002. "The Promise of Indigenous Scholarship." Keynote address to the First Aboriginal Policy Research Conference, Ottawa.

——. 2008. "Ganigonhi:oh: The Good Mind Meets the Academy." In "Indigenous Knowledges and the University," special theme issue of *Canadian Journal of Native Education* 31, 1: 184–97.

Regnier, Robert. 1995. "The Sacred Circle: An Aboriginal Approach to Healing Education at an Urban High School." In Marie Battiste and Jean Barman, eds, *First Nations Education in Canada: The Circle Unfolds*, 313–29. Vancouver: University of British Columbia Press.

Restoule, Jean-Paul. 2004. "Aboriginal Identity in Urban Areas: Shifting the Focus from Definition to Context." Ph.D. dissertation, Ontario Institute for Studies in Education, University of Toronto.

Royal Commission on Aboriginal Peoples (RCAP). 1996. *Report, vol. 1, Looking Forward, Looking Back; vol. 3, Gathering Strength*. Ottawa: Canada Communications Group. http://www.collectionscanada.gc.ca/webarchives/20071115053257/http://www.ainc-inac.gc.ca/ch/rcap/sg/sgmm_e.html.

Sanderson, Lillian. 1996. Oral presentation cited in *Report of the Royal Commission on Aboriginal Peoples*, vol. 3, *Gathering Strength*. Ottawa: Canada Communications Group.

Thomas, Jake. Personal communication.

Valaskakis, Gail Guthrie. 2005. *Indian Country: Essays on Contemporary Native Culture*. Waterloo, Ont.: Wilfrid Laurier University Press.

——, Madeleine Dion Stout, and Eric Guimond, eds. 2008. *Restoring the Balance: First Nations Women, Community and Culture*. Winnipeg. University of Manitoba Press.

VanEvery-Albert, Caroline. 2008. "An Exploration of Indigenousness in the Western University Institution'. In "Indigenous Knowledges and the University," special theme issue of the *Canadian Journal of Native Education* 31, 1: 41–55.

Chapter 5

Aboriginal Healing Foundation. 2006. *Final Report of the Aboriginal Healing Foundation: Promising Healing Practices in Aboriginal Communities*, vol. 3. Ottawa: Aboriginal Healing Foundation.

Adelson, N. 2005. "The Embodiment of Inequity: Health Disparities in Aboriginal Canada." *Canadian Journal of Public Health* (Mar.–Apr.): 45–61.

Adoption Council of Canada. 2009. "Canada's Waiting Children." www.adoption.ca.

Allen, S., and K. Daly. 2007. *The Effects of Father Involvement: A Summary of the Research Evidence*. Research review for the Public Health Agency of Canada Population Health Fund Project: Fathers Involvement. Ottawa: Fathers Involvement Initiative.

——, ——, and J. Ball. 2012. "Fathers Make a Difference in Their Children's Lives: A Review of the Research Evidence." In Jessica Ball and Kerry Daly, eds, *Father Involvement in Canada:*

Diversity, Renewal, and Transformation. Vancouver: University of British Columbia Press.

Anderson, Karen. 1991. *Chain Her by One Foot: The Subjugation of Native Women in Seventeenth-Century New France*. New York: Routledge.

Anderson, Kim. 2000. *A Recognition of Being: Reconstructing Native Womanhood*. Toronto: Canadian Scholars' Press.

——. 2007. "Giving Life to the People: An Indigenous Ideology of Motherhood." In A. O'Reilly, ed., *Maternal Theory: Essential Readings*, 761–81. Toronto: Demeter Press.

——. 2011. *Life Stages and Native Women: Memory, Teachings and Story Medicine*. Winnipeg: University of Manitoba Press.

——, Robert Alexander Innes, and John Swift. 2012. "Indigenous Masculinities: Carrying the Bones of Our Ancestors." In Christopher Greig and Wayne Martino, eds, *Canadian Men and Masculinities: Historical and Contemporary Perspectives*, 266–84. Toronto: Canadian Scholars' Press.

Arnott, J. 2006. "Dances with Cougar: Learning from Traditional Skills Parenting Programs." In D.M. Harvard-Lavell and J. Corbiere Lavell, eds, *Until Our Hearts Are on the Ground: Aboriginal Mothering, Oppression, Resistance and Rebirth*, 94–104. Toronto: Demeter Press.

Assembly of First Nations (AFN). n.d. "Fact Sheet: The Reality for First Nations in Canada." www.afn.ca/article.asp?id=764.

——. 1988. *Tradition and Education: Towards a Vision of Our Future*. Ottawa: AFN.

——. 2006a. *Leadership Action Plan on First Nations Child Welfare*. Ottawa: AFN.

——. 2006b. *Royal Commission on Aboriginal Peoples at Ten Years: A Report Card*. Ottawa: AFN.

——. 2013. *Annual Report, 2012–2013.* http://www.afn.ca/uploads/files/afn_ annual_report_2012-13_en_final.pdf.

Atleo, E.R. 2004. *Tsawalk: A Nuu-chah-nulth Worldview.* Vancouver: University of British Columbia Press.

Bala, N., et al. 2004. *Canadian Child Welfare Law: Children, Families and the State.* Toronto: Thompson.

Ball, J. 2005. "Early Childhood Care and Development Programs as Hook and Hub for Intersectoral Service Delivery in Indigenous Communities." *Journal of Aboriginal Health* 1: 36–49.

——. 2006. 'Developmental Monitoring, Screening and Assessment of Aboriginal Young Children: Findings of a Community–University Research Partnership." Paper presented at the Aboriginal Supported Child Care Conference, Vancouver, Nov.

——. 2008. 'Promoting Equity and Dignity for Aboriginal Children in Canada." *IRPP Choices* 14, 7: 1–30.

——. 2009. "Centring Community Services around Early Childhood Care and Development: Promising Practices in Indigenous Communities Canada." *Child Health and Education* 1, 4: 183–206. http://www.journals.sfu.ca/che/index.php/english/index.

——. 2010. "Indigenous Fathers Reconstituting Circles of Care." *American Journal of Community Psychology*, special issue on "Men, Masculinity, Wellness, Health and Social Justice–Community-Based Approaches." doi 10.1007/s10464-009-9293-1.

——. 2014. "Improving the Reach of Early Childhood Education for First Nations, Inuit and Métis Children." *Moving Child Care Forward.* www.movingchildcareforward.ca.

—— and R.T. George. 2007. "Policies and Practices Affecting Aboriginal Fathers' Involvement with Their Children." In J.P. White, S. Wingert, D. Beavon, and P. Maxim, eds, *Aboriginal Policy Research: Moving Forward, Making a Difference*, vol. 3, 123–44. Toronto: Thompson.

—— and K. Moselle. 2007. *Fathers' Contributions to Children's Well-being.* Research review for the Public Health Agency of Canada Population Health Fund Project: Fathers' Involvement. Ottawa: Fathers' Involvement Initiative.

Bennett, M., and C. Blackstock. 1992. *A Literature Review and Annotated Bibliography Focusing on Aspects of Aboriginal Child Welfare in Canada.* Winnipeg: First Nations Child and Family Caring Society.

Blackstock, C., et al. 2005. *Wen:de: We Are Coming to the Light of Day.* Ottawa: First Nations Child and Family Caring Society of Canada. www.cwrp.ca/sites/default/files/publications/en/WendeReport.pdf.

—— et al. 2006. *Reconciliation in Child Welfare: Touchstones of Hope for Indigenous Children, Youth, and Families.* Ottawa: First Nations Child and Family Caring Society of Canada.

——, with M. Bennett. 2003. *National Children's Alliance: Policy Paper on Aboriginal Children.* Ottawa: First Nations Child and Family Caring Society of Canada.

——, D. Bruyere, and E. Moreau. 2005. "Many Hands, One Dream: Principles for a New Perspective on the Health of First Nations, Inuit and Métis Children and Youth." www.manyhandsonedream.ca.

Brown, J.S.H. 1980. *Strangers in Blood: Fur Trade Company Families in Indian Country.* Vancouver: University of British Columbia Press.

Bourgeois, Robyn. 2006. "A National Epidemic: The Scope of Violence against Aboriginal Women in Canada." *Making Waves: An Ecumenical Feminist Journal* 6, 1: 19–20.

Campbell, Maria. 2008. Personal communication (summer).

Canada Council on Learning. 2007. *State of Learning in Canada: No Time for Complacency*. Report on Learning in Canada 2007. Ottawa: Canada Council on Learning.

Canadian Institute for Health Information (CIHI). 2004. "Aboriginal Peoples' Health." In Canadian Institute for Health Information, ed., *Improving the Health of Canadians*, 73–102. Ottawa: CIHI.

———. 2013. "Treatment of Preventable Dental Cavities in Preschoolers: A Focus on Day Surgery under General Anesthesia." https://secure.cihi.ca/free_products/Dental_Caries_Report_en_web.pdf.

Canadian Incidence Study of Reported Child Abuse and Neglect—First Nations Component. 2008. http://cwrp.ca/fn-cis-2008.

Canadian Institute of Child Health. 2000. *The Health of Canada's Children*, 3rd edn. Ottawa: Canadian Institute of Child Health.

Carter, S. 1997. *Capturing Women: The Manipulation of Cultural Imagery in Canada's Prairie West*. Montreal and Kingston: McGill-Queen's University Press.

Castellano, M. Brant. 2002. *Aboriginal Family Trends: Extended Families, Nuclear Families, Families of the Heart*. Ottawa: Vanier Institute of the Family. www.vifamily.ca/library/cft/aboriginal.html.

Claes, R., and D. Clifton. 1998. *Needs and Expectations for Redress of Victims of Abuse at Residential Schools*. Ottawa: Law Commission of Canada.

Cooke, M., D. Beavon, and M. McHardy. 2004. "Measuring the Well-being of Aboriginal People: An Application of the United Nations Human Development Index to Registered Indians in Canada, 1981–2001." In J.P. White, P. Maxim, and D. Beavon, eds, *Aboriginal Policy Research: Setting the Agenda for Change*, vol. 1, 47–70. Toronto: Thompson.

Correctional Services Canada. 2006. "Strategic Plan for Aboriginal Corrections: Innovation, Learning and Adjustment." www.csc-scc.gc.ca/text/prgrm/abinit/plan06-eng.shtml.

de Leeuw, S., J. Fiske, and M. Greenwood. 2002. *Rural, Remote and North of 51: Service Provision and Substance Abuse Related Special Needs in British Columbia's Hinterlands*. Prince George: University of Northern British Columbia Task Force on Substance Abuse.

Di Tomasso, L., S. de Finney, S., and K. Grzybowski. 2015. "Honouring Our Caretaking Traditions: A Review of Custom Adoptions." *First Peoples Child & Family Review* 10, 1: 19–38.

Dion Stout, M., and G. Kipling. 2003. *Aboriginal People, Resilience and the Residential School Legacy*. Ottawa: Aboriginal Healing Foundation.

Dickason, O.P., with D.T. McNab. 2009. *Canada's First Nations: A History of Founding Peoples*, 4th edn. Toronto: Oxford University Press.

Driskill, Quo-Li, Chris Finley, Brian Joseph Gilley, Scott Lauria Morgensen, eds. 2011. *Queer Indigenous Studies: Critical Interventions in Theory, Politics and Literature*. Tucson: University of Arizona Press, 2011.

Emmerich, L. 1991. "'Right in the Midst of My Own People': Native American Women and the Field Matron Program." *American Indian Quarterly* 15, 2: 201–16.

Farris-Manning, C., and M. Zandstra. 2003. "Children in Care in Canada: A Summary of Current Issues and Trends with Recommendations for Future Research." Ottawa: Child Welfare League of Canada. www.cecw-cepb.ca/publications/574.

First Nations and Inuit Regional Health Survey National Steering Committee. 1999. *First Nations and Inuit Regional Health Survey: National Report 1999.* First Nations and Inuit Regional Health Survey National Steering Committee.

First Nations Centre. 2005. "First Nations Regional Longitudinal Health Survey (RHS) 2002/03: Results for Adults, Youth and Children Living in First Nations Communities." www.naho.ca/firstnations/english/regional_health.php.

First Nations Child and Family Caring Society of Canada. 2005. "A Chance to Make a Difference for This Generation of First Nations Children and Young People: The UNCRC and the Lived Experience of First Nations Children in the Child Welfare System of Canada." Submission to the Standing Senate Committee on Human Rights, 7 Feb.

First Nations Information Governance Centre. 2012. First Nations Regional Health Survey (RHS), Phase 2 (2008/10). *National Report on Adults, Youth and Children Living in First Nations Communities,* June. http://www.rhs-ers.ca/sites/default/files/First_Nations_Regional_Health_Survey_2008-10_National_Report.pdf.

Fournier, S., and E. Crey. 1997. *Stolen from Our Embrace: The Abduction of First Nations Children and the Restoration of Aboriginal Communities.* Vancouver: Douglas & McIntyre.

Gionet, L., and S. Roshanafshar. January, 2013). "Select Health Indicators of First Nations People Living Off Reserve, Métis and Inuit." Jan. Catalogue no.82-624-X. http://www.statcan.gc.ca/pub/82-624-x/2013001/article/11763-eng.pdf.

Greenwood, M. 2006. "Children Are a Gift to Us: Aboriginal-Specific Early Childhood Programs and Services in Canada." *Canadian Journal of Native Education* 29, 1: 12–28. www.accel-capea.ca/pdf/FinalGreenwood.pdf.

Guimond, E., and N. Robitaille. 2008. "When Teenage Girls Have Children: Trends and Consequences." *Horizons* 10, 1: 49–51.

Health Canada. 2003. *A Statistical Profile on the Health of First Nations in Canada.* Ottawa: Health Canada, First Nations Inuit Health Branch.

——. 2005. "First Nations Comparable Health Indicators." www.hc-sc.gc.ca.

Indian and Northern Affairs Canada. 2008. "Early Childhood Development: Programs and Initiatives." www.ainc-inac.gc.ca/hb/sp/ecd/index-eng.asp.

—— and Canada Mortgage and Housing Corporation. 2007. *Aboriginal Demography: Population, Household and Family Projections, 2001–2026.* Ottawa: Indian and Northern Affairs Canada and Canada Mortgage and Housing Corporation.

Inukshuk, Rhoda. 2007. Personal communication (winter).

Innes, Robert Alexander, and Kim Anderson, eds. 2015. *Indigenous Men and Masculinities: Identities, Legacies, Regeneration.* Winnipeg: University of Manitoba Press.

Jacobs, Margaret. 2011. *White Mother to a Dark Race: Settler Colonialism, Maternalism and the Removal of Indigenous Children in the American West and Australia.* Lincoln: University of Nebraska Press.

——. 2007. "Working on the Domestic Frontier: American Indian Domestic Servants in White Women's Households in the San Francisco Bay Area, 1920-1940." *Frontiers: A Journal of Women's Studies* 1 and 2: 165–99.

John, E. 2003. Presentation to the Aboriginal Leadership Forum on Early Childhood Development, University of British Columbia, Vancouver, 10–11 Mar.

Lavell-Harvard, D.M., and J. Corbiere Lavell, eds. 2006. *Until Our Hearts Are on the Ground: Aboriginal Mothering, Oppression, Resistance and Rebirth.* Toronto: Demeter.

LeClaire, N., and G. Cardinal. 1998. *Alberta Elder's Cree Dictionary.* ed. E. Waugh. Edmonton: University of Alberta Press.

Link, B.G., and J. Phelan. 1995. "Social Conditions and Fundamental Causes of Disease." *Journal of Health and Social Behaviour* 35: 80–94.

Loppie Reading, C., and F. Wien. 2009. *Health Inequalities, Social Determinants and Life Course Health Issues among Aboriginal Peoples in Canada.* Prince George, BC: National Collaborating Centre for Aboriginal Health.

Macdonald, D., and D. Wilson. 2013. *Poverty or Prosperity: Indigenous Children in Canada.* Ottawa: Canadian Centre for Policy Alternatives, Save the Children Canada. www.policyaltneratives.ca.

McDonald, R.J., and P. Ladd. 2000. *First Nations Child and Family Services Joint National Policy Review: Final Report.* Ottawa: Assembly of First Nations, First Nations Child and Family Service Agency Representatives, and Department of Indian Affairs and Northern Development.

Mashford-Pringle, A. 2012. "Early Learning for Aboriginal Children: Past, Present and Future and an Exploration of the Aboriginal Head Start Urban and Northern Communities Program in Ontario." *First Peoples Child and Family Review* 7, 1: 127–40.

Miller, J.R. 1996. *Shingwauk's Vision: A History of Native Residential Schools.* Toronto: University of Toronto Press.

Minister of Indian Affairs and Northern Development. 1997. *Gathering Strength: Canada's Aboriginal Action Plan.* Ottawa.

Minister of Public Works and Government Services. 2002. *Aboriginal Head Start in Urban and Northern Communities: Program and Participants 2001.* Ottawa: Minister of Public Works and Government Services.

Mussell, W.J. 2005. *Warrior-Caregivers: Understanding the Challenges and Healing of First Nations Men.* Ottawa: Aboriginal Healing Foundation.

National Council of Welfare. 2007. *First Nations, Métis and Inuit Children and Youth: Time to Act.* Ottawa: National Council of Welfare Reports, vol. 127.

Native Council of Canada. 1990. *Native Child Care: The Circle of Care.* Ottawa: Native Council of Canada.

Native Women's Association of Canada. 2012. *Good Relations: Supporting Aboriginal Women and Families Who Have Experienced Violence.* Ottawa.

Newhouse, D., and E. Peters, eds. 2003. *Not Strangers in These Parts: Urban Aboriginal Peoples.* Ottawa: Indian and Northern Affairs Canada.

Norris, M.J., and S. Clatworthy. 2006. "Aboriginal Mobility and Migration in Canada: Factors, Policy implications and Responses." Paper presented at the Second Aboriginal Policy Research Conference, Ottawa, Mar.

Office of the Correctional Investigator. 2013. "Backgrounder: Aboriginal Offenders—A Critical Situation." Modified 16 Sept. 2013. http://www. oci-bec.gc.ca/cnt/rpt/oth-aut/ oth-aut20121022info-eng.aspx.

Office of the Prime Minister of Canada. 2008. "Prime Minister Offers Full Apology on Behalf of Canadians for the Indian Residential Schools." Press release, 11 June. http://pm.gc.ca/eng/ media/asp?id2149.

Ontario Federation of Indian Friendship Centres. 2002. "Aboriginal Approaches to Fetal Alcohol Syndrome/Effects."

———. 2015. "Akwe:go Wholistic Longitudinal Study (AWLS)." http:// www.ofifc.org/research/research/

ongoing-projects/akwego-wholistic-longitudinal-study-awls.

Palkovitz, Robert. 2002. "Involved Fathering and Child Development: Advancing Our Understanding of Good Fathering." In C.S. Tamis-LeMonda and N. Cabrera, eds, *Handbook of Father involvement: Multidisciplinary Perspectives*. New York: Routledge.

Peers, L., and J.S.H. Brown. 2000. "There is No End to Relationship among the Indians: Ojibwa Families and kinship in historical perspective." *History of the Family* 4, 4: 529–55.

Perry, A. 2005. "Metropolitan Knowledge, Colonial Practice, and Indigenous Womanhood: Missions in Nineteenth-Century British Columbia." In K. Pickles and M. Rutherdale, eds, *Contact Zones: Aboriginal and Settler Women in Canada's Colonial Past*, 109–30. Vancouver: University of British Columbia Press.

Preston, J. 2014. "Early Childhood Education and Care for Aboriginal Children in Canada." *Moving Child Care Forward*. www.movingchildcareforward.ca.

——, M. Cottrell, T. Pelletier, and J.V. Pearce. 2012. "Aboriginal Early Childhood Education in Canada: Issues in Context." *Journal of Early Childhood Research* 10, 1: 3–18.

Public Health Agency of Canada and Canadian Institute for Health Information. 2011. *Obesity in Canada: A Joint Report from the Public Health Agency of Canada and the Canadian Institute for Health Information*. https://secure.cihi.ca/free_products/Obesity_in_canada_2011_en.pdf.

Ralstin- Lewis, D. Marie. 2005. "The Continuing Struggle against Genocide: Indian Women and Reproductive Rights." *Wicazo S.A. Review* 20, 1: 71–95.

Red Horse, J. 1997. "Traditional American Indian Family Systems." *Family Systems and Health* 15, 3: 243–50.

Richmond, C. 2009. "Explaining the Paradox of Health and Social Support among Aboriginal Canadians." *Canadian Issues* (winter): 65–71.

—— and N.A. Ross. 2008. "Social Support, Material Circumstance and Health Behaviour: Influences on Health in First Nation and Inuit Communities of Canada." *Social Science and Medicine* 67: 1423–33.

Royal Canadian Mounted Police (RCMP). 2014. *Missing and Murdered Aboriginal Women: A National Operational Overview*. Ottawa: Her Majesty the Queen in Right of Canada.

Royal Commission on Aboriginal Peoples (RCAP). 1996. *Report of the Royal Commission on Aboriginal Peoples*. Ottawa: Canada Communication Group.

Rutherdale, M. 2002. *Women and the White Man's God: Gender and Face in the Canadian Mission Field*. Vancouver: University of British Columbia Press.

Salee, D., with D. Newhouse and C. Levesque. 2006. "Quality of Life of Aboriginal people in Canada: An Analysis of Current Research." *IRPP Choices* 12, 6: 1–38.

Sinha, V., N. Trocmé, B. Fallon, B. MacLaurin, E. Fast, and S. Prokop. 2011. *Kiskisik Awasisak: Remember the Children. Understanding the Overrepresentation of First Nations Children in the Child Welfare System*. Ontario: Assembly of First Nations. http://cwrp.ca/sites/default/files/publications/en/FNCIS-2008_March2012_RevisedFinal.pdf.

Smith, Andrea. 2005.*Conquest: Sexual Violence and American Indian Genocide*. Cambridge, Mass.: South End Press.

Smylie, J., and P. Adomako. 2009. *Indigenous Children's Health Report: Health Assessment in Action*. Toronto: Centre for Research on Inner City Health. www.crich.ca.

Statistics Canada. 2001. *A Portrait of Aboriginal Children Living in Non-Reserve*

Areas: Results from the 2001 Aboriginal Peoples Survey. Catalogue no. 89-597-XIe. Ottawa: Statistics Canada.

———. 2003. Aboriginal Peoples of Canada: Highlight Tables, 2001 Census. Ottawa: Statistics Canada.

———. 2006. "Census of Population 2006." www.statcan.gc.ca.

———. 2009. "Selected Findings from 2006 Aboriginal Children's Survey. First Nations People, Métis in Canada, Inuit in Canada." Canadian Social Trends, special issue. Catalogue no. 11-008. Ottawa: Statistics Canada.

———. 2011a. Population Projections by Aboriginal Identity in Canada, 2006–2031. Catalogue no. 91-552-X. http://www.statcan.gc.ca/pub/91-552-x/91-552-x2011001-eng.pdf.

———. 2011b. The Educational Attainment of Aboriginal Peoples in Canada. Catalogue no. 99-012-X2011003. http://www12.statcan.gc.ca/nhs-enm/2011/as-sa/99-012-x/99-012-x2011003_3-eng.pdf.

———. 2013. Aboriginal Peoples in Canada: First Nations People, Métis and Inuit. National Household Survey, 2011. www12.statcan.gc.ca/nhs-enm/2011/as-sa/99-011-x/99-011-x2011001-eng.pdf.

Stote, Karen. 2012. "The Coercive Sterilization of Aboriginal Women in Canada." American Indian Culture and Research Journal 36, 3: 117–50.

Stremlau, R. 2005. "To Domesticate and Civilize Wild Indians: Allotment and the Campaign to Reform Indian Families, 1875–1887." Journal of Family History 30, 3: 265–86.

Tjepkema, Michael, and Russell Wilkins. 2011. "Remaining Life Expectancy at Age 25 and Probability of Survival to Age 75, by Socio-economic Status and Aboriginal Ancestry." Health Reports 22, 4. Ottawa: Statistics Canada Catalogue no. 82-003-X. http://www.statcan.gc.ca/pub/82-003-x/2011004/article/11560-eng.pdf.

Torpy, Sally J. 2000. "Native American Women and Coerced Sterilization on the Trail of Tears in the 1970s." American Indian Culture and Research Journal 24, 2: 1–22.

Trocme, N., et al. 2005. The Experience of First Nations Children Coming into Contact with the Child Welfare System in Canada: The Canadian Incidence Study on Reported Child Abuse and Neglect. Ottawa: First Nations Child and Family Caring Society.

——— et al.. 2006. Mesnmimk Wasatek—Catching a Drop of Light. Understanding the Overrepresentation of First Nations Children in Canada's Child Welfare System. CIS-2003. http://www.fsin.com/healthandsocial/childportal/images/mesnmimk%20wasatek%20Catching%20a%20Drop%20of%20Light.pdf.

UNICEF Canada. 2009. Canadian Supplement to the State of the World's Children 2009: Aboriginal Children's Health: Leaving No Child Behind. Toronto: UNICEF Canada.

Truth and Reconciliation Commission of Canada. 2012. TRC Interim Report. Ottawa: Government of Canada.

———. 2012. Canada, Aboriginal Peoples and Residential Schools: They Came for the Children. Ottawa: Government of Canada.

Van Kirk, S. 1980. Many Tender Ties: Women in Fur-Trade Society in Western Canada, 1670–1870. Winnipeg: Watson and Dwyer.

Volo, J.M., and D.D. Volo. 2007. Family Life in Native America. Westport, Conn.: Greenwood.

Weitzman, M. 2003. "Low Income and Its Impact on Psychosocial Child Development." In Encyclopedia on Early Childhood Development, 1–8. Montreal: Centre of Excellence for Early Childhood Development.

Wemigwans, J., prod./dir. 2002. Seven Fires (feature video). Available from V-tape.org, Toronto.

Wesley-Esquimaux, C.C., and M. Smolewski. 2003. *Historic Trauma and Aboriginal Healing.* Ottawa: Aboriginal Healing Foundation Research Series.

Chapter 6

Acoose, Janice. 1995. *Iskwewak—kah' ki yaw ni wahkomakanak: Neither Indian Princesses nor Easy Squaws.* Toronto: Toronto Women's Press.

Albers, Patricia, and Beatrice Medicine, eds. 1983. *The Hidden Half: Studies of Plains Indian Women.* New York: University Press of America.

Allen, Paula Gunn. 1992. *The Sacred Hoop: Recovering the Feminine in American Indian Traditions.* Boston: Beacon Press.

Ambler, Stella. 2014. *Invisible Women: A Call to Action. Report on Missing and Murdered Indigenous Women in Canada.* Ottawa: Queen's Printer.

Amnesty International. 2006. *Stolen Sisters.* Ottawa: Amnesty International. http://www.amnesty.ca/campaigns/sisters_overview.php.

Atcheson, M. Elizabeth. 1984. *Women and Legal Action: Precedents, Resources and Strategies for the Future.* Ottawa: Canadian Advisory Council on the Status of Women.

Brown, Judith. 1982. "Cross-cultural Perspectives on Middle-aged Women." *Current Anthropology* 23: 143–53.

Boyer, Yvonne. 2009. "The First Nations Women's Contribution to Culture and Community through Canadian Law." In Gail Guthrie Valaskakis, Madeleine Dion Stout, and Eric Guimond, eds, *Restoring the Balance: First Nations Women, Community, and Culture,* 69–96. Winnipeg, University of Manitoba Press.

CBC News. 2000. "Full Text of Jack Ramsay Sentence," 4 May. Accessed 30 Aug. 2014. www.cbc.ca/news/canada/full-text-of-jack-ramsay-sentence-1.204386.

———. 2001. "Ramsay Sentenced to Probation, Community Service," 16 Oct. Accessed 30 Aug. 2014. www.cbc.ca/news/canada/ramsay-sentenced-to-probation-community-service-1.26955.

Connell, R.W. 2002. *Gender: Short Introductions.* Oxford: Polity Press.

Dickason, Olive Patricia. 1992. *Canada's First Nations: A History of Founding Peoples from Earliest Times.* Toronto: McClelland & Stewart.

Ezzo, David A. 1988. "Female Status and the Life Cycle: A Cross-cultural Perspective from Native North America." In William Cowan, ed., *Papers of the Nineteenth Algonquian Conference,* 137–44. Ottawa: Carleton University Press.

Faludi, Susan. 1991. *Backlash: The Undeclared War against American Women.* New York: Anchor Books.

Fiske, Joanne. 1990–1. "Native Women in Reserve Politics: Strategies and Struggles." *Journal of Legal Pluralism* 30–1: 121–37.

Francis, Daniel. 1993. *The Imaginary Indian.* Vancouver: Arsenal Pulp Press.

Gerber, Linda M. 1990. "Multiple Jeopardy: A Socio-economic Comparison of Men and Women among the Indian, Métis and Inuit Peoples of Canada." *Canadian Ethnic Studies* 22, 69–80.

Harper, Anita Olson. 2009. "Sisters in Spirit." In Gail Guthrie Valaskakis, Madeleine Dion Stout, and Eric Guimond, eds, *Restoring the Balance: First Nations Women, Community, and Culture,* 175–99. Winnipeg: University of Manitoba Press.

Hogg, Peter W. 1992. *Constitutional Law of Canada.* Scarborough, Ont.: Carswell.

Holmes, Joan. 1987. *Bill C-31 Equality or Disparity: The Effects of the New Indian Act on Native Women.* Ottawa: Canadian Advisory Council on the Status of Women.

Indian and Northern Affairs Canada. 1990. *Impacts of the 1985 Amendments,* Vol. 5, *Summary Report.*

——. 2009. "Minister Chuck Strahl Speech, Government of Canada Reintroduces Legislation to Provide Matrimonial Real Property Rights on Reserves." Ottawa: Indian and Northern Affairs Canada. http://www.ainc-inac.gc.ca/ai/mr/nr/j-a2009/nr000000176-eng.asp.

Jamieson, Kathleen. 1978. *Indian Women and the Law in Canada: Citizens Minus.* Ottawa: Minister of Supply and Services Canada.

Justice Canada. 1995. *Technical Report. Violence against Persons Who Prostitute, the Experience in British Columbia.* Ottawa: Justice Canada.

Kehoe, Alice. 1983. "The Shackles of Tradition." In Patricia Albers and Beatrice Medicine, eds, *The Hidden Half: Studies of Plains Indian Women,* 53–76. New York: University Press of America.

LeBlanc, Daniel. 2014. "List of Missing, Killed Aboriginal Women Involves 1200 Cases." *Globe and Mail,* 1 May: A1.

McDonald, Michael. 1987. "Indian Status: Colonialism or Sexism?" *Canadian Community Law Journal* 9: 23–48.

Mann, Barbara Alice. 2000. *Iroquian Woman: The Ganowisas.* New York: Peter Lang.

Native Women's Association of Canada. 1991. *Native Women and the Charter: A Discussion Paper.* Ottawa: Native Women's Association of Canada.

——. 2007. *Reclaiming Our Way of Being: Matrimonial Real Property Solutions Position Paper.* Ottawa: Native Women's Association of Canada.

——. 2008. *Sisters in Spirit Initiative Literature Review.* Ottawa: Native Women's Association of Canada. www.nwac.ca/en/documents SIS Literature Review _March2008_Final.pdf.

Paul, Pamela Marie. 1993. "The Trojan Horse: An Analysis of the Social, Economic and Political Reaction of First Nations People as a Result of Bill C-31." Master's thesis, University of New Brunswick.

Quinless, Jacqueline. 2012. "Aboriginal Women in the Canadian Economy— The Links between Education, Employment, and Income." Ottawa: Statistics Canada, Catalogue no. R3-161/2012 E.

Royal Canadian Mounted Police (RCMP). 2014. *Missing and Murdered Aboriginal Women: A National Operational Overview.* Ottawa: RCMP, Catalogue no. PS 64-115/20148E-PDF.

Silman, Janet. 1987. *Enough Is Enough: Aboriginal Women Speak Out.* Toronto: Women's Press.

Stacey-Moore, Gail. 1993. "In Our Own Voice." *Herizons, Women's News and Feminist Views* 6, 4: 21–3.

Statistics Canada. 2008. *Aboriginal Peoples in Canada in 2006: Inuit, Métis and First Nations, 2006 Census.* http.//www12.statcan.ca/census-recensement/2006/as-sa/97-558/p17-eng.cfm#02.

——. 2008. "Aboriginal Women in Canada, a Statistical Profile from the 2006 Census." *Census of Canada, 2006.* Ottawa: Statistics Canada.

——. 2010. "Projected Life Expectancy at Birth by Sex, by Aboriginal Identity, 2017." Catalogue no. 91-547-XIE. Ottawa: Minister of Industry.

Supreme Court of Canada. 1970. *Drybones v. Canada (Minister of Indian and Northern Affairs),* [1970] 2 S.C.R., 282.

——. 1974. *Attorney General of Canada v. Lavell and Bedard,* [1974] 2 S.C.R., 1349.

——. 1999. *Corbiere v. Canada (Minister of Indian and Northern Affairs),* [1999,] 2 S.C.R., 203.

Tsosie, Rebecca. 1988. "Changing Women: The Cross Currents of American Indian Feminine Identity." *American Indian Culture and Research Journal* 12, 1: 1–31.

Venne, Sharon. 1981. *Indian Act Amendments, 1868–1975.* Saskatoon: University of Saskatchewan Native Law Centre.

Voyageur, Cora J. 1993. "An Analysis of the University of Alberta's Transition Year

Program, 1985–1992." Master's thesis, University of Alberta.

———. 2008. *Firekeepers of the 21st Century: First Nation Women Chiefs*. Montreal and Kingston: McGill-Queen's University Press.

Wesley-Esquimaux, Cynthia. 2010. "Trauma to Resilience: Notes on Decolonization." In Gail Guthrie Valaskakis, Madeleine Dion Stout and Eric Guimond, eds, *Restoring the Balance: First Nations Women, Community, and Culture*, 13–34. Winnipeg: University of Manitoba Press.

Wherret, Jill. 1996. *Indian Status and Band Membership Issues*. Ottawa: Library of Parliament, Parliamentary Information and Research Service. Catalogue no. BP-410 E.

Williams, Robert. 1990. "Gendered Checks and Balances: Understanding the Legacy of White Patriarchy in an American Indian Cultural Context." *Georgia Law Review* 24: 1019–44.

Chapter 7

Alfred, T. 2000. "Deconstructing the British Columbia Treaty Process." http://web.uvic.ca/igov/uploads/pdf/GTA.bctreatyprocess.pdf.

———. 2005. *Wasáse: Indigenous Pathways to Action and Freedom*. Toronto: University of Toronto Press.

Allen, Paula Gunn. 1986. *The Sacred Hoop: Recovering the Feminine in American Indian Traditions*. Boston: Beacon Press.

Anderson, K. 2000. *A Recognition of Being: Reconstructing Native Womanhood*. Toronto: Sumach Press.

———. 2011. *Life Stages and Native Women: Memory, Teachings, and Story Medicine*. Winnipeg: University of Manitoba Press.

Borrows, J. 2007. *Recovering Canada: The Resurgence of Indigenous Law*. Toronto: University of Toronto Press.

Campbell, M. 1998. "Jacob." In Daniel David Moses and Terry Goldie, eds, *An Anthology of Canadian Native Literature in English*, 2nd edn, 129–36. Toronto: Oxford University Press.

Connell, R.W. 2005. "Change among the Gatekeepers: Men, Masculinities and Gender Equality." *Signs: Journal of Women in Culture and Society* 30, 3: 1801–25.

———. 2011. *Confronting Equality: Gender, Knowledge and Global Change*. Cambridge: Polity Press.

Corntassel, J. (2008). "Toward Sustainable Self-Determination: Rethinking the Contemporary Indigenous-Rights Discourse." *Alternatives* 33: 105–32.

Fanon, F. 1963. *The Wretched of the Earth*. New York: Grove Press.

———. 1969. *Toward the African Revolution*. New York: Grove Press.

Hokowhitu, B. 2012. "Producing Elite Indigenous Masculinities." *Settler Colonial Studies* 2, 2: 2–22.

Kennedy, Mark. 2014. "Stephen Harper Blasted for Remarks on Missing and Murdered Aboriginal Women." *Ottawa Citizen*, 23 Aug. http://ottawacitizen.com/news/national/stephen-harper-blasted-for-remarks-on-missing-and-murdered-aboriginal-women.

Manuel, George, and Michael Posluns. 1974. *The Fourth World: An Indian Reality*. Don Mills, Ont.: Collier Macmillan Canada.

Maracle, Lee. 1996. *I Am Woman: A Native Perspective on Sociology and Feminism*. Vancouver: Press Gang.

Memmi, A. 1991. *The Colonizer and the Colonized*. Boston: Beacon Press.

Palmater, P. 2011. *Beyond Blood: Rethinking Indigenous Identity*. Saskatoon: Purich.

Swift, J. 2011. "Si:ya:m Governance, Colonial Interference, and Contemporary Challenges Facing Cheam Leadership." http://web.uvic.ca/igov/index.php/igov-598-community-governance-project.

Tengan, T.P.K. 2008. *Native Men Remade: Gender and Nation in Contemporary Hawaii.* Durham, NC: Duke University Press.

United Nations General Assembly. 1948. *Convention on the Prevention and Punishment of the Crime of Genocide.* http://www.hrweb.org/legal/genocide.html.

Chapter 8

Aboriginal Affairs and Northern Development Canada (AANDC). 2013. "Registered Indian Population by Sex and Residence, 2012." Ottawa: Statistics and Measurement Directorate, AANDC.

Angel, L. 1984. "Health as a Crucial Factor in the Changes from Hunting to Developed Farming in the Eastern Mediterranean." In M.N. Cohen and G.J. Armelagos, eds, *Paleopathology at the Origins of Agriculture,* 51–73. Orlando, Fla: Academic Press.

Atleo, Shawn. 2009. "AFN National Chief Responds to Prime Minister's Statements on Colonialism," press release. http://www.afn.ca.

Beaujot, Roderic, and Don Kerr. 2004. *Population Change in Canada,* 2nd edn. Toronto: Oxford University Press.

Belshaw, John Douglas. 2009. *Becoming British Columbia: A Population History.* Vancouver: University of British Columbia Press.

Boserup, Ester. 1965. *The Conditions of Agricultural Growth.* Chicago: Aldine.

Boxhill, W. 1984. "Limitations of the Use of Ethnic Origin Data to Quantify Visible Minorities in Canada." Working paper prepared for Statistics Canada, Housing, Family and Social Statistics Division.

Boyd, Robert. 1992. "Population Decline from Two Epidemics on the Northwest Coast." In *Disease and Demography in the Americas.* Washington: Smithsonian Institution Press.

Boyd, Robert. 1990. "Demographic History, 1774–1874." In W. Sturtevant, ed., *Handbook of North American Indians,* vol. 7: *Northwest Coast,* 135–48. Washington: Smithsonian Institution.

Chackiel, Juan, and Alexia Peyser. 1993. "Indigenous Population from Latin American National Censuses." Paper presented at the International Union for Scientific Study of Population Conference, Montreal, Aug.

Charbonneau, Hubert. 1984. "Trois siècles de dépopulation amérindienne." In L. Normandeau and V. Piché, eds, *Les populations amérindienne et Inuit du Canada,* 28–48. Montreal: Les presses de l'Université de Montréal.

—— and A. Larose. 1979. *The Great Mortalities: Methodological Studies of Demographic Crises in the Past.* Liège: Ordina.

Clatworthy, S.J. 2003. "Re-assessing the Population Impacts of Bill C–31 Section 6." In Jerry White, Paul Maxim, Paul Whitehead, and Dan Deavon, eds, *The Aboriginal Condition: Research Foundations for Public Policy.* Vancouver: University of British Columbia Press.

——. 2009. *Recent Trends in the Demographic Characteristics of First Nations Populations in Canada.* Ottawa: Strategic Research, Indian and Northern Affairs Canada.

Cooke, Martin, and Dan Beavon. 2007. "The Registered Indian Human Development Index, 1981-2001." In Jerry White, Dan Beavon, and Nicholas Spence, eds, *Aboriginal Well-Being: Canada's Continuing Challenge.* Toronto: Thompson Educational Publishers.

—— and Éric Guimond. 2009. "Measuring Changing Human Development in First Nations Populations: Preliminary Results of the 1981–2006 Registered Indian Human Development Index." *Canadian Diversity* 7: 53–72.

——, P. Wilk, K. Paul, and S. Gonneville. 2013. "Predictors of Obesity among

Métis Children: Socio-economic, Behavioural and Cultural Factors." *Canadian Journal of Public Health* 104, 4.

Cybulski, J.S. 1994. "Culture Change, Demographic History, and Health and Disease on the Northwest Coast." In C.S. Larsen and G.R. Milner, eds, *In the Wake of Contact: Biological Responses to Conquest*, 75–85. New York: Wiley-Liss.

Daniels, J. 1992. "The Indian Population of North America in 1492." *William and Mary Quarterly* 49: 298–320.

Department of Health and Social Services, Nunavut. 2004. *Nunavut Report of Comparable Health Indicators*. Iqaluit: Government of Nunavut, Nunavut Health and Social Services.

Dickason, Olive Patricia. 1992. *Canada's First Nations: A History of Founding Peoples from Earliest Times*. Toronto: Oxford University Press.

Dickason, Olive Patricia, and William Newbigging. 2015. *A Concise History of Canada's First Nations*, 3rd edn. Toronto: Oxford University Press.

Dobyns, H. 1983. *Their Number Become Thinned: Native American Population Dynamics in Easter North America*. Knoxville: University of Tennessee Press.

Eschbach, Karl. 1995. "The Enduring and Vanishing American Indian: American Indian Population Growth and Intermarriage in 1990." *Ethnic and Racial Studies* 18: 89–108.

Frideres, James S. 1998. *Aboriginal Peoples in Canada*. Scarborough, Ont.: Prentice-Hall.

—— and Rene Gadacz. 2012. *Aboriginal Peoples in Canada*. Toronto: Prentice-Hall.

Goddard, I. 1996. *Languages: Handbook of North American Indians*. Washington: Smithsonian Institution Press.

Goldmann, Gustave. 1998. "Shifts in Ethnic Origins among the Offspring of Immigrants: Is Ethnic Mobility a Measurable Phenomenon?" *Canadian Ethnic Studies* 30: 121–48.

Goldmann, Gustave, and Andy Siggner. 1995. "Statistical Concepts of Aboriginal People and Factors Affecting the Counts in the Aboriginal Peoples Survey." In *Towards the Twenty-First Century: Emerging Socio-Demographic Trends and Policy Issues in Canada*, 265–80. Ottawa: Federation of Canadian Demographers.

Guimond, Eric. 2003. "Fuzzy Definitions and Population Explosion: Changing Identities of Aboriginal Groups in Canada." In David Newhouse and Evelyn Peters, eds, *Not Strangers in These Parts: Aboriginal People in Cities*, 35–50. Ottawa: PRI.

Harris, M., and E. Ross. 1987. *Death, Sex and Fertility: Population Regulation in Pre-industrial and Developing Societies*. New York: Columbia University Press.

Health Canada. 2009. *Drinking Water Advisories in First Nations Communities in Canada—A National Overview*. Ottawa: Health Canada, Catalogue no. H34-208/2009E.

Hout, Michael, and Joshua Goldstein. 1994. "How 4.5 Million Irish Immigrants Became 40 Million Irish Americans: Demographic and Subjective Aspects of Ethnic Composition of White Americans." *American Sociological Review* 59: 64–82.

Indian and Northern Affairs Canada (INAC). 1999. *Basic Departmental Data 1998*. Ottawa: INAC.

——. 2000. *Registered Indian Population Projections for Canada and Regions, 1998–2008*. Ottawa: INAC.

——. 2005. *Basic Departmental Data 2004*. Ottawa: INAC.

——. 2009. "Discussion Paper on Needed Changes to the Indian Act Affecting Indian Registration and Band Membership McIvor v. Canada." Ottawa: Minister of Indian Affairs and Northern

Development and Federal Interlocutor for Métis and Non-Status Indians.

Jain, A., and J. Bongaarts. 1981. "Breast-feeding: Patterns, Correlates and Fertility Effects." *Studies in Family Planning* 12: 79–99.

Jenness, D. 1977. *The Indians of Canada*. Toronto: University of Toronto Press.

Katzenburg, M.A., and S.R. Saunders, eds. 2000. *Biological Anthropology of the Human Skeleton*. New York: Wiley-Liss.

Lieberson, Stanley, and Mary C. Waters. 1988. *From Many Strands: Ethnic and Racial Groups in Contemporary America*. New York: Russell Sage Foundation.

—— and ——. 1993. "The Ethnic Responses of Whites: What Causes Their Instability, Simplification, and Inconsistency." *Social Forces* 72: 421–50.

Loh, S., R. Verma, E. Ng, M.J. Norris, M.V. George, and J. Perreault. 1998. "Population Projections of Registered Indians, 1996–2021." Working paper. Ottawa: Statistics Canada.

Malenfant, Éric Caron, and Jean-Dominique Morency. 2011. *Population Projections by Aboriginal Identity in Canada 2006 to 2031*. Ottawa: Statistics Canada, Catalogue no. 91-552-X.

Martel, Laurent. 2013. "Mortality Overview." In *Report on the Demographic Situation in Canada*. Ottawa: Statistics Canada, Catalogue no. 91-209-X.

Mercredi, Ovide. 1997. "Written Transcript of Conversation, Subject: Royal Commission on Aboriginal Peoples." National Press Theatre, 30 Apr.

Meuvret, J. 1965. "Demographic Crisis in France from the Sixteenth to the Eighteenth Century." In D. Glass and D. Eversley, eds, *Population in History*. London: Edward Arnold.

Mooney, J. 1928. *The Aboriginal Population of America North of Mexico*. Washington: Smithsonian Miscellaneous Collections 80: 1–40.

Morrison, W. 1984. *Under One Flag: Canadian Sovereignty and the Native Peoples of Northern Canada*. Ottawa: Treaties and Historical Research Centre.

Muckle, Bob. 2007. *The First Nations of British Columbia*. Vancouver: University of British Columbia Press.

Nault, F., J. Chen, M.V. George, and M.J. Norris. 1993. *Population Projections of Registered Indians, 1991–2016*. Ottawa: Statistics Canada.

Norris, Mary Jane. 2000. "Contemporary Demography of Aboriginal Peoples in Canada." In David Long and Olive Patricia Dickason, eds, *Visions of the Heart: Canadian Aboriginal Issues*. Toronto: Harcourt Canada.

——, Don Kerr, and François Nault. 1995. *Technical Report on Projections of the Population with Aboriginal Identity, Canada, 1991–2016*. Report prepared by the Population Projections Section, Demography Division, Statistics Canada, for the Royal Commission on Aboriginal Peoples. Ottawa: Statistics Canada.

Passel, Jeffrey. 1997. "The Growing American Indian Population, 1960–1990: Beyond Demography." *Population Research and Policy Review* 16: 11–31.

Peters, Paul A. 2013. "An Age and Cause Decomposition of Differences in Life Expectancy between Residents of Inuit Nunangat and Residents of the Rest of Canada, 1989 to 2008." *Health Reports* 24: 3–9.

Penney, Christopher. 2013. *Aboriginal Data as a Result of Changes to the 2011 Census of Population*. Ottawa: Strategic Research Directorate with the collaboration of Statistics Canada and the Statistics and Measurement Directorate of AANDC.

Ram, Bali. 2004. "New Estimates of Aboriginal Fertility, 1966–1971 to 1996–2001." *Canadian Studies in Population* 31: 179–96.

Robitaille, N., and R. Choinière. 1985. *An Overview of Demographic and Socioeconomic Conditions of the Inuit in Canada.* Ottawa: Department of Indian and Northern Affairs.

Romaniuc, Anatole. 1981. "Increase in Natural Fertility during the Early Stages of Modernization: Canadian Indian Case Study." *Demography* 18: 157–72.

——. 2000. "Aboriginal Population of Canada: Growth Dynamics under Conditions of Encounter of Civilizations." *Canadian Journal of Native Studies* 20: 95–137.

Royal Commission on Aboriginal Peoples (RCAP). 1996. *People to People, Nation to Nation: Highlights from the Report of the Royal Commission on Aboriginal Peoples.* Ottawa: Indian and Northern Affairs Canada. Catalogue no. Z1-1991/1-6E.

Saunders, S., P. Ramsden, and D. Herring. 1992. "Transformation and Disease: Pre-contact Ontario Iroquoians." In J. Verano and D. Ubelaker, eds, *Disease and Demography in the Americas.* Washington: Smithsonian Institution Press.

Savard, R., and J. Proulx. 1982. *Canada: derrière l'épopée, les autochtones.* Montreal: L'hexagone.

Siggner, Andy, and Gustave Goldmann. 1995. "Statistical Concepts of Aboriginal People and Factors Affecting the Counts in the Census and the Aboriginal Peoples Survey." *In Towards the Twenty-First Century: Emerging Socio-Demographic Trends and Policy Issues in Canada.* Ottawa: Federation of Canadian Demographers.

——, Annette Vermaeten, Chris Durham, Jeremy Hull, Eric Guimond, and Mary Jane Norris. 2001. "New Developments in Aboriginal Definitions and Measures." Presentation at the Canadian Population Society meetings, Quebec City.

Singman, Jeffrey. 1999. *Daily Life in Medieval Europe.* Westport, Conn.: Greenwood Press.

Snipp, Matthew. 1989. *American Indians: The First of the Land.* New York: Russell Sage Foundation.

Statistics Canada. 1999. "Life Expectancy." *Health Reports* 11: 9–24.

——. 2008a. *Aboriginal Peoples in Canada in 2006: Inuit, Métis and First Nations, 2006 Census.* Ottawa: Statistics Canada, Catalogue no. 97-558-XIE.

——. 2008b. CANSIM Table 051-0004.

——. 2009. "Persons Registered under the Indian Act, by Province and Territory." Census of Population Special Table.

——. 2012a. *Births.* Ottawa: Statistics Canada, Catalogue no. 84F0210X.

——. 2012b. *Final Report on 2016 Census Options: Proposed Content Determination Framework and Methodology Options.* Ottawa: Census Management Office, 2016 Census Strategy Project.

——. 2013a. National Household Survey (NHS), "Aboriginal Population: Data Tables Aboriginal Ancestry." Catalogue no. 99-011-X2011029.

——. 2013b. National Household Survey (NHS), *Aboriginal Peoples in Canada: First Nations People, Métis and Inuit.* Ottawa: Statistics Canada, Catalogue no. 99-011-X2011001.

——. 2013c. *Annual Demographic Estimates: Canada, Provinces and Territories.* Ottawa: Statistics Canada, Catalogue no. 91-215-X.

Steckel, Richard H., and Jerome C. Rose, eds. 2002. *The Backbone of History: Health and Nutrition in the Western Hemisphere.* New York: Cambridge University Press.

Stewart, T. 1973. *The People of America.* New York: Scribner's.

Sturtevant, W.C. 2006. *Handbook of North American Indians.* Washington: Smithsonian Institution Press.

Teillet, Jean. 2010. *Métis Law in Canada 2010*. Toronto: Pape Salter Teillet LLP.

Thornston, R. 1987. *American Indian Holocaust and Survival: A Population History since 1492*. Norman: University of Oklahoma Press.

———. 2000. "Population of Native North Americans." In M. Haines and R. Steckel, eds, *A Population History of North America*. Cambridge: Cambridge University Press.

Tjepkema, Michael, Russell Wilkins, Sacha Senécal, Éric Guimond, and Christopher Penney. 2009. "Mortality of Métis and Registered Indian Adults in Canada: An 11-Year Follow-up Study." *Health Reports* 20: 1–21.

Trovato, Frank. 2000. "Canadian Indian Mortality during the 1980s." *Social Biology* 47: 135–45.

———. 2001. "Aboriginal Mortality in Canada, the United States and New Zealand." *Journal of Biosocial Science* 33: 67–86.

Ubelaker, D.H. 1976. "Prehistoric New World Population Size: Historical Review and Current Appraisal of North American Estimates." *American Journal of Physical Anthropology* 45: 661–6.

———. 2000. "Patterns of Disease in Early North American Populations." In M. Haines and R. Steckel, eds, *A Population History of North America*, 51–98. Cambridge: Cambridge University Press.

United Nations Development Program (UNDP). 2012. *United Nations Development Report*. New York: UNDP.

Van Lerberghe, Wim, and Vincent De Brouwere. 2001. "Of Blind Alleys and Things That Have Worked: History's Lessons on Reducing Maternal Mortality." In Vincent De Brouwere and Wim Van Lerberghe, eds, *Safe Motherhood Strategies: A Review of the Evidence*, 7–33. Antwerp, Belgium: ITG Press.

Waldram, James, Ann Herring, T. Kue Young. 2006. *Aboriginal Health in Canada: Historical, Cultural and Epidemiological Perspectives*. Toronto: University of Toronto Press.

Weiss, K. l973. "Demographic Models for Anthropology." *Memoirs of the Society for American Archaeology*, no. 27. Washington: American Antiquity.

Wells, Spencer. 2010. *Pandora's Seed: The Unforeseen Cost of Civilization*. New York: Random House.

Wilkins, Russell, Michael Tjepkema, Cameron Mustard, and Robert Choinière. 2008a. "The Canadian Census Mortality Follow-up Study, 1991 through 2001." *Health Reports* 19: 25–43.

———, Sharanjit Uppal, Philippe Finès, Sacha Senécal, Éric Guimond, and Rene Dion. 2008b. "Life Expectancy in the Inuit-inhabited Areas of Canada, 1989 to 2003." *Health Reports* 19, 1: 7–19.

Williamson, R.F., and S. Pfeiffer. 2003. *Bones of Our Ancestors: The Archaeological and Osteobiography of the Moatfield Ossuary*. Mercury Series, Archaeology Paper 163. Ottawa: Canadian Museum of Civilization.

Young, K.T. 1994. *The Health of Native Americans: Towards a Biocultural Epidemiology*. New York: Oxford University Press.

Chapter 9

Abley, Mark. 2003. *Spoken Here: Travels among Endangered Languages*. Toronto: Random House of Canada.

Ball, Jessica. 2009. "Aboriginal Young Children's Language Development: Promising Practices and Needs." *Canadian Issues* (winter).

———, Ken Moselle, and Sarah Moselle. 2013. *Contributions of Culture and Language in Aboriginal Head Start in Urban and Northern Communities to Children's Health Outcomes: A Review of Theory and Research*. Prepared for Division of Children, Seniors & Healthy Development, Health Promotion and Chronic

Disease Prevention Branch. Ottawa: Public Health Agency of Canada.

Beck, David, and Thom Hess. 2014. *Tellings from Our Elders: Lushootseed syeyehub*, Vol. 1: *Snohomish Texts*. Vancouver: University of British Columbia Press. http://www.ubcpress.ca/search/title_book.asp?BookID=299173834.

Blair, Heather, Jacqueline Filipek, and Martin Zeidler. 2013. "Addressing Joshua Fishman's Ideological Clarification: Working with Pre-service Teachers." In Norris et al. (2013: 146–9).

Blythe, J., and R. McKenna Brown. 2003. *Maintaining the Links: Language, Identity and the Land*. Proceedings of the 7th Conference of the Foundation for Endangered Languages. Broome, Western Australia, 22–4 Sept.

Canadian Heritage. 2005. *Towards a New Beginning: A Foundation Report for a Strategy to Revitalize First Nation, Inuit and Métis Languages and Cultures*. Report to the Minister of Canadian Heritage by the Task Force on Aboriginal Languages and Cultures, June 2005. Catalogue no. CH4-96/2005. Ottawa: Canadian Heritage.

Carl, John, and Marc Belanger. 2012. *Think Sociology*, 1st Canadian edn. Toronto: Pearson.

Chandler, M.J. 2006. "Cultural Continuity in the Face of Radical Social Change: Language Preservation as a Protective Factor against Suicide in First Nations Youth." Paper presented at Raising Our Voices, Language Conference, Cornwall, Ont., 15 Aug.

Chandler, M.J., and C.E. Lalonde. 2008. "Cultural Continuity as a Protective Factor against Suicide in First Nations Youth." *Horizons* 10, 1: 68–72.

Clatworthy, Stewart. 2003. "Impacts of the 1985 Amendments to the Indian Act on First Nations Populations." In *Aboriginal Conditions: Research as a Foundation for Public Policy*, ed. Jerry P. White, Paul S. Maxim and Dan Beavon, 63-90. Vancouver: UBC Press.

Cloutier, Stéphane. 2013. "Uqausivut: Our Language—Implementing Made-in-Nunavut Language Legislation." In Norris et al. (2013: 14–17).

Crystal, David. 2000. *Language Death*. Cambridge: Cambridge University Press.

Fillerup, M. 2000. "Racing against Time: A Report of the Leupp Navajo Immersion Project." In J. Reyhner, J. Martin, L. Lockard, W. Gilbert, eds, *Learn in Beauty: Indigenous Education for a New Century*, 21–34. Flagstaff: Northern Arizona University.

Fishman, J.A. 1996. "What Do You Lose When You Lose Your Language?" In G. Cantoni, ed., *Stabilizing Indigenous Languages*, 86–91. Flagstaff: Northern Arizona University.

Fonda, Marc. 2009. "Towards Cultural Well-being: Implications of Revitalising Traditional Aboriginal Religions." *Canadian Issues* (winter).

Grenoble, Lenore A. 2013. "The Arctic Indigenous Language Initiative: Assessment, Promotion, and Collaboration." In Norris et al. (2013: 80–7).

Grenoble, L.A., & Whaley, L.J., eds. 1998. *Endangered languages: Current issues and future prospects*. Cambridge, UK: Cambridge University Press.

Guèvremont, Anne, and Dafna Kohen. 2012. "Speaking an Aboriginal Language and School Outcomes for Children and Adults." *International Journal of Bilingual Education and Bilingualism* 15, 1: 1–27.

Hare, Jan. 2011. "Learning from Indigenous Knowledge in Education." In David Long and Olive P. Dickason, eds, *Visions of the Heart: Canadian Aboriginal Issues*, 3rd edn, 90–112. Toronto: Oxford University Press.

Harrison, Brian, and Mary Jane Norris. 2012. "Influences on Aboriginal and Immigrant Language Groups in Canada: Some Similarities and Differences." *Canadian Issues* (summer).

Hinton, L. 2001. "The Use of Linguistic Archives in Language Revitalization."

In L. Hinton and K. Hale, eds, *The Green Book of Language Revitalization in Practice*, 419–23. San Diego and London: Academic Press.

Kinkade, M.D. 1991. "The Decline of Native Languages in Canada." In Robert H. Robins and Eugenius M. Uhlenbeck, eds, *Endangered Languages*. Oxford: Berg.

McCarty, Teresa L. 2012. "Indigenous Languages and Cultures in Native American Student Achievement." In Beverly J. Klug, ed., *Standing Together: American Indian Education as Culturally Responsive Pedagogy*, 97–119. Lanham, Md: Rowman & Littlefield.

McIvor, Onowa. 2013. "Protective Effects of Language Learning, Use and Culture on the Health and Well-being of Indigenous People in Canada." In Norris et al. (2013: 123–31).

Martin, K. 2003. "Ways of knowing, being and doing: A theoretical framework and methods for Indigenous and Indigenist re-search." *Journal of Australian Studies*, 76, 203-14.

Morris, Lori, and Marguerite Mackenzie, 2013. "Using all the Pieces to Solve the Puzzle: The Importance of Aboriginal Language Assessment in Child Populations." In Norris et al. (2013: 170–77).

Moseley, Christopher, ed. 2007. *Encyclopedia of the World's Endangered Languages*. London and New York: Routledge.

——, ed. 2010. *Atlas of the World's Languages in Danger*, 3rd edn. Paris: UNESCO. http://www.unesco.org/culture/en/endangeredlanguages/atlas.

Norris, M.J. 1998. "Canada's Aboriginal Languages." *Canadian Social Trends* 51 (winter). Catalogue. no. 11-008. Ottawa: Statistics Canada.

——. 2000. "Aboriginal Peoples in Canada: Demographic and Linguistic Perspectives." In D.A. Long and O.P. Dickason, eds, *Visions of the Heart: Canadian Aboriginal Issues*, 2nd edn. Toronto: Harcourt Brace Canada.

——. 2003. "From Generation to Generation: Survival and Maintenance of Canada's Aboriginal Languages within Families, Communities and Cities." In J. Blythe and R. McKenna Brown, eds, *Maintaining the Links: Language, Identity and the Land*. Proceedings of the 7th Conference of the Foundation for Endangered Languages, Broome, Western Australia, 22–4 Sept.

——. 2006. "Aboriginal Languages in Canada: Trends and Perspectives on Maintenance and Revitalization." In J.P. White, S. Wingert, D. Beavon, and P. Maxim, eds, *Aboriginal Policy Research: Moving Forward, Making a Difference*. Toronto: Thompson Educational Publishing.

——. 2007. "Aboriginal Languages in Canada: Emerging Trends and Perspectives on Second Language Acquisition." *Canadian Social Trends* 83 (summer):19–27.www.statcan.ca/english/freepub/11-008-XIE/2007001/pdf/11-008-XIE20070019628.pdf.

——. 2008. "Voices of Aboriginal Youth Today: Keeping Aboriginal Languages Alive for Future Generations." In "Hope or Heartbreak: Aboriginal Youth and Canada's Future." A joint collaboration between the Government of Canada's Policy Research Initiative and the Research and Analysis Directorate at Indian and Northern Affairs Canada. http://policyresearch.gc.ca/doclib/HOR_v1on1_200803_e.pdf.

——. 2009a. "Linguistic Classifications of Aboriginal Languages in Canada: Implications for Assessing Language Diversity, Endangerment and Revitalization." *Canadian Diversity: Quarterly Journal of the Association for Canadian Studies* 7, 3: 21–34.

——. 2009b. "The Role of First Nations Women in Language Continuity and Transition." In Gail Guthrie Valaskakis, Madeleine Dion Stout, and Eric

Guimond, eds, *Restoring the Balance: First Nations Women, Community and Culture.* Winnipeg: University of Manitoba Press.

——. 2010. "Canada and Greenland." In Moseley (2010).

——. 2011a. "Aboriginal Languages in Canada: Generational Perspectives on Language Maintenance, Loss and Revitalization." In David Long and Olive P. Dickason, eds, *Visions of the Heart: Canadian Aboriginal Issues*, 3rd edn, 113–48. Toronto: Oxford University Press.

——. 2011b. "Aboriginal Languages in Urban Canada: A Decade in Review, 1996 to 2006." *Aboriginal Policy Studies* 1, 2: 4–67. http://ejournals.library. ualberta.ca/index.php/aps/article/ view/8965.

——. 2013a. "Trends in the State of Aboriginal Languages in Canada, 1981 to 2011: A Census-based Analysis of Language Vitality and Endangerment." Unpublished paper, Department of Canadian Heritage, Ottawa.

——. 2013b. *Assessing the Vitality of Arctic Indigenous Languages: Development of a Canada-based Data and Mapping Approach.* www.articlanguages.com.

——, Erik Anonby, Marie-Odile Junker, Nicholas Ostler, and Donna Patrick, eds. 2013. *Endangered Languages beyond Boundaries: Community Connections, Collaborative Approaches and Cross-Disciplinary Research.* Proceedings of the 17th FEL Conference. Ottawa, 1–4 Oct. 2013. Bath, England: Foundation for Endangered Languages.

—— and L. Jantzen. 2002. Poster: "From Generation to Generation: Survival and Maintenance of Canada's Aboriginal Languages within Families, Communities and Cities." http://dsp-psd.pwgsc. gc.ca/Collection/R2-234-2002E.pdf.

—— and ——. 2003. "Aboriginal Languages in Canada's Urban Areas:

Characteristics, Considerations and Implications." In David Newhouse and Evelyn Peters, eds, *Not Strangers in These Parts: Urban Aboriginal Peoples*, 93–117. Ottawa: Policy Research Initiative.

—— and Karen MacCon. 2003. "Aboriginal Language Transmission and Maintenance in Families: Results of an Intergenerational and Gender-based Analysis for Canada, 1996." In Jerry White, Paul Maxim, and Dan Beavon, eds, *Aboriginal Conditions: The Research Foundations of Public Policy.* Vancouver: University of British Columbia Press.

—— and M. Snider. 2008. "Endangered Aboriginal Languages in Canada: Trends, Patterns and Prospects in Language Learning." In Tjeerd de Graaf, Nicholas Ostler, and Reinier Salverda, eds, *Endangered Languages and Language Learning.* Proceedings of the XII Conference of the Foundation for Endangered Languages, Fryske Academy and Mercator European Research Centre, Leeuwarden, The Netherlands, 24–7 Sept. http://recherchepolitique. gc.ca/doclib/AboriginalBook_e.pdf.

Perley, Bernard C. 2011. *Defying Maliseet Language Death: Emergent Vitalities of Language, Culture, and Identity in Eastern Canada.* Lincoln: University of Nebraska Press.

Royal Commission on Aboriginal Peoples (RCAP). 1996. *Report, vol. 3, Gathering Strength*, and vol. 4, *Perspectives and Realities.* Ottawa: Minister of Supply and Services Canada.

Sarkar, Mela, Janine Metallic, Beverly Baker, Constance Lavoie, and Teresa Strong-Wilson. 2013. "Siawinnu'gina'masultinej: A Language Revitalization Initiative for Mi'gmaq in Listuguj, Canada." In Norris et al. (2013: 39–46).

Soria, Claudia, Carlo Zoli, and Joseph Mariani. 2013. "Dwarfs Sitting on Giants' Shoulders: How LTS for Regional and

Minority Languages Can Benefit from Piggybacking on Major Languages." In Norris et al. (2013: 73–9).

Statistics Canada. 2003. *Aboriginal Peoples Survey 2001 Initial Findings: Well-being of the Non-Reserve Aboriginal Population.* Catalogue no. 89-589-XIE. Ottawa: Minister of Industry. www.statcan.gc.ca/pub/89-589-x/89-589-x2003001-eng.pdf.

——. 2008. *Aboriginal Peoples in Canada in 2006: Inuit, Métis and First Nations, 2006 Census.* Catalogue no. 97-558-XIE. Ottawa: Minister of Industry. http://www12.statcan.ca/english/census06/analysis/aboriginal/pdf/97-558-XIE2006001.pdf.

Tompkins, Joanne, Anne Murray-Orr, Sherise Paul-Gould, Starr Sock Roseanne Clark, and Darcie Pirie. 2013: "An Inquiry into Two Aboriginal Language Immersion Programs." In Norris et al. (2013: 138–44).

Tulloch, Shelley. 2005. "Inuit Youth: The Future of Inuktitut." In R.O. van Everdingen, comp., *Proceedings of the 14th Inuit Studies Conference*, 11–15 Aug. 2004, 285–300. Calgary: Arctic Institute of North America, University of Calgary. http://pubs.aina.ucalgary.ca/aina/14thISCProceedings.pdf.

——. 2008. "Uqausirtinnik annirusunniq—Longing for Our Language." *Horizons* 10, 1: 763–7.

UNESCO. 1996. *Atlas of the World's Languages in Danger of Disappearing.* Ed. Stephen A. Wurm. Paris: UNESCO.

——. 2003. "Language Vitality and Endangerment." Paper prepared by UNESCO Ad Hoc Expert Group on Endangered Languages submitted to the International Expert Meeting on UNESCO Programme Safeguarding of Endangered Languages, Paris, Mar. www.unesco.org/culture/ich/doc/src/00120-EN.pdf.

Wesley-Esquimaux, Cynthia, and Magdalena Smolewski. 2004. *Historic Trauma and Aboriginal Healing.* Ottawa: Aboriginal Healing Foundation

Chapter 10

Aboriginal Healing Foundation. 2009. *Response, Responsibility and Renewal: Canada's Truth and Reconciliation Journey.* Ottawa: Aboriginal Healing Foundation.

Alfred, A. 2004. *Paddling to Where I Stand.* Ed. M.J. Reid, trans. D. Sewid-Smith. Toronto: University of Toronto Press.

Alfred, T. 2009. "Restitution Is the Real Pathway to Justice for Indigenous Peoples." In Aboriginal Healing Foundation, *Response, Responsibility, and Renewal: Canada's Truth and Reconciliation Journey*, 179–87. Ottawa: Aboriginal Healing Foundation.

Amagalik, J. 2012. "Reconciliation or Conciliation? An Inuit Perspective." http://speakingmytruth.ca/v2a/?page_id=266.

Archibald, J. 2008. *Indigenous Storywork: Educating the Heart, Mind, Body, and Spirit.* Vancouver: University of British Columbia Press.

Archibald, Lundy, Reynolds, and Williams. 2010. *Accord on Indigenous Education.* Association of Canadian Deans of Education.

Assembly of First Nations (AFN). 1994. *Breaking the Silence: An Interpretive Study of Residential School Impact and Healing as Illustrated by the Stories of First Nations Individuals.* Ottawa: AFN.

Assembly of First Nations. 2011. "2011 AFN School Survey Results." http://www.afn.ca/uploads/files/education2/education-survey-results.pdf.

Barnhardt, R., and A.O. Kawagley. 2005. "Indigenous Knowledge Systems and Alaska Native Ways of Knowing." *Anthropology and Education Quarterly* 36, 1: 8–23.

Battiste, M. 2000. *Reclaiming Indigenous Voice and Vision.* Vancouver: University of British Columbia Press.

———. 2002. *Indigenous Knowledge and Pedagogy in First Nations Education: A Literature Review with Recommendations*. Ottawa: National Working Group on Education, Indian Affairs and Northern Development Canada.

———. 2005. "Indigenous Knowledge: Foundations for First Nations." *World Indigenous Nations Higher Education Consortium Journal*. www.win-hec.org/docs/pdfs/Journal/Marie%20Battiste%copy.pdf.

Bougie, E., K. Kelly-Scott, and P. Arriagada. 2013. *The Education and Employment Experiences of First Nations People Living Off Reserve, Inuit, and Métis: Selected Findings from the 2012 Aboriginal Peoples Survey*. Ottawa: Statistics Canada, Social and Aboriginal Statistics Division. http://www.statcan.gc.ca/pub/89-653-x/89-653-x2013001-eng.pdf.

Brayboy, B. Mc. J., and E. Maughan. 2009. Indigenous Knowledges and the Story of the Bean." *Harvard Educational Review* 79, 1: 1–21.

Cajete, G. 2000. *Look to the Mountain: An Ecology of Indigenous Education*. Durango, Colo.: Kivaki Press.

Canon, M. 2012. "Changing the Subject in Teacher Education: Centering Indigenous, Diasporic, and Settler Colonial Relations." *Cultural and Pedagogical Inquiry* 4, 2: 21–37.

Colleges and Institutes Canada. 2014. "Indigenous Protocol for Colleges and Institutes." http://www.collegesinstitutes.ca/the-issues/indigenous-learners/approaches-and-exemplary-practices-to-guide-implementation/.

Congress of Aboriginal Peoples. 2010. *Staying in School: Engaging Aboriginal Students*. http://www.abo-peoples.org/wp-content/uploads/2012/10/Stay-In-School-LR.pdf.

Corntassel, J., et al. 2009. "Indigenous Card on Aboriginal Education in British Columbia." *Studies in Education Policy Occasional Paper*. Vancouver: Fraser Institute.

Cowley, P., and S. Easton. 2004. *Report Embrace: The Abduction of First Nations Children and the Restoration of Aboriginal Communities*. Vancouver: Douglas & McIntyre.

Davin, N.F. 1879. *Report on Industrial Schools for Indians and Half-Breeds*. Ottawa.

Dickason, O.P. 1984. *The Myth of the Savage and the Beginnings of French Colonialism in the Americas*. Edmonton: University of Alberta Press.

——— and W. Newbigging. 2015. *A Concise History of Canada's First Nations*, 3rd edn. Toronto: Oxford University Press.

Fournier, S., and E. Crey. 2004. "Stolen from Our Storytelling, Truth-Telling, and Community Approaches to Reconciliation." *English Studies in Canada* 35, 1: 137–59.

Furniss, E. 1995. *Victims of Benevolence: The Dark Legacy of Williams Lake Residential School*. Vancouver: Arsenal Pulp Press.

Glavin, T. 2002. *Among God's Own: The Enduring Legacy of St. Mary's Mission*. Vancouver: New Star Books.

Grant, A. 2004. *Finding My Talk: How Fourteen Women Reclaimed Their Lives after Residential School*. Calgary: Fifth House.

Haig-Brown, C. 1988. *Resistance and Renewal: Surviving the Indian Residential School*. Vancouver: Tillicum Library.

Hallet, D., M. Chandler, and C. Lalonde. 2007. "Aboriginal Language Knowledge and Youth Suicide." *Cognitive Development* 22, 3: 392–9.

Hare, J. 2003. "September 11 and Its Aftermath: A Roundtable. Is the Bingo Palace Burning?" *Journal of Women in Culture and Society* 29, 2: 58991.

———. 2005. "To Know Papers: Aboriginal Perspectives on Literacy." In J. Anderson,

M. Kendrick, T. Rogers, and S. Smythe, eds, *Portraits of Literacy across Families, Communities and Schools: Tensions and Intersections*, 243–63. Mahwah, NJ: Lawrence Erlbaum.

——. 2007. "Aboriginal Education Policy in Canada: Building Capacity for Change and Control." In R. Joshee and L. Johnson, eds, *Multicultural Education Policies in Canada and the United States*, 51–68. Seattle: University of Washington Press/University of British Columbia Press.

——. 2011. "Learning from Indigenous Knowledge in Education." In D. Long and O.P. Dickason, eds, *Visions of the Heart: Canadian Aboriginal Issues*, 3rd edn, 90–112. Toronto: Oxford University Press.

—— and J. Barman. 2000. "Aboriginal Education: Is There a Way Ahead?" In D. Long and O.P. Dickason, eds, *Visions of the Heart: Canadian Aboriginal Issues*, 2nd edn, 331–59. Toronto: Harcourt Brace.

—— and ——. 2007. *Good Intentions Gone Awry: Emma Crosby and the Methodist Mission on the Northwest Coast*. Vancouver: University of British Columbia Press.

Harper, S. 2008. "Prime Minister Stephen Harper's Statement of Apology." http://www.cbc.ca/news/canada/prime-minister-stephen-harper-s-statement-of-apology-1.734250.

Hermes, M. 2007. "Moving toward the Language: Reflections on Teaching in an Indigenous Immersion School." *Journal of American Indian Education* 46, 3: 54–71.

Indian Chiefs of Alberta. 1970. *Citizens Plus*. Edmonton: Indian Association of Alberta.

Ing, N.R. 1991. "The Effects of Residential Schools on Native Child-rearing Practices." *Canadian Journal of Native Education* 18: 65–118.

Jaine, L., ed. 1993. *Residential Schools: The Stolen Years*. Saskatoon: University Extension Press, University of Saskatchewan.

Knockwood, I. 1992. *Out of the Depths: The Experiences of the Mi'kmaw Children of the Indian Residential School at Shubenacadie, Nova Scotia*. Lockeport, NS: Roseway.

Kulchyski, P., D. McCaskill, and D. Newhouse, eds. 1999. *In the Words of Elders: Aboriginal Cultures in Transition*. Toronto: University of Toronto Press.

Logan, T. 2012. "A Métis Perspective on Truth and Reconciliation: Reflections of a Métis Researcher." http://speakingmytruth.ca/downloads/AHFvol1/06_Logan.pdf.

McCarty, T. 2003. "Revitalising Indigenous Languages in Homogenising Times." *Comparative Education* 39, 2: 147–63.

McIvor, O. 2009. "Strategies for Indigenous Language Revitalization and Maintenance." http://literacyencyclopedia.ca/index.php?fa=items.show&topicId=265.

Manitoba Education. 2011. *Grade 12 Current Topics in First Nations, Métis, and Inuit Studies: A Foundation for Implementation*. http://www.edu.gov.mb.ca/k12/abedu/foundation_gr12/full_doc.pdf.

Mendelson, M. 2006. *Improving Education on Reserves: A First Nations Education Authority Act*. Ottawa: Caledon Institute of Social Policy.

Miller, J.R. 1996. *Shingwauk's Vision: A History of Native Residential Schools*. Toronto: University of Toronto Press.

Milloy, J.S. 1999. *A National Crime: The Canadian Government and the Residential School System, 1879–1986*. Winnipeg: University of Manitoba Press.

Morin, H. 2004. "Student Performance Data and Research Tools to Ensure Aboriginal Student Success." www.bced.gov.bc/abed/research/ab_student_success.pdf.

National Indian Brotherhood (NIB). 1972. *Indian Control of Indian Education*. Ottawa: NIB.

Nuu-chah-nulth Tribal Council. 1996. *Indian Residential Schools: The Nuu-chah-nulth Experience: Report of the Nuu-chah-nulth Tribal Council Indian Residential School Study, 1992–1994.* Port Alberni, BC: Nuu-chah-nulth Tribal Council.

Ontario Ministry of Education. 2007. *First Nation, Métis, and Inuit Education Policy Framework.* Toronto: Ontario Ministry of Education.

———. 2013. *A Solid Foundation: Second Progress Report on the Implementation of the Ontario First Nation, Métis, and Inuit Education Policy Framework.* Toronto: Ontario Ministry of Education.

Oritz, S. 1992. *Woven Stone.* Tucson: University of Arizona Press.

Preston, J.P., M. Cottrell, T. Pelletier, and J.V. Pearce. 2012. "Aboriginal Early Childhood Education in Canada: Issues of Context." *Journal of Early Childhood Research* 10, 3: 3–18.

Public Health Agency of Canada. 2012. "Evaluation of the Aboriginal Headstart in Northern Communities Program at the Public Health Agency of Canada." http://www.phac-aspc.gc.ca/about_apropos/evaluation/reports-rapports/2011-2012/ahsunc-papacun/index-eng.php#toc.

Royal Commission on Aboriginal Peoples (RCAP). 1996. *Report of the Royal Commission on Aboriginal Peoples, vol. 1, Looking Forward, Looking Back.* Ottawa: Minister of Supply and Services Canada.

Regan, P. 2010. *Unsettling the Settler Within: Indian Residential Schools, Truth Telling, and Reconciliation in Canada.* Vancouver: University of British Columbia Press.

Reyhner, J., O. Trujilio, R. Carrasco, and L. Lockard, eds. 2003. *Nurturing Native Languages.* Flagstaff: Northern Arizona University.

Saul, J.R. 2009. "Reconciliation: Four Barriers to Paradigm Shifting." In Aboriginal Healing Foundation, *Response, Responsibility, and Renewal: Canada's Truth and Reconciliation Journey*, 311–20. Ottawa: Aboriginal Healing Foundation.

Secwepemc Cultural Education Society. 2000. *Behind Closed Doors. Stories from the Kamloops Indian Residential School.* Kamloops, BC: Secwepemc Cultural Education Society.

Statistics Canada. 2013. Statistics Canada, Employment and Social Development Canada, and Council of Ministers of Education. *Skills in Canada: First Results from the Programme for the International Assessment of Competencies (PIAAC)*, Table B.3.1 "Literacy—Averages and Proficiency Levels of Population Aged 16–65, by Aboriginal Identification, Canada and Oversampled Populations, 2012." Catalogue no. 89-555-X. Ottawa, 2013.

——— and Council of Ministers of Education. 2006. *Education Indicators in Canada: Report of the Pan-Canadian Education Indicators Program 1999.* Ottawa: Statistics Canada.

Task Force on Aboriginal Languages and Cultures. 2005. *Towards a New Beginning: A Foundational Report for a Strategy to Revitalize First Nation, Inuit, and Métis Languages and Cultures.* Ottawa: Canadian Heritage, Aboriginal Affairs.

Teacher Education Office, University of British Columbia. n.d. "NITEP—The Indigenous Teacher Education Program." http://teach.educ.ubc.ca/bachelor-of-education-program/nitep.

United Nations. 2008. *United Nations Declaration on the Rights of Indigenous Peoples.* http://www.un.org/esa/socdev/unpfii/documents/DRIPS_en.pdf.

Usborne, E., J. Peck, D. Smith, and D. Taylor. 2011. "Learning through an Aboriginal Language: The Impact on Students' English and Aboriginal Language Skills." *Canadian Journal of Education* 34, 4: 200–15.

Villegas, M., S.R. Neugebauer, and K.R. Venegas, eds. 2008. *Indigenous Knowledge and Education: Sites of Struggle, Strength, and Survivance.* Cambridge, Mass.: Harvard Educational Press.

Chapter 11

Alcoff, Linda Martin. 1995. "The Problem of Speaking for Others." In Linda A. Bell and David Blumenfeld, eds, *Overcoming Racism and Sexism*, 229–54. Lanham, Md: Rowman & Littlefield.

Alfred, Taiaiake. 2005. *Wasáse: Indigenous Pathways of Action and Freedom.* Peterborough, Ont.: Broadview Press.

—— and Jeff Corntassel. 2005. "Being Indigenous: Resurgences against Contemporary Colonialism." *Government and Opposition* 40, 4: 597–614.

Armstrong, Jeanette. 1997. "Sharing One Skin: Native Canadian Jeanette Armstrong Explains How the Global Economy Robs Us of Our Full Humanity." *New Internationalist Magazine* (Jan.–Feb.). Accessed 10 Oct. 2014. http://newint.org/features/1997/01/05/sharing.

——. 1999. "Let Us Begin with Courage." Center for Ecoliteracy. Accessed 6 Mar. 2015. http://www.ecoliteracy.org/essays/let-us-begin-courage.

Belcourt, Christi. "Artist Description of 'Giniigaaniimenaaning.'" Aboriginal Affairs and Northern Development. Accessed 27 Oct. 2014. https://www.aadnc-aandc.gc.ca/eng/1339417945383/1339418457202.

Bennett, Jill. 2005. *Emphatic Vision: Affect, Trauma, and Contemporary Art.* Stanford, Calif.: Stanford University Press.

Boer, T.A. 2004. "Reconciling South Africa or South Africans? Cautionary Notes from the TRC." *African Studies Quarterly* 8, 1: 19–37.

Castellano, Marlene Brant. 2000. "Updating Aboriginal Traditions of Knowledge." In G.J.S. Dei, B.L. Hall, and D.G. Rosenberg, eds, *Indigenous Knowledges in Global Contexts: Multiple Readings of Our World*, 21–36. Toronto: OISE/University of Toronto Press.

——. 2006. *Final Report of the Aboriginal Healing Foundation, vol. 1: A Healing Journey: Reclaiming Wellness.* Ottawa: Aboriginal Healing Foundation.

——, Linda Archibald, and Mike DeGagné, eds. 2008. *From Truth to Reconciliation: Transforming the Legacy of Residential Schools.* Ottawa: Aboriginal Healing Foundation.

Chrisjohn, Roland, and Sherri Young. 1997. *The Circle Game: Shadows and Substance in the Indian Residential School Experience in Canada.* Penticton, BC: Theytus Books.

Dewar, Jonathan. 2011. David Garneau interview.

——. 2011. Armand Garnet Ruffo interview, 31 Oct.

——. Alex Janvier interview.

——. 2014. Christi Belcourt interview.

——. 2011. Jeannette Armstrong interview.

——. 2011. Maria Campbell interview.

Dickason, O.P., with D.T. McNab. 2009. *Canada's First Nations: A History of Founding Peoples from Earliest Times*, 4th edn. Toronto: Oxford University Press.

Gaertner, David. 2011. "'The Climax of Reconciliation': Transgression, Apology, Forgiveness and the Body in Conflict Resolution." *Journal of Bioethical Inquiry* 1, 1 (8 July). Accessed 16 Oct. 2014. http://rmooc.ca/wp-content/uploads/2013/07/gaertner.pdf.

Garneau, David. 2012. "Imaginary Spaces of Conciliation and Reconciliation." *Reconcile This! West Coast Line 74* 46, 2: 28–38

Gedi, Noa, and Yigal Elam. 1996. "Collective Memory—What Is It?" *History and Memory* 8, 1 (Spring–Summer): 30–50.

Gillis, John R. 1994. "Memory and Identity: The History of a Relationship." In Gillis, ed., *Commemorations: The Politics of National Identity*, 3–24. Princeton, NJ: Princeton University Press.

Gordon, Alan. 2001. *Making Public Pasts: The Contested Terrain of Montréal's Public Memories, 1891–1930*. Montreal and Kingston: McGill-Queen's University Press.

Govier, Trudy. 2003. "What Is Acknowledgement and Why Is It Important?" In Carol A.L. Prager and Trudy Govier, eds, *Dilemmas of Reconciliation: Cases and Concepts*, 65–89 Waterloo, Ont.: Wilfrid Laurier University Press.

Haig-Brown, Celia. 1988. *Resistance and Renewal: Surviving the Indian Residential School*. Vancouver: Arsenal Pulp Press.

Halbwachs, Maurice. 1992. *On Collective Memory*. Trans. Lewis Coser. Chicago: University of Chicago Press.

Handler, Richard. 1994. "Is 'Identity' a Useful Cross-Cultural; Concept." In John R. Gillis, ed., *Commemorations: The Politics of National Identity*, 27–40. Princeton, NJ: Princeton University Press.

Harper, Stephen. 2008. "Prime Minister Harper Offers Full Apology on Behalf of Canadians for the Indian Residential Schools System." Accessed 11 July 2013. https://www.aadnc-aandc.gc.ca/eng/1100100015644/1100100015649.

Hauss, Charles. 2003. "Reconciliation." In G. Burgess and H. Burgess, eds, *Beyond Intractability*. Boulder: University of Colorado Conflict Information Consortium. Accessed 16 Oct. 2014. www.beyond-intractability.org/essay/reconciliation.

Huffstetter, Stephen. 1998. *Lakota Grieving*. St. Joseph's Indian School, South Dakota: Tipi Press.

LaRocque, Emma. 2010. *When the Other Is Me: Native Resistance Discourse, 1850–1990*. Winnipeg: University of Manitoba Press.

Lederach, John Paul. 2005. *The Moral Imagination: The Art and Soul of Building Peace*. New York: Oxford University Press.

Levine, Stephen K. 1997. *Poiesis: The Language of Psychology and the Speech of the Soul*. London: Jessica Kingsley.

Levy, Daniel. 1999. "The Future of the Past: Historiographical Disputes and Competing Memories in Germany and Israel." *History and Theory* 38, 1: 51–66.

Llewellyn, Jennifer. 2008. "Bridging the Gap between Truth and Reconciliation: Restorative Justice and the Indian Residential Schools Truth and Reconciliation Commission." In Castellano et al. (2008).

McNiff, Shawn. 2004. *Art Heals: How Creativity Cures the Soul*. Boston: Shambhala.

Million, Dian Lynn. 2004. "Telling Secrets: Sex, Power and Narrative in the Rearticulation of Canadian Residential School Histories." Ph.D. dissertation, University of California, Berkeley.

Milloy, John. S. 1999. *A National Crime*. Winnipeg: University of Manitoba Press.

Minnow, Martha. 1998. *Between Vengeance and Forgiveness: Facing History after Genocide and Mass Violence*. Boston: Beacon Press.

Nora, Pierre. 1989. "Between Memory and History: Les Lieux de Memoire." Trans. Marc Roudebush. *Representations* 26: 7–25.

Osborne, Brian S. 1998. "Constructing Landscapes of Power: The George-Etienne Cartier Monument, Montréal." *Journal of Historical Geography* 24, 4: 431–58.

——. 2001. "Landscapes, Memory, Monuments, and Commemoration: Putting Identity in Its Place." *Canadian Ethnic Studies* 30, 3: 39–86.

Rice, Brian, and Anna Snyder. 2008. "Reconciliation in the Context of a Settler Society: Healing the Legacy of Colonialism in Canada." In Castellano et al. (2008: 43-61).

Ryan, Allan J. 1999. *The Trickster Shift: Humour and Irony in Contemporary Native*

Art. Vancouver: University of British Columbia Press.

Savage, Kirk. 1994. "The Politics of Memory: Black Emancipation and the Civil War Monument." In John R. Gillis, ed., *Commemorations: The Politics of National Identity*, 127–49. Princeton, NJ: Princeton University Press: 1994.

Simon, Roger I. 2004. "The Pedagogical Insistence of Public Memory." In Peter Seixas, ed., *Theorizing Historical Consciousness*, 181–201. Toronto: University of Toronto Press.

Smith, Linda Tuhiwai. 1999. *Decolonizing Methodologies: Research and Indigenous Peoples*. London: Zed Books.

Spivak, Gayatri Chakravorty. 1988. "Can the Subaltern Speak?" In Cary Nelson and Lawrence Grossberg, eds, *Marxism and the Interpretation of Culture*, 271–316. Champaign: University of Illinois Press.

Torpey, John. 2003. "Introduction: Politics and the Past." In Torpey, ed., *Politics and the Past: On Repairing Historical Injustices*, 5–7. Lanham, Md: Rowman & Littlefield.

Townsend-Gault, Charlotte. 1999. "Hot Dogs, a Ball Gown, Adobe, and Words: The Modes and Materials of Identity." In W. Jackson Rushing III, ed., *Native American Art in the Twentieth Century*, 113–33. New York: Routledge.

Truth and Reconciliation Commission of Canada (TRC). n.d. "Open Call for Artistic Submissions." http://www.trc.ca/websites/trcinstitution/index.php?p=194.

Vizenor, Gerald. 1999. *Manifest Manners: Narratives on Postindian Survivance*. Lincoln: University of Nebraska Press.

Weaver, Jace. 1997. *That the People Might Live: Native American Literatures and Native American Community*. Oxford: Oxford University Press.

Webster's Revised Unabridged Dictionary. 2009. Accessed 10 Apr. 2009. http://dictionary1.classic.reference.com/browse/reconciliation.

Wolschke-Bulmahn, Joachim, ed. 2001. *Places of Commemoration: Search for Identity and Landscape Design*. Washington: Dumbarton Oaks.

Chapter 12

Aboriginal Affairs and Northern Development Canada (AANDC). 1964 [1876]. *Copy of Treaty No. 6 between Her Majesty the Queen and the Plain and Wood Cree Indians and Other Tribes at Fort Carlton, Fort Pitt and Battle River with Adhesions*. Last modified 30 Aug. 2013, accessed 27 Feb. 2015. https://www.aadnc-aandc.gc.ca/eng/1100100028710/1100100028783.

——.2013. Aboriginal Demographics from the 2011 National Household Survey. https://www.aadnc-aandc.gc.ca/eng/1370438978311/1370439050610.

Adelson, Naomi. 1998. "Health Beliefs and the Politics of Cree Well-being." *Health* 2, 1: 5–22.

Anderson, Ian. 2007. "Understanding the Processes." In Bronwyn Carson et al., eds, *Social Determinants of Indigenous Health*, 21–40. Crows Nest, New South Wales: Allen and Unwin.

Assembly of First Nations (AFN). 2006. *Royal Commission on Aboriginal Peoples at 10 years: A Report Card*. Ottawa: AFN.

Berkman, L.A., and I. Kawachi. 2000. "A Historical Framework for Social Epidemiology." In Berkman and I. Kawachi, eds, *Social Epidemiology*, 3–12. New York: Oxford University Press.

Blackstock, C. 2003. Interview at Canadian Council on Social Development Social Inclusion and Social Policy Conference.

Bonilla-Silva, E., and T. Zuberi. 2008. "Toward a Definition of White Logic and White Methods." In T. Zuberi and E. Bonilla-Silva, *White Logic, White*

Methods: Racism and Methodology, 3–30. Plymouth, UK: Rowman & Littlefield.

Bramley, D., et al. 2004. "Indigenous Disparities in Disease-Specific Mortality, a Cross-Country Comparison: New Zealand, Australia, Canada, and the United States." *New Zealand Medical Journal* 117, 1207: U1215.

Caldwell, John. 2006. *Demographic Transition Theory*. Dordrecht: Springer.

Cammer, Alison Lee. 2006. "Negotiating Culturally Incongruent Healthcare Systems: The Process of Accessing Dementia Care in Northern Saskatchewan." In *College of Community Health and Epidemiology*, 116. Saskatoon: University of Saskatchewan.

Canadian Institute for Health Information (CIHI). 2003. *Seven Years Later: An Inventory of Population Health Policy since the Royal Commission on Aboriginal Peoples 1996–2003*. Ottawa: CIHI.

Canadian Public Health Association. 1996. "Action Statement for Health Promotion in Canada." www.cpha.ca/en/programs/policy/action.aspx.

Clark, M., P. Riben, and E. Nowgesic. 2002. "The Association of Housing Density, Isolation and Tuberculosis in Canadian First Nations Communities." *International Journal of Epidemiology* 31: 940–5.

Clement, J. 2008. "University Attainment of the Registered Indian Population, 1981–2001: A Cohort Approach." *Horizons* 10, 1: 34–48.

Cooke, M., et al. 2007. "Indigenous Wellbeing in Four Countries: An Application of the UNDP's Human Development Index to Indigenous Peoples in Australia, Canada, New Zealand, and the United States." *BMC International Health and Human Rights* 7: 9.

Dyck, R.F., H. Klomp, and L. Tan. 2001. "From 'Thrifty Genotype' to 'Hefty Fetal Phenotype': The Relationship between High Birth Weight and Diabetes in Saskatchewan Registered Indians." *Canadian Journal of Public Health* 92: 340–4.

Eggertson, Laura. 2006. "Safe Drinking Water Standards for First Nations Communities." *Canadian Medical Association Journal* 174: 1248.

Eichler, M. 1997. *Family Shifts: Families Policies and Gender Equality*. Toronto: Oxford University Press.

Episkenew, Jo-Ann, and Winona Wheeler. 2002. "A Brief to Propose a National Indigenous Research Agenda." Presented to the Social Science and Humanities Research Council.

Fee, Margery. 2006. "Racializing Narratives: Obesity, Diabetes and the 'Aboriginal' Thrifty Genotype." *Social Science and Medicine* 62: 2988–97.

Ferris, P., et al. 2005. *Promising Practices in First Nations Adolescent Child Welfare Management and Governance*. Weechi-it-te-win Family Services, Sept.

Flicker, Sarah, et al. 2008. "A Snapshot of Community-based Research in Canada: Who? What? Why? How?" *Health Education Research* 23: 106–14.

Fox, T., and D. Long. 2000. "Struggles with the Circle: Violence, Healing and Health on a First Nations Reserve." In D. Long and O. Dickason, eds, *Visions of the Heart: Canadian Aboriginal Issues*, 2nd edn, 271–301. Toronto: Harcourt Canada.

Go, C.G., et al. 1995. "Ethnic Trends in Survival Curves and Mortality." *Gerontologist* 35: 318–26.

Guimond, Eric, Don Kerr, and Roderic Beaujot. 2004. "Charting the Growth of Canadian Aboriginal Populations: Problems, Options and Implications." *Canadian Studies in Population* 31: 33–82.

Hawe, P., and A. Shiell. 2000. "Social Capital and Health Promotion: A Review." *Social Science and Medicine* 51: 871–85.

Health Canada. 2005. "Ten Years of Health Transfer First Nation and Inuit Control." Ottawa: Health Canada.

——. 2009. "Non-Insured Health Benefits for First Nations and Inuit." www.hc-sc.gc.ca/fniah-spnia/nihb-ssna/index-eng.php.

——. 2014. "First Nations and Inuit Health: Drinking Water Advisories in First Nations Communities." http://www.hc-sc.gc.ca/fniah-spnia/promotion/public-publique/water-dwa-eau-aqep-eng.php.

Indian and Northern Affairs Canada. 2005. *Basic Departmental Data 2004.* Ottawa: First Nations and Northern Statistics Section, Corporate Information Management Directorate, Information Management Branch.

Interagency Advisory Panel on Research Ethics. 2011. *TCPS 2–2nd Edition of the Tri-Council Policy Statement: Ethical Conduct for Research Involving Humans.* Ottawa: Interagency Secretariat on Research Ethics. http://www.pre.ethics.gc.ca/eng/policy-politique/initiatives/tcps2-eptc2/Default.

Lalonde, Marc. 1972. *A New Perspective on the Health of Canadians.* Ottawa: Department of National Health and Welfare.

Littlechild, Wilton, and Danika Littlechild. 2009. *The Treaty Right to Health: The Case of Treaty No. 6 in Alberta and Saskatchewan.* Brief presented to the Assembly of Treaty Chiefs. Feb.

Liu, Juan, et al. 2006. "Lifestyle Variables, Non-Traditional Cardiovascular Risk Factors, and the Metabolic Syndrome in an Aboriginal Canadian Population." *Obesity* 14: 500–8.

Long, D. 2004. "On Violence and Healing: Aboriginal Experiences, 1969–1993." In Jeffrey Ian Ross, ed., *Violence in Canada: Socio-political Perspectives*, 2nd edn, 40–77. Toronto: Oxford University Press.

——. 2009. *All Dads Matter: Towards an Inclusive Vision for Father Involvement Initiatives in Canada.* Guelph, Ont.: Father Involvement Research Alliance.

http://www.fira.ca/cms/documents/176/April7.Long.PDF.

—— and B. LaFrance. 2004. "Pursuing the Truth with Care: Aboriginal Research Issues." *Canadian Journal of Native Studies* (Spring): 1–5.

Macaulay, A., L.E. Commanda, W.L. Freeman, N. Gibson, M.L. McCabe, and C.M. Robbons. 1999. "Participatory Research Maximises Community and Lay Involvement." *British Medical Journal* 319: 774–8.

McDowell, I. 2008. "From Risk Factors to Explanation in Public Health." *Journal of Public Health* 30: 219–23.

MacMillan, H.L., et al. 2003. "The Health of Ontario First Nations People: Results from the Ontario First Nations Regional Health Survey." *Canadian Journal of Public Health* 94: 168–72.

McNaughton, Craig, and Darrel Rock. 2004. "Opportunities in Aboriginal Research: Results of SSHRC's Dialogue on Research and Aboriginal Peoples." *Canadian Journal of Native Studies* (spring): 37–60.

McPherson, Dennis. 2005. "Indian on the Lawn: How Are Research Partnerships with Aboriginal People Possible?" *American Philosophical Association Newsletter* 5, 2: 1–12.

Marmot, M.G., M.J. Shipley, and G. Rose. 1984. "Inequalities in Death—Specific Explanations of a General Pattern?" *Lancet* 1, 8384: 1003–6.

Michelle, Chino, and DeBruyn Lemyra. 2006. "Building True Capacity: Indigenous Models for Indigenous Communities." *American Journal of Public Health* 96: 596.

Munro, Gordon. 2004. "Comparing Risk Behaviours among Urban and Rural Youth by Grade, Grades 7 to 12: The Alberta Youth Experience Survey 2002." *Canadian Research Index.*

Muntaner, C., and J. Lynch. 1999. "Income Inequality, Social Cohesion, and Class

Relations: A Critique of Wilkinson's Neo-Durkheimian Research Program." *International Journal of Health Services* 29: 59–81.

——, ——, and G.D. Smith. 2001. "Social Capital, Disorganized Communities, and the Third Way: Understanding the Retreat from Structural Inequalities in Epidemiology and Public Health." *International Journal of Health Services* 31: 213–37.

National Aboriginal Health Organization. 2006. *First National Regional Longitudinal Health Survey (RHS) 2002/3: Report on Process and Methods*. Ottawa: National Aboriginal Health Organization.

Nechi Institute, Four Worlds Development Project, Native Training Institute, and New Direction Training. 1988. *Healing Is Possible: A Joint Statement on the Healing of Sexual Abuse in Native Communities*. Alkalai Lake, BC: Nechi Institute.

Neel, J.V. 1962. "Diabetes Mellitus: A 'Thrifty' Genotype Rendered Detrimental by 'Progress'?" *American Journal of Human Genetics* 14.

Newbold, K. Bruce. 1998. "Problems in Search of Solutions: Health and Canadian Aboriginals." *Journal of Community Health* 23: 59–74.

Newhouse, David. 2004. "Ganigonhi:oh: The Good Mind Meets the Academy." Department of Indigenous Studies, Trent University.

Nuu-chah-nulth Tribal Council. 1989. *Nuu-chah-nulth First Family Proposal*. Vancouver: Nuu-chah-nulth Tribal Council.

Olshansky, S.J., and A.B. Ault. 1986. "The Fourth Stage of the Epidemiologic Transition: The Age of Delayed Degenerative Diseases." *Milbank Quarterly* 64: 355–91.

Omran, Abdel R. 1971. "The Epidemiologic Transition: A Theory of the Epidemiology of Population Change." *Milbank Memorial Fund Quarterly* 49: 509–38.

O'Neil, John, Jeffrey R. Reading, and Audrey Leader. 1998. "Changing the Relations of Surveillance: The Development of a Discourse of Resistance in Aboriginal Epidemiology." *Human Organization* 57: 230–7.

O'Riley, Patricia. 2004. "Shapeshifting Research with Aboriginal Peoples: Toward Self-Determination." *Canadian Journal of Native Studies* (spring): 83–102.

Peters, Evelyn. 2000. "Aboriginal People in Urban Areas." In D. Long and O. Dickason, eds, *Visions of the Heart: Canadian Aboriginal Issues*, 2nd edn, 237–70. Toronto: Harcourt Canada.

Public Health Agency of Canada. 2003. "Population Health Approach: What Determines Health?" www.phac-aspc. gc.ca/ph-sp/determinants/determinants-eng.php#social.

Raphael, D. 2006. "Social Determinants of Health: Present Status, Unanswered Questions, and Future Directions." *International Journal of Health Services* 36: 651–77.

Royal Commission on Aboriginal Peoples (RCAP). 1993. *Public Hearings: Focusing the Dialogue. Interim Report of the Royal Commission on Aboriginal Peoples*. Ottawa: Supply and Services Canada.

——. 1996. *Looking Forward, Looking Back. Report of the Royal Commission on Aboriginal Peoples*. Ottawa: Canadian Communication Group.

Reidpath, D.D., and P. Allotey. 2003. "Infant Mortality Rate as an Indicator of Population Health." *Journal of Epidemiology and Community Health* 57, 5: 344–6.

Retnakaran, Ravi, et al. 2005. "Cigarette Smoking and Cardiovascular Risk Factors among Aboriginal Canadian Youths." *Canadian Medical Association Journal* 173: 885–9.

Richmond, C.A., and N.A. Ross. 2009. "The Determinants of First Nation and Inuit Health: A Critical Population Health Approach. *Health and Place* 15: 403–11.

Rose, Geoffrey. 1985. "Sick Individuals and Sick Populations." *International Journal of Epidemiology*: 32–8.

Rosenberg, T., et al. 1997. "Shigellosis on Indian Reserves in Manitoba, Canada: Its Relationship to Crowded Housing, Lack of Running Water, and Inadequate Sewage Disposal." *American Journal of Public Health* 87: 1547–51.

Rowse, Tim. 2009. "Official Statistics and the Contemporary Politics of Indigeneity." *Australian Journal of Political Science* 44: 193–211.

Salée, Daniel. 2006. "Quality of Life of Aboriginal People in Canada: An Analysis of Current Research. *IRPP Choices* 12, 6.

Saulis, M. 2003. "Program and Policy Developments from a Holistic Aboriginal Perspective. In Anne Westhues, ed., *Canadian Social Policy*, 3rd edn, 285–300. Waterloo, Ont.: Wilfrid Laurier University Press.

Shah, B.R., N. Gunraj, and J.E. Hux. 2003. "Markers of Access to and Quality of Primary Care for Aboriginal People in Ontario, Canada." *American Journal of Public Health* 93: 798–802.

Sinha, Samir K., et al. 2004. "The Incidence of *Helicobacter pylori* Acquisition in Children of a Canadian First Nations Community and the Potential for Parent-to-Child Transmission." *Helicobacter* 9: 59–68.

Statistics Canada. 2003. *Aboriginal Peoples of Canada: A Demographic Profile*. Catalogue no. 96F0030XIE2001007. Ottawa: Statistics Canada.

——. 2008a. *Aboriginal Peoples in Canada in 2006: Inuit, Métis and First Nations, 2006 Census*. Ottawa: Statistics Canada.

——. 2009. "Life Tables, Canada, Provinces and Territories." Catalogue no. 84-537-XIE. www.statcan.gc.ca/bsolc/olc-cel/olc-cel?catno=84-537-XIE&lang=eng.

Steenbeeck, Audrey. 2004. "Empowering Health Promotion: A Holistic Approach in Preventing Sexually Transmitted Infections among First Nations and Inuit Adolescents in Canada." *Journal of Holistic Nursing* 22: 254–66.

Steffler, Jeanette. 2008. "Aboriginal Peoples: A Young Population for Years to Come." *Horizons* 10, 1: 13–20.

Stephens, C., et al. 2005. "Indigenous Peoples' Health—Why Are They behind Everyone, Everywhere?" *Lancet* 366: 10–13.

Susser, M. 1998. "Does Risk Factor Epidemiology Put Epidemiology at Risk? Peering into the Future." *Journal of Epidemiology and Community Health* 52: 608–11.

Trovato, F. 2001. "Aboriginal Mortality in Canada, the United States and New Zealand." *Journal of Biosocial Science* 33: 67–86.

Tuhiwai Smith, Linda. 1999. *Decolonizing Methodologies: Research and Indigenous Peoples*. London: Zed Books.

Verma, R., M. Michalowski, and R.P. Gauvin. 2003. "Abridged Life Tables for Registered Indians in Canada, 1976–80 to 1996–2000." Presentation at the annual meeting of the Population Association of America, Minneapolis.

Waldram, James B., D. Ann Herring, and T. Kue Young. 2006. *Aboriginal Health in Canada: Historical, Cultural, and Epidemiological Perspectives*. Toronto: University of Toronto Press.

Walker, Ryan. 2008. "Aboriginal Self-Determination and Social Housing in Urban Canada: A Story of Convergence and Divergence." *Urban Studies* 45: 185–205.

Wilkins, R., P. Finès, S. Senécal, and E. Guimond. 2006. "Mortality in Urban and Rural Areas with High Proportion of Aboriginal Residents in Canada." Presentation at the annual meeting of the Population Association of America, 31 Mar.

Wilkins, R., S. Upal, P. Finès, S. Senécal, E. Guimond, and R. Dion. 2008. "Life Expectancy in the Inuit-inhabited

Areas of Canada, 1989 to 2003." *Health Reports* 19: 7–19.

Wilkinson, R.G. 1999. "Health, Hierarchy, and Social Anxiety." *Annals of the New York Academy of Sciences* 896: 48–63.

Willows, N.D. 2005. "Determinants of Healthy Eating in Aboriginal Peoples in Canada: The Current State of Knowledge and Research Gaps." *Canadian Journal of Public Health* 96 (supp. 3): S32–41.

Willows, N.D., et al. 2009. "Prevalence and Socio-demographic Risk Factors Related to Household Food Security in Aboriginal Peoples in Canada." *Public Health Nutrition* 12, 8: 1150–6.

Wilson, Kathi, and M.W. Rosenberg. 2002. "The Geographies of Crisis: Exploring Accessibility to Health Care in Canada." *Canadian Geographer* 46, 3: 223–34.

—— and T. Kue Young. 2008. "An Overview of Aboriginal Health Research in the Social Sciences: Current Trends and Future Directions." *International Journal of Circumpolar Health* 67: 179–89.

World Health Organization (WHO). 1986. *Ottawa Charter for Health Promotion.* Ottawa: WHO.

Young, T.K. 1994. *The Health of Native Americans: Toward a Biocultural Epidemiology.* New York: Oxford University Press.

——. 2003. "Review of Research on Aboriginal Populations in Canada: Relevance to Their Health Needs." *British Medical Journal* 327: 419–22.

—— et al. 2000. "Type 2 Diabetes Mellitus in Canada's First Nations: Status of an Epidemic in Progress." *Canadian Medical Association Journal* 163: 561–6.

Zuberi, T. 2008. "Deracializing Social Statistics: Problems in the Quantification of Race." In T. Zuberi and E. Bonilla-Silva, *White Logic, White Methods: Racism and Methodology,* 172–85 Plymouth, UK: Rowman & Littlefield.

Chapter 13

Aboriginal Affairs and Northern Development Canada (AANDC). 2013. "Aboriginal Demographics from the 2011 National Household Survey: Long Descriptions for the Demography Deck." Planning Research and Statistics Branch. Last modified 5 June 2013. https://www.aadnc-aandc.gc.ca/eng/1370440209795/1370440350563#-fig7.

——. 2014. "Aboriginal Demographics from the Statistics Canada 2011 National Household Survey (NHS)." Planning Research and Statistics Branch. Last modified 5 June 2013. http://www.aadnc-aandc.gc.ca/eng/1370438978311/1370439050610.

Berkhofer, R.F. 1979. *The White Man's Indian: Images of the American Indian from Columbus to Present.* New York: Vintage.

Carli, V. 2012. "The City as Space of Opportunity: Urban Indigenous Experiences and Community Safety Partnerships." In D. Newhouse and K. Fitzmaurice et al., eds, *Well-Being in the Urban Aboriginal Community: Fostering Biimaadiziwin, a National Research Conference on Urban Aboriginal People,* 1–21. Toronto: Thompson Educational Publishing.

Carter, S. 2007. *Aboriginal People and Colonizers of Western Canada to 1900.* Toronto: University of Toronto Press.

Chrisjohn, R., and S. Young, with M. Maraun. 2006. *The Circle Game: Shadow and Substance in the Residential School Experience in Canada,* rev. edn. Penticton, BC: Theytus Books.

Clatworthy, S. 2003. "Impacts of the 1985 Amendments to the Indian Act on First Nations Populations." In J.P. White, P. Maxim, and D. Beavon, eds, *Aboriginal Conditions: Research as a Foundation for Public Policy,* 63–90. Vancouver: University of British Columbia Press.

Environics. 2010. *Urban Aboriginal Peoples Study*. http://www.uaps.ca/wp-content/uploads/2010/03/UAPS-Main-Report_Dec.pdf.

FitzMaurice, K., and D. McCaskill. 2013. *Case Studies Report: Toronto Aboriginal Research Project*. Toronto: Toronto Aboriginal Support Services Council.

Francis, D. 1992. *Imaginary Indian: The Image of the Indian in Canadian Culture*. Toronto: Arsenal Pulp Press.

Guimond, E. 2003. "Fuzzy Definitions and Population Explosion: Changing Aboriginal Groups in Canada." In Newhouse and Peters (2003: 35–48). Ottawa: Policy Research Initiative.

Hanselmann, C., and R. Gibbins. 2002. *Another Voice Is Needed: Intergovernmentalism in the Urban Aboriginal Context*. Kingston, Ont.: Institute of Intergovernmental Relations.

Heisz, A. 2007. *Income Inequality and Redistribution in Canada: 1976 to 2004*. Ottawa: Statistics Canada.

Institute on Governance. 2005. *Roundtable on Urban Aboriginal Governance: Summary of the 5th IOG Aboriginal Governance Roundtable*. Ottawa.

La Prairie, C. 2002. "Aboriginal Over-representation in the Criminal Justice System: A Tale of Nine Cities." *Canadian Journal of Criminology* (Apr.): 181–208.

———. 2003. "Exile on Main Street: Some Thoughts on Aboriginal Over-representation in the Criminal Justice System." In Newhouse and Peters (2003: 179–91).

Loxely, J., and F. Wein. 2003. "Urban Aboriginal Economic Development." In Newhouse and Peters (2003: 217–42).

McCaskill, D. 1981. "The Urbanization of Indians in Winnipeg, Toronto, Edmonton and Vancouver: A Comparative Analysis." *Culture* 1, 1: 82–9.

——— and K. FitzMaurice. 2007. *Urban Aboriginal Task Force: Final Report*. Ontario Federation of Indian Friendship Centres, Ontario Métis and Aboriginal Association, and Ontario Native Women's Association. http://ofifc.agiledudes.com/publication/urban-aboriginal-task-force-ontario-final-report.

——— and ———. 2014. *Life Histories Report: Toronto Aboriginal Research Project*. Toronto: Toronto Aboriginal Support Services Council.

———, ———, and J. Cidro. 2011. *Toronto Aboriginal Research Project: Final Report*. Toronto: Toronto Aboriginal Support Services Council. http://www.councilfire.ca/Acrobat/tarp-final-report2011.pdf.

Malloy, Jonathan. 2001. "Double Identities: Aboriginal Policy Agencies in Ontario and British Columbia." *Canadian Journal of Political Science* 34, 1: 131–55.

National Aboriginal Housing Association. 2009. *A Time for Action: A National Plan to Address Aboriginal Housing*. http://www.cwp-csp.ca/wp-content/uploads/2011/07/NAHA_Action_Plan_July_2009_FINAL.pdf.

Newhouse, D. 2003. "The Invisible Infrastructure: Urban Aboriginal Institutions and Organizations." In Newhouse and Peters (2003: 243–52).

——— and E. Peters, eds. 2003. *Not Strangers in These Parts: Urban Aboriginal Peoples*. Ottawa: Policy Research Initiative.

——— and K. FitzMaurice. 2012. *Well-Being in the Urban Aboriginal Community: Fostering Biimaadiziwin*. National Research Conference on Urban Aboriginal People. Toronto: Thompson Educational Publishing.

Norris, M.J. 2003a. "Aboriginal Languages in Canada's Urban Areas: Characteristics, Considerations, and Implications." In Newhouse and Peters (2003: 93–110).

———. 2003b. "Aboriginal Mobility and Migration within Urban Canada: Outcomes, Factors, and Implications." In Newhouse and Peters (2003: 51–78).

Peters, E. 2006. "We Do Not Lose Our Treaty Rights outside the . . . Reserve: Challenging the Scales of Social Service Provision for First Nations Women in Canadian Cities." *GeoJournal* 65: 315–27.

Royal Commission on Aboriginal Peoples (RCAP). 1996. *Report of the Royal Commission on Aboriginal Peoples, vol. 4: Perspectives and Realities.* Ottawa: Canada Communications Group.

Schouls, T. 2003. *Shifting Boundaries: Aboriginal Identity, Pluralist Theory and the Politics of Self-Government.* Vancouver: University of British Columbia Press.

Siggner, A.J., and R. Costa. 2005. *Trends and Conditions in Census Metropolitan Areas: Aboriginal Conditions in Census Metropolitan Area, 1981 to 2001.* Ottawa: Statistics Canada.

Walker, R. 2008. "Aboriginal Self-determination and Social Housing in Urban Canada: A Story of Convergence and Divergence." *Urban Studies* 45: 185. http://usj.sagepub.com/content/45/1/185.full.pdf+html.

Chapter 14

Aboriginal Justice Implementation Commission. 1999. *Report of the Aboriginal Justice Inquiry of Manitoba.*

Ahluwalia, Seema. 2009. *Supporting Aboriginal Literacy: A Guide for Decolonizing Curricula.* Surrey, BC: Kwantlen Polytechnic University.

Alfred, Taiaiake. 2005. *Wasáse: Indigenous Pathways of Action and Freedom.* Toronto: University of Toronto Press.

——. 2013. "From Idle No More to Indigenous Nationhood." Presentation at Communication and Global Power Shifts: An International Conference in Celebration of the 40th Anniversary of the School of Communication, Simon Fraser University, Vancouver, 8 June.

—— and Jeff Corntassel. 2005. "Being Indigenous: Resurgences against Contemporary Colonialism." *Government and Opposition* 40, 4.

Amnesty International. 2004. *Stolen Sisters: A Human Rights Response to Discrimination and Violence against Indigenous Women in Canada.* Ottawa: Amnesty International.

——. 2013. "Invasive Surveillance of Human Rights Defender Cindy Blackstock." Accessed 14 May 2014. http://www.amnesty.ca/news/news-updates/invasive-surveillance-of-human-rights-defender-cindy-blackstock.

Atkinson, Judy. 2002. *Trauma Trails: Recreating Song Lines: The Transgenerational Effects of Trauma in Indigenous Australia.* North Melbourne: Spinifex Press.

Barron, F. Laurie. 1988. "The Indian Pass System in the Canadian West 1882-1935." *Prairie Forum* 13, 1: 25–42.

Borrows, John. 2002. "Wampum at Niagara: The Royal Proclamation, Canadian Legal History, and Self-Government." In Michael Asch, ed., *Aboriginal Treaty Rights in Canada*, 155–72. Vancouver: University of British Columbia Press.

Brennan. Shannon. 2011. *Violent Victimization of Aboriginal Women in the Canadian Provinces, 2009.* Ottawa: Ministry of Industry.

Brokenleg, Martin. 2013. "Spiritual Restoration among Native Peoples." Lecture hosted by Spirit of the Children Society, Douglas College, New Westminster, BC, 20 Apr.

Bryant, Colleen, and Mathew Willis. 2008. *Risk Factors for Indigenous Violent Victimization.* Canberra: Australian Institute of Criminology.

Brzozowski, Jodi-Anne, Andrea Taylor-Butts, and Sara Johnson. 2006. "Victimization and Offending among the Aboriginal Population in Canada." *Juristat* 26, 3: 1–31.

Burczycka, Marta. 2013. *Police Resources in Canada 2012.* Ottawa: Statistics Canada, Ministry of Industry.

Canadian Bar Association Committee on Imprisonment and Release. 1988. *Locking Up Natives in Canada*. Ottawa: Canadian Bar Association.

Cannon, Martin J., and Lina Sunseri. 2011. "Conclusion." In Cannon and Sunseri, eds, *Racism, Colonialism, and Indigeneity in Canada*. Toronto: Oxford University Press.

Carter, Tom. 2004. *Literature Review on Issues and Needs of Aboriginal People*. Winnipeg: Federation of Canadian Municipalities. Accessed 19 May 2014. http://geograph.uwinnipeg.ca/Carter/Publications/Background/Final_Lit_review_Issues.pdf.

Chamberlin, J. Edward. 2004. *If This Is Your Land, Where Are Your Stories? Finding Common Ground*. Toronto: Vintage.

Chrisjohn, Roland, and Sherri Young, with Michael Maraun. 2006. *The Circle Game: Shadows and Substance in the Indian Residential School Experience in Canada*, rev. edn. Penticton, BC: Theytus Books.

Cohen, Stanley. 1985. *Visions of Social Control*. Cambridge: Polity Press.

Comack, Elizabeth. Lawrence Deane, Larry Morrissette, and Jim Silver. 2013. *"Indians Wear Red": Colonialism, Resistance, and Aboriginal Street Gangs*. Black Point, NS: Fernwood.

Correctional Services Canada. 2013. "Correctional Service Canada Healing Lodges." Accessed 16 May 2014. http://www.csc-scc.gc.ca/aboriginal/002003-2000-eng.shtml.

Coyle, Michael. 1986. "Traditional Indian Justice in Ontario: A Role for the Present?" *Osgoode Law Journal* 24, 3: 605–33.

Cummins, Bryan D., and John L. Steckley. 2003. *Aboriginal Policing: A Canadian Perspective*. Toronto: Prentice-Hall.

Dickason, Olive Patricia. 2002. *Canada's First Nations: A History of Founding Peoples from Earliest Times*, 3rd edn. Toronto: Oxford University Press.

Environics Institute. 2010. *Urban Aboriginal People Study: Main Report*. Toronto: Environics Institute.

Erasmus, Georges. 1996. "Address for the Launch of the *Report of the Royal Commission on Aboriginal Peoples*." Accessed 17 May 2014. http://www.aadnc-aandc.gc.ca/eng/1100100014639/1100100014640.

Farrington, David, and Brandon Welsh. 2007. *Saving Children from a Life of Crime: Early Risk Factors and Effective Interventions*. New York: Oxford University Press.

Ferguson, Lynn. 2011. "The Hudson's Bay Company." In Léo-Paul Dana, ed., *World Encyclopedia of Entrepreneurship*, 238–46. Northampton, Mass.: Edward Elgar.

Fleming, Thomas, Subhas Ramcharan, Ken Dowler, and Willem de Lint. 2008. *The Canadian Criminal Justice System*, 2nd edn. Toronto: Pearson Prentice-Hall.

Furniss, Elizabeth. 1995. *The Victims of Benevolence: The Dark Legacy of the Williams Lake Residential School*. Vancouver: Arsenal Pulp Press.

Garland, David. 2001. *The Culture of Control: Crime and Disorder in Contemporary Society*. Chicago: University of Chicago Press.

Gehl, Lynn. 2011. "Indigenous Knowledge, Symbolic Literacy and the 1764 Treaty at Niagara." Federation for the Humanities and Social Sciences. Accessed 19 May 2014. http://www.ideas-idees.ca/blog/indigenous-knowledge-symbolic-literacy-and-1764-treaty-niagarax.

——. 2014. *The Truth that Wampum Tells: My Debwewin on the Algonquin Lands Claims Process*. Black Point, NS: Fernwood.

Hansen, John G. 2012. "Countering Imperial Justice: The Implications of a Cree Response to Crime." *Indigenous Policy Journal* 23, 1.

Heckbert, Doug, and Douglas Turkington. 2001. *Turning Points: A Study of the Factors Related to the Successful Reintegration of Aboriginal Offenders.* Ottawa: Correctional Service of Canada.

Helena Fennig, Tami. 2002. "Sentencing Aboriginal Offenders: Section 718.2(e) of the Criminal Code of Canada and Aboriginal Over-Representation in Canadian Prisons." Master's thesis, Simon Fraser University.

Hickman, Alexander T., Chief Justice, Associate Chief Justice Lawrence A. Poitras, and the Honourable Mr. Gregory T. Evans, QC. 1989. *Royal Commission on the Donald Marshall, Jr., Prosecution* (Province of Nova Scotia).

Human Rights Watch. 2013. *Those Who Take Us Away: Abusive Policing and Failures in Protection of Indigenous Women and Girls in Northern British Columbia, Canada.* New York: Human Rights Watch.

Iacobucci, Frank. 2013. *First Nations Representation on Ontario Juries: Report of the Independent Review Conducted by The Honourable Frank Iacobucci.*

Jolly, S. 1983. *Warehousing Indians: Fact Sheet on the Disproportionate Imprisonment of Native People in Ontario.* Toronto: Ontario Native Council on Justice.

Kelling, George L., Tony Pate, Duane Dieckman, and Charles E. Brown. 1974. *The Kansas City Preventative Patrol Experiment: A Summary Report.* Washington: Police Foundation.

Lame Deer, John (Fire), and Richard Erdoes. 1994. *Lame Deer, Seeker of Visions.* New York: Pocket Books.

La Prairie, Carol, and Phillip Stenning. 2003. "Exile on Main Street: Some Thoughts on Aboriginal Over-Representation in the Criminal Justice System." In David Newhouse and Evelyn Peters, eds, *Not Strangers in These Parts: Urban Aboriginal Peoples,* 179–93. Ottawa: Policy Research Initiative.

Law Reform Commission of Canada. 1991. *Aboriginal Peoples and Criminal Justice: Report on Aboriginal Peoples and Criminal Justice.* Ottawa: Law Reform Commission of Canada.

Lilley, P.J., and J. Shantz. 2013. "From Idle No More to Indigenous Nationhood." *Upping the Anti: A Journal of Theory and Action* 15: 113–27.

Ling, Justin. 2013. "Snooping Idle No More: When Native Protestors Were Talking Last Year, CSIS Was Paying Close Attention." *Maclean's.* Accessed 14 May 2014. http://www.macleans.ca/news/canada/the-spooks-werent-idle-either.

Lyons, Oren. 1997. "Epilogue: The Year of the Indigenous Peoples: Oka Revisited (with Extracts of the 1991 Proceedings of the Standing Committee on Aboriginal Affairs." In Andrea P. Morrison, *Justice for Natives: Searching for Common Ground.* Montreal: Aboriginal Law Association of McGill University.

Martel, Joane, Renée Brassard, and Mylène Jaccoud. 2011. "When Two Worlds Collide: Aboriginal Risk Management in Canadian Corrections." *British Journal of Criminology* 51: 235–55.

Maté, Gabor. 2012. *In The Realm of Hungry Ghosts: Close Encounters with Addiction.* Toronto: Vintage Books.

Milloy, John S. 1999. *A National Crime: The Canadian Government and the Residential School System 1879 to 1986.* Winnipeg: University of Manitoba Press.

Monchalin, Lisa. 2012. "Reducing Crime Affecting Urban Aboriginal People: The Potential for Effective Solutions in Winnipeg." Ph.D. dissertation, University of Ottawa.

Mohawk Council of Akwesasne. 2014. "The Kaswentha (Two Row Wampum)." Akwesasne: Mohawk Council of Akwesasne. Accessed 19 May 2014. http://www.akwesasne.ca/node/118.

Monture, Patricia. 2007. "Race and Erasing: Law and Gender in White Settler

Societies." In Sean P. Hier and B. Singh Bolaria, eds, *Race and Racism in 21st Century Canada.* Peterborough, Ont.: Broadview Press.

——. 2011. "The Need for Radical Change in the Canadian Criminal Justice System: Applying a Human Rights Framework." In David Long and Olive Patricia Dickason, eds, *Visions of the Heart: Canadian Aboriginal Issues,* 3rd edn. Toronto: Oxford University Press.

Morito, Bruce. 1999. "The Rule of Law and Aboriginal Rights: The Case of the Chippewas of Nawash." *Canadian Journal of Native Studies* 19, 2.

Morrison, Woody. 2014. Presentation to CRIM 4240, "Aboriginal Peoples and Justice Class." Kwantlen Polytechnic University, Surrey, BC, 20 May.

Muller, Kathryn V. 2007. "The Two 'Mystery' Belts of Grand River: A Biography of the Two Row Wampum and the Friendship Belt." *American Indian Quarterly* 31, 1: 129–64.

Native Women's Association of Canada. 2010. *What Their Stories Tell Us: Research Findings from the Sisters in Spirit Initiative.* Ohsweken, Ont.: Native Women's Association of Canada.

Office of the Correctional Investigator. 2012. *Spirit Matters: Aboriginal People and the Corrections and Conditional Release Act.* Ottawa: Office of the Correctional Investigator.

Pearce, Maryanne. 2013. "An Awkward Silence: Missing and Murdered Vulnerable Women and the Canadian Justice System." Ph.D. dissertation, University of Ottawa.

Palys, Ted. 1993. "Considerations for Achieving 'Aboriginal Justice' in Canada." Paper presented at the annual meetings of the Western Association of Sociology and Anthropology. Vancouver, BC. Accessed 18 May 2014. http://www.sfu.ca/~palys/WASA93.pdf.

Paul, Daniel N. 2006. *We Were Not the Savages: Collision between European and Native American Civilizations,* 3rd edn. Black Point, NS: Fernwood.

Perreault, Samuel. 2009. "The Incarceration of Aboriginal People in Adult Correctional Services." *Juristat* 29, 3.

——. 2011. "Violent Victimization of Aboriginal People in the Canadian Provinces, 2009." *Juristat* 30, 4: 1–35.

——. 2014. "Admissions to Adult Correctional Services in Canada, 2011/2012." *Juristat.*

Reiman, Jeffrey. 2007. *The Rich Get Richer and the Poor Get Prison: Ideology, Class, and Criminal Justice.* Boston: Allyn and Bacon.

Royal Canadian Mounted Police (RCMP). 2014. *Missing and Murdered Aboriginal Women: A National Operational Overview.* Ottawa: Her Majesty the Queen in Right of Canada.

Royal Commission on Aboriginal Peoples (RCAP). 1995. *Bridging the Cultural Divide: A Report on Aboriginal People and Criminal Justice in Canada.* Ottawa: Minister of Supply and Services Canada.

——. 1996. *Report of the Royal Commission on Aboriginal Peoples.* Ottawa: Minister of Supply and Services Canada.

Savard, Rémi. 2003. "Les peuples américains et le système judiciaire canadien: Spéléologie d'un trou de mémoire." *Revue Canadienne Droit et Société* 17, 2: 123–48.

Siegfried, Christine B., Susan J. Ko, and Ann Kelley. 2004. *Victimization and Juvenile Offending.* Los Angeles: National Child Traumatic Stress Network. Accessed 22 May 2014. http://www.nctsnet.org/nctsn_assets/pdfs/edu_materials/victimization_juvenile_offending.pdf.

Simpson, Leanne. 2011. *Dancing on Our Turtle's Back: Stories of Nishnaabeg Re-Creation, Resurgence and a New Emergence.* Winnipeg: Arbeiter Ring.

Smart, Carol. 1989. *Feminism and the Power of Law*. London and New York: Routledge.

Solicitor General Canada. 1975. *Native Peoples and Justice: Reports on the National Conference and the Federal–Provincial Conference on Native Peoples and the Criminal Justice System, both held in Edmonton, Feb. 3–5, 1975*. Ministry of the Solicitor General, Communication Division.

Statistics Canada. 2013. *Aboriginal Peoples in Canada: First Nations People, Métis, and Inuit, National Household Survey, 2011*. Ottawa: Statistics Canada.

Steckley, John L, and Bryan D. Cummins. 2008. *Full Circle: Canada's First Nations*. Toronto: Pearson Prentice-Hall.

Story, Rod, and Tolga R. Yalkin. 2013. *Expenditure Analysis of Criminal Justice in Canada*. Ottawa: Office of the Parliamentary Budget Officer.

Wagamese, Richard. 2013. "Wagamese: 'All My Relations' about Respect." *Kamloops Daily News*, 11 June 2013. Accessed 4 June 2014. http://www.kamloopsnews.ca/article/20130611/KAMLOOPS0304/130619980/-1/kamloops/wagamese-all-my-relations-about-respect.

Waller, Irvin. 2008. *Less Law, More Order: The Truth about Reducing Crime*. Ancaster, Ont.: Manor House.

———. 2014. *Smarter Crime Control: A Guide to a Safe Future for Citizens, Communities and Politicians*. Lanham, Md: Rowman & Littlefield.

Waziyatawin and Michael Yellow Bird. 2012. "Introduction: Decolonizing Our Minds and Actions." In Waziyatawin and Michael Yellow Bird, eds, *For Indigenous Eyes Only: A Decolonization Handbook*. Santa Fe, NM: School of American Research Press.

Wesley-Esquimaux, Cynthia C., and Magdalena Smolewski. 2004. *Historic Trauma and Aboriginal Healing*. Ottawa: Aboriginal Healing Foundation.

Williams, Robert A. Jr. 1986. "The Algebra of Federal Indian Law: The Hard Trail of Decolonizing and Americanizing the White Man's Jurisprudence." *Wisconsin Law Review*: 219–99.

Chapter 15

Atwood, Margaret. 1985. *The Handmaid's Tale*. Edinburgh Gate, Essex: Heinemann.

Du Bois, W.E.B. 1903. *The Souls of Black Folk*. Chicago: A.C. McClurg and Company.

Fontaine, Phil. 2008. Speech made to the Standing Senate Committee on Aboriginal Peoples. Issue 11, *Evidence*, 16 Apr.

McLeod, Neal. 2001. "Coming Home through Stories." In Armand Garnet Ruffo, ed., *(Ad)dressing Our Words: Aboriginal Perspectives on Aboriginal Literatures*, 5–36. Penticton, BC: Theytus Books.

Regan, Paulette. 2011. *Unsettling the Settler Within: Indian Residential Schools, Truth Telling, and Reconciliation in Canada*. Toronto: Penguin.

Saul, John Ralston. 2009. *A Fair Country: Telling Truths about Canada*. Toronto: Penguin.

———. 2014. *The Comeback: How Aboriginals Are Reclaiming Power and Influence*. Toronto: Penguin.

Credits

Index